A Companion to the Works of Grimmelshausen

Studies in German Literature, Linguistics, and Culture

Edited by James Hardin
(*South Carolina*)

Camden House Companion Volumes

The Camden House Companions provide well-informed and up-to-date critical commentary on the most significant aspects of major works, periods, or literary figures. The Companions may be read profitably by the reader with a general interest in the subject. For the benefit of student and scholar, quotations are provided in the original language.

A Companion to the Works of
Grimmelshausen

Edited by
Karl F. Otto, Jr.

CAMDEN HOUSE

First published 2003
by Camden House

Camden House is an imprint of Boydell & Brewer Inc.
PO Box 41026, Rochester, NY 14604–4126 USA
and of Boydell & Brewer Limited
PO Box 9, Woodbridge, Suffolk IP12 3DF, UK

ISBN: 1–57113–184–1

Library of Congress Cataloging-in-Publication Data

A companion to the works of Grimmelshausen / edited by Karl F. Otto, Jr.
     p. cm. — (Studies in German literature, linguistics, and culture)
Includes bibliographical references and index.
ISBN 1–57113–184–1 (alk. paper)
     1. Grimmelshausen, Hans Jakob Christoph von, 1625–1676 — Criticism
and interpretation. I. Otto, Karl F., Jr. II. Studies in German literature,
linguistics, and culture (Unnumbered)

PT1732 .C66 2002
833'.5—dc21

                                                                                                2002006594

A catalogue record for this title is available from the British Library.

This publication is printed on acid-free paper.
Printed in the United States of America.

Contents

Illustrations   vii

Acknowledgments   ix

Chronological List of Grimmelshausen's
Works and Their First English Translation   xi

Introduction
Karl F. Otto, Jr.   1

I. Basics

Problems in the Editions of Grimmelshausen's Works
Christoph E. Schweitzer   25

Grimmelshausen's "Autobiographies"
and the Art of the Novel
Italo Michele Battafarano   45

Allegorical and Astrological Forms in the
Works of Grimmelshausen with Special
Emphasis on the Prophecy Motif
Klaus Haberkamm   93

Grimmelshausen and the Picaresque Novel
Christoph E. Schweitzer   147

Grimmelshausen's *Ewig-währender Calender:*
A Labyrinth of Knowledge and Reading
Rosmarie Zeller   167

Grimmelshausen's Non-Simplician Novels
Andreas Solbach   201

In Grimmelshausen's Tracks:
The Literary and Cultural Legacy
Dieter Breuer 231

II. Critical Approaches

Engendering Social Order: From Costume
Autobiography to Conversation Games in
Grimmelshausen's Simpliciana
Lynne Tatlock 269

The Poetics of Masquerade: Clothing and the
Construction of Social, Religious, and Gender
Identity in Grimmelshausen's *Simplicissimus*
Peter Hess 299

"To see from these black lines":
The Mise en Livre of the Phoenix Copperplate
and Other Grimmelshausen Illustrations
Shannon Keenan Greene 333

The Search for Freedom: Grimmelshausen's
Simplician Weltanschauung
Alan Menhennet 359

Notes on the Contributors 379

Index 383

Illustrations

1. Copperplate from *Landstörtzerin Courage* 44

2. Grimmelshausen's "family" from *Simplicissimus Redivivus* 92

3. Engraved title page from *Vogelnest, Zweiter Theil* 146

4. Copperplate engraving from *Ewigwährender Calender* 166

5. Sample page (5), from the *Calender* 196

6. Sample page (122) from the *Calender* 197

7. Sample page (123) from the *Calender* 198

8. Sample page (221) from the *Calender* 199

9. Frontispiece copperplate from *Proximus und Lympida* 200

10. Copperplate from *Ratio Status* 228

11. Renchen celebrates the bicentennial of Grimmelshausen's death (1876) 230

12. and 13. "Grimmelshausen money" 265

14. Renchen celebrates Grimmelshausen (1924) 266

15. Copperplate from first edition of *Springinsfeld* (1670) 268

16. Copperplate from a later edition of
Springinsfeld (1684)   297

17. Copperplate from *Simplicissimus Redivivus*   298

18. Frontispiece copperplate (the "Phoenix"
copperplate) from *Simplicissimus Teutsch* (1668)   332

19. and 20.   Grimmelshausen's sketches of Schloß
Hohengeroldseck   357

Acknowledgments

I WOULD LIKE TO THANK THE AUTHORS of the individual essays for contributing their work to this volume as well as for their patience with me. The same thanks go to the two students from the University of Pennsylvania who were involved in translating some of the contributions from German to English (Vance Byrd and Christine Dombrowski). The Faculty Master's Research Fund of the University of Pennsylvania graciously provided financial support for portions of the work on this volume. To my colleagues in the Department of Germanic Languages and Literatures at the University of Pennsylvania, I also say "thanks" for the occasional assistance with difficult translations from the German. I would also like to thank the Fink Verlag (Munich) for permission to translate and publish the contribution of Dieter Breuer, which was translated from his recently published *Grimmelshausen Handbuch*.[1] Special thanks are also due to the series editor, James Hardin, for his continued guidance, suggestions, and forethought and the production editor, Jim Walker, for his help and assistance. In addition, I wish to thank Reth Touch and Edward Dixon, of the School of the Arts and Sciences Computing Services at the University of Pennsylvania and the Educational Technology section of the Penn Language Center, respectively, for their assistance with the illustrations for the volume. Finally, I wish to thank my friend (he knows who he is) for his understanding during the many hours I was involved with Grimmelshausen!

K. F. O.
July 2002

---

[1] Dieter Breuer. *Grimmelshausen Handbuch*. Munich: Fink, 1999. The title of the original chapter (Chapter VII) in the German edition is, "Wirkungsgeschichte," found on pp. 245–268 in the original.

Chronological List of Grimmelshausen's Works and Their First English Translation

THE ABBREVIATIONS FOLLOWING THE TITLES, two to four letters each, are the ones used in the body of all texts in this volume to indicate the source of quoted passages.

Satyrischer Pilgram, Das ist: Kalt und Warm, Weiß und Schwartz, Lob und Schand, über guths und böß, Tugend und Laster, auch Nutz und Schad vieler Ständt und Ding der Sichtbarn und Unsichtbarn der Zeitlichen und Ewigen Welt. Beydes lustig und nützlich zulesen, von Neuem zusammen getragen durch Samuiel Greifnson, vom Hirschfeld. Leipzig: Printed by Hieronymus Grisenius for Georg Heinrich Frommann, 1666. (SP)

Exempel der unveränderlichen Vorsehung Gottes. Unter einer anmutigen und ausführlichen Histori vom Keuschen Joseph in Egypten, Jacobs Sohn. Vorgestellet so wol aus Heiliger als anderer Hebreer, Egyptier, Perser, und Araber Schrifften und hergebrachter Sag, erstlich Teutsch zusammen getragen durch den Samuel Greifnson vom Hirschfeld. Nuremberg: Wolf Eberhard Felsecker, 1667 [i.e., 1666]; enlarged as *Des Vortrefflich Keuschen Josephs in Egypten, Erbauliche, recht ausführliche und vielvermehrte Lebensbeschreibung, zum Augenscheinlichen Exempel der unveränderlichen Vorsehung Gottes, so wol aus heiliger Schrifft, als anderen der Hebreer, Perser und Araber Büchern und hergebrachter Sage auf das deutlichste vorgestellt, und erstesmals mit grosser und unverdroßner Mühe zusammen getragen von Samuel Greifnson von Hirschfeld. Numehro aber wiederumb aufs neue vom Autore übersehen, verbessert, und samt des unvergleichlichen Josephs getreuen Schaffners Musai Lebens-Lauff. Vermehret, dem Curiosen Leser sehr anmuthig, lustig und nutzlich zubetrachten wolmeinend mitgetheilet.* Nuremberg: Wolf Eberhard Felsecker, 1670. (KJ)

Satyrischer Pilgram Anderer Theil, Zusammen getagen durch Samuel Greifnson vom Hirschfelt. Leipzig: Printed by Hieronymus Grisenius for Georg Heinrich Fromann, 1667. (SP-2)

Der Abentheuerliche Simplicissimus Teutsch, das ist: Die Beschreibung deß Lebens eines seltzamen Vaganten, genant Melchior Sternfeld von Fuchshaim, wo und welcher gestalt Er nemlich in diese Welt kommen, was er darinn gesehen, gelernet, erfahren und außgestanden, auch warumb er solche wieder freywillig quittirt. Überaus lustig und männiglich nützlich zu lesen. An Tag geben von German Schleifheim von Sulsfort. Monpelgart:

Printed by Johann Fillion, 1669 [i.e., Nuremberg: Wolf Eberhard Fel-
secker, 1668]. (ST); translated by A. T. S. Goodrick as *The Adventurous
Simplicissimus: Being the Description of the Life of a Strange Vagabond
Named Melchior Sternfels von Fuchshaim*. London: Heinemann, 1912;
New York: Dutton, 1913.

Continuatio des abentheurlichen Simplicissimi oder Schluß desselben. [as
German Schleifheim von Sulsfort]. Monpelgart: Johann Fillton [*sic*] [i.e.,
Nuremberg: Wolf Eberhard Felsecker], 1669. (Cont)

*Dietwalds und Amelinden anmuthige Lieb- und Leids-Beschreibung, sammt
erster Vergrösserung des Weltberühmten Königreichs Franckreich. Den
Gottseeligen erbaulich curiosen lustig Historicis annemlich Betrübten tröstlich Verliebten erfreulich Politicis nützlich und der Jugend ohnärgerlich
zulesen zusammen gesucht und hervorgegeben von H. J. Christoffel von
Grimmelshausen, Gelnhusano.* Nuremberg: Wolf Eberhard Felsecker,
1670. (Diet)

*Simplicianischer Zweyköpffiger Ratio Status lustig entworffen unter der Histori
des waidlichen Königs Saul, des sanfftmütigen König Davids, des getreuen
Printzen Jonathae, und deß tapffern Generalissimi Joabi.* Nuremberg:
Wolf Eberhard Felsecker, 1670. (RS)

*Trutz Simplex: Oder Ausführliche und wunderseltzame Lebensbeschreibung
der Ertzbetrügerin und Landstörtzerin Courasche, wie sie anfangs eine
Rittmeisterin, hernach eine Hauptmännin, ferner eine Leutenantin, bald
eine Marcketenterin, Mußquetirerin, und letzlich eine Zigeunerin abgege-
ben, meisterlich agiret, und ausbündig vorgestellet: Eben so lustig, annemlich und nutzlich zu betrachten, als Simplicissimus selbst. Alles miteinander
von der Courasche eigner Person dem weit und breitbekanten Simplicissimo
zum Verdruß und Widerwillen, dem Autori in die Feder dictirt, der sich
vor dißmal nennet Philarchus Grossus von Trommenheim, auf Griffsberg
&c.* Utopia: Printed by Felix Stratiot [i.e., Nuremberg: Wolf Eberhard
Felsecker], 1670. (Cour)

*Der seltzame Springinsfeld, das ist kurtzweilige, lusterweckende und recht
lächerliche Lebens-Beschreibung. Eines weiland frischen, wolversuchten und
tapffern Soldaten, nunmehro aber ausgemergelten, abgelebten, doch dabey
recht verschlagnen Landstörtzers und Bettlers, samt seiner wunderlichen
Gauckeltasche. Aus Anordnung des weit und breit bekanten Simplicissimi
verfasset und zu Papier gebracht von Philarcho Grosso von Trommerheim.*
Paphlagonia: Printed by Felix Stratiot [i.e., Nuremberg: Wolf Eberhard
Felsecker], 1670. (Spr)

*Der erste Beernhäuter, nicht ohne sonderbare darunter verborgene Lehrreiche
Geheimnus, so wol allen denen die so zuschelten pflegen, und sich so schelten
lassen, als auch sonst jedermann (vor dißmal zwar nur vom Ursprung*

dieses schönen Ehren-Tituls) andern zum Exempel vorgestellet, sampt Simplicissimi Gauckeltasche. Von Illiterato Ignorantio, zugenannt Idiota. Nuremberg: Wolf Eberhard Felsecker, 1670.

Des Abenteuerlichen Simplicissimi Ewig-währender Calender worinnen ohne die ordentliche Verzeichnus der unzehlbar vieler Heiligen Täge auch unterschiedliche curiose Discursen von der Astronomia, Astrologia, Item den Calendern, Nativitäten, auch allerhand Wunderbarlichen Wahr- und Vorsagungen, mit untermischter Bauren-Practic, Tag- und Zeitwehlungen, &c. Nicht weniger Viel Seltzame, jedoch Warhaffte Wunder-Geschichten, und andere Merckwürdiuge Begebenheiten, samt Beyfügung etlicher Künst- und Wissenschaften befindlich. [Anonymous] Nuremberg: Published by Wolf Eberhard Felsecker, printed by Marcus Bloss in Fulda, 1670 [i.e., 1671]. (EC)

Des Abenteuerlichen Simplicissimi Verkehrte Welt. Nicht, wie es scheinet, dem Leser allein zur Lust und Kurzweil: Sondern auch zu dessen aufferbaulichem Nutz annemlich entworffen von Simon Lengfrisch von Hartenfels. Nuremberg: Wolf Eberhard Felsecker, 1672. (VW)

Rathstübel Plutonis oder Kunst Reich zu werden, durch vierzehen unterschied licher namhafften Personen richtige Meynungen in gewisse Reguln verabfasset, und auß Simplicissimi Brunnquell selbsten geschöpfft, auch auffrecht Simplicianisch beschrieben von Erich Stainfels von Grufensholm, Sambt Simplicissimi Discurs, Wie man hingegen bald auffwannen; und mit seinem Vorrath fertig werden soll. Samaria [i.e., Nuremberg: Wolf Eberhard Felsecker or Strasbourg: Georg Andreas Dolhopff], 1672. (RP)

Der stoltze Melcher, sambt einer Besprecknuß von das Frantzoß Krieg mit der Holland. Welches durch Veranlassung eines Saphoyers der Fridens-satten- und gern-kriegenden teutschen Jugend zum Meßkram verehret wird. [anonymous] (Strasbourg [?]: Dolhopff [?]), 1672.

Des Printzen Proximi, und seiner ohnvergleichlichen Lympidae Liebs-Geschicht-Erzehlung. Strasbourg: Dolhopff, 1672. (PL)

Das wunderbarliche Vogel-Nest, der Springinsfeldischen Leyrerin, voller Abentheurlichen, doch Lehrreichen Geschichten, auff Simplicianische Art sehr nutzlich und kurtzweilig zu lesen außgefertigt durch Michael Rechulin von Sehmsdorff. Monpelgart: Printed by Johann Fillion [i.e., Strasbourg: Dolhopff (?)], 1672. (WV–I)

Bart-Krie, oder Des ohnrecht genanten Roht-Barts Widerbellung gegen den welt-beruffenen Schwartzbart deß Simplicissimi darinnen er zu Erhaltung der reputation aller zwar fälschlich Rohtgenanten Bärt die Goldfarb, wie billich, dem Kühnruß, das frewdenreiche Gelb, des Teuffels Leibfarb vorziehet. Strasbourg: Dolhopff or Nuremberg: Wolf Eberhard Felsecker, 1673.

Deeß Weltberuffenen Simplicissimi Pralerey and Gepräng mit seinem Teutschen Michel, jedermänniglichen, wanns seyn kan, ohne Lachen zu lesen erlaubt von Signeur Meßmahl. Nuremberg: Wolf Eberhard Felsecker, 1673.

Simplicissimi Galgen-Männlin, oder Ausführlicher Bericht, woher man die so genannte allräungen oder Geldmännlin bekommt, und wie man ihrer warten und pflegen soll; auch was vor Nutzen man hingegen von ihnen eigentlich zugewarten. Erstlich durch Simplicissimum selbsten seinem Sohn und allen andern, so die Reichthum dieser Welt verlangen, zum besten an tag geben. Nachgehends mit nutzlichen Anmerck- und Erinnerungen erläutert durch Israël Fromschmit von Hugenfelß. Strasbourg: Dolhopff or Nuremberg: Felsecker, 1673. (GM)

Deß Wunderbarlichen Vogelnessts Zweiter theil, an tag geben von A c eee ff g hh ii ll mm nn oo rr sss t uu. Strasbourg: Dolhopff, 1675. (WV–II)

Deß possirlichen, weit und breit bekannten Simplicissimi sinnreicher und nachdencklicher Schrifften Zweiten Theils. Nuremberg: Wolf Eberhard Felsecker, 1683.

Der aus dem Grab der Vergessenheit wieder erstandene Simplicissimus; dessen abentheurlicher, undmit allerhand seltsamen, fast unerhörten Begebenheiten angefüllter Lebens-Wandel. Nuremberg: Wolf Eberhard Felsecker, 1683.

Deß aus dem Grabe der Vergessenheit wieder erstandenen Simplicissimi, mit kostbaren, zu dieser Zeit hochwerthen und dero Liebhaber fest an sich ziehenden Waaren an- und ausgefüllter Staats-Kram, statt deß auf seinen jüngsthin hervorgegebenen Lebens-Wandel, nunmehr ordentlich folgenden dritten und letzten Theils. Nuremberg: Wolf Eberhard Felsecker, 1684. [Grimmelshausen and other authors]

Introduction

Karl F. Otto, Jr.

JOHANN (HANS) JACOB CHRISTOFFEL VON GRIMMELSHAUSEN (1621 or 1622–17 August 1676) is deservedly the best known and most often read German novelist of the seventeenth century. In fact, he is the only author who can act as a bridge between the first and second classical periods of German literature, the first being that of high medieval literature, which reached its peak around 1200, with works such as the anonymous heroic epic *Nibelungenlied* and the courtly epics of Wolfram von Eschenbach and Gottfried von Strasbourg, and the second that of German Classicism around 1800, which includes among its major writers Goethe and Schiller. Grimmelshausen is furthermore a writer whose works have stimulated an enormous quantity of scholarly studies over the past thirty years. This virtually unique activity in German Baroque studies has to do with a series of "discoveries" about several aspects of his works that mark them not as the naïve productions of an unlearned, "natural" author, but as the creations of a writer who consciously used exceedingly sophisticated and subtle modes of characterization, expression of symbolic meaning, and of narrative structure. His best known novel, *Der Abentheurliche Simplicissimus Teutsch* (1668; first translated as *The Adventurous Simplicissimus,* 1912) is Germany's only early modern contribution to the canon of world-class literature. Because of the details that they provide about the times, especially about the Thirty Years' War, Grimmelshausen's picaresque novels are widely read by historians as well as by students of literature. That novel forms the focus of the Simplician cycle of novels (a total of five different novelistic works), but the figure of Simplicius Simplicissimus is found in many of his other works as well.

Biographical Sketch

Grimmelshausen's exact date of birth is not known.[1] Although many assume he was born in 1621, some evidence in *Simplicissimus* indicates he was born in 1622, and, using astrological data presented there, some scholars hold that he was born on 17 March 1622. His hometown was

Gelnhausen (Hessia), although his family originally came from Suhl (Thuringia). His father died when Grimmelshausen was very young. Although the exact date of death is not known, we do know that Grimmelshausen's mother remarried in 1627. As did most boys of his class and age, Grimmelshausen attended the local Lutheran-oriented "Lateinschule" for some six or seven years (ca. 1627–28 to 1633–34). This public city school had a curriculum based on the recommendations of Philipp Melanchthon (1497–1560), who stressed religion and the classical languages, particularly Latin. Students were to be trained in grammar as well as in the works of the classical authors. There is no evidence to support any further formal education, although it is clear that Grimmelshausen (at least later in life) was abundantly familiar with classical literature and contemporary literature in various vernaculars. Volker Meid notes that Günther Weydt was able to compile a list of approximately 150 works (literature, history, and the like), with which Grimmelshausen was definitely acquainted (86). The remainder of Grimmelshausen's early life is shrouded in uncertainty. From the earliest days of Grimmelshausen scholarship it has been suggested that his early life was reflected in the adventures of the hero of his *Simplicissimus,* but more recent scholarship has found more of the book and less of the autobiographical in the literary productions of Grimmelshausen.

In 1639, Grimmelshausen joined the regiment of Colonel Hans Reinhard von Schauenburg, and between February and May 1645 he joined the regiment of Johann Burkhard von Elter, Schauenburg's brother-in-law. In July 1649, not long after the Peace of Westphalia, which concluded the Thirty Years' War, Grimmelshausen left the military and returned to Offenburg.

It was in Offenburg that he married Catharina Henninger on 30 August 1649. Their marriage record in the church registers reveals that he had in the meantime converted to Catholicism. He also began, once again, to use the more elegant name "von Grimmelshausen," which his grandfather had earlier abandoned. Between 1649 and 1669, Grimmelshausen and his wife had ten children, the majority of whom lived beyond infancy.

In the same year in which he married, Grimmelshausen became a steward for the Schauenburg family in Gaisbach (today part of Oberkirch). In 1653, he bought property in that town and erected two buildings, one of which contained the inn he owned and operated, "Zum silbernen Stern" (The Silver Star). He ran the inn from 1656 to 1658 and again from 1665 to 1667. In the intervening years, he continued to live in Gaisbach. In the earlier years he managed without employment. In the latter years he was steward in the Ullenburg, a castle which the Strasbourg physician Johann Küffer the Younger (1614–1675) frequented in the summer months.[2] Küffer had close contacts with many important German writers from the southwestern part of the country, for example, Jesaias Rompler von Löwenhalt (1605–after 1672), who in 1633 founded the Aufrichtige Tannengesellschaft, a patriotic linguistic society (*Sprachgesellschaft*) based ultimately on similar Italian societies. Küffer was probably also responsible, at least indirectly, for any contact that Grimmelshausen had with the prominent and influential writer Johann Michael Moscherosch (1601–1669). It seems that these were also the years in which Grimmelshausen began his creative phase as a writer and novelist.

Income from the inn was insufficient to support his family, and so he applied for, and received, the position as mayor in Renchen, a village of some seven hundred inhabitants. In that capacity, he was judge, police chief, notary public, and tax collector. If it had been difficult for Grimmelshausen earlier to combine work as an innkeeper and as an author, it must have been even more difficult for him to pursue his literary career while serving as mayor, although he did continue to hold the position until his death in 1676.

Simplicius Simplicissimus

Grimmelshausen's true stature as a writer did not become readily apparent until the literary detective work done, individually, but more or less at the same time by a number of scholars in the first half of the nineteenth century.[3] These scholars, some of the earliest Germanists, were, with the exception of Karl Hartwig Gregor von Meusebach (1781–1847), called on to review the first "modern" edition of Grimmelshausen's *Simplicissimus* (1836), edited and published by Karl Eduard von Bülow (1803–1853). Bülow had been spurred on to do an edition of the novel by his friend Ludwig Tieck, one of the most important Romantic authors in Germany, who, along with other authors of Romanticism, was interested in earlier German literature as it had originally appeared. These scholars were, in addition to Meusebach, Hermann Kurz (1813–1873), Julius Ludwig Klee (1807–1867), Theodor Echtermeyer (1805–1844), and Wilhelm Arthur Passow (1814–1864). Although Kurz was the first to publish his results in 1837, he did not realize all the connections between the various novels of Grimmelshausen, and he used only the initials at the end of the novel *Simplicissimus* to arrive at the true name of the author of that novel. In that same year, Klee also published his findings, but he was, again, somewhat limited, as he recognized the connections between individual names but assumed that the common name, Grimmelshausen, was also a pseudonym. The real detective was Echtermeyer, who, in 1838, finally solved the riddle and identified Grimmelshausen, who had written two works under his real name, but all his Simplician works under a variety of pseudonyms. He is, therefore, responsible for "discovering" Grimmelshausen as we know him today, that is, as the author of an extensive oeuvre. Passow, in turn, had arrived at many of the same conclusions as Echtermeyer, but stumbled on the latter's work just shortly before publishing his own investigations. He then added several biographical details to what Echtermeyer had shown, including things like the death entry from the church register in Renchen and many other details as well. The investigations of Meusebach never reached the printed stage, although he may well have been the first to realize that "Greifnson" was really Grimmelshausen. He wrote a letter to the Minister of the Interior Hassenpflug to that effect on 8 April 1837. These scholars, collectively, are responsible for the identification of Grimmelshausen as the author of several works that had been published under different pseudonyms. These anagrammatic pseudonyms all turned out, as Echtermeyer had shown, to be anagrams for various forms of the author's true name. These pseudonyms include German Schleifheim von Sulsfort, Samuel Greiffnsohn von Hirschfeld, Melchior Sternfels von Fuchshaim, Philarchus Grossus von Trommenheim auf Griffsberg, Michael Reculin von Sehmsdorff, Erich Stainfels von Grufensholm, Simon Leugfrisch von Hertenfels, Israel Fromschmidt von Hugenfels, and Signeur Messmahl. In addition, one novel appeared under a list of letters (a c eee ff g hh ii ll mm nn oo rr sss t uu), which, when re-arranged, also indicate that Grimmelshausen was the author. There are, of course, hints in several of Grimmelshausen's own works, but all the older reference works and encyclopedias, including Zedler's famously informative sixty-eight volume *Universal-Lexikon aller Wissenschaften und Künste* (1732–1754, reprint 1961–64) listed basically only one work each under (each of) these pseudonyms.

Grimmelshausen's acknowledged masterpiece, *Der abentheuerliche Simplicissimus Teutsch,* tells the life story of the hero, Simplicius Simplicissimus. The work is written in part on the model of the Spanish picaresque novel, so that the viewpoint is that of the boy, though the ultimate vantage point is that of a much older man writing in melancholy isolation. Particularly interesting are the descriptions of various scenes and battles from the Thirty Years' War, many of which were so realistically portrayed that readers and scholars thought, mistakenly as it turned out, that Grimmelshausen must have experienced them himself. Indeed, many readers and scholars have, again mistakenly, considered the life of the hero of the story to be the life of Grimmelshausen himself, perhaps the more so since the novel covers a period during which we know little of Grimmelshausen's own life. The arrangement of the lengthy novel is in six books. The first five books of the novel appeared in the first edition (1668), but the sixth book appeared almost immediately afterward (1669). Discussion in the research literature has centered around the structure of the novel. There have been lengthy controversies about whether or not the sixth book is an integral part of the whole or whether it is more an interesting, but perhaps not wholly essential appendage.[4] Curt von Faber du Faur even noted that Grimmelshausen had "spoiled the harmony of the original make-up" of the novel by adding a sixth book, and he lays the blame squarely on the "ordinary and greedy publisher of the novel" (Felssecker) (Faber du Faur 1 286).

Simplicissimus relates the life story of the hero, practically from his birth till he dies as a hermit on a remote island. We see Simplicius, the young boy, meeting with a hermit in the woods after he was forced to flee from his "Knan" and "Meuder" (figures one might regard as parents). For some time, he lives with the hermit, who teaches him to read, to pray, to value Christian virtues. The hermit also gives him a considerable amount of advice, including an important maxim: "Kenne dich selbst." After the hermit dies, Simplicius leaves the "home" he has had in the woods and ends up (not voluntarily, one might add) with the forces of Governor Ramsey in Hanau. It turns out that Ramsey knew of the hermit (had even seen to it that the hermit received food and other items necessary for life), and a series of coincidences allow Ramsey to discover who Simplicius really is, although he does not reveal this information to the young lad. In the meantime, Simplicius takes on the clothes and demeanor of a fool, during which time he realizes that the "fools" are the "real" people and the so-called real people are actually the fools. He is introduced to life in Hanau, but is shy; he does not know how to act in society.

Gradually he learns the rules of the game and begins to make his way in the world. However, as he learns more of the world and how to conduct himself, he begins, in an inverse proportion, to forget the rules of Christian virtues taught him by the hermit. During the time in which he takes on the role of "Jäger von Soest," and during which he is at the height of his worldly power and wealth, he is, at the same time, at the very nadir of his life as a Christian. Along the way, Simplicius meets with a number of influential characters, including the "fool" Jupiter, from whom he learns how things might be, how the world might be governed. A similar learning experience is provided for Simplicius in the "Mummelsee" episode, when he meets with the sylphs. They, too, describe for him an ideal community type of life, quite unlike that to which he has become accustomed on earth. Although these two sections do not belong to the "action line" of the novel, they are important, as is the later description of the Anabaptist community in Hungary. All three provide utopian visions of what might be, visions of alternatives to the life that Simplicius and his contemporaries live in Germany during the Thirty Years' War. Simplicius also has a pleasurable stint in Paris, during which he assumes the role of "Beau Alman," and during which his sexual experiences dominate. As the story continues, however, he gives up that role, as he had given up the role of Jäger von Soest, and decides to return to a hermit-like existence on a desert island.

There, he will be free of the temptations of the world and free to live a life devoted to Christian virtues. In a way, Simplicius goes full circle, from a hermit-like existence in the woods with the hermit, who turns out to be his father, to a hermit-like existence on an island, after he has gone through various stages of development. Still, he does not learn to live *in* the world, but returns instead to a hermit's existence on a deserted island. The manuscript of the novel, *Simplicissimus,* was supposedly taken back to civilization by the captain of a Dutch vessel that visited the island where Simplicissimus had been residing. The entire novel is filled with clever and funny incidents, but they are often taken from other sources and, hence, they have more a representational character than that they tell us specifically about Simplicissimus as an individual or, even much less, about Grimmelshausen himself.

Because of the five books in the novel, early research posited a kind of dramatic structure within the novel. This, of course, had to leave out the sixth book, the *Continuatio,* from the interpretation. This interpretation was basically the work of the Dutch scholar, Jan Hendrik Scholte, who equated each book of *Simplicissimus* with one act of a five-act tragedy. The idea of the dramatic structure is perhaps the oldest of the attempts to interpret the novel from a structural viewpoint, but others have continued to appear. Johannes Alt (1936) developed Scholte's interpretation further and found a certain "Typenfolge" in the five books. Rather than one book being the equivalent of one act, Alt saw the dividing lines more or less at the middle of each book, rather than at the end of the book. Some scholars have regarded the novel as a satire, with emphasis on the episode in which Simplicius is dressed like, and acts like, a fool, as well as with reference to the entire style of writing. Others have considered it a utopian novel, with the utopian sections being the Jupiter episode, the Mummelsee episode, and the description of the Anabaptists in Hungary. The possibility that it is an *Entwicklungsroman* has also been considered, but based on the hero's failure to return to the real world and come to terms with it, this interpretation is probably not viable. Faber du Faur termed it a "combination of the novel of adventure with the picaresque novel and the educational novel" (I 288).

The latest, and perhaps the most controversial, theory has to do with a planetary structure. Both the American Germanist Helmut Rehder and the German academic Günther Weydt proposed this theory more or less simultaneously.[5] Particularly important in this regard are the "Planeten-kindschafts-Bilder," a series of woodcuts illustrating each of the known planets and a number of characteristics of each as well. These illustrations seem to have originated in Italy, and then came to Germany where they "stellen [. . .] den jeweiligen Sterngott in verschiedenen Haltungen über einer Genreszene mit seinen 'Kindern' dar" (Berghaus und Weydt 156). Weydt believed that the illustrations done by Georg Pencz, a student of Albrecht Dürer, probably represent one of the series of illustrations that served Grimmelshausen as a source.

Using a slight variation on the Chaldean system of the planets (the series thus becomes Saturn, Mars, Sun, Jupiter, Venus, Mercury, and Moon), Weydt begins his interpretation by associating Cologne with the planet Jupiter. This fits in with the depiction in his *Ewig-währender Calender* and with the ancient system of assigning various geographical areas to certain planets. Cologne is, of course, one of the main settings for some of the important action within the novel. There are, to be sure, additional reasons for assigning Cologne to Saturn, including the fact that the fool, interestingly enough named Jupiter, lives there as well. From there, Weydt goes on to show how there are seven parts to the *Simplicissimus* novel, each based on, and centered around, one of the planets. The hero of the novel, Simplicius, is caught up in the antithesis between constancy, a characteristic of Saturn, and inconstancy, a characteristic of the Moon. The whole idea of constancy is central not only to this novel ("there is nothing more constant than inconstancy") but also to literature of the seventeenth century in general.

The influence of the planets on the structure of the novels of Grimmelshausen, especially in, but not limited to his main novel, *Simplicissimus,* is perhaps most clearly summed up by Klaus Haberkamm. He writes "Sieht man von kleineren Verwertungen des einschlägigen Wissens wie in seiner Schrift 'Gauckel-Tasche' (1670) ab, findet sich nach dem gegenwärtigen Forschungsstand insbesondere im 'Simplicissimus' und im 'Springinsfeld,' also in den sechs ersten und im achten Buch des simplicianischen Zehnerzyklus, bedeutsame Integration der Astrologische ins Epische: Die Strukturen des großen Romans und der kleinen, mit ihm eng verbundenen Simpliciade sind nicht zuletzt astrologisch bestimmt" (Haberkamm 151). There have been two very strong opponents of this theory in the research literature, one in Germany, one in the United States. The former is Gerhard Lemke, the latter Blake Lee Spahr.[6] Volker Meid, who has written one of the most useful reference works on Grimmelshausen, refers to Lemke's article as a "fundierte Auseinandersetzung," and to Spahr's as a "gelegentlich polemische Auseinandersetzung" (Meid, 96 and 98). Although other scholars also remain unconvinced as to whether Grimmelshausen consciously used an astrological structure in his Simplician novels, students of Weydt have continued to hold fast to the theory. Haberkamm, who was cited above and is a student of Weydt, continues his investigations into the planetary structure in Grimmelshausen's novels in his contribution to this volume, although in this contribution considerable emphasis is placed on the role of prophecies.

Other areas of investigation of the *Simplicissimus* include questions as to the literary sources of the novel: not only Moscherosch's *Gesichte Philanders von Sittewald* of 1640, the Spanish picaresque novel, Sidney's *Arcadia,* and possibly even Wolfram's *Parzifal* have been demonstrated as certain or likely sources. Also of scholarly interest is the "Erzählhaltung," that is, the narrator's role in the telling of the tale. The latter interest stems from the fact that we find various levels of narration within the novel, for example, Simplicissimus as a young man, Simplicissimus as an older man remembering his youth and reflecting on it, the perspective of the author himself, and others. Many articles have also been written about the engraved copperplate, the satyr-like figure and the rhymed verses below it (see especially Paas, Habersetzer, and Penkert). It was perhaps fitting that the Deutsche Bundespost picked a stylized reproduction of this satyr-like figure from the *Simplicissimus* frontispiece as the topic for the postage stamp commemorating Grimmelshausen on the occasion of the 300th anniversary of his death in 1976. Although the stamp is clearly based on the copperplate, much of the design is very different. The open book carries Grimmelshausen's name, and some of the individual items originally portrayed in the open book now grace the top of the postage stamp. The possible role of Grimmelshausen in designing some of his title pages and engravings as well as interpretation of these images are among the subjects covered in Shannon Keenan Greene's essay in this volume.

Grimmelshausen's masterpiece, his *Simplicissimus,* is surely the only Baroque novel, perhaps the only German novel at all, to be the subject of a rather lengthy and hefty debate in the Prussian (German) parliament.[7] It was the so-called "Simplicissimus-Debate" that occurred within the *Kulturkampf* associated with the beginnings of the Second Empire and Otto von Bismarck-Schönhausen (1815–1898). The entire affair was precipitated by a decree of the Prussian State Minister of Culture, Adalbert Falk (1827–1900), dated 22 January 1876, according to which a number of literary works were recommended for purchase and use by schools in Prussia. As Minister of Culture, Falk was directly involved in translating into law the measures dealing with culture that had been recommended by Bismarck, in particular those that were aimed at diminishing the influence of the Roman Catholic Church (*Kulturkampf*). Among the books that Falk recommended we find Grimmelshausen's novel, not, of course, as it had originally been published, but in a reworking for use by Prussia's youth, edited by Elard Hugo Meyer. When it came time for the budgetary discussions (including funds for the purchase of these literary works), there was considerable debate as to whether Falk had correctly recommended the "purified" version of the work or whether it ought not instead to be condemned as "seelenmörderisch," the word used by the centrist member of the parliament, Baron von Schorlemer-Alst. Interestingly, the representatives seem at first to have been less interested in the novel itself than in this particular version of the novel for this particular purpose. Later, however, the novel as such was the subject of debate, and the *Germania,* organ of the central party, recommended that the book not be read by Prussia's youths, "weil es eben nichts Anderes ist, als eine Zusammenstellung von Zoten und Unlauterkeiten aus dem wüsten Leben eines Landknechtes des 30 jährigen Krieges" (cited in Berghaus and Weydt 218). It even almost came, in the ensuing discussions, to the point that von Schorlemer-Alst would ask that the public be barred from the discussions, in case he had to provide some quotes from *Simplicissimus* to make his point! When it came to the actual debate, he noted that the novel contained more than two hundred pages of "Irrfahrten, Liebesabenteuer, Diebstahl, Unzucht, Mord, Bruch des Fahneneides" and the like, whereas the conversion and atonement was given "nur sehr wenige Seiten" (both cited in Berghaus and Weydt 218). Needless to say, Baron von Schorlemer-Alst was a representative of the aristocratic, conservative wing of parliament. At one point, it was recommended that all members of parliament read the novel, in order that they might be able to make a reasoned judgment. There were certainly several factors involved in the debate, not the least of which might well be the fact that the Roman Catholic Church had put the *Simplicissimus* on its *Index librorum prohibitorum*. Recommending precisely such a book would have a definite impact on the relations between the church and the state in Prussia and was meant to minimize, if not strangle, the influence of the church. Not only in the parliament did discussions take place, as we see in the daily press of the time. A few days after the debate, a letter appeared in *Kladderadatsch,* a letter supposedly by Melchior Sternfels von Fuchsheim to Baron von Schorlemer-Alst. He writes:

> Ich sag'es Euch rund heraus, Herr, daß Ihr mich schwer gekränkt habt. Nach dem Reinigungsprocesse, dem mein Bearbeiter mich unterzogen hat, war ich wohl der Art, um auch einer Jungfer — und eine solche seid Ihr doch sicher nicht — unter die Augen treten zu können. [. . .] Aber ich darf Euch verzeihen, da Ihr [. . .] meine Geschichte nicht gelesen habt und nur vom Hören-sagen urtheilt. Leset meinetwegen das ungesäuberte Original des alten Grimmelshausen; es wird Euch so wenig schaden wie einem berliner Professor der Medizin, der doch auch sonst nicht so zipp ist. Und Ihr wart ein Reiter!" (cited in Berghaus and Weydt 220–21 from Kladderadatsch 29 [21 March 1876], 59)

Needless to say, the popularity of Grimmelshausen's novel was assured after all the attention caused by the debate, and that popularity has continued to the present day.

Grimmelshausen's Other Works

The second most popular novel, *Courasche* (probably 1670), deals with a female hero, a pícara in her own right, whose chief characteristic seems to be that she has more husbands and partners than one can easily count. The structure of this novel has elicited much comment, and indeed the planetary or astrologically influenced structure has been suggested for it as well (see especially the work of Haberkamm 1972). However, there is also an excellent study dealing with the "vierfacher Schriftsinn," an exegetical interpretation based on the fourfold interpretation, or understanding, of Jerusalem in the bible. The story concerns Courasche, a suttler, who follows the troops throughout the war. She continues to lose one husband after another, is in part a whore, but she also appears to be much more faithful and loyal to those husbands who treat her as an individual rather than as a sex object. The continuing downfall of the heroine is clearly reflected in the diminishing rank of each of her successive husbands, until, finally, she marries a gypsy. The tale was no doubt influenced by the Spanish *Pícara Justina* of Andreas Pérez (see the work of Christoph E. Schweitzer in this volume), although the main influence seems to be that he chose a female hero. The story itself, set as with many of Grimmelshausen's works against the backdrop of the Thirty Years' War, seems to have been more strongly influenced by the works of Georg Philipp Harsdörffer (1607–1658) and historical works dealing with the war. Much has been made of the title, *Trutz Simplex,* as Courasche seems to want to "outdo" Simplicissimus, who made the mistake of insulting her in *Simplicissimus Teutsch.* In contrast to Simplicissimus, Grimmelshausen does not use the same type of reflection on the part of the hero. There are, to be sure, the introductory lines preceding each chapter, and there is the "Zugab des Autors" at the end. The difference lies not in the fact that Grimmelshausen has a different attitude, but rather that the hero here (Courasche) is not at all the same type of hero we see in Simplicissimus. He regretted his earlier life, made amends, and became a "good guy," whereas Courasche indicates no regret at all. Indeed, she seems to revel in her life, and in all that that life brought her. The "Zugab des Autors" does contain words of warning for young men and older men, but, interestingly, not for young women, who might be instrumental in leading the men astray. Meid refers to the "Frauenfeindlichkeit" (161) of Grimmelshausen, but there has been at least one attempt to "save" Courasche and put some, if not most, of the blame on the men in the novel.[8]

The remaining works of Grimmelshausen are much less well known than these works, but the other Simplician works are quite important in understanding the message of the entire work, which can be considered to consist of ten books, not just six. The works that are considered part of the Simplician complex, to which Grimmelshausen himself makes reference, are *Courasche, Springinsfeld* (1670) and the two parts of the *Wunderbarliches Vogelnest.* The reference of Grimmelshausen himself is found in his introduction ("Vorrede") to the second part of the *Wunderbarliches Vogelnest* (1675), where he writes:

> Sonsten wäre dieses billich das zehende Theil oder Buch deß Abentheuerlichen Simplicissimi Lebens-Beschreibung/ wann nemlich die Courage vor das siebende/ der Spring ins Feld vor das achte/ und das erste part deß wunderbarlichen Vogel-Nests vor das neundte Buch genommen würde/ sintemahl alles von diesen Simplicianischen Schriften aneinander hängt/ und weder der gantze Simplicissimus, noch eines auß den obengemeldten letzten Tractätlein allein ohne solche Zusammenfügung genugsam verstanden werden mag. (WV II 150)

There is considerable question as whether the ten books actually form a true cycle or not. Meid, for example, notes that there are major differences in "Erzählweise und Kompositionsprinzipien der einzelnen Bücher" (155), but also says that one cannot expect the same kind of inner unity in seventeenth-century works that one might expect in the twentieth century (Meid 155).

Springinsfeld is one of the husbands, perhaps better, partners of Courasche, a man whose name stems from the first command given him by Courasche ("Spring ins Feld"). He is really not her equal in any way and their partnership contract reflects her status as the one who "wears the pants." In the novel itself, Simplicissimus has returned to Europe and he meets his old soldier buddy, Springinsfeld, whose life story is every bit as picaresque as that of either Simplicissimus himself or of Courasche. Springinsfeld is pictured on the engraved title page as a cripple, playing the violin (or fiddle). This characterizes his state when he and Simplicissimus meet in the novel. There is here, as in most of Grimmelshausen's works a clear moral, since Simplicissimus returns as a Christian who has made good, whereas Springinsfeld has neither repentance nor guilt about his life. Indeed, the contrast is so clear that every reader sees the moral, without Grimmelshausen having to call it to our attention. This novel bridges in a way the *Courasche* with the *Wunderbarliches Vogelnest*. The two parts of the *Wunderbarliches Vogelnest* relate the adventures (both good and bad) of the person who is in possession of the enchanted or magical bird's nest, which makes the owner invisible. This bird's nest had been mentioned in *Springinsfeld,* but here it becomes the center of the story. In contrast to the other parts of the Simplician cycle, these two novels take place during times of peace. At the heart of the novels is the motto "Der Wahn betrügt." Earth and especially its pleasures are intent on tricking man into believing that they represent significant and lasting values. Eternity, God is repeatedly shown to be, or to be the key to, the true meaning of the universe. The hero of the story attempts to destroy the nest at the end of the novel, because he has been converted from his godless ways, but another character still takes up the remains of the nest. That leads us to the second part of the novel, which is the last work of Grimmelshausen (1675). This part is less moralizing, but in the end the hero also returns to the fold, giving up his evil ways and asking a cleric to destroy the nest.

Simplician writings outside the narrower confines of the Simplician cycle are many in number. Let us consider those briefly, before we move on to the non-Simplician works. In 1670 two works appeared: *Beernhäuter* and *Gauckel-Tasche.* The *Beernhäuter* tells of a mercenary who, in return for wearing the bearskin for seven years without washing and without doing several other things, ends up rich and famous. The story is not new with Grimmelshausen; it is an old fairy-tale motive. The *Gauckel-Tasche,* on the other hand, which appeared together with the *Beernhäuter,* is meant as a help or an aid for traveling entertainers, barkers, and minstrels as well as those who read horoscopes and otherwise entertain the public. The work is really a series of individual illustrations and accompanying verses that deal with various vices and evils. Those researchers who support the astrological and planetary structure of *Simplicissimus* and *Courasche* also have found support in the *Gauckel-Tasche* for their theories, especially in the various astrological signs within the illustrations. The year 1672 was a most productive one for Grimmelshausen, as several of his works appeared that year. *Des Abenteuerlichen Simplicii Verkehrte Welt* (1672) deals with the change of this world into an infernal life. The punishment to be dealt out to sinful mankind is painted in allegorical fashion. The author denounces various vices and sins of humankind, but also points out what fate might await those who reprint, in pirate fashion, his volume! His *Rathstübel Plutonis oder Kunst, reich zu werden* (1672) is written in the form of a *Gesprächspiel,* based on the example of Harsdörffer. The influence of Harsdörffer's work can even be seen in the engraved copper plate at the front of the book. Grimmelshausen claims on the title page that the work stems "aus Simplicissimi Brunnquell" and that it is "auffrecht Simplicianisch beschrieben." The palette of topics ranges from satire to polite conversation, to moral teachings. The particular appeal of the work, however, lies in the fact that it begins to approach the "Lebenswirklichkeit des Dichters und die souveräne Verbindung von Dichtung und Wahrheit" (Weydt 1971, 84) as almost no other work except the *Simplicissimus* itself. The *Stoltzer Melcher* (1672) relates the tale of an idler who, suffering from homesickness, listens to the conversation of three soldiers. The manner in which Melcher tells of the horrors of war is enough to scare the idler from considering a life as soldier. The work was a timely piece, for Louis XIV was attempting to hire mercenaries for the French army to assist him in the war against the Netherlands.

Grimmelshausen's *Bart-Krieg* appeared the following year (on 1 January!) and is unusual in that the name of the author is not contained in it at all. Gustav Könnecke, however, on the basis of parallels with other works of the author, was able to determine that the work was that of Grimmelshausen. Some characters, for example, the inn-keeper Schrepffeisen, appear in the *Ewig-währender Calender* as well as in *Wunderbarliches Vogelnest I.* Simplicissimus and the author (who has a yellow-colored beard) get into a fight about the appearance of red beards. The *Teutscher Michel* also appeared in 1673, one of the more interesting theoretical works of the author. This is the only publication of Grimmelshausen in which he deals with the German language itself. Most all the contemporary problems facing German come to life, including those with which the so-called *Sprachgesellschaften* were forced to grapple, namely, the knowledge of other languages, the purity of the contemporary German language, and others. As in some of his other writings, Tomaso Garzoni's *Allgemeiner Schauplatz* as well as writings of Hans Michael Moscherosch (1601–1669) and Georg Philipp Harsdörffer (1607–1658) seem to have been Grimmelshausen's main sources. Finally, in the same year, the author's *Galgen-Männlin* appeared. In terms of theme and form it seems related to the *Teutscher Michel*, but in terms of overall content, *Courasche* (Chapter 18) and *Springinsfeld* (Chapter 13) seem more closely related to it. The main topic of conversation here is the mandrake root, which appears in the works of many other authors in the seventeenth century as well, perhaps most clearly in those of Johannes Praetorius (1630–1680). The work also includes items that show its relationship to Simplicissimus, namely a letter that Simplicissimus supposedly wrote to his son. The work actually functions as a warning against becoming involved in magic and related areas of endeavor.

There are, of course, a number of works in which the figure of Simplicius plays no role whatsoever. The very first work that Grimmelshausen published, *Satyrischer Pilgram* (1667), picks up a motive that one sees already in the work of the famous Reformation era poet from Nuremberg, Hans Sachs (1494–1576) and other authors. There, a pilgrim is able to use his breath not only to warm his cold hands, but also to cool a hot drink. It is this aspect of two-sidedness that is the topic of Grimmelshausen's work.[9] More interesting perhaps is the structure, because Grimmelshausen provides the positive aspects of a given item, then the negative ones, and, finally, in a third section a summary, which generally gives us the author's own opinion. Within the two volumes, there are ten different topics with which the author deals.

One of the best-known novels of Grimmelshausen, apart from the cycle of Simplician novels, is his treatment of the biblical story of Joseph, *Histori vom Keuschen Joseph* (1667), and a heavily revised second edition, *Des Vortrefflich Keuschen Josephs in Egypten [. . .] Lebensbeschreibung* (1670), to which Grimmelshausen added the story of Musai, an architect at the Pharaoh's court. Interestingly, this figure of Musai resembles more closely the picaresque figures of Courasche or Springinsfeld than he does the courtly figure of Joseph. Grimmelshausen's contemporary Adam Olearius (1603–1671) provided the source for many of the tidbits of information about the strange and exotic places that we find here (the majority of which have only a secondary or tertiary connection with the plot). The first edition of the novel was the first treatment in a German novel of the figure of Joseph, whom we know from Genesis (v. 37–50), and it was followed rather quickly by another novel, *Assenat* by Philipp von Zesen (1619–1689). Both Grimmelshausen's *Histori vom keuschen Joseph* and Zesen's *Assenat* are among the few German baroque novels that were translated early on into other Germanic languages. Grimmelshausen's novel was rendered into Swedish (1690, 1696, and 1767), and Zesen's into Danish (a handwritten translation by Morton Nielsen from 1680 and another, printed translation that was published in 1711, 1729, 1746, 1755, 1767, and 1776). It is surely no coincidence that in this novel, as well as in the two to be discussed shortly, humility is the virtue that plays the most important role.

This first courtly novel of Grimmelshausen was then followed by two later novels, *Dietwalts und Amelinden anmuthige Lieb- und Leids-Beschreibung* (1670) and *Proximi und Lympidae Liebs-Geschicht-Erzehlung* (1672). Although the *Histori vom keuschen Joseph* appeared under one of Grimmelshausen's many pseudonyms (Samuel Greifnson vom Hirschfeld), both of these novels carried some version of his real name, Hans Jacob Christoffel von Grimmelshausen, and both indicate that he was born in Gelnhausen ("Gelnhusano"). Various scholars have seen in the use of Grimmelshausen's actual name an attempt on his part to ingratiate himself with members of the lesser nobility from his own area. Grimmelshausen could not, of course, claim to belong to that nobility, but he seems anxious to legitimize himself in their eyes. Both of the novels are dedicated to members of the lesser nobility, more particularly to members of the family who employed him for many years. His *Dietwalt und Amelinde* is dedicated to Philipp Hannibal von Schauenburg, to whom he owed much, and his *Proximus und Lympida* to Maria Dorothea von Schauenburg. These are not Simplician novels, but they do not fall into any other generally recognized class of novels either. Generally, scholars refer to them as "Idealromane" (e.g., Meid, 184 and passim). Meid notes, however, that the term generally used to describe them structurally, "Idealromane" is not really an accurate descriptor, but instead little more than a "Verlegenheitslösung" (184). Because "Idealromane" is used to describe or characterize these novels, we know that they, in some way, do not fulfill the definition of "höfische" or "höfisch-historische" novels that are used as the generic category for other seventeenth-century novels (Meid 185). Meid notes that Grimmelshausen is not alone in attempting to bridge novels with edificatory writings (186), as we see similar attempts in the works of Aegidius Albertinus (ca. 1560–1620) and Andreas Heinrich Buchholtz (1607–1671). Grimmelshausen's *Dietwalt und Amelinde,* set during the era of the great migrations, is clearly more than a novel that bridges fiction and edification. It is a political novel as well as other things, since the title page indicates it deals with the "*Vergrösserung des Weltberühmten Königreichs Franckreich*" (DA, title page).

Grimmelshausen takes care to provide, as was the tradition going back to at least the Middle Ages (one need only think of Wolfram von Eschenbach and his *Parzival*), an accounting of the sources he used in writing the work. The novel was considered to be "den Gottseeligen erbaulich, Curiosen lustig, Historicus [*sic*] annemlich, Betrübten tröstlich, Verliebten erfreulich, Politicis nützlich und der Jugend ohnärgerlich zu lesen" (PL, title page), and hence was meant for a wide range of readers. *Proximus und Lympida* seems to have had the same purpose, as the title page of this work notes it is "Vornemlich den vorhandenen Alten und Jungen: Aeltern und Kindern/ zur Richtschnur/ Lehr- und Nachfolgung: den Betrübten und Verliebten zum tröstlichen Beispiel: den Curiosen und Müssigen zur Ergetz- und Ehrlichen Zeitvertreibung: sonst jedermänniglich aber zum Nutzen und Christlicher Aufferbauung" (PL, Title page). It is really an edificatory work, but it is based on a legend that Grimmelshausen also uses in his *Rathstübel Plutonis*. Here in *Proximus und Lympida,* too, we have the world of the court, but it is the court of the Eastern Roman Empire, later the Ottoman Empire. We see the same things, however, that one sees in the west: murder, political intrigue, attempts to grab power, lack of trust, as well as other traits that sometimes characterize the world of the nobility in the baroque era. Those who are steadfast in virtue (especially the parents of Proximus, Modestus und Honoria — their names are not accidental — as well as Proximus und Lympida themselves) have to contend with the temptations of the world in order that they might finally participate in the glory of a virtuous life at a virtuous court.

The only other work that carries the real name of Grimmelshausen is the *Ratio Status* (1670), in which he investigates four biblical characters: Jonathan, Saul, Joab, and David. The basis for the discussion is, as one might expect from the title, an attempt to take into account the theories of Machiavelli, to see how one might separate politics from religion. Saul is portrayed as the ineffective Machiavellian in contrast to David, who is pictured as the person whose example we should follow in terms of politics. It is the absolute trust in God that provides David with whatever he needs, whenever he needs it. The same topic is, of course, taken up in *Simplicissimus,* in the figure of Olivier. The article of Andreas Solbach in this volume deals not only with *Ratio Status,* but also with the non-Simplician novels in general.

A separate category altogether has to be reserved for Grimmelshausen's *Ewig-währender Calender* (1670 [recte 1671]). Rosmarie Zeller's essay in this *Companion to Grimmelshausen* deals extensively with the work, which has been investigated in its own right only in the last twenty or so years. As Zeller points out in her essay, the complete calendar is not contained in either of the collected works or standard editions. Haberkamm did edit a reprint, and he provided an excellent introduction to the work as well. Still, overall, research on the calendar has been rather scant, despite its relative importance within the corpus of Grimmelshausen's works. This is especially true when we consider the large amount of information one finds there dealing with the planets and hence the opportunities for finding additional information to support the hypotheses about an astrological structure for the novels of Grimmelshausen. In this regard, the conversations with Johannes Indagine (Johann Rosenbach vom Hayn) are probably the most fruitful. The "ewig-währende" or perpetual calendars precede our annual calendars by quite some time. The Christian martyrologies and the calendar of saints' feast days seem to have served as models for Grimmelshausen. The calendar also contains a wealth of biographical information, probably more important for the biography of Grimmelshausen himself than for that of Simplicissimus (Berghaus und Weydt 130). The literary importance of the calendars of Grimmelshausen is probably seen most clearly in the "Kalendargeschichten," a number of short mostly prose pieces, which seem to elude precise description and classification (Meid 173). Grimmelshausen himself calls them either "Stücklein" or "Schwänke," but they are both more and less than either of these. Weydt refers to them as apophthegmata and he perhaps comes closest in trying to define them. It is "eine kurze und pointierte Form der Äußerung, die vornehmlich in der Konversation der gehobenen Gesellschaft gepflegt wird, zu der 'vermittelst gesunder menschlicher Vernunft' aber auch der 'gemeine Mann' befähigt ist" (Weydt, 368).

The *Companion to Grimmelshausen*

The contributions included in this *Companion to Grimmelshausen* are written by many of the foremost scholars interested in Grimmelshausen, as well as by younger scholars with a similar bent. They do not present a total or unified *Stand der Forschung* with regard to Grimmelshausen today, nor is that the intention of the volume. Rather, the articles focus on individual problems and approaches to the study of the author. Some of the essays are truly seminal, while others take a known approach and apply it to a different work. Each of them can and, I hope, will function as an impetus to further research. Some of these studies deal with a particular aspect within the corpus of Grimmelshausen's works. Schweitzer's work on the editions discusses problems in editing as well as touching on various translations. His second contribution (on the Spanish influence in the works of Grimmelshausen) points out the degree to which Grimmelshausen was indebted to Spanish sources and the degree to which he operated independently. Battafarano, on the other hand, provides a detailed investigation of the convergence of biography and novel narrative, in an attempt to show the degree to which they are intertwined. Haberkamm, as noted above, offers a well-argued case for the astrological and planetary structure in the works of Grimmelshausen, based on the original work by his mentor Günther Weydt. Haberkamm's main concern in his contribution is the role that prophecy plays in *Simplicissimus Teutsch*. Zeller delves into the world of Grimmelshausen's calendar, showing us what such calendars looked like and how we can best understand them. Solbach tackles the interpretation of the non-Simplician works, especially the three novels. The essay by Dieter Breuer — perhaps the one with the greatest breadth — shows the influence that Grimmelshausen has had since his own day in literature, in art, in music, in history, and in general. Tatlock and Hess both use very modern approaches in their articles, Tatlock taking a feminist perspective and Hess discussing in detail the role of clothing and the construction of gender in the Grimmelshausen's *Simplicissimus*. Greene provides fresh insight into the often-discussed dilemma of the copperplate engravings for Grimmelshausen's works. She spends some time dealing with the satyr-like figure in *Simplicissimus*, but provides detailed analyses, too, of other title pages, e.g., *Springinsfeld* and *Courasche*. Menhennet looks at the Simplician Weltanschauung, characterized in part by philosophy, but in part, too, by the vicissitudes of life in general. Breuer's essay is the only one that has appeared previously, albeit in German. It was translated for the first time for inclusion in this volume. All other articles were invited essays, written especially for this volume.

Notes

[1] There are two rather differing biographies of Grimmelshausen of relatively recent vintage. One is Günter Weydt. *Hans Jacob Christoffel von Grimmelshausen*. Metzler Realienbücher. 2nd ed. Stuttgart: Metzler, 1979 and the biography section of Volker Meid. *Grimmelshausen: Epoche — Werk — Wirkung*. Munich: Beck, 1984. In addition, the biography by Eberhard Mannack, "Hans Jacob Christoffel von Grimmelshausen," *Deutsche Dichter des 17. Jahrhunderts. Ihr Leben und Werk*. Ed. Benno von Wiese und Harald Steinhagen. Berlin 1984, 517–52 can be strongly recommended as well. There are also two basic bibliographies. For works of Grimmelshausen see Gerhard Dünnhaupt. *Bibliographisches Handbuch der Barockliteratur*. Stuttgart: Hiersemann, 1980–81 and for the works about Grimmelshausen see, Italo Michele Battafarano (und Hildegard Eilert). *Grimmelshausen-Bibliographie 1666–1972. Werk — Fiorschung — Wirkungsgeschichte*. Neapel: Istituto universitario orientale, 1975. A new updated version of the last mentioned work is scheduled to appear, and in fact may appear either before or simultaneously with this volume.

[2] There is a short biographical sketch of Küffer in Berghaus und Weydt, 80, and a copperplate engraving of him is in the same volume, 83.

[3] See the excellent discussion of the entire unraveling of the story in Berghaus and Weydt, 225–30. This section of the introduction relies heavily on the Berghaus and Weydt presentation.

[4] One of the better and more successful attempts to show the ways in which the sixth book does indeed belong to the story as a whole is the work on *Geheimpoetik* by Hubert Gersch, even though one might not agree with all the details. Gersch showed how the sixth book might actually function as a key to understanding the first five books.

[5] Helmut Rehder, "Planetenkinder: Some Problems of Character Portrayal in Literature," *The Graduate Journal* (Austin TX) 8 (1968): 69–97; Günther Weydt, "Planetensymbolik im barocken Roman. Versuch einer Entschlüsselung des Simplicissimus Teutsch," *Doitsu Bungaku. Die deutsche Literatur* 36 (1966): 1–14. Both articles deal with the planetary structure, albeit in a differing series of planets (the same planets in both cases, but the order differing in the two articles).

[6] The literary discussion among these scholars is to be found in their various contributions to *Argenis,* a journal edited by John D. Lindberg, and of which only two volumes appeared. Spahr's article is entitled "Grimmelshausen's Simplicissimus. Astrological Structure," *Argenis* 1 (1977), 7–26; Lemke's carries the title "Die Astrologie in den Werken Grimmelshausen und seine Interpreten. Zur Diskussion über den Sternenglauben in der barocken Dichtung," *Argenis* 1 (1977), 61–105. Weydt's response appeared in the following volume under the title "*Und sie bewegen sich* [leider?] *doch!* Zu B. L. Spahrs — und G. Lemkes — Zweifeln an der Planetenstruktur des Simplicissimus," *Argenis* 2 (1978), 3–17.

[7] Again, I am indebted in this section to the work by Berghaus and Weydt, 216–24.

[8] John W. Jacobson. "A Defense of Grimmelshausen's *Courasche*," *German Quarterly* 41 (1968): 42–54.

[9] See the list of topics in the title of the book (chronological list of Grimmelshausen's works above).

Works Cited

Battafarano, Italo Michele (with Hildegard Eilert). *Grimmelshausen-Bibliographie: 1666–1672. Werk, Forschung, Wirkungsgeschichte.* Quaderni degli Annali dell' Istituto universitario orientale, Sezione germanica 9. Naples: Istituto universitario orientale, 1975.

Berghaus, Peter and Günther Weydt. *Simplicius Simplicissimus. Grimmelshausen und seine Zeit.* Ausstellungskatalog des Westfälischen Landesmuseum für Kunst und Kulturgeschichte Münster im Zusammenarbeit mit dem Germanistischen Institut der Westfälischen Wilhelms-Universität. Münster: Landschaftsverband Westfalen-Lippe, 1976.

Faber du Faur, Curt von. *German Baroque Literature, a Catalog of the Collection in the Yale University Library.* Two volumes. New Haven: Yale UP, 1958–1969.

Haberkamm, Klaus. "Grimmelshausen am Wendepunkt der astrologischen Tradition." In: Peter Berghaus and Günther Weydt. *Simplicius Simplicissimus. Grimmelshausen und seine Zeit.* Ausstellungskatalog des Westfälischen Landesmuseum für Kunst und Kulturgeschichte Münster im Zusammenarbeit mit dem Germanistischen Institut der Westfälischen Wilhelms-Universität. Münster: Landschaftsverband Westfalen-Lippe, 1976. 141–61.

———. *Sensus astrologicus. Zum Verhältnis von Literatur und Astrologie in Renaissance und Barock.* Abhandlungen zur Kunst-, Musik-, und Literaturwissenschaft 124. Bonn: Bouvier, 1972.

Habersetzer, Karl-Heinz. "'Ars Poetica Simpliciana.' Zum Titelkupfer des *Simplicissimus Teutsch*." *Daphnis* 3 (1974): 60–82 and 4 (1975): 51–78.

Meid, Volker. *Grimmelshausen. Epoche — Werk — Wirkung.* Beck'sche Elementarbücher: Arbeitsbücher für den literaturgeschichtlichen Unterricht. Munich: Beck, 1984.

Paas, John Roger. "Applied Emblematics: The Figure on the Simplicissimus-Frontispiece and its Place in Popular Devil-Iconography." *Colloquia Germanica* 13 (1980): 303–20.

Penkert, Sibylle. "Grimmelshausens Titelkupfer-Fiktionen. Zur Rolle der Emblematik-Rezeption in der Geschichte poetischer Subjektivität." *Dokumente des Internationalen Arbeitskreises für deutsche Barockliteratur.* Vol. 1. Wolfenbüttel: Herzog August Bibliothek, 1973. 52–75.

Rasch, Wolfdietrich, Hans Geulen, and Klaus Haberkamm, ed. *Rezeption und Produktion zwischen 1570 und 1730. Festschrift für Günther Weydt zum 65. Geburstag.* Bern and Munich: Francke, 1972.

Schäfer, Walter Ernst. "Der Satyr und die Satire. Zu Titelkupfern Grimmelshausens und Moscheroschs." *Rezeption und Produktion zwischen 1570 und 1730. Festschrift für Günther Weydt zum 65. Geburtstag.* Bern and Munich: Francke 1972. 185–193.

Wagener, Hans. "Johann Jacob Christoffel von Grimmelshausen." *Dictionary of Literary Biography* 168, *German Baroque Writers, 1661–1730* ed. James Hardin. Detroit, MI: Gale Research, 1996. 121–39.

Weydt, Günther. "Apophthegmata Teutsch. Über Ursprung und Wesen der 'Simplicianischen Scherzreden.'" *Festschrift für Jost Trier.* Ed. William Foerste and Karl Heinz Bock. Cologne and Graz: Böhlau, 1964. 364–85.

———. *Hans Jacob Christoffel von Grimmelshausen.* Sammlung Metzler 99. Stuttgart: Metzler, 1971.

I. Basics

Problems in the Editions of Grimmelshausen's Works

Christoph E. Schweitzer

Simplicissimus: A Survey of the Editions

THE INTEREST THE ROMANTICS SHOWED in *Simplicissmus* brought about the desire to make the novel available to the contemporary reader. With Ludwig Tieck's encouragement, Karl Eduard von Bülow published *Die Abenteuer des Simplicissimus* in 1836. It contained only the first five books and offered a rather altered text, which is discussed in more detail below. A number of scholars took issue with the edition and, as a consequence of their research, were able to establish the real name of the author. Von Bülow still thought that German Schleifheim von Sulsfort, the anagram Grimmelshausen used on the title page, was the author's real, given name.

Difficult, too, was the matter of finding out which of the editions of *Simplicissimus* that appeared during Grimmelshausen's lifetime was the first edition, the *editio princeps*. Wilhelm Ludwig Holland (1851) thought that the edition published by Georg Müller in 1669 was the first, the one on which to base his edition of the text. Rudolf Kögel used the same edition (1880) because he believed that the 1669 edition was based on an earlier edition that had been lost to posterity. According to Kögel, the text was revised — with Grimmelshausen's consent — to modernize the language and to reduce the number of dialect passages. We now know that Georg Müller published the novel without Grimmelshausen's knowledge and that he published his edition after the first edition, which had been printed by Wolff Eberhard Felssecker in Nuremberg. Just the same, as we shall see below, Georg Müller's text was to play a significant role in later editions of the novel that were, as far was we can ascertain, authorized by Grimmelshausen.

Basing their editions on the 1671 edition of Grimmelshausen's works were Heinrich Kurz (1863–64) and Felix Bobertag (*Deutsche National-Litteratur*, vols. 33–35, 1882–83). The first scholarly edition of *Simplicissimus* based on the 1668 Felssecker appeared in the "Bibliothek des Litterarischen Vereins in Stuttgart" in 1854 (vols. 33–34). Adelbert von Keller, the editor of this work, also included most of Grimmelshausen's other works and listed variants found in subsequent editions. Thus, Keller's text is still a valuable edition even today. In 1922, Hans Heinrich Borcherdt brought out an annotated edition of the so-called Simplician works, that is, *Simplicissimus Teutsch* (here he used the first edition), *Courasche, Springinsfeld,* and *Das wunderbarliche Vogelnest I* and *II,* but he also included two texts not written by Grimmelshausen. It has been shown that Balthasar Venator is the author of these two texts, *Seltzame Traum-Geschicht von Dir und Mir* and *Kurtze und Kurtzewilige Reise-Beschreibung nach der obern neuen Monds-Welt.* However, these two texts had both been included in the three posthumous editions of Grimmelshausen's works that appeared between 1683 and 1713.

Jan Hendrik Scholte, who specialized in research on Grimmelshausen, edited the most important works for the series *Neudrucke Deutscher Literaturwerke* between 1923 and 1943. Scholte's texts, based on careful justification for his readings, are still highly regarded. Since Scholte maintained that the end of Book V of *Simplicissimus* formed the true conclusion of the novel, he printed the *Continuatio* separately. The works published by Scholte were re-edited in the same series by Rolf Tarot, who, with the collaboration of Wolfgang Bender and Franz Günter Sieveke, added to the number of titles. Also, each decision as to how to read a certain word or passage was re-examined for this edition. Tarot's 1967 edition of *Simplicissimus* was analyzed by Ernst E. Müller, who came to the conclusion, after a thorough discussion of the various options, that some of Tarot's readings in which he disregarded Scholte's emendations and restored the original text, were ill advised, while others were a real improvement. Among the instances in which Müller disagrees with Tarot's restoration of the original text is the sentence in the *Continuatio* that describes how Julus treats his guests not "mit Kraut oder Stüben: Sonder mit theuren frantzösischen Bottagien [. . .]" (ST, 493). Tarot keeps "Stüben" whereas Scholte, and Keller before him, replaced the word with "Rüben." In a note, Tarot explains that "Stüben" is a "Name für Felchen im 2. Jahr" (ST 493). Müller, however, shows that "Stüben" is a technical term that is used exclusively in the Lake Constance area. Furthermore, manuscripts from the sixteenth and seventeenth centuries show that "St" and "R" are at times indistinguishable. Finally, Müller argues, only a word for something inexpensive would make sense in the sentence in question. "Felchen," though, would not be considered inexpensive (Müller 337–38). In 1984 Tarot published, again in the *Neudrucke* series, a revised edition of *Simplicissimus*. The latest critical edition of Grimmelshausen's works has been edited by Dieter Breuer in three volumes in the Deutscher Klassiker Verlag between 1989 and 1997. Since Tarot's and Breuer's editions are the only critical editions available at present and clearly also the most comprehensive, I will compare them below so as to delineate their characteristics.

A Chronology of the Early *Simplicissimus* Editions

As mentioned above, there was uncertainty for some time as to which of the six editions that appeared during Grimmelshausen's life should be considered the original one. With the help of the catalogues of the Frankfurt and Leipzig book fairs, it is possible to establish that the one printed by Wolff Eberhard Felssecker in Nürnberg is the first edition, the real *editio princeps*. This edition is dated 1669 but was already on the market in 1668; it carries the words "Monpelgart/ Gedruckt bey Johann Fillion" on the title page. That edition is referred to as E^1. It contains only the first five books, not the *Continuatio*. Its success made Felssecker rush into print another edition, which shows a number of new errors; this new edition is referred to as E^2. However, it includes the *Continuatio*, which was also printed separately, but at the same time, so that the owners of the original edition, the E^1, could also purchase it. The first printing of the *Continuatio* is normally referred to as Co. Then follows the unauthorized printing by Georg Müller (Frankfurt / Main 1669). It is referred to as E^{3a}. Georg Müller himself seems to have been responsible for the revision of E^1, supposedly using the recently published grammar by Christian Gueintz (1592–1650) as a guide. The result was a carefully edited text that did away with some of the dialect phrases of the original, revised certain grammatical forms, clarified some of the obscure passages, and standardized the orthography. Also, for the first time, the chapter summaries were moved to the beginning of each chapter. In the original, they were placed at the beginning of each book. Felssecker, in response, tried to beat the competition by stating in the title of the next edition that it contained a revised *Simplicissimus* "Mit seinem ewigwehrenden wunderbarlichen Calender/ auch anderen zu seinem Lebens-Lauf gehörigen Neben-Historien." However, the book as printed did not have either the "Calender" or the "Neben-Historien"; this edition, with the new title page, is referred to as E^4. The edition follows E^{3a} as to the placement of the chapter summaries. Edition E^4 also has an added preface in which the author takes issue with the emendations in the edition known as E^{3a}.

In 1671 Felssecker came out with a major revision of the text of *Simplicissimus,* thus creating the edition known as E^5. In addition to the famous frontispiece found in E^1 and subsequent editions, E^5 has a plate showing the four members of the Simplicissimus family (Simplicius himself is depicted twice, once as a boy and once as an adult). There are also twenty illustrations with rhymed verses at the bottom that explain the meaning of the picture above. Edition E^5 has a new and expanded preface in which "Simplicius Simplicissimus" again chides the unauthorized publication and draws attention to his other writings. Still, the 1671 printing incorporates many of the phrasings and other aspects of that unauthorized edition! Two examples will suffice to show the kinds of changes involved. The *editio princeps* has in ST 1, 13 and 34 "daß mir alle Berg gen Haar stunden." Edition E^{3a} and edition E^5 change the phrase to "daß mir alle Haar gen Berg stunden." The original wording "den Wirbel/ und das Knick"(ST II, 5) is changed in these editions to "den Wirbel/ und das Genick." In the edition E^5, we also find three "Continuationen" and a "Zugab/ des Wunderbarlichen Weltstreichenden Artzts Simplicissimi," all taken from the *Wundergeschichten Calender,* of which Grimmelshausen was supposedly the author. The text of the novel itself was expanded by three longer passages and many short additions. Some add to the characterization without offering new information as at the end of the second chapter of the first book. Simplicius's father is unhappy with his adopted son because, as he says, "mein grober Verstand könte seine subtile Unterweisungen nicht fassen" (Tarot, 14). The phrase is expanded to:

> mein grober und ungehobelter/ durch seine Unterweisung noch nicht genugsam auspolirter Verstand könte seine subtile Unterweisungen nicht fassen/ noch zu dieser Zeit derselbigen fähig seyn. (Breuer, 763)

Other passages tend to explain further a given situation. Thus, when Simplicius yields to temptation in Paris and remembers "daß ich wol ein Ploch hätte seyn müssen/ wenn ich keusch hätte darvon kommen sollen" (IV, 5 [Tarot, 307]), his statement is augmented by:

> über das operierten die Würste/ die mir mein Doctor zu fressen geben hatte/ daß ich mich von selbst stellte/ als ob ich ein Bock worden wäre. (Breuer, 770)

In the same year (1671), the edition was reissued; it is known as E^6. It shows a few additional misprints, but is otherwise identical with E^5.

The 1671 edition of *Simplicissimus* has been called the "Ausgabe letzter Hand" by several scholars. The matter of which text, E^1 or E^5, should be preferred has not been settled for good, just as little as it has been in the case of Goethe's *Die Leiden des jungen Werthers* (Saine). In a series of studies Manfred Koschlig tried to show that Grimmelshausen had a falling out with Felssecker before the issuing of E^5. That would mean that he was not responsible for the various changes and additions, that the edition E^5 was Felssecker's way of cashing in on Grimmelshausen's success without sharing the profits with him. Two pieces of evidence disprove such a hypothesis. In *Das wunderbarliche Vogelnest I* the narrator says: "Gibt mich dannoch nicht Wunder/ daß der alte Simplicissimus in alle Kupfferstück so sich in seiner Lebens-Beschreibung befinden/ gesetzt hat: Der Wahn betreugt!" (72). The illustrations containing the motto "Der Wahn betreügt" are not found in any edition prior to E^5. The other piece of evidence is found in a letter Quirin Moscherosch wrote to Sigmund von Birken, a letter Birken received on 27 January 1673, recte 1674:

> Es hat der beruffene Simplicissimus sonsten mein Nachbar, u. nur ein geringer Dorfschultes, aber ein Dauß Eß, u. homo Satyricus in folio, bey H. Felßeckern vor weynachten ein Tractätlein trucken lassen, deßen Titel des Teutschen Michels Sprachengepräng [. . . .] (Spahr, 51–52)

The break, then, between Grimmelshausen and Felssecker that Koschlig assumed, did not take place and the E^5 edition of *Simplicissimus* must be considered an edition that had the approval of Grimmelshausen.

There were in all six editions of *Simplicissimus* during Grimmelshausen's life. In 1683–84, 1685–99, and 1713 Felssecker's son and then his grandson published three-volume editions of most of Grimmelshausen's works, including some that were not written by him. These editions are referred to as C^1, C^2, and C^3. They present a *Simplicissimus* text with many additions in both prose and in verse that emphasize the moral message of the novel. Thus, at the end of Book I, Chapter 1, there are about ten additional lines, followed by:

> Simplicissimus hält dafür daß es redlicher und feiner sey/ mit der Warheit heraußgehen/ und lieber Edel von Gemüth/ als Geblüt zu seyn.

> So weist hier Simplex seinen Adel/
> Ein Einfalt-Leben ohne Tadel/
>   Er lieget nicht daß sich Balcken biegen/
> Und läst sich mit dem schlechten Stande/
> Jn seinem edlen Spessert Lande/
>   Treuhertzig-auffrecht wohlvergnügen.

> Du/ der du dieses auch wirst lesen/
> Denck welch ein Adel diß gewesen/
> Prang nicht mit eitlen Kalck und Steinen/
> Die/ so da Edel von Gemüthe/
> Gelangen offt durch Gottes Güte/
> Zu höhern Würden/ von den feinen.

It is obvious that such didactic moralizing is so heavy handed as to destroy the artistic integrity of the text. The illustrations and the verses at the bottom are new; missing is "Der Wahn betreügt."

Later Adaptations

The *Simplicissimus* adaptations begin in 1756 when an anonymous editor reduced the novel to fifty-three chapters and gave it the title *Der Wechsel des Glücks und Unglücks im Krieg, oder Wunderbahre Begebenheiten Herrn Melchior Sternfels von Fuchsheim, Eines gebohrnen Edelmanns.* Subsequent known editors (Christian Jacob Wagenseil 1785 and Christian Ludwig Haken 1810) as well as an anonymous editor (1790) all point to Lessing as having encouraged the reissue of *Simplicissimus.* As we noted above, added textual matter was already included in the 1671 edition of Grimmelshausen's works. Even more additions can be found in the three last printings done by Felssecker. Beginning with the 1756 edition, however, all adaptations of *Simplicissimus* have an abridged version of the text. The main goal was to make the novel readable. Thus the title of one edition mentioned above reads *Der im vorigen Jahrhundert so weltberufene Simplizius v. Einfaltspinsel, in einem neuen Kleide nach den [sic] Schnitt des Jahres 1790.* While the late Felssecker texts had added moral advice, such advice and the passages with enumerative display of learning were all omitted in these later editions. To be sure, there was acknowledgment of the author's vocabulary as presenting authentic older German words, yet it was still considered advisable to modernize the style. In the process, new words and phrases were introduced. Sometimes these new words and phrases were simple substitutes for Grimmelshausen's own version, while at other times they elaborated on the original style in the belief that this would actually improve the original. The theme of Robinson Crusoe was in vogue at the time, and several of the early editors pointed to the fact that Simplicissimus's stay on the island constituted an early Robinson Crusoe-like episode.

A detailed study by Lieselotte E. Kurth-Voigt of the *Simplicissimus* adaptations published prior to the 1810 Haken edition appeared in 1986. Haken stressed the many adventures of the protagonist and the insight that the novel provided into the period of the Thirty Years' War. That period with its many horrors seemed to Haken to parallel his own time. Still, as he states in the preface, he felt obliged to omit the many "Plattheiten, Obscönitäten und Ungeschmacktheiten." Jörg-Ulrich Fechner has made a substantial analysis of Haken's adaptation of the novel. I will return to Haken's version below, where I compare it to von Bülow's adaptation.

With each of the late eighteenth and early nineteenth century editions, we find there is more understanding for the author and his involvement in the story as well as more respect for the text. The 1836 edition by Eduard von Bülow constitutes the last one before the discovery of the author's real name and before the appearance of the first scholarly edition. Von Bülow was a friend of Ludwig Tieck, who, like several other Romantic poets, was well acquainted with Grimmelshausen's works and encouraged von Bülow to make *Simplicissimus* available to the educated reader. Von Bülow agrees with Haken's comments and editorial decisions in several respects. Both give a careful account of the various editions known to them and both make the first edition, i. e., E^1 the basis of their texts, thus limiting it to five books. In addition, they both assume that the author hides his name behind various anagrams. Von Bülow surmises that the initials found at the end of the *Continuatio* are those of the author, but he is unable to come up with Grimmelshausen's name. To be sure, von Bülow criticizes his predecessors for having modernized the language and praises Grimmelshausen by stating that "Seine Art zu schreiben ist in ihrer derben deutschen Althertümlichkeit fast klassisch zu nennen" (vii). Still, he decides against "denselben etwa wie einen klassischen Autor in einer todten Sprache anzusehen, und wortgetreu wieder abdrucken zu lassen" (xv). He, too, then makes stylistic changes, tones down expressions that he considers too strong or offensive, and, like editors before and after him, omits passages replete with the author's sterile learning ("mit unfruchtbarer Belesenheit" [xvi]). In contrast to Haken, who arranged the novel in a series of chapters of his own design, von Bülow adheres to Grimmelshausen's divisions into books and chapters. Neither he nor Haken is especially interested in the religious aspects of *Simplicissimus*. Thus, Haken's adaptation ends with Book V, Chapter 22, von Bülow's with Book V, Chapter 23, thereby omitting all of the long "Adjeu Welt" quotation from Antonio de Guevara (1480?–1545). Haken's interest in the novel comes from his anti-French feelings during the Napoleonic occupation. Von Bülow's primary interest was the depiction of the ruination of his country and of the customs and views of the time of the Thirty Years' War.

A number of scholars now set out to ascertain the author's true name and his life as well as to publish an unchanged text. Among the learned few, Grimmelshausen's fame spread through a series of scholarly editions. On a wider scale, that fame was also enhanced by more than 150 adaptations. Most of them were of *Simplicissimus,* some were of *Courage,* and a few were of *Springinsfeld.* They appeared in the course of the nineteenth and twentieth centuries. All of them shorten the text, at times reducing it to a bare minimum, but their purposes vary greatly. As in the late eighteenth and the early nineteenth century editions, the twentieth century text is changed so as to make it accessible to the contemporary reader. While orthography and interpunctuation are modernized, stylistic changes are generally made only in those cases where it seemed absolutely necessary. The prefaces and postscripts prepare the reader to see the author's message in certain aspects of the works, be it an autobiographical account of the horrors or war, the depiction of the time and customs of the Thirty Years' War, or an indictment of social injustice. Some editors stress the humorous scenes and those in which bawdiness plays a major role, while others give prominence to the religious message, namely the protagonist's sinful life that ends in repentance. We have bibliophile editions, often printed with old-fashioned lettering and with illustrations that support the editor's approach to the work. These are also found in many of the other adaptations. They come either from the Baroque editions or older prints or were commissioned by the publisher. The many school editions omit, of course, the various passages universally found unsuitable for the young. A good example is the *Simplicissimus* edition by Klaus Haberkamm in "Schöninghs deutsche Textausgaben." The clearly written preface touches on Grimmelshausen's life and works and stresses the novel's universal appeal and its astrological structure (following the interpretation of Günther Weydt). Also mentioned are the echoes the novel has had in recent times. The text is that of the first edition, thus excluding the *Continuatio.* Orthography and punctuation are modernized and the novel is reduced to forty-seven chapters that take up 133 pages. The famous frontispiece is not reproduced. There are summaries of what has been left out, for example, the extreme cruelties committed by soldiers and peasants in Book I. Haberkamm also omits the scene in which Simplicissimus witnesses the sexual encounter in the goose pen, his amorous conquests in Lippstadt, and his being a male stud in Paris. Haberkamm uses Kelletat's notes and includes eight of the wonderful "Der wahn betreügt" illustrations from the 1671 edition. Still, one might question why Haberkamm or, more likely, his publisher, includes the illustration showing Olivier with the cat on his head and the two dogs jumping as they try to reach it, when that great episode is not part of the text itself. All in all, the editor has succeeded in the difficult challenge of making the novel accessible to younger students.

The fame and sales of *Simplicissimus* and Grimmelshausen's works in general received a significant boost in 1876. That year was the height of the "Kulturkampf," the conflict between the newly founded German Empire and the Catholic Church. In that year, members of the Center Party objected, in the Prussian Chamber of Delegates, to the inclusion of Elard Hugo Meyer's adaptation of *Simplicissimus* among the books recommended for acquisition by the schools in Germany. Meyer immediately "purified" his text even further. Italo Michele Battarafano has shown how, in the preface to their *Simplicissimus* editions, the novelist Erwin Guido Kolbenheyer (1919) and Hans Heinrich Borcherdt (1922) compared Germany's devastation at the end of the Thirty Years' War to that at the end of the First World War. He also notes that both saw in the novel a call for a new and strong Germany.

As one might expect, works of Germany's most well-known seventeenth-century author are also on the internet. Except for the biblical and heroic novels, Grimmelshausen's works are available on-line. The name of the editor is not given. The *Simplicissimus* text is that of Alfred Kelletat, which modernizes spelling and punctuation. However, the explanatory notes of Kelletat are missing. There are also other omissions, for example, the verses at the bottom of the frontispiece, the omission of the illustration on the title page of the *Continuatio* (both of these are also missing in the Kelletat edition itself) as well as the frontispiece from *Courage*.

The Critical Editions: Tarot and Breuer

As I mentioned above, the editions published in the nineteenth century wavered among E^1, E^{3a}, and E^5 for the basis of the text. All presently available editions of *Simplicissimus* are based on E^1. That holds true also for the one prepared by Alfred Kelletat, available both in the Winkler Verlag and dtv, and for the one by Volker Meid (Reclam). Both Kelletat and Meid present a slightly modernized text and offer excellent aids for the understanding of the novel. Both editions are highly recommended for instructional purposes. If we compare Kelletat's text of the first paragraph of the novel with the original, we find the removal of the virgules and the insertion of commas whenever necessary. Also, Kelletat disregards italics as in *Guinea*. He also consistently modernizes the original spelling in words like "Aufferziehung," "tausenderley," "bekant," "Rittermässige," "uhralten," "seyn," and "Vor-Eltern." He likewise modernizes forms and gender: "etwan," "Kupplerin" (changed to "Kupplerinnen"), and, to use an example from the second paragraph, "den Werckzeug." I will show below, when comparing Rolf Tarot's handling of textual problems with the way Dieter Breuer handled them, how Kelletat decided more substantive cases.

Also basing their editions on E^1 are Rolf Tarot (Niemeyer, 1967, revised 1984) and Dieter Breuer (Volume One of the three-volume edition of Grimmelshausen's *Werke,* Deutscher Klassiker Verlag, 1989–99). However, there are significant differences between these two exemplary scholarly editions.

Rolf Tarot sketches the editorial history since 1713, explains his decision to use E^1, including the *Continuatio,* and gives minute bibliographical descriptions of E^1 through E^5, listing in each case the libraries at which copies were checked. Tarot's text has at the bottom of the page variants found in E^2 and E^4. His intention to publish E^5 has as yet not been carried out. There is a list of corrected misprints and of the abbreviations that were dissolved as well as a select bibliography followed by photos of a page each from E^1, E^2, the *Continuatio,* and E^4.

While Tarot's edition has the title page in color, Breuer's has it in black and white. Breuer's text changes that of E^1 in that the chapter summaries are placed not only at the beginning of each book and of the *Continuatio,* as E^1 and the *Continuatio* have it, but also at the beginning of each chapter (here in square brackets). Footnotes provide explanations of words that present difficulties to the modern reader. More extended explanations are placed in the commentary, where sources are given, historical information supplied, parallels to a given motif in *Simplicissimus* or other works pointed out, and references to contemporary events, personages, mores and the like explained. Some of the comments seem a bit far-fetched, as when Don Quijote's Rosinante is said to be a possible model for the run-down horse of the dragoon (II, 29) or "Läuse und Flöhe (vgl. dazu ST III, 6) werden zu den saturnischen Kreaturen gezählt, die Simplicissimus immer wieder befallen werden" (in connection with the battle Simplicius wages with the lice in II, 28). While Breuer profited from the work of previous editors, such as Kurz, Bobertag, and especially Borcherdt, he clearly surpasses them in thoroughness. Breuer sketches Grimmelshausen's life and delineates an approach to the meaning of his works. Here he stresses that one must read the *Simplicissimus* within the spirit of the author's oeuvre. To be sure, Grimmelshausen claims such an approach for the Simplician works in the *Wunderbarlicher*

Vogelnest I (WV, 150), but this claim was, of course, written *after* he had such success with the less than exemplary *Simplicissimus* and *Courasche*. Also, to keep in mind such novels as *Keuscher Joseph* or *Dietwald und Amelinde* while reading *Simplicissimus* seems difficult to me, to say the least.

In a short survey of the editions printed up to 1713 Breuer reproduces the title pages of those through C^1. For printing errors that were corrected and for the dissolution of abbreviations, he directs the reader to the editions by Scholte and Tarot. The list of variants supplied by Breuer is restricted to those cases where previous editors changed the text of E^1. Tarot lists all deviations from E^1 found in E^2 and E^4, while Breuer lists variants only in problematic cases. For those, however, Breuer includes all editions through C^3. Of the twenty-one pages devoted to variants, as many as fifteen refer to the *Continuatio,* showing either the poor condition of the manuscript or the haste with which the *Continuatio* was printed, or possibly both. Breuer also includes the text of all the passages that were added in E^5. As stated above, most of the additions are shorter, a few somewhat longer. One of the longer ones to the text of E^1 found in E^5 is of special interest. In the first edition, in Book V, Chapter 8, the "Knan" tells Simplicius that he had been brought up with "Gaiß-Milch." Whoever was responsible for the revised text of E^5 must have read the novel with extreme care, since that person added not having sucked a woman's milk as the condition for obtaining the treasure in Book III, Chapter 12. Indications point to Grimmelshausen himself as being that person. Breuer also includes the illustrations of both E^5 and C^1 — they are repeated in C^2 and C^3 — and samples of the textual expansion of the posthumous editions. Breuer adds a useful explanation of the value of coins mentioned in the novel and a bibliography of primary and select secondary works.

At this point it will be instructive to give a few examples of how Tarot and Breuer resolve specific readings where there are problems. Even though Breuer tends to preserve the text of E^1 as faithfully as possible, he decided against the original "Stüben" mentioned above which was kept by Tarot. Breuer replaces it with "Rüben," as later contemporary editions, including E^{3a} and E^5, was well as Scholte and Kelletat, had done. Breuer's principle of keeping the original text leads to the identical rhyme ("Macht") in lines fourteen and fifteen of "*Komm Trost der Nacht*" (ST I, 7). The variant states that previous editors replaced the second "Macht" with "Nacht." Breuer's conservative approach to the text leads to occasional difficulties for the reader. Scholte and Tarot supply "voll" in the sentence "war es voll dem/ so unden und oben weg gangen" (ST II, 2). As Breuer states, the addition of "voll" is without basis in any edition up to and including C^3. Kelletat follows Scholte's reading, except, of course, for "unten." In ST 5, 16, both Tarot and Breuer keep "seyn" in the phrase "wolte ich aber [. . .] in seinem Reiche eins und andere beschauen/ daß meines gleichen ohne zweifel selten seyn würde," whereas Scholte had replaced "seyn" with "sehen." There are similar difficulties for the reader of Breuer's text when he retains the original "aber ich schlug die Annehmung ab/ und liesse mich mehr als gehen nur mit einem Früstuck abfertigen" (*Continuatio,* 13). Breuer lists the variants found in E^{3a}, E^5, and C^1. Scholte and Tarot replace "gehen" with "geren," Kelletat has "gern." In chapter 14 of the *Continuatio* we find a number of misspelled place names. Breuer believes they might be Grimmelshausen's way of satirizing books of travel literature that are filled with incorrect information and exaggerations. He therefore keeps the original spelling as in "Berbeti" and "Tydia," while Scholte and Tarot have "Berberi" and "Lydia."

As mentioned earlier, the *Continuatio* presents special problems for the editor. There are many corrupt passages that both Tarot and Breuer emended so as to make them intelligible, although their emendations are not identical. In chapter 8 we read about Julus: "'bald hatte er Gäst/ und bald wurde er wider zu Gast geladen; fast täglich zu/ er führte zu Wasser oder Land anderer Leuth Töchter und Weiber nach Engelländischen Gebrauch spatziren." Tarot emends the passage to "[. . .] geladen; er führte fast täglich zu [. . .]," while Breuer, basing his reading on later editions has "[. . .] geladen; und nam seine conversation fast täglich zu/ er führte [. . .]." Kelletat had already made the same emendation as Breuer. Another instance in which both Tarot and Breuer needed to supply a missing word is in ST V, 6, where the first edition had "massen er den berühmten Teufelsbanner aus der Geißhaut kommen liesse/ der durch seinen den Dieb dergestalt tribulirte/ [. . .]." Tarot, following Scholte, adds "spiritum familiarem" after "seinen" on the basis of a reference to it later in the chapter. Breuer supplies "Bann," in agreement with later editions, and in agreement with his predecessor Kelletat.

There are a few minor mistakes in Breuer's edition. He is not consistent in listing all additions to E^1. The explanatory phrase "der war ich" in the sentence "Nach dem Nacht-Essen wurde mein Herr (der war ich) in ein Bette gelegt" (ST I, 23) was added in E^{3a} and repeated in E^5. Of course, the irony is undercut by the addition, but Breuer should have listed the phrase in the "Texterweiterungen." Interestingly enough, Kelletat explains in a note to the passage: "*mein Herr*— ich ." In the scene in which Simplicius is fighting a battle with lice (ST II, 28), E^5 adds to the first edition, as Breuer notes in the "Texterweiterungen," a verse relating to the plague. However, in the commentary pertaining to the same passage in E^1 he says about that addition:

> Die erste posthume Gesamtausgabe erläutert durch die nachstehenden, vermutlich vom Nürnberger Lektor Johann Christoph Beer (1638–1712) eingefügten Verse eines Meistersingerliedes, welche Quälgeister Simplicissimus meint. (Breuer, 869)

Then follows the same text as in the addition to E^5, except that the posthumous edition has the usual changes as to both spelling and interpunctuation. It was Manfred Koschlig who tried to make Beer responsible for the additions found in E^5, a hypothesis that is not supported by any evidence. In any case, Breuer's assertion that the addition referred to above is new in C^1 is incorrect, since it is already found in E^5. Finally, at the end of Book I, Chapter 11, E^1 reads "ein solcher elender Tropff in die Welt war" (Tarot, 34). Tarot's variant lists "der" in E^4, Breuer "der" in E^{3a}, E^4, E^5, but the Yale copy has "die" in E^5. Kelletat has "der" in his edition.

Breuer refers to Scholte and Tarot for a list of misprints and of abbreviations that have been spelled out. As will have become evident from the above, each editor of Grimmelshausen's works faces problems that require considered judgment. There are undoubtedly some readings in both Tarot's and Breuer's texts that do not correspond to what Grimmelshausen had written, but the disputed cases rarely affect our understanding of the passage. Tarot's text contains some questionable readings as Müller has shown. Breuer makes occasional mistakes, as I have pointed out above. In addition, he claims in a note to a passage in ST II, 8 ("weil ich mit meisterlichem Betrug und seiner Kunst durch geschloffen") that Tarot had replaced "seiner" with "feiner," when Tarot had actually kept "seiner." Tarot's and Breuer's editions represent superior scholarly achievements. Both consistently note any divergence from the first edition; Breuer is especially good in informing the reader about various possibilities and in explaining his reading.

Simplicissimus: First Edition vs. Edition of 1671

There is still the unresolved issue of why we do not read the revised version of *Simplicissimus* of 1671 (E^5). To be sure, Breuer includes in his edition the additions of E^5 in a special section. This means, however, that one has to leaf back and forth to incorporate the additions when reading the novel and thus break the flow of the story. Furthermore, Breuer does not record the myriad orthographic and grammatical changes from E^1 to E^5. It will be best to give a concrete example of the changed text of E^5 by listing in the first paragraph of the novel those words in E^5 that differ in any way from E^1. It should be noted that after "offt befindet" there is an addition of some six lines recorded by Breuer:

> eröffneten (the letters "ten" are poorly aligned) . . . glaubet . . . sey . . . Patienden . . . wan . . . Bändern . . . Adeliche . . . uralten . . . Kuplerinnen . . . des . . . sie diese . . . selbest

Stefan Trappen's plea, then, to make E^5 available to the modern reader (Trappen, 415) has been answered only partially by Breuer. Would an edition of E^5 even be feasible? In all likelihood not, now that we have accepted the first edition as the one to read and have the additions of E^5 as supplied by Breuer. Also, as Breuer points out, there is still the suspicion that Grimmelshausen might not have been responsible for all the changes in the edition of 1671 (Breuer, 721–22). Ultimately, it is a matter of taste that we prefer E^1 to E^5. All that E^5 does is to tone down some dialect phrases of E^1 (as Goethe did in the second version of *Werther*), standardize some spellings, and add to certain passages. I suspect that we will continue to prefer the first edition of *Simplicissimus*.

The Remaining Works

The second part of volume one of Breuer's edition of Grimmelshausen's works contains the so-called "Simplicianische Schriften" (Simplician Writings) as well as *Ratstübel Plutonis*. The second and final volume has all the other works, except for the *Ewig-währende Calender*, of which Breuer has only the third column of pages 92–204, consisting of a collection of "lustige Erzehlungen" and "Stücke." The original, published as a facsimile by Klaus Haberkamm (Constance: Rosgarten 1967), is printed in three columns each on opposing pages and thus requires a special size paper. Haberkamm is also the author of an accompanying fascicle that contains explanatory notes.

In the two other volumes of Breuer's edition, the same principles apply as for *Simplicissimus*. In the case of *Courasche*, Breuer could not inspect the unauthorized edition published by Georg Müller in 1671 and he had to rely on Scholte's list of variants. Georg Müller's edition has a text that parallels the revision of *Simplicissimus* (E^1) by the same publisher (E^{3a}) discussed above. Klaus Haberkamm and Günther Weydt (Reclam) also both edited *Courasche*. Breuer's principle of always basing his text on the first edition is questionable in the case of *Keuscher Joseph*, of which Felssecker published a second, revised edition with the addition of *Musai* in 1671. Wolfgang Bender's text (Niemeyer 1968) is based on that revised edition.

For all the remaining works, just as for the *Simplicissimus,* Breuer's extensive commentary is most impressive. When one considers Grimmelshausen's wide reading in works that are today not easily located and the many obscure names and events to which he alludes, one must admire the Herculean labors performed by Breuer and his assistants. In the last volume of the edition, the many cross-references to other writings by Grimmelshausen are especially useful. The maximum I counted comes in connection with the section "Der Melancholiker" of the *Ewig-währender Calender,* for which motif there are no less than one hundred cross-references. All but one of the texts in the Breuer edition are also available in *Gesammelte Werke in Einzelausgaben,* as edited in such a careful and reliable manner by Rolf Tarot in collaboration with Wolfgang Bender and Franz Günter Sieveke. Dieter Breuer excels in the consideration of later editions, including their illustrations, and in the commentary.

Chronological Listing of the Critical Editions Mentioned

1851 — Holland. *Der abenteuerliche Simplicissimus. Versuch einer Ausgabe nach den vier ältesten Drucken.* Von Dr. W. L. Holland. Tübingen: Laupp, 1851.

1854–1862 — Keller. *Der abenteuerliche Simplicissimus und andere Schriften von Hans Jakob Christoph von Grimmelshausen.* Hrsg. von. A. von Keller. Stuttgart: Litterarischer Verein, 1854 and 1862. Four volumes. (= Bibliothek des Litterarischen Vereins in Stuttgart 33–34 and 65–66)

1863–1864 — Kurz. *Hans Jacob Christoffels von Grimmelshausen Simplicianische Schriften.* Hrsg. und mit Erläuterungen von Heinrich Kurz. Leipzig: Weber, 1863–1864. Four volumes. (= Deutsche Bibliothek 3–6)

1880 — Kögel. *Der abenteuerliche Simplicissimus. Von H. J. Chr. V. Grimmelshausen. Abdruck der ältesten Originalausgabe 1669.* Hrsg. von Rudolf Kögel. Halle / Saale: Niemeyer, 1880. (= Neudrucke Deutscher Literaturwerke 19–25)

1882–1883 — Bobertag. *Grimmelshausens Werke.* Hrsg. von Felix Bobertag. Berlin and Stuttgart: Spemann, 1882–1883. Three volumes. (= Deutsche National-Litteratur 33–35)

1922 — Borcherdt. *Grimmelshausens Werke.* Hrsg., mit Einleitung und Anmerkungen von Has Heinrich Borcherdt. Berlin: Bong, 1922. Four volumes. (= Bongs Goldene Klassiker Bibliothek)

1923 — Scholte. *Grimmelshausens Courasche. Abdruck der ältesten Originalausgabe (1670) mit den Lesarten der beiden anderen zu Lebzeiten des Verfassers erschienenen Drucke.* Hrsg. von J. H. Scholte. Halle / Saale: Niemeyer, 1923. (= Neudrucke Deutscher Literaturwerke 246–48)

1928 — Scholte. *Grimmelshausens Springinsfeld. Abdruck der ältesten Originalausgabe (1670) mit den Lesarten der anderen zu Lebzeiten des Verfassers erschienenen Ausgaben.* Hrsg. von J. H. Scholte. Halle / Saale: Niemeyer, 1928. (= Neudrucke Deutscher Literaturwerke 249–52)

1931 — Scholte. *Grimmelshausens Wunderbarliches Vogelnest erster Teil. Abdruck der ältesten Originalausgabe mit den Lesarten der anderen zu Lebzeiten des Verfassers erschienenen Ausgaben.* Hrsg. von J. H. Scholte. Halle / Saale: Niemeyer, 1931. (= Neudrucke Deutscher Literaturwerke 288–91)

1938 — Scholte. *Grimmelshausens Simplicissimus Teutsch. Abdruck der editio princeps (1669) mit der stark mundartlich gefärbten, nicht von einem berufsmäßigen Korrrektor überarbeiteten Originalsprache des Verfassers.* Hrsg. von J. H. Scholte. Halle / Saale: Niemeyer, 1938. (= Neudrucke Deutscher Literaturwerke 302–9)

1939 — Scholte. *Continuatio des abentheuerlichen Simplicissimi, oder der Schluß desselben.* Hrsg. von J. H. Scholte. Halle / Saale: Niemeyer, 1939. (= Neudrucke Deutscher Literaturwerke 810–14)

1943 — Scholte. *Simpliciana in Auswahl. Weitere Continuationen des abentheurlichen Simplicissimi, Rathstübel Plutonis, Bart-Krieg, Teutscher Michel.* Hrsg. von J. H. Scholte. Halle / Saale: Niemeyer, 1943. (= Neudrucke Deutscher Literaturwerke 315–21)

1967 — Haberkamm. *Des Abenteurlichen Simplicissimi Ewig-währender Calender. Faksimile-Druck der Erstausgabe Nürnberg 1671 mit einem erklärenden Beiheft.* Hrsg. von Klaus Haberkamm. Constance: Rosgarten 1967.

1967–1976 — Tarot Edition. The following individual volumes form part of *Grimmelshausen. Gesammelte Werke in Einzelausgaben.* Unter Mitarbeit von Wolfgang Bender und Franz Günter Sieveke herausgegeben von Rolf Tarot.

1967 — Tarot. *Grimmelshausen. Der Abentheurliche Simplicissimus Teutsch und Continuatio des abentheurlichen Simplicissimi.* Hrsg. von Rolf Tarot. Tübingen: Niemeyer 1967.

1967 — Tarot. *Grimmelshausen. Dietwalts und Amelinden anmuthige Lieb- und Leids-Beschreibung.* Hrsg. von Rolf Tarot. Tübingen: Niemeyer, 1967.

1967 — Sieveke. *Grimmelshausen. Des Durchleuchtigen Printzen Proximi und Seiner ohnvergleichlichen Lympidae Liebs-Geschicht-Erzehlung.* Hrsg. von Franz Günter Sieveke. Tübingen: Niemeyer, 1967.

1967 — Bender. *Grimmelshausen. Lebensbeschreibung der Ertzbetrügerin und Landstörtzerin Courasche.* Hrsg. von Wolfgang Bender. Tübingen: Niemeyer, 1967.

1968 — Tarot. *Grimmelshausen. Simplicianischer Zweyköpffiger Ratio Status.* Hrsg. von Rolf Tarot. Tübingen: Niemeyer, 1968.

1968 — Bender. *Grimmelshausen. Des Vortrefflich Keuschen Josephs in Egypten Lebensbeschreibung samt des Musai Lebens-Lauff.* Hrsg. von Wolfgang Bender. Tübingen: Niemeyer, 1968.

1969 — Sieveke. *Grimmelshausen. Der seltzame Springinsfeld.* Hrsg. von Franz Günter Sieveke. Tübingen: Niemeyer 1969.

1970 — Bender. *Grimmelshausen. Satyrischer Pilgram.* Hrsg. von Wolfgang Bender. Tübingen: Niemeyer, 1970.

1970 — Tarot. *Grimmelshausen. Das wunderbarliche Vogelnest.* Hrsg. von Rolf Tarot. Tübingen: Niemeyer, 1970.

1973 — Tarot. *Grimmelshausen. Kleinere Schriften.* Hrsg. von Rolf Tarot. Tübingen: Niemeyer 1973.

1973 — Sieveke. *Grimmelshausen. Die verkehrte Welt.* Hrsg. von Franz Günter Sieveke. Tübingen: Niemeyer, 1973.

1975 — Bender. *Grimmelshausen. Rathstübel Plutonis.* Hrsg. von Wolfgang Bender. Tübingen: Niemeyer, 1975.

1976 — Tarot. *Grimmelshausen. Deß Weltberuffenen Simplicissimus Pralerey und Gepräng mit seinem Teutschen Michel.* Hrsg. von Rolf Tarot. Tübingen: Niemeyer, 1976.

1989–1997 — Breuer. *Hans Jacob Christoffel von Grimmelshausen. Werke.* Hrsg. von Dieter Breuer. Frankfurt / Main: Deutscher Klassiker, 1989–1997. Two volumes in three. (= Bibliothek der frühen Neuzeit. Zweite Abteilung. Literatur im Zeitalter des Barock, 4/1 and 4/2 and 5)

Works Cited

Battafarano, Italo Michele. "Erwin Guido Kolbenheyers und Hans Heinrich Borcherdts Grimmelshausen-Ausgaben im Zeichen nationaler Aufbaustimmung nach dem Ersten Weltkrieg." *Simpliciana* 18 (1996): 217–25.

Breuer, Dieter. "'Ein erschreckliches Monstrum:' editorische Probleme mit dem barocken 'Klassiker' Grimmelshausen." *Etudes Germaniques* 46 (1991): 121–35.

Fechner, Jörg-Ulrich. "Rezeption als Interpretation. Hakens *Simplicissimus*-Ausgabe von 1810." *Daphnis* 5 (1976): 677–97.

Kurth-Voigt, Lieselotte E. "Grimmelshausens *Simplicissimus* in Aufklärung und Vorklassik." *Simpliciana* 8 (1986): 19–50.

Müller, Ernst E. "Editionsprobleme bei Grimmelshausen und anderswo." *Zeitschrift für deutsches Altertum*, 107 (1978): 330–44.

Koschlig, Manfred. *Grimmelshausen und seine Verleger: Untersuchungen über die Chronologie seiner Schriften und den Echtheitscharakter der frühen Ausgaben.* Leipzig: Akademische Verlagsanstalt, 1939. (= Palaestra 218)

———. *Das Ingenium Grimmelshausens und das "Kollektiv": Studien zur Entstehungs- und Wirkungsgeschichte des Werkes.* Munich: Beck, 1977.

Saine, Thomas P. "The Portrayal of Lotte in the Two Versions of Goethe's *Werther.*" *Journal of English and Germanic Philology* 80 (1981): 54–77.

Schier, Manfred. "Simplicissimus im preußischen Abgeordnetenhaus." In: *Simplicius Simplicissimus. Grimmelshausen und seine Zeit Ausstellungskatalog.* Ed. Peter Berghaus and Günther Weydt. Münster: Landschaftsverband Westfalen-Lippe, 1976. 217–22.

Scholte, J[an] H[endrik]. *Der Simplicissimus und sein Dichter: Gesammelte Aufsätze.* Tübingen: Niemeyer, 1950.

Spahr, Blake Lee. *The Archives of the Pegnesischer Blumenorden: A Survey and Reference Guide.* Berkeley and Los Angeles: California UP, 1960. (= University of California Publications in Modern Philology 57)

Tarot, Rolf. "Notwendigkeit und Grenzen der Hypothese in der Grimmelshausen-Forschung. Zur Echtheitsfrage des Barock-Simplicissimus." *Orbis Litterarum* 25 (1970): 71–101.

Trappen, Stefan. "Edition und Interpretation von Grimmelshausens *Simplicissimus:* Zur ausstehenden Edition der zweiten Fassung von 1671." *Germanisch-Romanische Monatsschrift* NF 39 (1989): 403–23.

Engraved copperplate for Landstörtzerin Courage (1670).
Reprinted with permission of the Herzog August Bibliothek, Wolfenbüttel.

Grimmelshausen's "Autobiographies" and the Art of the Novel

Italo Michele Battafarano

The New Element in Narrative Form

WITH GRIMMELSHAUSEN'S SIMPLICIAN novel cycle, which consists of *Simplicissimus Teutsch, Continuatio, Courasche, Springinsfeld,* and *Vogelnest* I–II, the German novel of the early modern age attains the level of world literature. The novels, appearing in rapid succession over a period of seven years (1668–1675), present a goldmine of masterfully narrated biographies and successfully executed fictional autobiographies. This is all the more surprising since before Grimmelshausen the novel in the German-speaking world, especially in the form of first person narratives, was without support in the poetic handbooks of the time and actually did not exist in any form worth mentioning. The only narrative tradition accessible to Grimmelshausen was that of the *pícaro* in the German variation of Aegidius Albertinus (1560–1620), *Der Landstörtzer Gusman von Alfarche oder Picaro genannt* (Munich 1615) and the anonymous translation of *Lazarillo de Tormes* in *Zwo kurtzweilige lustige vnd lächerliche Historien* (Augsburg 1617).[1] Both, however, constitute only one aspect of Grimmelshausen's narrative universe and cannot by themselves reveal the multiplicity of Simplician interwoven autobiographies in novel form. The narratives of Grimmelshausen, which revolve around characters who thematize themselves, are based on other presuppositions and have other goals.

War as Theme

Grimmelshausen announces his first novel *Der Abentheurliche Simplicissimus Teutsch* (1668) at the end of the tract entitled *Satyrischer Pilgram* (1667).[2] There one can read what follows in the "Nachklang" to "Zehenden Satz / vom Krieg":

Jch gestehe gern / daß ich den hundersten Theil nicht erzehlet / was Krieg vor ein erschreckliches und grausames *Monstrum* seye / dann solches erfordert mehr als ein gantz Buch Papier / so aber in diesem kurtzen Wercklein nicht wohl einzubringen wäre / Mein *Simplicissimus* wird dem günstigen Leser mit einer andern und zwar lustigern Manier viel *Particularit*äten von ihm erzehlen. (160)

Grimmelshausen's announcement that he prefers the novel for treating the theme of the war stems from his conviction that one cannot get at the horror of war only by reasoning. Even a critically engaged discussion, as found for example in pamphlets written by Erasmus von Rotterdam (1466–1536) and Sebastian Franck (1499–1542 or 1543) at the beginning of the sixteenth century, must have seemed insufficient to Grimmelshausen after a thirty-year war.[3] He must have arrived at the realization that this war, which depleted and demoralized the civil population like no earlier conflict in European history, cannot be spoken of as an object. In order to have a better approach to the monstrosity of war and to expose it as a phenomenon that was simultaneously desired, created, experienced and suffered by people, Grimmelshausen makes his personal experience of the war the theme, while making use of the form of the autobiographical novel.

Grimmelshausen chose no heroes as protagonists for his novels. Instead he tells the life stories of ordinary individuals, who, voluntarily or involuntarily, participated in the war, who hoped they would lose nothing in and with the war, and who perhaps even sought to make a fortune. This is exposed in his novels as a grand illusion. All his characters, after all, have to fight for mere survival, and when they are able to save themselves, they are either physically injured like Springinsfeld, or morally traumatized like Simplicius and Courasche. Thus, with Grimmelshausen the war ceases to be a stage for heroes in German baroque literature as had been the case in the courtly novels. With their heroes battling gods, fate and enemy warriors, neither Homer nor Virgil could serve as role models for this German poet of the baroque era, nor could Torquato Tasso with his Christian heroes who liberated Jerusalem from the clutch of the Mohammedans. He had to create something new so as to illustrate the modern chimera of war by way of narrative.

In order to solve adequately the self-imposed task in a literary manner, Grimmelshausen invents a double narrative perspective in the first person, a first person narrator. Simplicius the island dweller and mature skeptic removed from the world as such, the disillusioned Springinsfeld, or the untamable Courasche in gypsy costume — all tell their life story only in advanced years. They narrate their lives beginning with their younger years and how they naively set foot into the world, how they became fascinated by its many attractions, how they experienced fortune and misfortune, and finally how they found themselves with a skeptically distanced or disillusioned attitude toward the world. *However,* Simplicius also tells in the *Continuatio* of a newly won personal relationship to God and of a belief in eternal values, which, however, pose imminent obligatory character. Each first person narrator also is given a clerk or an editor, who prepares for print the material read or heard. That individual's evaluation of the narrated material is also made explicit, to varying degrees, in the individual novels.

The change from *Satyrischer Pilgram* to *Simplicissimus Teutsch,* that is, the change from treatise to autobiographical novel, implies a change in the relationship between author-reader and addressees. Instead of an omniscient and lecturing author, we have a searching, insecure, personal narrator, who is capable of admitting mistakes and who is remorseful. Not abstract knowledge, but the evaluation of situated action is asked of the reader, whereby the reader's experience and exposure is called upon, but not directly thematized. With the choice of a fictive narrative form Grimmelshausen addresses a wider audience. He reaches all those who have limited schooling in and little interest for abstract thought processes that have as their theme a cogent consideration of the different theses regarding war. He can convince such individuals of the monstrosity of the war only if his narration captures, entertains, and stimulates them to contemplation.

The title pages with the promise that the novels are "überauß lustig/ und männiglich nutzlich zu lesen"[4] indicate that Grimmelshausen was quite aware of the possibilities and dangers inherent in addressing a wider readership with a first person narrator from the Thirty Years' War. Perhaps because of this, unlike almost any other later German author, he was able to exhaust the possibilities of a genre without falling prey to the danger of simplification. He understood how to narrate a difficult theme like the behavior of people in war without being overly didactic and pedantic. He neither offers a banal treatment of the problems nor does he loudmouth heroism, but rather narrates in an entertaining manner, drawing on the emotion and reason of his readers.

In the "Vorrede an den geneigten Leser" in *Wunderbarliches Vogel-Nest II,* the last novel in the cycle of Simplician novels, Grimmelshausen picks up on the poetological reflections on the connection between pleasure and usefulness, which he had already developed at the beginning of the *Continuatio* of *Simplicissimus.* Looking back, he comments that among seventeen readers, it was unlikely to find anyone who would have perceived his use of "Zeit-Verkürtzung" (VN II 149) as a strategy of sweetening bitter pills, who would have understood that utility and pleasure are inseparable. At the same time, Grimmelshausen makes it clear that the close relationship of these two elements is neither a sales strategy nor a clever moral and didactic method, but rather that it is situated in the nature of the author and in the object itself. He actually defends satirical writing as an expression of a worldview that is not melancholic, which derives its justification from the justice and compassion of the Almighty. Grimmelshausen argues that heaven and hell, sin and salvation must be seen as belonging together. Thus, neither a rejoicing Democritus nor a mourning Eraclitus alone is sufficient in the eyes of Grimmelshausen as a model for contemplation and knowledge of the world (cf. *Springinsfeld* 18–19).

The Narrative Perspective of the First Person Ich-Form

The continual alternation of the view of the narrating "I," between the acting view and the reflecting view, is one of the essential characteristics of the Simplician novels. This is readily seen in the titles, which characterize the works as biographies of a person, namely *Simplicissimus Teutsch, Courasche*[5] and *Springinsfeld*.[6] It is thus worthwhile to take a more careful look at this technique.

On the narrative level it eases the author of the burden of simultaneously narrating the war entertainingly and didactically, because the events of the war are presented from the view of the actively participating first person "I." At the same time, though, they are also being reflected from a distance by a matured and, at any rate, aged, and now no longer participating first person narrator. In no way do his comments automatically possess authorial character. In reference to this, the opening of *Simplicissimus* will serve as an example.

The attack by soldiers on his Knan's farm is told from the view of the young and extremely naive Simplicius. The shepherd boy isn't able to interpret the event. Since he does not know who the strangers are who suddenly appear in the forest, their action remains incomprehensible to him. Simplicius draws parallels to the daily routine of the farm in order to describe the events that took place. In this manner, Grimmelshausen succeeds impressively in presenting the blind destructive mania of the soldiers, who "Bettladen / Tisch / Stühl und Bänck verbrannten [. . .] / da doch viel Claffter dürr Holtz im Hof lag" (18). Since the naive shepherd boy Simplicius only understands what he sees, the attack on the farm of his parents appears to him as a strange celebration, or a "lustig Panquet" (18). Simplicius even considers the torture of his Knan a funny game, because the latter is literally being tickled to death and must constantly laugh. Without using a lot of words, Grimmelshausen makes the reality of war in all of its cruelty all the more clear by setting it in contrast with the background of a happy get-together.

The aged Simplicius summarizes these events and his situation at that time succinctly in the following words: "Mitten in diesem Elend wendet ich Braten" (19). The role of the old Simplicius does not exhaust itself in this alone. Before the soldiers destroy Knan's farm, he justifies the story of the horrible event with the meaning of the event for his life. He interprets it traditionally as the expression of divine providence and punishment. The old Simplicius claims that thanks to "der Güte deß Allerhöchsten" (17), he was lead in this way out of the state of innocence and ignorance, while his step-parents were punished for allowing him to grow up without a Christian education. The depiction of the event from the perspective of the young Simplicius, the rape of the innocent girls and his stepsister, as well as the torture of the servant and the other farmers, make such an evaluation of the event seem, at the very least, insufficient.[7]

The incongruity between traditional Christian teaching and the unheard of cruelty of the war, which is illustrated through the double I-perspective, presents the reader with a central theme throughout the entire cycle of novels. That theme is how perception, conviction, and knowledge relate to reality. Through the doubling of the first person perspective in a novel, the point of view of each first person narrator in the novels is shown to be changeable and capable of being confronted with and mirrored in each of the others. The particular ages, the respective levels of knowledge and experience, and the resulting specific courses of action in the world are made evident and relativized. Unexpected external events occur throughout Grimmelshausen's novels that strongly determine the journey through life of the main characters. These events constantly demand new behaviors of them, and frequently they force the main characters to adopt new perspectives and convictions. Let us look at an example. Although the war suddenly ends a protected childhood for Simplicius and Libuschka-Courasche, both, throughout their lives, find themselves unexpectedly in situations that fundamentally change their existence. The individual person is thus as subject to change as everything else in the world. The enumeration of the various military ranks of Courasche on the title page of *Courasche* clearly indicates this.

Through his Simplician cycle of interconnected fictive autobiographies, Grimmelshausen expands his project of relativizing human perception, experience, and knowledge, and thus demonstrates impressively his belief that every human viewpoint is limited and has a unique perspective. None of the first-person narrators can claim to have exclusive possession of the truth or even to have an objective viewpoint. Therefore, according to her biography, and thus her viewpoint, the older Courasche attempts to correct the false claims made by Simplicius in his autobiography, while he wants to expose Courasche by way of writing down Springinsfeld's biography. Through the telling of his biography, Springinsfeld hopes not to have to continue as a docile servant of Courasche. In the prologue to *Wunderbarliches Vogel-Nest II* Grimmelshausen stresses that none of the novels "allein ohne solche Zusammenfügung genugsam verstanden werden mag" (150).

In spite of a noticeable contrast with the preceding novels in terms of narrative style and theme, the two parts of *Das Wunderbarliche Vogel-Nest*, which first appeared in 1672 and 1675, are to be interpreted in the context of the cycle as well. *Wunderbarliches Vogel-Nest I* explicitly ties in with the *Springinsfeld* novel (VN I 5), but, just as *Wunderbarliches Vogel-Nest II*, its action does not occur during the Thirty Years' War but in its aftermath.

The connection to *Springinsfeld* has to do with the first-person narrator, a young halberdier who receives from Springinsfeld's wife, a hurdy-gurdy player, a bird's nest that makes its wearer invisible. The main characters of *Wunderbarliches Vogel-Nest I* and *II*, the halberdier of part one and the rich businessman of part two, are pale in comparison with Simplicius, Courasche, and Springinsfeld. As their namelessness already indicates, it is difficult to speak here of an "I" being constituted through the act of narrating or writing down one's life. There is thus no complex first person perspective to speak of here. Instead, Grimmelshausen experiments in these two novels with the two extreme possibilities of the first person narrator: the erosion versus the absolutizing of the first person narrative perspective. In Grimmelshausen's last two volumes the polyperspectivism as an ideal center of the Simplician cycle is in this manner turned into the theme of narrating itself.

He makes it believable in a narrative sense by making the first person narrators owners of a bird's nest with the power of making invisible. This possession, however, simply amplifies a stance, which has already been expressed through the jobs they hold, toward the world and their fellow humans. The simple soldier-guard merely watches critically and unnoticed with the aid of the bird's nest the activities in his colorful surroundings and interferes in order to punish or praise. The businessman, by contrast, appropriates whatever he wants. Whereas in the first half of the work the reader, together with the first person narrator, casts a wide and impersonal eye toward a panoramic view of the world, in the second half the view becomes largely focused on the one of the businessman, since he absolutizes his perspective.

After a series of episodes, the halberdier's observational stance towards life turns into both self-doubt and doubt about the possibility of acting properly. Beliefs in God and in a Christianity characterized by active charity finally provide him with new support. Grimmelshausen reminds us through his simple halberdier that the awareness of the perspectivism of human thought, emotion, and action, and his Simplician cycle as well do not have impartiality and incapacity to act as their goal.

On the other hand, in the figure of the corrupt, cynical businessman, Grimmelshausen presents in an unusually stark manner a human being who thinks in pre-fashioned categories, who questions neither himself nor the world, and who is even incapable of relativizing anything, precisely because he only follows his own interests. Even when, after making it through a life-threatening situation, he remorsefully turns away from his prior way of life, he remains caught within a formal and traditional religiosity, which serves him more or less as life insurance on the hereafter.

Grimmelshausen therefore takes leave of the reader of the Simplician cycle by underscoring the positive meaning of both skepticism and irony as an attitude toward not only the world, but also toward oneself and by, indirectly, trying once again to justify his satirical novels. Grimmelshausen himself manifests this attitude when he treats the figure of the wealthy tradesman with ironic distance in the prologues and in the chapter headings (see also below).

The doubling of the first person perspective in the individual novels and the plurality of first person perspectives in the cycle as a whole make it clear that Grimmelshausen was not concerned with depicting the inner world of individual subjects, as by contrast the future *Entwicklungsroman* would do. Rather, he wanted to narrate the dramatic life of man in the world. In a world governed by war and thus by force, by hate, envy, greed, and deceit, Grimmelshausen's heroes learn quickly that neither solidarity nor cooperation governs the actions of humankind. This they learn in a world that, however, claims to be a Christian world and that claims to be fighting war in the name of a true Christianity. Yet, in the long run they fail to assert themselves in the world. In order to save themselves they start to withdraw more or less and in differing fashion.

Simplicius leads a harmonious life on a South Sea island with nature and God. Courasche leaves an allegedly civilized Europe and enters the community of Gypsies. Springinsfeld, by contrast, withdraws to the farm of Simplicius, and the rich tradesman and the halberdier turn into authors of didactic treatises.

Every withdrawal from the world in the novels, however, is neither total nor permanent and every private idyll comes to a sudden end. None of the figures enters a monastery or chooses the ascetic hermitage. Even Simplicius returns to Europe from his South Sea island in *Springinsfeld*. Even the religious dimension of man is not one that can be realized against the world. As the novel cycle with its rich range of perspectives shows, religion itself cannot claim sole possession of absolute truth, for otherwise it could not serve as the salvation of man.

Instead, the perspectivism and relativism of human perception and insights must be taken seriously so as to keep the unavoidably tense relationship between man and the world from becoming destructive. This is emphasized *ex positivo* in several passages of Grimmelshausen's novels that present a peaceful cooperation (for example, the farmer's paradise of the young Simplicius or the youth of Courasche, the Anabaptist episode or the world of the sylphs, Switzerland or the few successful marriages of Courasche). Still, it becomes especially apparent that *Courasche* enforces this notion. As the title *Trutz Simplex* announces, not only is the view of a woman set consciously against the view of a man, but also the genre of the picaresque novel, which stems from the tradition of the "Heiligenvitae" and the Augustinian *confessiones,* is declared insufficient.

Courasche refuses at the outset to view her biography as a remorse-filled general confession. According to the queen of the Gypsies, a remorse of that kind would deny the necessity and contingency of the situation in which she makes her decisions in favor of not fulfilling norms, which support neither the instinct for self-preservation nor the vitality of a young woman. Grimmelshausen the author makes his readers aware that such a general remorse would appear unmotivated and unjustified in the face of a biography that indicates the opposite. He thus removes himself from the edifying and picaresque tradition. His fictive autobiographies constitute *in toto* novels, which are organized according to literary rules. One of them demands of the narrator the precise characterization and motivation of the thoughts, feelings, and actions of his figures. One should not deny Grimmelshausen's masterful success, simply out of fear of undertaking the task of offering a modern psychological interpretation of the characters of a baroque novel. One should not forget, however, that Grimmelshausen invented a literary first person "I," long before it was defined psychologically and scientifically in our age.

Writer and Narrator

In the Simplician cycle, the perspective narration of the world does not exhaust itself in a series of interconnected biographies that are written down or allowed to be written down, in each respective case, by a different "I." In addition to this, there are autobiographies that are told orally and that are organized and written down by the first person narrator in the biography. An example of this is contained in the biography of the highway robber Olivier, whose story Simplicius listens to at a particular time and then subsequently writes down. In addition, *Simplicissimus* contains a non-autobiographical counterpart to Olivier's self-depiction. It concerns the two Englishmen, Julus and Avarus, whose biographies have a tragic end. These offspring of a rising bourgeoisie and its servants are the victims of a bet for their souls, a bet that Lucifer concocted in hell between envy and wastefulness, as we see portrayed in a dream of Simplicius.

Thus while the first person narrators do not merely appear as narrators of their own lives, Grimmelshausen pushes between their biographies and the writing down of them and/or their revision for print a professional writer or a scribe. In *Simplicissimus,* he is called Melchior Sternfels von Fuchshaim. In *Courasche* and in *Springinsfeld* he is called Philarchus Grossus von Trommenheim. In *Wunderbarliches Vogel-Nest* his name is Michael Rechulin von Sehmsdorff.[8] The name is in each case an anagram of Hans Jakob Christoffel von Grimmelshausen, who was not merely playing hide and seek. His real purpose is to separate explicitly his role as narrator from his historical self and in so doing to underscore the fictional nature and autonomy of that which is being narrated. In addition, he gives the reader to understand that an additional perspective is there, beyond the narrated first person perspective. That is, he shows how another stratum overlies the first person perspective.

According to the story, Simplicius, on the island in the Indian Ocean, cannot oversee the printing of his autobiography and neither Courasche nor Springinsfeld has the time, the interest or the ability for such matters. Hence, the reader is left with no guarantee that no one has tampered with, or otherwise falsified, the biographies. That the fictive publisher of the Simplician novels has made changes is readily apparent to the reader in that *Simplicissimus Teutsch* is not identical to the biography of Simplicius. The Dutch captain Melchior Sternfels von Fuchshaim has expanded that biography in the reports in *Continuatio*.

At the end of *Courasche* the reader comes up against an epilogue as well. In the "Zugab des Autors" (140), according to the title page, "Philarchus Grossus von Trommenheim/ auf Griffsberg" voices his negative opinion of Courasche. In contrast to *Simplicissimus,* the reader learns nothing in the novel *Courasche* about the way in which this biography from the time of the Thirty Years' War came to be written and published. Rather, from the very beginning there is a feminine first person "I," which narrates, in her more mature years, her adventurous life. Although her life was classified as sinful according to the norms of time, Courasche refuses to use the autobiography as a general confession. Instead, she uses her story to defy the hypocritically pious Simplicius and his biography as it appears in *Simplicissimus.*

The critical "publisher" Philarchus Grossus also appears in the next book of the cycle, namely *Springinsfeld*. Curiously, this eighth book in the cycle begins not with the "I" of the title page, but with Philarchus Grossus. It is he who speaks in the first person. In a tavern he first meets Simplicius, who has just returned to Europe, and then Springinsfeld. He tells them about himself and how the gypsy princess Courasche solicited him to be her scribe and how she subsequently cheated him of the salary she had promised. Only then does Simplicius Simplicissimus invite Springinsfeld, who has been disappointed in life, to tell those who are present about his life as well. The novel *Springinsfeld* ends as Simplicius takes his comrade from the time of Soest to his farm. At the same time, Simplicius asks Philarchus Grossus to write down the biography of Springinsfeld he has just heard and to have it printed. For this he pays him — unlike with Courasche — six Reichsthaler in advance. Yet, Simplicius's motives are far from altruistic. Just as Courasche allegedly wrote her autobiography so as to defy Simplicius, he in turn wants to prove with the autobiography of Springinsfeld, "daß sein Sohn der leichtfertigen *Courage* Huren-Kind nicht seye" (Spr 132).

This is, of course, not exactly what Courasche claimed, but the opposite. The motives of both of them for the compilation of the autobiographies are thus threadbare, and not to be taken literally. In this way Grimmelshausen justifies the cycle within the fiction and points out once more that statements are always influenced by gender, age, opinions, and situations and are therefore limited. Grimmelshausen the author is thus not to be identified with any person in the cycle, not even with Philarchus Grossus. While his name is an anagram of Grimmelshausen, and he is therefore at least nominally identical with Grimmelshausen, he is only distantly related to him with regard to age and wisdom. In speaking of himself as a cheated writer, Grimmelshausen nevertheless relates himself to the critical and ironic problematics of the narrative flow.

Grimmelshausen, in his function as narrator, intervenes explicitly in this respect through chapter titles and also in the prologues in *Wunderbarliches Vogel-Nest II*. In the brief prologue: "*Privilegia* und Freyheiten/ so diesem *Tract*ätlein verliehen" (145–47), Grimmelshausen parodies the usual documentation from the emperor or the lord of the land, which was suppose to protect printed material from unlawful reprinting. Since his work appeared anonymously he could not have owned such documentation. He proceeds in a consistently formal-nihilistic manner when he parodies the typical concluding formula for the documentation in the following manner:

> alles laut mehr — angeregter *Originalia,* so gebcn unter eygenhändiger Unter-Schrifft deß offtmahlig ermeldten grossen Königs / *de dato* in der Haupt- und *Residen*tz-Statt *Invisibilis,* den 33. Monatst. *Inauditae, Anno post nihil 00000.*
>
>> *Nullander Rex Selenitide.*
>> *(L.S.)*
>> *Nemonius Secretar.* (147)

These *Privilegia* as well as the subsequent and for the Simplician novel cycle unique "Vorrede an den geneigten Leser," in which Grimmelshausen defends his satirical style, warn the reader right from the beginning not to assume blindly the perspective of the first person narrator.

With the aid of the chapter titles Grimmelshausen then continually sets up new warning signals. For example, chapter 12 carries the heading: "Das beste Mittel vor die Kriegs-Läuffe wird gesucht und gefunden / das schlimmste aber wird erwöhlet" (VN II 217). In that chapter, the businessman has nothing more urgent to do than to take his money out of the country and to hide it with a rich Portuguese Jew, about whom he produces all of the traditional anti-Semitic prejudices, but whose money and daughter he nevertheless does not resist.

In the rest of the cycle of novels Grimmelshausen continues to help the reader gain a more distanced posture toward the narrated material. Using irony, he summarizes the chapter content in the chapter heading. The third chapter of *Courasche,* for example, is summarized as follows:

> Janco vertauschet sein Edles Jungfer-Kräntzlein bey einem resoluten Rittmeister umb den Nahmen Courasche. (21)

The heading refers to the patriarchal tradition in which the woman receives the surname of the husband in marriage, thus becoming his property. The new name of Libuschka, who was dressed up as a boy and called Janco, indicates that she has apparently lost her virginity without being married. The name "Courasche" is a euphemism for the male genitals, which she lacks, and it defines the male gender as being superior to her. The resolute "Rittmeister" has courageously used his genitals with the inexperienced but in no way reluctant girl. She becomes a woman and she is ironically defined as such in that she is defined as not being a man. Her new name is supposed to remind her constantly about what has become obvious. As the resolute "Rittmeister" has proven, regardless of what she does or how she behaves, she belongs, in the eyes of the men, to the weaker sex. The masculine self-definition and the feminine foreign definition that are both indicated in the chapter title are shown to be untenable in the course of the narration, for the "Rittmeister" is anything but resolute and Courasche is anything but weak. The seemingly neutral summarizing heading proves to be a valuable reading aid for an understanding of the text, which goes well beyond the personal view of the feminine first person narrator and the narrow-minded male writer.

The heading of chapter 6 of the first book of *Simplicissimus* serves as an additional example:

> Jst kurtz / und so andächtig / daß dem *Simplicio* darüber ohnmächtig wird. ([5])

The attentive reader notices that Grimmelshausen is blurring the levels of the narrative fiction, for shortness and devoutness of the chapter can not possibly pertain to the helplessness of Simplicius. The innkeeper from Oberkirchen and the mayor of Renchen reminds the reader in a skillfully double coded but nevertheless lucid manner that the world, like the world of the Simplician novel cycle, is *a narrated* one.

Since the totality of life cannot be comprehended we should not explicitly shorten it. That is the message of the creative and imaginative poet from the Upper Rhine.

Autobiography and Novel

The Simplician cycle of novels shows, as indicated, a division into two parts that can be seen with regard to both form and content. Only the first four novels, *Simplicissimus Teutsch, Continuatio, Courasche* and *Springinsfeld,* take part during the Thirty Years' War or thematize that war. But they present themselves, on the title page, as biographies. Hence, the rest of this essay will be devoted exclusively to these works, so as to determine the relationship between novel and autobiography.

Simplicissimus Teutsch und *Continuatio*

It is astonishing that a cycle of novels, which constantly thematizes anew and from varying perspectives the life of the people during and immediately after the Thirty Years' War, should begin, as we read on the title page, with the biography of a man who claims to have "freywillig quittirt" the world. Must not the obvious negative judgment of the world, which underlies such a decision, lead every declared perspective in the narration of the life of people in the world *ad absurdum*? It is therefore appropriate to take a closer look at both the justification of the first person narrator and his escape "outside" the world.

It has already been pointed out that within the cycle the retreat of Simplicissimus is not definitive. Nevertheless, the claim made in the title of *Simplicissimus Teutsch* must be taken seriously. On the other hand, the autobiographical character of the novel urgently demands for its full understanding that the *Continuatio* must be taken as the sixth book of *Simplicissimus*. Both works, as the title already indicates, are more closely related to one another than are the remaining works in the cycle. Only in the *Continuatio* do we understand how the biography came to be written and what its purpose and goal are. Only here do we experience Simplicius as a voluntary exile.

The stay on the island is initially in no way voluntary. Rather, it is the result of a shipwreck, which Simplicius experiences on his return from Arabia back to Europe. After an initial despair of remaining definitely separated from his fellow humans, Simplicius experiences, exposed to the fruitfulness of nature, the unfamiliar dimension of being human. In contrast to his father, who led a lonely and ascetic life in the forest, Simplicius, following the quick death of those who were shipwrecked with him, lives a good but solitary life in the midst of lush nature. Lack of conflict and a plentitude of nourishment compensate for lack of social opportunities. Without being forced to swear allegiance to any religion, Simplicius finds a new and personal relationship to God.

In contrast to his father, he requires no books in order to get to know his God.[9] The book of nature announces God in abundant measure. Reflection on his earlier life offers him occasion to think about himself in the world. Thus his autobiography is the only book he needs and so he writes it down. In Europe he will have it put to print as a view of the world from the perspective of one who has left the world.

The harmony of God-nature-man turns the island, far from Europe, into a utopian locality where Simplicius re-experiences the bucolic paradise from his early childhood at a higher level.[10] Clearly, the locality as such does not have utopian quality. The island metaphor underscores instead the individual character of the harmony that has been achieved. Grimmelshausen thus allows for the presence of temptation and death on the island and contrasts the experience of Simplicius with that of the Dutch seamen.

Their arrival and their hunt for Simplicius as if in pursuit of a wild animal strengthen his resolution not to return to Europe. At the end of his report in the *Continuatio,* the Dutch captain reproduces a long speech given by Simplicius. In that speech, Simplicius provides detailed reasons why he remained on the island. Simplicius begins by saying, "Hier ist Fried/ dort ist Krieg" (584) and then explains that he did not view the war as God's punishment, but instead viewed the peace on the island as God's gift. No one in Europe knew what to do with peace, however, for all pursue one goal, "durch Unterdruckung deß andern sich groß zumachen" (584). Since they also use religion for their goal, there is no hope for improvement according to Simplicius, who explains:

> und was das allerärgste/ ist dieses/ daß keine Besserung zuhoffen/ in dem jeder vermeinet/ wann er nur zu acht Tagen wanns wol geräth dem Gottesdienst beywohne/ und sich etwan das Jahr einmahl vermeintlich mit GOtt versöhne/ er habe es als ein frommer Christ/ nit allein alles wol außgerichtet/ sondern GOtt seye ihm noch darzu umb solche laue Andacht viel schuldig. (584)

The church-bound religion of Europe reduces God in the eyes of Simplicius to *one single* human perspective and degrades Him as an instrument in the rationalization of human weaknesses. True divine service, by contrast, should bring people closer to God and enable them to see beyond themselves.

This is what Simplicius has learned in the "stillen Ruhe" (Co 584) on the lonely, but fruitful island. Liberated from the daily fight for survival and from daily competition he finds, by reflecting on his life, his way to God and to himself. Simplicius's "one-man-project" represents a clear repudiation not of the world as such, or as a place of diabolic temptation, but of civilized Europe and a church-bound religiosity. It is thus the appreciation of nature in its bounty that manifests to Simplicius the endless kindness of God and that leads him to realize the greatness and omnipotence of God. By looking back on his life, in viewing his thoughts, feelings, and actions, he also comprehends his own weaknesses and the subjectivity of his and all human worldviews.

It has been frequently emphasized that Simplicius does not undergo a development in the sense of the later "Entwicklungsroman." This is correct insofar as Simplicius is one more agent who acts in the world, but this does not pertain to the narrating Simplicius, who is reflecting back on the events of his life. This is evident in his religiosity. Although Simplicius on the island still refers to the traditional thought of war as punishment by God while relating the attack by soldiers on the farm of his "Knan," he no longer holds that view when speaking with the Dutch captain. Instead, he emphasizes the responsibility of the individual. In other words, the religiosity of the narrated Simplicius at the end of the fifth book of *Simplicissimus,* clearly characterized by tradition in its reference to Francisco de Quevedo y Villegas (1580–1645) and the hermitage of his father, ripens with the writing down of his life. At that same time, it leads to his becoming aware, on the island, of his individual relationship to God, which centers around his belief in the omnipotence and mercy of the Almighty. If Grimmelshausen's own view of the world can be identified with that of any of his figures, then most likely it would be with that of the old Simplicius at the end of *Continuatio,* of which the Dutch captain reports.

It is the stance that Simplicius gained on the island that explains his detached narrative position with regard to his own biography. We see this particularly in the fact that he speaks about himself, but he does not rationalize his behavior, nor does he justify it, nor does he accompany it with stereotypical acknowledgements of repentance. Instead, he comments very precisely on his errors and where he lost his way. The islander stands by his past, *in toto,* and that lends the narrative a bit of distance as well as an air of authenticity — with regard to the life of Simplicius.

Grimmelshausen hence disguises the useful or didactic aspect of his novel as self-reflection of the narrating first person. This indirect didacticism, however, always remains under his control, as he is the real narrator who pulls all the strings. Since Grimmelshausen does not intend to announce any general truths, but rather wants to challenge the reader to reflect on the possibilities of the realization of such general truths in human life, he allows the narrating Simplicius to report on certain behaviors, without having him comment on them explicitly. This would have only created extra motivation, which would have appeared superfluous and would have destroyed the fiction of the novel. As a talented narrator, however, Grimmelshausen knows that the important difference

between a sermon and a piece of literature lies in playing with a complicated story. Whatever warns too directly or has the effect of being too
direct in its message loses its charm for the reader, and the attention of
the reader declines. Furthermore, no didactic message can be carried
over hundreds of pages. On the other hand, that which lies hidden in a
closely woven text provokes the curiosity of the reader and moves the
reader to decipher the message.

We will use three examples, each different in its importance, to show
how Grimmelshausen puts the fictive autobiography in the service of an
overarching reflection, without allowing the narrative to suffer. The three
are Simplicius's pilgrimage with Herzbruder to Einsiedeln, his trip to the
world of the sylphs, and his last meeting with Olivier.

The islander Simplicius relates at one point how he, no longer so
young and no longer naive at all, accompanies his friend Herzbruder on
a penitent pilgrimage to Einsiedeln in Switzerland (Book 5, chapter 1).
In contrast to his friend, he used cooked peas in his shoes. On the island
Simplicius does not dissociate himself from the way he cheated during
the pilgrimage back then. By not commenting on the former comfort
and joy at his ingenious and funny trick, he actually makes a basic renunciation of asceticism as a demonstration of religiosity that only hurts
oneself. The context of the novel supports such an additional reading of
the trick that Simplicius once played on the pilgrim Herzbruder. The old
Simplicius namely also provides the reader with the reproachful sermon
that Herzbruder gave Simplicius when he became aware of the latter's
trick. However, this only reveals the problematic life strategy of Herzbruder, for whom Christianity and war are automatically connected.
Herzbruder, the professional soldier, actually goes on a strictly peniten-
tial pilgrimage when he happens not to have a job as a soldier. He tor-
ments himself, when he cannot frolic against the enemy on the battlefield
with his weapons. However, he throws away the hair shirt immediately
when Mars reigns and calls him back to the battlefield.

The biography of Simplicius is hence used, in this case, functionally
so as to clarify the contradictions present in another individual in the
novel. In presenting Herzbruder, Grimmelshausen gives us a character
who is in no way evil, but who belongs to that group of people who, by
their uncritical, conformist behavior, made possible a war that lasted
thirty years. Simultaneously, Herzbruder serves to make more precise the
religiosity of Simplicius on the island.[11]

A further example is the journey of Simplicius to the world of the
sylphs. In answering the question of the king of the sylphs about the life
of mankind on earth, Simplicius draws an ideal picture with regard to

ethics and to Christianity. However, he presents this picture as reality (Book 5, chapter 15; the speech itself in on 426–27). In addition, he attempts to make his speech believable by delivering it in an ostensibly dispassionate manner. Finally, when Simplicius is allowed to ask for something from the king of the sylphs as a parting gift, he does not ask for "etliche grosse Smaragd" (432), but rather for "einen rechtschaffenen *Medicinali*schen Sauerbrunnen auff meinen Hof" (432). Simplicius's pretended modesty impresses the king, who comments: "jetzt sehe ich/ daß kein Geitz bey euch Christen ist" (432). The autobiographical narration then makes absolutely clear that Simplicius at that time was in no way modest, but that he wanted the Sauerbrunnen "zu Nutz machen" (433), that is to say, he wanted to use it to become rich. Simplicius is not straight-forward with the pious king of the sylphs, because he knows that his large-scale, bustling activity, as well as the bribes for the doctors who would recommend his spa to their patients, would not please the king.

This scene is really not of further importance in the assessment of the narrated first person narrator. The reader has already been sufficiently informed about the art of dissimulation employed by Simplicius, and this scene sheds no new light on his wickedness. The hypocrisy is, in one way, actually not even problematic, because Simplicius does not enrich himself at the cost of the king of the sylphs. The narrator Grimmelshausen here quite obviously uses instrumentally the biography of Simplicius, in order that he might, through the deception of the king of the sylphs, open the eyes of the reader about the condition of the world. The quickly sketched utopia of a Christian society based on justice and charity should make the reader aware of the difference between the ideal and the real. It should show readers that they should have no illusions about the condition of the Christian western world. Whoever thinks that one would find there the best of all communities on earth, is mistaken, and whoever makes such a view known to others, is lying — this is the message Grimmelshausen wants his readers to take from the episode dealing with the world of the sylphs. The story-telling mayor of Renchen sets up the remainder of the action such that the grand scale plans of the would-be spa owner Simplicius are thwarted in a very ridiculous manner. Thus Grimmelshausen provides a comic, literary equivalent and an ethical balance to the proverb: He who sets a trap for others will fall into it himself.

The last example we will consider in terms of mutual influence of autobiography and novel in *Simplicissimus* is the last meeting of Simplicius with Olivier. It includes chapters fourteen through twenty-four

(Book IV); of those, chapters eighteen to twenty-two, which contain the long life story of Olivier, told in first person narration, deserve our special attention. These two figures are closely connected to one another, due to a prophecy of the elder Herzbruder shortly before the battle of Wittstock. The elder Herzbruder had prophesied that Simplicius would avenge the brutal death of Olivier by killing the latter's murderer (Book 2, chapter 24). After long years of separation, Simplicius and Olivier meet again, quite by chance. Olivier, who has become a highwayman or street thief, assaults Simplicius, whom he does not recognize. The violent duel, which develops between the two, finally allows them to discover, by accident, with whom they are dealing. The bodily fight therefore gives way to a verbal one.

In the course of the discussion with Olivier, for whom "die Rauberey das aller-Adelichste *Exercitium* ist" (338), Simplicius presents rather simple convictions, asks naive questions, and makes critical observations that do not correspond to his station in life at that time. The discussion deals partially with philosophical and political ideas, partially with social and pedagogical ones. When he meets Olivier, Simplicissimus has become sufficiently disillusioned that he still believes in abstract concepts of value and worth, which, however, have lost their relevance in the course of the lengthy war. His naiveté is therefore only feigned.

Simplicius, reacting piously and upright to the ruthless, egotistical and utilitarian self confidence of Olivier, is justified in terms of the plane of action because he in no way trusts Olivier, the highwayman who ostensibly wishes him well. He plays the part of a naive person, because he figures he has a better chance to survive if he does so.

> Jch gedachte/ was will das werden/ du must ander Wort hervor suchen/ als bißher/ sonst möchte dich dieser Unmensch/ [. . .] erst *caput* machen. (339; cf. 341)

There are several reasons why the naiveté of Simplicissimus does not arouse the suspicion of the highwayman. First, he has confidence in the fate that was announced to him, and he accepts that fate in a virile fashion, just as did the heroes of antiquity whom he so admires. Secondly, the naiveté of Simplicius only serves to prove to Olivier that the former is still the inexperienced youth from the camp in Magdeburg (cf. 337–339 and 358). This feigned naiveté, which however corresponds to Olivier's expectations, has the following result: the more naively Simplicius contradicts him, the more sincere and radical Olivier becomes in his self-portrayal. It is particularly attractive to the highwayman that he can appear ostentatious and as a loudmouth regarding his criminal successes in front of Simplicius, whom he considers gullible. The reason is that he will be able to revel in Simplicius's horror or, as the case may be, his astonishment.

In addition to the internal motivation for the successful posing of Simplicius, there are additional motives that have to do with the narration. Olivier receives from Grimmelshausen an unlimited opportunity to give voice to a ruthless settling of accounts with a society that, in his eyes, consists of sanctimonious, lazy, and corrupt Christians. That, in turn, allows him to portray his existence as a highwayman as a social and ideological protest. This former son of a middle class family thus becomes a negative point of orientation, while Herzbruder, who is described as a friend, portrays for the time being a positive pole. However, in retrospect, Simplicius on his island also questions that portrayal. Thus, with the help of Olivier and Herzbruder, Grimmelshausen clarifies the position of Simplicius.

For the soldier Herzbruder there is no conflict between the war and his Christian ethics; he loyally carries out his duty, without asking questions, with regard to Church and religion as well as with regard to his soldier status. Olivier, of course, sees the contradiction, but negates it nevertheless, because he cannot justify the existence of a Christian ethic, since the majority of the people do not respect it anyhow. For Simplicius on the island, however, the contradiction between Christian ethics and war is, as he reviews his life, the central problem that he attempts to solve. His decision to remain alone on the island makes clear that for him, as for Olivier, there is no compromise. However, in contrast to Olivier, he decides for the Christian ethic of charity and against the so-called Christian Europe.

In addition, Grimmelshausen uses the autobiographical excursus of Olivier instrumentally within the genre "novel," which strives for totality. The naiveté of Simplicissimus actually allows Olivier to tell his entire life story willingly. That takes up a good five chapters (18–22) of Book IV of the novel. Thus, in addition to Simplicius's childhood on a farm, we also have the world of the bourgeoisie, although this is given in a very specialized situation.

From a formal point of view, the biography of Olivier is perfectly placed in the narrated autobiography of Simplicius Simplicissimus. In the church building of a deserted village on the Upper Rhine, Olivier, accompanied by Simplicissimus, waits for passers-by so that he can rob them. He asks Simplicius, whom he values as the future avenger of his death, what has happened to him since their separation after the Battle of Wittstock. Simplicius, however, by appealing to Olivier's pride, manages to have Olivier tell his life story first. His request to Olivier was "er wolte mir doch zuvor seinen Lebens-lauff erzehlen/ der vielleicht possierliche Schnitz in sich hielte" (345).

The life story of Olivier, presented as a first person narrative, is thus justified from the point of view of narrator as well as from the point of view of narration. First, it keeps Simplicius from repeating what the reader already knows. Second, the empty, *de facto* de-sanctified church in a village ravaged by war somewhere in southern Germany on the border with France seems the ideal location for the *confessio* of a non-repentant robber and murderer with "gut Alt-Teutschen" (338) and Machiavellian airs.[12]

Olivier's autobiography charms the reader as the consistently related self-portrayal of a criminal. Olivier was the son of a well-to do businessman in Europe in the middle of the seventeenth century. He then became a criminal because his parents spoiled him and because he lacked a proper upbringing. Olivier sees himself as the result of an "Affen-Liebe" (346), which at first forgave him for everything, only to be followed by an exaggerated strictness. He accuses his father, who finally threatened him with prison, of being the cause of his son's ruin:

> Solche und dergleichen *Lectiones* muste ich täglich hören/ biß ich zuletzt auch ungedultig wurde/ und zu meinem Vatter sagte: Jch wäre an allem nit schuldig/ sondern er und mein *Praeceptor,* der mich verführet hätte; daß er keine Freud an mir erlebe/ wäre billich/ sintemal seine Eltern sich auch seiner nicht zu erfreuen/ als die er gleichsam im Bettel verhungern lasse. (350)

Olivier, who is not at all stupid, combines a lack of self-criticism with an ideology of power and force, which he shores up with arguments relating to power politics stemming from Machiavelli. This combination he uses to justify his dissolute and predatory life. Olivier tells his story with a cold indifference, making it seem an appropriate strategy for a wolf among the wolves, which fight over their booty, the naive sheep that have no idea what is going on. The indifference with which Olivier speaks of murder, deception, force, and rape is unique in the entire Simplician cycle. Olivier's self-thematization culminates in the last chapter of his biography. In that chapter, he speaks of his ill fate with cats and dogs (Book 4, chapter 22, 356–58). Olivier's touching, scarred face bears witness in a platonic fashion to the hideousness of Olivier's soul, which will never again be beautiful or pure, because Olivier is not capable of any positive feeling, least of all the feeling of repentance. He supposedly does not believe in the ethical values of a Christian community, since he sees them flagrantly disregarded everywhere. Basically, though, this fits in well with his egotistical principles of life, which do not consider other human beings.

It is astonishing how consistently Olivier's slide into a life of crime is socially motivated in the novel. His biography hence becomes the model of a story of middle-class decline. This instance of criminality expands to an exemplary social study, which is carried out without any palliation, but also without any false-sounding moralizing. The islander Simplicius never comments on the cold, distant narrative style of Olivier, this street hero. Nor is this style interrupted with warnings to the reader. Thus, Grimmelshausen ensures that Olivier's criticism of a hypocritical Christianity, and of the egoism and coldness of his parents, does not lose its justification. On the other hand, Olivier's responses to that criticism (as seen in his words, his life, and his violent death) are sufficiently repudiated.

All the more inappropriate, however, are the attempts Simplicius the listener makes at converting Olivier. His moralizing comments never place doubt on or jeopardize the ideological justification of the highwayman. Simplicius's helplessness when confronted with Olivier's existential flow of speech makes clear how unresolved Simplicius's convictions are at that point in the story. It also shows how difficult it has become in time of war to defend values, to withdraw from the corrupting flow of events, and how senseless it is to represent ethics with weapons. Of course, this all supports the decision of the narrator, Simplicius, to stay on the island.

The weight of Olivier's autobiography is strengthened within *Simplicissimus* by the fact that it anticipates or foreshadows the story of Julus and Avarus in the *Continuatio*.[13] The two Englishmen, the one a weak son of a rich trading family and the other his instructor, especially in matters of corruption and lack of responsibility, finally end up on the gallows during the Puritan revolution. However, they are not criminals like Olivier, but instead big spenders who shun work, individuals who perish in luxury and vice. However, their life story is not presented as an autobiography, but instead is told by Simplicius. He had had a dream about a bet between the two vices of greed and wastefulness, a bet which took place in front of Lucifer, the prince of darkness, and the victims of which were Julus and Avarus. Dream and the kind of dream underscore the exemplary nature of their biography and indirectly of that of Olivier, since the two stories differ from one another only in a few details.

The lengthy autobiography of Olivier, which represents a compact literary unit and which is taken up again in the dream about Julus and

Avarus, leads us to assume that Grimmelshausen might originally have considered a plan for giving Olivier his own novel within the Simplician cycle about the "Krieg als Monstrum." Olivier, the badly raised son of a citizen, is a figure who, like Simplicius, Courasche, Springinsfeld, the halberdier or the merchant in *Wunderbarliches Vogel-Nest*, is suited to be the main character in an independent novel. In any case, the life story of Olivier is without a doubt the most compact autobiography of a minor character in *Simplicissimus*.

The narration of the biography of Olivier as a spontaneous act of speech was, within the fictional autobiography of Simplicius, only possible if it was told to the writing Simplicius, who thematizes himself. The only way to achieve this was to have Simplicius once again speak and act like a naive young man. Simplicius himself later maintains, after the Olivier-episode, that it had been an act of providence that Olivier related his life story before Simplicius related his. This was the only way that Simplicius was saved from having to acknowledge that he was the hunter from Soest [Jäger von Soest] at whose hands Olivier had suffered disgrace (cf. chapter 22).

Grimmelshausen uses this interpretation of events by a main figure, which stresses God's saving grace, to demystify the routine of daily life, because it presents to the reader the course of events in the story as a necessary result of the construction of the novel. Thus he justifies the autonomy of the novel, which does not need any extra-literary dimension in order to exist. The life of the figures and the biographies of invented characters in the novel develop independently. They cross each other's paths, they quarrel with other individuals, and they try to outdo the others. They fail or they become successful within the literary immanence of the author, who has invented them and who moves them around within the cycle of novels. Within that cycle, all have the right to speak, to report about themselves. They either repent or do not, are mostly defeated and crippled, disillusioned or grim, but they are never so successful that they might maintain that they had tamed the war and in so doing had done something which would be of lasting value.

With this type of novel construction, which instrumentally changes the function of the constitution of the "I" within the flow of the narration, Grimmelshausen sends a clear signal in this, his first novel, that he has opted for the totality of life and against the exemplary nature of any single individual. In the course of the Simplician cycle, he keeps the promise inherent in *Simplicissimus* that he would present the multiplicity of human being through a series of great and small protagonists, who either tell about themselves or whose lives are reported by a given "I" narrator. They all lived from 1618 to 1648 and beyond, under Mars, the reigning god of the sun. Mars, with the assistance of Venus and Mercury, fascinates, confuses and blinds these humans with Eros and money, with honor and success, and leads them down false paths again and again, unceasingly. All this, Grimmelshausen had promised, will be "exceedingly droll and very advantageous to read."[14]

Courasche

Courasche certainly has to be counted among the great protagonists of the Simplician cycle. It shows like almost nothing else the acuity and sensibility of Grimmelshausen that he has a woman narrate the second independent autobiography within the Simplician cycle. In so doing he clearly points to the very basic fact that the gender to which one belongs, masculine or feminine, defines one's way of thinking, of feeling, of dealing with others; indeed that it is more important than societal, geographical and historical matters. This was done at a time when women were not considered equal to men, certainly not independent; Grimmelshausen was clearly aware of the extraordinariness of his undertaking in giving a woman a public voice. This is clear not only in the figure he created and in her life, but even in the title of the novel.

The woman, who relates her life, is introduced as an *outlaw*, as an "Ertzbetrügerin," and as a "Landstörtzerin." She speaks out publicly, not to praise God or to defend herself against unjustified accusations,[15] but rather to show "Verdruß und Widerwillen" (title page) to a man, Simplicius Simplicissimus. This task could only be given to a woman who traveled through the country as a Gypsy, who lived outside the law, outside of justice, indeed, outside the Christian order. The first part of the title, *Trutz Simplex,* therefore gains a significance that goes well beyond the purely narratological function of linking the novels together. It shows the right of a woman, who is a marginal figure in *Simplicissimus* and who is depicted there as a liberal female, to present her view of events, to become a protagonist, and to portray the world of the Thirty Years' War from a female perspective. In so doing she denies the male first person narrator any claim that he alone represents the human race. *Trutz Simplex* also captures something else: the biography of a woman arises as a reaction, just as her decisions and her conduct in life consist, for the most part, of reactions, since, as a woman, she does not play any independent societal role. The status of the husband determines the social position of the woman, as the series of military ranks in the title of the novel about Courasche makes clear.

The autobiography of Simplicissimus ends as the lonely hero on the island consciously decides against Europe and war. The autobiography of Courasche also ends with the protagonist leaving the Christian, western society. However, Courasche enters a new community, a community of Gypsies, where she lives freely, is recognized and satisfied. As the reader discovers in the next novel of the cycle, *Springinsfeld,* people in her new society also use her real name once again, Libuschka, whereas she had previously tried again and again without success to rid herself of her nickname, Courasche. This was the name given to her by the soldiers as they discovered that the groom Janco, whom Libuschka pretended to be, was really not a man at all. Therefore they called her Courasche, and in so doing referred to the male genitalia, in order to remind her constantly that as a woman she was really not a man.

Even through the title and naming of his main character, Grimmelshausen signals his readers that the biography of Courasche does not report the life of just any woman, but that in the story of her life we find general feminine conditions of life and feminine perspectives. We are, hence, dealing in the autobiography of Courasche with an autobiographical novel. Of course, one does have to ask whether such an unusual life can really claim to be valid for women in general.

Without a doubt it shows us the greatness of Grimmelshausen as a writer that he created a unique woman with his figure of Courasche and yet in narrating her life story he pointed out the way her life is controlled by her gender. The fate of Courasche has a consistency that is due not to her wishes or her actions but rather to her gender. This becomes clearer in view of the fact that Libuschka grew up without a family and as far as we know does not belong to a given class as such. She is actually the illegitimate daughter of an influential count in Bohemia, who fought against the emperor in Vienna for the independence of Bohemia. For that reason, she grew up, protected, under a false name, in a village. There the war surprised her and her nurse, whereupon her stepmother dressed her up as a boy so that she would not be raped. Hence, Libuschka begins her socialization under the name Janko, as a horse-groom for an officer. However, as she begins to mature, her femininity brings her increasingly into conflict with this role. Having fallen in love with her officer, she announces to him that she is a woman, before the soldiers, who had discovered it while playing cards, make that announcement. Shortly thereafter, she becomes the mistress of the officer and, with him on his deathbed, his wife as well.

As the illegitimate daughter of a nobleman and as the widow of an officer, Courasche at first hopes to balance the taint of her birth with her exceptional beauty and still land up in a good match. However, the story about the Danish captain in chapter 13 shows the reader in two instances that she is mistaken. The captain brings the roughed-up and raped Courasche to one of his houses, thinks of marriage, and becomes her lover, because he likes her. However, the knowledge about her origins in a Bohemian noble family was of more importance for his decision. On the other hand, Courasche is not noble enough for the parents of the captain. Therefore, they thwart the planned marriage of their son with deceptive tactics.

Gradually, Courasche learns that money is often a more deciding factor than love in moving men to marry her. After that point, everything in her life has to do with men and money, because only as a rich, married woman is she able to have a relatively good and secure life during the Thirty Years' War. Her biography makes this clear, at least indirectly, on two occasions. As a widow, Courasche is twice attacked and repeatedly raped, although she knows how to use weapons and often has proven her extraordinary courage on the battlefield.

Now, however, acquisition of money and the securing of a husband are connected to one another in a rather peculiar way. Courasche, who has not learned a trade of any sort, can get money most simply by means of prostitution. The numerous men who woo her make this step rather easy for her. On the other hand, her bad reputation endangers her desire to marry just as much as her money functions in a way to attract men, who, of course, are not to be trusted.

Her second marriage already makes this connection clear. A captain saves Courasche, who has been attacked and raped, and, impressed with her beauty, he offers her marriage and wants to share her possessions. She does not agree right away, because she tells him that according to the laws of war, he has no claim to her possessions. However, he threatens to leave her and her possessions for the young men to fight over. Against all odds, the marriage with the captain is a happy one. Although he proves to be impotent, he is very liberal as far as Courasche's sexual needs are concerned. Not really worried about what others might say, he also allows her to fight on the battlefield and to win booty. Their good fortune is, however, short-lived. Courasche quickly becomes a widow once again, and she has to begin seeking a new husband.

Marriage and widowhood continue to characterize the life of Courasche like accented and unaccented syllables in a line of poetry. However, her increasing self-confidence and independence, which are based on her accumulated riches as well as on her successes on the battlefield, where she fights along as if she were an Amazon, make her appear less and less attractive as a spouse. Courasche's decline therefore begins once she is able to maintain her position in a man's world. The men continue to desire her as a sex object and would not despise her as a rich spouse, but they stand united against her as a vigorous and successful woman. In so doing, they always reach for the two old tried and true means: violence and defamation. There are negative consequences for Courasche when her former Italian husband is shot as a deserter, just as there are when she single-handedly captures a major. It was her Italian husband, who, the morning after their first night together, demanded that they fight to see who would "wear the pants." He had been so sure of his success that he had invited his officer colleagues to the spectacle! After that, no one wants to have anything to do with her, they defame her as a witch, and, when the occasion arises, they rape her in a bestial fashion.

In view of this situation, Courasche has to change her strategy. She finds a musketeer, who, in terms of class is beneath her and who is blinded by her beauty, her money, and her position. She attempts to convince him to live with her, according to a contract they would make. He would be *pro forma* boss and owner of her sutlery, but would actually recognize her as boss and owner. Her superior position would actually be clear to everyone, because he would be known by a name that would be formed from the first command that she would give him. In this way, Courasche would avenge herself for her nickname and would consciously turn the practices of the Christian patriarchal society upside down. Her plan succeeds, but the secret changing of the traditional gender roles does not, in the long run, have the desired consequences. Springinsfeld (the name Courasche gave the musketeer) does not put up with her gentle reign for very long, because his comrades begin to tease him about being a hen-pecked husband. In order to save his male honor, he tries to subdue Courasche by beating her. When this has no effect, he, too, falls back on the reproach of witchcraft.

At this point, Courasche's social decline takes a definitive turn. Expelled from the army, she seeks her fortune in prostitution, but this time she loses both health and money. Only when she crosses over into a completely different social dimension, into the world of the Gypsies, does she once again begin to blossom. Here she is no longer forced to try and win, in a world which is ruled by war and the laws of which are clearly written for the advantage of one single gender, namely that of the male, her place in the sun. Among the Gypsies, Courasche can actually do as she pleases. That, of course, is what she shows the readers in the play that she produced so magnificently in a Lothringian village in order to earn money for food.

Among the Gypsies Courasche develops more than a criminal creativity — she also composes her autobiography. She becomes a narrator, just like her author. Like his first figure, Simplicius, she, too, looks over her whole life from an external perspective. She regrets nothing, because she could not have acted much differently, and of that she is sure. Instead she indicts the clergy, who now demand repentance of her, but who during her entire life to date had left her alone. This programmatic rejection of repentance removes the autobiography of Courasche from the picaresque tradition and underscores Grimmelshausen's literary search for a religiosity outside the institutions of a church.

Although Courasche's autobiography is, with regard to length, considerably shorter than that of Simplicius, many researchers — quite in contrast to the reading public — had major problems right from the beginning, with the text and with its main character, a female. Her strong personality contradicted the idea about the role of the woman, and this not only in the seventeenth century. The allegorical and moral-didactic interpretation solved this contradiction in that it declared Courasche an object of Grimmelshausen's criticism. The argument went as follows: Courasche is the negative counter-image of Simplicius, an allegory of evil, Dame World, woman who follows her uncontrolled instincts, woman who upsets the Christian, patriarchal order with her attitude and with her behavior. Therefore, she was designated a witch, and the mass rapes that she suffered foreshadowed the eternal punishment in hell that justifiably awaited her.[16]

This interpretation, which is presented over and over again with new arguments, assumes *a priori* a definition of that epoch, which is characterized by a negative evaluation of the female, who, according to a divine *ordo*, is subject to the male. Witch-hunting is considered as the extreme expression of this Zeitgeist. However, it is precisely the witch-hunting that ought to lead us to caution. The *Disquisitiones Magicae* (1599) of the Jesuit priest, Antonio Martino Delrio, is one of the most important theoretical works on witchcraft. The *Cautio Criminalis* (1631) of another Jesuit priest, Friedrich von Spee, is the most important critical treatise about witch-hunting and witch-trials. These two works show that, even within the same Catholic religious order, there existed conceptions of witchcraft, witch-hunting and witch-trials that differed completely from one another.[17]

One cannot overlook the subliminal sympathy of the author for his female first person narrator, and this fact allows doubts to arise. The narrative strategy of the author, who describes her actions as a reaction to a war-torn world, lets such an interpretation appear highly questionable. In that war-torn world, a young girl paid doubly for naiveté and feelings, if she did not quickly learn to defend herself with all possible means. The hypothesis, according to which Courasche is Dame World and the destroyer of the divine *ordo,* fails to take into consideration that from the very beginning of the novel there is nothing of this *ordo* left at all. Libuschka never gets to experience a family situation, where family structures serve as the basic cells of a Christian community. Her protected childhood is nevertheless abruptly destroyed by male soldiers, who apparently have nothing other in mind than robbing, pillaging, raping, and murdering. Grimmelshausen goes one step further. His female protagonist is within the novel the only figure who is capable of completely positive relationships (we will get to that shortly), and also formulates a theological basis for her conception of a harmonious relationship in which both genders operate on equal footing. She tries to talk the Italian lieutenant, who wants to fight with her about who will "wear the pants," out of such a plan. Courasche has recourse to the biblical account of creation, and she says:

> gleich wie ich wol weiß/ daß das Weib nicht aus des Manns Haubt/ aber wol aus seiner Seiten genommen worden/ also habe ich gehofft meinen Hertzliebsten werde solches auch bekand seyn/ und er werde derowegen sich meines Herkommens erinnern/ und mich nicht/ als wann ich von seinen Fußsohlen genommen worden wäre/ vor sein Fuß-Thuch/ sondern vor sein Ehe-Gemahl halten. (42)

The creation of woman from a bent rib of man was, in the demonology one of the arguments used for the inferiority of the woman. This designated her as a being that somehow was lacking something, as an "unvollkommenes Tier," and pointed to the fact that the woman was, just like the curved rib, "gleichsam dem Mann entgegen geneigt."[18] Hence, she always wanted to do harm to the male and for that reason made a pact with the devil. Courasche counteracts that with a completely different interpretation. The episode that provokes this conversation confirms her opinion. Grimmelshausen shows that it is the man who has deceived the woman about his true intentions, and that it is he who wants to do her harm.

We have already alluded to the fact that Courasche is classified as a witch within the novel. It is the men who are not her equal who intentionally classify her as such. We cannot identify that with Grimmelshausen's own concept. However, since we often find this stance in the research on this novel, and since this thesis is offered as support for the fact that Courasche is an allegory of Dame World, that Courasche is evil incarnate, we need to take a closer look. The relevant scene shows how Courasche is tortured and raped by the soldiers and officer colleagues of the major whom she had subdued and captured in a fair combat, one on one.

The episode occurs as Courasche, after her clearly happy fourth marriage, becomes a widow once again, during the siege of Schloß Hoya. The officer mentioned uses the opportunity, and he leads away the sad, crying Courasche as the defeated soldiers surrender. Immediately he insults her as a "Blut-Hex" (61) and announces his intention of revenge. Courasche later remembers that "Er sahe so gräßlich aus / daß ich mich auch nur vor seinem Anblick entsetzte" (61). That she had every reason to do so we read in the next scene, the rape scene, which leaves nothing to be desired in terms of brutality. It shows that Courasche was correct when she adjudged that these "Viehischen Unmenschen" (Cour 63) had forgotten "aller Scham / und Christlichen Erbarkeit" (63). Finally the attackers confer as to whether they ought, as the crowning finality of their revenge, to have Courasche "als einer Zauberin den Proceß durch den Hencker machen lassen" (63). Even though the initial situation speaks for the fact that calling Courasche a witch was absolutely unfounded and intentional, Grimmelshausen underscores it once again by making clear that the officers are obviously thinking of "lynch justice" and not of an objective, legal process. Some may still want to think of the rape as a brutal, but just punishment of Courasche (she as a woman had offended a man, an officer who was a member of the nobility, and thus had breached the divinely ordained social order). However, they then have to deal with the question of how to interpret the end of that chapter.

At the end of that chapter, another captain appears on the scene. Courasche had also captured him in the past. The major leads him to her, because he thinks that the captain would also want to use this opportunity to take revenge on Courasche. It turns out quite differently, however. The captain is horrified at the state of the roughed-up Courasche, and asks for an explanation of what has happened. The major, who in the meantime has gotten drunk, thinks he will get rid of all the captain's scruples if he explains that they are dealing with a witch. The captain will have none of it, and instead reports that it is not the devil, who is Courasche's father, but rather one of the closest allies of the Danish king, who happens to be the superior officer of the major. The chapter ends with the major and the other officers, for opportunistic reasons *on their knees,* asking Courasche for forgiveness, which she, crying, grants.

Since nowhere in the novel does Grimmelshausen have Courasche working with magic practices, the chapter described above allows only one reasonable conclusion: Courasche is a witch only in the eyes of a few *male* characters in the novel, not in the eyes of Grimmelshausen! The foes of the self-confident Courasche define her as such in order to excuse the fact that they failed to defeat a woman, in order to be able to give vent to their lowest human desires and still remain innocent of wrongdoing. This they can only do by accusing this woman as being the magical cause of their actions. In other words, Grimmelshausen thinks that during the war Lucifer rules over the male figures.

Courasche's autobiography actually forbids us, on both the level of the story told and on that of the narrating itself, from seeing in its protagonist an ally of the devil, of considering Courasche the negative pole and Simplicius as the positive pole of the entire cycle. Basically, one can take issue with an antithetical grouping of Simplician figures by noting that such an interpretation negates the formation of relativity of human thought and action as the creative center of the entire anti-war cycle of Grimmelshausen's novels. The author himself points inescapably to that fact through the Simplician narrative fiction of having figures from the novel in competition with each other and carrying on controversies with each other. This he accomplishes by giving them all a similar position and importance, that is, each of them appears as a first person narrator.

Since Grimmelshausen does not stand behind *one individual* figure, but rather behind the entire corpus of Simplician writings, we are not allowed to see Courasche through the eyes of Simplicius, of Springinsfeld, or of Philarchus Grossus. We are particularly forbidden to view her through the eyes of all her important and unimportant enemies, her military foes, her economic competitors or disappointed lovers and rivals within the novel. Nor can we define her through their eyes. If we do, we simplify that which Grimmelshausen intentionally formed in a complex and multi-perspective fashion. Only in such a fashion could he portray the war as a piece of inhumane and unchristian handiwork.

If one still, in keeping with the teaching from *Wunderbarliches Vogel-Nest I,* wants to make value judgments about the figures in the novel, it is perhaps more appropriate to compare Courasche with those characters in the cycle who are clearly negative characters. Those include Olivier, Julus and Avarus, the hurdy-gurdy woman, the lyre player, and the merchant from *Wunderbarliches Vogelnest II.* That would be more appropriate than a comparison with Simplicius, whose positive role first has to be determined, because that which might be valid for Simplicius on the island is scarcely valid for the Hunter von Soest, for Beau Alleman or for the quack doctor who deceives the farmers. Even for these negative characters we have to keep in mind that Grimmelshausen does not depict them as representative of evil incarnate. Rather, he is interested in the genesis and development of evil in mankind on the basis of specific external conditions.

Let us take the figure of Olivier for a short comparison, since he also appears as a first person narrator and operates during wartime as well. If you compare the autobiography of Olivier with that of Courasche, it becomes clear that the latter, apart from the immediate similarities, which lie particularly in the pride of self-portrayal, diverges significantly from the former. Olivier continually justifies himself, and he makes others, beginning with his parents, responsible for his ill fortune and his wickedness. He even tries to pass off his misdeeds as heroic actions. He doesn't repent, because he considers the system of values itself to be dishonest. For that reason, he fights everyone and tries to deceive everyone. He uses his life story to try and convince Simplicius, whom he considers naive, of those things. That autobiography reveals a hardened, pessimistic man, who is concerned only with himself, who stops at nothing to acquire whatever it is that he wants. Although other paths were open to him, Olivier chose war, because he thought he had recognized that only the god of power and the god of deception rule the world. War becomes his basic principle of life, because it corresponds to his conception of life. In the final analysis, he pays for his attitude with a violent death.

Courasche's autobiography on the other hand makes clear that she would have liked to lead a different life, even though she does not deny that the war fascinated her just as it did young Simplicius. War seemed to her as though it promised a fullness of life. Even as it is expressed in this error, it is the positive attitude toward life in Courasche's autobiography that captivates us. It is revealed again and again in her gregarious, her generous, and her considerate nature, as seen, for example, in her regard for her stepmother. Courasche, who was violently drawn into the war as a child therefore tries, repeatedly, to draw back from the war and to lead a private life that is not based on fighting, on domination and subjugation. Her attempts always fail, due to intervention from external sources. One need only think of her life with her Danish officer, which fails because his family takes violent actions against her, or her marriage to the good-looking Italian, which ends even as it begins. He, after all, immediately turned out to be a man who insisted on his male prerogatives and wanted to construct his authority with a whipping cane. Let us quote here the description of her fourth marriage as an example of Courasche's ability to form a positive relationship:

> Jch und mein Mann bekamen einander je länger je lieber/ und schetzte sich als das eine glückseelig/ weil es das andere zum Ehegemahl hatte/ und wann wir uns nit beyde geschämt hätten/ so glaub ich/ ich wäre Tag Nacht in den Lauffgräben auf der Wacht und in allen occasionen niemahl von seiner Seiten kommen; wir vermachten einander alles unser Vermögen/ also/ daß das letzt-lebende (wir bekämen gleich Erben oder nicht) das Verstorbene erben: Meine Säugamme oder Mutter aber/ gleichwohl auch ernehren solte. (59)

This marriage, however, was also not meant to last, because the Danes shot her husband to death during the siege of Schloß Hoya.

Grimmelshausen neither lets Courasche boast about her autobiography nor does he let her "sell" the insights that she gained in the course of her eventful life as the ideal solution. Instead, Courasche shows herself as aware of her mistakes, and she does not gloss over her way of life, which is clearly not edificatory. However, she also knows that she often could not have acted differently if she wanted to survive in the world of war. She regrets nothing, because as a woman she became the object of desire, and victim of the power, of men and she received neither familial nor spiritual assistance. During the war, she learned to rely solely on herself, on her strength, her wisdom, her beauty, and above all her money.

For that reason, Courasche is also not ready to pay any hypocritical tribute in her old age to Christian morality and confess her sins. On the contrary, her autobiography is the written confirmation of an independence that was forced upon her by circumstances. She does not give it any exemplary function, but rather sees in it her last act of self-assertion when faced with male authorities. These have lost all authority in her eyes, because they did not perform their legal responsibilities of taking care of her and did nothing to stop the war, as she says *expressis verbis* in the first chapter of her autobiography. She denies that they have any right to judge Courasche. *Trutz-Simplex* therefore turns against the first person narrator in *Simplicissimus* and indirectly warns the reader about considering as truth itself the word of any one single human being, in this case, namely, the narrator Philarchus Grossus von Trommenheim, alias Grimmelshausen.

With the autobiography of the *un*-repentant Courasche, Grimmelshausen goes beyond the picaresque and thematizes not an individual sin, the a-historical evil, but rather the *un*-Christian world of the Thirty

Years' War. The victims of that war were primarily women, even though women did not complain about it, just as Grimmelshausen's main character does not. Rather, those women surrendered themselves to the war and tried to enjoy it in spite of everything. Grimmelshausen related, through the autobiography of a woman named Libuschka-Courasche, the general conditions of life for a woman in the time of the Thirty Years' War. His novel is therefore the first attempt to depict the world from a woman's perspective and at the same time to undertake a revision of theories inimical to women through a narrated life.

Springinsfeld

In contrast to *Simplicissimus Teutsch, Continuatio,* and *Courasche,* the novel entitled *Der seltzame Springinsfeld* is not centered on the autobiography of the title figure. Although it is like the other novels in the Simplician cycle in that the title announces that the reader will be offered a "Kurtzweilige/ lusterweckende und recht lächerliche Lebens-Beschreibung," the reader quickly is able to see that someone else relates the story in the first person, namely Philarchus Grossus von Trommenheim. The scribe, who is given almost exclusively an instrumental function in *Courasche,* reveals himself at the beginning of *Springinsfeld* as someone who gladly and eagerly talks about himself. He speaks at first about his Swiss origins, then about his failed attempts to secure a position as a scribe in the Upper Rhine area, then about how he chanced, in an inn on an ice-cold winter's day, to meet up with Simplicius, who was most unusual in appearance, as well with Springinsfeld, and, finally, how he came into conversation with the both of them. Philarchus, presenting himself as an "armer Schüler" (Spr 27), relates how he met Courasche and was hired as a scribe to write her autobiography which is directed against Simplicissimus, how he lived among the Gypsies, and finally, how Courasche left him and how he was then swindled out of his salary. Not until chapter 10 (out of a total of twenty-seven chapters) does Springinsfeld begin with his life story. Before we get that far, the group, after Simplicius has related still another prank from his youth, has moved to the marketplace in the village, where Simplicius is introducing his marvelous book. Back at the inn, "Knan," "Meuder," the son of Simplicius, the latter's friend, and a servant join them. Since they cannot seem to sleep at night, Springinsfeld, urged on by Simplicius, helps them pass their time by telling his life story. The next day, Simplicius engages Philarchus Grossus, for six Reichstaler, to write down the autobiography of Springinsfeld and to publish it, so that the whole world will know that his son is not the child of Courasche.

We see that the autobiography of one single figure is not the central point of *Springinsfeld*. Nor are we simply dealing with a doubling of first person narrators. Instead of a self-portrait, consciously told later in life as an expression of self and as an act of self-assertion, we have the writing down of one, no, of two, biographies, which arise from a conversational situation. That is to say, we are dealing with occasional narratives, told in the presence of other individuals. These individuals influence the narrator as they are the direct addressees, and, in addition, they enter into the narrative flow and even direct it.

The differences between this novel and the two earlier autobiographies in the Simplician cycle become clear in the fact that the story of Springinsfeld and that of Philarchus Grossus both actually come to an end within the novel. Grimmelshausen emphasizes the difference, insofar as he again lets Courasche dominate the scene in the first part of *Springinsfeld* and completes her story on the narrative level because her scribe, Philarchus Grossus, begins to take on contours here. Thus his interventions and explanatory notes in the autobiography of the gypsy woman subsequently lose, after the fact, any aura of authorial authenticity they might have had. Philarchus Grossus turns out not to be an independent thinker, but rather a man totally bound up in clichés, who is fearful and, as a result, very trusting in authority. His judgment about Courasche is mixed with the anger of someone who has been deceived and with an excitement about a woman, who ought not to excite him, as she is considerably older and is a Gypsy.

His detailed descriptions of the richly bejeweled Courasche, who is dressed in a snow-white blouse and who lives in a white tent, reproduce very well the fascination that the Gypsy leader and the free life of the Gypsies have on him. The luminous figure Philarchus Grossus draws of the women, whom, as he says, "bis auf diese Stund in meiner Einbildung sehen kan / wann ich will" (Spr 26), contrasts noticeably with the comparisons he uses to characterize her. Courasche is like the whore of Babylon, she reminds him of a devilish ghost, of a witch.[19] In so doing, he is like Springinsfeld, who, on the one hand praises the beauty of Courasche and admits to having had "bey derselbigen [. . .] ein güldene Herrnsach" (54) while on the other hand cursing her as "Blut Hex" (24) and "Teuffelsvihe" (24). Simplicius, while he admonishes Springinsfeld to be more circumspect, refuses to make a definitive judgment about Courasche. He does see Courasche "bis über die Ohren im Sündenschlam" (38), but he does not want to exclude the possibility of a conversion on her part. Simplicius acts as though the thought of the gypsy woman no longer upsets him. In her failed attempt at revenge he wants only to see an example of the deceived deceiver. However, his request that Philarchus Grossus write down the life story of Springinsfeld and confirm that his son is not the child of a "losen Zigeunerin" (29) shows that his serenity is only feigned. Since Courasche's revenge consisted in her revealing that she was not the mother of Simplicius's son, we do not need Springinsfeld's autobiography to prove it, especially since in his autobiography he excludes the part of his life where he lives together with Courasche.[20]

In *Springinsfeld,* therefore, the narrative fiction of *Courasche* is, as is that of *Simplicissimus Teutsch* in the *Continuatio,* cleared up after the fact, so to speak. Readers had experienced and meditated on the life of the protagonist step by step and had formed an initial judgment. Then, they are forced to look back once again on the life that had been narrated and perhaps to revise those earlier judgments. In the *Continuatio,* the report of the Dutch sea captain served that purpose. Here with regard to Courasche we have divergent opinions from three individuals, particularly the opinion of Philarchus Grossus.

As noted, Grimmelshausen works differently with the autobiography of Springinsfeld. The extrinsic motivation for the narrative has its effect on the narration. Since that figure stands with regard to itself without any distance and is not self-critical, the doubled first person narrator perspective, which characterizes the autobiographies of Courasche and Simplicius, is reduced to a purely temporal perspective, and therefore it is almost totally lost. The tale of Springinsfeld shows us an individual for whom looking back on his life does not really cause him to reflect on that life. His story therefore ends without any radical decisions. More for reasons of comfort than out of conviction does Springinsfeld accept Simplicius's offer that he stay on the latter's farm. There, supposedly having mended his ways due to Simplicius, he dies the following spring.

In the narration of his life story, Springinsfeld sticks much more closely to externals than do his predecessors. He seldom comments on or makes value judgments about his actions; when he does, it is only superficially. To relate his life story means to him primarily to list the important stages and events or to relate in a somewhat more detailed manner for the enjoyment of his listeners the unusual events. He, too, would like to get rich off the war and to have a position in the military, but he plans neither for the short nor the long term. Instead, he enjoys his life when things go well, and he suffers adversities as if they were strokes of fate over which he has no control. Thus, he reports about the good times:

> Von dannen gelangten wir in das Mayländische und so fort zu Land durch Saphoiam/ Burgund/ Lotharingen/ ins Land von Lützenburg und also in die Spanische Niderlande/ allwo wir neben andern Völckern mehr under dem berühmten Ambrosio *Spinola* wider des Königs Feinde *agir*ten; um dieselbige Zeit befande ich mich noch zimlich wol *content;* ich war noch jung/ mein Herr liebte mich/ und liesse mir allen Muthwillen zu; ich wurde weder durch strenges *marchirn,* noch andere Kriegs-Arbeiten abgemattet. (Spr 59)

When fate is less favorable to him, he describes his situation in the following manner:

> Diese Schlacht und darinn erlittener Verlust war nur der Anfang und gleichsam nur ein *Omen* oder *praeludium* des jenigen Unglücks/ das noch länger bey mir *continui*ren solte; dann nachdem mich die Altringische erkanten/ muste ich wieder under dem jenigen Regiment ein Tragoner seyn/ worunder ich mich anfänglich vor einen underhalten lassen; und solcher Gestalt hatte nicht allein meine Freyreuterschaft ein End/ sonder weil ich auch alles verloren/ ausser dem was ich am Leib darvon gebracht/ so war auch die Hoffnung pritsch ein Officier zu werden. (Spr 78)

Springinsfeld criticizes the war when it works to his disadvantage, whereas he praises the life of a soldier when he makes a profit at it. Hence he rejects the reproach of Simplicius's adoptive mother that he violated the farmers because, as he explains, soldiers exist to keep the farmers in line. As a justification, he points besides to Simplicius, who did not act any differently. Finally, he criticizes the custom, common to both the Turkish and the German armies, of having poor soldiers fighting in the front lines, because in this manner he is robbed of potential booty. Springinsfeld follows ruthlessly his own interests in the war, just as Olivier did, but without the ideological superstructure of the latter. Thus he kills an injured, unarmed Swedish officer, who is seeking his help, so that he can rob him. He justifies this inhumane conduct as an act of reparation against repressive military structures (Spr 82–83). He would most like to take part in the war as an unattached soldier, as a free lance.

Springinsfeld is not really able to process intellectually his experiences in war. He prefers to speak of the war in the form of general examples, which at one point even take up an entire chapter (chapter 11). Several times, Simplicius has to remind him that he and the other people listening are interested in his life and in his experiences, and not in generic thoughts about the war.

Simp: fiele ihm in die Rede und sagte/ entweder redestu im Schlaf oder wilst wieder aus dem Weg tretten/ du wilst den Krieg underscheiden und vergist abermal deiner eignen Person/ sage darvor wie es dir selbst gangen? (Spr 66)

It is actually a paradox that Springinsfeld's inability to portray his life results from an exaggerated concentration on himself. Such a concentration degrades everything around it down to the level of an object. A change in perspective is no longer possible. Hence, he can either speak about himself or he can speak in generalities. This is especially clear in his relationships with the opposite sex. He is actually a misogynist, because in his relationships with women, to whom he considers himself superior (in line with tradition), he always is the loser. He condemns the majority of females as allies of the devil and the remaining few honest women he considers, unjustifiably, as an expensive burden, because each of their services costs money. "Spinnet sie mir und ihr ein Stück Tuech an Leib / so mus ich Flachs / Woll und Weberlohn bezahlen" (Spr 55), is the way he explains it to Simplicius, who would like to talk him out of his misogynist ways of thinking.

Grimmelshausen gives his readers to understand, less through the arguments of Simplicius than through the course of action in the novel, that injured male honor has blinded Springinsfeld. For example, he allows an enraged Springinsfeld to go after Philarchus Grossus, when the latter reveals the origin of the name Springinsfeld. Later, when Simplicius attempts to find out the cause of Springinsfeld's misogyny, Springinsfeld demurs:

ja Bruder/ sagte Springinsfeld/ wann du wüsstest/ wie übel mirs mit einem Weib gangen/ so würdest du dich gar nit verwundern/ wann verbrente Kinder das Feur förchten; *Simplicius* fragte/ villeicht mit der leichtfertigen *Courage*? wohl nein/ antwortet Springinsfeld/ bey derselbigen hatte ich ein güldene Herrnsach/ ohnangesehen sie mir gleichsamb offentlich aus dem Geschirr schlug; aber was geheyte es mich/ sie war doch nicht meine Ehefrau. (Spr 54, 30)

We see that Springinsfeld does not possess the human greatness of a Simplicius or of a Courasche. Grimmelshausen expresses this very clearly by not having an entire novel devoted to Springinsfeld's autobiography. Instead, he allows Philarchus Grossus the freedom of using the first nine chapters for his own self-portrayal. This is noteworthy, because, as the reader learns in the last lines of the work, Simplicius, in contrast to Courasche, has paid Philarchus Grossus to write down the life story of Springinsfeld.

In spite of a less significant human greatness in the title character and in spite of the resultant reduced literary tightness, *Der seltzame Spring-insfeld* is not an uninteresting novel. Its place and role within the Simplician cycle is not unimportant. The central characters of the earlier novels meet one another again through him or, as the case may be, become the objects of a discussion, whereby they are, once again, seen in a new light. Simplicius and Courasche prove to be the central characters in the cycle, because they are the ones who, directly or indirectly, steer the life and the narration of the other figures from the novel.

If we look closely, we see that Courasche has a special role. She is the actual connector between Simplicius, Philarchus Grossus and Springins-feld and she provokes the narrative of Philarchus Grossus as well as, indirectly, the life story of Springinsfeld. Springinsfeld's misogyny, which manifests itself at the very mention of Courasche's name, causes Simplicius to request that Springinsfeld narrate his life story and through that autobiography, which he orders Philarchus to write down, he wants to answer Courasche. However, Springinsfeld doesn't speak of his life with Courasche in his narration. Instead, his second wife, the lute player with her bird's nest, is revealed as the real source of his hatred of women. In this way, on the one hand, his tale announces the novels to follow. On the other, it offers an indirect challenge to the reader to compare the lute player with Courasche, with whom Philarchus Grossus had previously dealt in detail.

Grimmelshausen hence steers the reader by placing the subject of witchcraft at the center of attention. It turns out that Springinsfeld has called both Courasche and the lute player a witch. However, their behavior with regard to the supposedly magical and devilish objects is basically very different.[21] Courasche acquires, innocently and in a drunken state, an unusual object, the *spiritus familiaris*, from a poor, old soldier. The lute player, on the other hand, is immediately interested in the nest that makes one invisible and that Springinsfeld had discovered. Not only does she cast to the winds the warnings of her husband, she insults him and then leaves him so that she can become rich through dishonest means without having to share the wealth with him. The lute player carries things to such an extent that she is finally burned at the stake as a murderer, a witch, and a magician. Courasche, too, keeps the *spiritus familiaris* in spite of the warnings of her nurse. However, she does not ignore the dangers that are involved with it. Instead, she accepts the risks for quite some time, since she thinks that simply through her possession of it she will sell more goods, will acquire lovers more easily, and will enjoy the goodwill of her fellow citizens. At the first possible opportunity however, she sells the object, to Springinsfeld. He is able to rid himself of the object without any difficulties, in contrast to the supposed conditions of ownership. Thus, it seems that the magical and devilish quality of the *spiritus familiaris* is rather far-fetched, and this is confirmed by the poverty of its first owner.

The comparison of Courasche with the lute player not only exonerates Courasche, but it also suggests to the reader that the simple possession of an object is less decisive in judging a person than is the individual's attitude and behavior. However, it is difficult to make definitive judgments about such things, as is clear from Grimmelshausen's multi-perspective cycle of novels. Thus, Grimmelshausen makes relative the reproach of witchcraft. This we notice with regard to Courasche as well as in the *Springinsfeld* novel. It is, in the final analysis, uncertain whether it was really the lute player about whose death as a magician some innkeeper had reported to Springinsfeld. He, in turn, is the victim of a corresponding defamation, by people who are jealous of his prosperity.[22] Within the Simplician cycle of novels, *Springinsfeld* has the position of a switch or reversal, because in it, one looks back on the previous novels and also prepares for the forthcoming ones. This applies, by the way, not only to the content. Even though Springinsfeld is less striking than Simplicius or Courasche, in terms of either human qualities or of literary ones, his figure is nevertheless still sufficiently full that it can function as a title character. This is, of course, true for neither the halberdier in *Wunderbarliches Vogel-Nest I* nor for the businessman in *Wunderbarliches Vogel-Nest II.*

The gradual withdrawal of the first person narrator as the main character underscores in retrospect and as a point of comparison the personality of the two great figures of the Simplician cycle. It lends their life stories, in spite of their general validity, their uniqueness. This also causes the meta-literary construction to emerge even more clearly, as if it were a game, confidently conducted by Grimmelshausen with his individual figures. These figures complement each other, because they carry on their controversies from novel to novel, they cuss each other out and fight with one another. Still, they are closely tied to each other, like close relatives and old friends. In the conversations held in *Springinsfeld,* this internal logic of the Simplician cycle is pictorially conveyed, as if on a multiple stage.

Hence, I consider it misleading, even fallacious, if we do not consider this meta-literature characterized by figures that are claiming a place in literature for themselves. We would then be thinking that we would hear the voice of the author Grimmelshausen instead of that of the good, middle-class Philarchus Grossus, or the pious, repentant Simplicius who has returned to Europe. In addition, we would be ascribing to these figures the authority to make value judgments about the other characters and about the world that is portrayed in the novels. Quite the contrary, the selection of the autobiography as the narrative form of the Simplician cycle suggests that none of these persons is identical to Grimmelshausen and that no figure from the cycle, whether a central or a marginal one, represents *in toto* the opinion of the innkeeper from Oberkirchen. Were that so, then the cycle as a construction desired by Grimmelshausen would have no justification whatsoever, and his literary battle against the war as an extreme form of the maintenance of an opinion would be senseless right from the start.

Translated by Karl F. Otto, Jr.

Notes

[1] Cf. H.-G. Rötzer: *Picaro — Landstörtzer — Simplicius.* — G. v. Gemert: *Die Werke des Aegidius Albertinus.* — G. Hoffmeister: *Niclas Ulenhart: Historia.* — D. Ynduráin: *La autobiografía y el Lazarilo.* — G. v. Gemert: *Funktionswandel des Pícaro.* — I. M. Battafarano: *Picari simpliciani tedeschi.* —A. Martino: *Il Lazarillo de Tormes.*

[2] The complete title of the seventeenth-century first edition is: *Der Abentheurliche SIMPLICISSIMUS Teutsch/ Das ist: Die Beschreibung deß Lebens eines seltzamen Vaganten/ genant Melchior Sternfels von Fuchshaim/ wo und welcher gestalt Er nemlich in diese Welt kommen/ was er darinn gesehen/ gelernet/ erfahren und außgestanden/ auch warumb er solche wieder freywillig quittirt. Überauß lustig/ und männiglich nutzlich zulesen. An Tag geben Von GERMAN SCHLEIFHEIM von Sulsfort. Monpelgart/ Gedruckt bey Johann Fillion/ Jm Jahr M DC LXIX* [= Nürnberg: Wolff Eberhard Felßecker 1668]. The *Continuatio* appeared one year later. Its complete title is: *CONTINUATIO des abentheurlichen SIMPLICISSIMI Oder Der Schluß desselben. Durch GERMAN SCHLEIFHEIM von Sulsfort. Mompelgart/ Bey Johann Fillion/ 1669* [= Nürnberg: Wolff Eberhard Felßecker]. — The novels of Grimmelshausen are quoted from the edition of Rolf Tarot (according to the abbreviations in the Introduction, with page numbers).

[3] Erasmus published his *Querela Pacis* in Basle (1517) and Sebastian Frank his *Krieg Büchlin des Friedes* in Augsburg (1539).

[4] From the title page of *Simplicissimus Teutsch. Courasche* has "Eben so lustig/ annemlich uñ nutzlich zu betrachten als Simplicissimus selbst." *Springinsfeld* on the other hand claims to be a "Kurtzweilige/ lusterweckende und recht lächerliche Lebens-Beschreibung." The title pages of *Wunderbarliches Vogel-Nest* I and II make no references to biographies. Their baroque titles are: *Das wunderbarliche Vogel-Nest/ Der Springinsfeldischen Leyrerin/ Voller Abentheurlichen/ doch Lehrreichen Geschichten/ auff Simplicianische Art sehr nutzlich und kurtzweilig zu lesen außgefer-*

tigt Durch Michael Rechulin von Sehmsdorff. Monpelgart/ Gedruckt bey Johann Filli-on/ Jm zu Endlauffenden 1672 Jahr [= Strasbourg: Dollhopff]. The second part carries the title: *Deß Wunderbarlichen Vogelnessts Zweiter theil An tag geben von Aceeeffghhiillmmnnoorrssstuu.* The work also appeared in the Dollhopff publishing house in Straßburg (1675).

[5] The complete title of the first edition is: *Trutz Simplex: Oder Ausführliche und wunderseltzame Lebensbeschreibung Der Ertzbetrügerin und Landstörtzerin Coura-sche/ Wie sie anfangs eine Rittmeisterin/ hernach eine Hauptmännin/ ferner eine Leutenantin/ bald eine Marcketenterin/ Mußquetirerin/ und letzlich eine Zigeunerin abgegeben/ Meisterlich agiret/ und ausbündig vorgestellet: Eben so lustig/ annemlich uñ nutzlich zu betrachten/ als Simplicissimus selbst. Alles mit einander Von der Coura-sche eigner Person dem weit und breitbekanten Simplicissimo zum Verdruß und Wider-willen/ dem Autori in die Feder dictirt, der sich vor dißmal nennet PHILARCHUS GROSSUS von Trommenheim/ auf Griffsberg/ etc. Gedruckt zu Utopia/ bei Felix Stratiot* [= Nürnberg: Wolff Eberhard Felßecker 1670].

[6] The complete title of the first edition is: *Der seltzame Springinsfeld / Das ist Kurt-zweilige / lusterweckende und recht lacherliche Lebens-Beschreibung. Eines weiland frischen / wolversuchten und tapffern Soldaten / Nunmehro aber ausgemergelten / abgelebten doch dabey recht verschlagnen Landstörtzers und Bettlers / Samt seiner wunderlichen Gauckeltasche. Aus Anordnung des weit und breit bekanten Simplicissimi Verfasset und zu Papier gebracht Von Philarcho Grosso von Tromerheim. Gedruckt in Paphlagonia bey Felix Stratiot. Anno 1670.* [= Nürnberg: Wolff Eberhard Felßecker 1670].

[7] Grimmelshausen dealt in a similar way with tradition when the young Simplicius sang his song about the peasants. He allows the soldiers to interrupt Simplicius right at that point in the song when he is praising the evil custom of the soldiers who appropriate all the worldly possessions of the peasants because the peasants would otherwise become too arrogant. However, the young Simplicius, in his dream about the "Ständebaum" (Book I, Chapter 15–18), offers a considerably more fundamental sociological explanation for the enmity between peasants and soldiers. In *Springins-feld* (Chapter 13) the Meuder criticizes Springinsfeld's view that soldiers are the scourge of the peasants, just as God would have it. Springinsfeld, on the other hand, emphasizes that Simplicius, too, would not have acted differently as a young soldier, and he notes that the peasants have themselves killed soldiers and have stolen from their neighbors. The aged Simplicius puts forward as an alternative that it is not whether peasants or soldiers are better, but simply that war spoils everything and everyone. In *Wunderbarliches Vogel-Nest* II the justification of war as a punishment of God is again criticized as a comfortable way out of responsibility.

[8] In *Wunderbarliches Vogel-Nest* II the narrator hides behind a simple series of letters, which, however, again produce the name Grimmelshausen.

[9] The total lack of books on the island represents a conscious attempt to present a world other than that which is based on interpretation of the bible and which had lead to a split within the church. Compare with this Simplicius's attempts to "extin-guish the fire" in Book One (30–31).

[10] Compare Book One, Chapter One, where an express comparison with paradise is made (12).

[11] The following chapter with its exorcism and Simplicius's temporary conversion deepen this aspect even more.

[12] Cf. 338 and 339, where Machiavelli is listed by Olivier as his ideological point of reference.

[13] Cf. Co, Chapter 5–9. The story of Julus and Avarus however, is related as a third person narrative in a dream of Simplicius the islander.

[14] Cf. the title page of *Simplicissimus The Vagabond*. Translated by A. T. S. Goodrick, with an introduction of William Rose. — London: George Routledge & Sons, New York: E. P. Dutton & Co. [1924].

[15] The witch hunts show us how limited such actions were. To the degree that I have knowledge of archival material, there is not extant a single public defense written by a woman.

[16] For a discussion of the critical literature cf. I. M. Battafarano: *Erzählte Dämonopathie in Grimmelshausens "Courasche."*

[17] Cf. I. M. Battafarano: "Hexen, Hexenlehre, Kritik der Hexenverfolgung: Bodin, Binsfeld, Delrio Remy, Spee." — "Barocke Typologie femininer Negativität und ihre Kritik bei Spee, Grimmelshausen und Harsdörffer." — "Mit Spee gegen Remigius: Grimmelshausens antidämonopathische Simpliciana im Strom nieder-ober-rheinischer Vernunft." — "Absentia dei in Spees Cautio Criminalis?"

[18] Sprenger / Institoris: *Der Hexenhammer*, 99. — The *Hexenhammer* or, in Latin *Malleus Maleficarum*, was published for the first time in 1487. It is the most important book of witch hunting. Jean Bodin, Antonio Martino Delrio and Nicolas Remy (Remigius), the most famous demonologists in the late sixteenth century, still based their reasoning on it.

[19] Cf. Chapter Five in *Springinsfeld*, 26, 29; 27, 14 and 27, 15.

[20] Of course it is true that Simplicius lets Courasche know that the child foisted upon him was indeed his son, since he had produced it together with the servant girl. However, this announcement makes sense only as revenge on Courasche, because, as Philarchus expressly says, the similarity between son and father is so great that no one would be able to negate the fact that he was the father, cf. Spr 50.

[21] The references are to chapters 18 and 22 of *Courasche* as well as chapter 13 of *Springinsfeld*. With regard to the lute player, see also chapters 23, 24, 26, and 27 of *Springinsfeld*.

[22] Cf. Chapter 22. It is not coincidental that it is precisely in the two chapters (7–8, 38–50) that separate the autobiographical report of Philarchus Grossus von Trommenheim from that of Springinsfeld that Simplicius delves into the problems associated with a belief in witchcraft and magic.

Works Cited

Aylett, R. P. P. *The Nature of Realism in Grimmelshausen's "Simplicissimus" cycle of Novels.* Bern and Frankfurt: Lang, 1982. (= European University Studies, Series 1: German Language and Literature 479)

Battafarano, Italo Michele. *Grimmelshausen-Bibliographie 1666–1972. Werk — Forschung — Wirkungsgeschichte.* With assistance of Hildegard Eilert. Naples 1975. (= Quaderni degli Annali dell'Istituto Universitario Orientale di Napoli, Sezione Germanica 9). [An updated version of this bibliography (1666–2002) is expected to appear soon]

———. *Glanz des Barock. Forschungen zur deutschen als europäischer Literatur.* Bern: Lang, 1994. (= IRIS 8)

———. "Die Faszination des Monstrums Krieg in Grimmelshausens Simplicianische Schriften." In: I. M. B. *Glanz des Barock,* 13–32.

———. "Leben vor der Schöpfung Adams: Präadomiten und Nicht-Adamische: Isaac de Lapeyère / Paracelsus / Grimmelshausen." In: I. M. B. *Glanz des Barock,* 161–85.

———. "Der seltsame Pilger, der wilde Mann, der gute Wilde: Garzoni, Montaigne, Grimmelshausen." In: I. M. B. *Glanz des Barock,* 238–79.

———. "Der barocke Pegasus: Grimmelshausens literarisches Selbstverständnis." In: I. M. B. *Glanz des Barock,* 280–88.

———. "Hexen, Hexenlehre, Kritik der Hexenverfolgung: Bodin, Binsfeld, Delrio, Reme, Spee." In: I. M. B. *Glanz des Barock,* 338–58.

———. "Barock Typologie femininer Negativität und ihre Kritik bei Spee, Grimmelshausen und Harsdörffer." In: I. M. B. *Glanz des Barock,* 392–412.

———. "Mit Spee gegen Remigius: Grimmelshausens antidämonopathische Simpliciana im Strom nieder-ober-rheinischer Vernunft." *Simpliciana* 18 (1996): 139–64.

———. "Erzählte Dämonopathie in Grimmelshausens 'Courasche.'" *Simpliciana* 19 (1997): 55–89.

———. "Absentia dei in Spees Cautio Criminalis? Wesen und Wirkung einer epochemachenden Schrift." *Morgen-Glantz* 8 (1998): 385–400.

———. "Garzoni und Grimmelshausen." In: I. M. B. *Von Andreae zu Vico. Untersuchungen zur Beziehung zwischen deutscher und italienischer Literatur im 17. Jahrhundert.* Stuttgart: Heinz, 1979. 55–105. (= Stuttgarter Arbeiten zur Germanistik 66)

———. "Vom polyhistorischen Traktat zur satirischen Romanfiktion. Garzonis 'Piazza Universale' bei Albertinus und Grimmelshausen." In: I. M. B., ed. *Tomaso Garzoni.* Bern: Lang, 1991. 109–24. (= IRIS 3)

————. "Picari simpliciani tedeschi. Crisi e stravolgimento del modello ideo-poetologico della narrative picaresca nell'opera de Grimmelshausen." In: I. M. B. and P. Taravacci. *Il Picaro nella cultura europea*. Trento: Reverdito, 1989. 243–89. (= Apollo 3)

Berns, Jörg Jochen. "Die 'Zusammenfügung' der Simplicianischen Schriften. Bemerkungen zum Zyklus-Problem." *Simpliciana* 10 (1988): 301–25.

————. "Libuschka und Courasche. Studien zu Grimmelshausens Frauenbild." *Simpliciana* 11 (1989): 215–60 and *Simpliciana* 12 (1990): 417–41.

————. "Buch der Bücher oder Simplicianischer Zyklus. Leserprovokation als Erzählmotivation im Gutenbergzeitalter." *Simpliciana* 12 (1990): 102–22.

————. "Erzählte und erzählende Bilder. Porträttechniken im simplicianischen Zyklus." *Simpliciana* 20 (1998): 105–22.

Breuer, Dieter. "Grimmelshausens politische Argumentation. Sein Verhältnis zur absolutistischen Staatsauffassung." *Daphnis* 5 (1976): 303–32.

————. "Krieg und Frieden in Grimmelshausens 'Simplicissimus Teutsch.'" *DU* 37 (1985): 79–101.

————. "Der sinnreiche Poet und sein ungewöhnlicher neuer Stil. Grimmelshausen und die europäische Argutia-Bewegung." *Simpliciana* 15 (1993): 89–103.

————. "Der Erzähler Grimmelshausen als Historiker und die 'Vollkommenheit der Histori.'" *Simpliciana* 20 (1998): 37–48.

————. *Grimmelshausen-Handbuch*. Munich: Fink, 1999 (= UTB für Wissenschaft 8182)

Feldmann, Linda Ellen. "The rape of 'Frau Welt:' Transgression, Allegory and the Grotesque Body in Grimmelshausen's 'Courasche.'" *Daphnis* 20 (1991): 61–80.

Gaede, Friedrich. "Grimmelshausen." In: F. G. *Realismus von Brant bis Brecht*. Munich: Francke, 1972. 39–43.

————. "Grimmelshausen und die Tradition des Skeptizismus." *Daphnis* 5 (1976): 465–82.

————. "Grimmelshausen scepticus: Urteil als Wahn." In: F. G. *Poetik und Logik. Zu den Grundlagen der literarischen Entwicklung im 17. Und 18. Jahrhundert*. Bern and Munich: Francke, 1978. 69–82.

————. "Homo homini lupus et ludius est. Zu Grimmelshausens 'Der seltzame Springinsfeld.'" *Deutsche Vierteljahrsschrift für Literaturwissenschaft und Geistesgeschicht* 57 (1983): 240–59.

————. *Substanzverlust: Grimmelshausens Kritik der Moderne*. Tübingen: Francke, 1989.

Gemeret, Guillaume van. *Die Werke des Aegidius Albertinus (1560–1620). Ein Beitrag zur Erforschung des deutschsprachigen Schrifttums der katholischen Reformbewegung in Bayern um 1600 und seiner Quellen.* Amsterdam: Holland UP, 1979.

———. "Funktionswandel des Pícaro. Albertinus' deutscher 'Gusman' von 1615." In: *Il Picaro nella cultura Europea.* Ed. I. M. Battafarano and P. Taravacci. Trento: Reverdito, 1989. 91–120.

Geulen, Hans. "Positionen und Auffassungen pikaresken Erzählens vor Grimmelshausen und Beer." In: H. G. *Erzählkunst der frühen Neuzeit.* Tübingen: Rotsch, 1975. 189–208.

Grimmelshausen, Hans Jakob Christoffel von. *Gesammelte Werke in Einzelausgaben.* Ed. Rolf Tarot, with assistance from W. Bender and F. G. Sievecke. Thirteen vols. Tübingen: Niemeyer, 1967–1976.

———. *Werke.* Ed. Dieter Breuer. Three vols. Frankfurt: Deutsche Klassiker, 1989–1997. (= Bibliothek deutscher Klassiker 44 and Bibliothek der frühen Neuzeit 16/1 and Zweite Abteilung, 4/1)

Heckmann, Andreas. "Melancholie in Grimmelshausens 'Courasche.'" *Simpliciana* 14 (1992): 9–34.

Hesselmann, Peter. "'Dessen Schwall mache Jesuiten verstummen.' Grimmelshausen und die Rhetorik." *Simpliciana* 15 (1993): 105–22.

Hoffmeister, Gerhart, ed. *Niclas Ulenhart: Historia von Isaac Winckelfelder vnd Jobst von der Schneid. 1617. Nach Cervantes'* Rinconete y Cortadillo. *Kommentiert und mit einem Nachwort von G. H.* Munich: Fink, 1983. (= Literatur-Kabinett 1)

Jacobson, John W. "A Defense of Grimmelshausen's Courasche." *GQ* 41 (1968): 42–54.

Joldersma, Hermina and Elke Wickeert. "Moraldidaktik, Erzählform und Autorintention in Grimmelshausens 'Landstörtzerin Courasche.'" *GR* 64 (1989): 158–66.

Kaminski, Nikola. "Narrator absconditus oder der Ich-Erzähler als 'verschwundener Kerl.' Von der erzählten Utopie zu utopischer Autorschaft in Grimmelshausens 'Simplicianischen Schriften." *Deutsche Vierteljahrsschrift für Literaturwissenschaft und Geistesgeschichte* 74 (2000): 367–94.

Krebs, Jean-Daniel. "La pícara, l'aventurière, la pionnière. Fonctions de l'héroïne picaresque à travers les figures de Justina, Courage et Moll." *Arcadia* 24 (1989): 239–52.

Mannack, Eberhard. "Grimmelshausen und das Monströse." *Simpliciana* 15 (1993): 149–62.

———. "Politische und verfassungsgeschichtliche Aspekte im Werk von Grimmelshausen." *Daphnis* 5 (1976): 333–41.

Martino, Alberto. *Il Lazarillo de Tormes e la sua ricezione in Europa*. Two vols. Pisa and Rome: Instituti Editoriali e poligrafici internationali, 1999.

Meid, Volker. *Grimmelshausen. Epoche — Werke — Wirkung*. Munich: Beck, 1984 (= Arbeitsbücher für den literaturgeschichtlichen Unterricht. Beck'sche Elementarbücher)

Menhennet, Alan. *Grimmelshausen the Storyteller: A Study of the "Simplician" Novels*. Columbia, SC: Camden House, 1997 (= Studies in German Literature, Linguistics, and Culture)

Ornam, Vanessa van. "No Time for Mothers: Courasche's Infertility as Grimmelshausen's Criticism of War." *Women* 8 (1992): 21–45.

Petersen, Jürgen Hans. "Formen der Ich-Erzählung in Grimmelshausens simplicianischen Schriften." *Zeitschrift für deutsche Philologie* 93 (1974): 481–507.

Rötzer, Hans Gerd. *Picaro — Landstörtzer — Simplicius. Studien zum niederen Roman in Spanien und Deutschland*. Darmstadt: Wissenschaftliche Buchgesellschaft, 1972. (= Impulse der Forschung 4)

Schade, Richard E. "Junge Soldaten alte Bettler: Zur Ikonographie des Pikaresken am Beispiel des 'Springinsfeld'-Titelkupfers." In: Gerhart Hoffmeister, ed. *Der deutsche Schelmenroman im europäischen Kontext. Rezeption, Interpretation, Bibliographie*. Amsterdam: Rodopi, 1987. 93–112 (with 10 illustrations). (= Chloe. Beihefte zum Daphnis 5)

Schäfer, Walter Ernst. "Der Dreißigjährige Krieg aus der Sicht Moscheroschs und Grimmelshausens." *Morgen-Glantz* 9 (1999): 13–30.

Schmitt, Axel. "Intertextuelles Verwirrspiel — Grimmelshausens Simplicianische Schriften im Labyrinth der Sinnkonstitution." *Simpliciana* 15 (1993): 69–87.

Schweitzer, Christoph E. "Grimmelshausen, Philarchus Grossus von Tromerheim, and 'Simplicianische Schriften.'" *Monatshefte* 82 (1990): 115–22.

———. "Multiple Perspective and the Issue of Truth in Grimmelshausen's Fiction." In: Barbara Becker-Cantarino and Jörg-Ulrich Fechner, eds. *Opitz und seine Welt: Festschrift für George Schultz-Behrend zum 12. Februar 1988*. Amsterdam: Rodopi, 1990. 455–68. (= Chloe. Beihefte zum Daphnis 10)

Shepphard, Richard. "The Narrative Structure Of Grimmelshausen's 'Simplicissimus.'" *Forum for Modern Language Studies* 8 (1972): 15–26.

Solbach, Andreas. "Erzählskepsis bei Grimmelshausen im 'Seltsamen Springinsfeld.'" *Simpliciana* 12 (1990): 323–50.

———. "Macht und Sexualität der Hexenfigur in Grimmelshausens 'Courasche.'" *Simpliciana* 8 (1986): 71–87.

Speier, Hans. "Courage, the Adventuress." In: H. S. *The Truth in Hell and Other Essays on Politics and Culture 1935–1987*. New York and Oxford: Oxford UP, 1989. 245–55.

Sprenger, Jakob and Heinrich Institoris. *Der Hexenhammer, zum ersten Male ins Deutsche übertragen und eingeleitet von J. W. R. Schmidt.* Berlin: Barsdorf, 1906 Reprint: Darmstadt: Wissenschaftliche Buchgesellschaft, 1980.

Stadler, Ulrich. "Satire und Romanform. Zur immanenten Poetik des Hans Jacob Christoffel von Grimmelshausen." *Daphnis* 9 (1980): 98–107.

Stein, Alexandra. "Die Hybris der Endgültigkeit oder der Schluß der Ich-Erzählung und die zehn Teile von 'deß Abentheuerlichen *Simplicissimi* Lebens-Beschreibung.'" *Deutsche Vierteljahrsschrift für Literaturwissenschaft und Geistesgeschichte* 70 (1996): 175–97.

Streller, Siegfried. "Rollensprechen in Grimmelshausens Erzählen." *Simpliciana* 12 (1990): 89–99.

Tarot, Rolf. "Formen erbaulicher Literatur bei Grimmelshausen." *Daphnis* 8 (1979): 3–4, 95–121.

———. "Grimmelshausens 'Simplicissimus' und die Form autobiographischen Erzählens." *Etudes Germaniques* 46 (1991): 55–77.

———. "Grimmelshausen als Satiriker." *Argenis* 2 (1978): 115–42.

———. "Grimmelshausens Realismus." In: Wolfdietrich Rasch, Hans Geulen, Klaus Haberkamm, eds. *Rezeption und Produktion zwischen 1570 und 1730. Festschrift für Günther Weydt zum 65. Geburtstag.* Berne and Munich: Francke, 1972. 233–65.

Valentin, Jean-Marie. "Théologie et esthétique. Sur le chapitre premier de la 'Landstörtzerin Courasche' de Grimmelshausen." *Études Germaniques* 42 (1987): 278–90.

Verweyen, Theodor. "Der polyphone Roman und Grimmelshausens 'Simplicissimus.'" *Simpliciana* 12 (1990): 195–228.

Wagener, Hans. "Perspektive und Perspektivismus in Grimmelshausens 'Wunderbarlichem Vogelnest.'" *GQ* 49 (1976): 1–12.

Wiedemann, Conrad. "Die Herberge des alten Simplicissimus. Zur Deutung des 'Seltzamen Springinsfeld' von Grimmelshausen." *Germanisch-Romanische Monatsschrift* 64 (1983): 394–409.

———. "Zur Schreibsituation Grimmelshausens." *Daphnis* 5 (1976): 702–32.

Ynduráin, Domingo. "La autobiografia y el Lazarilo." In: *Il Picaro nella cultura Europea.* Ed. I. M. Battafarano and P. Taravacci. Trento: Reverdito, 1989. 37–53.

Zeller, Rosmarie. "Fabula und Historia im Kontext der Gattungspoetik." *Simpliciana* 20 (1998): 49–62.

Grimmelshausen's "family" from the Simplicissimus Redivivus *(1683).*
Reprinted with permission of the Herzog August Bibliothek,
Wolfenbüttel

Allegorical and Astrological Forms in the Works of Grimmelshausen with Special Emphasis on the Prophecy Motif

Klaus Haberkamm

I. Fundamentals

A. Grimmelshausen as Author between the Middle Ages and the Enlightenment

1. Predecessor of the Enlightenment?

NOT ONLY IN OUR progressive times does literary and historical research on the seventeenth century edge toward the Enlightenment. This approach gained legitimacy after the rediscovery of the literary Baroque by scholars of German in the 1920s and 1930s. Should we project Leibniz exclusively into the eighteenth century, not only because of his life span (1646–1716)? Was the universal philosopher, who made differential equations known long before Newton, rather not representative of many of his future-oriented contemporaries, including poets?

Johann Jakob Christoff von Grimmelshausen, whose novel *Der Abentheurliche Simplicissmus Teutsch* can be viewed as seventeenth century German literature's contribution to the world canon, offered himself as a candidate for such a movement toward reorientation. As one of the most important baroque authors, he is highly eligible. Even if his astonishingly vigorous reception proved itself as relatively weak in the eighteenth century, it (= the reception) should encourage this view. Several details seem to advance the argument that Grimmelshausen was at the very least a forerunner of the Enlightenment. Grimmelshausen, as a "Volkspädagoge," intended to spread "Bildung in populärer Form," according to Hubert Gersch, whose comments preceded the reforms of 1968. This can be recognized in the

Vorzeichen jener neuen Geistesbewegung [. . .], die ein Dutzend Jahre
später von Thomasius eingeleitet wurde. [. . .] Im Hinblick auf diese
Bildungsrevolution wird man Grimmelshausens Kommunikationsarbeit
als Vorform aufklärerischer Publizistik einschätzen dürfen. (Gersch
1966, 56–57)

The author approaches "dem liberalen Standpunkt [. . .], den die
Gesellschaftskritik der Aufklärung beziehen sollte," in his Simplician
calendar stories. He uses a narrative technique "die als die klassische
Methode der Aufklärer gilt: das detektivische Erzählverfahren, das eine
Illusion zuläßt, um sie dann abzutragen." Gersch comes to the conclusion that this seventeenth-century author with "seinen Versuchen in
einer rationalistischen Weltschicht" has "merklichen Anteil an einer
Bewegung, die noch vom Geist des Humanismus getragen ist und sich
als Vorspiel der Aufklärung abzeichnet" (Gersch 1966, 60–61).[1] Jan
Knopf, writing after 1968, claims that Grimmelshausen emancipated
himself from the Middle Ages (162).

One might have expected that Grimmelshausen would adopt the
model of the Spanish picaresque without alterations in his *Trutz Simplex,
die Lebensbeschreibung der Ertzbetrügerin und Landstörtzerin Courasche*
(1670). On the contrary, he deviates innovatively. This is valid not so
much for his introduction of the female protagonist, since the prototype
of that heroine was already present in the German translation of López
de Úbeda's *Pícara Justina* (1608). Grimmelshausen's title character was
nevertheless actually the first modern heroine of German literature, a
much superior model. The author shows genuine innovation in the
absence of the prologue — as in *Simplicissmus* — something that was
actually characteristic of the period. The "Zugab des Autors" does not
replace it, although the engraved title page possibly does. Moreover,
details about Courasche's descent and identity, which are only sparingly
mentioned, are no longer found in the beginning chapter, in accordance
with the norms for the genre. The genre concentrates on the birth and
somewhat innocent youth of the pícaro, here picara, but Grimmelshausen emphasizes the age and perniciousness of his heroine instead (Valentin 91). Above all it was a work in which "die Heldin sich weigert, jene
Tat der Reue und Umkehr zu vollziehen, die seit [Mateo] Aleman für
einen zentralen und unentbehrlichen Bestandteil des christianisierten
Modells gehalten wurde" (92).

This important modification is signaled already on the intricate engraved title page of the novel: Courasche does not rid herself of the vain
trifles out of pure remorse and insight, but because it is simply unnecessary for the woman who becomes a Gypsy by choice. She does not hum-

bly dismount from the horse to continue on by foot. Allegorically, she makes "folglich, gegen jede puristische Erwartung des 'scholastischen' Lesers, die *via pedestris* als vorgegebenen Heilsweg zur *via equestris,* die nur zur Verdammnis führen kann" (Haberkamm 1991, 93). The iconographical Y-sign, integrated as a forked branch on the title page, sets off the outside perspective of the observer against the normal occu-pation of values of a left-right dichotomy. What seems to be the symbol of the rider's willingness to repent by deciding for the right, narrow path to heaven turns out to be the way to a luxuriant and sinful existence until death. According to Simplicus's words from the novel, Courasche goes "zu weit auff die lincke Hand" (197). Although the classical paradigm is of Hercules at the crossroads, one should not underestimate a female character standing in opposition to this tradition. Grimmelshausen fol-lows "an seinem — literarhistorischen — Scheideweg sozusagen selbst den linken Weg, den er zum im doppelten Wortsinn rechten erklärt, um dem 'simplicianischen stylus' unpoetische Knebelung zu ersparen."[2]

2. Grimmelshausen in the Tradition of Allegory and Allegorism

The reevaluation of the Y-sign in its allegorical meanings results in an interesting dialectical case. If we view Grimmelshausen historically, it seems paradoxical: the author's sporadic, flexible usage of allegory, which has a tendency toward the modern, makes recognizable his comprehen-sive and deep knowledge of its tradition, as well as its logic. It has such a presence in his total work that Grimmelshausen can be rightly consid-ered a "vornehmlich allegorischer Erzähler" (Haberkamm 81). Viewing allegory and its interpretations as central literary and exegetical methods during the Middle Ages puts the Baroque author closer to the past than to the future. Again, he is a reformer of tradition, not a revolutionary in this intellectual and literary historical area. This definitely applies to the allegorical system of the *mehrfacher Schriftsinn,* which actually functions as a double level of significance, a *sensus duplex:* a second, allegorical meaning has to be imagined, as it were, above the literal meaning of the narrative. Historically, this second meaning can be differentiated on several levels. Clemens Heselhaus pointed out relatively early (1963) that Grimmelshausen used the intensifying allegory of the *mehrfacher Schriftsinn* in *Simplicissimus.* He even recognized the "Dispositions-schema" of the novel in this allegorical form (Heselhaus 27–31).[3] Alle-gory appears in many forms and to a large degree continuously in all of Grimmelshausen's works, especially in *Simplicissimus Teutsch.*

Peter Hesselmann (1988) offers a comprehensive overview of its varying usage in the ten-book cycle of Simplician writings, while appropriately taking into consideration the closeness of allegory to emblem. An especially poignant example would be the Mars allegory, a personal allegory, at the beginning of *Simplicissimus*. Grimmelshausen is also clearly aware of the various allegorical interpretations of images that can be shown with a tulip, which refers to the resurrection. The author also knows the variations of similes (parables) like the sugar pill, which, by virtue of the relationship between the shell and the kernel, makes clear to the reader how the *sensus duplex* functions. The author utilizes this concrete parable in the plot for explanation of his own allegorical narrative process: some readers are so ignorant that they only consume the narrative on the sugar level. The "sweetness" actually should make it easier for the more intelligent reader to understand the story, that is, the external, which is enjoyable, should make easier the reception of the internal kernel, which is healthy and useful. Many of Grimmelshausen's title pages, which he may have created himself, have indisputably allegorical characteristics. Hence, as was shown, the Y-sign (a figuratively interpreted *littera Pythagorae*) which is artistically integrated into the emblematic engraved title page of *Courasche,* is an allegorical indicator of the existentially human act of choice, with far reaching allegorical consequences (Haberkamm 1991, 79–95).

B. Grimmelshausen as an Allegorist

1. The discovery of multiple levels of meaning in the text of *Simplicissimus*

An entire chapter of Hesselmann's work is reserved for an introduction to Grimmelshausen's "Allegorie und Allegorese nach dem Modell des mehrfachen Schriftsinns." The interpretations in the ensuing chapters offer, in conjunction with the research literature, concrete evidence for such opinions in the ten-book cycle of Simplician writings. While this allegorical framework provides for an ever increasing layering of various levels of meaning, and, at the same time, the presence of all allegorical possibilities, Heselhaus is more concerned with the changing dominance of individual layers of meaning. This can simply be exclusively the "historische" level, the narrative content without any allegorical meaning whatsoever. Partial simultaneous layering of several levels is by no means ruled out. Heselhaus interprets "Bedeutung" as allegorical in its narrowest interpretation. Figuratively speaking, this is found directly above the "Historie" in the story, and, as an additional level of meaning, it apparently does not coincide with the mere semantics of the narrative. Heselhaus refers to the moral meaning, which is one level higher and was originally referred to as *sensus moralis* or *tropologicus,* as "Anwendbarkeit." As the fourth, and appropriately highest level of meaning of the hierarchy in *Simplicissimus Teutsch,* we have the *sensus anagogicus sive eschatologicus,* which, with Heselhaus, has to do with salvation and thus is called "Heilsbedeutung."

Looking at this concretely, we see that Heselhaus attributes to the Jupiter episode an allegorical function. The moral level of meaning, which has to do with usefulness, seems to have the upper hand throughout almost the entire work. The hermit framework, which has "ein ganz anderes geistig-geistliches Niveau als die eigentlichen simplicanischen Geschichten" (Heselhaus, Grimmelshausen 27), has spiritual significance quite aside from its moral meaning. Heselhaus concludes especially from these hermetic sections "daß es in diesem Roman weniger um eine kontinuierliche Entwicklung als um Schichten der Bedeutung geht" (29). In Book V of *Simplicissimus,* as a further example, Heselhaus sees how the four levels of meaning accumulate into an entangled sequence of motifs. The unity of varying levels is once again successful in "der phantastischen Existenz dieses philosophierenden und lesenden Bauern (= Simplicissimus)":

> Auf der Ebene der 'Histori' ist es Herzbruders Krankheit, die Simplicissimus überhaupt nach Griechenland führt. Auf der moralischen Ebene ist es die Ansiedlung auf einem Schwarzwälder Bauernhof und die damit verbundene Beschränkung. Auf der allegorischen Ebene ist es das geheimnisvoll-elementische Wesen um die Natur des Sauerbrunnens. Die sinnbildliche Bedeutung wird im Bekehrungsmotiv, das dies Buch von der Wallfahrt nach Einsiedeln bis zum einsiedlerischen Weltabschied durchzieht, deutlich. (29)

Withdrawal from the world, complemented by a theological level of meaning, forces itself into the forefront "durch die Anordnung der Kapitel am Anfang und Ende" (Heselhaus 47–48). In summarizing, Heselhaus concludes the following with regard to the prominent reflections of Simplicissimus in the narration: "Als eine besondere Methode dieses erörternden Stils wird die theologische Interpretation nach den vier Schriftsinnen verwendet" (58). Heselhaus names no source for Grimmelshausen's knowledge of the productional and exegetical framework of the *mehrfacher Schriftsinn.* In this regard, of course, the translation of Tomaso Garzoni's encyclopedic compendium *Piazza Universale* (Frankfurt 1619), the German translation of which Grimmelshausen used intensively, is clearly important.

2. The *mehrfacher Schriftsinn:*
a Systematic and Historical Outline

The productional and interpretive system of the *mehrfacher Schriftsinn,* which is actually only *sensus duplex,* holds "hidden" as well as at least partially accessible allegorical levels. One spoke in the Middle Ages of the reserved (spiritual) meaning of the *sensus mysticus* and of the *sensus spiritualis* in relation to openness. Whereas in the former case the narration is explicit solely as *sensus historicus* or *litteralis,* in the latter case one or more, less often all additional levels of meaning are articulated *expressis verbis.* In the beginning, these levels of meaning are — as always in western-Christian cultures — divine in nature and are found in the story of the creation, the *Buch der Natur,* and in the Bible. In the Middle Ages, one referred particularly to the Epistle of Paul to the Galatians (Gal 4, 24). Luther's translation of the passage is "Die Worte bedeuten etwas" (Freytag 27–43). Consequently, within or rather above the semantic meaning we find hidden the allegorical meaning. Moreover, God gives meaning not only to things (*res*) but also to words (*verba*). The allegorical semantics of both words and things can be decoded by mankind via the exegesis according to the *mehrfacher Schriftsinn* of interpretation. The historical, narrative level of meaning can be open (*sensus spiritualis*) or closed (*sensus mysticus*), and this level can again be subdivided in different ways. The dominant system consists of three levels of meaning, which are thought of in a hierarchical fashion: the *sensus allegoricus* in its most restricted meaning (this is a sub-unit of the more all-inclusive allegorical level of meaning), the *sensus tropologicus* or *moralis* and the *sensus anagogicus* or *eschatologicus.* The historical presents itself to the interpreter in the *sensus historicus;* later, after the expansion of the system to religious and spiritual texts other than the Bible, this also applies to fictional texts. The allegorical meaning, in its strict sense, transmits to us the meaning of the text in terms of salvation. Often it does this typologically, in that it puts one thing (type) into relation with its (mostly positive) opposite. "Allegorie meint hier dasselbe wie der moderne Begriff der Typologie, also den Bedeutungsbezug zwischen Präfiguration und Erfüllung wie zwischen dem Alten und dem Neuen Testament" (Ohly 10).

A classical example is sinful Adam's victory through his opposite, Christ, in the New Testament. The tropological or moralistic meaning provides one with assistance for leading a pious Christian life and forms a transition to anagogical and eschatological meaning. This level of meaning has to do with the Last Judgment, which is a prophecy fulfilled.

However, not every religious text needs to be structured according to this model. Moreover, not every passage of a religious text must contain all four interpretive levels. In seeking a method of interpreting Grimmelshausen's *Simplicissimus,* Heselhaus draws certain conclusions from this flexibility: he modified the hierarchically structured vertical system into a horizontal one, which looks at the meanings separately. This conclusion implies, first of all, that, in the course of the continuing development of its exegetical approach, secular texts could be taken into consideration. The interpretation that Dante provided for his *Divina Commedia* is a well-known example of this. Secondly, it implies that the original religious-theological method of interpretation could more or less be secularized. According to Heselhaus, the continuous use of satire as the basis of levels of meaning in Grimmelshausen's novel represents such a possibility. Dante's example shows us that not only do the texts fit into our framework of allegorical interpretation according to levels of meaning, but that they were conceived in this structure from the very beginning.

Early non-Christian works by Homer, Virgil, or Ovid could be accepted through this "liberalization" into the historical framework of reception. Luther, who believed in the literal meaning of the Bible, did not abandon the conventional interpretation according to multiple levels of meaning. Here we have an important prerequisite for the methodological tradition up into the seventeenth century. Luther merely wanted to battle the misuse of this type of allegorical exegesis for ecclesiastical purposes, a continuing practice of the Catholic Church up into the eighteenth century and beyond. Biblical parables provided a strong impulse for such allegorical interpretation.

Interpretation according to the *mehrfacher Schriftsinn* continues to be dominant during the Baroque era, although there is an increasing tendency toward purely philological textual interpretation ever since the Renaissance. That can be proven not only in literature, but also for the visual arts. As is well known, Dutch paintings during the Golden Age were not created as merely realistic. Allegorical details, which occasionally are visible to a modern viewer only after more study of the picture, can make a seemingly naturalistic picture into an emblem. Still-lives of flowers with wilting leaves are generally categorized under *memento mori.* Hans Sedlmayr has shown this to be true, apart from the works of Pieter Breughel, especially for the works of Jan Vermeer (169–77). It is especially effective in certain literary genres: "Eine eminent wichtige Rolle in der Vermittlung und Popularisierung des hermeneutischen Verfahrens des 'sensus duplex' spielen nicht nur die Predigten, sondern darüber hinaus die Erbauungsschriften" (Hesselmann 33). The poetics of the epoch assume a literature based on multiple levels of meaning whenever they make authors into exegetes of the "Book of Nature." Creation is to be both understood and imitated in its levels of meaning in one's own work. Even when poetic handbooks did not consider levels of meaning as a structural principle of literary works, there was a widespread awareness of their complexity: "Bei Opitz, Harsdörffer, Zesen, Schottel, Buchner und andern wird [. . .] mit einer mehrschichtigen Bedeutung des Kunstwerks gerechnet. Ja die Theoretiker sehen das, was die Dichtung als Kunstwerk auszeichnet, gerade in den mehrfachen Bedeutungen" (Feldges 15).

Several of those who provided Grimmelshausen with literary material were acquainted with *sensus duplex* interpretations and offered him relevant information concerning it. The Nuremberg polymath, Georg Philipp Harsdörffer, repeatedly wrote that there should "unter der Geschichte ein heimlicher Verstand gesuchet werden" (cited in Hesselmann 35). Both Tomaso Garzoni with his extremely influential and eclectic work *Piazza Vniversale,* who principally presented the theory of the exegetic system, and the Bavarian court secretary Aegidius Albertinus, from whom Grimmelshausen learned the concrete methodology, were among his most prominent sources. In the twenty-fifth discourse of the Italian encyclopedia, he learned that the interpretation of the Bible, and of the world, too, the *mundus symbolicus,* was based principally on the concept of "zweierlei Verstandt." This *sensus duplex* is differentiated "nach den viererley fürnembsten Verständtnussen oder sensibus, nemblich Literali, Morali, Tropologico, vnd Anagogico" (Garzoni 154)[4]. The religious and theological terminology in use since Scholasticism points out that every word or thing can be understood on a second level, as spiritual or mystical. We are hence dealing with the allegorical level of meaning within the *sensus duplex,* in the form of *sensus mysticus.* Garzoni encourages creative use of the interpretive methods as compositional principles, because poets are, according to Plato, "messengers," interpreters of the Gods.

Albertinus demonstrates in descriptive allegorism what will be in spiritual, but also in secular texts "Geistlicher weiß zuuerstehen gegeben" (36). Representative of this is the interpretation of the Circe adventure of Odysseus in his work entitled *Christi vnsers Herrn Königreich vnd Seelengejaidt* (1614). Whenever the sea is interpreted as the "Meer dieser Welt," on which people go out on as pilgrims, and Circe as the allegorical embodiment of gluttony, it alludes to the *sensus moralis,* which easily leads to the *sensus anagogicus* (Hesselmann 40–41). The protestant cleric Hartmann Creidius differentiates between the *sensus proprius* and the *sensus mysticus* in his work entitled *Danck-Buß vnd Bet-Altar* (1650), from which a longer "Dedication" passage is almost literally transferred to Grimmelshausen's *Ewig-während Calender*. Creidius separates the "Verstandt/ den der Buchstaben mit sich bringet," on the semantic level, from the "geistlichen Deutung" of the allegory (53–54).

3. Selective Demonstrations of the *mehrfacher Schriftsinn* in Grimmelshausen's Works

Grimmelshausen shows us again and again that he is well acquainted with the theory of multiple levels of meaning. He lets his protagonists view "verschiedentlich die Dinge der Natur als Träger eines spirituellen Sinnes" (Jöns 385). In the *Continuatio* all "Dinge der Natur, die Simplex auf der Insel sieht, [become for him] fortan zu Sinnbildern der Heilsgeschichte." He understands them "als Mahnung zu gottgefälligem Leben" (Jöns 385).

> also! Sahe ich ein stachelecht Gewächs/ so erinnerte ich mich der dörnen Cron Christi/ sahe ich einen Apffel oder Granat/ so gedachte ich an den Fall unserer ersten Eltern und bejammert denselbigen; gewanne ich ein Palmwein auß einem Baum/ so bildet ich mir vor/ wie mildiglich mein Erlöser am Stammen deß H. Creutzes sein Blut vor mich vergossen; sahe ich Meer oder Berg/ so erinnerte ich mich des einen oder andern Wunderzeichens und Geschichten/ so unser Heyland an dergleichen Orthen begangen; fande ich einen oder mehr Stein so zum Werffen bequem waren/ so stellte ich mir vor Augen/ wie die Juden Christum steinigen wolten; war ich in meinem Garten/ so gedachte ich an das ängstig Gebett am Oelberg/ oder an das Grab Christi und wie er nach der Aufferstehung Mariae Magdalenae im Garten erschinen/ etc. [. . .] ich asse nie daß ich nicht an das letzte Abendmahl Christi gedachte; und kochte mir niemahl keine Speiß/ daß mich das gegenwertige Feur nicht an die ewige Peyn der Höllen erinnert hätte. (Cont 568–69)

The allegorical interpretation, in the strict sense, dominates although a tendency toward tropological and eschatological interpretation is evident in certain points of the text. When he sees a cautious bird building its nest, the hero of the *Wunderbarliches Vogel-Nest I* comes to the realization that God has created animals "nicht allein zu unserer Speise und zu unserem Wollust" (VN I, 129). The implications of this immediately become apparent when the nest carrier must watch a snake devour a rather clumsy toad. He learns from this

daß ein Mensch der mit Hoffart beladen (an welche mich ihr graviteti-
scher Gang ermahnte) oder einer der wie ein Schwein sich Tag und
Nacht mit übrigem Fressen und Sauffen mästet: oder einer der dem
gifftigen Neid/ Haß und Zorn ergeben: oder einer der immer den
fleischlichen Wollüsten abwartet: oder einer der sich auß Geitz mit zu-
vielen zeitlichen und vielleicht unrechtmässigen Reichthümen beladen
hat/ oder einer der auß fauler Trägheit die Himmel-strasse nicht laufen
mag/ beinahe dieser Krotten gleiche/ und der Schlang/ dem hölli-
schen Drachen schwerlich entrinnen mög. (WV I, 130)

This "offene" allegorical interpretation is predominantly morally and
tropologically oriented, but nevertheless branches out to a possible eschatological interpretation. Inasmuch as the snake alludes to the myth of
temptation in paradise, the *sensus allegoricus* becomes clear. With this last
example, the full quartet of classical levels of meaning is brought together in this significant episode. This paradigm demonstrates moreover
that each individual characteristic of the animals can serve as a basis for
interpretation. Consequently, the breadth of the allegorical interpretation depends on the number of traits of the observed object. The context
determines the interpretational perspective. It can be principally positive — "in bonam partem" — or negative — "in malam partem." The
episode of the raid in the forest, as it is told in *Wunderbarliches Vogel-
Nest I,* can be interpreted tropologically and anagogically. In it are lay-
ered the lessons of the diverging paths according to the gospel of Matthew (7, 13), the model of Hercules's liaisons at the crossroads, and the
tradition of the Y-sign in "verlandschaftlichter" form. The wandering
students allegorically represent "den sündigen Menschen auf seinem Weg
durch die Welt zu seinem ewigen Ziel [. . .] Er droht es durch die Versu-
chung des Satans, den der heuchlerische Wegweiser signifiziert, zu verlie-
ren, wird aber von der Gnade Gottes, die hier der unsichtbare Held
allegorisch vertritt, gerettet" (Haberkamm 1972a, 128; cf. Haberkamm
1972b, passim). In accordance with the liberal crossing over of various
traditions of the motif of choice, which is in accord with Grimmelshausen's intentions, we can observe in this paradigmatic case the gradual
weakening of orthodox interpretations of a work. It is symptomatic of
the gradual turn from the development of exegesis away from the classical interpretative system of the *vierfacher Schriftsinn.*

4. The *mehrfacher Schriftsinn* in the Works of Grimmelshausen: The Example of a Complete Simplician Work

Not only single objects or the plot and connections with the course of events in a story, but entire works of Grimmelshausen are structured according to the system of the *vierfacher Schriftsinn*. For example, Mathias Feldges's interpretation of the *Courasche* is based on this theory. In the Baroque era lies "das, was die Dichtung als Kunstwerk auszeich-net, gerade in den mehrfachen Bedeutungen" (15). This means that it is irrelevant that contemporary poets did not explicitly mention the exegetical method of interpretation. Nor should we be concerned with the ancient question of whether the theory of the *furor poeticus,* which came to Grimmelshausen from Garzoni, is related to the quartet of the allegorical interpretation of levels of meaning. Feldges is certain that the "furores" described by the author of the Simplician works caused the author to put pen to paper and that they have to "[. . .] sich in entspre-chenden mehrfachen Schriftsinnen niederschlagen" (31). One then has to assume that this applies not only to *Courasche,* but that it is valid for all ten books of Grimmelshausen's Simplician cycle. Grimmelshausen, after all, postulated in the prologue to *Wunderbarliches Vogel-Nest II* that "alles von diesen Simplicianischen Schrifften aneinander hängt/ und weder der gantze *Simplicissimus,* noch eines auß den obengemeldten letzten Tractätlein ohne solche Zusammenfügung genugsam verstanden werden mag" (150).

According to Feldges's interpretation, the figure of the runagate Courasche is "vom Dichter als Weib katexochen gestaltet worden" on the level of the *sensus historicus* (47) and this occurs within the context of the class-system and political and military activity of the Thirty Years' War. On the allegorical level *stricto sensu,* the protagonist represents the traditional position of "Frau Welt" in the Middle Ages; added to this is a combination of the two dominant types, the demon and the lady. The author had knowledge of both traditions. Feldges suggests that he inte-grated the allegory into the narration when he transformed the canon of distinguishing attributes of the "Frau Welt" into "menschliche, wirklich-keitsnahe Eigenschaften" (92). In this way, Grimmelshausen keeps the character from fossilization in the form of a personal allegory. Raising the allegorical meaning to the tropological level results in the emergence of a moral lesson, namely avoid the world and especially womankind. Fi-nally, the author, who viewed himself as a prophet of sorts, concealed a message about the fate of the world's end in the anagogic level. Accord-ing to this, Courasche is "die den ewigen Tod bringende, antichristliche

Frau Welt" (Feldges 181). As such, she is prefigured by the whore of Babylon.

5. Profane Variations of the *mehrfacher Schriftsinn*

The classical quartet of four levels of interpretation, still quite common in the baroque era, could be further subdivided. Up to eight levels of meaning have been proven, for example, in the work of the prolific Jesuit writer Athanasius Kircher (1602–1680). His work *Oedipus Aegyptiacus* (1652) makes use of the "physische," "medizinische," "tropologische," "anagogische," "allegorische," "politische," and finally "chemische" significance of the text, in addition, of course, to the "historische." Creidius, the Protestant cleric mentioned above, achieves a variation of the allegorical system by subdividing the "sensus mysticus." The roses of Salomon's temple refer to Christ, the "Rose im Thal," and moreover to the church as Christ's "Rosengarten," and finally to individual members of the church who are comparable to the "Rosen vnder den Dornen" (Creidius 53–54). There is no longer, so to speak, a vertical differentiation, but rather a horizontal one. The transition to such a vertical expansion of the levels of meaning and their structure is especially well demonstrated in the works of Albertinus. He shows an additional one, the *sensus politicus,* which is closely connected to the tropological and analogical exegesis. He repeatedly sets "seine Deutungen mit politischen Ereignissen und Sachverhalten in Beziehung" (Hesselmann 41). Grimmelshausen's important source, Garzoni, expands the system of four levels by two additional ones. He stresses that the hermeneutic interpretation according to the *mehrfacher Schriftsinn* has more or less been preserved up to his time, but that it then has been modified. "Die species aber solcher [allegorischer] Erklärungen vnd wie dieselbige anzustellen/ werden von vnterschiedlichen auch vnterschiedlich angedeutet" (158). Hieronymus had argued for the division into three parts "interpretatio Historialis, [. . .] tropologica, [. . .] Spiritualis." Hugo von St. Victor had described this triad slightly differently: "historialis, mystica, & moralis." However, Augustine decided on a four part division: "Historialis," "Allegorica," "Anagogica," and "Aethiologica." The last of these levels, that is, Aethiologica, is said to show "auß was Vrsachen dieses oder jenes geschehen/ oder gered ist worden [. . .]" (158). As Albertinus's example shows, this expansion of the number of levels of meaning, since the time of the Church Fathers, is really equivalent to a turn away from strict allegory and allegorical interpretation. It reflects the tendency toward secularization.

If art history has proven, as shown above, that the structural system of the *mehrfacher Schriftsinn* can be determined in the works of Velasquez, Brueghel, and Vermeer, then it manifests itself "statt in geistlicher in humanistisch säkularisierter Fassung." Similarly, it would explain in the Cavalieri papers of Michelangelo "'wörtlich' die antike Fabel, allegorisch eine Anspielung auf das Verhältnis Michelangelos zu Cavalieri, spirituell und 'tropologisch' geistige Vorgänge (Ganymed ist nach Alciat die 'Ekstase,' die Erhebung der Seele)" (Sedlmayr 170).

Even Grimmelshausen can turn the spiritual meaning of an emblem into a worldly one. The general eschatological meaning of the allegorical object is made completely profane in chapter two of *Wunderbarliches Vogel-Nest II*. The unhappy owner of the bird's nest, who has been cheated out of his money, derives from a flower bulb resting in the ground the hope that he will again be restored to the good graces of the Almighty. He is, of course, not thinking of this in a spiritual sense. After all, for the accumulation of new riches, he still possesses "den Samen/ das ist/ die Mittel und Gelegenheit/ gleich wie diese Blumen-Zwiebeln die Art ihres Wachsthumbs" (VN II, 158–59; cf. Jöns 386). The trivialization of the original spiritual system occurs in an even more drastic fashion in Grimmelshausen's *Ewig-während er Calender*. Here, we can scarcely fail to recognize a sexual meaning in the seemingly harmless "Monatssprüchen":

> Ob gleich das Blum-Gewächs
>   Mit Lobe wird berühret/
> Jhr Blat fält auff die Erd: Mein
>   Korn wird eingeführet
> Mit meiner dürren Frucht gedient
>   Ist jederman.
> Jst deine Rose dörr/ so bringstu
>   Niemand dran.
>   (EC II, 160; cf. Haberkamm 1967, 19–23)

There is a clear connection between the warning about "allerley geschlecht der Pflaumen" and the same fruits in the *Continuatio*. These "sein ein Speiß der Säw/ und taugen wann die rote Ruhr regieret/ sehr trefflich den Menschen auffzuopffern" (II, 162). Simplicissimus advises in the continuation of the novel in relation to a group of mentally confused people that these individuals "nur von den Pflaumen darin sie ihren Verstand verfressen/ die Kernen essen [zu] lassen/ so würde es sich mit allen in einem Augenblick wider bessern [. . .]" (Cont 77). With his reference to the difference between actual fruit and the seed Grimmelshausen obviously offers the reader an allegory in terms of *sensus duplex,* that is, the type of allegory he demands, a sort of visual introduction to the allegorical interpretation of his texts. Siegfried Streller completed the interpretation in this case: "Es ist also die Fleischeslust gemeint, die ärgste Gefährdung des Seelenheils, wenn man nicht auch den Kern ge-nießt, wenn man nicht durch dieses äußere irdische Leben zu Gott vor-dringt" (44).

6. The *sensus astrologicus*

In view of the variations and modifications of this patristic and medieval system of exegesis, it should come as no surprise that, in the epoch be-tween Renaissance and baroque that was largely determined by astrology, there develops a special level of interpretation, namely that of the *sensus astrologicus.* The interest of this era in nature, which subsequent to the invention of telescope was devoted even more strongly to cosmic occur-rences, goes hand in hand with this type of allegorical interpretation.

The *Dialoghi d'amore* (appeared posthumously in 1635) of the Portuguese-Jewish philosopher Leone Ebreo (Jehuda Abrabanel) (ca. 1460–ca. 1525) can serve as a paradigm for considering and using the heuristic category of the *sensus astrologicus.* He had contact with the great philosophers of the Florentine renaissance and his main treatise was widely read and received, up to Spinoza, Cervantes, and Schiller. Leone Ebreo had maintained the view of his father, the Bible commentator Jizchaq Abrabanel that the fate of individuals, peoples, and nations de-pends on the influence of the stars. His dialogues, which are in the same vein as those of the Florentine philosopher, Marsilio Ficino (1433–1499), the opponent of Pico della Mirandola (1463–1494), teach of an astrological system that includes all the constellations of the planets and stars. It deals especially with the influence of the firmament on humans, according to astrology. This thought construct is based on the teachings about love, which stem from Plato. It is poetologically interesting that Ebreo sees in the myths about the gods of antiquity literary fictions that refer to the allegorical quality of the planet deities. "Die Liebe der klassi-chen Götter bezeichne die Liebe der Sterndämonen; über einem mytho-logischen 'sensus litteralis' baut sich ein, allgemein gesprochen, astral orientierter 'sensus allegoricus' auf" (Haberkamm, 1972a, 135). It is hermeneutically important that, in order to have an astrological level of meaning, not every characteristic of a mythical narration needs to have an equivalent within that astrological level of meaning. The *sensus duplex* is not limited to the astrological level above the mythical, but also is differentiated by Ebreo: "Li poeti antichi non una solo ma, molte inten-tioni implicono ne suoi poemi, il qua chiamano sensi" (Dialogo II, 26v). In the Christian system as with the humanistic thinker Leone Ebreo, moral meaning is most important, even if it is particularly oriented to-ward the idea of the *vita activa* rather than of final salvation. According to Leone Ebreo, authors of antiquity refer to "qualche uera intelligentia de le cose naturali, o celesti, astrologali, o uer' theologali" (Dialogo II, 26v). Two or even all three *sensi scientifichi* are occasionally contained in the fable like the core beneath the fruit skin.

In this sense, we can have a division of meaning along five levels, in which the astrological level of meaning is set directly next to the theo-logical. Ebreo demonstrates his exegesis framework with the myth of Perseus and Gorgo. The Latin translation of the *Dialoghi* by Johannes Carolus Saracenus (Sarasin) develops the astrological component more strongly. In accord with the stability of the astrological tradition, we find that Leone's contextual attributions to the gods in the stars correspond, even in the finest of details, to the later depictions of Grimmelshausen in his *Ewig-währender Calender*. In addition, it is important that the astro-logical interpretation of a myth, that is, of a story, can be applied not only to the deities but also to human beings. Finally, just as the different amours of Jupiter can be in reference to astrological constellations and signs, so these constellations and signs can also be interpreted on the level of literal meaning. This interchanging relationship among the levels of meaning is relevant for the Simplician author.[5]

The heuristic exegetic category of the *sensus astrologus* can be shown in several academic tracts from the University of Leipzig. These tracts, dealing with Ebreo's *Dialoghi* stem from the end of the seventeenth century. It is irrelevant that, in this pre-Enlightenment era, the authors of these tracts viewed both the interpretation method according to the *mehrfacher Schriftsinn* and astrology rather critically. For even in the first half of the eighteenth century, Johann Heinrich Zedler points to astro-logical discourse in his encyclopedia *Universal-Lexicon aller Wissenschaf-ten und Künste* and explicitly to "Verstand," that is, "Sinn." These academic treatises deal with allegorical interpretations by other authors, such as the "physische," which is separated from the "astrologische," the "ethische" and the "politische." They all prove the modification and, above all, the secularization of the traditional system in the seventeenth century.

Not only the theory, but also literary practice of the seventeenth century is acquainted with the astrological level of meaning. *Sensus astrologicus* can function as the literal meaning or as a component of higher-level, allegorical level of meaning. Johann Valentin Andreae's *De Christiani Cosmoxeni Genitvra, Ivdicivm* (1615) describes the fathers of the church as planets, whereby both luminaries, the sun and the moon, are reserved for Christ and the Church, of course. On the other hand, Gotthilf Treuer's poetic lexicon, *Deutscher Dädalus* (1675), calls to our attention that "Etliche von denen Außlegern der Fabeln" interpret the Hercules myth astronomically and astrologically in respect to the zodiac. They understand, he says, "durch den Herculem die Sonne. Durch seine zwölff schwere Bemühungen die zwölff himmlische Zeichen/ welche die Sonne jährlichen durchkreiset" (962). On the one hand, then, the stars have the allegorical meaning of things holy and are concerned with the history of the Church, while on the other hand, something mythical signifies the stars. One must remember, Treuer reminds us, that any object to be interpreted possesses just as many interpretations as characteristics; because "es der Eigenschaften aber gute und schlechte gibt, kann dasselbe Ding gute und schlechte Bedeutungen haben" (Ohly 6). In this way, the sun's passage through that sign of the zodiac known as the poisonous scorpion refers to Christ, "da ihn das Gifft der Sünden ans Kreutz brachte/ daß Er endlich freywillig starb/ und der Höllen eine Gifft/ dem Tode eine Pestilentz ward" (Treuer 966). The poison is also an antidote, according to one's frame of reference. One last piece of evidence: Heinrich Kornmann's tract *Mons Veneris* (1614), which Grimmelshausen may have employed as a source, uses a text from late antiquity for the astrological interpretation of the myth of Venus's adultery with Mars:

> Plutarchus im Buch de audienda Poetica deutet diese Allegorien auff Astrologische Vrsachen/ dann er schreibt daß die jenigen von Natur geneigt sein zum Ehebruch in deren Geburtsstunde Venus vnnd Mars zusammen kommen/ vnnd daß deren Ehebruch nicht verborgen blieben/ wann die Sonn darzu käme [zur Konstellation]. (148–49)

7. The *sensus astrologicus* in Grimmelshausen's Works

Using Heselhaus's thesis as a point of departure, Müller-Seidel notes: "In Wirklichkeit gibt es im *Simplicissimus* keinen Realismus ohne Allegorie. [. . .] Nicht allein Einzelnes, nicht nur bestimmte Personifikationen und Episoden sind allegorisch, sondern die Darstellung im Ganzen verfährt so" (275). This conclusion is valid at least for all ten books of the Simplician cycle and applies especially to the level of the *sensus astrologicus*. A requirement for this conclusion is the fact that Grimmelshausen was a writer of calendars. Disregarding those calendars where there is some doubt as to authorship, we know he published the *Ewig-währender Calender* in 1671, although its origins certainly go back many years. One finds here the raw material Grimmelshausen needed for his astrological allegorization. According to the title page, this comprehensive collection contains among other things "unterschiedliche *Curiose Discursen* von der *Astronomia, Astrologia,* Jtem den Calendern/ Nativitäten/ auch allerhand Wunderbarlichen Wahr- und Vorsagungen/ mit untermischter Bauren-Practic/ Tag- und Zeitwehlungen/ etc." Müller-Seidel's statement maintains that in addition to the meaning of the allegorical word and thing, there is "eine mit dieser grundsätzlich verwandte Ereignisbedeutung" (Ohly 6). Such occurrences need not be real, they can also be fictional. With respect to the Simplician narration and its astrological allegorical interpretation, one should also be aware of the analogy that Hans Robert Jauss recognizes for Guillaume de Lorris's *Rosenroman* from the thirteenth century. He says, it "wird vom Leser gefordert, daß er den *sensus litteralis* nicht als bloßen Verweisungszusammenhang abtut, sondern [. . .] als bildhafte Deutung des *sensus allegoricus* ständig vor Augen hält" (181). A similarly interdependent relationship results in the works of Grimmelshausen from the specific situation of the allegory: the planets affect the earthly events, that is, here the narrative events, and these point back toward the planets.

A theoretical defense of the *sensus astrologicus* in Grimmelshausen's Simplician cycle is transmitted through his *Ewig-währender Calender.* Assorted verbs like "versuchen" or "regieren" express, in the astrological sections of the "Zweiten Tages" of fifth "Materie" of the report, the causal relationship between the seven classical planets and the sublunary world. Saturn, as one example out of many, "verursacht ein gewaltig scharff Gedächtnuß" (V, 103). The verbs "bedeuten" and "bezeichnen" stand out from the abundance of these words: the example of Saturn "bedeut Gefängnuß" (V, 103). The sun — in another brief proof — "bezeichnet/ die Reichthumb/ Verstand und Reinigkeit" (V, 121). Both verbs function as hermeneutic terms and concentrate on the meaning of a *res significans* in the sense of "significare," in this case on the meaning of each planet. Jail, or serving time in jail, belongs to the astrological allegorical aspect of the significance of the planet Saturn. The sun represents wealth. The conviction of the mythical pair Venus and Mars by Vulcan, as Grimmelshausen might have read by Kornmann, "bedeut daß der Ehebruch viel vnd ja die Grösten zu schaden gebracht" (147). Creidius asks his congregation in his *Bet-Altar:* "Was bedeuten die güldnen Rosen/ die in dieser Kirchen vber und neben vns in groser

Anzahl gesehen werden?" (54). An allegorical typological interpretation follows that question. In the *Pícara Justina,* which Grimmelshausen might well have used for his *Courasche,* we find the question about whether the "Schlang allein etwas böses bedeute vnd [. . .] einen Vnfall verkündige." This is answered inasmuch as one can find "auch in der Schlangen etwas glücklichs verborgen ligen" and that it "ein Gnad bedeute" (40–41). Clearly this is an allegorical interpretation "in malam partem" and "in bonam partem," as there also is for the astrological exegesis of Grimmelshausen's texts.

Each planet, as outlined in his calendar, "bedeutet" something in the sublunar world. This "etwas" is, in the systematic order of astrology, a section of the world as a whole and in detail. A section of the world, to be more precise, which according to the number of "Wandelsterne" encompasses one seventh of the earth, is addressed. The *Ewig-währender Calender* provides an excellent example of this principle. Concretely

> erscheint im astrologischen Weltbild das Ganze der Zeiten und Lebens-
> alter, der Qualitäten und Elemente, der Körper- und Geisterwelt, der
> Charaktere und Temperamente nach dem gleichen Modell aufgebaut,
> das sich uns in der Gestaltung der Planetenwelt nur am klarsten ent-
> hüllt, weil es hier gleichsam in deutlichster räumlicher Projektion, in
> übersichtlichster Anordnung aller Grundverhältnisse vor uns steht.
> (Cassirer 34–35)

Accordingly, this astrological edifice is based on the principle of "'pars pro toto,' wonach jeder Teil das Ganze, dem er angehört, nicht nur vertritt, sondern wonach er, im kausalen Sinne, dieses Ganze tatsächlich ist" (Cassirer 42). In this crystal-like structure, Venus represents love in the entire astrological tradition just as in mythology. However, this also applies in the other direction, if we consider it logically—*pars pro toto, totum pro parte* — then love also represents Venus. From the hermeneutic standpoint, this results in the relationship of literal meaning and allegorical astrological meaning being reversible within the *sensus-duplex* framework. The plot, which Grimmelshausen or his first-person narrator provides, is originally on the astrological level of meaning, because it was created out of all those particles that the calendar lists as raw material from an astrological and epic perspective. It is transformed to the narrative, literal meaning because of its crystalline reversibility and points to the representative astrological planetary patron. This becomes especially clear in those sections that have an explicit equivalent in the calendar. Once again, according to Grimmelshausen's *Ewig-währender Calender,* the planet Venus represents "der Welt Frewd/ und das

Gesang" (V, 127). Hence, the erotic pleasures of Simplicissimus in the Parisian "Venus-Berg" and his surprising entrance as a stunning opera singer for the king in the Louvre (288) show, considered from the reverse perspective, that Venus was responsible. When Simplicissimus, quite independent of all psychological development, abruptly turns to love in Lippstadt, we know that the entire plot is under the influence of Venus.

II. Interpretation

A. The Astrologically Based Motif of Prophecy in the Simplician Cycle

1. Astrologically Prophesied Intrigue in the *Wunderbarliches Vogel-Nest*

The motif of prophecy, in the sense of predicting the future, counts as dominant structure-building element in *Simplicissimus Teutsch* and throughout the Simplician cycle. It is linked to the practice of reading horoscopes and is thus astrologically based. From the hermeneutical standpoint, this motif and the exegetical category of *sensus astrologicus* are related. According to astrological views held in Grimmelshausen's era and earlier, the future life of a person can be ascertained from the position of heavenly bodies, above all the planets. The first part of the *Wunderbarliches Vogel-Nest* demonstrates impressively this "teaching" of the baroque author. The elder Simplicissimus can precisely predict, exactly to the day, danger for his son from his "Nativitätenbuch." He views himself as the "Nativitäten-Steller," and reads his son his horoscope. He foresees a disaster because of confusion of two inns, which have a similar name and are found in the same area. One is the pub "Zum schwartzen Roß" (I, 98); the other a tavern, "welches in seinem Schild eine Rabe führte/ dannenhero zum Rappen genannt wurde" (I, 98). Simplicius junior mistakenly applied the description black bird to the black horse. This humorous incident of confusion is closely tied to astrology: the old Simplicissimus is in no way surprised by the news that his son has innocently been caught in an awkward and dangerous situation in the "Schwarzen Roß." Seeing the youth had already been a victim of intrigue, the father has

> deßwegen in seinem [d.h. des Sohnes] nativitäten-Buch nachgeschlagen/ und befunden/ daß er umb diese Zeit/ vornemblich aber heut wegen seiner Redlichkeit und Neigung jedermann bedient zu seyn/ auß

Neid/ Jrrung und Mißtrauen in äußerste Gefahr Leibs und Lebens kommen werde. (I, 99)

The young Simplicius helps the landlady of the "false" tavern carry a sack of flour, "über welcher Arbeit beyde sich mit Meel bestäubten" (I, 105). The jealous innkeeper, arriving on the scene, is suspicious and reports the young man, who is "ein schöner gerader Mensch" (I, 105) to the town council. The predictions from the "Nativitätenbuch," of the horoscope based on his birth, were thus fulfilled for the immediate past as well as for the present ("heut"). Simplicissimus is identified as an infallible astrologer, who foresaw the fate of his child because of the position of the planets. His son's fate proves to be unavoidable; representative of classical tragedy, as it were, the father reaches for defensive measures: "derohalben [d.h. auf Grund des astrologischen Befundes] habe ich ihm [. . .] befohlen/ daß er sich auff diesen Tag hier in diesem Hauß einstellen/ und meiner erwarten sollen/ zu sehen/ wie ihm etwann zu helffen seyn möchte" (I, 99). By following these directions, the younger Simplicius enters the "Schwarze Roß" instead of the "Rappen," where he will be accused of adultery. The astrologically structured plot stresses that the older Simplicissimus makes his entrance into the plot almost exclusively for the purpose of the horoscope, since afterwards he steps back. We can conclude that the unavoidable situation can be predicted from the stars, is determined by them, and refers back to them. There exists a relation between the two levels, namely, the contextual-narrative one and the astrological one. According to the *sensus duplex,* a literal and allegorical astrological level of meaning results from the intertwinement of planetary causality.

2. The Infallible Prophecies of the Old Herzbruder

The author already implements the astrologically based prophecy motif in *Simplicissimus,* which leads to certain hermeneutical consequences for the interpretation. If the astrological structure is adequately established and the *sensus astrologicus* is presented as a layer above the Simplician plot, it can no longer be suspended according to astrological views. The claim of astrology to validity must be a total one; it is not allowable to apply it at one point and not at another. This means, from the point of view of interpretation, that if it has been established, then we have to reckon with it even in those situations where clear signals are not given. However, Grimmelshausen works very hard to weave such signals into the narrative. Sometimes, this even happens *en passant.* During Simplicissimus's visit to the Mummelsee, the king of the sylphs asks if God is not readying himself to give "der Welt ihr Endschafft" (425) because of mankind's depraved way of life. The monarch, whose kingdom would certainly be destined for destruction, is confident. His water spirits could namely "auß dem Gestirn noch nichts dergleichen abnehmen [. . .]/ daß ein so nahe Veränderung obhanden seye" (45). Simplicissimus later begins his autobiography with the claim that many believe of the present time, "daß es die letzte seye" (9). In spite of that, however, the world obviously continues to exist. The sylphs' astrological analysis and prognosis have been confirmed. The mirroring function of the stars is proven *ex negativo* in the empty prophecy. It shows what God had predetermined for the world, according to the King of the Sylphs. The stars serve as instruments of correct prophecies. As a result when Simplicissimus, after the change to a fool, has to laugh about his "Unstern" (110), or when his "star" (270) leads him to the woman who will later be his wife, or when in his judgment "deß einen Unstern [eintritt] Staffelweis und allgemach" (279), whereas another person is hit abruptly by bad luck, he is not simply speaking in metaphors. He wants to be understood literally and gives linguistic signals, which, over and above their characteristics as *topoi,* indicate the effects of the constellations. These occasional statements are of particular importance for understanding the course of events in the novel.

The astrological motif of prophecy surrounding the elder Herzbruder carries larger exegetical weight than the statements of the Sylphen King in *Simplicissimus Teutsch.* The twenty-first chapter of the second book relates that the elder Herzenbruder, the foster-father and confidant of the protagonist, "ihm selbst und seinem Sohn einen grossen bevorstehenden Spott *prognostici*rte" (159). We are not informed about the specific method of prediction; however, Simplicissimus's foster-father has already been introduced as a palmist:

> Er beschaute meine Händ/ und verwundert sich beydes über die verwichene und künfftige seltzame Zufälle; Wolte mir aber durchauß nicht rathen/ daß ich in Bälde mein Narrn-Kleid ablegen solte/ weil er/ wie er sagte/ vermittelst der *Chiromantia* sahe/ daß mir mein fatum eine Gefängnus androhe/ die Leib- und Lebensgefahr mit sich brächte. (151)

Moreover, Herzbruder is characterized as a "vortrefflicher *Phisiognomist*" (164) as well as a "guter *Mathematicus* und *Nativit*äten-Steller," that is, as an astrologer just like the older Simplicissimus. In accordance with the spirit of the times, all three methods of prognosis were equally reliable. This statement gains strength in the novel through the correctness of the prophecies, which are presented through Herz-bruder. All three practices are intimately related to one another and find — according to the beliefs of the time and examination of Grimmel-shausen's sources — their common denominator in astrology. One need only consult a passage from Grimmelshausen's *Keuscher Joseph* for evidence proving the relationship between chiromancy and astrology. There, Musai reads the palm of the title character and predicts his fate exactly: "Joseph hätte sich einbilden können/ der Kerl sey unsinnig worden/ wann dessen Reden mit seiner Nativität nicht überein gestimmt/ zumahlen auch eingetroffen hätten/ was ihm Musai vor drey-zehn Jahren gesagt" (J 81). This connection of both "disciplines" is also present in the narrower sense of the word. For example, Johannes ab Indagine, in his *Stern-Kunst,* a source which Grimmelshausen consulted extensively, assigns, with reference to "die alten Lehrer dieser Kunst" (6), each part of the hand to a specific planet. The ball of the "Goldfin-ger," i.e., the ring finger, is attributed to the shining sun in accordance with the analogical way of thinking in this era. Among the metals, gold belongs to the sun. We are dealing not with a formal attribute, but rather the connection "nach himmlischem Jnfluß" (6).

The following example from Indagine's *Stern-Kunst* proves the as-trological functionalization of physiognomy — generally it is true:

> dz weñ man eines Menschen Complexion weiß/ man auch auß dessel-ben Geberden vnd Sitten erkeñen möge/ was für einen Planeten/ auch an was für gutem: oder bösem Ort/ er in seiner Geburtsstund habe? Vnd alsdañ auß Wissenschaft des Planeten sein gantzes Leben vnd We-sen errathê möge. (208)

When Indagine stresses that he uses all three ways of predicting, it becomes clear why Grimmelshausen's Herzbruder character possesses all of these qualifications which are based on astrology. He is the perfect "Stern-Künstler" noted in the title of Indagine's book: *Natürliche Stern-Kunst/ Oder Gründlicher Bericht wie auß Ansehen des Gesicht/ der Händ/ vnd gantzer Gestalt des Menschen Wahr gesagt werden könne [. . .].*

The elder Herzbruder soon understands what the seemingly foolish Simplicius is doing in the Magdeburg camp, as "er denn zuvor auch etwas gemerckt/ und von mir auß meinem Angeschicht ein anders ge-urtheilet hatte/ weil er sich wol auff die *Phisiognomiam* verstund" (150). Herzbruder realizes with the help of chiromancy that Simplicissimus's fate threatened him with a stint in prison, in addition to "Leib- und Lebensgefahr" (151), if he were to remove his fool's clothing. The prognosis of the elder to Simplicius is fulfilled in the episode dealing with cross-dressing. The peculiarity of Herzbruder's prediction confirms what had already been proven in connection with the alleged adultery of the young Simplicius: the prophecies relevant for the structure of the novel are not only fulfilled, they are fulfilled in two-fold fashion. When Simplicius ignores the warning of the Herzbruder and dons women's clothing, the prediction becomes reality. As the prognosis first begins to become reality, Simplicissimus is wooed as a "girl" by both the captain of the cavalry and by his servant. The officer's wife, however, recognizes that he is a boy merely dressed as a girl, and she, too, is interested in him. This constellation creates a strange, though still comical situation. "Damal (aber viel zu spat) gedachte ich fleissig an meines Seel. Hertzbruders Weissagung und Warnung/ und bildete mir nichts anderes ein/ als daß ich schon würklich in der jenigen Gefängnus auch Leib- und Lebensgefahr steckte/ davon er mir gesagt hatte" (170). However, while the hero thinks he can escape the predicament, the prophecy actually begins to turn into reality. Because of his clothing, he is suspected of committing espionage and is threatened with torture and the stake. "Jn dieser Gefangenschafft dachte ich stetigs an meinen Pfarrer zu Hanau/ und den [. . .] alten Herzbruder/ weil sie beyde wahr gesagt/ wie mirs ergehen würde/ wenn ich wieder auß meinem Narrenkleid käme" (175). The clergyman had told Simplicissimus on the occasion of the "Narrenverwandlung," that he had "mit Gefahr deiner Vernunfft in diese Narren-Kappe geschloffen," but it was uncertain "ob du ohne Verlust deines Lebens wieder herauß kommest" (114). The first person narrator does not want his apprehension viewed only metaphorically as a prediction and, hence, the motif of prophecy in *Simplicissimus* increases. Thus an additional person, who takes on the role of Simplicius's father, is actually integrated into the structure-building motif.

Captivity and endangerment of life help create the basic chords within the prophecy motif. Herzbruder had already warned the boy against both before the episode dealing with the cross-dressing:

> demnach lage uns nichts härter an/ als wie wir meines Narren-Kleids mit Ehren loß werden [. . .] möchten; welches aber der alte Herzbruder [. . .] nicht gut hiesse/ sondern außtrücklich sagte: Wenn ich in kurtzer Zeit meinen Stand änderte/ daß mir solches ein schwere Gefängnus und grosse Leib- und Lebensgefahr gebären würde. (158–59)

Surprisingly, there is an amalgamation of the prophecy with Herzbruder's own fate:

> Und weil er auch ihm selbst und seinem Sohn einen grossen bevorstehenden Spott *prognostici*rte/ und dahero Ursach zu haben vermeynte/

desto vorsichtiger und behutsamer zu leben; Als wolte er sich umb so
viel desto weniger in einer Person Sachen mischen/ deren künfftige
grosse Gefahr er vor Augen sehen konte. (159)

Herzbruder, as Simplicissimus's accomplice, fears that he will be
forced to be a witness. The prediction contains again the criteria of
double fulfillment. First the plot against the younger Herzbruder, the
son of the older one, was spun. It is only a preliminary phase in the
realization of the complex prophecy. As it begins to come to fruition, the
element of astrology, which up to this time had been present at best only
implicitly, becomes much clearer. Worrying about the humiliation of his
innocent son, which could at first not be controlled, brought the older
Herzbruder to the sickbed — the conditions for the fulfillment of a
prophecy made about him (that is, the older Herzbruder) have thus been
created. He had "sich selbst prognosticirt [. . .]/ daß er den 26. Julii
Leib- und Lebensgefahr außstehen müste," indeed, he "versahe [. . .]
sich seines Todts" (162). An officer, who although turned away, insists
on having Herzbruder read him his horoscope, stabs Herzbruder to
death because of frustration from a warning that he should guard against
being hanged "in dieser Stund" (166). This fulfills not only Herzbruder's prophecy concerning himself, but the motif involves also the
officer, who is hanged immediately after this deed. "Zwo Wahrsagungen
werden auff einmal erfüllt" (94), announces the title of the chapter. One
notices, as in *Wunderbarliches Vogel-Nest I*, that prophecies will be fulfilled even when precautions are taken against them: Herzbruder, no
longer ill, decides to stay in bed in order not to risk facing his own prognosis and paradoxically finds death right there. All of the old man's
prophecies are infallible. He

> nennete sogar den Tag/ an welchem die Schlacht vor Wittstock nach-
> gehends geschahe/ sintemal ihm viel zukamen/ denen umb dieselbige
> Zeit einen gewaltthätigen Todt zu leiden angedrohet war; Die Obristin
> versichert er/ daß sie ihr Kindbett noch im Läger außhalten würde/
> weil vor Außgang der sechs Wochen Magdeburg an die Unserige nicht
> übergeben würde. (164)

In particular, Herzbruder predicts in exact detail the death of his enemy Olivier who pulled the strings in the case of the intrigue against his
son. The ramifications of such predictions make us even more conscious
of the astrological determination of the event. Herzbruder does not
allow his son to seek vengeance against his adversary, because "der jeni-
ge/ der den Olivier todt schlüg/ wieder von mir dem Simplicio den Rest
kriegen werde" (163f). The father knows anyway that "ihr beide [Herz-

bruder and Simplicius] einander nicht umbringen werdet/ weil keiner von euch durch Waffen umbkommen solle" (164). The younger Herzbruder is actually poisoned. Simplicissimus, warned of the dangers of water by the Elder, "weil er besorgte/ ich würde meinen Untergang darinn leiden" (165), faces the danger of drowning multiple times in his life. Olivier, who will die "eines gewaltthätigen Todts" (164), learns from Herzbruder, that Simplex "seinen Todt/ er geschehe wann er wolle/ rächen/ und seinen Mörder wieder umbbringen würde" (165). All these predictions come true, right down to the most intricate details. While raiding Oliver's hide-away, one of the soldiers slays the other with the butt of his rifle. Simplicius, who is staying with Olivier according to predicted circumstances, kills the soldier out of self-defense in the tumult. The fulfillment of the prophecy is the more astonishing because Simplicissimus had doubted it, in spite of the trust he had in Herzbruder:

> ich betrachtete auch/ wie weislich und obscur Hertzbruder seine Weißsagungen geben/ und gedachte bey mir selber/ ob zwar seine Wahrsagungen gemeinlich unfehlbar einzutreffen pflegten/ daß es dennoch schwer fallen würde/ und seltzam hergehen müste/ da ich eines solchen Todt/ der Galgen und Rad verdient hätte/ rächen solte. (355)

The "Obskurität," which Simplicissimus notes, does not change the reliability of the prognoses, which are based on astrology. On the contrary, it picks up once again the theme of double fulfillment. As the plot progresses, the protagonist learns only later from Olivier's story that Herzbruder has made a complex prediction for his dear friend:

> "Du weist dich zu erinnern/ wie richtig der Alte Hertzbruder mit seinen Prophezeyhungen zugetroffen," continues Olivier, trustingly, "schaue/ derselbe hat mir vor Magdeburg diese Wort geweissagt/ die ich bißhero fleissig im Gedächtnus behalten: *Olivier,* sihe unsern Narren an wie du wilt/ so wird er dannoch durch seine Dapferkeit dich erschröcken/ und dir den grösten Possen erweisen/ der dir dein Lebtag je geschehen wird/ weil du ihn darzu verursachest in einer Zeit/ darinn ihr beyde einander nicht erkennet gehabt/ doch wird er dir nit allein dein Leben schenken/ so in seinen Händen gestanden/ sondern er wird auch über ein Zeit lang hernach an das jenig Ort kommen/ da du erschlagen wirst/ daselbst wird er glückseelig deinen Tod rächen. Dieser Weissagung halber/ liebster *Simplici,*" Oliver explains, "bin ich bereit mit dir das Hertz im Leib zu theilen/ dann gleich wie schon ein Theil davon erfüllt/ in dem ich dir Ursach geben/ daß du mich als ein dapfferer Soldat vor den Kopff geschossen/ und mir mein Schwerd genommen/ (das mir freylich noch keiner gethan) mir auch das Leben gelassen/ da ich unter dir lag/ und gleichsam im Blut erstickte; Also

zweiffle ich nicht/ daß das übrige von meinem Todt auch [nicht] fehl schlagen werde." (340)

Olivier's trust in the reliability of Hertzbruder's predictions is very much justifiable as he soon learns for himself, phsyically. Luckily for Simplicissimus, he is incorrect when he interprets the duel in the Endinger forest as Herzbruder's announced "gröster Posse." Olivier is excused so to speak, because all of the criteria named by the older man are correct in every detail right up to this struggle. The mechanism of double fulfillment is present here, too, because Herzbruder additionally aims for the "Jäger von Soest's" former settling of accounts with his arrogant challenger, the "Jäger von Werl," otherwise known as Olivier. It's not just losing the sword, as Olivier thinks, that demonstrates Oliver's strong humiliation; it is actually also the crude punishment he receives in the pastoral scene at the hand of Simplicissimus's partner at the time, Springinsfeld. He does not know he faced Simplicissimus at the time. The protagonist now understands: "Damals sahe ich erst, was ich dem Olivier vor ein Possen erwiesen darvon ihm der Alte Hertzbruder prophezeyet/ welches er Olivier aber selbst [. . .] zu meinem grossen Vortel anders außgelegt" (355). Because of this, the relevant chapter is entitled: "Wie er Hertzbruders Weißsagung zu seinem Vorthel außlegt/ und deßwegen seinen ärgsten Feind liebet" (289). The recognition of the alleged or actual fulfillment of a central prophecy of the elder Herzbruder may depend on the interpretive perspective of each of the characters in the novel — there is not any doubt about its actual fulfillment. Because this absolute accuracy of the prognoses is only possible with the astrological basis in *Simplicissimus,* it does not matter whether "der leichte Sinn so vieler Unterschiedlicher Menschen/ oder das Gestirn selbst/ wie etliche wollen" (VN I, 137) is the cause of earthly inconstancy, as the nest carrier thinks. The answer is definitively given for the astrologically structured novel, particularly as the carelessness of humans is based on planetary determination, as is thoroughly presented in Grimmelshausen's calendar. One example out of many:

> "Lieber *Simplici,*" Indagine tells his eager student, "vor allen sey erinnert/ daß die himmlische Jnfluß (und zwar vff einen weniger oder mehr je nach dem sich die Planeten befinden) mit jhren Würkungen wohl starck herab striemen/ und starcke Neigungen erwecken; Es können aber dannoch solche Neigungen den vernünfftigen und weisen Menschen keineswegs zum bösen zwingen/ sondern es kan der Mensch jhnen mit guthen begegnen und vorseyn; Will er aber der Natur welche ohne daß zum bösen geneigt/ in solchen seinen Neigungen jhren Zaum lassen/ so vollstrecken sie jhre Würckung kräfftiglich/ und

folgt alsdann der Mensch seiner verderbten Natur wie ein Vieh und nicht seiner vernunfft als ein Mensch." (V, 41)

This passage, in which Grimmelshausen additionally solves the explosive issue of determinism in astrology, could be a paraphrase of the narration contained in the *Wunderbarliches Vogel-Nest*. There the jealous innkeeper represents a category of individual that yields to affectionate tendencies or leanings and thereby allows the planetary influence to play a more important role. The young Simplicissimus is indeed the pure one, whom the stars actually cannot harm. He is at the same time led into temptation through various circumstances, including disastrous verbal misunderstandings, only to be even more brilliantly rehabilitated. As a witness to the event and as someone who listens to the astrological explanations of the elder Simplicissimus, the carrier of the bird's nest (*Vogelnest-Träger*) cannot downgrade the astrological effectiveness of the prognosis, even independent of the remarks in the calendar. He merely asks whether the heavens can be effective, either directly or, through the disposition of humans, indirectly. With each case of double fulfillment there is almost an over-fulfillment of the prognoses so that the motif of prophecy, which has remained relatively unnoticed in research, takes on the function of a dominating structural element. It may even be the most dominant tectonic component of the novel in the terms of its very effectiveness. Together with recurring characters, who cannot be separated from the prophecy motif, this astrological chain of motives decisively distances itself from the loose genre schemata like that of the Pícaro novel.

3. The Council of Gods in the *Wunderbarliches Vogel-Nest* as a Prediction of the Future

A further narrative complex highlights the astrological foundation of the prognosis motif in the Simplician texts, although it may be different from what we have seen so far. It deals with the casting of a spell, which functions as the means of prophecy. It is found in a context heavy with "Propheten," "Chaldaeer," and "*Prognosticanten*" (VN II, 211). It is about "Ertz-Schwartz-Künstler" who want to produce a "lustiges Spectacul, so sie/ vermittelst ihrer Künst zurichten" (VN II, 275). It is so created, "daß man vergangenes/ gegenwärtiges und zukünfftiges darbei sehen könte" (VN II, 275). Concretely, it deals with a vision of the council of gods that will serve as a narrative illustration of the influence of the planets on the earth. The clairvoyant "Gauckelei" is noticeably embedded in the narration: this narration, actually the "historische" substratum, appears as the realization of the allegorical and astrological levels of meaning. The allegory appears as its reference. In a club of smokers in Amsterdam, at which the bird's nest carrier is a guest, the punishment of the political arrogance of the Dutch through a war is mentioned as something to be feared. In the course of the story, the French-British invasion of the Netherlands follows. Indeed, the council of gods takes place between these passages, and the participants complain of the general state of the moral ruin of mankind, specifically that of the Dutch. This happens by stressing the correspondence between both levels of action, at times in literal agreement with the debate in the earthly discussion. Finally, the gods summon Mars, the god of war, to earth. The signifying and signified levels of meaning of the narration are hence obvious; "da thät sichs voneinander" (VN II, 275) as it is called most clearly with the evocation of the "Gesicht." No longer from the allegorical-astrological but rather from the astrological-causal perspective we can say that the narrative events outside of the vision should be seen as the effects of the council's resolutions. Since Jupiter, rather than Apollo, is serving as head of the council, there is widespread Jovial blossoming on earth. This, however, is superceded by warlike destruction when Mars is sent to mankind.

Hermeneutically, the author opens up an allegorical level of meaning for the reader in order to demonstrate the results of the gods' decision and make them clear. The causal relationship of *sensus allegoricus* and *sensus litteralis* is made transparent through the narrative stance that Grimmelshausen adopts. It is relevant that the *sensus allegoricus* specifically is the *sensus astrologicus* here. First, Jupiter subordinates himself and his colleagues and their will to god, which would be absurd for autonomous mythological gods. Secondly, and more importantly, he characterizes the whole bunch of them expressly as planetary gods. Apollo's (the Sun's) intention of scarring the Earth as punishment is not possible for Jupiter: "solche *procedur* wäre zu streng/ und wider die Güte deß grossen *Numinis,* und wann er *Apollo*" — a genuinely biblical thought — "sich deren auß eygenem Willen unterfangen würde/ so wäre sie auch straffbar" (VN II, 278). One would have to instigate mankind's improvement, so that "das schöne Gebäu der Welt/ mit welchem auch sie die Planeten selbst auffhören müssten, noch länger in seinem Flor stehen bleiben könte" (VN II, 278). The gods, this has to be emphasized, are not mythological, that is, sovereign rulers of an independent world, but rather subjugated to a biblical god. They, too, would have to face the end of the world, just as everybody else, if it were so decided by God. They are therefore undoubtedly astrological gods, although not all gods introduced in the text might be identified this way. The sun god, to give just one example, explains that God had "ihm befohlen/ meinen Schein beydes guten und bösen mitzutheilen" (VN II, 278). This biblical reminiscence cannot be connected to the mythical gods of the classical antiquity. Jupiter or Apollo, as mythological gods, could represent God allegorically, but could not act along with Him, no, they could only act under Him. There are indications, like the kindness of Jupiter, that correlate to passages concerning planets in Grimmelshausen's *Ewigwährender Calender*. Mercury, who was considered originally in both mythology and astrology "vor den schlauesten *Vocativum* unter allen Göttern" (VN II, 279), names money as the root of all moral evil while being interrogated by Jupiter, exposing illuminating astrological information. He ostentatiously counts "Kupffer/ Zinn/ Bley/ Ganza" (a type of iron) as well as leather in addition to gold and silver as pecuniary raw material (VN II, 280). They are the metals and materials of all seven of the planetary gods. Mercury thus signals that the rest of the planets, aside from the obviously recognizable ones, should be included in Jupiter's overall characterization of the planets. The sun, moon, Venus, Jupiter, Saturn, Mars, and Mercury, the only "planets" known at that time, correlate exactly to the sequence of the metals and the leather. The leather naturally substitutes for quicksilver, which was unsuitable for coins. Its malleability offers the *tertium comparationis* to the flexibility of the god Hermes-Mercury.

4. Jupiter the Fool as a Planet God in *Simplicissimus*

Jupiter, who sits on the council of gods in *Wunderbarliches Vogel-Nest II* as a sidereal god, has a predecessor in *Simplicissimus Teutsch*. This character appears in the sixty-ninth of 169 chapters in the novel, practically in the middle of the narration. While at the end of Grimmelshausen's total work, with an experienced audience, the astrological characteristics may seem meager and apodictic — "sie die Planeten" — Jupiter, who appears chronologically as the first one, must show more extravagance: he introduces himself as a "grosser GOtt," and afterwards as the "Gott Jupiter" (209). His astrological origins only become clear from his gifts, which he wishes to bestow upon the "Teutscher Held" "in seiner Geburt-Stund" (210). The "Geburt-Stund" is a synonym for the term "Nativität" in this case. This indicates, as in the *Wunderbarliches Vogel-Nest,* the astrologically important position of the planets at the time of birth of a person, one's horoscope. The word "Nativität" is presented in the text shortly thereafter: the planet god Jupiter wants to view (= "anblicken") the goddess Venus "in seiner [d.h. des Teutschen Helden] Natività̈t desto freundlicher" (211). What with the mythological god of the same name would appear as a flirtation of the notorious charmer with the goddess of love, is in this context a "Kon-Stellation," a definite sidereal "A-spekt," "An-Blick." All combinations of the astrological positions of Jupiter and Venus are for the greater good of the earthly inhabitants, except for the hostile "Opposition," which is excluded by Jupiter's utterance. Grimmelshausen's *Ewig-währender Calender* confirms this fact precisely. The planetary gods Jupiter and Venus represent the "Großes" and the "Kleines Glück" according to the teachings of astrology. The goddess should give the hero extraordinary beauty, a part of such missions already in the Middle Ages; she is after all, "ein ursach [. . .] der Schönheit" (V, 129). The hero should receive "zu allen seinen Tugenden ein sonderbare Zierlichkeit/ Auffsehen und Anmüthigkeit" in accordance with Jupiter's wishes (211). The *Calender* is literally in agreement with this:

> Venus hat gar nahe mit dem Jove gleiche Eigenschafften/ doch etwas geringer/ und was der Planet Jupiter von Tugenden/ Künsten/ Geschicklichkeiten und allem Guten im Thun und Lassen inflösset/ demselben gibt Venus hinzu eine Zierlichkeit besonders Auffsehen und Anmuth; und solches umb so viel destomehr/ wann Jupiter sie freundlich anblickt. (V, 195)

The German hero will be "mit Fürsichtigkeit/ Weisheit und Verstand überflüssig geziert" (210), since Jupiter offers especially "Ruhm der Rathgebung/ Weißheit/ Fürsichtigkeit" according to the *Ewig-währender Calender* (V, 193). In addition to possessing these traits, a hero, according to the treatise, can only be a jovial type of individual. From the many other clear astrological indications in the novel, let us consider just one more: the formula "in Hora Martis" (211). The hours of the day and the week are ruled, from the astrological point of view, by specific planets. Up to the present time, European clocks of this era, especially those in churches, illustrate the principle and practice of astrological selection of time. A sword of wonders was to be cast for the German hero in the "Stunde des Kriegsgottes Mars" in *Simplicissimus*. This god of war can only be the planet Mars in conjunction with the mythologically meaningless choice of hour, although Vulcan — as mythological god without a correlating astrological pendant — is viewed as Jupiter's blacksmith. The mythological apparatus of the context — we have to keep this in mind in terms of methodology — is subordinate to astrology. The singular turn of phrases quoted, "sie die Planeten," serves as an overall turn. An opposite subordinate relationship would be absurd. Historically, the attributes of the mythological gods have been transferred, almost completely, to the concept of astrological gods. Additional astrological attributes and functions, for example, the choice of time here, can, however, not be integrated into mythology. It is impossible that the Olympic Jupiter could give in to the goddess of love in a similar fashion as in Grimmelshausen's novel in an "An-Blick" or a "Kon-Stellation."

No reasonable doubt can exist that both Jupiters (in *Simplicissimus* and the *Wunderbarliches Vogel-Nest*) consider themselves astrological gods, regardless of the epical contextual usage of parts of mythology. The verbatim citations of sections of the calendar, which preclude an ironic perspective, speak for themselves. An alternative interpretation would assume that the author, because of his own ignorance, could not differentiate between the 'disciplines' of mythology and astrology. How should the collective self-characterization of the Jupiter-figure: "sie die Planeten" be tied in with a mythological exegesis?

On the contrary, the intention of the text is clear. The type of madness with which Jupiter is suffering shows this conclusively. It is an intermittent state of lunacy. During the time periods in which he is mentally ill, he functions as the god of the planets. In such a case, the narrative is clearly marked as jovial through and through. For example, Jupiter moves to Cologne, while still sick. This city is categorized under the same planet according to the *Calender* (III, 8, and V, 111). On the other hand, when Simplicissimus visits Jupiter, "so damals gantz klug war" (280), the title of the chapter indicates the city is "nur pro forma Cöln" (199). When the protagonist later passes through Cologne once again, Jupiter, who is in the meantime "wiederumb gantz hirnschellig" (387), addresses him as "Merkur" on several occasions. He views the hero as a companion planet functioning as a messenger of the gods. For example, Jupiter asks: "O Mercuri [. . .]/ was bringst du neues von Münster?" (387), that is, from the peace negotiations taking place there. The sick one reactivates the *sensus astrologicus* hermeneutically. Cologne no longer carries its name "pro forma." The *sensus astrologicus*, however, has increasingly acquired a mercurial structure. One should note for the unrestricted jovially significant phase of narration that Jupiter serves in astrological literature and iconography as the master of the hunt. Accordingly, the *Calender* recommends hunting "hohes Wild" (V, 113) during the hours of this planet. Hence, the hunt becomes both literally and figuratively a dominating motif for the entire narrative period which deals with the fool Jupiter. Simplicius, strongly favored by good fortune, hunts the enemy and receives the spoils, and carries the significant name "Jäger von Soest." The rival "Jäger von Werl" doubles the designation and the motif.

Grimmelshausen chooses a narrative technique similar to that of the council of gods in the *Wunderbarliches Vogel-Nest*. Such a technique allows him to demonstrate the allegorical structure of his work. In a sense, the plot unfolds on the lower level, while above it lies the astrological superstructure of the *sensus astrologicus*, which, in this case, is revealed by a "fool." On the basis of his being sane or ill, Jupiter can evidently be seen either in his function as a mere character in the foreground or in his function as a planetary god with allegorical significance. This functional illness does not in any way detract from the astrological utterances of Jupiter, which all make sense by themselves. The author creates derision differently. Ridicule — which is directed less at astrology than at a specific character — can be seen in Grimmelshausen's *Courasche*. There the crafty Springinsfeld introduces, on the occasion of an astrological prognosis that obviously should not be taken seriously, the hedgehog as a sign of the zodiac, even though such a sign does not exist.

5. The Prognosis Motif within the Central Complex of Astrological Prophecy

Additional prophecy motifs have been established in the astrological prophecy complex surrounding the old Herzbruder. These constitute a narrative component of the novel, which cannot be ignored. It begins in the twelfth chapter of the first book of the novel. Before his death, the hermit bases his moral instructions to Simplicius on the fact that he can see his "Lebens künfftige Begegnussen beyläuffig" and that he knows well that Simplicissimus will "in dieser Einöde nicht lange verharren" (34). However, this rather obvious appraisal of the situation, taken together with the testamentary letter to Simplicius, actually becomes a prophecy. The prediction of an emergency situation for the neighboring pastor, which only occurs long after the death of the hermit, goes well beyond simple assumptions or fears. This is more true, since it comes to pass only at the time the letter is accidentally found. "Lieber Simplici, wann du diß Briefflein findest/ so gehe alsbald auß dem Wald/ und errette dich und den Pfarrer auß gegenwärtigen Nöthen/ [. . .] Gott [. . .] wird dich an ein Ort bringen/ das dir am bequemsten ist" (51). Even as Simplicius leaves the forest, the pastor is still not in any difficult or dangerous situation. The "Gegenwart" of the danger is measured in terms of the language use of the time; it is valid only in Hanau, in the predicted place, which the youth in the forest does not even know by name. The pastor is taken prisoner when he raises the suspicions of the governor of the fortress, who is a brother-in-law of the hermit, by selling the jewelry, which he had legally acquired from the hermit. It almost seems as though the hermit was more or less involved in his own prognosis. In point of fact, Günther Weydt identified the hermit as the allegorical representation of the planet Saturn, even to the point of his external appearance. The outer and inner characteristics of Saturn for the comparison with the figure in the novel are found in Grimmelshausen's *Ewig-währender Calender.*

Another complex of prediction motifs surrounds "die bekante Wahrsagerin zu Soest" (208). She advises Simplicius to bury his fortune in the fertile plain, because he has more enemies among his comrades than among his opponents. He takes to heart, "was mir die berühmte Wahrsagerin zu Soest ehemals gesagt" (247), and profits from this precautionary measure after his capture. He will have access to the spoils in the free countryside. The hero additionally learns from the seeress that his comrades would murder him if he returns to Soest, "weil du ihnen beym Frawenzimmer bist vorgezogen worden" (260). This clue gives occasion to a new prediction: love would soon awaken in Simplicius, even though now he "dem Frauenzimmer nichts nachfrage" (261). The seeress argues with reference to him who had been honorably held prisoner in Lippstadt:

> du hast mich jederzeit verlacht, wenn ich dir etwas zuvor gesagt habe/ woltest du mir abermal nicht glauben/ wann ich dir mehr sagte/ findestu an dem Ort/ wo du jetzt bist/ nicht geneigtere Leut als in Soest? Jch schwöre dir/ daß sie dich nur gar zu lieb haben/ und daß dir solche übermachte Lieb zum Schaden gereichen wird/ wann du dich nicht nach derselbigen *accomodi*rest. (261)

The "Freyherr" promptly learns "mit der Leimstangen lauffen" from the books of love (262): "wo meine Lieb hinfiel/ da erhielte ich leichtlich und ohne sonderbare Mühe/ was ich begehrte" (262). The suddenness of this change of heart in the hero, the fact that he learns of love from "Helden-Gedichten" and similar "Gattungen" (262), and the efforts involved in using a prophecy motif for an expected natural course of events speak against a psychological interpretation. All criteria emphasize the prophecy motif and point to the beginning of Venus' rule, which culminates in Simplicius's nonvoluntary (!) adventures on the "Venus-Berg" in Paris (288). However, Venus, seen in the context of a prophecy which is certain to be fulfilled in the future — the prophecies of the seeress of Soest are, without exception, fulfilled — can only be a planetary god. The infallibility of the predictions proves itself once more, when these are seen in conjunction with the motif of the search for parents. She informs him: "[. . .] ich solte alsdann nach meinen Eltern fragen, wann mir mein Pflegvatter unversehens begegne/ und führe meiner Säug-Ammen Tochter am Strick daher" (261). This facetious sibylline Simplician prognosis confirms itself in the anagnorisis scene in the eighth chapter of the fifth book, in which Simplicius meets the Knan with a goat, a descendant of that "Amme," and learns from him the truth about his real parents.

The characteristic of unlimited reliability of the prophecies, which is either explicitly or implicitly determined by astrology, is stressed through the reflections of the protagonists. These reflections clearly demonstrate the relationship to astrology. Because of their programmatic significance for the novel they should be cited in full:

> AUß dieser warhafftigen Histori [i.e. the murder of the older Herz-bruder and the acts preceeding it] ist zu sehen/ daß nicht so gleich alle Wahrsagungen zu verwerffen seyen/ wie etliche Gecken thun/ die gar nichts glauben können. So kan man auch hierauß abnehmen/ daß der Mensch sein auffgesetztes Ziel schwerlich überschreiten mag/ wann ihm gleich sein Unglück lang oder kurtz zuvor durch dergleichen Weis-sagungen angedeutet worden. Auff die Frag/ die sich ereignen möch-te/ obs einem Menschen nötig/ nützlich und gut seye/ daß er sich wahrsagen/ und die Nativität stellen lasse? Antworte ich allein dieses/ daß mir der Alte Hertzbruder so viel gesagt habe/ daß ich offt gewün-schet/ und noch wünsche/ daß er geschwiegen hätte/ dann die un-glückliche Fäll/ die er mir angezeigt/ hab ich niemals umbgehen können/ und die jenige die mir noch bevor stehen/ machen mir nur vergeblich graue Haar/ weil mir besorglich dieselbige auch/ wie die vorige/ zu handen gehen werden/ ich sehe mich gleich für denselben vor oder nicht. (167)

Simplicius is, as he says, more skeptical about the realization of for-tunate prophecies. He toys with them, though, when he dismisses Herz-bruder's suggestion that he is of noble descent (his foster parents being "Knan" and "Meüder"), and playfully substantiates his "Zweifel" with the example of Wallenstein (who was murdered rather than crowned). Sim-plicius actually believes in the fulfillment of other prophecies of the old Herzbruder, which lie beyond his narrative position. He uses a past situation to confirm the infallibility of his mentor:

> mir selbsten aber erzehlet er meinen künfftigen gantzen Lebenslauff so umbständlich [i.e. detailed]/ als wenn er schon vollendet/ und er alle-zeit bey mir gewesen wäre/ welches ich aber wenig achtet/ und mich

jedoch nachgehends vielen Dings erinnert/ das er mir zuvor gesagt/ nachdem es schon geschehen oder wahr worden. (165)

The result is noteworthy: Herzbruder had predicted the course of events for Simplicius's entire life, even beyond his narrative stance, with the help of astrologically based techniques. The stars thoroughly determine Simplex's life. The *Simplicissimus Teutsch* is, as the title page informs us, nothing less than the "Beschreibung deß Lebens eines seltzamen Vaganten" by the name of Simplicissimus. The description also includes other characters, whom Herzbruder integrated into his prophecies. The narrative possesses in its totality, independent of the abundance of other explicit astrological evidence, an allegorical level of meaning, a *sensus astrologicus*.

6. The "*Conjunction Saturni* und *Mercurii*"

Grimmelshausen's astrological method, which emphatically reveals the planetary background of the seemingly autonomous Simplician plot, is one of the most important structural characteristics of the Simplician cycle. The parallel between *sensus litteralis* and *sensus astrologicus* is particularly obvious in the *Simplicissimus Teutsch* in the section dealing with the camp in Magdeburg. It is told in the twenty-second chapter of Book II that Olivier and the disciplinary officer of the regiment have conspired against the younger Herzbruder. It must be stressed that the relevant elements of this narration, as far as we know, are not found in any of Grimmelshausen's sources. The narrator describes this malicious alliance of both schemers as "die *Conjunction Saturni* und *Mercurii*" (160). Similarly, and with far reaching implications and consequences, we find the curious usage of the title of the second chapter of *Seltzsamer Springinsfeld:* "*Conjunctio Saturni, Martis & Mercurii*" (Sp 12).

Simplicissimus provides the contemporary reader in advance with a clear clue for understanding the metaphor in the larger novel. The first named deity in his use of the connection between Saturn and Mercury points toward the disciplinarian, because "Sein Bildnus sahe natürlich auß/ wie uns die Mahler und *Poëten* den *Saturnum* vorstellen/ ausser daß er weder Steltzen noch Sensen trug" (160). While the attribute of the scythe could also be ascribed to a mythological god, in which case it would be understood as an attribute of the god of time, Chronos, stilts or crutches in literature and iconography are attributes of the astral god Saturn. Moreover, the astronomical "Konjunktion" as an astrological term has been proved through analysis of the astrological Jupiter character in *Simplicissimus*. Olivier is convincingly identifiable with the sidereal god Mercury. A given god of mythology (much less two such gods) cannot sensibly be ascribed to an astrological concept. Indeed, the secretarial position of Olivier confirms this; after all, the planetary god Mercury is, not only according to the *Ewig-währender Calender,* the patron of language and of writing, the god of the writers. According to Grimmelshausen's *Calender,* he holds "in der Lincken eine *Chartam:* und in der rechten Hand ein Schreibfeder" (V, 133). Finally, the astrological treatise counts among Mercury's subjects the "*Secretarios*" (V, 135). In conjunction with this, the title of the second chapter of the *Springinsfeld* aims with the mention of the planet Mercury for the writer-character, to whom Courasche dictates the story of her life. The *Continuatio* of the novel explains the negative impact of the god in *Simplicissimus.* It characterizes the spirits of hell, who come marching by, as "so tückisch und dockmäusig wie *Mercurius*" (478). This "Steckbrief" is too pejorative for the mythological cattle thief. Thus, when Simplicissimus concludes from the "Verträulichkeit" between Olivier and the disciplinary officer, "daß die *Conjunction Saturni* und *Mercurii* dem redlichen Hertzbruder nichts guts bedeuten würde" (160), he alludes to the astrological constellation between both planets with their sinister effects.

His fears are not indeed unfounded, because he knows the old master as a merciless, "abgefäumten Ertz-Vogel und Kern Bößwicht" (159) and Olivier, "der ein arger Gast und durchtriebener Schalck war," as a totally jealous and false "Speyvogel" (157). Because he definitely wants to obtain the "Secretariat-Stell" of the regiment, which is reserved for the young Herzbruder, he has a motive for the intrigue, but he needs the support of the disciplinary officer, who is a "rechter Schwartzkünstler/ Siebdreher und Teuffelsbanner" (160). This sorcerer "convicts" his innocent rival by magical means of alleged theft and gets rid of him with these machinations according to his wishes. The planet Saturn, described as "zaubersüchtig" (V, 101), rules over the "listige/ heimbdückische Menschen die mit allerley Betrug und Schelmerey umbgehen" (V, 103) and sets traps for others according to the *Calender.* Individuals controlled by Mercury "haben gemeiniglich lange Finger," are "listig/ verschmitzt und handeln selten offentlich" (V, 133). This planetary god is also the "Herr der Verbindnuß" (V, 135).

Everything that is mentioned here about the so-called "Kinder" of the planets and their activities is also true for the astral gods themselves, due to the astrological structuralism. Their characteristics and functions are brought moreover into the narrative game. If, according to the *Calender* Saturn means "heimbliche Feind" and "Gefängnuß" (V, 103), then "die arme gefangene Soldaten" (160) are, by virtue of his office, subject to the disciplinarian, who at first keeps his animosity secret from Herzbruder. As a suspected spy, Simplex himself will soon be "[dem] alten Provosen gefänglich überliefert" (173). The repeated emphasis on the age of the disciplinarian can be explained by astrological circumstances, namely that Saturn's "Bild" is "[. . .] gleich einê alten Mann" (V, 101). Simplicius's designation of the older man as a "Wendenschimpff" (160) is even stronger evidence, because the calendar treatise speaks of "Wendenschimpff *Saturnus*" (IV, 113). Herzbruder acquiesces in this situation: "Er als ein weiser/ verständiger und tieffsinniger Mann ermaß ohnschwer auß den Umbständen/ daß *Olivier* seinem Sohn diß Bad durch den Provosen hatte zurichten lassen/ was vermochte er aber wider einen Zauberer?" (162). Being powerless in the face of magic is a motive for Herzbruder's actions on the narrative level. As a versed and infallible "Nativitäten-Steller," he knows that he has no chance against the influence of the planetary god Saturn, especially in conjunction with the evil Mercury. Olivier, on the other hand, employs the astrological rules for his own purposes, whenever he takes up contact with the disciplinarian in an hour of Saturn, a time beneficial for dealing with "Zauberern und andern verläumbten Leuthen" (V, 105). As a planet, that is, on an allegorical level, he is attracted to Saturn in any case: "dieser unbeständige Wetterhan," according to the *Calender,* which "den Mandel nach dem Wind henckt," assimilates easily with the other "Wandelsternen." This is especially true of those, "so jhm zugethan oder mit denen er sich *conjungirt*" (V, 133).

An astrological textbook, with which Grimmelshausen might well have been acquainted, states: "Mercurius ist sehr wandelbar/ vnd richtet sich wie ein rechter Wendehut oder Wetterhahn/ nach eines jeden Planeten Natur/ kömpt er zum Saturno, so nimpt er Saturni Natur an sich/ vñ sterckt also des Saturni Natur" (Hildebrand 44). Hence, Olivier lets himself "so vest als Stahl machen" (351) by the disciplinary officer, who is "von sich selbsten [. . .] so vest als Stahl" (160). Grimmelshausen's *Calender* warns directly and correctly of a "*Conjunction Saturni* und *Mercurii*": "Jst bequem zu geschwinder heimblicher listiger Practic/ darumb sihe dich vor daß du nit auffs Eyß gesetzt werdest" (V, 145). The magical "Vbunge" of the disciplinarian, which lead to ostracism of the younger Herzbruder, is exactly the epic equivalent of a secret and deceitful "Practic," in which term magic is implicit. Olivier needs the support of this type of conjunction; he could do nothing alone against his rival. The drastic metaphor of the astrological prognosis corresponds to the vividness of the title of the chapter: it promises "Diebs-Kunst," "einander die Schuh außzutretten" (94). Grimmelshausen continues a long tradition of including astrological views in narrative works and could expect certain background knowledge from his readers even before his *Ewig-währender Calender* appeared. In the chapter "Von Coniunctio vnd zusammenfügung der Planeten vnd jren bedeutungen" in the *Teutsche Astronomie* (1545) we read: "Mercurius mit Saturno bedeut das die leute sich underwinden der schwartzen kunst/ und geucherei/ vnd geschehen auch hinderung den schreibern/ dann sie werden geschnödet" (leaves LII^v and LIII^v). Thus, the fate of the young Herzbruder is precisely formulated beforehand. January passes gently according to the astrologer and astronomer Johannes Kepler (1571–1630) in his *Prognosticum Vber das Jahr MDCXXIII,* "obwohl Mercurius dem Saturno zugegen lauffent, seiner heimblichen Tücke darbey nit vergisset" (690).

Olivier and the disciplinarian are on the one hand as scribes, or officers and magicians, respectively, characters in the concrete plot, that is, on the level of the *sensus litteralis.* On the other hand, they are as anthropomorphous planetary gods actors in the area of the second level of the narration, the *sensus allegoricus.* These two levels of meaning, according to the structural logic of the allegory, are basically separate from each other. Still, as far as the paradigm of astrology is concerned, the second layer of the narrative crosses over into the first, because of causal necessity. On the level of literal meaning, we have the tale of intrigue against Herzbruder by two resentful individuals; on the level of allegorical meaning, we have the conjunction of two planets, Mercury and Saturn.

The terminological formula, the "*Conjunction Saturni* und *Mercurii*" points explicitly to the astrological level of meaning, which, appropriately enough, is placed on the upper level. Both of these planets, which are clearly marked in this way, affect the fate of Herzbruder. The intermittent insanity of Jupiter possesses the same transparent function as the astrological formula here. Only when the illness is acute does Jupiter rule, as we can see in specific narrative events. Only at this point, viewed hermeneutically, does the mostly jovial *sensus astrologicus* come into play. Only sporadically is the god Jupiter, who considers himself a "Großer Gott," really healthy. When this rare situation occurs, other textual factors keep the astrological level of meaning alive, for example, the venereally important prognoses of the fortune-teller of Soest.

7. The Effects of the "*Conjunction Saturni* und *Mercurii*"

The "*Conjunction Saturni* und *Mercurii*" — in the structural function of the *sensus astrologicus* — determines not only the narrower content area of the intrigue surrounding the young Hertzbruder. It affects, over and above that, a rather lengthy section of the plot as well. It is that section of the work in which Simplicius is addressed as "Mercurius" by the foolish Jupiter and is emphatically marked by the charlatan Simplicius when he gets rid of the "Mercurius Sublimatum" (315). Thus, in addition to his explicit reference to the constellation between the two planets, the author presents additional "sublime" allusions to the jurisdiction of Mercury in the course of the story. We have to keep in mind that the disciplinary officer is killed in the battle of Wittstock at the behest of the young Herzbruder; that is to say, from an allegorical perspective the influence of Saturn is over.

Interestingly enough, Olivier disappears, or so it seems, from the plot for a lengthy period of time. From the reader's standpoint, he enters into the narrative again for the first time during the attack on Simplicius in the Endinger Forest (IV, 14). Just two chapters earlier, the young Herzbruder also reappears suddenly. As was the case beforehand in the camp in Magdeburg, the two characters are closely linked to one another; this proves true for the duration of the novel. The correlation is apparent: both happen to be writers who never finished their studies and both strive to hold the same position of secretary within the regiment. If Olivier stops in the Westphalian town of Werl, Herzbruder is in Westphalia, if not in a closer neighboring area; he even has a conversation with the "Commandanten in Soest" (328). Both antagonists participate in the battle of Wittstock, significantly enough on different sides. The Swedes capture Olivier, the imperial troops Herzbruder. Both characters battle near Breisach, one on the side of those laying siege, the other is among the relief troops. That both are forced to join the Merode-Brüder only serves to emphasize the parallel structure of their lives. It is the Merode-Brüder who make it clear that this has to do with equality, considered from a mercurial aspect. In a lengthy and detailed passage the narrator characterizes the Merode-Brüder almost as absolute representatives of mobile and restless mercurial types in general. For him, they represent real riff-raff:

> so sich mit nichts besser als mit den Zügeinern vergleicht/ weil es nicht allein nach seinem Belieben vor/ nach/ neben und mitten unter der Armee herumb streicht/ sondern auch demselben beydes an Sitten und Gewonheit ähnlich ist. (331)

Formally, too, the text type of this passage is interesting from a mercurial point of view, because Simplicius considers himself, with this apparent digression, to be an original author, that is a mercurial type. He has, he claims, "bißher noch keinen *Skribenten* angetroffen/ der etwas von ihren [i.e., the Merode-Brüder] Gebräuchen/ Gewonheiten/ Rechten und *Privilegien/* seinen Schrifften einverleibt hätte" (330). Removed from the context of the novel, however, this is incorrect, because Grimmelshausen is utilizing another source for this passage.

The mercurial element is even more strongly emphasized within the plot by the fact that Simplicius falls into the hands of the Merode-Brüder, although the otherwise rather noble Herzbruder could have prevented that. In general, the protagonist of the novel can be found anywhere that the two opponents, Olivier and Herzbruder, are staying, and, of course, at the same time as they are there. In the camp in Magdeburg after the death of the elder Herzbruder, he has Olivier as a "Hofmeister" (168), and in Book Five Herzbruder trains him in this role (cf 381). Later, Simplicius himself will hold this position (cf. 444). Near Wittstock, in Westphalia, and in the Breisach siege, the hero is always in close proximity to both teachers. His "pilgrimage" to Switzerland corresponds to the trip with Olivier "an die äusserste Grentzen der Schweitzer" (360). After Olivier's death Simplicius reaches the nearby town of Villingen, only to find that Herzbruder also turns up there in the same chapter! In general, the three characters move on the same temporal plane within the narrow territory between the Upper Rhine and the Black Forest, and indeed they even meet each other there, too. According to the *Ewig-währender Calender,* "Theil am Rhein" and "Basel" are subject to the zodiacal signs of "Zwilling" and "Jungfrau," which, in turn, are dominated by the planet Mercury (III, 6). The "Seckel von dem Olivierschen Erbgut" (394) has its counterpart in the possessions that the dying young Herzbruder bequeaths to Simplicius. Herzbruder and Simplicius openly address each other often as "Bruder"; although one would not expect it, the same thing happens between Simplicius and Olivier. On each occasion a "Bund" (158) exists between the pairs. From the obvious similarity in important aspects of their lives it follows that Herzbruder and Olivier both allegorically represent the planet god Mercury. The latter — and only because of this is the hypothesis at all tenable — is, according to the calendar, "mit den guten Planeten [. . .] gut/ und mit den bösen auch böß" (V, 133). Herzbruder naturally points to the positive function of the god.

Grimmelshausen shows the ambivalence of the planet by creating two figures in the novel who, although conceived quite differently (even as opposites), are understandable only in relation to each other. The reader sees them, after an early introduction in the camp in Magdeburg, for the first time again precisely in the Mercury phase of *Simplicissimus Teutsch*. If, in their hermeneutic role as allegorical representatives of a complex dualistic conception of an astrological Mercury, both characters accompany the hero of the novel on a permanent basis, then it is because they represent for us the mercurial state of that hero on the level of the *sensus astrologicus*. That planet is not only "ein Herr der Verbindnuß" (V, 135), but also "ein Herr der jungen Brüder" (5, 133).

That is, of course, the reason for the moral vacillations of Simplicius, especially in the Mercury phase of the novel. He is always aligned with one of the two companions, which is to say, he is steered by one of the two polar astrological halves or sides. Olivier, one-time intimate friend of the evil disciplinary officer, wants to turn the hero of the novel to a Machiavellian way of thinking; Herzbruder, earlier the arch-enemy, urges the hero to repent and do penance. His frequent and short-lived vacillations between the troops in Weimar and those of the Emperor, precisely in this section of the narrative, are, taken together with Simplicius's "unlustig Bad im Rhein" (289), in effect an allegory of mercurial inconstancy. The allusion to the ball of Fortuna underscores this allegorical content:

> Ob ich mich nun zwar auß allen Kräfften spreitzte/ und alle Vörtel der guten Schwimmer brauchte/ so spielte dennoch der Strom mit mir wie mit einem Ballen/ in dem er mich bald über- bald undersich in Grund warf [. . .]. Jch versuchte offt ans Ufer zu gelangen/ so mir aber die Würbel nit zuliessen/ als die mich von einer Seite zur andern warffen. (320)

After his unexpected rescue, Herzbruder, who appears quite without warning, frees Simplicius from his miserable barracks. When the former suggests that the latter pretend to be his cousin, so that he "desto mehr geehrt würde" (329), the astrological significance of this affinity is readily apparent. It is thus no surprise that the fool Jupiter addresses Simplicius in Cologne as Mercurius. Cologne is a city which is not only so named simply "*pro forma*" (199) but which had also been "zwischen den kriegenden Partheyen Neutral" (387), that is, it has been "neutralized" as a Jupiter city within the mercurial phase of the novel. This happens no less than three times. It is also not coincidental that as a messenger *Simplicissimus* appears in Cologne, just as his planetary patron often does. In Lippstadt, too, he functions as a "fremder Bott" (389). Simplicius delivers his own letters to his brother-in-law, without the latter knowing who he is, because he wanted him to find out from "einem Botten [. . .]/ was Stands *Simplicius* seye" (389).

The Mercury phase of the novel ends with the death of Olivier and Herzbruder, both of whom allegorically represent this god. After the murder of Olivier there follows, surprisingly enough, but as a matter of course, within a relatively short time span, the poisoning of Herzbruder. This fact is all the more important when we consider that, according to the prophecy of the elder Herzbruder, the death of Olivier was to be expected within the novel. However, that prophecy did not mention anything at all about the death of Herzbruder's son. Research has called our attention to the fact that Gemini is one of the two signs of the zodiac associated with the planet Mercury (Rehder 91).

Simplicius's mercurially functional digression about the Merode-Brüder finds — still within the mercurial phase — a supplement, or rather a counterpart, in the life story of Olivier. Even that life story has, in accordance with the astrological significance of the connection between Herzbruder and Olivier, its correlative in the story of his adversary; thus, in keeping with the system, Simplicius gets ready to tell his "Lebens-Lauff" (358) to the robber. From a purely formal point alone, Olivier's oral report, which meshes later with Simplicius's written recapitulation of the story, is in keeping with his allegorical role as the god of writing, of authors, of speech, and, in general, of communication. Thus, Grimmelshausen, when working with his sources, replaces "Verß/ oder Reimen dichter" (Hildebrand 13) with "Poëten" and "Bücherschreiber" (V, 135), both of which seemed more appropriate to him. For the context of the novel it is also fitting that Olivier comes from a businessman's family — the planetary god is, like his mythological counterpoint, the god of merchants and of trade. In his story, Olivier includes in some detail the school system and student milieu. It is precisely here that he proves to be particularly mercurial, "ein *Disputir*er und Schnarcher/ der sich einbildete/ er verstehe trefflich viel!" (349). He finds himself stealing more and more — the astral Mercury is after all the patron saint of the appropriate brotherhood — so that he can then take on the duties of a writer.

In the gruesome tale dealing with the killing of one's comrades we have a macabre confirmation of the affinity of Mercury to arithmetic. Although there were originally eight soldiers, that number continues to be cut in half while the monetary profit for those remaining continues to double; finally, Olivier is the only one still alive. During a long march, Olivier flees first to the imperial troops, from there he goes to the Hessians, subsequently to the Dutch, and finally to the Bavarians — all this as the epitome of the mercurial state of transience and change. With his acceptance among the Merode-Brüder and subordination to the troops of the Duke of Weimar we find the parallelization of his life with those of both Herzbruder and Simplicius, all of which has been explained above.

8. The Conjunction of Saturn and Mercury within the Context of the Solar Narrative Phase in *Simplicissimus Teutsch*

Günther Weydt's astrological exegesis of Grimmelshausen's novel has shown that there is a significant solar narrative phase within the novel. In accord with the system it is principally determined by the courtly milieu of the "herrliche[n]" fortress and residence of Hanau. It stands in marked contrast to the life on the farm and in the woods, which Simplicius had led up to that point. The important heuristic indicator of this phase is, for Weydt, the treasure of "dreyhundert und etlich sechtzig Ducaten" (141), which the hero takes from the "Schnapphanen." The number of gold coins — gold is after all the metal of the "planet" sun — points to the number of days within the solar year. The lack of an absolute number of coins leaves room for leap years.

Now the sun is, according to astrological teachings, just as ambivalent as the planet Mercury. To be sure, it approaches Jupiter and Venus in terms of its good influence, but still it is of a double nature, which results from its constellations with favorable and unfavorable planetary companions. In an explanatory note of a sheet dealing with the sun, contained in an astrological manuscript in Tübingen, which stems from 1404, we read: "die sonne ist eyn planet by andern planeten ungluckhafftig und bose und mit angesichte der planeten auch gut."[6] In *Keuscher Joseph,* the titular hero, in his fight against the robbers, functions as Apollo, "von welchem sie Glück hofften und Unglück besorgten" (KJ 32). In accord with that, Grimmelshausen's calendar notes that only a person who has "die Sonn in ziemlichen Orten [. . .] in seiner Geburt" (V, 193) will consider the sun "ein guten Planeten." In *Simplicissimus,* the officer on watch, whom Simplicius apostrophizes as a hermaphrodite, points to the ambivalence of the "planet" sun. The young boy is not sure whether the military person "Sie oder Er wäre," and finally concludes the person is "Mann und Weib zugleich" (54). The allegorical scene at the city gates obviously functions as an initiation of the inexperienced hero into that phase of the narrative which the author structured acccording to the sun. Thus, Simplicius, who was to be thrown into jail as a suspected spy, is, in an abrupt change, named the page of the governor. In general, the behavior of the Swedish governor changes from the most brutal cruelty to the most gracious favor. Generally speaking, there is a distinct discrepancy between the moral claims of Hanau society and their, at times, rather uncouth and bestial way of life. The entire Hanau section of the novel is structured in a remarkably ambiguous manner. The essence of the astrologically determined two sided being is the "change" of the naive, truth-loving hero, who, however, is viewed by the governor as a disobedient and unruly, insubordinate child, into a fool. Simplex learns confidentially that this change is a "Schul/ darinn du deine Vernunfft verlernen solt" (105).

This grotesquely gloomy procedure seemingly results in the governor's favorite becoming an animalistic fool, whose miserable fate then informs a significant section of the plot. This metamorphosis occurs "eben umb die Winterliche Sonnenwende" (112). This dating, which seems to be lacking any pragmatic value, divides the Hanau events into two opposing parts, the positive section dealing with the governor's page and the negative part dealing with the "calf." It has an astrological function. Beginning on 21 December, the actual day of the winter solstice, the days get longer and the sun shines more brightly. In an analogous fashion, according to Grimmelshausen's *Calender*, the sun designates the intellectual capabilities of human beings. It confers on them "guten Verstand" (V, 123), "auch Vernunfft" (V, 97), and this "mehr als die anderen Planeten all" (V, 123). Sure enough, quite in contrast to the governor's intentions, the process of change makes Simplicissimus "allererst witzig" (115). He suddenly learns to disguise himself: "Damals fieng ich erst an/ in mich selbst zu gehen/ und auff mein Bestes zu gedencken. Jch setzte mir vor/ mich auff das närrischte zu stellen/ als mir immer möglich seyn möchte" (110). The pastor in Hanau, who is "in" on the whole situation, advises him to imagine "als ob du gleich dem *Phoenix*, vom Unverstand zum Verstand durchs Feuer/ und also zu einem neuen menschlichen Leben auch neu geboren worden seyest" (114). In astrology, too, the power of giving life and intellectual growth is attributed to the sun. The governor notices with astonishment that the boy

> zuvor so unwissend gewesen/ nunmehr aber von Sachen zu sagen weiß/ solche auch so perfect daher erzehlet/ dergleichen man bey älteren/ erfahrneren und belesneren Leuten/ als er ist/ nicht leichtlich finden wird. (133)

In a similar fashion, Simplicius's purity, subsequent to his having been freed "von mehr als drey- oder vierjährigem Unlust" (59), is, along with the change into a fool, once again switched back to impurity, while his intellectual and moral purity continues to increase. Domagalla already recognized, albeit without knowledge of an astrological perspective, that the change in Hanau was "ziemlich unvermittelt, durch seine innere Entwicklung nicht bedingt" (14). The change is accounted for astrologically, since the sun according to the *Calender* means "Reinigkeit" (V, 121). There is, therefore, from an astrological perspective, a two-fold solstice. After a glowingly positive period, Simplex externally gets into a kind of "Höll" (114) at this juncture; internally, however, he chalks up a rather large improvement and quasi overnight seems to come to his senses.

Chiastically, the intellectual climb runs counter to his social decline, whereby the crossing point of the two lines is marked exactly by the calendar's solstice. Aside from that, the quite conspicuous chronology of events in the novel, upon which the narrated events are based, is "durchaus widerspruchsvoll und unsicher" (Könnecke, I, 164). The date of 21 December falls between two signs of the zodiac, namely Sagittarius and Capricorn, which are the astrological "houses" of the planets Jupiter and Saturn. Therefore, the sun, prior to the crossover of the winter solstice, is in a jovial sphere, afterward in a saturnine one. At first, then, the influences of the sun and of Jupiter occur, later those of the sun and of Saturn. In accord with that, the fate of the protagonist prior to the solstice is diametrically opposed to his fate after the solstice. Prior to the solstice, Simplicissimus is the perfect solar-jovial type; he is, after all, "bey grossen Herren" and "liebet gute Kleyder" (V, 127). The peasants refer to him as a count. Numerous characteristics, which are in accord with the details in the *Calender,* constitute the narrative picture of a sun-like individual. The similarities extend even into bodily details; for example, Simplex's hair was, here after his having neglected it during his time in the forest, "von Natur krauß" (53)—the sun-type of individual is according to the Calender "krauß Haars" (V, 123)—while much later, once outside the solar phase, "meine schöne krause Haar [. . .] meiner schämten/ und ihre Heimat verliessen" (311). The new hair of the hero resembles that of "Säuborsten" (311). "Ja ich glaube schwerlich/ daß ich mein Lebtag einiges mal einen grössern Wollust empfunden/ als eben damals" (59) are the words the hero uses to sum up that luxurious, solarly significant time of his life in Hanau. After his first night with sufficient sleep, Simplicius awakens just as "die liebe Sonn wieder leuchtet" (60). In this seemingly insignificant comment of the narrator, we see reflected the winter solstice, after which Simplex, in a figurative sense, "awakens." After a caesura of night, which symbolizes the saturnine way of life in its extreme neediness and intellectual stagnation, Simplicius becomes, on that very next day, the page of the governor. The sun "verleyhet [. . .] herrliche und Königliche *Digni*teten" (V, 123).

In the second half of this phase of the novel, after the hero has changed into a fool, the sun, which has been in the saturnine sign of Capricorn, proceeds immediately into the similarly saturnine sign of Aquarius. From an astrological standpoint, this stands for a lengthy phase filled with disastrous events. During this time we have the appearance of the disciplinarian, who allegorically refers to the planet Saturn. The miserable external fate of the hero is manifested in the witches' ride, the very essence of the magical-saturnine. Until this adventure, Simplicissimus lives as he had lived with his "Knan" and with the hermit, principally in the forest, and as in the episode with the robbers, in the "finstern Einöde" (140). Torn from the community in Hanau by the Croats, he lives, and this is important, totally alone ("wieder überall ein Einsidlerisch Leben wie hiebevor" [141]). In the end, he also loses his solarly significant ducats, which, against all odds, he had previously managed to save in various precarious situations. That fits in with the bitter irony that in the context of the intrigue in the camp at Magdeburg, Herzbruder's "That so Sonnen-klar am Tag lag" (161). The illustration of the so-called *Barock-Simplicissimus* (edition E[5] 1671) pictures that situation: it puts the young Simplex on the magical circle of the disciplinary officer, right next to the sign of the sun.

The winter solstice in *Simplicissimus* has a counterpart in *Courasche*. The heroine awaits her cavalier at the Danish castle, where she is, typically enough, "wie ein Princessin unterhalten" (65): "der stellte sich auch bey mir ein/ ehe die längste Nacht gar vergiengen/ weil er der lieblichen Frühlingszeit so wenig als ich mit Gedult erwarten konte" (65). This dating occurs in Chapter Thirteen (out of twenty-eight chapters), almost in the exact center of the novel. In this case, too, the *sensus astrologicus* is obvious: after extreme misery, Courasche enjoys, beginning with the winter solstice, a period of extreme happiness and good fortune. In viewing this Simplician work as a whole, however, we find the exact opposite, because the winter solstice forms a boundary between a first, positive section and a second, essentially negative part of the life of the protagonist. After this turning point, we see the actual onset of Courasche's social decline and moral descent.

III. Conclusion: The Total Astrological Structure of *Simplicissimus Teutsch*

The arguments presented here were based on various astrologically structured major phases of the *Simplicissimus Teutsch,* namely the jovial, the mercurial, and the solar phases. The venereal phase, too, was discussed. The narrative sections are structured in such a way that the literal meanings of the plot are overlaid with an astrological level of meaning, for example, the solar one. These larger phases can be further subdivided; as a concrete example: when the solar phase in accord with the ambivalence of the "planet" sun is halved into a jovial section prior to the winter solstice and a saturnine one following that solstice. The four large segments listed form a linear sequence within the total series of seven segments of the novel, which Weydt postulated in his work. Each of these seven phases comes under the jurisdiction of one of the seven planets from a series known as the Chaldean order since early times, a series which was still valid in the seventeenth century. The series included the following "Wandelsterne": Moon, Mercury, Venus, Sun, Mars, Jupiter, and Saturn (or vice-versa). That order is based on the relative distance from the earth, whereby the earth is the center of a geo-centric conception of the universe. The luminaries, that is the sun and the moon, the latter actually being a satellite of the earth, were also viewed as planets according to the astrological orientation of this period. Several works of world literature, from the ancient Persian poet Nizami via Dante to Milton, and we will stop the enumeration with works of the seventeenth century, are structured in a similar fashion. According to Weydt — and Rehder was, at the same time, of the same opinion — there is a slight deviation from the classical version in *Simplicissimus Teutsch.* Jupiter has the central position rather than the sun. That is not unusual. In the *Wunderbarliches Vogel-Nest II,* Jupiter takes over the position of the Sun-god, who usually presides at the Council of the Gods. Other deviations from the Chaldean order are also known. For example, the grouping of the planetary sculptures on the garden façade of the castle of the prince-bishop in Münster in Westphalia still contains the sun in the middle of the group, but otherwise it is quite different from the model, because the artist wished it so. Weydt suggested that the prominent positioning of Jupiter in *Simplicissimus* might have to do with homage being paid to the birth planet of the author, there being, after all, several allusions to the zodiacal sign of Pisces within the whole oeuvre of Grimmelshausen. If in such a case the author were to subject himself at least artistically to "his" planetary god, then without a doubt we would also be dealing with astrological specification of the basic Baroque concept of "Vanitas" for the protagonist Simplicissimus. The picaresque structural scheme has also been modified to the extent that the changeability seen in Simplicius's life story results from the successful intervention of the seven gods of the stars. The "*Conjunction Saturni und Mercurii,*" which Grimmelshausen demonstrably has worked into his epic structure, stands paradigmatically for the general astrological structure of the novel; it is its *sensus astrologicus.* That the structure goes throughout the entire novel is seen in the motif of prophecy, especially from the central part of the story dealing with the infallible elder Herzbruder, to which is subjected the constellation which includes Olivier and the disciplinarian. With all the astrologically based techniques of prophesying, Herzbruder makes absolutely reliable prognoses. Simplicissimus affirms that he cannot avoid any of Herzbruder's prophecies. He extends this feeling of certainty well beyond the events in the narrative, carrying it into the future on the far side of that which is being related. The certainty of the prophecies is proven, last but not least, in the failed attempts, including those of Herzbruder himself, to hinder their fulfillment. It is precisely these attempts which result in the realization of the prophecies themselves:

> Die bisher unerkannte Planetenfolge vermittelt dabei mit dem Spiel der reinen Symbolik auch den Ernst einer tiefen Einsicht in Beständigkeit und Unbeständigkeit des Daseins. Sie fördert nicht nur die Darstellung im einzelnen, sondern öffnet auch den Blick auf die Welt im ganzen. Die Planeten geleiten den Helden — und den Leser bei der Betrachtung der Welt — von der Anschauung der äußersten Beständigkeit (unter Saturn) über das Erlebnis hohen, aber trügerischen irdischen Glücks (vorwiegend unter Jupiter und Venus) zur Einsicht in die Wandelbarkeit und Unbeständigkeit der Welt (unter Merkur und Mond). Der Dichter lehnt sich mit dieser Gestaltung an ein altes System an. Er zeigt sich also systematisch und traditionell in seinem Vorgehen, aber auch möglichst individuell durch die geistreiche Ausnahme, die er zu Gunsten eines "Leitplaneten," des Jupiter, macht. Gerade damit ist Grimmelshausen in besonderem Sinne "barock," hegt doch seine Zeit sowohl den Glauben an das "System" als auch den an die hervorragende Rolle des Individuellen und Exzeptionellen. (Weydt, 300)

The "reine Symbolik" referred to at the beginning of this quote has to do with astrological allegorism, which manifests itself in the *sensus astrologicus.*

Let us be clear: not only do the phases of the changing planets Mercury and the moon demonstrate the changeability of life for the protagonist in *Simplicissimus Teutsch*. They do it quite emphatically. The sequence of the seven planets as a whole has precisely this function. The attentive reader of the novel cannot but notice seven distinct major sections within the entire narrative, and each has specific motifs in individually and clearly formed contexts. Slowness and intellectual lethargy, poverty and the secluded life, comtemplativeness and spirituality, constancy and battling against darkness characterize the farmer-hermit milieu at the beginning of the novel. The astute reader will easily differentiate that from the dynamism, the abrupt changeability, the worldliness, and the massive dominance of water near the end of the novel.

That same astute reader will never confuse the glittering courtliness and desire for showing off (in the narrative section dealing with Hanau) with the broad description of courtly life in Paris. The latter, particularly after the amorous events in Lippstadt, occurs for the most part in the sign of the "Venusberg" and its erotic and sexual adventures. Simplicissimus, on the one hand, experiences various episodes in Hanau without understanding them, for example, metaphorically how "ein Ganser und eine Gänsin" (92) become a couple. On the other hand, in Paris of all places, he himself experiences love and sex to the extent that he becomes "endlich auß Unvermögen der Narrenpossen gantz überdrüssig" (307). The "eiserne Männer," dominated by Mars, break into the peaceful world of the young boy with terrible deeds, and they are strengthened by the effect of surprise and newness as well as by the Mars-allegory of the "Ständebaum." Even though the novel deals with war, these characters create a different effect than we see when Simplicius travels throughout the land as a charlatan and deceiver, trying to peddle his self-brewed tinctures to an unsuspecting public. The section in the middle of the novel, a section made up of several chapters centered around the fool Jupiter, is quite different from each of these individually contoured narrative events. In that section, we have a climax in worldly fortune of the hero of the novel and its hunting motifs, which are to be taken literally and figuratively as well. Everything, that is Simplicius's entire life, is subsumed by the author — and this needs to be repeated for didactic purposes — into an astrological complex of motifs dealing with prophecy and its absolute certainty about the future. One can make reliable prognoses by using astrological means only when the gods of the planets determine human fate. It is precisely in such situations that we find signals that Grimmelshausen provides, for example with the "*Conjunction Saturni* und *Mercurii*." The *Simplicissimus Teutsch* is, therefore, in accord with the number of classical planets, structured around seven astrological phases. The deviation in the position of the Jupiter-phase from the otherwise valid Chaldean system makes even more possible from a structural point of view the extremely important changeability within the course of events narrated. In his experience of this change-ability, Simplicius becomes an emblem for people of the seventeenth century along with their "vanitas," the novel itself becomes a reflection of the cosmos according to the times in which it was conceived, namely a correspondence of macrocosm and microcosm. There are seven masks at the foot of the fabulous being on the engraved copper title page of the novel. Scholarly research has yet to come up with a satisfactory explanation for them, but that explanation, when found, should certainly take an astrological interpretation into consideration.

Translated by Vance Byrd and Karl F. Otto, Jr.

Notes

[1] Representative of others who share these opinions are Wilhelm Engelbert Oeftering, "Eine weitere Quelle zu Grimmelshausens *Ewigwährender Kalender*," *Euphorion* 27 (1926): 184ff. and Gerhard Lemcke, "Die Astrologie in den Werken Grimmelshausens und seiner Interpreten: Zur Diskussion über den Sternenglauben in der barokken Dichtung," *Argenis* 1 (1977): 63–105.

[2] Haberkamm 1991, 93. In *Wunderbarliches Vogel-Nest II,* there is also an episode about which path to choose, and it too confirms Grimmelshausen's rather free use of the traditional schemata. The Y-sign there is also in the "verlandschaftlichten" form (Erwin Panofsky). The Simplician author "steht in der allegorischen Tradition und emanzipiert sich von ihr zugleich" (Haberkamm 1991, 82). Cf. Haberkamm 1972b, 285–318. In his dissertation (1973), Hubert Gersch also decidedly opts for an allegorical approach.

[3] Heselhaus calls our attention to the fact that *Simplicissimus* has also been interpreted "als Beispiel barocken Stils und als Gegenbeispiel bürgerliche Strömungen" (15). Heselhaus differentiates the satire of *Simplicissimus Teutsch* from that of the picaresque novel in general; the former he says, is always directed toward a specific morality and spirituality within the novel, which is manifest particularly in the framework that the hermit-motif provides. This proves to be a distinct departure from the traditional picaresque formula.

[4] The Bible, as "Buch des Lebens" is "inwendig beschrieben nach dem sensu Mystico oder seinem verborgenen Verstandt/ oder außwendig/ nach dem sensu literali, dem Buchstabischen Verstandt beschrieben/ wie man siehet Apocal. 5." According to Garzoni, additional examples of this type of exegesis can be found in Exodus 4, Jeremias 1, and Matthew 11.

[5] Grimmelshausen mentions — probably due to his source, Garzoni — Leone Ebreo in his *Calender.*

[6] Universitätsbibliothek Tübingen. Signatur: M.d.2, Blatt 269ᵛ.

Works Cited

Albertinus, Aegidius. *Hirnschleiffer*. Ed. Lawrence S. Larsen. Stuttgart: Hiersemann, 1977. (= Bibliothek des Literarischen Vereins, Stuttgart 299)

Anonymous. *Astronomia. Teutsch Astronomie*. Frankfurt/Main: Jacob, 1545.

Cassirer, Ernst. *Die Begriffsform im mythischen Denken*. 2nd ed. Leipzig and Berlin: Teubner, 1922. (= Studien der Bibliothek Warburg 1)

Creidius, Hartmann. *Danck-Buß vnd Bet-Altar*. Frankfurt: Beyer, 1650.

Domagalla, Leo. *Der Kalendermann Grimmelshausen und sein "Simplizissimus."* Würzburg: Triltsch, 1942.

Feldges, Mathias. *Grimmelshausens "Landstörtzerin Courasche": Eine Interpretation nach der Methode des vierfachen Schriftsinnes*. Bern: Francke, 1969. (= Basler Studien zur deutschen Sprache und Literatur, 38)

Freytag, Hartmut. "'*Quae sunt per allegoriam dicta*.' Das theologische Verständnis der Allegorie in der frühchristlichen und mittelalterlichen Exegese von Galater 4, 21–31." In: Hans Fromm, Wolfgang Harms, and Uwe Ruberg, eds. *Verbum et Signum. Friedrich Ohly zum 60. Geburtstag überreicht. 10. Januar 1974*. Munich: Fink, 1975. 27–43.

Garzoni, Tomaso. *Piazza Vniversale, das ist Allgemeiner Schauwplatz [. . .]* Frankfurt / Main: Jennis, 1619.

Gersch, Hubert. 1966. "Vorspiel aufklärerischer Publizistik." Afterword in: Hubert Gersch, ed. *Grimmelshausen: Simplicianische Kalendergeschichten*. Frankfurt: Insel, 1966. (= Insel-Bücherei 884)

———. 1973. *Geheimpoetik: Die* Continuatio *des abentheurlichen Simplicissimi interpretiert als Grimmelshausens verschlüsselter Kommentar zu seinem Roman*. Tübingen: Niemeyer, 1973. (= Studien zur deutschen Literatur 35)

Haberkamm, Klaus, ed. 1967. [Grimmelshausen] *Des Abenteurlichen Simplicissimi Ewig-währender Calender*. Faksimile-Druck der Erstausgabe Nürnberg 1971. Mit einem erklärenden Beiheft. Constance: Rosgarten 1967.

———. 1972a. *"Sensus allegoricus." Zum Verhältnis von Literatur und Astrologie in Renaissance und Barock*. Bonn: Bouvier, 1972. (= Abhandlungen zur Kunst-, Musik- und Literaturwissenschaft 124)

———. 1972b. "'Fußpfad' oder 'Fahrweg?' Zur Allegorese der Wegewahl bei Grimmelshausen." In: *Rezeption und Produktion zwischen 1570 und 1730. Festschrift für Günther Weydt zum 65. Geburtstag*. Ed. Wolfdietrich Rasch, Hans Geulen and Klaus Haberkamm. Bern: Francke, 1972. 285–318.

————. 1991. "Verkehrte allegorische Welt. Das Y-Signum auf dem Titelkupfer von Grimmelshausenns 'Courasche.'" In: Eckehard Czucka, Thomas Althaus, and Burkhard Spinnen, eds. *"Die in dem alten Haus der Sprache wohnen": Beiträge zum Sprachdenken in der Literaturgeschichte. Helmut Arntzen zum 60. Geburtstag.* Münster: Aschendorff, 1991. (= Literatur als Sprache. Supplementband)

Heselhaus, Clemens. "Grimmelshausen. Der abenteuerliche Simplicissimus." In: Benno von Wiese, ed. *Der deutsche Roman. Vom Barock bis zur Gegenwart. Struktur und Geschichte. Bd. 1.* Düsseldorf: Bagel, 1963.

Hesselmann, Peter. *Gaukelpredigt: Simplicianische Poetologie und Didaxe. Zu allegorischen und emblematischen Strukturen in Grimmelshausens Zehn-Bücher-Zyklus.* Bern: Lang, 1988. (= Europäische Hochschulschriften I, 1056)

Hildebrand, Wolfgang. *Ein new außerlesen Planeten-Buch* [. . .]. Erfurt: Schmuck, 1613.

————. *Magiae Naturalis Ander Theil. Hortus Deliciarum. Das ist Paradiß Lustgarten* [. . .]. Leipzig: Groß, 1625.

Indagine, Johann von. *Natürliche Stern-Kunst* [. . .]. Straßburg: Paulli, 1664.

Jauss, Hans Robert. "Form und Auffassung der Allegorie in der Tradition der 'Psychomachia' (von Prudentius zum ersten 'Romanz de la Rose')." In: *Medium Aevum Vivum. Festschrift für Walther Bulst.* Ed. Hans Robert Jauss and Dieter Schaller. Heidelberg: Winter, 1960.

Jöns, Dietrich. "Emblematisches bei Grimmelshausen." *Euphorion* 62 (1968): 385–91.

Kepler, Johann. *Astronomi.* Opera Omnia. Bd. 7, ed. Ch. Frisch. Frankfurt / Main: Heyder & Zimmer, 1868.

Knopf, Jan. *Frühzeit des Bürgers: Erfahrene und verleugnete Realität in den Romanen Wickrams, Grimmelshausens, Schnabels.* Stuttgart: Metzler, 1978.

Könnecke, Gustav. *Quellen und Forschungen zur Lebensgeschichte Grimmelshausens.* Ed. J. H. Scholte. Two vols. Weimar: Gesellschaft der Bibliophilen, 1926–28.

Kornmann, Heinrich. *Mons Veneris, Fraw Veneris Berg Das ist/ Wunderbare vnd eigentliche Beschreibung der* [. . .] *Göttin Venere* [. . .] Frankfurt / Main: Fischer, 1614.

Lemcke, Gerhard. "Die Astrologie in den Werken Grimmelshausens und seiner Interpreten: Zur Diskussion um den Sternenglauben in der barocken Dichtung." *Argenis* 1 (1977): 63–105.

Müller-Seidel, Walter. "Die Allegorie des Paradieses in Grimmelshausens *Simplicissimus.*" In: *Medium Aevum Vivum. Festschrift für Walther Bulst.* Ed. Hans Robert Jauss and Dieter Schaller. Heidelberg: Winter, 1960.

Oeftering, Wilhelm Engelbert. "Eine weitere Quelle zu Grimmelshausens *Ewigwährender Kalender*." *Euphorion* 27 (1926): 184–95.

Ohly, Friedrich. "Vom geistigen Sinn des Wortes im Mittelalter." *ZfdA* 89 (1958–59) 1–23. Reprint: Darmstadt: Wissenschaftliche Buchgesellschaft, 1966. (= Libelli 218)

Pérez, Andreas (= López de Úbeda). *Die Landstörtzerin Ivstina. Dietzin Picara genanndt* [. . .]. Frankfurt/Main: Weiss, 1626.

Rehder, Helmut. "Planetenkinder: Some Problems of Character Portrayal in Literature." *The Graduate Journal* 8 (1968): 69–85.

Sedlmayr, Hans. 1951. "Der Ruhm der Malkunst. Jan Vermeer 'De schilderkonst.'" In: *Festschrift für Hans Jantzen*. Berlin: Gebr. Mann, 1951. 169–77.

———. 1959. *Kunst und Wahrheit: Zur Theorie und Methode der Kunstgeschichte*. 2nd ed. Hamburg: Rowohlt, 1959. (= rowohlts deutsche enzyklopädie 71)

Streller, Siegfried. *Grimmelshausens Simplicianische Schriften: Allegorie, Zahl und Wirklichkeitsdarstellung*. Berlin: Rütten & Loening, 1957. (= Neue Beiträge zur Literaturwissenschaft 7)

Treuer, Gotthilf. *Deutscher Dädalus/ Oder Poetisches Lexicon [. . .] Ander Theil* [. . .]. Berlin: Völcker, 1675.

Valentin, Jean-Marie. "'Wann du nicht im Sinn hast, dich zu bekehren, warumb willst du dann deinen Lebenslauf beichtsweis erzählen und aller Welt deine Laster offenbarn?' Zu den theologischen und ästhetischen Implikationen des Anfangskapitels von Grimmelshausens *Landstörtzerin Courasche*." *Simpliciana* 10 (1988): 89–104.

Weydt, Günther. *Nachahmung und Schöpfung im Barock: Studien um Grimmelshausen*. Bern: Francke, 1968.

Engraved title page from Vogelnest, Zweiter Theil (1675).
Faber du Faur Collection, Beinecke Library, Yale.

Grimmelshausen and the Picaresque Novel

Christoph E. Schweitzer

T HE BASIC STRUCTURE OF Grimmelshausen's picaresque novels, including *Courasche, Springinsfeld* and his masterpiece, *Simplicissimus Teutsch,* goes back to the picaresque novels that originated in Spain in the sixteenth century. Among the Spanish examples it is Mateo Alemán's *Guzmán de Alfarache* (part one 1599, part two 1604) that has been called the prototypical picaresque novel. Aegidius Albertinus (1560–1620), who left his native Holland to settle in Munich where he held a variety of positions at the court, adapted the first part of Alemán's novel and parts of an unauthorized continuation by an otherwise unknown writer, Juan Martí. Albertinus gave his version the title *Gusman von Alfarche* (1615). Since this adaptation is the most important antecedent for *Simplicissimus* and since Grimmelshausen apparently did not know Spanish, I will discuss below the many striking parallels as well as the radical differences between the two works.

Spanish literature played a major role in seventeenth-century Germany. Although few were able to read the texts in the original, there were translations into German. In addition, the works were often also available in French, Italian, and Latin.[1] Here one must keep in mind that, while some of the versions followed the original fairly accurately, others departed from it, some in radical ways, as in the case of Albertinus's *Gusman von Alfarche.* Spanish literature of the sixteenth and seventeenth centuries is often referred to as being of the "Golden Age." Early on we have the ever so popular prose romance of chivalry, *Amadís de Gaula,* the first extant version (by Montalvo) of which was printed in 1508. This work, filled with adventure, magic, and love, inspired innumerable variations, translations, such as that of Herberay des Essarts (8 volumes, 1527) and more continuations than any other novel known in literary history. It reached 24 books in the German version completed by 1595. Later on, there were the playwrights like Lope de Vega (1562–1635), who wrote close to 500 plays, and Calderón de la Barca (1600–1681), who is best known for his *autos sacramentales* (one-act religious plays) and the philosophical *La vida es sueño.* Among the poets there were Luis de Góngora (1561–1627), whose unfinished pastoral idyll, *Las soledades* (1613), is considered his masterpiece, and Francisco de Quevedo y Villegas (1580–1645) whose *Los sueños* (1627), a bitterly satiric account of the inhabitants of hell, served as the basis for Johann Michael Moscherosch (1601–1669) when he translated, or, better said, adapted (from a French version) *Les Visiones de Don Francesco de Quevedo Villegas Oder Wunderbahre Satyrische gesichte Verteutscht durch Philander von Sittewalt* (first edition, undated, 1640) and whose *La vida del buscón* (1626) I will take up below. Miguel de Cervantes Saavedra's *Don Quijote* (part one 1605, part two 1615) was not translated into German until 1648, and then only a small fragment of the original was translated. However, the novel's fame had reached Germany via translations into other languages well before that date. In addition, there was the renowned Jesuit priest and philosopher Baltasar Gracián (1601–1658) author of *El criticón* (1651–1657), a philosophical novel and allegory of human existence, to mention just a few of the authors who had an enormous impact on seventeenth-century German literature and in particular on Grimmelshausen.

In the second half of the sixteenth and in the seventeenth century, another Spanish author gained greater fame than any of those mentioned above: Antonio de Guevara (1480?-1545), a Franciscan who was the court preacher and chronicler of Emperor Charles V and who had a long ecclesiastical career. While he is practically forgotten today, his voluminous treatises, including a spurious work supposedly written by Marcus Aurelius, combined Christian morality with stoicism and were translated into the main European languages, including Latin. It is Albertinus who translated the corpus of Guevara's oeuvre into German. At the end of the fifth book of *Simplicissimus,* the end of the original version of that novel, Grimmelshausen has Simplicius quote at length from Guevara's ("Quevarae") *Menosprecio de corte y alabanza de aldea,* in Albertinus's translation, *Verachtung des Hoflebens und Lob des Landlebens* [Contempt of the Courtly and Praise of the Rural Life]. In a rhetorical tour de force the narrator takes leave of this world: *Quédate adiós, mundo* which becomes in Grimmelshausen's text "Adjeu Welt," "Behüt dich Gott Welt," and similar phrases. They introduce nineteen paragraphs that contain Simplicius's reasons, taken over almost verbatim from Albertinus's text, for quitting the worldly life and for becoming a hermit. In 1554 the first picaresque novel, the anonymous *La vida de Lazarillo de Tormes y de sus fortunas y adversidades,* appeared. The title would have made the reader think of an idealized knight like Amadís, who proudly calls himself "of Gaule." Lazarillo, however, takes his name as a literary figure from the fact that his mother, the wife of a dishonest miller, gave birth to her son on the River Tormes. While knights will accomplish great deeds on their ladies' behalf, Lázaro, Lazarillo's real name, threatens to fight to the death anyone who questions his wife's virtue, even though it is well known that his wife is an archpriest's mistress and that Lázaro benefits from the arrangement. *Lazarillo de Tormes* is a masterpiece of first-person storytelling in which the narrator, the son of less than reputable parents, has to use his wits to survive in a hostile world. He not only begged, but was, according to his own account, even forced to resort to thievery to keep from starving in what he describes as a hypocritical and corrupt society in which people only watch out for themselves. A blind beggar to whom the boy Lázaro serves as a guide initiates him into the ways of the world. As they leave Salamanca and cross a bridge, the blind man asks Lázaro to put his head to a stone monument so as to hear a loud noise inside. When the unsuspecting Lázaro obeys, the blind man hits Lázaro's head against the monument so that the boy feels the pain for days. From then on, Lázaro relies on his own resources while serving a number of masters, mostly less than honest priests and an impoverished nobleman. The latter was to become famous as the epitome of Spanish honor. In *Lazarillo de Tormes,* the nobleman is described at one point as standing in front of his house using a toothpick, even though he hadn't eaten meat for days and had been living off Lázaro's begging. Finally, Lázaro obtains the position of town crier in which he is protected by the *ménage à trois* arrangement mentioned above. Thus, he insists, he is just as good a person as any of his neighbors. In other words, according to him society is basically immoral. The novel's critical portrayal of the clergy and various negative remarks about the court meant that in 1573 a revised text was the only approved version that could be published in Spain until 1812, when censorship was suspended. The German translation of 1617 is based on such a revised version; however, the translator made further, sometimes radical changes and added material as well. That *Lazarillo de Tormes* was so attractive even in these bowdlerized adaptations and continuations proves the enormous power of its original conception.

Mateo Alemán's *Guzmán de Alfarache* (first part 1599, second part 1604) is generally considered the most important Spanish picaresque novel. Before Alemán had finished the second part, Juan Martí, much to Alemán's annoyance, published a continuation of inferior quality. Aegidius Albertinus had by 1615, the date of his adaptation of Alemán's novel, already published a great variety of translations, adaptations, and compilations primarily from Spanish, but also from French and Italian works as well.[2] These writings, mostly of a moral nature, served to promote the teachings of the Counterreformation. In the first nineteen chapters of his translation of Alemán, Albertinus follows the first part of Alemán's novel fairly closely, except for interspersing the original text with a few moralizing sections. For some of the other episodes of his first part, Albertinus uses Juan Martí's continuation of Alemán's first part. The remaining text of the German version comes from a variety of sources; some of the passages clearly express Albertinus's own ideas. In the second part, which comprises a bit less than one third of the total text, Albertinus departs completely from his Spanish sources. Here Gusman meets a hermit who instructs him on how to reach the heavenly Jerusalem. Since Albertinus's adaptation of Alemán's novel with its sequel and its various additions is the work that presents the closest parallel to *Simplicissimus*, I will first continue with a description of some of the other Spanish picaresque novels before returning to a consideration of *Gusman von Alfarche*, and *Simplicissimus*.

Francisco López de Úbeda's *La Pícara Justina* (1605) is, with its female protagonist, a parody of Alemán's *Guzmán de Alfarache*. The Spanish novel was translated via an Italian version into German under the title *Justina Dietzin Picara* (1620–1627). The protagonist demonstrates as little remorse about her sinful life as does Grimmelshausen's Courasche. We know that Grimmelshausen knew the *Justina Dietzin Picara* (Zaenker 643–53).

Another example of the picaresque is Francisco de Quevedo's *La vida del buscón* (1626), in which the author's linguistic virtuosity and biting satire permeate the story. Satire is achieved using such strategies as inversion of religious ritual. This is achieved by using Christian imagery in a parodistic manner. The protagonist, ashamed of his parents — his mother is a whore and a witch — leaves home, and tries to make a name for himself by flattery and every other means possible. However, he fails time and time again. He chooses different names as he chooses picaresque disguises, but he is utterly humiliated in his attempts to improve his lot and to gain entry into the ranks of the respectable. At the end, he is a defeated man who escapes with his whore to America. In a famous grotesque, surrealistic sequence the protagonist depicts the consequences of extreme starvation at a boarding school. Hunger is a theme that occurs in most picaresque novels. Different from other authors of picaresque novels, the conservative aristocrat Quevedo does not empathize with his protagonist, but rather condemns him as an upstart who should not have tried to improve his low stature in society by devious means.

While the etymology of the word *pícaro* remains uncertain, its meaning is clear: it means rogue, swindler, juvenile delinquent. In his *Gusman*, Albertinus uses *Landstörtzer*, *Schwarack*, and *Schelm*, as well as a few other equivalents of the Spanish *pícaro*. Since the first two terms are not in current usage and since the word "Schelm," used by some for *pícaro*, has acquired a rather endearing connotation in connection with the antics of boys, many critics have preferred to use the original Spanish word.

The definition of what constitutes a picaresque novel is still disputed, as are indeed the definitions of most all such literary terms. Still, it is possible to enumerate some common features, as long as one keeps in mind that each novel has its peculiar characteristics.[3] There is, first of all, a narrator who tells his or her life story.[4] Usually the "I" tells the story in retrospect, from the point of view of a person who has mended his ways or is ready to do so. Thus, the flow of the account can be interrupted by comments which the narrating "I" makes about his former self. Often these comments refer to foolish and sinful past behavior. Most first-person narrators are unreliable, since they tend to paint as favorable an image of themselves as possible and therefore try to underplay their own culpability. At the same time, of course, they try to make society responsible for their misfortunes. It should be obvious that Courasche is an exception since, to spite Simplicissimus, she wants him to think that she is a truly evil person. In *Lazarillo de Tormes* we see most clearly how the narrator subtly tries to ingratiate himself with the person to whom he writes up his case, and, thus, also to ingratiate himself with the reader. As a consequence, readers have found Lazarillo traditionally more charming than a close reading of the text would warrant.[5]

The protagonist of a picaresque novel is in most cases the child of disreputable parents, the father often being a one-time criminal and the mother taking up with several men. The *pícaro* lacks the moral background which most other children would receive from, or see in, their parents. All *pícaros* leave home at a very early age and experience life from the point of view of the poor, the underdog, and even the imprisoned. Being ignorant of the ways of the world, they are given a rude awakening in their first encounter with strangers. Soon, the *pícaro* learns to watch out for himself and he tries to get the upper hand in dealing with others. In the course of their lives, *pícaros* have a great variety of ways of making a living, at times being part of a band of beggars or of petty thieves or being in the service of different masters, including innkeepers, merchants, physicians, lawyers, the clergy, and officials. The *pícaro*/narrator exposes society as cruel, corrupt, and hypocritical. To make his point as effectively as possible, he often uses satire.

The picaresque novel is characterized by an episodic structure that consists of the various adventures of the protagonist. Some of these are humorous, a few scatological, but all of them entertaining. Just as the way they are making a living changes, so do the places. *Pícaros* move from Spain to Italy and even to the Near East. While there might be sexual episodes, there never is idealistic love, and just as rarely do we encounter depictions of family life. *Pícaros* are by nature restless, they cannot settle down. All the episodes center around the protagonist and there is always stated or implicit tension between his worldly ways and his — and the reader's — awareness that he should reform. Some *pícaros* show early on that their life of sin, of trying to climb the social ladder by illicit means, their thievery, gambling, and whoring, is wrong and that they should change. Others come to that realization late in life, a few write their story without having repented.

The main characteristics of a picaresque novel are that it is a pseudo-autobiography by the protagonist/narrator, who is of low birth, and who uses his wits, resorting at times to criminal acts to survive. Since *Simplicissimus* and its two sequels, *Courasche* and *Springinsfeld,* have these characteristics, it is clear that they belong to the picaresque genre.

We have no direct evidence that Grimmelshausen ever read Albertinus's *Gusman von Alfarche.* However, the parallels between this adaptation of Mateo Alemán's novel and Juan Martí's continuation of Alemán's first part, on the one hand, and *Simplicissimus* on the other, go beyond the general features discussed above and will be described below.

The tone and contents of the two titles are similar. Here is Albertinus's title:

> Der Landstörtzer: *Gusman* von *Alfarche* oder *Picaro* genannt/ dessen wunderbarliches/ abenthewrlichs vnd possirlichs Leben/ was gestallt er schier alle ort der Welt durchloffen/ allerhand Ständt/ Dienst vnd Aembter versucht/ vil guts vnd böses begangen vnd außgestanden/ jetzt reich/ bald arm/ vnd widerumb reich vnd gar elendig worden/ doch letztlichen sich bekehrt hat/ hierin beschriben wirdt.

Let us look at Grimmelshausen's title for the sake of comparison:

> Der Abentheuerliche Simplicissimus Teutsch/ Das ist: Die Beschreibung deß Lebens eines seltzamen *Vagan*ten/ genant Melchior Sternfels von Fuchshaim/ wo und welcher gestalt Er nemlich in diese Welt kommen/ was er darinn gesehen/ gelernet/ erfahren und außgestanden/ auch warumb er solche wieder freywillig quittirt. Überauß lustig/

und männiglich nutzlich zu lesen. An Tag geben Von German Schleifheim von Sulsfort.

As we see, both authors juxtapose the name of the protagonist with that
of a "Picaro" (Albertinus) and its German equivalent, "Landstörtzer" in
the case of Albertinus, "*Vaganten*" in that of Grimmelshausen. Also,
both titles are clearly intended to arouse the prospective buyer's curiosity
about the adventurous lives of the protagonists, with their many ups and
downs and, finally, their conversions, their quitting this world. Just as
Albertinus has added a long, descriptive title to Alemán's short one —
that one consisted only of the protagonist's name — so, too, did he
introduce irony into the summaries of the contents of the first two
chapters. He refers to Gusman's father as an "erbarer Mann" when he
was everything but that and to his mother as an "erbare Fraw" when it
turns out that two men claim to be Gusman's father. However, Albertinus ceases to use such irony in the chapter summaries after the first two
chapters. Grimmelshausen, in contrast, uses irony throughout. He also
often adds to the chapter summaries plays on words, and brings out the
humorous implications of what is to come, poking fun at both the protagonist and the story itself. There is, then, distance between the narrating "I" and its former self, a distance that is much more noticeable in
Simplicissimus than in *Gusman*. Günther Weydt has pointed out the
similarities between Cervantes in *Don Quijote* and Grimmelshausen in
Simplicissimus in that both tease the reader in some of their chapter
summaries (153–54). Most striking, but not mentioned by Weydt, is the
following parallel. The summary for II, 56 of *Don Quijote* is "Que trata
de lo que verá el que lo leyere, ó lo oirá es que lo escuchare leer," which
deals with what the reader of the pages will see, or someone will hear
when listening to what is being read. The summary for *Simplicissimus,*
II, 13, is "Hält allerley Sachen in sich/ wer sie wissen will/ muß es nur
selbst lesen/ oder ihm lesen lassen." A study of the many different implications of the wording of the chapter summaries found in *Simplicissimus*
will reveal the fertile mind of its author.

Gusman and Simplicius introduce their parents in a round-about
manner. Both point out how others claim to be of noble ancestry, when
in reality they are descended from Jews, tinkers, fools, scribes, usurers,
or merchants (Albertinus). Grimmelshausen has them descended from
common, even disreputable people, including witches. He mentions
among such people Zuckerbastel's gang of thieves, a name found in
Niclas Ulenhart's free and superb German rendering of Cervantes' *Rinconete y Cortadillo,* a tale that describes the two protagonists' life with a

gang of *pícaros*. To be sure, Simplicius learns much later that his parents were not the ignorant peasants who raised him but rather were members of the nobility. However, that knowledge has relatively little bearing on his life.

Both Gusman and Simplicius leave home at a very early age and are immediately confronted with the reality of a cruel world. Both receive religious advice early on, Gusman from a pious priest, Simplicius from a hermit. Neither one follows the advice given him; both become deeply involved in sin, with pride being their most serious and recurrent offense. The basic structure of both *Gusman* and *Simplicissimus* rests on the constant tension between two things. On the one hand, we have the pleasures and enjoyments of this world, that is, eating and drinking, outwitting others, and consorting with fellow outcasts of society and with a variety of women. On the other hand, we have promises to reform one's life and admonitions in that direction as well.

Albertinus in the dedication of his book to an abbot and via Gusman throughout the text and Grimmelshausen through the verses that are found under the frontispiece as well as via Simplicius throughout *Simplicissimus* stress that instability governs the world. We read again and again that everything is in constant flux, that as soon as good fortune smiles on you and you are on top of the world, misfortune will bring you down.

However, there is a marked difference in the way the two protagonists move on from adventure to adventure. In Gusman's case it is at times his restlessness, his desire to be some place else where he might find something better than what he had at the time that makes him move on. More often than not, though, he is forced to leave a position because his master finds out that he is a thief. He needs the extra money to support his uncontrollable gambling addiction and his consorting with women. To be sure, in hindsight the narrator is fully aware of his former sinfulness and compares himself in several instances to the prodigal son. At the time he seems to be completely oblivious to the pious priest's admonitions he heard as early as in the fifth chapter. Gusman will bounce from one position to the next without ever regretting his criminal acts. Only when he is finally imprisoned, condemned to be hung, and then pardoned to the galleys, does he finally repent. Simplicius, on the other hand, realizes his failings early on. Thus, when, toward the beginning of the novel, he is put in prison as a spy in Hanau and threatened with torture, he condemns himself bitterly for having left the forest where he would have lived like the hermit, turning his thoughts to God. Instead, he accuses himself of having yielded to his shameful desire to see the world. He asks God for forgiveness and entrusts his soul to Him. In this moment of despair he is recognized by the minister who knew both him and the hermit when they were in the forest, and he is freed from prison. He is cleaned thoroughly and dressed in fine clothes, so that he says of himself: "Da sasse mein Herr *Simplicius* wie ein junger Graf / zum besten *accomodi*rt" (ST 59). This expression of pride is the beginning of Simplicius's renewed involvement in worldly matters. Periods of remorse followed by adventures and transgressions characterize the structure of *Simplicissimus.*

There is another similarity between Albertinus' *Gusman von Alfarche* and Grimmelshausen's *Simplicissimus* that needs to be mentioned. We already saw that moral comments about his sinful past always come from the Gusman who is telling his life story in retrospect. The same is true of an allegorical tale found at the beginning of chapter 16, a tale that comes from part one, chapter 7, of the third book of Alemán's novel. The narrator first makes the observation, as he does repeatedly, that everything constantly changes. He ends with the traditional complaint about how women no longer sit at the spinning wheel and attend to the household chores. Rather, he says, today they are unable to live without their little lap dogs, their monkeys, parrots, and especially without their admirers. This leads the narrator to relate a tale in which Truth has been dethroned and Lying put in its place. Truth is then ordered by Queen Lie to follow her. Queen Lie, with the help of her courtiers, tries to cheat an innkeeper out of the money she owes him, but Truth makes her pay up. Then Queen Lie tries again to cheat those from whom her courtiers bought provisions. Now, however, Truth, fearing its enemies, keeps quiet. In the conclusion the narrator compares Truth to a tough nail and Lying to a beautiful sounding string and claims that ultimately Truth will triumph.

For a similar allegorical tale, we turn to chapters 2 through 8 in the *Continuatio.* Simplicius, asleep, sees Lucifer in a dream. He is furious because he fears that with the ending of the Thirty Years' War and the signing of the final peace treaty, people will be more pious than before. He admonishes other spirits of hell to work as hard as possible so that the flow of souls to hell will not be diminished. A dispute arises between Extravagance, a sumptuously dressed woman on a richly decorated horse, and Avarice, an old and starved man in rags, as to who is the better servant of hell. They attach themselves to an English lord and his steward. As a consequence, the lord squanders away a fortune, while the steward gains one by extreme avarice. In the end, both Extravagance and Avarice are executed and Simplicius wakes up. There is, then, at least an attempt by Grimmelshausen to integrate the allegory into the story. Also, it is believable that Simplicius at this stage of his life could have had such a vision. In Albertinus' case, the tale is clearly the addition of the narrating "I" who, after the story has been told, says that if he had at that time of his life considered and understood the meaning of the allegory, he would not have gone on lying and deceiving.

Today we tend to appreciate most of all the author's vivid and often satirical description of contemporary life, the exciting adventures, the pranks, and the humor, even the petty thievery of the *picaros*. We excuse their less than exemplary actions on the basis of their low background and lack of moral education and are taken by the lively depiction of a great variety of episodes. Every picaresque novel vibrates with life. At the same time, we tend to dismiss the admonitions found in various places in the text as unfortunate additions to an otherwise great story. Admittedly, Albertinus failed to integrate the religious message into his story, at least in the second part but also in sections of the first part of the novel. Nevertheless, we still find the clearly stated or at least implicit tension between the worldly and the holy in the first part of *Gusman*. The worldly and the religious are, of course, superbly intertwined in *Simplicissimus*, even though Grimmelshausen, via Simplicius, felt it necessary to call the readers' attention in the beginning of the *Continuatio* to his true purpose. That purpose was to instruct the readers by giving them "sugar-coated pills," that is, the bitter moral message contained in the entertaining adventures of the protagonist.

Having to take on so many different roles, both Gusman and Simplicius become successful actors at some stages of their lives. Gusman spends some time with a company of actors in Spain. Simplicius acts the fool in calf's skin in Hanau, acts the role of a girl and as such has to fend off two men and a woman, and impresses the ladies as Orpheus in the operatic performance in Paris. Both Gusman and Simplicius describe themselves as being quite intelligent as they learn various trades quickly, they are well spoken and are thus able to endear themselves to many different masters. They are also musically gifted, with Gusman playing the flute and Simplicius playing first the bagpipe and then also the flute in the cloister Paradeis as well as in Paris. In addition, he shows in Paris that he has a wonderful voice, if we can trust his reporting the reaction of the music director.

The two authors were able to view the world through the eyes of the disenfranchised. Alemán, the author of the Spanish text on which the first part of Albertinus's adaptation is based, was the son of a *converso*, that is, of a Jew who had converted to Catholicism. As a *converso*, he was not fully accepted by Spanish society. Some critics use this as an explanation for his ability to empathize with the outcast. Gusman and Simplicius experience extreme poverty and, as a consequence, extreme hunger. In these circumstances, being clad in rags, they meet with the contempt people have for those at the bottom of the social ladder. Acquiring riches and dressing in fine clothes to gain respectability are, therefore, among their main goals. The variety of garments worn by the two protagonists at different times of their life is truly remarkable and indicative of the lack of stability of their character. Both authors thus emphasize the fickleness of this world as contrasted to the permanence of the divine. Grimmelshausen combines in a masterly fashion deeper significance with the type of garment Simplicius wears (Müller, 25–43). To give just one example: after the hermit's death, Simplicius wears the hermit's patched and repatched coat, but Simplicius's moral conviction is only superficial. He is soon seduced by the snares of this world. It will take years and years before he finds the "Rhue" (Ruhe, peace) mentioned in the verses accompanying the frontispiece. Appropriately enough, "Rhue" is the last word of those verses.

As the clothes of the two protagonists change, so do their names. Gusman calls himself after the place where he was born — von Alfarche. When he has money and wants to impress others, he claims to be Don Iohan de Guzman. In Madrid, when he is poor and in rags, a stranger addresses him as Gusmändl, an endearing term that is reminiscent of the protagonist of *Lazarillo de Tormes* whose real name is Lázaro. In both cases the diminutive serves in the eyes of the reader to take away from the responsibility of Lázaro and Gusman for their actions. The differences among Simplicius's names are even greater: according to the title page and to his foster father, it is Melchior Sternfels (or Sternfelß) von Fuchshaim (or Fuchsheim). Simplicius is the name given him by his hermit father, the Simplicissimus is added when his name is recorded in the muster roll in Hanau. When he is wearing women's clothes, one of his admirers calls him Sabina; at the cloister Paradeis he is known as "det Jäjerken," then the "Jäger von Soest"; finally, in Paris, he is called Beau Alman, the handsome German. Just as in the case of the variety of clothes, the multiplicity of the pícaro's name reveals the instability of his persona that is contrasted with God's permanence.[6]

From the above it become clear that *Simplicissimus* shares with *Gusman* important structural elements in that their first-person narratives combine adventurous episodes with moral admonitions, some of which take the form of allegorical tales. Both works end with the conversion of the protagonist and in neither case do we know whether the conversion is final. However, such a comparison also reveals the superior quality of

Simplicissimus over *Gusman*. Earlier on, we saw that Albertinus was unable to integrate the moral aspects into the story, with the second part of the novel being devoid of any action. Furthermore, the various adventures and criminal acts become increasingly more predictable in *Gusman*.

Even though it is justified to call *Simplicissimus* a picaresque novel, as was explained above, one must also note significant differences between this work and the Spanish picaresque tradition. It is not so important that in the first five books of *Simplicissimus* the Thirty Years' War forms the background of much of the action while armed conflict is largely absent from the Spanish model. More to the point is that Simplicius knows true friendship. Hertzbruder rescues Simplicius when the latter is down and out, and Simplicius rescues Hertzbruder from certain ruin. Simplicius sacrifices his own money and career in the army to help his friend get to Sauerbrunnen for the cure of his ailment. There is the touching scene in which both Simplicius's and his son's noses start bleeding when Simplicissimus has to say good-bye to him in Lippstadt. Such emotional involvement is foreign to the Spanish picaresque. Also foreign to that tradition is the concern his uncle, the governor of Hanau, has for Simplicius in whom, though he cannot be sure, he recognized the features of his sister, the mother of Simplicius who, upon the governor's instructions, has been made to believe that he is a calf. The trust Simplicius has in his foster parents also belongs to such emotional relationships that are not present in the Spanish prototype. Finally, Jupiter and his vision of a parliamentary monarchy as well as the utopia described in the Mummelsee episode do not belong to the Spanish picaresque, nor would it ever occur to Gusman to contemplate joining a model community such as the Hungarian Anabaptists, as Simplicissimus does (V, 19). Unique to the German novel is also the poetry. Then, there are also the significant allegorical signs that are especially prominent toward the end of the *Continuatio,* and, last not least, there is the protagonist's ever present search for a life that will please God and thus also mankind.

Alemán's *Guzmán de Alfarache* was even more popular than *Don Quijote*. Indeed, the success of the first part of that novel was unprecedented, as eleven editions appeared within the first two years. Also being published in many editions were Albertinus's *Gusman* and Grimmelshausen's *Simplicissimus*. One must ask what made these three and other picaresque works so successful. At the time, books were expensive and the ability to read was limited to a small portion of the population. For most, the Bible and religious texts would come first, followed by calendars and instructional books, including those for students. Literature as such could be purchased only by the privileged few. Books were relatively expensive: to purchase a copy of *Simplicissimus*, teachers or maids had to spend approximately what they earned in one to two weeks. It has been estimated that even if one assumes that five or six people read a book, the number of readers for the *Simplicissimus* editions that appeared between 1668 and 1671, making up a total of 10,000 to 12,000 copies, was just below one percent of the total population.[7] In the case of *Gusman*, one would need to have studied Latin to understand the frequent quotations in that language, for only some of which Albertinus added a paraphrase in German. The success of *Guzmán*, *Gusman*, and *Simplicissimus* and other picaresque novels can only be explained by the interest readers had in participating vicariously in a life style quite different from their own. Coming from established families and having enjoyed a good education so as to obtain positions of importance in society or having married men in such positions, the reader had not lived the life of an outcast and did not have to perform the various menial tasks of a pícaro. When Gusman, penniless and in rags, gets to Madrid, he loses all shame and joins a band of boys and learns how to beg, to play at cards and dice as well as any of the other members of the gang. He loves his picaresque or roguish life because, as he says, while merchants, lawyers, and highly placed officials toil to achieve honor and while they endure constant worry, he enjoys noble freedom and is without care (Albertinus, VIII).

In *Simplicissimus* the clearest indication of how those outside the established society value their freedom comes from the description of the marauding soldiers who are said to live scot-free, like barons (IV, 13). The marauding Olivier uses the same term to praise his life as a robber and claims that it is even nobler than that of a baron (IV, 16). Simplicius, having been forced to marry the girl with whom he has been found in bed and having been asked how he would from now on arrange his life and household, realizes that he has lost his noble freedom (III, 22). He now has to live with someone else in command. Would any reader not envy Simplicius for his exciting adventures, some of them in far-away places, for his success with women, and for his ability to survive? Thus, readers tend to be fascinated by a life style that at least temporarily provides for exciting adventures and frees the individual from the daily routine of civic and family obligations.

The two sequels to *Simplicissimus*, *Courasche* and *Springinsfeld*, can also be characterized as picaresque novels. The term *Landstörtzer*, introduced by Albertinus as the equivalent of *pícaro*, is used in the title of both novels. The title pages also list the typical ups and downs of a picaresque life. Courasche is an illegitimate child and Springinsfeld the son of social outcasts. Also, in the course of their lives, the two protagonists are known by various names, just as Gusman and Simplicissimus had been known by various names. Again, they resemble Gusman and Simplicius in that they frequently change their appearance and their roles, and, in so doing, point to their protean nature. The two novels, in the case of *Springinsfeld* the last two thirds, to be specific, consist of a series of episodes, some of which are humorous, some bawdy, and most of them entertaining. These episodes tell of the fortunes and misfortunes, the triumphs and defeats of the two protagonists.

As in the prototypes, the stories told by Courasche and Springinsfeld are told in retrospect. However, differing from Alemán's *Guzmán de Alfarache* and Albertinus's adaptation of that novel, and differing, too, from *Simplicissimus,* neither Courasche nor Springinsfeld feels remorse when telling their stories. On the contrary, they both praise their picaresque way of living as Gusman had done when he first joined the gang of boys. Gusman noted how he enjoyed this "edle Freyheit/ welche von den Gelehrten so sehr gelobt/ von vilen verlangt/ vnnd von den Poeten besungen wird vnd gegen dern alles Goldt vnnd Reichthumb der Erden nit zuschetzen ist" (ch. 8, 57–58). The scribe to whom Courasche dictates her life story observes that in her gypsy band there was neither sadness nor worry, not even grief; the gypsies reminded her of weasels and foxes that live in freedom and without care (Spr ch. 6). Courasche tells the scribe that none of them would ever go to the highest potentate, even if that person had offered to make them gentlemen; no, they would esteem as nothing any such princely favor, something that, according to her, other servile people so much desire (Spr ch. 6). Springinsfeld, at the end of his story, tells his listeners that he doesn't see any reason for changing his life, since there are always those who feel pity for him and since in that way, he has at all times something to eat. Thus, he can enjoy his freedom.

Courasche remains defiant to the end, that is, to the time when she is dictating her story to the scribe, but we learn in a postscript added by the scribe that Springinsfeld, with the encouragement of Simplicissimus, finally reformed. Already when Springinsfeld was telling his story, there were indications that he knew right from wrong. His story is also interrupted by moral comments from both Simplicissimus and the latter's foster mother. Thus, in the case of Springinsfeld, the tension between the protagonist's actions and what these actions should have been like is present, even if in a more indirect manner than in *Gusman* or *Simplicissimus.* Courasche paints such a sinful picture of herself that readers who might admire her unbelievable strength as a woman in a hostile environment also see that her life is after all just as little to be held up as a paragon as is that of Lázaro, Guzmán, Gusman or Simplicius.

As mentioned above, it has been shown that Grimmelshausen knew Francisco López de Úbeda's *Pícara Justina,* translated as *Die Landstört-zerin Justina Dietzin Picara genandt* (1620–27). As Úbeda exploited the fame of Alemán's *Guzmán de Alfarache,* so did Grimmelshausen that of his own *Simplicissimus* to create their protagonists' female counterparts, making them rivals of their male predecessors. There are a number of striking parallels between Courasche and Justina Dietzin: They are both barren, both contract syphilis, they are superior to many of the men they encounter, and they ride mules. In the end, though, it is the basic structure that makes *Springinsfeld* and *Courasche* as well as Grimmelshausen's greatest work, *Simplicissimus Teutsch,* examples of the picaresque. That structure centers on a story told by a protagonist about a low birth (that is, low societal origins) and adventurous life, a life that is ultimately found wanting by the narrator, the listeners, and the "author."

Grimmelshausen used the possibilities inherent in the picaresque novel in a remarkably creative, indeed unique manner. The first-person narrative meant that he could have Simplicius tell his story from various perspectives. At the beginning of the novel, he looks at the world with the eyes of a young boy, thus gaining the reader's sympathy. As in other novels of the genre, the beginning of *Simplicissimus* is a brilliant display of wit, humor, and satire. Grimmelshausen, again like other authors of picaresque novels, had more difficulties with a proper ending, as the controversy about the *Continuatio* and whether or not it belonged to the original plan shows. He used the picaresque framework to include a great diversity of material not found in the traditional picaresque tale. Examples of this material include the devastating consequences of the Thirty Years' War with its battles and the hordes of marauding soldiers and deserters and, on the other side, the suffering peasants. The authenticity and vividness of these scenes is such that they have shaped our view of that war. Also beyond the picaresque is the depiction of a utopian government under a strong ruler and a look at an imaginary, perfect community when Simplicissimus descends into the Mummelsee. Throughout *Simplicissimus,* there is the underlying, or also sometimes openly stated, tension between the moral voice of the narrator and the various, often worldly adventures of the former "I." New in *Simplicissimus* is the broad spectrum of members of various social classes and the ways in which they cope with the vicissitudes of life in times of both war and peace. Ultimately, the novel deals with Simplicius, as it shows us the ways in which, in him, the forces of good and evil play out, with good prevailing at the end.

Ever since its inception in Spain the picaresque novel has flourished throughout Europe. In seventeenth-century Germany, we find, in addition to Grimmelshausen's novels, the many works by Johann Beer and, at the end of the seventeenth century, Christian Reuter's hilarious *Schelmuffsky*. Thomas Mann's wonderful *Die Bekenntnisse des Hochstaplers Felix Krull* and Günter Grass' *Die Blechtrommel* can both be considered modern examples of the picaresque tradition.

Notes

¹ See Martino 1997b for the various ways by which Spanish literature reached the German-speaking countries.

² Gemert provides a complete listing of Albertinus' works.

³ Among the many books on the picaresque novel, those of the following authors stand out as particularly good: Parker, Miller, Rötzer, and Bjornson. Bauer is also very good, but he restricts himself to German literature.

⁴ For the sake of simplicity, I shall refer to the *pícaro* in the masculine form, except, of course, for references to Courasche.

⁵ Riggan discusses the implications of first-person narratives. See also Schweitzer (1991).

⁶ For a discussion of the protean aspects of baroque literature, see Spahr, especially 255–56.

⁷ Meid summarizing the findings of other scholars (62–65).

Works Cited

Albertinus, Aegidius. *Der Landstörtzer Gusmann von Alfarche oder Picaro genannt.* Munich: Heinrich, 1615. (Reprint 1975).

Bauer, Matthias. *Der Schelmenroman.* Stuttgart: Metzler, 1994. (= Sammlung Metzler 282)

Bjornson, Richard. *The Picaresque Hero in European Fiction.* Madison: Wisconsin UP, 1977.

Feltre, Marta. "La traduizione del termine Pícaro nel Gusman di Aegidius Albertinus." *Prospero* 3 (1966): 117–44.

Gemert, Guillaume van. *Die Werke des Aegidius Albertinus (1560–1620). Ein Beitrag zur Erforschung des deutschsprachigen Schrifttums der katholischen Reformbewegung in Bayern um 1600 und seiner Quellen.* Amsterdam: Rodopi, 1979.

Grimmelshausen, Hans Jacob Christoffel von. *Werke.* Two vols. Ed. Dieter Breuer. Frankfurt / Main: Deutscher Klassiker, 1989. (= Bibliothek deutscher Klassiker 44; Bibliothek der frühen Neuzeit. 16/1; Bibliothek der frühen Neuzeit. Zweite Abteilung, Literatur im Zeitalter des Barock. 4/1)

Hoffmeister, Gerhart. *Spanien und Deutschland. Geschichte und Dokumentation der literarischen Beziehungen.* Berlin: Schmidt, 1976. (= Grundlagen der Romanistik 9)

Martino, Alberto. 1997a "Die Rezeption des 'Lazarillo de Tormes' im deutschen Sprachraum (1555/62–1760)." *Daphnis* 26 (1997): 301–99.

——. 1997b "Von den Wegen und Umwegen der Verbreitung spanischer Literatur im deutschen Sprachraum (1550–1750)." In: *Studien zur Literatur des 17. Jahrhunderts.* Ed. Hans Feber. Amsterdam: Rodopi, 1997. 285–344. (= Chloe 27)

Meid, Volker. *Grimmelshausen. Epoche — Werk — Wirkung.* Munich: Beck, 1984. (= Arbeitsbücher für den literaturgeschichtlichen Unterricht. Beck'sche Elementarbücher)

Miller, Stuart. *The Picaresque Novel.* Cleveland: Case Western Reserve UP, 1976.

Müller, Klaus-Detlev. "Die Kleidermetapher in Grimmelshausens 'Simplicissimus.' Ein Beitrag zur Struktur des Romans." In *Deutsche Vierteljahrsschrift für Literaturwissenschaft und Geistesgeschichte* 44 (1970): 20–46.

Parker, Alexander A. *Literature and the Delinquent: The Picaresque Novel in Spain and Europe 1599–1753.* Edinburgh: Edinburgh UP, 1967. (= Norman Maccoll Lectures 1965)

Riggan, William. *Pícaros, Madmen, Naïfs, and Clowns: The Unreliable First-Person Narrator.* Norman: Oklahoma UP, 1981.

Rötzer, Hans Gerd. *Picaro — Landstörtzer — Simplicius. Studien zum niederen Roman in Spanien und Deutschland.* Darmstadt: Wissenschaftliche Buchgesellschaft, 1972. (= Impulse der Forschung 4)

Schweitzer, Christoph E. 1981. "Antonio de Guevaras 'Adjeu Welt' in der deutschen Literatur." *Daphnis* 10 (1981): 195–209.

————. 1987. "Der Pikaroroman als Selbstrechtfertigung und Selbstbestätigung am Beispiel von *Lazarillo de Tormes, Simplicissimus* und *Moll Flanders.*" In: *Der deutsche Schelmenroman im europäischen Kontext: Rezeption, Interpretation, Bibliographie.* Ed. Gerhart Hoffmeister. Amsterdam: Rodopi, 1987. 49–60. (= Chloe 5)

Spahr, Blake Lee. "Protean Stability in the Baroque Novel." *GR* 40 (1965): 253–60.

Weydt, Günther. *Nachahmung und Schöpfung im Barock. Studien um Grimmelshausen.* Bern and Munich: Francke, 1968.

Zaenker, Karl F. "Grimmelshausen und die *Pícara Justina.*" *Dapnhis* 27 (1998): 631–53.

Copperplate engraving for Ewigwährender Calender
(1670, recte 1671). Including Grimmelshausen's "family."
Reprinted with permission of the Herzog August Bibliothek,
Wolfenbüttel.

Grimmelshausen's
Ewig-währender Calender:
A Labyrinth of Knowledge and Reading

Rosmarie Zeller

Introduction to the Work and Previous Research

WITH REGARD TO ITS CONCEPTION and uniqueness, Grimmelshausen's *Ewig-währender Calender* is probably the least acknowledged work of the author. For quite some time, even up to the 1990s, the work has been viewed only as a collection of "calendar stories." Jan Rohner and Ludwig Knopf had devoted studies to the work in the 1970s and 1980s, but they also analyzed the work chiefly as "calendar stories," that is, as short, entertaining stories that pretended to be true and were published in calendars. They, and many other scholars as well, saw Grimmelshausen's calendar as a by-product of *Simplicissimus,* the most important novel of the author (Berns, 1994, 23). Only in the last few years, due in large part to the workshop conducted by Jörg Jochen Berns in 1994, which was dedicated solely to the calendar, has it become clear that we are really dealing with an independent literary work with its own organizational principles.[1]

It would be useful before proceeding to a study of Grimmelshausen's calendar to look at calendars in general in the seventeenth century. Calendars had been, of course, widely distributed ever since the invention of the printing press, particularly in rural areas. It goes beyond the scope of this presentation to trace the whole history of printed calendars.[2] However, let us at least look at the various types of calendars which probably served as a background, even as a basis for Grimmelshausen's *Ewig-währender Calender.* There are four types that have to be mentioned: martyrologies, continuous calendars, farmer's almanacs, and annual calendars. The martyrologies provide a complete list of saints to be honored on every day of the year; they have primarily an ecclesiastical audience. Those who used this kind of calendar most frequently were certainly not the laity (even though they were written in German), but rather the priests. The priests had to know, for example, on which day of the year the patron saint of the parish or of the numerous chapels within the parish was to be honored. The names of certain saints who were of greater than regional importance were, in the martyrologies as in other calendars, printed in red. They were celebrated at the national, or international, level and also served to orient the farmers with regard to agricultural tasks such as planting. These are the saints who were then listed in the early continuous calendars, which begin to appear at the end of the fifteenth century.[3] The first calendars of this type served mainly medical and medicinal purposes, that is, they listed the good and the bad days for bleeding. These were the first calendars to contain the so-called Sunday letters, with the help of which one could determine the Sundays and the moveable feasts and, in this way, change the continuous calendar into an annual calendar. In the beginning these calendars were to last for only nineteen years, but later there were hundred-year calendars. In the farmer's almanac we find the calendar combined with meteorological forecasts as well as with prognoses about political events, especially war and peace. The weather forecasts in these almanacs are based primarily on the so-called "Lostage," as, for example, Christmas, New Year's Day, and the feast days of certain saints, on the basis of which one would then make prognoses about the weather for the entire year. Political prognoses were generally based on astrological interpretations of the various constellations of the planets, but occasionally on various celestial events, for example, the sunrise on certain days.[4] In these almanacs, the farmers also received a lot of practical information, for example, when they ought to plant and when they ought to harvest, or when they ought to get a haircut or when they ought to have their nails trimmed. Already during the seventeenth century the farmer's almanacs were mocked as being superstitious; however, they continued to appear regularly and they seem to have been profitable for those who wrote them as well as for the printers and publishers. The annual calendars, on the other hand, could take on various formats. For example, some might be printed, like the farmer's almanacs, as broadsides while others might appear in book form. There were also other types of calendars, including those on which one could write additional information and others that contained a substantial amount of historical information. In those calendars in which one could write we find the calendar itself on the left-hand side (one month on each page) and the right-hand side was left free for notes. This free page was then often used in many a calendar for notes about matters of health, recipes for various foods and drinks, notes about supplies as well as for practical tips for agricultural work. In the course of time, various other kinds of information pushed its way onto these blank pages, including tales about behavior of various animals or anecdotes or other types of short narratives. Such stories were also frequently printed in an appendix to the calendars.

With that in mind, let us begin our consideration of Grimmelshausen's calendar. Most of the scholars in recent times thought that Grimmelshausen's calendar simply corresponded to the typical norms for calendars (Haberkamm, 17; Michelsen, 447; Wimmer, 243, van Ingen, 137), that is, that it was a calendar of the kind we know today. This view is reflected in the fact that neither of the editions of Grimmelshausen's collected works includes his calendar.[5] It is readily accessible only in a reprint edited by Klaus Haberkamm (1967), which has been out of print for some time.[6] Unfortunately, few scholars felt intrigued enough to undertake additional scholarship on the calendar itself. On the other hand, there has been a considerable amount of research on the question of which of the calendars purported to be written by Grimmelshausen are actually his work (Sodmann 1976). In the 1670s there appeared a number of publications, especially under the title of *Wunder-Geschichten Calender,* that contain fragments of the biography of Simplicius and which were therefore ascribed to Grimmelshausen. After a lengthy discussion begun by Jan Hendrik Scholte's book *Zonagri Discurs Von Waarsagern. Ein Beitrag zu unserer Kenntnis von Grimmelshausens Arbeitsweise in seinem Ewigwährenden Calender* that was continued by Hertha von Ziegesar in 1924 and finally was resurrected as a research topic in the late 1960s with the work of Günther Weydt, scholars today generally accept that only one work can be ascribed to Grimmelshausen with absolute certainty; that work is his *Ewig-währender Calender.*[7]

Those who compare the organizational principles of the *Ewig-währender Calender* with those of the *Wundergeschichten Calender* see immediately that the latter are genuine calendars, whereas the former (Grimmelshausen's work) is not a typical calendar, as we shall soon see.[8] The *Wundergeschichten Calender* contains, as is typical for calendars with stories, the actual calendar on the left hand side, and the stories on the right hand side, in contrast to that of Grimmelshausen's *Ewig-währender Calender,* in which they are mixed. A second question posed in this study is, comparatively speaking, rather unimportant, namely the question of the actual date of publication. In spite of the chronogram on the title page, which provides us with the date of 1670, the calendar seems to have appeared in 1671. Internal evidence suggests that it appeared immediately after *Simplicissimus Teutsch.*[9] That means that it stands within

Grimmelshausen's oeuvre between, on the one hand, *Courasche* and *Springinsfeld* and, on the other, the *Wunderbarliches Vogelnest* (Berns 1988, 304). The *Ewig-währender Calender* is not included among those works enumerated as part of "deß Abentheurlichen Simplicissimi Lebens-Beschreibung." Since it was composed by Simplicius, it is clearly a Simplician work, but it does not belong, strictly speaking, to the Simplician cycle of works. As such, it has a standing similar to works like *Der erste Beernhäuter* (1670), *Das Galgen-Männlin* (1670), or *Die Gauckel-Tasche oder die Verkehrte Welt* (1672). However, it differs from these shorter works in several ways, principal among which is the fact that its organizational principles are much more refined. Such refinement is most clearly evident where Grimmelshausen introduces a mutual modification of points of view and introduces us, in a most concentrated way, to the cryptic world of the Simplician cycle. This is also seen in the fact that the calendar is printed in several columns, which is indeed typical for calendars. That composition, however, is used here for quite a different purpose: it allows for a togetherness and yet for a jumbling of materials not possible in the narrative works, which are primarily thought capable of providing a linear reading. In the remainder of this investigation, the calendar will be investigated in its rather complicated composition as a Simplician work.

Division of the Calendar

The calendar contains six columns (see illustrations). The left column, with the heading "Erste Materie" or "First Matter," corresponds most closely to that which one usually thinks of in a calendar, namely, a calendar of saints, of dates with particular saints assigned to each date. In typical calendars, numerous saints are emphasized in red printing; obviously those are the ones whose feast days are being celebrated in some particular fashion and on the basis of which the common people oriented the passage of time within a given year. The second and third columns, with heading of "Chaos oder Verworrenes Mischmasch," contain the most varied materials, "as in a maze or perhaps better in a pleasant labyrinth": stories, rules for the weather, curious events, and recipes. The second column is organized according to the principles and numbering system of the Roman calendar, and the dates in this column are given according to the Roman calendar. This calendar counts the days somewhat backward, so that, for example, 16 December according to our system would appear in the Roman calendar as xvii. Calendas Januarii. That is to say, the calends of January are the first of the month, and 16

December is 17 days before that. On the opposite page of this calendar, which is printed as a quarto and which in a normal calendar would be blank, there are, first of all, various "discourses," conversations Simplicissimus has with Zonagri (an acronym for Tomasa Garzoni (1549–1589), the well-known author of Grimmelshausen's source, *Piazza Universale: Allgemeiner Schauplatz*) and Indagine (Johannes von Indagine [1467–1537], the famous expert on physiognomy). In the sections dealing with the later months of the year (after about 10 August), these columns are in part filled with the stories of miracles, until, beginning with 4 October, the two-column wide actual calendar takes up the entire page. Although the fact that the calendar, beginning with October, is printed in only two columns does not point to a careful printing,[10] this in no way takes away from Grimmelshausen's confusing games; however, one could have done it a little more cleverly, had one printed the book more carefully.

The Order of the Calendar

With regard to the ecclesiastical calendar, annual calendars and perpetual calendars are actually quite similar (Matthäus, Petrat). All the calendars upon which I drew for comparisons with that of Grimmelshausen contain an ecclesiastical calendar. In such an ecclesiastical calendar we have on the left the date of the new calendar, on the right the date of the old calendar, and in the middle the name of the saint being honored on that day.[11] Often there are also additional details, for example, the sign of the zodiac in which the moon can be found, the phase of the moon, the time of sunrise and sunset and the so-called "signs of choice," which provide information about various matters.[12] These matters include, for example, the favorable time to get one's hair cut, favorable times for bleeding, etc., as well as details about the weather forecast.[13] In many calendars there are also quoted for Sundays the biblical texts about which the sermon is to be held or, as the case may be, the selections from both the epistles and gospels to be read on that day.[14] The perpetual calendar, of which Coler's housekeeping book is an example, functions in the same way; of course, the perpetual calendar does not list those things that change from year to year.[15] Instead, they usually provide a register, covering several years, even decades, of the days on which Easter falls. Beginning with Easter, one can always figure out all the remaining moveable feasts, so that normally a perpetual calendar can also function as an annual calendar. The fact that housekeeping books like that of Coler contain calendars shows that the calendar contains those data which the farmers need in order to have a smooth running chain of events during the year. The calendar tells the farmers when the favorable days are for sowing and for harvesting, when they have to pay taxes, when they are to undertake certain hygienic tasks, e.g., cutting their nails, bathing, etc. Heinz Moritz Grellmann very accurately describes the function of the calendar in the eighteenth century:

> Der Kalender diente dem gemeinen Mann zur Richtschnur seines Gewerbes, wie seiner Gesundheit; er fand darin einen vom Himmel geholten Unterricht, wenn er seine Äcker düngen, säen, pflantzen und erndten, wenn er kaufen und verkaufen, Geld zahlen, bey grossen Herren etwas suchen, oder andere Dinge vornehmen sollte. Und wie er nächstdem daraus lernte, zu welcher Zeit er Purgirgetränke und Latwergen nehmen, Schröpfköpfe setzen und zu Ader lassen, seine Kinder entwöhnen, Haare und Nägel abschneiden, oder neue Kleider anziehen mußte; so hatte er an dem Kalender auch in politischer Hinsicht, über Krieg und Frieden, einen beständigen Astrologen und Hauspropheten, wie sein Fürst. (cited in Rohner 70)

The calendar in this sense is, therefore, above all an instrument that provides for *order* in the course of events during a given year. Simplicissimus also considers it such, for example, when he defends the purchase of calendars to his mother as something that is useful.[16] Zonagri, too, explains to Simplicissimus that a calendar is nothing other than "ein ordentliche Außtheilung und Entscheidung der Zeiten durchs Jahr hindurch/ nach deren man sich beydes in der Kirchen und auff dem Rathhause zurichten hat" (9). One can actually understand most of the information in the calendars as an attempt to project some sort of order and regularity into the chain of events, which is, at first glance, deemed to be chaotic. An example might be the weather, to which the author attempts to attribute some regularity by positing rules that allow one to predict it. It seems astonishing that neither the fact that the old and the new calendars were printed next to each other, nor the close proximity of various chronological orders (the year in question was always considered with regard to the beginning of creation and to the birth of Christ), seemed to be problematic to the people living in the seventeenth century. On the contrary, one could even see in these proximities a certain sort of guarantee that a given year participated in various kinds of order.

In Grimmelshausen's *Ewig-währender Calender* it is obvious that the days are unequally divided on the page, that is, where the date and the various saints are listed, there are varying numbers of days, sometimes two, sometimes three. There is no overall picture of the month, one has to leaf through the book, until, after a certain number of pages, one happens on the name of the next month.[17] This uneven division on the pages is due to the fact that Grimmelshausen always lists more than a single saint; if there are only a few, it might be six, but often there are ten or twelve listed, or even more. The saints are, of course, an excellent way of orienting oneself, not only in a conventional calendar, but also on an everyday basis. Writers tended to describe the course of a given year in terms of the names of various saints, even in those calendars that appeared in Protestant areas. We have, for example, in a calendar that appeared in Basle the following: "Von St. Michels tag [= 29 September] bis auf Martini seind allwegen sechs Wochen/ vnd zween tag. Von Martini/ biß auf Weynacht auch so viel. Von Weynacht/ biß zur Liechtmeß [= 2 February] seind fünff Wochen vnd vier tag," etc.[18]

Everything depends on the saints: rules for the weather, rules for the plants, the indications of when one ought to hunt for certain animals, when one ought to slaughter them, etc. The names of those saints on whom such things depend are, for the most part, printed in red in the calendars. They are therefore essential in the orientation of the user of such calendars. Grimmelshausen naturally knows these rules quite well, he provides every now and then short verses as an indication of such things, for example, for the change of seasons.[19] That Grimmelshausen provides numerous saints for each day actually hinders the primary function in the naming of these saints: one often has to search out the important saints in this jumble of names, whereas in other calendars they are printed in red. Klaus Haberkamm's theory that Grimmelshausen mentions many saints so as not to hurt the feelings of any single potential purchaser of his calendar, is not convincing (17). Indeed, it is even less convincing when one sees that numerous saints were added by hand in the copy of the calendar that he reproduces in his work. In addition, we see, on the other hand, that the user(s) underlined the more common saints or feast days, for example, the Epiphany or the feast of John the Baptist. This was obviously done in order to provide a point of departure. In addition, a comparison of several calendars from various areas, which were also meant to be sold, shows that the saints are for the most part identical; the deviations are at an absolute minimum.[20] Precisely because the saints were an aid for the users in orienting themselves, the publishers had to maintain a certain uniformity. Grimmelshausen's calendar counts the saints not according to the principles of a calendar, but rather according to the *Martyrologium;* the latter served clerics as a reference work, so that they would know when the feast days of the numerous local saints were to be celebrated. The *Martyrologium,* which Grimmelshausen indeed used as a source for his enumeration of saints, has, however, in contrast to Grimmelshausen's calendar, at the beginning "ein gemainer Christlicher Catholischer Kalender/ sampt den fürnembsten Festen/ mit roten Buchstaben verzaichnet." This provides precisely the orientation to the normal user which Grimmelshausen's calendar lacks. There are also other details, which one expects to find in a calendar, which are either lacking in Grimmelshausen's calendar or which can only be found in unexpected places. It is essential in a perpetual calendar, for example, that one know the "Sunday letter" for an entire year, because only then can one determine which days are Sundays. In addition, one needs the so-called "golden number" in order to be able to determine Easter and all the other moveable feasts.[21] Grimmelshausen or, as the case may be, Zonagri explains in the calendar (35, I) how one can find the "Sunday letter." He gives instructions for a calendar maker, but not for the user of a perpetual calendar, who does not want to have to figure out such "Sunday letters" on the basis of a complicated system but instead wants them easily accessible, directly at the beginning of the calendar. In a perpetual calendar one expects a listing of these "Sunday letters" for several years, and one expects the listing right near the beginning of the calendar.[22] How is the user of a calendar to know that on page 39, close to the entry for 14 February, there is a table of moveable feasts? Even when the user has found this table, it is of little help, because it is arranged according to the "Sunday letters," and these would have to be figured out before the table itself could be used!

There exists a similar situation with the houses of the moon. One needs these in order to know in which sign of the zodiac the moon can currently be found, which, in turn, is important for certain hygienic tasks or medical treatments, for example, bleeding or cutting one's nails. This table is located near the end of August and is really not useable, because one first has to figure it out for any given day. The author instructs little Simplicius not, as one might expect, to use the present calendar that was written for him, but rather to use a normal calendar: "Wann du begehrest zu wissen in welcher Mansion der Mon sey/ so nimb deinen Calendar für diech den du alle Tage brauchest/ schaue in welchem Zeichen der Mond desselbigen Tag lauffe usw" (177, II).

The "signs of choice," which are among the oldest components of calendars and which show the favorable and unfavorable days for medical and hygienic tasks like bleeding, are also lacking in Grimmelshausen's calendar. For the months of January through September, there are, in the calendar, only the signs for "verworfene Tage." The precise instructions about what one ought to do in which signs of the zodiac begin in the month of July (145, II).

Near the end of the calendar, the reader finds once again a list ("Canon aller Anfänge/ Erwehlungen/ oder Täfelein deß Glücks und Unglücks/ auff die zwölff himmlischen Zeichen gerichtet"). However, this list is such a mass of various activities that the reader is probably more likely to be confused than not (224–29).[23] In addition, the activities are listed in alphabetical order, that is without any sense of hierarchy, so that the reader has to read through a pile of unimportant things until perhaps stumbling on a fact or issue that could be of use. There are hundreds of activities listed by which one either has no choice of day or where the choice of day is really not important, for example, sending messengers so that they will deliver the right information. It is as if the sender could keep the information until there were a favorable moment to send it! Another example has to do with the selling of jewelry, as if the reader often had to worry about the best day on which to sell jewelry. Still another example has to do with sending children to school, so that they will actually become learned, again, as if one could choose the time to send children to school. Finally, there are certain days for wearing new clothes for the first time! That Grimmelshausen is making fun of things here is clear — earlier in the book he explains to the little Simplicius where the moon has to be when one undertakes certain activities, like purging, cutting nails, etc. For cutting hair, for example, he advised him: "werest du aber gern bald Glatzköpfig/ so lasse dir das Haar abschneyden," when the moon is both in Aries and on the wane (155, III). Even more ironically does Grimmelshausen treat those rules that have to do with bleeding. Bleeding is listed as the very last activity, even after the weaning of babies, whereas it is usually listed as the very first activity. The irony is compounded as Simplicissimus explains that he has "bey nahe vergessen/ zu erinnern/ was etliche vor ein sonderbahr Art haben einen Tag zum Aderlassen zuerkiesen" (157, III).[24] Simplicius counts off no fewer than thirty days that are favorable or unfavorable for bleeding, and in so doing accompanies many of them with funny comments, for example, on the twenty-fifth day:

> Ist gut/ dienet auch zur Klug- und Weißheit; Ach warumb hab ich doch diß nicht gewust/ da ich noch übrig Geblüth hatte/ wie wollte ich doch so ein witziger Kerl seyn worden; Weil es aber nunmehr mit mir zu spath/ mein lieber Simplice, so lasse dir bey leib diesen Tag wol befohlen seyn/ ob ich vielleicht einen Sohn bekäm/ der auß der Art schlüg/ und witzig würde. (161, III)

On the sixteenth day, which is the most dangerous for bleeding, he notes that this day comes around twelve or thirteen times a year and asks which of them is then the most dangerous of all (EC, 161, III). On the twenty-eighth day, he notes "Jst gar gut/ ich kann aber nicht wissen/warumb?" (161, III). He concludes his enumeration of the days for bleeding with the following observation: "Schaue mein lieber Simplice, dieses schewen sich unsere Calenderschreiber nicht in ihre Calender zu setzen/ auß was Grund sie aber solches haben/ kann ich dir nicht sagen/ und ich glaub/ sie wissens auch selber nicht" (163, III). Finally, he provides Simplicius with instructions which all boil down to this: use these rules as a guide, but when you are really sick, it is better to have the bleeding immediately than to wait for a favorable date and to be in danger of death in the meantime. That is to say, he actually rescinds or revokes all those rules which took up more than two columns and he makes the reader aware that one can often not determine the choice of time, that a concrete course of action depends on factors other than favorable or unfavorable days. However, it is not enough that Grimmelshausen seems not to believe in these rules and still in all uses column after column to list them — he returns to them in the conversation that Simplicissimus has with Indagine. Indagine explains to Simplicissimus about the man who bleeds the sick, the man who is present in most of the calendars, and in so doing he refers once again to the calendars in which one finds information about when it is good to do bleeding and when not.[25] While Indagine passes on without reservation the information about the rules with reference to the signs of the zodiac, the temperaments, and the age of the person as well as the unfavorable days, Zonagri is critical with regard to the unfavorable days:

> Dieses lieber Simplici, erzehle ich nit daß ichs eben glaube/ oder dichs zuglauben überreden wolle/ sondern darumb/ damit du sehst wie weit die beschreibung der unglückseligen Täge von einander stimme/ und was sich dessentwegen von einer gewißheit gegen ihnen zu versehen. (29, I)

As we know, the author amassed all kinds of information for the calendar, much of it contradictory. The contradictory data are present in all areas, including the name of saints, the listing of various dates for the creation of the world (29, I), the enumeration of rules for the weather, and rules for bleeding. Hence, the above quote is another piece of evidence for the fact that the amassing of information, typical for the *Ewigwährender Calender*, shows that all these data are relative. It confirms the judgment given in the introduction, namely that calendars either lie or are unable to provide us with the truth.

Miracles, Farmers' Almanac, Funny Stories

The second and third columns of the calendar carry the heading "Chaos, oder Verworrenes Mischmasch" (Breuer passim). The second column contains the days of the week according to the Roman calendar. This, of course, contributes to the confusion, because the Roman calendar counts the days, at least in part, with reference to the following month, so that the names of two months exist right next to each other. The kinds of information assigned to each day are quite varied. On the one hand, biblical events are connected to each day, which is strange, because these, if they are mentioned at all, are connected to the Christian calendar and not to the Roman way of counting.[26] However, we do find information about rules for the weather, stories of miracles, historical events, testaments about prophecies, about the meaning of comets, and about the calculations of the length of time during which the moon shines (8, II; 10, II). All of this information is about things that really belong in the fourth to the sixth columns. Actually, the comets are mentioned again in the sixth column; there they deal with what the comets announce in terms of coming events (75, III). Not only does one not find in the ecclesiastical calendar the sought for information, but even the other data are not to be found in those places where one would expect them; thus, themes sort of creep into rubrics in which they do not belong. Although Zonagri is extremely skeptical with regard to prophecies, both prophecies and stories of miracles are included in the material for the second and third columns, and they are treated as fact. It seems as though the right hand did not know what the left hand was printing and vice versa, as if the two sides of the calendar had nothing in common. This, too, is a way of making the information presented seem less important.

Many of the miraculous stories reported by Grimmelshausen are found in the *Book of Miracles* by Lycosthenes.[27] Lycosthenes, whose real name was Konrad Wolfhart (1518–1561), was a humanist and professor of grammar and dialectics at the University of Basle. His book is, as its title indicates, ordered according to years, as in a chronicle. Grimmelshausen puts individual events together with specific days; in the chronology, however, he jumps around wildly, something which in most cases would not be necessary since the events are often not tied to a specific day. If a specific date is given, then it does not correspond to the date on the calendar; for example, on 9 May there is a report of an event which occurred on 24 June 1474. Grimmelshausen seems to avoid at all costs any sort of clear ordering of materials in his text.

The third column is for the most part dedicated to the so-called farmers' almanac, that is, the rules. The farmers' almanac contained astrological prognoses of all kinds; it predicted the weather, the amount of the harvest, but, then, war and peace, too. The rules for the weather have continued to be used, even up to our day.[28] The farmers' almanac actually determined the everyday life of many people, especially farmers. First of all, one has in the third column those sayings enumerated which recall for the farmers their activities within the course of the year, by virtue of the saints' days. Then, however, we have the first disturbance in the system, because there follows a list of the signs of the zodiac and the countries which belong to each. Although this is important in the interpretation of the comets, it really has nothing to do with the overall theme of the farmers' almanac. Such information actually belongs in the fourth through sixth columns, namely, astrology. Here we are not dealing with a concrete application to a certain comet. The list makes sense only when it is tied to a specific comet and its course through the constellations. Of course, broadsides dealing with the comets frequently carry the same data as the farmers' almanac, since the comets also have an influence on the weather and, therefore, on the prospects for a good harvest. Here, they are not included.

The topic of the farmers' almanac is also dealt with on a meta plane, since Simplicissimus discusses for a long time with his mother the use of such a farmers' almanac. His mother finds such an almanac unnecessary, because one finds out about the feast days from the pastor in the chancel and the weather is not right in the calendars anyhow. The mother can predict the weather much better from the conduct of the animals than the "Herrn Doctor Calendermacher" (44, III). That is to say, the mother, too, has a system of prognosis, but it rests on different assumptions, namely on the conduct of animals rather than astrology. One finds such rules, as the mother has, in popular books like the *Silva de varia leccion* of Petrus Mexía (1497–1551) and similar writings, which are excerpted from the writers of antiquity.[29] The underlinings in the original of the Haberkamm reprint show that the rules the mother uses obviously appeared worthy of memorizing by some early user. However, the mother can also observe celestial phenomena, like the brightness of the moon, the sunset and similar things. At the end, she recommends that Simplicissimus use as toilet paper the otherwise useless farmers' almanac he has purchased.

The Knan, who picks up the conversation, proves to be a real expert in astrological prognoses. He knows, for example, "Donnerts in der Waag/ so wird Krieg und Unglück genug/ auch Verderbung aller

Früchten. Ist der Mon dann im Scorpion wann es donnert so wird grosser Hunger/ aber viel Vögel" (66, III). These rules, too, were underlined by the unknown user of the book. The Knan knows the so-called super days, that is, those days on the basis of which one can make predictions about the weather an entire year in advance. Thus, he explains to Simplicissimus the consequences for weather and politics for each day of the week on which New Year's Day might fall. "Gefält daß Jahr [Neujahr] vff den Sontag/ wo wird der Winter warm/ der Frühling feucht/ ein winterlicher Herbst/ gut Korn genug/ viel Wein/ viel Garten-Kraut/ junge Leuthe sterben/ viel gefechts under den Soldaten/ newe Mähr kommen von Königen und anderen landen her" (68, III). He knows, too, what thunder means in each of the months. Simplicissimus invites Knan to tell him all about these things, and he gives as a reason, "ich höre gern so alte Geschichten erzählen" (72, III). The data, therefore, which interested the users of these calendars are referred to by Simplicissimus as "old tales" and not as useful data. While Simplicissimus is convinced after the talk with his mother that the farmers' almanac he purchased is useless, he argues with Knan about whether the farmers or the scholars know more about such things and whether the scholars might not have their knowledge from the farmers or vice-versa. As proof that the scholars also know all about the farmers' almanac, Simplicissimus provides examples, just as both his mother and Knan had done before. Knan finds the rules, which Simplicissimus brings, quite accurate. Nevertheless he is astonished that the scholars would write "so geringe Sachen in ihre Bücher" (84, III), whereby he, on the one hand, devalues the information and on the other, passes judgment about the *Ewig-währender Calender*, which is, of course, full of such information.

The controversy never is resolved. Simplicissimus defends the scholars and "Naturkündiger," from whom the farmers have learned and Knan represents the opposite side of the argument. As an example of how stupid the scholars are, Knan relates a farce about a scholar who was commanded to keep silent while hunting but who then speaks Latin, because he thinks that the birds will not understand Latin! One can relate this conversation about the farmers' almanac to the opposite page in the text, where the scholars Zonagri and Indagine initiate Simplicissimus into their realms of knowledge. This is rather obvious, because the farmers' almanac has the same claim as other phenomena that have to do with astrology. With this presentation of the opposing sides of scholars and farmers, Grimmelshausen undermines the constant reference to authority that was still so common in the seventeenth century. He does this by allowing his mother and Knan the same authority that the scholars have. On the one hand, he dismisses the farmers' almanac as useless; on the other hand, however, he allows as valid the rules from his mother and Knan. These rules are supposedly based on experience but actually they are taken from precisely such a farmers' almanac. When we set up such connections, according to the instructions to the little Simplicius, we almost get dizzy, because there is nothing anymore that is secure, nothing that is constant; the binding norms that provide us with a certain orientation no longer exist.

In this third column we also find the story about how the calendar was saved by Brandsteller before it was re-used as butter paper, as well as various "stories" by Simplicissimus. In this way, this column becomes the one in which we find the most biographical information. The telling of so-called calendar stories only gradually comes about in the seventeenth century; most of the time, stories are taken from the reservoir of multifaceted writings by writers such as Georg Philipp Harsdörffer (1607–1658), Erasmus Francisci (1627–1694), Johann Lauremberg (1590–1658), and Martin Zeiller (1589–1661). Sometimes the stories are simply put at the end of the actual calendars. In his *Märtzens-Unterredungen* (1644) the third in his series of monthly conversations, Johann Rist (1607–1657) relates how European printers are now printing all sorts of tomfoolery in the calendars, a practice that was, he indicates, well liked by the populace. Rist further admonishes calendar makers in Germany to print in the third or fourth part of their calendars stories that "der Spielende" (that is, Harsdörffer) or Martin Zeiller had translated from the French. This is done "mit der schönen Vertröstung/ das der fernere Verlauf solcher Geschichte/ in den negstfolgenden Jahren/ dem begierigen Leser gahr gewisse solle mitgetheilet werden" (Rist V, 66). Here, too, we see differences between Grimmelshausen's calendar and the typical ones. First, Grimmelshausen orders the information differently, namely by not putting the stories at the end of the calendar but rather in one of the columns. Secondly, he relates exclusively stories of which Simplicissimus is the hero. Finally, these stories, due to their extreme shortness, do not anticipate further installments.

Astronomy, Astrology, Lies, and Truth

The fourth to the sixth columns contain conversations that Simplicissimus has had with either Zonagri or with Indagine. Four sections from Tomaso Garzoni's *Piazza universale* form the basis for the conversation with Zonagri. These are in part taken over verbatim.[30] The four sections are according to the numbering in the original by Garzoni, the sixth discourse "Von Calenderschreibern/ unnd was darzu gehört," the eighth discourse "Von Practick vnd Prognosticstellern/ Wetterzeyger/ vnd was denselbigen abhängig," the thirty-ninth discourse "Von den Astronomis und Astrologis," and, finally, the fortieth discourse "Von Waarsagern." The *Astrologia naturalis* of Johannes ab Indagine and the *Planeten-Buch* by Wolfgang Hildebrand (fl. 1622–1631) form the basis for the conversation with Indagine (Bauer). In all three of these columns, Simplicissimus plays the role of the naive one, who knows absolutely nothing, not even how one is to read the signs in the calendars. Zonagri reproaches him again and again because of his lack of knowledge and he mocks him, whereas Indagine adopts a very different attitude, namely he informs him very objectively about both astronomy and astrology. That is to say, in the fourth through the sixth columns, we are dealing with a type of meta-text of the far left-hand column. This column is contrasted with the premises of calendar making in that left-hand column. Although Grimmelshausen has taken his astronomical and astrological knowledge verbatim from his sources, one can nevertheless ask what kind of knowledge he wanted to transmit and what function the transmission of this knowledge has within the text. Those sources of Grimmelshausen which have been traced, at least to date, show that we are dealing with a popularized scientific literature that was not on a par with the most recent investigations, but which was nonetheless widely disseminated through numerous treatises and broadsides.

One of the few scholars who has done research in this area is Sara Schechner Genuth in her *Popular Culture, and the Birth of Modern Cosmology,* an investigation of the comets and modern cosmology (1997). Schechner Genuth shows that there was indeed a culture among those who were less well educated and another, different culture among those who were more well educated. She goes on to show, however, that the boundaries are not clearly drawn between the two and that even up until the end of the seventeenth century, scholars built traditional ideas about comets into their learned writings. Inasmuch as Garzoni's *Piazza universale,* a kind of popular encyclopedia, was reprinted in 1664, and just five years later a work like Mexía's *Silva de varia Leccion* appears in a German translation, we can assume that these works in Grimmelshausen's age were read by a rather broad public. That public was indeed probably the same public that was engaged in reading the calendar. The amazing increase of knowledge in the sixteenth and seventeenth centuries led to publications like calendars and at the same time was responsible for their huge success because people were interested in reading them. On the one hand they served the cause of expanding the knowledge of the population and on the other hand they were most interesting in conversational circles because they did not have a particularly systematic approach. I can not agree with Barbara Bauer, who speaks of a "scientific theory" of Grimmelshausen (84); rather, I agree more with Battafarano that Grimmelshausen's main purpose was not the transmittal of knowledge, but a general relativization of knowledge in the areas of astronomy, astrology, and prophecy (1994, 62). This Grimmelshausen does by placing various ideas or theories about a particular item next to each other without making any judgment as to his own position regarding the actual truth of the statements, ideas, or theories. It is, therefore, unimportant that Grimmelshausen uses outdated scientific literature, as do both Garzoni and Indagine; the data he presents do not really belong in a calendar, but no matter, because that was not his intention. His main goal was not to present an accurate, or truthful, calendar, or, for example, to spread correct astronomical knowledge. Rather, he was interested in presenting various theories. Hence, he need not always be presenting the most modern, or the newest, insights on any given topic. Grimmelshausen is much more interested in unmasking or exposing a single aspect of this world, which continues to want to be deceived.[31] This already becomes clear in the dedication of Melchior Sternfels von Fugshaim to his son Simplicius, for he states that he has written the calendar for his son, not so that the latter can study astrology, but rather that he "gereitzt und angefrischt [wird]/ höhern Dingen nachzusinnen" (4).

A dominant theme in the entire work is that of lying and deception. One has the feeling that no one deceives more than does the calendar maker himself. On the dedication page we see the first occurrence of this theme. Melchior Sternfels von Fugshaim writes a letter to his son. In it, he tells his son that if someone should ask why he had written this "fool's work," he should answer that his father had been afraid that the world would change so much that no one would be allowed to lie anymore. In that case, the "Wetter-Practic und Prognostic-schreiberey" would cease and only his perpetual calendar would survive. Calendar writers by their very nature have to lie, says Zonagri to Simplicissimus; this after he had explained the characteristics of the planets and their effects. He thinks that he can work out calendars, almanacs, even horoscopes with this sort of information:

> wiewohl man sich auf diese Kunst nit viel zuverlassen/ dann sie ist ungewiß/ und so unbeständig als der Mercurius und der Mon selbsten; und wirst du manchen Phantasten mit deinen phantastischen Calenderen betriegen: sonderlich wann du der heutigen Art und gewohnheit

nach der ungewissen Calenderschreiber/ dich auch zweyffelhaffter Reden gebrauchest/ und dich sonderlich dieser Worte gebrauchest; es
möchte/ köndte/ dörffte, vielleicht/ auch wohl: [. . .] und was der
gleichen Wörter der Ungewißheit seyn/ dadurch die Practicanten
gleichwohl der Kunst ungewißheit anzeigen muß. (83, I)

Precisely here we find the most interesting things in those columns
that are next to each other. In the second column namely Grimmelshausen deals with the casting of horoscopes and the influence of the planets
on the character of an individual, in the third we find the tale about a
swindler with an artificial stomach. A little further along, Simplicius
protests against the fact that fortune telling should be punishable. If that
were to happen, the fortune tellers would have to wander about like
persons unable to speak, but in the final analysis they would come to the
conclusion that the clerics published so many calendars because they
wished to spoil fortune telling for the people in general (71, III).[32]

Various topics are then mixed with one another: one is the question
as to whether the stars have an influence on humankind, the other is the
question as to the reliability of the calendars. Even if the stars have an
influence, that does not mean that the calendars are reliable, particularly
when they are put together as quickly as the one Simplicius executed in
a single night, even though he makes no prognoses. It is surely no accident that one of the last comments that Simplicius makes about the topic
of an influence of the stars on humankind compares the astronomers and
calendar writers with the poets:

Man müste es halt machen wie die närrische Poeten/ welche ihr Müt-
lein damit kühlen/ wann sie in ihren wiederwertigen Buhlschaften
über unglückliche Stern/ über ein crudele fatum sich beklagen/ wann
Himmel und Erde sich über ihrem Unglück vereinigt hätten. (207)

Simplicissimus complains about calendar writers, but makes one himself in order to show that calendars are filled with lies; this in turn proves
that he is a poet, and poets have the privilege of lying without fearing
punishment. Taken from this point of view, the "perpetual" in the title
has still another meaning: one can apply it to the claim that an artistic
work makes for immortality.[33] Criticism of calendars as a conversational
topic was not invented by Grimmelshausen; it can be found in the *Märtzens-Unterredungen* of "der Rüstige" (= Johann Rist), where a series of
arguments appear that one later finds in Grimmelshausen's work. Thus,
it is noted that calendars are useful, although in the preparation of the
same there is so much idiocy that one is amazed about it all (Rist V, 66).
Rist also complains about the preparation of calendars by ignoramuses:

dieweil Kalender-Schreiben/ bei dieser Zeit so gemein wurde/ das auch etliche grobe Ignoranten/ oder nichtes wissende Grillenfänger sich nicht scheueten/ dieses Falles die Feder anzusetzen/ und ihre närrische Phantaseien an das offne Tages Licht zu geben/ unangesehen sie den rechten Grund dieser Edlen Wissenschaft so wenig verstünden/ als Ich die Spanische Sprache verstehe." (Rist V, 66)

It almost sounds like a criticism about the conduct of Simplicissimus. We are tempted to see the calendar as literature, because we see both its origin and its discovery as literary.

The Calendar as a Biographical Document

The most conspicuous characteristic of Grimmelshausen's calendar is that it takes on aspects of a biography. He builds his calendar around the biography of Simplicissimus and then works into that biography numerous quotations, which he has copied from various texts. This procedure is the same one that was used in *Simplicissimus,* because there, too, Simplicissimus passes off that which he has read as something that he himself has experienced, and he does this expressis verbis (ST 527). The biographical situation in which the calendar must have been written is the following (Wimmer, 242): Simplicissimus discusses, as noted above, in the third section with his mother and Knan both calendars and the farmers' almanac. This episode must have taken place on the farm near Sauerbrunnen, after Simplicissimus has again found his foster parents and his wife has died (V, chapter 8). After he has given the farm over to his foster parents, he has time for all sorts of contemplation. When he has returned from the Mummelsee his time is completely taken up with books: "mein gröste Freud und Ergetzung war/ hinter den Büchern zu sitzen/ deren ich mir dann viel beyschaffte" (ST 439). He had a sufficient number of books dealing with grammar, arithmetic and music, and so he turned to astronomy and astrology, "welche mich dann trefflich delectirten/ endlich kamen sie mir auch falsch und ungewiß vor" (ST 439), so that he again gave up interest in those fields. During this time, before he began his world trip to Russia, he obviously wrote the calendar for his son Simplicius, the child who was left at his doorstep. This at least is the story told by Brandsteller, who saved the calendar from its being used as butter paper:

Ich berichte euch allerseyts freundlich/ daß dieser Calender nicht geschrieben oder verfertigt worden/ ihne in offnen Truck zugeben/ sonder es hat ihn der so genandte Abentewrliche Simplicissimus, dessen Lebens-Beschreibung vorm Jahr daß erste mahl gedruckt worden/ sei-

nem jüngsten Sohn *Simplicio,* welchen er neben seinem Knan und
Meuder zu Erben und Besitzern seines Bauerhoffs an Schwartzwalt
hinderlassen/ umb dessen Verstand darinn zu üben/ und ihn zu höhe-
ren Gedancken dardurch zu reitzen/ vermög der Vorrede/ zugefallen
geschrieben/ wann er etwann in seinen Wittwerstand eine übrige Stund
hätte/ darinn ihn die *Melancholia* überfallen und plagen: oder besser
zusagen/ wann er seine Zeit nit müssig zubringen wollen. (92, III and
Breuer, II, 357)

In this sense the calendar fills a lacuna in the biography of Sim-
plicssimus in the same manner that *Courage* and *Springinsfeld* fill such
lacunae, gaps that were actually not noticed by the readers of *Simplicissimus Teutsch.* This method of observation brings some problems into the
discussion, because Simplicissimus appears much more naive here in the
calendar than he appears to be in *Simplicissimus Teutsch.* Whereas he
pretends in his conversation with Zonagri and Indagine to know nothing, but then makes a calendar immediately after the first lesson, he
appears in the corresponding passage in *Simplicissimus Teutsch* to be
quite well-versed. He emphasizes the fact that he understood both "Phy-
siognomiam [and] Chiromantiam" (ST 436) and that in Sauerbrunnen,
where he passed himself off as a traveling student, he boasted about his
knowledge. When speaking with Garzoni on the other hand, he pretends
not to know what calendars are and says that at first he considered them
to be news items from strange lands, but then when he saw the signs, he
considered them to be books of magic.[34] Inasmuch as calendars were
widely available in the seventeenth century, it is quite unlikely that Simplicius does not know what they are. It seems instead that he is simply
playing a role here, namely that of the innocent, of a "Simplex," so that
he can clothe the informative exchanges of the two scholars into a dialogue and make the whole thing seem literary.

Only rather late in the story (92, III) do we find out how the calendar that Simplicius wrote was actually sold to the public. We probably
would not have even asked a question about this, were it not for the
report about it in the calendar. Christian Brandsteller, who spent time in
Sauerbrunnen and was supposed to eat butter every day as a medicine,
received his butter packaged in such a calendar. He immediately noticed
"weil alles mit rothen und schwartzen Buchstaben überschrieben war/
daß es Schrifften seyn müssten/ die in eines Bawren Krautgarthen nicht
gewachsen" (96, III). Brandsteller therefore considers calendars to be
something which farmers could not make, although the calendar itself
seems to suggest the opposite in several places. Responding to Brandsteller's inquiries, Simplicius's mother says,

es wären so alte Schriften von ihrem Sohn/ die er etwann hierbevor
beschrieben/ weil er aber nun jetzunder wie sie gehöret häte/ sich
in der newen Welt befünde/ und sein Lebtag wohl nimmermehr zu
Land kommen würde/ und also auch diese Brief niemand nichts nutz-
ten/ so hätte sie selbige angegrieffen und ihre Butter hinein gepackt.
(96, III)

This passage is interesting from a variety of viewpoints, particularly
because it offers a very refined game in which fiction and illusion are
combined. It confirms the reality of Simplicissimus' life, which we can
substantiate from another source, namely the novel. His mother relates
only those things that we already know from the novel, namely that he
had been a soldier, that he had led a contemplative life in the forest, and
that he had then left. She had seen neither hide nor hair of him since
(92, III). She continues, however, that she has heard that he has departed for the New World, and this is a foreshadowing of that which is
subsequently reported in the *Continuatio*. In an allusion to the title of
the novel, she says that one calls Melcher at this time "den offendürli-
chen Simplicissimus." Brandsteller had up to this time only read the
biography and so he correctly deduces that the woman who wants to sell
him butter must be the mother (Meuder). Reality here confirms the
novel. He then wants to see whether the description of Knan, with a wart
on his forehead, also conforms to reality, and he hopes to be able to find
the father in the facial features of young Simplicius. However, neither of
them is at home, so he cannot undertake this important examination;
once again, in a manner typical of Grimmelshausen, the truth of the
description in the novel cannot be confirmed, but it cannot be proven
false either and so everything remains undecided. However, the mother
can show him a portrait of Simplicissimus, which for its part has been
copied, just as the little Simplicii seem to multiply. At the same time,
then, Brandsteller gets the manuscript of the famous hero and, in the
next step, the calendar, which is lacking a title page that seems to stem
from Brandsteller himself.

The explanation about why the calendar has become wrapping paper
for butter is not very clear, because Simplicissimus did not write the
calendar for himself, but rather for the little Simplicius, who was supposed to get it from his grandmother. With its foreword written to the
little Simplicius, it takes on the character of a last will and testament.
When it is saved through the actions of Brandsteller, who by the way also
has to purchase all the butter that is wrapped in the calendar, the value
of the calendar is obviously increased. This rather complicated transac-
tion should have led scholars to see that the calendar, even solely on the

basis of its author, is worth more than the wrapping paper usually made out of calendars and the farmers' almanac. The story goes even further: Brandsteller has found some empty spaces on the paper which he can fill with tales about Simplicissimus, which he has collected now and then from people who knew Simplicissimus (104, III). Many of these stories he has from the "butter letters," which stem from Simplicissimus's pen and were taken to market by his mother along with the butter.[35] In many of these tales, which are really epigrammatic sayings rather than stories in the literal sense, there are express references to the biography, which is said to be historical (122, Nr. IX, XI and 142, Nr. XX, XXXV).

From the type of story, Brandsteller deduces that Simplicissimus "ein Man von ziemlicher Conversation und ein Apophthegmatischer Mensch gewesen sei" (104 and Breuer, II, 361). These are all elements that support the illusion that in Simplicissimus we are dealing with a person who really lived. Scholars who have investigated Grimmelshausen often set Simplicissimus as the equivalent of Grimmelshausen; they have, for the most part, also been taken in by this. The title page of the calendar is part of the biographical game, too, inasmuch as it pictures Simplicissimus, Simplicius, Meuder, Knan (of course with the wart), and Ursula, the daughter of Meuder and Knan. We have to assume that Simplicissimus is pictured in line with the portrait found with his mother. It is not unusual for calendars to portray the calendar writer either on the cover or inside the calendar. Once more, though, Grimmelshausen uses the multiplier effect and portrays the entire family, which brings with it a certain parodistic effect. It is possible that Meuder and Knan should be pictured, because they can be seen in conjunction with tidbits of knowledge drawn from the farmers' almanac part of the calendar. That the addressee of the calendar, Simplicius, is also pictured shows clearly the divergence from normal practice. Zonagri notes ironically that Simplicissimus could put his "Adelich Brust-Bild sambt Schild und Helm [. . .] mit einem Quadranten oder ein Astrolabio neben sich" on the calendar, as if he had always gone around looking like that (55, I). Interestingly, there is an astrolabe on the title page, but it is not an attribute of Simplicissimus; he has a fool's cap, a sword, a flail, a rosary, and an inkwell as attributes. A bearded man carries the astrolabe; he also holds a crown. A woman, on the other hand, who is crowned with a laurel wreath, is carrying a panel on which the zodiac is represented. It is difficult to discern who else is pictured on the title page; they are all inside the snake (Uroboros),[36] which represents the passage of time over the years. Still, one can say that in addition to Meuder and Knan there are obviously representatives of various nations and classes, all of which are especially characterized by their headgear. On the edge of the snake sit the allegories of the four seasons, although a coherent reading of these images is not possible. On the bottom we have, sitting across from each other Bacchus, representing autumn and an old man, who is warming himself by the fire, representing winter. On top there are two women, who represent spring and summer. No matter in which direction one goes, there are always next to each other two figures who represent seasons which in reality do not follow each other. The "orderly disorder," therefore, begins right on the title page.

The Calendar as Miscellanies

If the calendar therefore is not really a calendar, or is a calendar only to a limited degree, the question arises as to what it really is, whether one can make connections between it and any recognized genre. Making the calendar literary does not simply mean that Grimmelshausen added calendar stories. Instead he gives the calendar a function which is appropriate for a literary work, but not for a calendar or a newspaper. He has, as he says in the foreword to his natural son Simplicius, "mixed up" the things in the calendar, so that Simplicius can not just read it superficially, but rather that he has to read it repeatedly. He is, after all, to sharpen his wits with the calendar and not simply learn, as one might anticipate, astrology and astronomy. Instead, he is to prodded to reflect on "higher things" (cf. 82, III).

That is also the reason for his having made the calendar a perpetual calendar, namely so that one would look at it more than once and in so doing, we have to assume, discover the deeper meaning. The confusion, the chaos that Grimmelshausen presents in this work is therefore thematized in the para-text of both title page and foreword. It would seem at first glance as though the confusion, the mixing would not be in line with that of a work of art, the basic criterion of which is a clear intentionality. If one is clear however that in the sixteenth and seventeenth centuries there is a whole list of genres which rely on change as the basic principle, then the situation is a different one. I am thinking here of genres like Miscellanies, for which Mexía's *Geschicht — Natur — und Wunderwald* [Sylvae, dealing with History, Nature, and the Miraculous] would be a good example, where the change of topic becomes the organizational principle. One can think, too, of the genre of Conversations, or *Gesprächspiel* (Parlor Conversations), for which change is also the organizing principle.

It is characteristic, too, for both of these genres that they spread the most varied kinds of knowledge, historical, scientific, or even those kinds of chic knowledge which characterize the seventeenth century, like astronomy, astrology, chiromancy and physiognomy. On the other hand, both of these genres also tell stories and provide epigrams of all sorts. Such works often have no other organizational principle than that of variety or change. Hence, it is no accident when Grimmelshausen uses the image of a "pleasant labyrinth" to characterize the materials presented in the third and fourth columns. He picks up on the image of the garden once again in the foreword to Simplicius, in which he emphasizes his method of diligently mixing together all kinds of material. In so doing, he follows his didactic purpose, for Simplicius in this manner is, on the one hand, supposed to keep everything together better in his memory and, on the other hand, he is almost required to read everything in the calendar. From another angle, he is, of course, also emphasizing the entertainment aspects of the work: "Ich vor mein theil gehe lieber in einen Garthen spatzieren darinnen allerhand Blumen undereinander stehen/ da mir bald diß bald jenes liebliche oder seltzame Gewächs zusehen wird/ als durch unterschiedliche Aecker deren jeder nur mit einerley Samen angeblümbt ist" (141, III). The image of the forest, which also occurs frequently in such works, is supported in a similar fashion: just as in a forest the trees are without any order, so, says Mexía, are the themes without any particular order in his miraculous forest. A forest, says his translator Lucas Zolekhofer (Zollikofer) in his introduction, consists of "allerhand böum gewächs vnd frucht."[37] Conversations exhibit the same characteristics. Francis Bacon uses a similar image in his essay "Von Unterhaltung und Gesprächen": "Dann vertreuliche Gespräche/ sollen wie offene Felder seyn/ in denen man lustwandeln kann und keine Landstrasse/ die nach Hause führt."[38]

The hallmark of conversations is, as has been noted over and over again, not that one finds truth, but that as much material as possible is covered. All topics in conversations are actually of equal, or equivalent value. But what differentiates Grimmelshausen's calendar from this type of miscellany is the manner in which it is made part of the life of Simplicissimus. Thus, the calendar is given a different character and must be compared with other Simplician works, in which the sequence of events is also often governed by chance. Chance is indeed one of the organizational principles of the picaresque novel, which, in its prototype, consists of a series of episodes. Satirical works, too, which often use the idea of travel as an organizational principle, are marked by principles of association and, therefore, of disorder. This is quite in contrast to the "höfisch-historisch" novel, following in the tradition of Heliodor, which at first glance seem to reflect the disorder of the world, but in the final analysis can be traced back to a very clear order. Disorder, or hotchpotch, is therefore not unknown to the more common genres of literature, even from very early times. Just as carnival represents an exception to the normal order, so one can consider the calendar to represent a carnivalesque genre, which lays open to question both the concept of order in the world and the meaning of the world in general.

Translated by Karl F. Otto, Jr.

Notes

[1] Cf. the articles in *Simpliciana* 16 (1994). Most early research on Grimmelshausen's calendar failed to take into account the literary qualities of the calendar. Since my discussion deals mainly with such literary qualities, I will cite such earlier research only in those cases where it relates to my arguments.

[2] See Matthäus (1969) for the history of calendars in Nuremberg.

[3] See Matthäus (1969), 978–80 as well as Hellmut Rosenfeld, "Bauernkalender und Mandelkalender als literarisches Phänomen des 16. Jahrhunderts und ihr Verhältnis zur Bauernpraktik," *Gutenberg Jahrbuch* 1964, 88–96 and the latter's "Kalender, Einblattkalender, Bauernkalender und Bauernpraktik. Mit dem Text der Bauernpraktik von 1508 und einem Bauernkalender von 1574," *Bayerisches Jahrbuch für Volkskunde* 1962, 7–24.

[4] Thus we find in one of the farmer's almanacs from 1574, which had been printed in Zurich, the following notation for January: "Wirts Morgenrot am Nüwen jar | So ists kriegs halben grosse gfaar. | [. . .] Gibt an Vincentz [= 24 January] die Sunn jrn schyn | So wird deß selben jars vil wyn."

[5] The *Gesammelte Werke,* ed. Rolf Tarot (Tübingen 1967ff.) contain no part of the *Calender,* while Breuer's edition (1997) contains only some story-like passages from the *Calender.*

[6] Klaus Haberkamm, ed. Johann Jakob Christoph von Grimmelshausen. *Des Abentheuerlichen Simplicissimi Ewig-währender Calender.* Faksimile-Druck der Erstausgabe. Nürnberg 1671 mit einem erklärenden Beiheft von Klaus Haberkamm. Konstanz: Rosgarten 1967. In the remainder of this article, this edition will be cited as EC with Roman numerals for the columns. If it is clear from the context that EC is the work cited from, then only number and column number will be given.

[7] Jan Hendrik Scholte. *Zonagri Discurs Von Waarsagern. Ein Beitrag zu unserer Kenntnis von Grimmelshausens Arbeitsweise in seinem Ewigwährenden Calender mit besonderer Berücksichtigung des Eingangs des Abentheuerlichen Simplicissimus.* Amsterdam: Müller 1921. (= Verhandelingen der Koninklijke Nederlandse Akademie van Wetenschappen, Afd. Letterkunde NS 22, 3); Hertha von Ziegesar. "Grimmelshausen als Kalenderschriftsteller und die Felßeckerschen Verlagsunternehmungen."

Euphorion. Ergänzungsheft 17 (1924): 50–79; Günther Weydt. *Nachahmung und Schöpfung im Barock. Studien um Grimmelshausen.* Berne: Francke 1968.

[8] Cf. the calendars reproduced in Sodmann (1976). Previous research did not recognize this fact because the composition of the calendars had never been investigated. Berns (1994) offers an overview of the scholarship on Grimmelshausen's calendar.

[9] EC 92, III: "der so genandte Abentewrliche *Simplicissimus,* dessen Lebens-Beschreibung vorm Jahr das erste mahl getruckt worden" is said to be the author of the *Calender.* See also below.

[10] It would certainly have been easily possible to keep the type size for columns four through six larger all the way through the book.

[11] Zeller (1994) provides a detailed analysis of various Swiss calendars.

[12] These data, the so-called *Mansiones,* serve to determine how positive or negative it is to carry out certain activities.

[13] Similar data can be found in very old calendars; originally they had a medicinal function.

[14] One such page from a calendar is reproduced in *Simpliciana* 16 (1994), 226.

[15] Michelsen surmises that Coler's *Calendarium oeconomicum* was Grimmelshausen's model; however, this cannot be substantiated without a thorough knowledge of calendars of the era.

[16] "Man muß gleichwol auch wissen wanns New wird/ wann Feyr- und Fastäg kommen/ und was es etwann vor Wetter geben möchte/ damit man sich beydes in der Haußhaltung und auff dem Feld mit der Arbeit darnach richten kann" (EC 42, III).

[17] Petrat considers the following to be "trust-building" in calendars: short lines, large spaces between lines, readily clear divisions, and practical format. Of these, Grimmelshausen's *Calender* has only the last mentioned characteristic.

[18] [Johann Georg Gross]: *Immerwährend-Järlicher Kalender: auff all vnd jede Jahr gestellt: alßlang die Welt nach Gottes Willen stehen wirdt.* [. . .]. Basel 1629.

[19] For example: "Clemens den Winter bringt herbey/ | Petrus vertreibt den wider frey.| Urban den Frühling: den Sommer Symphorian | Was übrig/ nimb vor die Herbstzeit an" (EC 19, I).

[20] The *Martyrologium,* too, speaks, as does Grimmelshausen, of "unzählbaren Heiligen." The copy to which I had access carries, significantly enough, notes of ownership by a church cleric.

[21] For example, Gross's calendar (see footnote 18) contains the dates for Easter for the years 1629–1640. The first perpetual calendar, by Regiomontanus, contains the dates for the years 1447–1531!

[22] Garzoni provides a table of "Sunday letters" and also provides the specific ones for 1568, so that one can figure out the feasts for other years as well.

[23] On these pages, the canon replaces the actual calendar!

[24] The rules for bleeding are among the oldest components of calendars. Cf. Matthäus, cols. 995 and 1069–1071.

[25] "Davon findestu ja in allen Calendern genugsambe Nachricht/ auch zuvorderist wann sonderlich gut Aderlassen sey" (EC, 195, II).

[26] For example, on "tertio nonas Januarii": "An diesem Tag hat unser Erlöser mit dem Samaritischen Weiblein beym Brunnen geredt/Joan. 4." (EC 4, II). Similar passages are found in the *Martyrologium,* from which Grimmelshausen probably excerpted them.

[27] Scholars have failed to recognize this; Michelsen (463) considers these stories to be inventions of Grimmelshausen. The fact that dates accompany these stories made them believable to Grimmelshausen as well as to his contemporaries.

[28] Examples include: "So viel Taw im Mertzen/ so viel Reiffen umb Pfingsten/ und Nebel im Augusto" (EC 50, II); "Wann es am Charfreytag regnet/ so soll es ein gut jahr bedeuten/ regnets aber am Ostertag/ solles die negste Sontäg zwischen Ostern und Pfingsten auch regnen" (EC 50 / 52, II); "Versetze jetzt Bäum beym zunehmenden Mon/ sonderlich solche die frühe Obs tragen" (EC 52, II).

[29] Chapter titles in Mexía's Wunderwald include "Daß dem Menschen die vernünfftigen Thiere von vielen Artzneien/ und anderer Dinge Eigenschafften/ Bericht ertheilen" (2. Teil, Kap. 37) and "Daß durch den Antrieb der Natur viel Thiere die zukünfftige Zeit und Gewitter wissen" (2. Teil, Kap. 37).

[30] As to the reception of Garzoni in Germany, see Battafarano 1990 und 1991.

[31] Bauer points out that the "M. V. D." on the title page stands for "Mundus vult decipi," and that these letters are frequently found in calendars (99).

[32] The citation comes from the sixth column, after the previous quote. Cf. van Ingen on the stance of the church with regard to fortune-telling.

[33] There is a slight ambiguity here in the translation; generally perpetual calendars are called "immerwährend" in German, whereas Grimmelshausen calls his "ewigwährend."

[34] "ich fande so seltzame Zeichen darinnen/ als ich etwann bey einem vff einem Zettel gesehen/ der solche vor hawen und stechen bey sich trug; da stunden rothe unnd schwartze Kuglen/ [. . .] und darbey stunden auch so seltzame unteutsche Wörter/ die mir allerdings vorkahmen wie die jenige/ so die Zäuberer brauchen/ wann sie den Teuffel auß der Höllen herauß bannen wollen; derowegen ichs vor nichts anders/ als vor ein Zauber-Buch halten könde" (EC 7 and 9, I).

[35] "Diß Stückgen ist auß einem Butterbrieff genommen worden/ der mit *Simplicissimi* aigner Hand überschrieben gewesen" (EC 106, III). "Dies obige ist auch auß einem Butter-Brief/ den *Simplicissimi* Meuder zu Marck gebracht/ und *Simpl.* hiebevor eigenhändig überschrieben/ extrahirt worden/ wie auch das nächstfolgende" (EC 140, III).

[36] In this regard, note Simplicissimus, who seems less than uneducated when he quotes Virgil in Latin and then translates into German: "Das Jahr sich in sich selbst verlaufft/ | Da es anlangt hörts wider auff," and then explains: "Dieses haben die Egyptier wie Orus Apollo meldet mit einer Schlang welche in einem Circkel gelegen/ und den Sch[w]antz im Maul hatte/ zuverstehen geben" (EC 95, I). In the

later imitations of Grimmelsdhausen's *Calender*, the snake appears on the title page in various forms. See the reproduction in *Simpliciana* 16 (1994), 245.

[37] *Petri Messiae Von Sibilia vilualtige beschreibung/ Christenlicher vnnd Heidnischer Keyseren/ Künigen/ weltweiser Männeren gedächtnuß wirdige Historien/ löbliche geschicht/ auch manicher Philosophen leben vnd sprüch/ zweyfelhafftiger dingen natürliche außlegungen/ nit alleyn kurtzweylig/ sonder jedem tugendliebhabenden menschen nutzlich vnd lustig zu lesen/ Vnd Jetz neüwlich auff das fleissigest verteütscht.* Gedruckt zu Basel durch Henricum Petri/ vnnd Petrum Pernam. 1564. See Zeller, 1999.

[38] Francis Bacon. [. . .] *Getreue Reden: die Sitten- Regiments- und Haußlehre betreffend. Aus dem Lateinischen gedolmetscht* [translated by Johann Wilhelm von Stubenberg]. Nuremberg 1654.

Works Cited

Battafarano, Italo Michele. 1991a. "L'opera di Tomaso Garzoni nella cultura tedesca." In: *Tomaso Garzoni. Uno zingaro in convento. Celebrazione garzoniane.* Ravenna: Longo, 1990. 35–79.

———. 1991b Ed. *Tomaso Garzoni. Polyhistorismus und Interkulturalität in der frühen Neuzeit.* Bern: Lang, 1991. (= Komparatistisches und rezeptionsgeschichtliches Arbeitsgespräch 2)

———. 1994 "Die simplicianische Literarisierung des Kalenders." *Simpliciana* 16 (1994): 45–63.

Bauer, Barbara. "'Es bleibt doch bey dem alten Brauch M(undus) V(ult) D(ecipi):' Veraltete Astrologie in Grimmelshausens *Ewig-währendem Calender.*" *Simpliciana* 16 (1994): 81–115.

Berns, Jörg Jochen. 1988 "Die 'Zusammenfügung' der Simplicianischen Schriften. Bemerkungen zum Zyklus-Problem." *Simpliciana* 10 (1988): 301–25.

———. 1994 "Kalenderprobleme der Grimmelshausen-Forschung. Ein Überblick." *Simpliciana* 16 (1994): 15–32.

Breuer, Dieter. "Die Geister unterscheiden lernen. Zur 4. bis 6. Materie von Grimmelshausens *Ewig-währendem Calender.*" *Simpliciana* 16 (1994): 65–79.

Canisius, Petrus. *Martyrologium. Der Kirchenkalender/ darinnen die Christlichen Feste vnd Hailigen Gottes bayder Testament begriffen/ wie dieselbigen durch das gantze Jar in der Christenhait/ von tag zuo tag begangen werden. Auch mit verzaichnuß unzalbarer Hailigen.[. . .] Mit deß Erwürdigen vnd Hochgelehrten Herrn D. Petri Canisij vbersehung/ auch Vorred vnd nothwendiger Erklärung* [. . .]. 3rd edition. Dillingen: Mayer, 1583.

Coler, Johann. *Calendarium oeconomicum & perpetuum. Vor die Haußwird / Ackerleut* [. . .] Wittenberg 1591. Nachdruck Weinheim: VCH, 1988. (= Acta Humaniora)

————. *Oeconomica ruralis et domestica. Das ist: Ein sehr Nützliches Allgemeines Hausz-Buch [. . .] hiebvorn von Ioanni Colero, zwar beschrieben / Jetzto aber/ auff ein Newes in vielen Bücheren mercklich corrigirt, vermehrt und verbessert.* [. . .] Mainz: Heyll, 1655.

Garzoni, Tomaso. *Piazza universale, das ist: Allgemeiner Schawplatz/ oder Marckt/ vnd Zusammenkunft aller Professionen/ Künsten/ Geschäfften/ Händlen und Handwercken/ so in der gantzen Welt geübt werden.* Frankfurt / Main: Iennis, 1619.

Grimmelshausen, Hans Jacob Christoffel von. *Werke.* Two vols. in three. Ed. Dieter Breuer. Frankfurt / Main: Deutscher Klassiker Verlag, 1989–1997.

————. *Des Abentheuerlichen Simplicissimi Ewig-während er Calender.* Faksimile-Druck der Erstausgabe. Nürnberg 1671 mit einem erklärenden Beiheft von Klaus Haberkamm. Konstanz: Rosgarten, 1967.

Haberkamm, Klaus. *Beiheft zur Faksimile-Ausgabe:* Des Abentheuerlichen Simplicissimi Ewig-währender Calender. Faksimile-Druck der Erstausgabe. Nürnberg 1671 mit einem erklärenden Beiheft. Constance: Rosgarten, 1967.

Henn-Schmölders, Claudia. "Ars conversationis. Zur Geschichte des sprachlichen Umgangs." *Arcadia* 10 (1975): 16–33.

Hildebrand, Wolfgang. *Ein new außerlesen Planeten-Buch* [. . .]. Erfurt: Schmuck, 1613.

Johannes ab Indagine. *Deß Hochgelehrten Astronomi Johannes Indagine Astrologia naturalis/* [. . .] *anjetzo aber In sechs Bücher vnd gewisse Capitel abgetheilt/ vnd mit ihren Summarien in gut verständig Teutsch vbergesetzt/* [. . .] *Durch Johann Friderich Halbmayen.* Straßburg: Simon Paulli, 1664.

Knopf, Jan. *Die deutsche Kalendergeschichte. Ein Arbeitsbuch.* Frankfurt / Main: Suhrkamp, 1983.

Lycosthenes, Conrad Wolfhardt. *Prodigiorum ac ostentorum Chronicum* [. . .]. Basel 1557. German translation by Johann Herold: *Wunderwerck Oder Gottes vnergründliches Vorbilden* [. . .]. Basel: Petri, 1557.

Matthäus, Klaus. "Zur Geschichte des Nürnberger Kalenderwesens. Die Entwicklung der in Nürnberg gedruckten Jahreskalender in Buchform." *Archiv für Geschichte des Buchwesens* 9 (1969). Col. 965–1396.

Mexía, Petrus. *Sylva variarum lectionum. Das ist Historischer Geschicht — Natur — und Wunder-Wald* [. . .]. Trans. Johann Andreas Mathe. Three vols. Nuremberg: Endter, 1669.

Michel, Paul und Rosmarie Zeller: "'. . . auß andern Büchern extrahirt.' Grimmelshausens Schwankvorlagen im *Simplicissimus*." In: *Wahrheit und Wort. Festschrift für Rolf Tarot zum 65. Geburtstag.* Ed. Beatrice Wehrli and Gabriela Scherer. Bern: Lang, 1996. 307–23.

Michelsen, Peter. "Der Wahn vergnügt. Grimmelshausen als Kalendermacher." *Simpliciana* 13 (1991): 443–76.

Pascher, Peter Hans. *Praktiken des 15. und 16. Jahrhunderts.* Klagenfurt: Armarium, 1980. (= Armarium 11)

Petrat, Gerhardt. "Der Kalender im Hause der Illiteraten und Analphabeten: seine Inanspruchnahme als Lebenshilfe vor Beginn der Aufklärung." In: *Literatur und Volk im 17. Jahrhundert. Probleme populärer Kultur in Deutschland.* Ed. Wolfgang Brückner, Peter Blickle and Dieter Breuer. Wiesbaden: Harrassowitz, 1985. 701–25. (= Wolfenbütteler Arbeiten zur Barockforschung 13)

Rist, Johann. *Sämtliche Werke.* Unter Mitwirkung von Helga Mannack und Klaus Reichelt ed. Eberhard Mannack. Vol. 5: *Epische Dichtungen. Die AllerEdelster Tohrheit Der gantzen Welt/ Vermittelst eines anmuhtigen und erbaulichen Gespräches/ welches ist diser Ahrt das Dritte/ und zwahr eine Märtzens/ Unterredung/ Beschrieben und fürgestellet von Dem Rüstigen.* Berlin: de Gruyte,r 1974.

Rohner, Ludwig. *Kalendergeschichte und Kalender.* Wiesbaden: Athenaion, 1978.

Schechner Genuth, Sara. *Comets, Popular Culture, and the Birth of Modern Cosmology.* Princeton NJ: Princeton UP, 1997.

Scholte, Jan Hendrik. *Zonagri Discurs Von Waarsagern. Ein Beitrag zu unserer Kenntnis von Grimmelshausens Arbeitsweise in seinem* Ewigwährenden Calender *mit besonderer Berücksichtigung des Eingangs des* Abentheuerlichen Simplicissimus. Amsterdam Müller, 1921. (=Verhandelingen der Koninklijke Nederlandse Akademie van Wetenschappen, Afd. Letterkunde NS 22, 3)

Sodmann, Timothy. "Die Kalenderschriften Grimmelshausens." In: *Simplicius Simplicissimus. Grimmelshausen und seine Zeit.* Ed. Peter Berghaus and Günther Weydt. Münster: Landschaftsverband Westphalen-Lippe, 1976. 129–39.

Van Ingen, Ferdinand. "Die "Ars prognostica" im *Ewig-währenden Calender* und im *Simplicissimus Teutsch.*" *Simpliciana* 16 (1994): 137–49.

Weydt, Günther. *Nachahmung und Schöpfung im Barock. Studien um Grimmelshausen.* Bern: Francke, 1968.

Wimmer, Ruprecht. "Chaos — Mischmasch — Labyrinth. Zur Poetik des *ewigwährenden Kalenders.*" *Simpliciana* 15 (1993): 241–51.

Zeller, Rosmarie. 1994 "Die "ordentliche Unordnung" als poetologisches Prinzip in Grimmelshausens *Ewig-währendem Calender.*" *Simpliciana* 16 (1994): 117–36.

———. 1999 "Wunderbares, Ingeniöses und Historien. Zu Pedro Mexías *Geschicht — Natur und Wunderwald.*" *Simpliciana* 20 (1999): 67–92.

Ziegesar, Hertha von. "Grimmelshausen als Kalenderschriftsteller und die Felßeckerschen Verlagsunternehmungen." *Euphorion.* Ergänzungsheft 17 (1924): 50–79.

ewigwehrender Calender. 5

Simplicissimi Discurs mit Zonagrio / die Calender-Macherey und was deme anhängig / betreffent.	Simplicissimi Discurs mit Joanne Indagine / darinnen er unterrichtet wird / wie vermittelst der Astrologia Naturali er einem jeden Menschen ohne Kopfbrechung die Natiwität stellen könne.	Zonagri Discurs von Waarsagern ins gemein / als Propheten / Sibyllen / Vatibus, Augutibus, Aruspicibus, und anderem dergleichen / davauf etwan die Alte viel gehalten.
Der erste Tag.	**Der erste Tag.**	**Der vierdte Tag.**
Die vierdte Materia.	*Die fünffte Materia.*	*Die sechste Materia.*
Simplicissimus.	**Simplicissimus.**	**Simplicissimus.**

Col. 1 — Simplicissimus.

Hochgeehrter Herr Zonagri / seine berühmte Weltbekandte Weisheit und Doctrinität in allen Dingen / neben dessen leutseligen und bereitfertigen Freywilligkeit solche habende hohe Talenta andern / ja auch den Geringsten mitzutheilen und zu communiciren / erkühnen mich denselben mit einer einfältigen Erzehlung und daranhangenden Frag zu beschwehre; um abermal etwas aus dem reichen Brunnen seiner Wissenschafften zu schöpffen.

Zonagrius. Mein Simplici, du wirst hierzu die Kühnheit der dreyen Helden Davids / die ihrem König zu Bethlehem mitten aus der Feinde Gewalt Wasser holeten / nicht bedörffea ; lasse nur deinen bekandten Fürwiz ohngescheut heraus ; zu sehen ob dir vielleicht das jenige so du in mir zu seyn vermeinest / aus deinem jetzigen Traum auch helffen möge? Worzu ich desto fertiger bin / weil deine Wurmbrändeische Einfäll und seltsame Fragen so artlich zu fallen pflegen / daß mich deren Erzählung offt mehrers delectirt / als dern Beantwort: und Erleuterung bemühet.

Simplicissimus. Die Wenigkeit meiner Person lässt sich von ihm nach seinem alten Gebrauch gern schärffen/weil auch seine Humanität und löbl. Gewonheit meiner Einfalt unterschiedliche Begierden etwas zu wissen ; zugleich Erleuterung und Concentament zu geben nicht unterlassen kan ; die Ursach der Erregung meiner jetzigen Grillen / die mich ansporen dem Herrn jetzmals molest zu seyn/ seynd unterschiedliche Jahr-Bücher samt den jenigen Leuten deren jeder eins oder auch wol mehr kauffen wolte / welche ich dieser Tagen in- und bey einem Buchladen fande; diese rieffen / langt mir her den

Col. 2 — Simplicissimus.

Bonus dies mein Herr Indagine / wohin beliebt ihm so frühe zu spazieren?

Indagines. Deo gratias mein lieber Simplici, woher wehet dich der Wind? Ich vermeine ich habe dich in 100. Jahren nicht gesehen ; glaube auch / ich hätte dich noch nicht zu sehen bekommen/wann du heint Nacht nicht irgents in einem Winckel gestecket: und dein Publichafft aufgewartet hättest / und mir also unversehens aufgestoßen wärest ; dann du sihest so trüb drein/daß ich unschwer aus deinen Augen abnehmen kan / daß du die verwicheneNacht wider die Anforderung deiner Natur / mehr gewacht als geschlaffen habest.

Simplicissimus. Mein Herr verzeihe mir wann ich eins gestehe und das ander läugne / ich hab zwar wenig geschlaffen / darumb aber doch nicht die Zeit so ich mit Wachen zugebracht / der Veneri: Sondern vielmehr der Minervæ gewidmet;

Indagines. Ey potz Hertz! das wäre eins / wann du dich abermal veränderst / und in so kurtzer Zeit vom Marte zur Venere, und wider so bald von denselben zu der Pallade dich geselletest ; aber in Ernst Simplici, wo hast du die heintig Nacht passirt / daß du so schläfferig drein sihest?

Simplicissimus. Gewißlich Herr/ sonst nirgends als auf meiner gewöhnlichen Liegerstatt; daß ich aber wie sonsten meinen gewöhnlichen Schlaff nicht gehabt / ist die einige Ursach / daß ich dieser Tagen mit Herrn Zonagrio nicht allein von der Calender-Macherey oder Calender-Schreiberey und was zum Prognostic. und Nativität-stellen auch den Praticquen und Wetters-Warsagungen gehörig ; Sondern auch so gar von der Astro-

Col. 3 — Simplicissimus.

Sintemal die Practickmacherey nur zu dem End angesehen / künfftigs warzusagen/ solches aber gleichwol zum öfftern gar ungewiß/ so bitte ich mein hochgeehrter Herr wolle belieben/ was er dann von den übrigen Warsagern halte/ ohnschwer zu communiciren.

Zonagrius.

Unter den Alten hat man etliche so grobe und unverständige Leute gefunden / welche sich beydes mit Worten und Schrifften so halsstarrig als thorechtig unterstanden zuverneinen / das doch so gewiß und klar ist / als die liebe Sonn am hellen Mittag ; welches dann ist gewesen die Gewißheit des Warsagens / so ins gemein von Xenophonto Colophonio und Epicuro / welcher doch sonsten nicht so gar uneben davon stamlet / in seinem Tractatu de natura Deorum, öffentlich ist verneinet worden ; desgleichen auch von Panetio / welcher des Possidonii Lehrmeister gewesen / geschehen ; und von Antipatro seinem Discipulo / welcher / ob er sich gleich nicht zu gar widersetzet / dannoch genugsamb zuverstehen giebt / das er sehr daran zweiffle.

Daß aber die Seele (wie St. Augustinus lib. de Confessionibus) eine Krafft habe warzusagen / oder zuvor zu verkündigen / es geschehe gleich solches durch die Gemeinschafft der Idearum nach Platonis Meinung / oder durch eine Einbildung und impression der Causarum superiorum wie Aristoteles will/ und daß man auf vielerhand Weisen erfahre / daß sie warhafftig zuvor mercke/ was da geschehen soll ; solches will ich dir nach Länge darthun und erzeblen.

Erstlich aber halten wir es für gewiß/ daß ins gemein der Propheten Warsagungen bey jederman ausser allem Streit und

A iij

Sample page (5) of the Ewigwährender Calender.
Reprinted with permission of the Herzog August Bibliothek,
Wolfenbüttel.

122   Deß Abenteurlichen Simpliciſſimi

Dugenas / Blaſius und Cantianus.
Dioſchorus und Marinus mart.
Helprandus Martyrer.
Nichrand⁹ uñ Martian⁹ mart.
Gudolph⁹ Biſch. zu Bituxica.
Hunrius Biſch. zu Emilia.
Veredemius Biſch. zu Avinió.

A Der 18. Brachmonath.

Eliſabeth Königin / Abbtiſſin im Cloſter Schoraw Tryer Biſtumbs.
Marina Jungf. zu Alexandria.
Syriacus Mart zu Maleta.
Paula Jungf. Märt. zu Male.
Amädus Biſch. zu Burdegalia.
Fortunatus der Landſchafft Senonico Biſchoff.
Colomannus Abbt in Irzland.
Kunera eine auß den 11000. Jungfrawen Martyrin.

B Der 19. Brachmonath.

GErvaſius und Prothaſius Gebrüder Zwilling Märt.
Urſicinus Martyrer.
Michelina Jungf.
Juliana Serviter Ordens.
Bonifacius Romualdi Jünger / Martyrer.
Johannes und Benedictus Camalduenſer Ordens / Mart.
Innocentius der Cenomaner Biſchoff.
Deodatus Niverlienſer Biſch.

C Der 20. Brachmonath.

MArinus Biſchoff zu Tryer Martyrer.
Sylverius Pabſt.
Latuinus Biſchoff.

Schwartze oder gelbe Zähn damit / ſo werden ſie weiß.

Wartzen an Händen zu vertreiben.

JEr kratz die Wartzen daß ſie bluten / wäſche ſie und ſchmiere ſie mit Haſen - Schweiß daß continuir biß ſie hinfallen; daß Blut vom Haſen Hertz macht ein lauter Angeſicht.

XIV. Calend. Julij.

Harnſtein zu vertreiben.

NJm guten Eſſig in ein Glaß leg Tauben Miſt darein / laß ein gantze Woche zugedeckt ſtehen / ſolchen Eſſig trincke nach und nach / wiltu es zuvor probiren / ſo leg ein Stein in den Eſſig / er zerbricht in dreyen Tagen.

Lutum.

HAmmerſchlag / venedisch Glaß / Beinäsche / Schleiffthon / jedes gleich viel / damit lutire die Schmeltztigel / es hält ſo feſt / daß es auch die Spiritus behält.

XIII. Calend. Julij.

JM Anno 278. vor Chriſti Geburth iſt Benner ein teutſcher Obriſter in Græciam gefallen / da er den Berg Parnaſſum ſtürmen und den Tempel Apollinis plündern wollen / da kam ein ſolcher grauſamer Erdbiebem daß ein ſtück vom Berg in ſeinen Hauffen gefallen / der viel umbbracht / gleich darauff folgt ein ſchröcklich Ungewitter von Hagel Platzregen / Plitz und Donner daß der meiſte Theil vom Hauffen umbkahm der Oberſt ward ſelbſt wund / daß ſchmertzte ihn ſo ſehr daß er ſich ſelbſt erſtach.

XII. Calend. Junij.

JM dieſem Tag hat Chriſtus der HErr 4000. Menſchen geſpeiſet und geſättiget / Matth. 15. Marci 17.
Als Dion Anno 357. eine Armee in

ſchäfften ſo hurtigen Beſcheid zugeben weiß. :

IX.

Das Pfaffenbiſſel.

ER nahme einsmahls im Läger vor Magdenburg einem Officier, als er in ſeinem Kalbs - Kleyd vorm Tiſch uffwartet / und ſich zugleich vor ein kurtzweiligen Rath gebrauchen lieſſe / ein gutes Stück vom Teller und ſagte / daß iſt ein delicat Pfaffenbiſſel / und mit ſolchen Worten verſchlang ers: Der Officier ſagte ja daß wars / es iſt aber ſchad daß es in einen Narren kommen ſoll: daß gedachte ich auch / antwortet Simpliciſſimus dann eben darumb nahm ichs / damits dem Herren nicht zu theil würde.

X.

Die Cupplerin.

ALs ſich ein ehrlicher Mann verwundert / daß ſich Simpliciſſimus an eine Bawren Dirne verheyrathet hatte / da er doch wohl etwas beſſers hätte kriegen mögen / ihn auch im Saurbrunnen fragte / wie er an diß Menſch kommen wäre / antwortet er / durch die Torheit.

XI.

Seine Magd.

ALs er dieſe / deren er / wie in ſeiner Lebens - Beſchreibung zu ſehen / ein Jungs angeheckt nach der Kindsbeth abſchaffte / und ſie ſich darüber beſchwerte / ſagte er zu ihr / liebs Menſch / der Friedensſchluß bringts mit ſich

---

Sample page (122) from Ewigwährender Calender.
From the Faber du Faur Collection, Beinecke Library, Yale.

dorus Siculus lib. 3. schreibt die für-
nehmbste Wissenschafft und Erfah-
rung dieser Kunst den Babyloniern
und Galdeern zu/ desgleichen thut
auch Philo Hebræus in seinem Buch
de Transmigratione Abrahami, dem
sey nun wie ihm wolle/ so erscheinet
die Würde dieser Kunst daraus/ daß
soviel vortreffliche Leuthe sie geliebt/
und mit ihren vielfältigen Schrifften illustrirt haben: Als unter dem
alten Anaximander Milesius so Ta-
letis Discipulus gewesen; und zu erst
die Sphæram gemacht darinn er die
Conversiones und Wendungen der
Sonnen beneben den Æquinoctijs
gezeiget; Eudoxus Gnydius, ein sehr
berühmter Astrologus so diese Wissenschafft mit künstlichen Versen beschrieben: Conon Ægyptius welcher
eben schöner und nutzlicher Volumi-
na hiervon geschrieben und hinder-
lassen/ dahero er auch von Virgilio
in seinen Bucolicis gerühmet wird/
da er von ihme sagt:

*In medio duo Signa: Conon (& quis
fuit alter)
Descripsit radio totum qui gentibus
orbem.*

Das ist:

Mitten stehen zwey Brüst-Bilder
drauff/ daß ein Conon ist der deß him-
mels Lauff
Beschrieben/ wie er ihm bekandt/
und kundt gethan im gantzen Land.

Julius Higinius so dem Quintilia-
no wohl bekandt gewesen/ und sechs
Bücher geschrieben von den himmlischen Zeichen. Hiparchus Nicæus
welches de Stellis fixis & motu lunæ,
von den ohnbeweglichen Sternen
und Bewegung deß Mons wiederPla-
tonem geschrieben/ und nach Plinij
vorgeben die erste Mathematica In-
strumenta erfunden hat. Manetus
Ægyptius, welcher wie Cælius erzeh-
let/ die Würckung der Stern mit
Versen beschrieb es/ vor welchem aber
und vor allen andern C Manilius An-
tiochenus lateinische Poëmata von
der Astrologia geschrieben; Publius
Nigidius Figulus ein erfahrner Astro-
lorus

ihren Lauff in einem Jahr/ macht
365. Tag/ in jedem Zeichen bleibt sie
30. Tag/ 10. Stund/ und so gradirt
sie ihren Circul in 29. Jahren/ wie
die Sonn den gantzen Tag über dem
Erdreich scheinet/ also scheinet sie
auch die gantze Nacht under der Er-
den/ bey unsern Antipodibus: der
Widder ist ihre Erhöbung/ darinn
sie grosse Gewalt hat/ und noch
grösser im Löwen/ der ist ihr Hauß/
sie hat kein Gewalt im Wasserman/
vielweniger in der Waag/ ist ihr Fall/
sie operirt in dem Menschen eine tem-
perirte Wärme und Tröckne/ ist
Männlicher Art/ dem Tag zugethan/
ist nit zu warm/ auch nit zu trucken
in guten Aspecibus/ bey den andern
Planeten ist sie auch gut/ hergegen
auch schädlich in bösen Aspecten
der andern Planeten/ ist sonderlich
glückselig wann sie wohl stehet im
sechsten Hause; Die Menschen so
under ihr geboren/ seynd gelber Far-
ben/ krauß Haars/ auch Kahlköpf-
sigt/ schöner Farb/ starck/ fromm/
herrlich/ behertzt/ tieffsinnig/ rühig/
sie verlehpet ihnen langes Leben/ ein
frischen gesunden Leib/ guten Verstand herrliche und Königliche Digni-
teten/ mehr als die andere Planeten
all: sie ist ein Herr über alle gewalti-
ge Potentaten/ als Käyser/ König/
Fürsten/ Graven/ und andere hohe
Obrigkeiten der Länder und Stätte/
auch alle fürnehme/ fürsichtiger/ lieb-
reicher/ ehrgeitziger/ hoffärtiger/ stol-
tzer/ schöner/ hochmütiger/ ver-
schmitzter Leuth/ und aller deren die
in einem grossem Ansehen seyn/ oder
seyn wollen/ ja deren die zu herrschen
Wollüsten unnd Ergetzungen: als
Schiessen/ Jagen/ etc. einen Lusth-
ben: mit diesen ists glücklich umbzu-
gehen wann sichs im Calender also
besindet/ ∆ ☉/ ⚹ ☉/ alsdann
seyn sie wanns also stehet/ ⚹ ☉/
□ ☉/ ☍ ☉/ die Sonn herrschet auch
selbsten über die Königreich/ gibt
Herrschafften/ Herrhafftigkeit
Stärck/ Ehr/ und ander dergleichen
Sachen; An Menschlichen Leib

treibet Abraham Sawr in seinem
Theatro Urbium diese Wort. Es
ist sich hoch zuverwundern/ daß Rodericus Toletanus Archiepiscopus
schreibet von einem Schlosse so vor
Zeiten zu Toler gewesen ist: Im Jahr
unsers HErrn 700, da Rodericus der
letzte König der Gothen regierte/ war
zu Toleto ein Palast/ von vieler Königen Zeiten hero immer zugeschlos-
sen/ und mit vielen eysenen Gittern
und Schlössern verriegelt und be-
wahrt: diß hat der König Rodericus
wider aller Spannier Willen eröff-
net/ damit er einmahl wisse was darinn wäre/ dann er hoffte einen ge-
waltigen Schatz daselbst zubekom-
men; aber er hat allein einen ver-
schloßnen Kasten/ und in demselben
ein gemahltes Tuch gefunden/ darauff Moren und Arabische Männer
mit ihrer Kriegs-Rüstung gewaff-
net/ entworffen waren/ sambt einer
lateinischen Schrifft diß Innhalts:
Wann dieser Pallast eröffnet und die
Rigel desselben zerbrochen werden/ so
soll man vor gewiß darvor halten/
das diß Volck so allhier abgemahlt/
Hispania überziehen und einnehmen
werde. Der König gantz bestürtzt
und verzagt/ liesse zwar den Pallast
zumauren/ aber im 3. Jahr Christi
714. andere setzen 717. haben die Sa-
racener nach gehaltener Schlacht
welche acht Tag ohn unterlaß ge-
wehret/ den König Rodericum umb-
gebracht/ seinen Adel vertilget/ das
Land mit gewalt eingenommen/ und
also diese Prophezeyhung erfüllt/ haben auch die Statt Toler die sie Anno 715. auff den Palmtag mit hilff
der Juden einbekommen biß Anno
1093. besessen/ in welchem Jahr sie
wider von Alphonso dem Vierdten
erobert worden.

**Grosse Erdbieben so sich vor
Enthörung der Juden und
Käyser Trasano zugetra-
gen.**

Anno Christi 107. wurden in Asia
vier Stätt: als Elea, Mirrhina,
Picane und Cime: wie auch Opun-

Ewigwährender Calender. 221

| E Der 16. Wintermonat. | XVI. Calend. Decembris. |

E Der 16. Wintermonat.

Othmar Abt in Teutschland.
Eucherius Bischoff zu Lion/sampt dessen Gemahl Galla/ und ihren Töchtern Consortia und Tullia.
Secundian9/Aurelianus und Marcell9/Märt.
Martinus ein Knab/Märtyrer zu Rom.
Secundanus und Marcellus/Beichtiger.
Benedicta Abtissin.
Margaretha Königin in Schottland.

F Der 17. Wintermonat.

Hugo Bischoff in Engelland.
Dionysius Bischoff zu Alexandria.
Anianus Bischoff zu Aurelia.
Felix Pabst und Märtyrer.
Gregorius Bischoff zu Turon.
Mamatus Bischoff zu Wien.
Amon zu Nicomedia Märtyrer.
Gregorius Thaumaturgus/ Bischoff zu Neo-Cæsarea

G Der 18. Wintermonat.

Odo Cluniacenser Abt.
Roman9 und Barulus/Märt. zu Antiochia.
Oriculus und seine Gesellen/Märtyrer.
Gelasius der Erste Pabst.
Mombolus Abt.
Tecla Jungfrau zu Corduba/Märtyrin.
Eusebia Jungfrau zu Rom/Märtyrin.
Electa Jungfrau und Märtyrin.
Maximus Bischoff zu Mäyntz.

A Der 19. Wintermonat.

Elisabeth Landgräfin zu Hessen.
Maximus Priester/Märtyrer zu Rom.
Severinus/Exuperius und Felicianus/Märtyrer zu Wien.
Faustus Diacon/Märtyrer zu Rom
Pontianus Pabst und Märtyrer/ so von etlichen auff folgenden Tag gesetzt wird.
Mechtildis von Honckeborn/ S. Gertrudis Schwester.

B Der

XVI. Calend. Decembris.

Vor Christi Geburt 346. hat sich der Zweykampff zwischen einem Gallier und Marco Valerio einem Römer zugetragen/in welchem mit Hülff eines Raben der Römer oblag/und den Namen Corvinus erwarb.

Krebs zu fahen.

Nim Frösch aus einem Weiher/ (und keine/die auff dem Land hoppen) so viel du wilt/ schind sie/ lege sie in Brantewein/ wan sie zuvor ein wenig gebraten seyn/ bind sie in ein Reuse oder Garn/ oder auch wol nur in eine Nebwelle/versenck/so kriechen die Krebs bald daran/alßdann zeuchs geschwind herauff.

XV. Calendas Decembris.

Glaß weich zu machen.

Nim Liebstöckel-Wasser und Sal gemmæ. siede das Glaß darinn/so wird es so weich/daß du es wie ein Tuch zusammen legen/unzerbrochen über Land führen und hernach wieder auffthun kanst/ daraus zu trincken. Wie man es aber wieder hart machen soll/ da laß ich dich sür sorgen. Den Safft aus Centaureum gedruckt/ glühend Kupffer darinn abgeleschet/machts so weich als Bley.

XIV. Calend. Decembris.

Heut haben zu Rom bey den Kauffleuten die Mercurialia angefangen/ und 3. Tage gewähret/ an welchen sie Mercurio opfferten.

Metall/ daß es wohl fliesse.

Wann das Metall aus dem Tiegel gegossen soll werden/ so thu den vierten Theil so viel Glaßgall darein/ das macht/ daß es schön glatt fällt / ohne Blasen oder Auffwerffung deren Löcherlein/ wie man bey dem Bley siehet.

XIII. Calend. Decembris.

Dieser Tag war zu Rom der Göttin Cybele/ aller Göttin Mutter/zugeeignet.
Anno Christi 50. ist der Vogel Phönix in Egypten gesehen worden. Es wurde gemeiniglich außgelegt/ daß solches den Tod des Käysers Tiberii bedeutet habe/der das folgende Jahr drauff gieng.

Vor die kalte Pisse.

Welchen dieser schmertzliche Zustand ankömpt/ der schmier alßbald den Nabel mit ein wenig Unschlit/ es höret gleich auff.

Ee ij   XII.

Sample page (221) from Ewigwährender Calender.
From the Faber du Faur Collection, Beinecke Library, Yale.

Folding copperplate frontispiece from Proximus und Lympida (1672).
Reprinted with permission of the Herzog August Bibliothek, Wolfenbüttel.

Grimmelshausen's Non-Simplician Novels

Andreas Solbach

GRIMMELSHAUSEN RESEARCHERS HAVE always made a distinction between the ten-book cycle of the *Simplicissimus Teutsch* and related material on the one hand, and the "non-Simplician" works on the other. There are in fact good reasons for such categorization. The novels in question, *Histori vom Keuschen Joseph* (1666), *Musai Lebens-Lauff* (1670), *Dietwalt und Amelinde* (1670) and *Proximus und Lympida* (1672), are quite different when compared to *Simplicissimus Teutsch* (1668–69). Still, they show some common features that indicate it may be sensible to group the first four mentioned novels together.

However, as much as it has been accepted that they are not Simplician, a common definition and denomination has been lacking. They have been labeled "galant," "höfisch," "höfisch-historisch," and, *faute de mieux*, "non-Simplician." Grimmelshausen's latest editor, Dieter Breuer, labels them "Legendenromane" und "Historische Romane" on the back of volume 2 of his edition, but does not categorize them within the text, and in his recent *Grimmelshausen-Handbuch* (1999) he simply calls them "Historische Romane." Whereas such a definition seems too wide, the other favorite description "Legendenromane" clearly is too narrow and misses the mark.

The whole question, however, seems academic in view of the persistent neglect that these works have experienced. Interpreters have shunned them, and when they were made the main focus of a monograph or an article, philological ground-work was most often the topic: influences, sources, reception, but hardly much by way of analysis or interpretation. The moralistic tone together with long passages of circumstantial narrative and a pronounced religious and didactic intention did not enhance the attraction toward this group of novels which was rigidly set apart from the Simplicissimus cycle as if two different authors had been at work. This procedure aggravated the problem considerably since it obscured and eventually destroyed important linkages between all parts of Grimmelshausen's oeuvre.

The "non-Simplician" writings, and I will include two supplementary tracts, *Satyrischer Pilgram* (1666–1667) and *Ratio Status* (1670), do not form a separate group within the works of Grimmelshausen. The *Keuscher Joseph* and *Satyrischer Pilgram* precede *Simplicissimus,* and the other non-Simplician novels are parallel to the Simplicissimus-cycle. Unless we want to assume that the author had a schizophrenic mind and two entirely distinct sets of literary instruments and intentions, we have to accept that the tedious *Dietwalt* peacefully coexists with the adventurous *Springinsfeld* and the highbrow, moralistic *Amelinde* with a racy *Courasche*. They all belong in one coherent and homogenous intellectual cosmos that is governed by one unified intention: to teach the ignorant by unfolding the eternal truths of Christian beliefs.

It has been argued that, in his *Simplicissimus Teutsch,* Grimmelshausen employed the established device of *docere et delectare,* of teaching and entertaining, visualized in the picture of the "sugared pill" containing the bitter truths of moral and religious instruction. The baroque author studiously tries avoiding what he calls the "theological style," and he attempts instruction and correction by satirical treatment. It seems, however, that even contemporary readers found a way to delight in the vivacity and persuasive entertainment of the story without digesting the bitter pill of pedagogic instruction. As soon as Grimmelshausen realized his narrative technique was not foolproof, he added the *Continuatio* to the first five books of *Simplicissimus,* a sometimes heavy-handed allegory to pin down the intended meaning of the preceding adventure-story.

Against this background it seems fruitful to assume that the "non-Simplician" novels present alternate ways of narrative instruction and that they are variations of the "theological style" that the author so carefully avoids elsewhere. In what follows, I will first treat *Satyrischer Pilgram* and *Ratio Status* as tracts that are laying the foundation for the novelistic work and in particular for the "non-Simplician" fiction before I continue with analyses of *Keuscher Joseph, Dietwalt und Amelinde* and *Proximus und Lympida*. Also, I will pay special attention to the edifying character of these novels that seem to be directed rather to the Christian believer who is disoriented and whose firmness is shaken than to the neglectful sinner who is slipping further and further into *superbia* and her dependent vices, thereby endangering both soul and eternal life. Consequently, the picaresque novel in the fashion that Grimmelshausen preferred could be regarded as "wake-up calls" of the admonitory kind whereas those using the "theological style" would be understood as edifying works, *Erbauungsromane*. As far as we know, *Satyrischer Pilgram* and *Keuscher Joseph* (both 1666) are Grimmelshausen's first publications until the first five books of *Simplicissimus Teutsch* followed two years later. The biblical history of virtuous Joseph has stimulated among the three novels in question about as much interest as the rest of them put together. This strong interest is no doubt due to the fact that this well-known topic has been treated by one of Grimmelshausen's famous contemporary competitors, Philipp von Zesen (1619–1689) in his *Assenat,* and more prominently, in modern times, by Thomas Mann (1875–1955) in *Joseph und seine Brüder* (1933–1943). Biblical histories of all sorts have enjoyed great popularity over hundreds of years, and it certainly helped that readers have found the *Keuscher Joseph* the most readable of the "non-Simplician" works. By comparison, *Satyrischer Pilgram* has not attracted much attention at all, no doubt owing to its particular tripartite structure that lists the pros and cons of a list of two times ten items each time followed by a "Nachklang," as summary judgment on things like God, mankind, farmers, money, dancing, women, poetry, priests, love and war among others. Many sources have been claimed for the tract but none is more important than the *Piazza Universale* (German version 1619, original 1586) of Tomaso Garzoni (1549?-1589), since Garzoni provides Grimmelshausen with his topics and also suggests the tripartite structure. To be sure, there are many other examples of dialogic deliberation of particular problems or questions, but in *Satyrischer Pilgram* something very particular shapes and moulds the literary from. Although it has been suggested that it is an example of inductive rhetorical reasoning allowing the readers to find their own answers as a result of counterbalancing arguments, close reading shows that there cannot be much doubt as to the intended meaning. The author does not argue both sides in good faith but he exhibits more or less clearly his own preferences, often long before the authorial summary at the end.

The major underlying structure thus seems to be a treatment of adiaphora, things that are neither good nor bad in themselves. With a few exceptions (for example, God) this can be said about all the topics in *Satyrischer Pilgram.* Grimmelshausen's standard procedure does not aim at establishing a dialectic equilibrium of arguments but at weighing the items under consideration in view of their active use. Thus the reader is offered affirmative and negative information concerning a certain topic such as "war," which has in reality already been evaluated and manipulated by the author. The affirmative voice claims war's value by citing a list of classical sources that maintain its necessity, whereas the negative voice speaks from the experience of the recent "German War" quoting all the losses and atrocities of war. The author explicitly criticizes those who yearn for war without having experienced it actively. The critical statement is obviously informed by the writer's own existence as a soldier and can be taken as the correct opinion that he intends to present to the reader; consequently, the "Nachklang" is often nothing more than an afterthought, as it is in this instance.

Under this appearance of providing critical information on a number of crucial items, a pocket dictionary based on religious commentary so to speak, there exists a deeper level of meaning, reflecting on the form and the method of the text itself. So far, interpreters of *Satyrischer Pilgram* have noted influences from rhetorical argumentation, a *syllogismus practicus,* or an even more modern skepticism that presents itself as dialectic. However, it has not been noticed that the tripartite structure opposes the two main epideictic modes, praise and punishment, in order to arrive at a judgment. The main notion, however, does not concern the argument but the discipline itself, rhetoric. Grimmelshausen takes his title from a scene in which a pilgrim meets a satyr; he breathes on his cold hands to warm them up and shortly thereafter blows on his hot soup to cool it down. The pilgrim's innocent use of the same thing for opposite purposes is nothing less than an allegory of rhetoric itself: in the words of the greatest rhetorician of ancient Greece, Gorgias, rhetoric has the power to turn black into white and vice versa. It is exactly this metaphor that the sub-title of the tract quotes: "Das ist: Kalt und Warm/ Weiß und Schwartz/ Lob und Schand/ über guths und böß/ Tugend und Laster/ auch Nutz und Schad vieler Ständt und Ding der Sichtbarn und Unsichtbarn der Zeitlichen und Ewigen Welt" (SP 3). The orator uses rhetoric for all purposes regardless of their intrinsic value; praise and criticism (Lob und Schand) can be applied to literally everything, leaving the audience disoriented and in doubt. It is this dubious epistemological status of the discipline that has been the focus of criticism ever since Plato's *Gorgias,* and it is exactly this criticism that Grimmelshausen cites in his tripartite foreword, beginning with a critical statement by Momus. Momus maintains that the following work is a "nichtiges Gewesch und lehres Wortgeplerr: ohne Lust/ Nutz/ Lehr und Frucht [. . .]. [U]nd findet sich im End/ daß man an statt verhofften Nutzens/ Lehr und Ergetzung nichts anders/ als eine spate Reu über die verlohrne Zeit erobert/ welche man in lesung dieser Narredey, unnütz verlohren und zugebracht" (SP 5–6). Language cannot help but be ambiguous and open to rhetorical manipulation, and Momus's attack on the author and his work, itself full of rhetorical devices, results in the virtual denial of the possibility of sincere communication. Here we see, already in the seventeenth century, the rather modern insight that literature is always rhetorically determined.

This relativism, tantamount to pre-modern nihilism, receives a strongly worded counterattack by the author who calls the mocking and skeptic satyr Momus a beast (Bestia) and associates him with the devil. Grimmelshausen needs to refute this relativism and to establish nothing less than a convincing argument to make sincere communication possible. Thus he embraces rhetoric claiming that there is a way out of epistemological ambiguity. First, however, he states his motive for writing, excluding interest-related purposes: he writes for his peers ("meinesgleichen einfältige Leut" 9) who are keen on learning something, but instead of resigning in the face of rhetorical relativism, he maintains: "Ich schreibe von schwartz und weiß dieweil eben so nöthig ist/ die tödtliche Würckung des Giffts: Als die heilsame Tugenden des Bezoars zuwissen/ umb mich vor des einen Schädlichkeit zu hüten/ und des andern Kräffte zugebrauchen; wer aber etwas weiß/ sols seinem Nebenmenschen communiciren" (SP 11). He wants to share his experiences with others in order to help them distinguish the good from the bad. He suggests that rhetoric does in fact provide a method of arriving at a fairly safe evaluation through its epideictic genre of praise and criticism, provided, however, that everything is seen from an empirical point of view. Excepting obvious vices and virtues, he regards all his topics not theoretically but in their practical use, and the measure of all things is, of course, a religious standard:

> In meinem Buch aber/ dieweil ich darinnen zuvernehmen zu geben schuldig wer/ was wir Menschen gegen Gott und umb seinet willen thun solten/ und lassen könten; Wie und warumb nehmlich wir Ihme dienen: Ihme dancken: Ihn loben: preisen: ehren/ und uns vorsichtiglich hüten und befleißigen solten/ daß wir nichts wider seinen allerheiligsten Willen vollbrächten oder im geringsten seine Göttliche Mayestät erörtern und beleidigen möchten. (SP 17)

We will see that the author carefully contrasts examples of good and bad use of various items in his edifying novels so that the reader is able to distinguish between acceptable and unacceptable behavior. Again, in novels such as *Keuscher Joseph,* the narrator concentrates on concepts that reflect the poetological maxims of the text, like "rhetoric." However, in his novels, he also uses concepts that are dealt with in an expository way, like "beauty." In this way, he transforms them into highly significant elements of the plot. In all cases, however, he follows the procedure set up in *Satyrischer Pilgram,* providing for the "black and white" of each item.

In his treatment of mankind in the third discourse, ["Vom Menschen"] Grimmelshausen has the affirmative voice claim God's love for the human race and its close relationship to its divine creator. The critical voice, however, points out the miserable shortcomings of human beings and their sorry state in view of their fleeting chances of redemption. The conclusion within the critical statement is foreseeable: man is the Supreme Being here in the universe as long as he obeys God's laws and strives for God's grace. Consequently Grimmelshausen's tract aims at those who are not fully cognizant of this condition since he is convinced that whoever really knows God ("Gott recht erkennet" 33) must love Him and wish to live according to His commands. Being able to love God in this way resembles eternal bliss already in this world. The author knows this and thus feels obliged to communicate it to his ignorant neighbors in his book:

> [M]ir ist genug wann der verkehrte Mensch hierin so viel findet/ das Ihn bewege in sich selbst zu gehen/ und zu seinem vergänglichen Madensack zu sprechen/ da: Vogel friß oder stirb; Wilstu das sanffte Creutz Christi nicht tragen sonder von dir werffen/ so wird dir der Teuffel hingegen ein so schweres uffladen/ daß du endlich darunter zur Höllen hinunter sincken wirst; Ob sich ein solcher villeicht bessere und bekehre; der Frome aber in Trost und Hoffnung hierinnen sich stärcke. (SP 32)

To better and convert the disoriented and fortify the pious by providing consolation and hope, this is his literary and religious program of which the first portion is dedicated to the Simplician-cycle and the latter position to the "Erbauungsromane." Both types of novels seek to instruct, which can be seen from the recurrence of the term "useful" ("nützliche," "mit Nutz") in the title of many novels. However, they approach the goal of *prodesse* (being useful) in two significantly distinct ways. The Simplician style is characterized by mediacy of instruction, using entertaining features (*delectare*) to hide, obscure, and sweeten the didactic message. The non-Simplician style is characterized by its immediate approach, using exemplary stories that depict idealized behavior in order to fortify, edify, and console the reader who can find hope in these stories. Although the examples are idealized, or maybe because they are, the edifying aspect does not aim directly at such a holy life but rather at its possible imitation. The *Imitatio Christi* (1418) of Thomas à Kempis (1379?-1471), arguably the most influential edificatory text ever written, addresses those pious believers who are plagued by doubt and disorientation and it asks for steps of imitation, not the heroic gesture of the all-or-nothing. Grimmelshausen's non-Simplician novels work in a similar way, although they integrate their didactic immediacy into a narrative plot that allows for secondary purposes. This argumentative figure recurs in the treatment of "poetry" (Poeterey) in which Grimmelshausen uses the ancient *ars-natura* controversy in order to argue for a natural *furor poeticus* which allows him to endow the poets with the power of prophecy ("Weissagungen und Prophezeyhungen," SP 89). In close analogy to the epideictic forms of praise and criticism, itself the traditional home of poetry in the rhetorical system, he assigns the highest position to those poets who sing God's praise using His natural gift to its highest end. The critical voice points out that the poetic *furor* often is empty and unfounded, producing vain and shallow fantasies, citing common criticism leveled against the decorous courtly novel. From his discussion in *Satyrischer Pilgram*, it seems clear that Grimmelshausen only acknowledges pious religious praise as poetry and that he does not fully accept novelistic forms as poetry although he demands clear religious guidelines for them.

Two more passages provide important insights for our analytic interest. One concerns the discussions of money that can be regarded as a close analogy to rhetoric: both can effect almost everything, both are universally usable, and both share the character of being a sign or representation for other things. The rich man thus resembles the poet since both can translate potentiality in actuality; but both are also equally dangerous and in danger. Money, then, seems to be an illustration of the ambiguous power of rhetorical language that has been shown to be a major concern of Grimmelshausen's entire tract.

Another instance of the same figure of thought can be found in the discussion concerning "disguises" ("Mummereyen") where the critical voice points out that the most atrocious use of dissimulation can be found in the theory of *ratio status*, the devilish Machiavellian doctrine to which Grimmelshausen dedicates an entire book.

Although published 1670, the *Simplicianischer zweyköpffiger Ratio Status* seems to predate the *Simplicissimus Teutsch* (1668–69) which is evident from its use of biblical material very much in the fashion of *Keuscher Joseph* (1666). Together with the poetological information and the methodological reflections of *Satyrischer Pilgram*, it can be regarded as the somewhat hidden theory of the Erbauungsromane to follow.

In contrast to the *Satyrischer Pilgram*, *Ratio Status* is clearly organized and divided into six parts ("Discurs") using the lives of Saul, Jonathan, David and Joab in order to illustrate the workings of good and bad *ratio status*. The first "Discurs" introduces the theoretical ramifications of the problem-ridden category, and the last "supplementary" part treats a non-related problem using the character of Sabud.

The lives of both Jonathan and Joab are less convincing examples of the respective good and bad *ratio status* (and shorter ones, too). The theoretical introduction and the lives of Saul and David form the core of the argument that is methodologically derived from the adiaphora technique of *Satyrischer Pilgram*. Grimmelshausen deviates significantly from the standard rejection of *ratio status* by affirming its character as an adiaphoron, that is, something that is neither good nor bad intrinsically, but only as the result of a specific use that is made of it. Also, the author claims that it should be understood as the general demand to practice *Selbst-Erhaltung*, a mixture of self-conservation and self-defense that applies equally to governments seeking to avoid civil war, destruction and strife, and to households seeking to secure the lives and welfare of its members. Grimmelshausen takes his cue from the divine law that regards everybody as equal; it is only human "positive" law that allows for hierarchies of power and domination, necessary after original sin. However, the master or king in such a situation of domination is obliged to show a whole battery of virtues, the most important of which is humility, the opposite of the cardinal vice, *superbia*. Since nobody can persist without using *ratio status*, the author stresses the importance of distinguishing between good and bad use of its dangerous devices. The necessary humility then translates into the acceptance of divine providence and a total confidence in God, which manifests itself in the relinquishing of one's own will. In such a fashion, *ratio status* must be used even by the church, particularly to overcome confessional separation and to preach the Christian faith among non-believers "[v]ornehmlich aber mit selbs vorleuchtenden Exempeln der Gottseligkeit (welches dann dessen Ratio Status erfordert)" (RS 11). Thus, the author will present good and bad use of *ratio status* by depicting "true" biblical histories.

The story of Saul then serves as a self-explanatory example of the fall from humble confidence in divine providence and the subsequent abuse of *ratio status*. Saul is described as a handsome young man who shows all the necessary virtues of a good king as they are listed in the first "Discurs" and repeated at length in the characterization of the king. Most of all, Saul possesses humility, the source of all other virtues: "Die Demuht/ wo sie sich findet/ da ist und vertritt sie das Fundament/ worauff alle andere Tugenden sich gründen/ worauff sie auch ruhen und beharren" (RS 12). In his early perfection, Saul is best described as being fine ("fein"), but, although "there was nobody finer than he was," Saul fell from grace. Grimmelshausen's entire tract is concerned with establishing a reason for this sharp turn of Saul's fortune. He finds it, not surprisingly, in his affirmed autonomy as a ruler who rejects the advice of his religious aide, the prophet Samuel:

> Josephus gibt diesem König das Lob/ daß er sehr schön/ gerad und starck von Leib: aber am Verstand und Klugheit viel vortrefflicher gewesen sey; woraus zu schliessen/ er werde sich ohne Zweifel eingebildet haben/ als er seinen Königlichen Stuhl genugsam befestiget zu sein vermeinet/ solches seye durch sein eigene gute Qualitäten und Geschicklichkeit geschehen/ vermittelst deren er auch seine Hohheit wol zu erhalten getraute; Samuelis Geschäfften waren/ daß er daß Volck lehre/ und vor sie bete [. . .]; Ihme aber selbst/ als dem König würde er hinförders in seinen Staats=Sachen und des Reichs Regierung keine Ordnung mehr zu geben haben; durch diese Gedancken/ die ihm seine angemaste selbst Erhaltung/ das ist/ sein Ratio Status, eingeben/ litte seine anfängliche Demuth gegen Gott: seine Ehrerbietung gegen der Religion: sein schuldiger Respect gegen dem Propheten: und sein Gehorsam gegen dem Gesetz/ den ersten Stoß! (RS 17)

Saul dissociates politics from ethics, thereby establishing the basic frame for a Machiavellian politics of dissimulation; consequently he starts slipping away from the path of humble obedience. However, his fate is not fully determined before he rejects Samuel's criticism of his "hoffärtige / übermütige und trotzige Gedancken" (RS 18) and defends his decisions against God's wishes. It is precisely this self-defense, born out of a feeling of rational autonomy, which overrides the precepts of divine providence, causing his final fall from grace:

> Gleich wie eine demühtige Bekanntnus begangener Ubertrettung leichtlich Vergebung erlangt; Also ist es ein gewisse Anzeigung der von GOtt verhassten und abscheulichen Hoffart/ wenn man sich unterstehet (wie Saul hier gethan/) die Sünden zuentschuldigen/ ja er wolte anfänglich noch recht haben/ eben als hette er die Sach gar wol ausgerichtet [. . .]. Ach warumb bittestu nicht vielmehr in deiner vorigen Demuht und selbst Verachtung umb Verzeihung/ deren dich der Gottselige Prophet [. . .] so treuhertzig erinnert [. . .]. Aber ach! dein Ratio Status den du dir an Statt GOttes erwöhlet hattest/ wolte solches nicht zu lassen; Sondern weil du dich einmal ein gewaltiger König zu sein wustest/ die Demuht gegen GOtt auch bereits dein Hertz quitieren müssen [. . .]. (RS 18–19)

Consequently, the rest of the second discourse is devoted to a full description of Saul's intensifying dependence on *ratio status* and the subsequent atrocities he feels compelled to pursue. *Ratio status,* it becomes clear, is nothing other than a form of secular *fortuna* and the exact opposite of divine providence. Personal hubris opposes God's wishes and plans, and it manifests itself as self-affirming autonomy; no wonder then that Saul is damned to hell and has to beg for his death in a situation of extreme humiliation. In his summary statement, the author leaves no doubt about the meaning of Saul's exemplary story:

> Und hat diesen seinen erbärmlichen Fall sonst nichts verursacht/ als daß er seine anfängliche Haupt-Tugenden der Demuht und Gottes-Forcht beyseits gesetzt/ und sich hingegen auf sich selbst/ auf sein Königlichen Gewalt und Politische Griff die ihm sein Ratio Status eingeben/ verlassen; welche ihn aber schrecklich betrogen: und von einer Staffel zur andern: von einem Laster ins ander: Ja biß endlich in die Verzweiflung hinunter gestürzt [. . .]. (RS 31)

Against this background, David's life and fate must be regarded as the counterpart. They offer an exemplary story that shows how deep humility and constant faith and confidence in divine providence are stronger than the rational machinations of *ratio status:*

> Nein der fromme König richtet sich nach keinem anderen Ratio Status, als nach dem jenigen/ den ihm seine Gottseelige Tugenden: sein Gelassenheit in GOttes Willen/ sein Demuht/ sein Gedult/ sein Sanftmühtigkeit/ etc. vorgemahlet und eingebildet hatten; allen Machiavellischen Statisten damit zuerkennen gebende/ daß der getreue GOtt deren ihme ergebenen Potentaten ärgste Feinde zu seiner Zeit auch ohne derselben GOtt ergebenen Fürsten Zuthun/ schon ernidrigen und nach seinem Göttlichen Belieben gar vertilgen könne/ massen auch allen seinen Feinden endlich widerfahren. (RS 39–40)

However, David was a strong sinner; adultery and murder for personal reasons were among the lesser offenses that culminated in cold-blooded mass murder, and as such he outdistances Saul by far. If the question concerning Saul was how he fell from grace, the question concerning David clearly is how he could retain or even regain God's grace. The author's answer is clear and to the point:

> Antwort; Sündigen ist Menschlich; darinnen verharren ist Teufflisch; viel abscheulicher aber/ wann der Gefallene sich noch unterstehet/ durch seine Vernunfft und GOtt widerstrebende spitzfindige Staats-Griff der Machiauellisten/ ihm selbst zu helffen; wie Saul gethan; Solches thät unser König David aber nicht/ sondern so bald er seinen Fall merckte/ stunde er mit hertzlicher und innbrünstiger Reu wider auf/ und ergriffe ohnverweilt rechtschaffene Wercke der Busse. (RS 45)

It is sincere contrition and immediate ("ohnverweilt") repentance that distinguish Saul and David, the latter being able to give up his own will in the face of divine providence. His sincere character ("aufrichtig

Gemüth") and constant confidence ("unveränderliches Vertrauen") in God's grace made him accept and seek "no other ratio status for his self-preservation than the sanctuary in God." Hubris vs. humility and autonomy vs. obedience are the religious coordinates which define good and bad usage of *ratio status;* and with self-preservation as the task for everyone, the fundamental preconditions for retaining God's grace are the renunciation of one's own will and the active acceptance of divine providence. The author understands that this angelic vision is far from reality, and he also accepts that kings and rulers will have to commit crimes and sin on a larger scale to achieve the goal of self-preservation; however, they can only save themselves through sincere and immediate repentance.

We do not need to see that this sincerity asks for active signs and proofs to realize the Catholic basis of the entire argument. It begins with the notion that worldly things have to be regarded mostly as adiaphora which can be evaluated morally only through the uses that people make of them. This, in turn, leads to the general conclusion that Christian humility, obedience and sincere repentance are the keys to salvation as exemplified by the problem of *ratio status.* These notions inform and guide the non-Simplician novels, which freely incorporate material from the theoretical tracts, bringing new perspectives and individual solutions to a common body of problems. Grimmelshausen's career is founded on precisely this argument for willing subjection under the law of divine providence. The *Satyrischer Pilgram* shows the root of the poetological and religious program by problematizing moral evaluation in an historical situation dominated by politics of dissimulation and fundamental uncertainties. How is it possible simultaneously to accept and criticize sinful behavior and how is it possible to have virtue punished and vice rewarded? In *Ratio Status,* Grimmelshausen subjugates the totality of worldly experiences to the notion of divine providence, a hidden and often illegible eschatological master plan that asks for unconditional cooperation. The renunciation of individual autonomy is then the pivotal point in Grimmelshausen's theory: acts in accordance with the divine design are to be regarded as good (*ratio status*), acts in defiance as bad. The argument is constructed in order to suspend rigid moral evaluation concerning specific, extremely important items such as money and *ratio status,* thereby alleviating the argumentative burden of proving the meaningfulness of the world.

The basic operation then declares human acts as the basis for moral evaluation and not their means, simultaneously establishing obedience to divine providence as the eternal and overriding measure. However, Grimmelshausen does not necessarily allow for innocent usage in every case, nor is he interested in the general application of this procedure. He is in fact only aiming at a small number of concepts revolving around the notorious *ratio status,* which he has reason to regard as the most prominent and powerful representation of his epistemological dilemma.

Ratio status shares this capability of being good or bad with some other key concepts such as rhetoric and literature, both of which are at the heart of Grimmelshausen's interest since he sincerely believes that "wer aber etwas weiß/ sols seinem Nebenmenschen communiciren" (SP 11). His motivation for writing lies entirely in this obligation to communicate what he regards as the most notable truth of utmost importance, that is, God will judge acts, not items, and His grace will consider the existence and sincerity of contrition and the accompanying acts of repentance. This is the truth that the author almost desperately wants to convey, and it is a Catholic mission, the Catholicism of which deeply penetrates into the poetological program.

In all its conservatism, Grimmelshausen's writing exhibits one particular feature that is very modern. It helps today's readers to appreciate his non-Simplician novels. He introduces *ratio status* and related concepts as the material content of his narratives and he simultaneously establishes an additional level of understanding that focuses on the self-reflective character of the various texts. The problematic distinction between good and bad in reality is the starting point for his mission to help enable his readers in making that distinction, and by introducing the model of rhetoric in the *Satyrischer Pilgram,* Grimmelshausen instrumentalizes the very problem that he has as a means to its solution. The same thing can be good and bad at the same time. It all depends on the particular use that is made of it. This observation is true first and foremost of the type of literature that the author is writing. Because of its epistemological status, which allows for more than one meaning, it is always open to misreading. This is true, no matter how directly and openly didactic the text appears to be.

Thus, the author confirms and stresses that he writes with the "Intent/ daß sich der Christliche Leser des guten gebrauchen; und des bösen eüsern möge" (SP 14). Telling good from bad is then not only the eventual, extra-textual goal, but it has its intra-textual counterpart in the narrative strategies to make sure the right meaning is extracted from the text. It is in the light of this hermeneutic double bind that the novels will have to be analyzed.

Keuscher Joseph (1667) marks then the temporary end-point in a series of authorial attempts to communicate "something useful." Grimmelshausen's insistence on such a communication leads him from theoretical exposition over strictly purposeful example stories to a serious application of the novel form to biblical history. However, the gradual development of his writing into narrative forms is dominated by the intention to propagate his message. *Keuscher Joseph,* although the liveliest of his edifying novels, is clearly a variation of the model of *Ratio Status,* assuming that the two texts were written simultaneously, regardless of their apparent dates of publication. *Keuscher Joseph* exhibits the methodological demands stated in *Satyrischer Pilgram* and *Ratio Status* and it may well have been begun as one of the exemplary stories in the latter tract. The remarkable narrative dexterity suggests that the author may have interrupted his work on *Ratio Status* in order to complete *Keuscher Joseph* once he realized that the Joseph-story broke the frame of the tract and would be best dealt with as a full and separate novel. These conjectures can of course not be substantiated but they outline a fairly plausible development in the early work of Grimmelshausen.

Be that as it may, the meaning of *Keuscher Joseph* rests on the opposition of good, "Christian" rhetoric and its bad counterpart, affective Machiavellian dissimulation. In the first part of the novel it is the counter-play between Ruben, "the oldest brother and best speaker," and the brothers who are determined to kill Joseph. Their rhetoric is dominated by passion and self-interest as well as on their resentment of their father's preference for Joseph and his alleged superiority that rests on prophecies and explanations of dreams. The brothers perceive Joseph as the main obstacle to their own welfare and prosperity, whereas Joseph stresses his humble obedience to God and his father although he finds himself described as the savior of the family. He learns the hermeneutic arts of prophecy and dream explication, both of which are also characteristics of the poet, from his father, and later he finds opportunities to complete and perfect this decisive knowledge that will be the tool of his eventual liberation.

In the beginning, however, Ruben's "Christian" rhetoric cannot persuade the passionate brothers to leave Joseph alone, but it is able to convince them not to kill him personally. Ruben uses all the techniques of Machiavellian dissimulation he can muster; basically he lies to his brothers and plans to save Joseph behind their backs. This obviously good and appropriate use of rhetorical dissimulation and *ratio status* is in stark contrast to the passionate deliberations of the brothers, but it is made null and void by divine providence when Joseph is suddenly and surprisingly sold into slavery.

The interplay of good and bad rhetoric reaches its apex, however, in the antagonistic attempts of Selicha to seduce Joseph and his efforts to remain virtuous. Here the tables are turned. Selicha uses all possible techniques of rhetorical seduction, stretching from promises, threats, and commands to the elocution of the (half-naked) body. Joseph, on the other hand, except for one occasional lie in the heat of the battle, stays with basically one argument only, that is, his determination to fulfill the divine laws of humble obedience to his superiors and God. Selicha is driven wholly by her own erotic passion, and the situation is clearly an elaboration on the chapters on "love" and "women" in *Satyrischer Pilgram*. The good counterpart is, of course, Joseph's wife-to-be, Asaneth, a paragon of virtue worthy of such a husband as Joseph.

Another item from the list of the *Satyrischer Pilgram* is "beauty," the opposite uses of which can be witnessed in Joseph and Selicha. Her sense of beauty is restricted to the erotic although she realizes that Joseph's angelic beauty is founded in his humility and virtue. The ambiguity of beauty is very cleverly explicated when the robbers threaten to plunder the caravan. The Odysseus-like Musai dresses Joseph in the richly ornate garments that were meant as a welcoming gift for the pharaoh. This neat trick saves the caravan and it also illuminates the good use of "disguise" ("Mummerey"), dealt with in chapter seven in part two of *Satyrischer Pilgram*, because the robbers can be persuaded that a God has descended from heaven and that they can pay tribute to him.

The novel is replete with allusions to the insincerity and ambiguity of signs, symbols, and texts. Joseph's father curses his (correct) dream explications because, unlike Joseph, he temporarily loses faith in providence; the robbers and Selicha misinterpret his beauty; Selicha misconstrues the meaning of Joseph's solicitation for his master Potiphar, who misreads a prophecy. All of these hermeneutic blunders originate in the dominance of passion, and Joseph's virtuous *constantia* opposes these seductive attempts by an unconditional reliance and trust in divine providence. Selicha's attacks on Joseph's virtue reach their apex in the notable scene of bodily seduction, and this "*argumentum ad corporem*," so to speak, is complemented by an open declaration of Machiavellian *ratio status*, in which she underlines the central problem of *ratio status*, namely, distrust. The basic premise of Machiavellian *politica* is the general distrust that makes simulation and dissimulation necessary in the first place, clearly a circular argument that Joseph and the author try to avoid by binding every decision to unconditional and humble obedience to divine providence. Thus, general distrust is counteracted by voluntary trust.

This argument is elaborated in two directions: it informs the poetological construction of the text, and it serves as the background to political and social deliberations. It is not surprising from a poetological point of view that the narrative structure reflects the cognitive problem from *ratio status,* that is, how is it possible to communicate something useful persuasively without being trapped in the circle of rhetorical uncertainty. Momus's demand, in *Satyrischer Pilgram,* that rhetoric be used effectively results in exactly the ambiguity of meaning that renders the reader helpless in judging whether the given advice is good or bad. The edifying novels avoid this problem by showing good and bad rhetoric coupled with unmistakable evaluations.

The chapter on poetry in *Satyrischer Pilgram* (II, 1) attributes two characteristics to the poet: he praises the Lord in his poetry and he possesses the gift of prophecy, which is nothing else but a heightened insight into divine providence. However, astrological and other mantic procedures can only be regarded as good if they serve the purpose of explaining providence. Musai, who is trained in the art of prophecy, uses his mantic powers for his own profit — and loses all his wealth. Only those insights that elucidate divine providence prove to be true and meaningful. By analogy, the same can be said for the literary text, which must be regarded as a prophecy of sorts. Poetry is permissible only insofar as it praises God (epideictic mode as explained in *Satyrischer Pilgram*) or shows the working of His divine plan. The latter then entails a contrast between good and bad *ratio status* and the argument for hermeneutic trust in narrative intention. Joseph uses his prophetic and hermeneutic powers only to interpret dreams and the fate of individuals as parts of the divine plan. Thus, he regards himself as a contributor who humbly obeys God's commands and exercises good *ratio status* in order to preserve the welfare of the nation.

The political meaning of *Keuscher Joseph* is then consequently bound to the argumentative pattern from *ratio status* since it shows how true and good, that is, Christian, *politica* will affect self-preservation ("Selbsterhaltung") for future needs. Joseph's dream hermeneutics explain that the renunciation of individual desires not only help to maintain a nation but can also be understood metaphorically as giving up individual autonomy in order to secure future redemption. The second part of *Keuscher Joseph* thus projects a political and economic situation resembling early absolutism, in which good *ratio status* is subservient to divine providence and aims at the welfare of the nation, not the king.

All the above tendencies culminate in the history of Joseph and his brothers who seek to buy grain from the stocks of the pharaoh. Their wish to participate in the wealth that Joseph's providential knowledge amassed can be regarded as an attempt to partake metaphorically of the wealth of providence itself. Joseph the provider is the agent of providence, and as such he is also a master of hermeneutics, providing the meaning of it all. The intersection of meaning and providence thus materializes in the symbol of far-sighted provisions, and Joseph tests his brothers as to whether they are worthy of being readmitted to the realm of meaningful providence.

He confronts them with his distrust accusing them of a misdeed that he maintains he sees written on their forehead. After Musai substantiates this accusation, the brothers are terrified and sincerely repent. Their second visit gives Joseph the opportunity to test their virtue when he falsely accuses Benjamin of having stolen the cup he uses for prophecies. The brothers stand by Benjamin and offer all possible kinds of retribution, even to suffer punishment in his stead. Whenever Joseph talks to his brothers, he cites divine providence as the universal law of mankind, and each time he is moved to tears. However, when he realizes that they sold him into slavery fulfilling God's plans, he bursts into tears and confesses his identity. The final tableau reaffirms the main maxim of the entire novel: everything that happens serves divine providence and only humble obedience can secure God's grace and redemption. This message forcefully and repeatedly elaborated in *Keuscher Joseph* and theoretically proven and legitimized in *Satyrischer Pilgram* and *Ratio Status* also informs the two remaining novels, *Dietwalt und Amelinde* and *Proximus und Lympida*. The thrust of the narrative argument changes, to be sure, and both novels can be regarded as focusing on specific elements of the general argument from *Keuscher Joseph*.

Between the dedication and the beginning of the novel, there is in *Dietwalt und Amelinde* a "Sonnet" by Sylvander, who also signs the dedication in *Proximus und Lympida,* praising the author's intention of teaching the way to virtue, regardless of the type of novel he is writing. The book ends with verses written by Urban von Wurmsknick auff Sturmdorff (an anagram of the author) in praise of the author who is directly quoted. Its more or less obvious (self-) laudatory tone is only partially ironic; Grimmelshausen seems to be trying to establish a solid reputation as an author of moralistic novels. His work is characterized as down to earth (it has "Händ und Füß") as opposed to the flighty illusions of the courtly novel. He defends *Simplicissimus* by explaining how "noble truth" appears in it in disguise. Grimmelshausen is then quoted as saying that his sole motivation for writing is his desire to instruct his neighbor ("zu des Nechsten Nutz") by describing the vices of the world. Only at the end of the poem does he devote four lines to *Dietwalt und Amelinde* stressing that it too will contribute to the author's fame making his name known among the intellectuals of the day ("dem gelehrten Volck").

Obviously, Grimmelshausen slightly alters his perspective here, still maintaining his overall tenets and the general appeal of his novels, but he also aims now directly at an educated audience for which *Simplicissimus* may not have been appropriate reading. The author uses a two-pronged strategy here; he defends his picaresque novel by explaining its pedagogic mechanism, thereby trying to ennoble it, on the other hand he proudly uses its popularity to identify himself as its author in trying to raise interest for *Dietwalt und Amelinde*. This project spectacularly misfired: interest in his non-Simplician novels has been so low from the beginning that Grimmelshausen's self-identification as the author of *Simplicissimus* was overlooked until the late nineteenth century.

The author clearly realized that his claim to fame rests on his Simplician works; however, he engages in an attempt to establish himself as a truly serious poet by catering to what he believes are the expectations of the educated readership — with fatal consequences. He introduces a wooden, historical, frame narrative giving a conspectus of medieval European history clearly designed both to prove his own illusory erudition and to rouse the interest of the educated reader. He did not understand or anticipate that his initial concept, non-picaresque novels for a broad and basically uneducated audience, would not tolerate erudite additives. Quantity, quality and thematic interest declare *Dietwalt und Amelinde* at first sight not to be a courtly novel. Still, it is equally obvious that it poses obstacles for the uninitiated reader with the result that the novel does not gain a new readership but loses its old readership.

Thematically, *Dietwalt und Amelinde* does not deviate significantly from the catalogue in *Keuscher Joseph*. The title page lists possible reader-types and their use, a device that *Proximus und Lympida* reproduces. The novel is edifying to the pious, interesting for the historian, consolatory, stimulating, and useful for the *politicus*. It also satisfies the curious and is without objectionable material. Grimmelshausen spends considerable effort on the plot-construction, making it perfectly symmetric with the pilgrimage of the main protagonists as the semantic axis. The symmetry of the plot development extends to the structure of the main episode that is in itself clearly organized. He invests much labor exploring the historical sources, but for his main plot he again uses prefabricated material, a "Meisterlied" by Hans Sachs (1494–1576). Upon closer scrutiny the historical parts and the narrative plot work together sufficiently well, although it is not evident that the historical allusions are aimed at the educated reader. However, W. E. Schäfer's suggestion (1957) that *Diet-*

walt und Amelinde as well as *Proximus und Lympida* should be regarded as a sustained criticism of courtly society, cannot be accepted on the available evidence; it would be more fruitful to regard them as a pronounced criticism of the courtly novel.

With respect to the didactic intention, *Dietwalt und Amelinde* narrows the scope of topics presented in *Keuscher Joseph*, again giving *ratio status* the most prominent position. Good and bad *ratio status* can be observed on two narrative levels, in the high discourse of kings and noblemen in the historical parts and in the more private world of Dietwalt und Amelinde themselves. Both are connected, since the princely pair is part of politics but also because high-profile advisors occur in both worlds. More important are, of course, the exemplary situations in the strictly narrative parts beginning with the hermeneutic problem of how to interpret the prophecies of a future, worldwide kingdom that has been achieved through victory in a decisive battle. Dietwalt and Amelinde indulge in fantasies of self-aggrandizement but are brought back to heaven so to speak by the criticism of a God-sent angel who suggests that they should rather spend ten years of their lives in humble repentance. The noble pair is brought back to their religious senses and readily agrees. When the devil tries to seduce them into a relativistic and skeptical reading of God's message, they already have enough determination and trust in divine providence to de-mask him.

This is, of course, the traditional situation of the problematical hermeneutics of rhetorical discourse as it has been explored in *Satyrischer Pilgram* and *Ratio Status*. The author's solution has not changed either: there has to be unconditional trust in divine providence and its orders to overcome this hermeneutic uncertainty. Accepting the angel's censure in sincere repentance assures their eventual salvation and reinstatement, and their ten-year absence from politics seems more a ploy of providence to keep them away from nasty political battles than necessary punishment for a fairly fleeting feeling of *superbia*.

On the level of grand politics, bad *ratio status* incites greed for power and its unavoidable consequences: simulation and dissimulation, betrayal, aggression, and war. Murder, and in particular fratricide, is rampant, whereas the pious king of France, Amelinde's natural father, excels in the right "Christian" *ratio status*. He makes a tacit distinction between *simulatio*, an active lie giving a false impression of one's motives, and *dissimulatio*, holding back and guarding one's true motives and interest. Only the latter poker-face politics is allowed, and the advice the king receives from his hermit-advisor, Warmund, literally "true mouth," is equally directed at passive conservation and far-sighted preservation of the status quo, thus implementing "Selbst-Erhaltung."

Warmund's negative counterpart is the advisor on board the ship where Amelinde is kept prisoner. While the sailors can hardly restrain their wishes to rape her, their elected advisor discusses the pros and cons of such an act. His deliberations are entirely free of moral notions and resemble the passionate discussion among Joseph's brothers who plot to kill their brother. Here it is not envy but sexual desire that drives the sailors, and their arguments exhibit the pitfalls of bad *ratio status* that is primarily concerned with short term personal gains and passions. Good *ratio status* is characterized by sincere trust in divine providence; here the sailors are beset by distrust and so blinded by their desires that only hard and irrefutable evidence, the portrait proving Amelinde's claim to be the king's daughter, can hold them back. Also, their surrender is not informed by willing consent to divine providence but by fear of punishment, a typical Machiavellian motive that ensures their eventual downfall.

As much as they cannot read the providential text, Dietwalt and Amelinde perfect their hermeneutic powers. Already at the outset of their pilgrimage, after they reject the devil's seductive reading of their situation as a satanic play to keep them away from their people, Dietwalt and Amelinde show that they have now correctly understood the true meaning of the prophecies of domination over the world. The devil practices simulation, disguising himself as a hermit (the sign of the king's advisor) and he actively lies to them. He tries to make them believe that God's advice was in fact a devilish trick. The consequences of this argument would necessitate that Dietwalt assume his princely powers and actively engage in interest-driven warfare and murder. However, Dietwalt's trusting interpretation embraces the true meaning of the prophecies, humbly accepting his subjection under God's will as evidence that he has overcome the world. The secure knowledge that domination over the world means the denial of the world and its passions guides the noble pair during their passage of repentance, and the second attempt of the devil to seduce Dietwalt is nothing more than an episode perfecting the symmetric narrative structure.

It is only at the very end of the story of *Dietwalt und Amelinde* that the historical frame narrative receives full recognition. The reformed couple has achieved the necessary Christian *ratio status,* and they are now able to practice "Selbst-Erhaltung" in accordance with divine providence and in order to secure the good of the people. Thus they can be reinserted in their old position like a spare part that needed to be changed.

Not surprisingly, *Proximus und Lympida* (1672) does not deviate far from the mold that the tracts and the two previous non-Simplician novels have formed. The title page again lists a number of uses for this novel that are only to be expected. It can serve as a consolatory example ("zum tröstlichen Beyspiel") for those in love and for the depressed ("den Betrübten und Verliebten"), as an unobjectionable, delightful pastime for the curious and idle readers and in general for everybody's good use and Christian edification ("christlicher Aufferbawung").

However, Grimmelshausen has one new classification precede this list, and we can assume its meaningfulness also for the other novels. Likening the novel to children's literature, he declares the novel to be a measure and a doctrine to be followed by young and older readers alike ("den vorhandenen Alten und Jungen: Aeltern und Kindern/ Zur Richtschnur/ Lehr/ und Nachfolgung"). To be sure, nothing like modern "literature for young adults," the more appropriate denomination for *Proximus and Lympida,* exists in the seventeenth century, either quantitatively or qualitatively. However, there does exist reading material for young adults, mainly heavily didactic and religious in its intention, and Grimmelshausen's non-Simplician novels do aim at such a readership. This is particularly the case because they can simultaneously serve as edificatory "house-books" for adult members of the household.

If we extrapolate this idea, it becomes obvious that Grimmelshausen's novelistic typology corresponds to the major readerships that he wants to differentiate from one another: the courtly novel for the noble and educated adult readers and his own Simplician cycle of novels for the sake of simple folk. The courtly novel he finds hazardous, and consequently he assumes his Simplician novels to be fitting reading material for elevated readers as well. In contrast to the later novels of courtly instruction *ad usum delphini,* such as *Télémaque* (1699) of François Fénélon (1651–1715), which are too restricted in scope, Grimmelshausen tries establishing the new and comprehensive genre of edificatory novels for the use of old and young readers alike. He can do that because the gap between older and younger readers is not as marked as one would assume today. Also, the given content and form are supposedly appropriate for a younger readership among the nobility. Excluded are only adult nobility and educated academics, it seems.

All novels present young adults as protagonists during a specifically difficult period of maturation. Driven by love and the desire for power and glory, the inexperienced and noble couples are easily manipulated by external forces, as is shown in *Dietwalt und Amelinde.* Proximus, on the other hand, is an extreme paragon of virtue, accepting the wise counsel of his father whose wish is that he should give his wealth to the poor and only keep a fraction for himself. This wish he faithfully implements after his father's death. Proximus had already exhibited his humility and devotion by neglecting to reap the fruits of his military valour, and consequently the courtly world regards his filial duty as stupendous stupidity.

It becomes clear, however, that his father's advice was in line with divine providence since assuming the most powerful position in the state after the king himself would have eventually cost him his life. While his father could be regarded as loyal to the king, Proximus's military achievements and popularity among soldiers and citizens alike must arouse suspicions. Ridding himself of this burden, Proximus disqualifies himself as a participant in the power game and saves not only his physical life.

His father had already known best that the present kingdom was not to last much longer and that it seemed wise to hide behind conspicuous poverty. The narrator allows for two instances when past events are summarily reported so that protagonists and readers have a chance to consider the fate of Proximus as a full-fledged repetition of his father's behaviour. Modestus relates his personal history to his son Proximus in order to make him aware of the noble ancient lineage of his family, reaching back into the earliest Christian communities, and to restore him for his future ordeals. On the surface, Modestus is arguing for Proximus to report to the king that his shield was hacked to pieces while he was fighting the most valiant Persian prince, whose shield he assumed as his own after he had defeated his enemy. Proximus needs to defend the loss of his shield and he has to ask for his king's permission to replace it. In order to be able to accept the new insignia on the shield he has won in battle, Proximus is obliged to identify with his proper family background. However, the true meaning of Modestus's narration of how he had to renounce his wealth and position for almost a decade, when he lived under cover of an humble artisan, lies in preparing Proximus for a similar fate.

The members of the family traditionally excel in piety, charity, and humility. Grimmelshausen is somewhat desperately trying to make this point when he allows Basilia, Proximus's former wet-nurse and the mother of Modestus the younger, his closest friend, to narrate the apparition of Jesus under the disguise of a beggar. Honoria, about to give birth to Proximus, humbly washes and dries the feet of the seemingly sick beggar. When she discovers and kisses the stigma on his feet, Jesus disappears leaving behind a heavenly scent.

Thus, Proximus could possibly claim Jesus as his godfather, which explains his almost intolerable piety and humility that at times leaves the reader exasperated. Basilia, again, explains the function of such excessive virtue, claiming that Modestus and Honoria taught without words only by their exemplary conduct:

> aber gegen dem ists schwerlich zuvergleichen/ das beydes ich und mein Man Seel. auß ihrer Beywohnung vnd Gegenwardt so geschwind andere Sitten an vns genommen! er wiße vns niemahl nichts! er beredet nichts! er corrigirt vns nit! er vermahnet: lehret vnd predigt vns nichts/ vnd dannoch verändert sich vnser Handel vnd Wandel in eine augenscheinliche Besserung vnsers gantzen Lebens! [. . .] in summa dise zwey Leüthe wisen vns ohne Wortlehr oder mündliche Vnderrichtung allein durch exemplarischen Vorgang [. . .] vilmehr als der güldene Mund eines Christlichen Predigers thun mögen! dan ihr Thun vnd Lassen war so gnadenreich vnsere Sinne ich weiß nit durch was vor einen himlischen Zwang nach sich zuziehen/ daß wir ihnen gleichsamb musten nachähmen. (PL 45)

This is nothing less than the poetological maxim for the entire novel and a reflection on rhetorical practice.

After *Dietwalt und Amelinde,* Grimmelshausen again focuses his novelistic themes along the lines of *Satyrischer Pilgram* and *Ratio Status,* elevating the topics of money and love to the level of *providentia.* Clearly the notion of self-preservation and the danger of self-assumed complacency inform the particularities of the plot of *Proximus und Lympida,* which follows the established structure of the interplay of rhetorical seduction and trustful reliance on divine providence. Again, the author turns rhetorical seduction into the seduction of rhetoric, and in so doing makes the text its own topic.

On his deathbed, Modestus is tempted to doubt whether Proximus will indeed enact the provisions in his testament. Asked if he would follow Modestus's wishes even if they seemed to be contradicting the divine order, Proximus answers that for him his father's wishes and God's wishes are identical and that he regards dissenting advice as the devil's work. This is another instance of unconditional trust in divine providence as it translates into filial duty and the acceptance of conscientious self-humiliation. The religious implications are manifest, and Modestus does not need to invoke Jesus Christ as Proximus's (legal) guardian. The trust in God, (and) the father, is paralleled by the necessary trust in the text. The reader needs to renounce entirely his scepticism and to put his fate, so to speak, into the hands of the narrator, whose moral duty it is to make sure that his advice does not harm. The immediate effect, however, is the edification of the reader, who suffers just like Modestus from the temptation of disbelief.

For the modern reader, this poetological argument suffers from circular reasoning, since the author-father demands as a precondition what he eventually promises as a reward. That is to say that if the reader surrenders himself to the text by total and unconditional affirmation of *providentia,* the text will help to contest the temptations of doubt by edification. However, this is not entirely true, since the act of a willing suspension of disbelief asks for a major investment on the side of the reader who needs to embrace the unlikely construction of a paragon of virtue.

When his uncle Orontaeus questions the decision to follow the testament's directive and distribute the entire wealth and estate among the poor as not only unwise but also as against the divine law of self-preservation, he uses the suggestive force of secular rhetoric, and his argument fulfils the paternal prophecy. To be sure, Orontaeus's motives are egotistical and he does not know that Proximus, twice blessed by Jesus, is compelled to complete his own *imitatio Christi.* Consequently, Proximus's heartfelt and sincerely irate counter-rhetoric wins the case, not least since the king is happy to see that a dangerous possible competitor disqualifies himself.

The second half of the novel develops the love-story between Proximus and Lympida. She is another example of virtue and a likely match for Proximus, except in the eyes of her materialistic mother. Lympida is first impressed by Proximus's bravery, but when she hears of his pious virtue, her admiration turns into love.

The moment she realizes that she is affectionately in love, she, too, is tempted to distrust divine providence since for her it means betraying her love for God. Consequently she withdraws completely from the world. Her parents try to cure her subsequent depression by presenting her with possible suitors, but all to no avail, since her doubts persist:

> warumb solte sich dan der Mensch nicht betrüben/ wann er selbst zweyfflen muß und nicht weiß/ ob solche seine schuldige Liebe rechtschaffen oder gefärbt: vollkommen oder zerteilt sey? [. . .] weil ich nemblich auß meiner schwachen zu Gott tragenden Liebe mich nicht versichern kan/ das solche volkommen/ unzertheilt/ auffrichtig und in summa also beschaffen/ daß sie GOtt auch angenehm sey. (PL 76)

Pressed by her parents, Lympida surrenders to divine providence when she declares that God will choose a spouse for her. She suggests that the only good measure for selecting a candidate would be his active

Christian behaviour: "an ihren Früchten solt ihr sie erkennen" (PL 110). Her father, slightly irritated, tries to vex her by suggesting she may then take as her husband the first nobleman she would meet in church the next morning, but of course divine providence provokes Proximus to go to church early in the morning, thus providing a partner for Lympida. Her solution certainly borders on the frivolous, but there does not seem to be another choice for her, given her own doubts and her mother's foreseeable resistance.

The declaration of *Proximus und Lympida* as a "love story" ("Liebs=Geschicht= Erzehlung") on the title page is obviously misleading, unless the author had the protagonists' love for God in mind; the two lovers do not even meet physically until thirty pages before the end of the novel. In fact, the novel is the exact counterpart of *Dietwalt und Amelinde* as an edificatory tale, written for young adults and an older readership alike. Both novels, and also *Der keusche Joseph,* try to anticipate the temptation of religious doubts concerning the working of divine providence by instilling in the readers a sincere feeling of trust and unconditional reliance on *providentia.*

All novels are built on Catholic beliefs concerning justice, guilt and redemption, and all novels incorporate topics from *Satyrischer Pilgram* and *Ratio Status,* the latter providing the central theory of self-preservation in a Christian sense. To be sure, doubt-ridden (young adult) readers do not find in these novels examples to be emulated. Instead, they find the lives of almost holy people who cannot lead the way to God's grace but whose example seem to suggest that providence rules the world and that it determines the destiny of all living creatures. Reading Grimmelshausen's non-Simplician novels, the modern reader has to acknowledge that the one-dimensionality of these texts is a carefully crafted mechanism that fortifies the pious reader and strengthens the inexperienced in their beliefs. They are narrativized and secularized "lives of saints" and "lives of the fathers" designed to witness the presence of God in the world, thus edifying the circle of readers. Their lasting value, however, resides in the manifold self-reflections of the novel and the narrator as agents of both good and bad rhetoric as it is described in *Satyrischer Pilgram.*

Works Cited

Breuer, Dieter. *Grimmelshausen-Handbuch.* Munich: Fink, 1999.

———, ed. *Hans Jacob Christoffel von Grimmelshausen. Werke.* Two volumes in three. Frankfurt am Main: Deutscher Klassiker Verlag, 1989–1997. (= Bibliothek der Frühen Neuzeit. Zweite Abteilung. Literatur im Zeitalter des Barock, 4/1 and 4/2 and 5)

Busch, Walter. "Biblisch-Mythische Erzählform und Darstellungsironie. Grimmelshausens *Lebens-Lauff des Musai.*" *Simpliciana* 10 (1988): 431–68.

Dallett, Joseph B. "*Satyrischer Pilgram* Triangulated." *Carleton Germanic Papers* 12 (1984): 11–22.

———. "'*diese achtzigjährige Zeit:*' Geschichtsgestaltung in der Vorrede zu *Proximus und Lympida.*" *Simpliciana* 10 (1988): 365–85.

Dinter, Rudolf. "Grimmelshausens *Musai:* 'Denck- und Lesewürdige[s]. . . Aus Uralten Scribenten.' Ein Quellenbeitrag." *Simpliciana* 4/5 (1983): 155–71.

Fischer-Bosshardt, Andrea. "Die erzählerischen Verfahrensweisen in Grimmelshausens *Keuschem Joseph.*" *Simpliciana* 12 (1990): 123–34.

Gaede, Friedrich. "Janusköpfiger Ratio Status. Grimmelshausens Beitrag zum Thema: Chaos wird Geschichte." *Simpliciana* 20 (1998): 77–91.

Gaggl, Edith Elisabeth. "Grimmelshausens höfisch-historische Romane." Diss. Vienna 1954.

Hesselmann, Peter. "*Entblösete Brüste* auch in Wolfenbüttel. Grimmelshausens *Keuscher Joseph* und seine Rezeption im 17. und 18. Jahrhundert." *Simpliciana* 11 (1989): 17–33.

von der Heyde, Andreas. "Die wahre und die falsche Ratio Status. Zur Machiavelli-Rezeption im 16. und 17. Jahrhundert und bei Grimmelshausen." *Simpliciana* 12 (1990): 503–16.

Hillenbrand, Rainer. "Restauration von Grimmelshausens *Ratio Status.*" *Simpliciana* 20 (1998): 307–17.

———. "Zu Grimmelshausens Satyrischem Pilgram." *Archiv für das Studium der neueren Sprachen und Literaturen* 148 (1996): 326–30.

Iber, Gudrun. "Studien zu Grimmelshausens Josef und Musai mit einem Neudruck des Musai-Textes nach der Erstausgabe von 1670." Diss. Bonn 1957.

van Ingen, Ferdinand. "Grimmelshausens *Keuscher Joseph* und seine Leser." *Simpliciana* 10 (1988): 405–20.

Janda, Otto. "Grimmelshausens Roman *Der keusche Joseph in Egypten.*" Diss. Graz 1928.

Kampel, Johanna. "Die höfischen Romane Grimmelshausens." Diss. Vienna 1932.

Köhler, Eberhard. "Die beiden Idealromane von Hans Jakob Christoffel von Grimmelshausen." Diss. Jena 1965.

Konopatzki, Ilse-Lore. *Grimmelshausens Legendenvorlagen.* Berlin: Schmidt, 1965. (= Philologische Studien und Quellen 28)

Kühlmann, Wilhelm. "*Syllogimus practicus.* Antithese und Dialektik in Grimmelshausens *Satyrischem Pilgram.*" *Simpliciana* 13 (1991): 391–405.

Lechler, Hans Heinrich. "Grimmelshausens Roman *Dietwalt und Amelinde.* Beiträge zu seinem Verständnis." Diss. Frankfurt 1975.

Meid, Volker. *Grimmelshausen. Epoche — Werk — Wirkung.* München: Beck, 1984. (= Arbeitsbücher für den literaturgeschichtlichen Unterricht)

Nieder, Horst. "Grimmelshausens *Simplicianischer Zweyköpffiger Ratio Status.* Fingerübungen eines im discurierenden Stil Befangenen oder simplicianische Satire?" *Simpliciana* 14 (1992): 59–104.

Ortel, Karl. Proximus und Lympida. *Eine Studie zum idealistischen Roman Grimmelshausens.* Berlin: Ebering, 1936. (= Germanistische Studien 177)

Ristow, Brigitte. "Grimmelshausen-Studien." Diss. Berlin 1953.

Schäfer, Walter Ernst. "Die sogenannten 'heroisch-galanten' Romane Grimmelshausens. Untersuchungen zur antihöfischen Richtung im Werk des Dichters." Diss. Bonn 1957.

———. "Laster und Lastersysteme bei Grimmelshausen." *Germanisch-romanische Monatsschrift* 12 (1962): 233–43.

———. "Tugendlohn und Sündenstrafe in Roman und Simpliciade." *Zeitschrift für deutsche Philologie* 85 (1966): 481–500.

Singer, Herbert. "*Joseph in Egypten.* Zur Erzählkunst des 17. und 18. Jahrhunderts." *Euphorion* 48 (1954): 249–79.

Stilgebauer, Edward. *Grimmelshausens* Dietwald und Amelinde. Gera (Reuss): Lentzsch, 1893. (= Diss. Tübingen)

Streller, Siegfried. "Grimmelshausens *Keuscher Joseph* und Zesens *Assenat.* Ein Vergleich." *Simpliciana* 10 (1988): 421–30.

Stucki, Clara. *Grimmelshausens und Zesens Josephsromane. Ein Vergleich zweier Barockdichter.* Horgen-Zürich: Münster, 1933. (= Wege zur Dichtung 15)

Tarot, Rolf: "Formen erbaulicher Literatur bei Grimmelshausen." *Daphnis* 8 (1979): 95–121.

———. "Die erzählerischen Verfahrensweisen in Grimmelshausens Legendenromanen." *Simpliciana* 10 (1988): 387–403.

Trappen, Stefan. *Grimmelshausen und die menippische Satire: Eine Studie zu den historischen Voraussetzungen der Prosasatire im Barock.* Tübingen: Niemeyer, 1994. (= Studien zur deutschen Literatur 132)

Welzig, Werner. "Ordo und verkehrte Welt bei Grimmelshausen." *Zeitschrift für deutsche Philologie* 78 (1959): 424–30 and 79 (1960): 133–41.

Wimmer, Ruprecht. "Grimmelshausens *Joseph* und sein unverhofftes Weiterleben." *Daphnis* 5 (1976): 369–413.

Zeller, Rosmarie. "Grimmelshausens *Keuscher Joseph, Dietwald und Amelinde* und *Proximus und Lympida* im Kontext zeitgenössischer Romantheorie." *Simpliciana* 15 (1993): 173–92.

Copperplate from Ratio Status *(1670).*
Reprinted with permission of the Herzog August Bibliothek,
Wolfenbüttel.

Celebrating the bicentennial of Grimmelshausen's death.
Reprinted from Simplicius Simplicissimus: Grimmelshausen und seine Zeit (1976).

In Grimmelshausen's Tracks:
The Literary and Cultural Legacy

Dieter Breuer

The Calendars

EVEN WHILE GRIMMELSHAUSEN WAS STILL ALIVE, his publisher, Felssecker, attempted to use the success of *Simplicissimus Teutsch* and the word "Simplician," quite independent of the author himself, for other books from his publishing house. In the same year he published Grimmelshausen's *Ewig-währender Calender* (1670), he published an additional annual "Simplician" calendar along with five other calendars which he had been publishing since 1661. This annual calendar appeared continually until 1747, and after that year, due to a change in publishers, in the Endter publishing house until 1807. It consists of two parts. The first part, entitled *Glücklicher und Unglücklicher seltzamer und notabler ganz neuer Europäischer Wundergeschichten Calender,* contains the calendar itself along with "Scherzreden deß Abentheurlichen Simplicissimi" and "Simplicianische Wunder-Geschichten" in two columns. These sections contain three further "Continuationen" of *Simplicissimus Teutsch,* which Felssecker then included in the fifth edition of *Simplicissimus Teutsch* (1671). The second part, entitled *Grosses astrologisches Jahrbuch,* contains various prognoses about the future in the form of a conversation between Simplicissimus, his son, the merchant Politicus, the innkeeper Schrepffeisen, and the charlatan Kugelmann. Beginning in 1673, various picaresque novel characters are also included in the conversation, including Don Buscon, Gusman, Jan Perus, and Gonella. The conversations deal with topics such as the seasons of the year, the months, signs of the zodiac, weather predictions, humorous tales, notes about solar and lunar eclipses, dangers of war, diseases, and, finally, predictions about the coming harvest. Of those annual calendars that appeared during Grimmelshausen's lifetime, the ones from 1670 and 1674 no longer exist, only the second parts (the predictions) from the calendars of 1671 and 1673 are available, and only the two years 1672 and 1675 are still available in their entirety.

The question about whether or not this calendar might be attributed to Grimmelshausen has long been the subject of scholarly debate (von Ziegesar 1924, Koschlig 1939 and 1977, Weydt 1979). The following considerations seem to indicate that they should not be considered works of Grimmelshausen. First, the Simplician calendars cannot really be distinguished from other annual calendars produced by Felssecker in terms of conception, material, or style. Second, it is clear that the humorous stories and tales in the supposedly Simplician sections are compiled from current collections of apothegma and narratives. Third, the three new "Continuationen," through their use of language and motifs borrowed from *Simplicissimus Teutsch* but used in a very flat manner and struggling to attain the comic effect present in the original, change the hero into an incorrigible and unconverted rogue, which is in stark contrast to the entire conception of the original Simplician cycle. Hence, we really have to consider them as typical serial products of the Felssecker publishing house in which Grimmelshausen was not really involved. In fact, Grimmelshausen had made such market-oriented calendars the subject of satire in his *Ewig-währender Calender*. In addition, two other publishing houses, Hoffmann (1675) and Endter (1681) also produced similar "Simplician" calendars (Sodmann 132–37).

As Grimmelshausen himself states, one recognizes an author "am besten auß seinen Schrifften" (W I/1, 319). The same thesis is valid here: the qualitatively different language, style, and narration cannot be ignored. It is not sufficient to argue for Grimmelshausen as the author solely on the basis of identical expressions, stylistic figures, motives, or figures from the novel *Simplicissimus* and other Simplician works. Instead, the deciding factor has to be the manner in which this material is presented in the context of the annual calendars. This occurs in an overpowering, schematic, manner. For example, the author of Felssecker's calendars has both Knan and Meuder speaking dialect, but not the Upper Hessian dialect that would be appropriate. Instead, they use the Nuremberg dialect with which the Felssecker author was himself acquainted (Sodmann, *Simplicius Simplicissimus* 1976, 136). In its Simplician sections, the *Europäische Wundergeschichten-Calender* offers only scanty attempts at imitation of Grimmelshausen's narrative techniques.

"Improved" and Expanded Editions

In view of the textual emendations of the *Simplicissimus* edition of 1671 (E^5), similar conclusions seem reasonable. This is the edition which, since Scholte (1938, 77), has been known as the "BarockSimplicissimus." In addition to a rather pompous title and a reworking of the language, which presents a text for a Protestant public from central Germany, this new edition has an extensive foreword. In addition, the former chapter headings have been replaced by rhymed summaries, the text has been expanded by numerous additions, and the sixth book, the *Continuatio,* has been "enhanced" by the three "Continuationen" mentioned above as well as by a "Zugab/ des wunderbarlichen Weltstreichenden Artzts Simplicissimi." In addition, there are twenty full-page copperplate engravings, eighteen in selected chapters of the original text and two in the "Continuationen," all having been taken from the *Wundergeschichten Calender.* The question still being debated today is this: are these additions and changes from the pen of Grimmelshausen or are they to be attributed to someone in the Felsecker's publishing house, someone like Johann Christoph Beer, the learned proofreader in that house, as Koschlig (1977, 297–534) suggests?

A comparison with the text of the first edition of *Simplicissimus Teutsch* and the other writings of Grimmelshausen tends to support the idea that a different hand was at work here. In the foreword, Simplicissimus takes the side of the Felsecker publishing house in an attempt to protect his work. It is done in such a crass manner that the likes of it cannot be found anywhere else in Grimmelshausen's oeuvre. The uniform, monotonously rhymed chapter headings, which replaced the ingeniously ironic prose headings of the first editions, do not contain the typical, ironic change in perspective characteristic of Grimmelshausen; instead, they provide a relatively flat summary of contents based strictly on the uniform perspective of "Simplex" (Wieckenberg 1969, 165). Thus the verse: "Simplex wird zu einem Hirten erwehlet/ Und das Lob selbigen Lebens erzehlet" replaces the original heading: "Das II. Capitel. Beschreibet die erste Staffel der Hoheit/ welche Simplicius gestiegen/ sampt dem Lob der Hirten/ und angehängter trefflichen Instruction." The numerous expansions of the text, and they are of differing lengths, give the impression of cheap imitations of the ingenious style of the author of *Simplicissimus Teutsch,* as for example, in the insertions in the fifth chapter of Book Four. In the first edition, we read: "Jch gedachte zwar heim an meine Liebste/ aber was halffs/ ich war leyder ein Mensch/ und fand eine solche wolproportionirte Creatur/ und zwar von solcher Lieblichkeit/ daß ich wol ein Ploch hätte seyn müssen/ wenn ich keusch hätte darvon kommen sollen." The person who reworked the "BarockSimplicissimus" adds after the word *sollen* the following: "über das operierten die Würste/ die mir mein Doctor zu fressen geben hatte/ das ich mich von selbst stellte/ als ob ich ein Bock worden wäre" (W I/1, 369 and 770). It seems as though the "love sausages" of Monsieur Canard got to the person reworking the text! He clarifies or, as the case may be, spoils two further sections with his shallow, associative comments. Right after the following sentence he returns to the sausages in another lengthy addition, and just a few sentences further on, at the end of the chapter, he refers a third time to the seasoned sausages. The "Continuationen" appended to Book Six, as well as the narratives from the calendars and the "Artzt-Zugab," actually the description of a picture separately published as a broadside by Felssecker, correspond exactly in both intention and style to these textual emendations.

The situation is somewhat different when we come to the accompanying illustrations. Eighteen of the twenty carry the inscription "Der Wahn betreugt." In *Wunderbarliches Vogel-Nest I*, the author refers specifically to this inscription as his own invention. The two illustrations in the appended "Continuationen" do not have this inscription, which not only calls into question the authenticity of these illustrations, but also that of the "Continuationen" themselves. It seems questionable that these simple pictures were produced specifically for the edition of 1671. Generally, Felssecker had more capable engravers at his disposal. It is possible that Grimmelshausen handed over these eighteen engravings together with the manuscript of the first edition and that the publisher first used them for a later edition. Still in all, the eighteen "genuine" engravings do not change significantly the re-working of the text, which, taken as a whole, trivializes the work. The changes were probably made by proofreaders of the publishing house, who paid no attention to the carefully conceived ten book cycle of Simplician works and who, in addition, were not really capable of imitating Grimmelshausen's ingenious, satiric Simplician style.

The same is true of the editing of the three-volume, posthumous edition of Collected Works published by Felssecker beginning in 1683. Volume One (C^1, presumably predated to 1684) had another printing in 1685 and in the same year a new edition (C^2), which itself was reprinted in 1701, 1703, and 1705. Finally, another new edition appeared in 1713 (C^3). This volume contains *Simplicissimus* and *Teutscher Michel*. Volume Two (1683), along with a new edition (C^2) in 1685, which was reprinted in 1699 and re-edited in 1713, contains *Springinsfeld, Coura-*

sche, Wunderbarliches Vogelnest I and *II, Keuscher Joseph,* and *Musai.* Volume Three (1684) contains the remaining writings of Grimmelshausen (except for *Anhang, Extract, Ewig-während er Calender* and *Bart-Krieg*) as well as six works which were not authored by Grimmelshausen. A new edition of this volume appeared in 1695 (C^2); it was reprinted in 1699 and, finally, a new edition appeared in 1713 (C^3).

This 1713 edition of the collected works is extolled as "neu verbessert" and "vermehrt." It contains a lengthy foreword of the publisher and an even longer "Vorerinnerung" of the editor. It is handsomely produced along with new title page copperplate engravings and numerous new illustrations of the text, each in the "recht lebhaften" style prevalent at the end of the seventeenth century (Wimmer, Hesselmann 1992, 117–30). In addition, it offers a smooth text with numerous additions in the form of edifying or moralizing comments in both prose and poetry; most often these are to be found at the end of the individual chapters. All texts are uniformly divided into chapters and have rhyming summaries as chapter headings; "epimythische" additions, found in individual chapters, make known the exemplary character of the chapters in terms of a super-imposed, uniform, narrow, orthodox set of morals. Their satirical meaning is limited to a single interpretation. Nevertheless, the editor limits his comments to volumes one and two; the *Simplicissimus Teutsch* edition contains the most commentaries. The desire to comment seems to have ebbed in volume three. Here we have only the rhyming summaries at the beginning of the chapters or, in the singular case of *Keuscher Joseph,* at the end of the chapters. There are even more extensive comments in the C^2 edition (cf. Hesselmann 1992, 109–17). The curious and discreet piety, which stood at a distance from the formal institution of the church, and which had imprinted its stamp so clearly on the Simplician cycle of novels as well as the shorter works of Grimmelshausen, is no longer present. Nor is the morality of the "weltstreichenden" doctor and runagate of the "Kalender-Continuationen." Missing, too, are the textual emendations of the Baroque *Simplicissimus.* Wolf Eberhard Felssecker had thought all these changes would make the novels more profitable. His son, Johann Jonathan, and his grandson, Adam Jonathan, who followed in his footsteps in the publishing trade, were obviously of a different opinion and they stuck closer to the strains of Lutheran orthodoxy prevalent in Nuremberg.

Editors of Grimmelshausen's works, beginning with Scholte, answered the query about greatest authenticity of the text by returning to the original, first editions, in which the author probably saw his intentions, rather than the interests of the publisher, most clearly realized.

That does not mean that the later emendations made by proofreaders and illustrators are of less value. They actually provided for the reputation of the author in the late seventeenth century as well as in the eighteenth century, because they were the editions through which readers knew the author and his novels at all. Those who reworked the editions in the eighteenth century based their texts on one of the editions of the collected works. The Romantic poets, too, who re-discovered the author of *Simplicissimus* around 1800 and provided for many new readers, read their "Greifnson" mainly in the versions of either the BarockSimplicissimus or of the collected works.

Imitations and Related Novels
Simpliciaden

It was not only the proofreaders of the Felssecker publishing house who noticed that Grimmelshausen had brought a new and fresh tone into the literary life of his times. They attempted to narrow the discrepancy between the new and the old, more desirable type of writing by their additions, changes, and comments. However, the figure of Simplicissimus and the use of first-person, ironic-satirical narratives, filled with the success stories of the protagonist, stimulated other writers and publishers to pursue imitations and continuations. The spectrum stretches from pirated editions of Grimmelshausen's novels in both Frankfurt and Hamburg through analogous novelesque presentations, calendars, letter-writing manuals and tracts to those authors whose only similarity with *Simplicissimus* consists of their use of the adjective Simplician for stories that are totally un-Simplician. Hesselmann (1992) offers an excellent overview of such works.

Johann Beer (1655–1700), the other great German storyteller of the seventeenth century, begins his list of novels, which are meant to entertain, with an imitation of Grimmelshausen's *Simplicissimus.* His *Simplicianischer Welt-Kucker* (four parts, 1677–1679), the adventurous biography of Jan Rebhu, makes use of certain suggestive moral episodes from *Simplicissimus,* for example the Beau-Alman adventures. However, he also includes the turning away from worldly things, the life of the hermit, a shipwreck combined with a stay on an island, use of the allegories of nature, as well as arguments and formulations meant to defend the use of satire. Imitations of these episodes as well as poetological statements occur in numerous other narrative works of Beer as well. In *Pokazi* (1680) and in the *Weiber-Hechel* (1680) we find a re-formulation of the didactic conversation between the hermit and the nameless child taken from Book One of *Simplicissimus*. In the *Narren-Spital* (1681), the lazy Lorenz has someone read aloud to him the paradise episode from Book Two of *Simplicissimus*, in the *Teutsche Winternächte* (1682), the country nobleman Ludwig reports that as a student he read *Simplicissimus*, in which, he says, "der ganze Teutsche oder Dreißigjährige Krieg" is described. In addition to his use of Grimmelshausen's main work, Beer seems to have found a number of ideas for his novels and tales in Grimmelshausen's *Wunderbarliches Vogel-Nest* (Hesselmann 1992, 135–51). However, the conception of these sections in Beer shows they are not simple imitations but rather, as, for example, his parodies of the turning away from worldly things show, an attempt to outdo the older author by playing on the emotions of the reader. Human nature, which is capable of almost anything, is supposed to be brought into a "gelinde" condition, quite in keeping with Christian norms and morals, but without the sharpness of the old dualism between God and the world.

In comparison with such independent use of Simplician narratives, the highpoints of which are seen in the "biographies" included in Beer's *Teutsche Winternächte* (1682) and *Kurzweilige Sommertäge* (1683), the so-called Simpliciaden, through which especially Matthäus Wagner, a publisher in Ulm, wanted to participate in the success of Grimmelshausen's *Simplicissimus*, clearly fall short. Johann Georg Schielen (1633–1684), the author involved, had understood *Simplicissimus* above all as a novel about the Thirty Years' War. A loquacious "cousin" of Simplicissimus narrates his novel, *Deß Französischen Kriegs-Simplicissimi hochverwunderlicher Lebens-Lauff* (1682–83), which appeared anonymously. He tells his picaresque life story in an inn, relating especially his adventures as a soldier in the service of France. His story includes broad didactic sections on geography and historical and political topics dealing with the war between France and the Netherlands.

Another anonymous work also appeared in Wagner's publishing house, the *Ungarischer oder Dacianischer Simplicissimus, Vorstellend Seinen wunderlichen Lebens-Lauff / Und sonderliche Begebenheiten gethaner Räisen* (1683, with a third edition in 1684). The work was written by "Dacianischer Simplicissimus," a pseudonym employed by the Silesian musician Daniel Speer (1636–1707). In the same year appeared a continuation, *Türckischer Vagant,* and in the next year, 1684, we find another offshoot, *Simplicianischer/ Lustig-Politischer Haspel-Hannß.* Following the example provided in Simplicissimus, Speer related in thirty chapters the life story of an orphaned Silesian child, who, after a short education in the school system, is employed in the service of a Polish nobleman. Along with other young people, he makes his way across the Carpathian Mountains to Hungary and there he is trained in music in the mining towns. He then joins the war against the Turks, is imprisoned, freed, and, as a trumpeter, sold or given from one Hungarian magnate to the next. Subsequently he is employed by noblemen in Siebenbürgen and finally lands in Constantinople. The continuation describes his travels through the Ottoman Empire. Stops along the way include Egypt, the Holy Land, Saudi Arabia, Cyprus, and, finally, once again, Constantinople. The major difference between his novel and those of Grimmelshausen lies in the linguistically clumsy narrative manner, which is pointless, and in the boring method of narration, which is totally lacking in irony. Such a narrative manner is reminiscent of the autobiographies of the time. The author's real goal is not satire at all, but rather an authentic description of the Hungarian landscape in time of war and crisis, written from a realistic, but picaresque perspective. Of particular interest is the detailed description of a descent from the Carpathian Mountains. Even today, the book ranks among the more important sources of Hungarian regional studies. When it appeared in 1683, it offered highly welcome information about the theater of war, in which the Turkish armies, unable to be stopped, were advancing toward Vienna.

An anonymous pamphlet, *Straßburgischer Staats-Simplicius* (1684), serves the cause of political agitation. It is a satire on the lack of reaction from the European powers to the annexation of the Imperial Free City of Strasbourg by France in 1681. It purportedly describes a trip of the aged Simplicius to twelve princely courts and is garnished with comic interludes and allusions to episodes of the original novel. Another Simpliciade, *Der Politische/ possierliche/ und doch manierliche/ Simplicianische Hasen-Kopff* (1689), appearing under the pseudonym Erasmus Grillandus, offers satirically conceived adventures in the milieu of the city bourgeoisie. These adventures, as the author (most certainly Johann Riemer) boldly maintains, might have stemmed, both in their variety and in the way the hero comes to terms with them, "aus des lächerlichen Simplicissimi Hirn." However, apart from the code word "simplicianisch," he offers nothing from the brains of Simplicissimus!

The anonymous author of *Simplicissimus Redivivus. Das ist: Der in Franckreich wieder belebte und curieus bekörperte alte Simplicius, welcher mit der Französischen Armée nach Prag marchiret ist, dabey viele wunderliche Abendtheuer erlebt hat* (1743) seeks a closer connection to Grimmelshausen's *Simplicissimus,* which he knew from the posthumous edition of collected works. The subtitle motivates the re-establishment of the genre. After reading *Simplicissimus,* a French magician has conjured up the spirit of Simplicissimus in his laboratory in Paris and "bekörpert" him. After serving as a laboratory assistant, this new being allows himself to be recruited into the French army and he goes with this army to Prague in order to participate in the War of Austrian Succession. Prague, of course, is captured, and Simplicissimus comes to the Austrian side as a result of the changing fortunes of war. Hence, we are dealing with reports, presented in a picaresque fashion, about the events of the war of 1741–42. The whole story is written in the style of Simplicissimus. The author characterizes Grimmelshausen's book as "curieus" and at the same time as a moral and satirical "zeitvertreibliches" book. In 1744, he published a sequel, which follows the course of the war: *Der [. . .] sich noch in dem Kriege befindliche Simplicissimus Redivivus, Schreibet von Straßburg an einen Vertrauten Caffée-Sieder nach Prag.* The hero comments on the relevant military and political developments from an Austrian point of view, although he no longer pays any attention to the fictional framework of the earlier novel.

The content of Grimmelshausen's *Continuatio* also continued to have its effect on other authors. The events narrated in chapters 19–27 of the *Continuatio* (shipwreck, rescue, and the existence of Simplicissimus on the island) are items Grimmelshausen had found in a work by the de Bry brothers (1601) and in *The Isle of Pines* by Henry Neville (German version 1668). Of course, he then reworked them to suit his purpose. Fifty years later, these same items found their classical form in Daniel Defoe's *Robinson Crusoe* (1719), although he, too, reworked them to suit his purpose. However, that was not the end of the influence of Grimmelshausen's *Continuatio.* In 1731, Johann Gottfried Schnabel's novel *Wunderliche Fata einiger Seefahrer* (later known as *Insel Felsenburg*) appeared, and it became the most successful German treatment of this topic. Schnabel did not find the models for the portrayal of the shipwreck of his hero, Albertus Julius, his rescue, his pious life on an island, and his refusal to return to a sinful Europe in Defoe's work, but rather in Grimmelshausen's *Continuatio.*

In addition to his *Simplicissimus,* Grimmelshausen's *Courasche* also influenced a later work: *Falsette/ Das ist: Eine Beschreibung Einer Ertzbetriegerin* (1686). The anonymous author allows an aging whore to tell the eventful story of her life in an attempt to outdo the picaresque and Simplician models. Falsette knows neither repentance nor conversion. Another author builds a story based on Falsette, *Falsetta rediviva inpunita* (1726). As the seventeenth century drew to a close, the *Erste Beernhäuter* also continued to draw some attention. Thus, Eberhard Werner

Happel includes the story, in slightly changed and moralizing form (the painting episode has been deleted), in a collection, entitled *Grösseste Denckwürdigkeiten der Welt oder so genandte Relationes curiosae* (1685). Among Grimmelshausen's other works, only the *Keuscher Joseph* inspired others to imitation. The author himself complained about Philipp von Zesen's *Assenat*. In 1690, Heinrich Anselm Ziegler von Kliphausen (1663–1697) used the corresponding passages from Grimmelshausen's *Keuscher Joseph* for the portrayal of the lascivious beauty of his heroine, Sephira, in his *Helden Liebe Der Schrift Alten Testaments/ in sechzehn Anmuthigen Liebes-Begebenheiten*. There also exists a drama manuscript from 1741 from the Swiss town of Steckborn, which deals with the Joseph figure as we know it from Grimmelshausen. Wimmer (1976) first reported on this drama, the *Historie von dem keuschen Jüngling Joseph in einer Comödie vorgestellet*.

Related Novels from the Romantic Period

During the course of the remainder of the eighteenth century there were no more imitations or re-workings of the narratives or figures from Grimmelshausen's works. The Romantic poets, who had gone through the Enlightenment and the Revolution, were the first ones who, after the old empire had fallen apart, recognized the value of the religiously based medieval and early modern culture for the national consciousness. They, too, re-discovered this ironic author from the baroque period along with his Simplician family. They then used his texts as they composed various montages. Jakob Koeman (1993) was the first to investigate this creative use of Grimmelshausen's texts.

During this phase of revolutionary changes in Europe, the Jupiter episode from Book 3 of *Simplicissimus* was the first item to precipitate direct copying. In his tale *Ein Tagebuch* (1798), Ludwig Tieck made the reading of Grimmelshausen by his narrator, the fictional diarist, a theme of the work. Hans Michael Moscherosch's *Gesichte Philanders von Sitte-wald* (1640) and Christian Weise's "political" novel, a kind of early, primitive educational novel, *Die drey ärgsten Ertz-Narren in der gantzen Welt* (1672), also played a role in this work, which takes place within the framework of an educational trip during which the narrator is searching for the greatest fools. Engaged in political discussions at a table d'hôte, Tieck's hero accidentally stumbles onto *Simplicissimus*. While reading, he discovers that the satirical portrayal of the political projects of Jupiter are "noch nicht unpassend geworden" and that a lasting peace can only by achieved by a hero similar to the one in that episode of the novel. He gets into a quarrel with a fanatical Republican, to whom he then reads aloud the text of the Jupiter episode "mit ironischer Ernsthaftigkeit." Their quarrel ends in a duel; the narrator, wounded, realizes in his pains that he himself was the greatest fool. The story attempts to show that the Jupiter episode was superior to the political dreams in the years prior to Napoleon's seizing of power. The narrator notes that the Jupiter episode had not only the greater truths and similarity to life on its side, but that it also offered "mehr Poesie" and a "besseren Styl" than the enlightened political journals.

Just as Napoleon came on the scene as a "Held," albeit not a "Teutscher Held," who would provide a new and lasting peace and order in Europe, another author, Johann Christian Ludwig Haken, once again posed, this time in the form of a sly satirical tract, the question about the timeliness of the Jupiter episode from *Simplicissimus*. In his work, *Der Held des neunzehnten Jahrhunderts, eine Apokalypse des siebzehnten: oder die erfüllteste Weissagung neuerer Zeiten* (1809), Haken publishes the entire text of the Jupiter episode, although he has made major revisions to it. He precedes the text with short explanations about how he found a prophecy from the seventeenth century that seems to have been realized in the present time. In order to make the prophecy apply to Napoleon, he has to change the "Teutscher Held" into a "Held" and play down the German aspect of the work. The author also provides commentary on individual parts of the text, and he proves with an ironic emphasis that the old prophecy could only have to do with Napoleon and his adherents in Germany. Since he was able to escape the censors, he then explains, in accord with the text, that the Napoleonic regime is really a reign of terror.

In his comedy, *Zerbino oder die Reise nach dem guten Geschmack* (1799), which is directed against the Enlightenment, Tieck provided a new arrangement of another episode from *Simplicissimus* which after that became one of the Romantics' regular motifs. It centers around the story of the hermit, who was the father of Simplicissimus, and his evening song, "Komm Trost der Nacht/ O Nachtigal." In one of the hermit scenes, which are strewn throughout the work, we find the dialogue between the hermit and a young visitor, Helikanus. It is here that Tieck, in accord with his source, incorporates the Simplician father-son constellation. The Nachtigall-Lied has its own scene in the third act. Other reworkings of the hermit episode and the Nachtigall-Lied can be found in Clemens Brentano's *Märchen von dem Schulmeister Klopfstock und seinen fünf Söhnen* (written ca. 1808) and in the works of Eichendorff. Actually, Eichendorff has two versions of the Nachtigall-Lied in his novel *Ahnung und Gegenwart* (1815). One of the versions is in the fairy tale about the water sprite and the beautiful Ida in chapter 5, the other in Leontin's song in chapter 13. In Eichendorff's tale *Eine Meerfahrt* (1816), Spanish sailors meet up with the hermit on a deserted island and the *Nachtigall-Lied* is sung, in still another version. The deserted island is clearly based on the "Kreuzinsel" of Simplicissimus from the *Continuatio*. Characteristic for the nineteenth century is that the song was set by music by a variety of composers. Wilhelm Heinrich Riehl (1855), Adolf Jensen (prior to 1879), Fritz Scheiding (1895), and later von Armin Knab (1941) wrote versions for a single voice and piano. In addition there were various versions of the song written for a choir.

The predilection of the Romantics for outsiders found material in different places in Grimmelshausen's work. They found the depictions of the Gypsies in *Courasche, Springinsfeld* and *Rathstübel Plutonis* interesting. In addition, they were attracted to the depiction of the harvesting and care of the mandrake root from both the *Galgen-Männlein* and the tale entitled *Erster Beernhäuter*. Achim von Arnim's novella *Philander unter streifenden Soldaten und Zigeunern im dreißigjährigen Krieg* (1809) proves to be a collage of lightly reworked texts from Moscherosch's *Gesichte Philanders von Sittewald* and Grimmelshausen's *Springinsfeld*. From Grimmelshausen's work he chose sections from chapters 4 to 6. These sections include the capture of the writer by Courasche's band of Gypsies, his obligation to write down her life story as she dictated it, his report about the living conditions among the Gypsies, his betrothal to the young Gypsy woman, and the deception and departure of the Gypsies. Eichendorff's portrayal of Gypsies in his novel *Dichter und ihre Gesellen* (1834) also harkens back to *Springinsfeld*, but here in a comic role-playing situation. In chapter 9 of Eichendorff's novel, the wandering theater troupe meets Otto, the friendly student, spies on him, plays out the Gypsy episode from *Springinsfeld,* and forces him to take on the role of the writer.

Grimmelshausen's description of the harvesting and care of the profitable mandrake root, as well as the *spiritus familiaris* which would also make one rich, was a favorite subject among the Romantic poets, beginning with Tieck's novella *Der Runenberg* (1804). We also find it in Friedrich de la Motte-Fouqué's novella *Das Galgenmännlein* (1810), which was later dramatized by Ferdinand Rosenau (*Vizlipuzli* 1817). Achim von Arnim's novella *Isabella von Ägypten, Kaiser Karl des Fünften erste Jugendliebe* (1812) makes use of it as well. Here, the Gypsy Bella wins her "financier" precisely according to Grimmelshausen's description; he gets the name Cornelius, and actually plays a role in the story.

Grimmelshausen's tale about the *Beernhäuter* actually gained, within the circle of the Heidelberg Romantics, the status of a programmatic work with which one could distance oneself from the camp of the rationalists (Voss, Cotta). Clemens Brentano's parodistic version appeared in several installments (1808) in their journal, *Zeitung für Einsiedler* — itself a nod in Grimmelshausen's direction. The work carried the rather baroque title *Geschichte und Ursprung des ersten Bärnhäuters Worin die Volkssage vom papiernen Calender-Himmel, und vom süßen breiten Gänsefuß nach Erzählungen einer alten Kinderfrau aufgeschrieben vom Herzbruder.* Brentano works into the existing narrative framework a plethora of episodes and motifs from the farcical tales of the sixteenth century, from Spangenberg's *Ganskönig*, from Pliny's *Historia naturalis*, from *Eulenspiegel*, and from Christian Reuter's short novel *Schelmuffsky* (1696–97). This results in a rather broadly drawn, fantastic literary satire. The additions and changes made to the originals make the Bärenhäuter into an allegory of the Romantic. He is a vagabond, an artist, a hermit, an unkempt scholar, who protects rejected animals from the Philistines, teaches them to write, and finally, is himself transfigured at the end of the story into the *Ursa Major* constellation (Koeman 399). Brentano goes even further. He gives the noble gentleman from Grimmelshausen's tale the name Cotta and in so doing provides for all sorts of possibilities of an aggressive satire, filled with contemporary allusions. The satire is, of course, strictly tied to the times, as it is directed at the publisher of the *Morgenblatt für gebildete Stände*. Nor could Achim von Arnim leave the *Beernhäuter* alone. In the previously mentioned novella, *Isabella von Ägypten, Kaiser Karl des Fünften erste Jugendliebe*, he has the entire story of the *Beernhäuter* told. He replaces the noble gentleman, however, with the pope, and he gives that pope three "natural" daughters: Past, Present, and Future. The Future is to become the bride of the Bärenhäuter. He revises the fairy tale ending present in Grimmelshausen's version. Instead, he has a "Bärenhäuter redivivus" function as the miserly guard of the mandrake named Cornelius.

The Grimm brothers likewise changed the *Beernhäuter* tale so that it would fit into their style and their special purposes in their famously influential collection of fairy tales, *Kinder- und Hausmärchen* (1812/14). Actually, there are three differing fairy tales which are connected to Grimmelshausen's tale: *Des Teufels rußiger Bruder* (1815), *Der Teufel Grünrock* (1815), and *Der Bärenhäuter* (1843). In the two versions from 1815 the original can only be recognized in individual motifs and strands of action. The Grimms, who claim to be preserving the oral traditions of the stories, have added other motifs and settings. These include a pact with the devil, the devil's money, a visit to hell, and a rescue from the power of the devil. Whatever did not fit in with the traditional oral version of the tale, for example historical dates or tidbits of knowledge, has simply been dropped.

Justinus Kerner has shown that the tale about the Bärenhäuter can also be dramatized. This change of genre has also found some followers in the twentieth century. Kerner's comedy, *Der Bärenhäuter im Salzbade: Ein Schattenspiel* (1811–1835) is directed, as was Brentano's reworking, against the rationalistic spirit of the times. Kerner enriched his plot by adding characters from a contemporary spa. The Bärenhäuter is no longer a farmhand but instead has become a crooked tailor. He is sent by the devil to chase the pious daughter of one of the guests at the spa. He never really has any success. In the end, he is taken by the devil, in whom now even the rational preacher at the spa is willing to believe. These Romantic adaptations of the baroque tale have in common that they bring in the devil and set up the religious world of the baroque in contrast to the enlightened present, and they do so in a provocative manner. Grimmelshausen, on the other hand, had suppressed somewhat the religious ideas and had only spoken of a "Geist" in a neutral way, in order to be able to portray a problem of contemporary art.

Newer Poetic Versions

As time passed, the Beernhäuter even became part of the genre of opera. In 1897, the opera *Der Bärenhäuter* appeared, with a libretto by Hermann Wette and music by Arnold Mendelssohn, a composer from Frankfurt who later taught Hindemith. Just one year later Siegfried Wagner, son of Richard Wagner, published his opera, for which he had also written the libretto. It too was called *Der Bärenhäuter;* it had its premiere at the Royal Theater in Munich in 1899. One of the newest versions of the original *Beernhäuter* tale stems from the pen of Hans Baumann: *Der Bärenhäuter: Ein Soldatenspiel* (1942). The composer Karl Amadeus Hartmann seems more clearly akin to the author of *Simplicissimus Teutsch*. His opera, *Des Simplicius Simplicissimus Jugend,* written between 1934 and 1936, had its first real premiere only in 1948 in Cologne, although concert versions had been performed in Munich. The opera follows Book One of *Simplicissimus Teutsch* and shows us the horrors of war and of bands of soldiers; it culminates in the dressing down of Simplicius at the fortress in Hanau. Hartmann combines the language of Grimmelshausen with a much more modern music, in order to expose the political realities of 1936, although it is clothed in an historical situation (cf. Bauer 1988).

Only with the rediscovery of Grimmelshausen by the Romantics and the creative re-workings of his literary figures did the canonization of the great baroque author begin. Interestingly it runs parallel with the establishment of "Germanistik" and the creation of German classes. The more progress this canonization made, the more his texts were read and interpreted, the more his biography was researched — these all seemed to make other authors less ready to imitate his works or to re-work them creatively, or at least to be able to resist them. This seems to have been possible only in the related artistic fields, like music or film. Still, the name Simplicissimus could be used as the name of a program, as the title of the satirical journal, *Simplicissimus,* shows (1897–1944, 1954–date).

Artists not only provided commissioned illustrations for editions of Grimmelshausen's works; they also provided independent folders of works and artists' books with graphics related to *Simplicissimus,* to *Courasche, Springsinsfeld, Wunderbarliches Vogelnest,* and *Beernhäuter. Simplicissimus* is the subject of Max Klinger's series of etchings entitled *Intermezzi* (1881), of August Macke's drawings (1909/1910), Walter Klemm's series of twelve stone drawings (1916), Erich Erler-Samaden's etchings (1921), Kare Schmidt-Wolfratshausen's linocuts (1921), Ernst Barlach's wood engraving "Simplicius bei dem Einsiedler" (1925), Hans Sauerbruch's pen-and-ink drawings (1934), Max Hunziker's 174 etchings, drawings, and paintings, Josef Hegenbarth's drawings (1961), A. Paul Weber's lithographs, pen-and-ink drawings, and charcoal sketches (1970), Fritz Eichenberg's wood engravings (1981), Jiri Anderle's drawings (1983), and Udo Claassen's drawings (1983). Other works of Grimmelshausen also provided artists with material. One thinks of Max Unold's woodcuts of *Springinsfeld* (1925), the drawings of Josef Hegenbarth (1939), of Bernhard Heisig (1969), and of Gerhart Kraaz (1970), all dealing with *Courasche,* and the colored wood engravings of Bruno Goldschmitt dealing with *Wunderbarliches Vogelnest I* (1917). Martin Bircher's exhibition (1990) was an impressive display of twentieth-century art related to Grimmelshausen (see Bircher).

Literary works of the twentieth century presuppose the canonization of Grimmelshausen. Here, too, as with other classical authors, the writers seek points of comparison with the contemporary situation. For most of them, it is the experience of war and the ability to deal with it critically via the written word that makes the reference to the work and the life of the classical author worthwhile. We clearly see the fruit of an identificatory reading of the much admired author in each of the following: Ernst Stadler's poem *Simplicius wird Einsiedel im Schwarzwald und schreibt seine Lebensgeschichte* (1914), Bertolt Brecht's drama *Mutter Courage und ihre Kinder: Eine Chronik aus dem Dreißigjährigen Krieg* (1941–49), to which Georg Tabori's *Mutters Courage* (1979) alludes, Johannes R. Becher's verse epic *Grimmelshausen 1625–1676* (1944), Thomas Mann's allusion to the language of Grimmelshausen in *Doktor Faustus* (1947), and Günter Grass's *Das Treffen in Telgte* (1979). However, the interest in Grimmelshausen, the classical author of the German baroque, has been expressed since Romanticism above all in the continuous run of new editions, in re-workings of his text for young readers, in illustrated editions, and in interpretations, which are almost too numerous to be counted. These interpretations are based on readings that are more or less closely tied to the Zeitgeist dominant at the time they were written.

New Editions and Translations

In the eighteenth century, too, there were, subsequent to the last post-humous editions of the collected works printed by Felssecker (1713), several new editions. However, due to the changing taste of the readers, most of these offered a re-worked text, so changed in most cases that it was almost unrecognizable. One such edition is *Simplicissimus: Der Wechsel des Glücks und Unglücks im Krieg, oder Wunderbahre Begebenheiten Herrn Melchior Sternfels von Fuchsheim, Eines Gebornen Edelmanns,* which was published in Leipzig (1756) and was clearly indebted to Gottsched, the literary pope reigning there at the time. Of the original 139 chapters, there remain only 53, in which the editor related the education of a young nobleman and his ever-changing fortunes during wartime. There is nothing left of the satirical or comical touch. Anything that the rationalistic editor considered repugnant, either in terms of content or in terms of language, is either stricken or made unobjectionable.

There is even less of Simplicissimus remaining in the "empfindsame" re-telling of the story by Christian Jacob Wagenseil. His first attempt was a thirteen-page summary of *Simplicissimus* in the fourth volume of Heinrich Reichard's *Bibliothek der Romane* (1779). His lengthier re-telling of the story appeared as *Der abentheuerliche Simplicissimus: Auch Melchior Sternfels genannt. Neu bearbeitet* (Leipzig 1785). Wagenseil replaces the first person narrative with an omniscient narrator, who wants to make "das ganze genießbarer" for his readers. It is certainly the exception when his wording corresponds to that of the original. It is no surprise that a review of this work (1787) called for an edition that has not been corrupted. An anonymous edition, which appeared in Frankfurt and

Leipzig three years later, comes close to that, despite its flowery title: *Der im vorigen Jahrhundert so weltberufene Simplicissimus v. Einfaltspinsel, in einem neuen Kleide nach dem Schnitt des Jahres 1790. Neue nach dem 1684 aufgelegten Original umgearbeitete Auflage in sechs Büchern.*

In his 876 pages, the editor struck, overall, only the "moralischen Betrachtungen," which the person who reworked the edition used (C^2) had actually added. In addition, he substantially reworked, in keeping with the taste prevalent at that time, the poems in Book One as well as the language in general. Only in the "je-pète" episode did he feel a footnote was necessary. Still in all, he attracted the anger of the critics (Hesselmann 230–36). One of them, comparing various editions of the seventeenth century, already realized that the editions beginning in 1684 had textual emendations not done by Grimmelshausen. All the critics reject the linguistic changes that made the work appear modern; they demanded a return to the early, individual editions, along with commentary on both words and things. Still, it was not yet time for that, as the new editions of *Springsinsfeld* and *Courasche* (1791) are, as was *Simplicissimus,* modernized with regard to language; the basis of these editions was also the text of the collected works. The title is of baroque length: *Lächerliche und unterhaltliche Lebensgeschichte des im vorigen Jahrhunderte allgemein bekannten tapfern Soldaten Kilian Springinsfeld, getreuen Kriegskammeraden des Simplizius, zuletzt aber verarmten Landstörtzers. Mit einem Anhange von der begünstigten Liebhaberin des Simplizius, Jungfer Courage.*

The Romantics, beginning with Ludwig Tieck, were not dependent on such editions for their textual re-workings. They went back directly to the editions of the seventeenth century, which, as one critic mentioned in the *Allgemeine Literatur-Zeitung* (1787), were still available for purchase in various bookstores (Hesselmann 1992, 224). Still, re-workings of *Simplicissimus* continued to appear, and every editor, without any scruples whatsoever, simply based his text on that edition which he happened to have at hand. Johann Christian Ludwig Haken published his re-working under the title of *Der Abentheuerliche Simplicissimus in zweckmäßigen Auszügen* (1810). Haken wanted to put out an entire library of such adventure novels, but he managed only this first volume of his planned series. His re-working offers an adventure novel, strong in terms of action, but in a language which has been modernized. However, the basis for his text is one of the early editions (either E^1 or E^2).

Whereas Haken responded to the needs of his readers in the era of Romanticism, Friedrich Christoph Weissen uses his free re-working of *Simplicissimus* as a satire on the Romantic writers themselves. This he does by using an ironic style and additions that really are commentaries. His work appeared in 1822 in Berlin under the title: *Schalckheit und Einfalt, Oder der Simplicissimus des 17. Jahrhunderts im Gewande des neunzehnten. Ein Roman in zwey Theilen.* The hermit episode, which was particularly important to the Romantic poets, and the nightingale song are presented in an ironic tone; Romantic poetry is mocked at every opportunity (Meid 214–15). In 1801, Tieck himself had given up his plans to re-work *Simplicissimus,* mainly because of the difficulties he expected from the critics. His young friend, Karl Edward von Bülow, made up for this just one generation later. Brockhaus in Leipzig published his re-working of the editio princeps with the title *Die Abenteuer des Simplicissimus: Ein Roman aus der Zeit des dreißigjährigen Krieges* (1836). Von Bülow, who had already edited re-workings of *Beernhäuter* (1834) and *Stolzer Melcher* (1836), criticized in his foreword the previous unsuccessful attempts to modernize the novel. Nevertheless, he also did not want to offer his readers an edition that corresponded word for word to the first edition; instead, he tried to "verbessern," linguistically, stylistically, and by omitting parts of the text. He wanted to meet the expectations of his readers for a vivid cultural portrait and a "Volksbuch" from the era of the Thirty Years' War. By virtue of such a "Restauration," von Bülow's edition was really no different than the ones that had preceded it.

Meantime, however, that other child of the Romantic poets, German literary science with its principles for editing works in a classical and philological manner (the method used for medieval works), had also grown up. Thus, the numerous reviewers of von Bülow's editions no longer had any understanding for dealing in such a high-handed way with these texts, which were, after all, part of the national tradition. They produced positive criticism, and two of them, Hermann Kurz (1837) and Theodor Echtermeyer (1838), were, for the first time, successful in decoding the many anagrams that Grimmelshausen had used. Hence, they were the first ones able to determine both the extent and the interconnectedness of Grimmelshausen's entire oeuvre, and they were able as well to shore it up from a biographical standpoint.

That was the beginning of research on Grimmelshausen, but, of course, it was only in the twentieth century that scholars of note, such as Jan Hendrik Scholte (1912), Artur Bechtold (1921), Hans Heinrich Borcherdt (1921), and Manfred Koschlig (1939) were able to provide a scientific analysis of the printing history of Grimmelshausen's works. The nineteenth century editors, all of whom wanted to edit the first edition of *Simplicissimus,* were still groping in the dark. Wilhelm Ludwig

Holland mistakenly used the pirated edition of 1669, which had appeared in Frankfurt and had been reworked in terms of language (E^{3a}), as the basis for his edition (1851). Rudolf Kögel (1880) did the same in his new edition, while Adalbert von Keller (*Der abentheuerliche Simplicissimus und andere Schriften von Hans Jacob Christoph von Grimmelshausen*, four vols., Stuttgart 1854–1862) decided to use the edition known as E^1. Heinrich Kurz, on the other hand, based his edition (1863) on the so-called "BarockSimplicissimus" (E^5), just as Felix Bobertag (1882) and Hans Heinrich Borcherdt (1921) did in their new editions. Each and every one of these editors thought he was offering the most authentic text possible. Scholte was actually the first one who was able to distinguish among the first editions. He based his own editions on the real first editions: *Courasche* (1923), *Springsinsfeld* (1928), *Wunderbarliches Vogelnest I* (1931), *Simplicissimus* (1938), *Continuatio* (1939), *Simplicissimus in Auswahl*, which included some *Continuationen* from the calendars, *Rathstübel Plutonis, Bart-Krieg*, and *Teutscher Michel* (1943). Rolf Tarot and his co-editors, Franz Günter Sieveke and Wolfgang Bender, followed Scholte's example in their standard edition of *Gesammelte Werke in Einzelausgaben* (thirteen vols., Tübingen 1967–1976), as did Dieter Breuer in his edition of the narrative works along with commentary (three vols., Frankfurt 1989–1997). There is still considerable debate as to whether the "BarockSimplicissimus" (E^5) is to be considered the *Ausgabe letzter Hand* and to be edited as such.[1] To date, there is still no standard edition of the *Ewig-währender Calender*.[2]

One should not overestimate the role of the standard editions when considering Grimmelshausen's effectiveness as an author. For the general reader it is still the reworked, re-edited, and often illustrated edition that keeps the classical author Grimmelshausen alive through the ages. Thomas Bürger (1976, 235) counted close to two hundred new editions during the years 1756–1976, not to mention well over a hundred new printings of these editions. These are all editions of *Simplicissimus*. Except for *Courasche*, none of the other works has had a significant audience. Only about one fourth of these editions could be termed scholarly editions. The majority of these editions come from the twentieth century, in which one also sees higher numbered printings than for those editions of the eighteenth and nineteenth centuries. The basic editorial principles, however, are the same as they were in the eighteenth century. The editors cut out the sections less important for the "story" and they modernize the language and style, often to the point where they simply re-tell the story rather freely. The latter is especially true for editions of *Simplicissimus* meant for children and younger readers. The drastically truncated edition, provided with pen and ink sketches by Henrich Kley, has been particularly successful. It first appeared in 1911, and, by 1940, over 206,000 copies were in circulation.

From the very beginning, Grimmelshausen's books were illustrated. However, only in the twentieth century did scholars begin to sense the value of the original baroque illustrations (Scholte 1912, Penkert 1973, Noehles 1976, Sestendrup 1983, Wimmer n.d., Hesselmann 1992). Numerous artists around the end of the nineteenth century and in the twentieth century, as shown above, illustrated the texts of Grimmelshausen. In doing so, they contributed to the widespread dissemination of his works, particularly of *Simplicissimus*, as reading material for children and young adults.

In comparison with the continually increasing number of editions of Grimmelshausen's works since 1850, translations were slow in coming. Only in the twentieth century, once Grimmelshausen was firmly entrenched in the German literary canon, do we find translations into other languages. The translations are limited to *Simplicissimus* and *Courasche;* most of them are more or less strongly reworked and shortened versions of the novels. The English translation by Alfred Thomas Goodrick, *The Adventurous Simplicissimus, Being the Description of The Life of a Strange Vagabond Named Melchior Sternfels von Fuchshaim. Written in German by Hans Jacob Christoph von Grimmelshausen and Now for the First Time Done into English* (1912), was the first. After the First World War there followed translations into French by Maurice Colleville (*La vagabond Courage*, 1922 and *Les aventures de Simplicius Simplicissimus*, two vols, 1926), into Russian by E. G. Guru (*Simplicissimus*, 1925), and into Italian by Angelo Treves (*L'aventuroso Simplicissimus*, 1928). The majority of the translations, however, appeared only after the Second World War. The translations of Colleville were reprinted (1951 and 1963) as was that of Goodrick (1962). Camilla Conigliani (1945) and Ugo Dèttore and Bianca Ugo (1945) produced new translations of *Simplicissimus* into Italian. The first Japanese translation of *Simplicissimus* was by Kiyonobu Kamimura (1951). A more complete translation by Ichie Mochizuki followed (1953) as did a translation of *Courasche* by Nakada Miki (1967). There are translations of *Simplicissimus* into Finnish, Czech (several different ones), Serbian, Flemish, Polish, Swedish, Slovenian, Danish, Hungarian, Russian, Rumanian and new English translations for the American book market by Hans Speier (1964), Georg Schulz-Behrend (1965), and Monte Adair (1986). All of these, together with the translation of *Simplicissimus* into Chinese by Ms. Li Shu (1984) have made Grimmelshausen a worldwide known representative of German culture.

Interestingly, early translations of Grimmelshausen's historical novels appeared in Swedish. In 1690 there appeared in Uppsala a Swedish *Keuscher Joseph*, in 1697 in Stockholm a Swedish *Musai*. In 1763 a Swedish translation of *Proximus und Lympida* appeared in Norrköping and in 1767 a new translation of *Keuscher Joseph* appeared in Uppsala.

Grimmelshausen: Mentioned, Honored, Remembered

Even though his true identity was not known for a long time, the author Grimmelshausen had always been in the public eye of the literary world. His contemporaries had, to be sure, underestimated his new way of writing. The educator and novelist Christian Weise (1642–1708) had called the author of *Simplicissimus* a "ledernen Salbader." Obviously he misunderstood the basic religious stance of the author. The novelist Philipp von Zesen (1619–1689) had found fault with Grimmelshausen's rather free use of historical sources, which quite angered Grimmelshausen, because he trusted his poetic genius more than sources. Quirin Moscherosch (1623–1675) felt that Grimmelshausen the satirist had attacked him, along with others, and he schemed against him. Grimmelshausen, quite oblivious to all of this, sent him a friendly dedicatory poem for his new volume of poetry.

However, the great reading public, composed of people from all walks of life, was of a different opinion about "Samuel Greifnson" as Hesselmann has shown (1992, 17–50). Johannes Praetorius, from Leipzig and holder of a master's degree, referred extensively in his works to *Satirischer Pilgram* and *Simplicissimus*. The Nuremberg poet, Sigmund von Birken (1626–1681), even sent several copies of *Simplicissimus* to a friendly book dealer in Bayreuth (1669). Duchess Sophie of Hannover had heard of this new novel in 1670 and asked her brother, the Prince Elector of the Palatinate, to have someone buy it for her. She received it along with the *Courasche*. She was particularly charmed by her reading of *Courasche*, less so by her reading of *Simplicissimus*. The latter work seemed to her to be too religious, as she noted in her thank-you letter. The Capuchin monk, Procopius von Templin (1608–1680), a convert to Catholicism, used episodes from *Simplicissimus* for his cycles of sermons and later for his printed collections of sermons (Kirchweihpredigten *Encaeniale* 1671 and *Patrociniale* 1674). Even the *Courasche* seemed worthwhile enough for him to mention to the faithful. On the other hand, Christian Selhammer, a preacher from Salzburg, strictly rejected the use of *Simplicissimus* as a source of examples to be used in sermons (1696). The novelist Wolfgang Caspar Printz (1641–1717) also mentions Greifnson (1675). Johann Ludwig Hartmann, the Lutheran superintendent from Rothenburg refers in his tract on superstition (1680) to Grimmelshausen's *Galgen-Männlin*. Daniel Georg Morhof (1639–1691), a university professor in Kiel, had, if one is to believe his handbook (*Unterricht Von der Teutschen Sprache und Poesie* [1682/ 1700]), at least heard of Greifnson's *Satirischer Pilgram*. Another professor from Kiel, the moral theologian Georg Pasch, refers in 1707 to the popularity of *Simplicissimus* and *Courasche*. The great philosopher, Gottfried Wilhelm Leibniz (1646–1716), who heard an episode from *Simplicissimus* during an Easter Sunday sermon in 1688 in Munich, went back and read the novel. He compares it, in a letter to Duchess Sophie (mentioned above), with the *Francion* of Charles Sorel. This was, as Manfred Koschlig was able to show (1957) an important reference for Grimmelshausen's own understanding of the genre in which he was writing. In the same year (1688), Christian Thomasius compares in his *Monats-Gespräche* (Januar 1688) the *Keuscher Joseph* with Zesen's *Assenat* and recommends Grimmelshausen's novel. The Breslau medical doctor, novelist, and apothecary Johann Christoph Ettner von Eiteritz (1650– 1724) discusses in his long novel *Der unwürdige Doktor* (1697) the Mummelsee episode as well as Simplicissimus's attempt to discover a medicinal spring with the help of a miraculous stone. In a later novel, *Der Verwegene Chirurgus* (1698), he takes up the motif of invisibility by referring to the *Wunderbarliches Vogelnest*.

Once set before the tribunal of the Enlightenment author, Johann Christoph Gottsched (1700–1766), Grimmelshausen's satirical works ceased to exist. He had already expressed his disapproval of Grimmelshausen in 1725 in his moral weekly, *Die Vernünftigen Tadlerinnen*, and in his *Critische Dichtkunst* he admits only that they were "bekannt und beliebt." We find similarly sparse information in Johann Heinrich Zedler's famous eighteenth-century encyclopedia *Großes vollständiges Universal-Lexikon Aller Wissenschaften und Künste*. In the entry entitled "Simplicissimus" (Vol. 8, col. 1524) we read that this invented name had been attached to the title of various books and there is a reference to the posthumous edition of collected works from the year 1713. Christian Gottlieb Jöcher's *Allgemeines Gelehrten-Lexikon* (1750) contains an entry under "Grimmelshausen" and one under "Simplicius." The former lists the two historical novels that had appeared under the real name of the poet; the latter lists *Simplicissimus, Ewig-währender Calender, Galgen-Männlin, Verkehrte Welt, Satyrischer Pilgram*, and two works by Johann

Beer. Nor do Gotthold Ephraim Lessing's notes on Jöcher's *Lexikon* lead us any further; they show only that he was aware of Greifnson's *Simplicissimus, Keuscher Joseph* and *Satyrischer Pilgram* as they appeared in the first edition of collected works.

Wagenseil's note (1785) that "der selige Lessing" had encouraged him to work on a new edition of *Simplicissimus* was much more important. Abraham Gotthelf Kästner, a professor of mathematics in Göttingen, took pride in his proof that the first "Robinsonade" was not *Robinson Crusoe*, but rather long before that another work, namely the *Continuatio* of the *Simplicissimus Teutsch*. Friedrich von Blankenburg, who re-worked Sulzer's *Allgemeine Theorie der Schönen Künste* (1792–94) mentions Greifnson's writings in the articles dealing with "Erzählung" and with "Satire." In the second edition (1795–98) of Erduin Julius Koch's *Compendium der Deutschen Literatur-Geschichte* (1790) all of Grimmelshausen's works are listed under Greifnson, including those that had appeared under his real name (Hans Jakob Christoph von Grimmelshausen). This combined listing played a more significant role with the Romantic authors and their turning to the writings of Greifnson. He also was able to differentiate among the early printings of *Simplicissimus* and he provides comments on the baroque imitations. Koch was the teacher and friend of Wilhelm Heinrich Wackenroder (1773–1798), who, in turn, had given his friend Tieck the impetus to begin work on Greifnson's writings and, in so doing, had initiated the Romantic phase of the Grimmelshausen reception. Goethe mentions "Simplicissimus" for the first time in his early "mikrokosmisches Drama" *Hans Wursts Hochzeit oder der Lauf der Welt* (1775). There Simplicissimus appears, with the notation "kommt von der Reise um die Welt" between the other wedding guests, "Claus Narr" and "Hans Tap ins Mus," who, according to the text, are "grose Namen" from the "deutsche Welt."

Goethe did not read *Simplicissimus* until December 1809 and then only in the version that had appeared in the collected works. He compared it with the French picaresque novel, *Gil Blas* by Alain René Lesage, but found it "tüchtiger und lieblicher" than that novel. On the other hand, he was annoyed with the commentated additions to the text, which he ascribed to a "Kollektiv" consisting of publisher and public.

Since then, every author writing in German who is to be taken seriously has paid homage to the author of *Simplicissimus* and *Courasche*. There are various reasons for that. Among them are the biography with its surprising turns and the lacunae in that biography that stimulate our fantasy, and the fresh, powerful, unspent, rich language; further the art of the realistic natural portrayal and the plasticity and freedom of his figures. In addition, Grimmelshausen had a supremely good way of working with materials and forms of literary tradition and we find an unerring view of the (miserable) condition of society and the differences among the classes in that society. The author also had a certain irony and skepticism about wishes to improve the state of the world and programs that might accomplish that, but he also was relentlessly opposed to war and those who instigated it. There is also a discreet and unobtrusive Christianity, a "Volkstümlichkeit," and an openness of his text to the most varied interpretations. All of these were — and are — reasons why this author from the distant seventeenth century has, ever since the Romantics, been a contemporary of all generations. Let us cite Hans Magnus Enzensberger's reasoning (1962) as representative of them all:

> Grimmelshausens Sprache ist ohne Vorbild in der Tradition; sie ist gänzlich frisch gemünzt und hat ihren unvernutzten Glanz bis heute bewahrt — vielleicht gerade deshalb, weil sie so folgenlos geblieben ist. Hört man ihr zu, so mag man kaum glauben, daß sie aufs Jahr genau so alt ist wie das Schloß von Versailles, so alt wie Racines Berenice und die Allonge-Perücke. (152)

The seemingly unlimited interpretability of the texts includes the possibility of misunderstanding them. Even the author himself complained about the thoughtlessness of his readers and he made them the object of an allegorical portrayal in the closing chapters of the *Continuatio*. Still in all, the possibility of one supposedly correct interpretation has been attractive ever since the commentators of the Felssecker publishing house started to seek it. Since the Romantics' turn toward patriotic and nationalistic goals there has been more and more of an instrumentalization of *Simplicissimus*. Haken's interpretation of the Jupiter episode with reference to Napoleon stands as the first on the list. After that, Grimmelshausen was understood as a poet whose roots were deeply within the German folk, and his "Volksbuch" *Simplicissimus* supposedly offered its readers "wahres" "deutsches" life and it was made to fit in with a Protestant-Prussian picture of German Literature and German History. Anything running counter to that concept (for example, the conversion of Grimmelshausen to Catholicism or his free use of Spanish tracts as sources) is simply disregarded (cf. Meid, 1984, 223–24). Robert König's popular illustrated *Deutsche Litteraturgeschichte* (1878, 12th ed. 1882), which is dedicated to "dem deutschen Hause" summarizes strikingly how one is to think of Grimmelshausen's *Simplicissimus* during the Wilhelminian Empire: "Der Simplicissimus ist ein echt deutscher Roman, nicht nur der beste und bedeutendste des siebzehnten Jahrhunderts, sondern einer der besten aller Zeiten" (1882, 293). In the detailed summary of the contents of the novel, the Jupiter episode receives, as one might anticipate, a correspondingly contemporary political interpretation:

> Doch auch für ernstere Dinge hatte er Sinn; er erkannte es mit scharfem Blick und mit Trauer im Herzen, die unter der ironischen Larve seiner Schilderung sich wohl durchfühlen läßt, was für ein Jammer es sei, daß sein Volk, anstatt in diesem greuelvollen Kriege einander in fremder Herren Namen zu zerfleischen, nicht lieber wie ein Mann wider die Fremden zusammenstünde. Seine Ideen zur Rettung seines Vaterlandes legt er einem Narren in den Mund, der sich für den Gott Jupiter hält [. . .]. Neben manchem Konfusen, das in seinen religiösen und politischen Ansichten sich ausspricht, leuchtet doch trostvoll die Überzeugung hervor, daß im deutschen Volke die edelsten Kräfte schlummern und daß man seine Stämme nur zu vereinigen brauche, um es wieder zur ersten Nation der Erde zu machen. (1882, 292)

During the debates in the Prussian Landtag of 1876, similar political assertions were made about the pedagogical value of *Simplicissimus*. The celebrations for the two hundredth anniversary of the death of the poet (held on 17 August 1876 in Renchen) took place against a background of imperial political topicalization of *Simplicissimus* and its author. The interpretation synthesized by König became, as Volker Meid has shown (1984, 230–244), in the following decades aligned ever more strongly with the "völkisch-germanentümelnde." We see this not only in the work of Arthur Moeller van den Bruck (1910) but also in the work of Friedrich Gundolf (1923) and Herbert Cysarz (1924). An intolerant Weltanschauung was demanded, and it was projected into Grimmelshausen's *Simplicissimus* just as it was into Wolfram's *Parzival,* Goethe's *Faust,* and the lyric poetry of Hölderlin. The possibilities of identification, which the reading of *Simplicissimus* had provided for the soldiers during the First World War, gave the nationalistic interpretations of the novel an additional existential authentication. The groundwork done by these interpretations provided for a seamless connection to the National Socialists' attempts to use Grimmelshausen's novel for their own purposes, as the writings of the Berlin Germanist, Julius Petersen, show (1924, 1935, 1939, 1941). He, too, makes a prophet out of the fool Jupiter, even a "Propheten des Dritten Reiches, der das Wunder ahnte, das über uns gekommen ist, und der die Wege voraussah, auf denen es als Fügung Gottes und Tat eines deutschen Helden zustande kommen werde" (1939, 45). Others were even clearer in their praise of the dictator. In the "Grimmelshausen-Runde," which the National Socialist and writer Herman Eris Busse founded in Offenburg (1940) and in which NS-giants met with German Literature scholars like Petersen and Borcherdt, the national-socialist veneration of Grimmelshausen received an institutional framework. Fortunately, serious philological investigations into Grimmelshausen's works continued in other quarters, even in countries outside of Germany. Jan Hendrik Scholte's research and editorial work and Manfred Koschlig's reconstruction of the printing history of the works of Grimmelshausen (1939), as well as the works of Lugowski (1934) or Zieglschmid (1939–40) on *Simplicissimus* lead away from such nationalistic mis-interpretations and distortions. Instead, the research of these individuals provided the basis for an appropriate understanding of the works of Grimmelshausen.

After 1945, this work was expanded and deepened, above all by Manfred Koschlig, Siegfried Streller, and Günther Weydt and his school. Koschlig, with his study *Der Mythos vom Bauernpoeten* (1957), had already freed the poet from the association with National Socialism and instead turned research toward the questions of the author's sources. In the same year, Streller tried to show, in spite of the handicaps imposed by the Socialist party, the importance of allegory and number for the portrayal of reality in the Simplician writings. In so doing, he had problematized the question of a cycle and the artistic methods of the baroque author. After decades of preliminary work, Weydt and his students were able to show a larger public, in connection with the 300th anniversary of Grimmelshausen's death, in the great exhibition "Simplicius Simplicissimus — Grimmelshausen und seine Zeit" (Münster in 1976), with justified pride, what great strides they had made. At the same time, the accompanying scholarly symposium set the course for future association with and investigation of the author. The founding of the Grimmelshausen-Gesellschaft e. V. (Münster 1979), a coming together of Grimmelshausen scholars and friends from all parts of the world, provided for the beginning of international and interdisciplinary research into the Early Modern Era. Since then, the triennial meetings of this literary society and its annual publication, *Simpliciana,* have become, under the leadership of Günther Weydt, Rolf Tarot, and Dieter Breuer, the center of Grimmelshausen research. At the same time, they have furthered an understanding for the culture, the questions of daily life, and the artistic problems of the Early Modern era in general. It is, of course, disturbing to note that since we have begun to know more about Grimmelshausen and his times, the canon has been revised, and the younger generation has turned more toward the visual media. Hence, the reading of Grimmelshausen's works by a broad segment of society is no longer automatic. Whether films might help in this regard is questionable, especially in view of the four-part series dealing with *Simplicissimus,* produced by ZDF in 1976.

The towns in which an author was born, wrote, and died, are, of course, not unimportant for making that author more popular. In Grimmelshausen's case, these places first had to be discovered. Only through the research of Arthur Passow (1843) did we come to know that the town in which Grimmelshausen worked and died was Renchen, located in Baden, and that his birthplace was the Hessian city of Gelnhausen. (The latter was not proven definitively until the work of Albert Duncker in 1882.) Hence towns could not really begin honoring Grimmelshausen until the middle of the nineteenth century. Renchen took the first step; it held a special function honoring the two hundredth anniversary of the death of the poet on 17 August 1876. Three years later, on 17 August 1879, it erected a monument to its mayor Grimmelshausen. That monument was a commemorative obelisk, purchased with donations made by the city and its residents, honoring the victims of the 1848 revolution in Baden. The monument was not actually erected to honor Grimmelshausen specifically, but rather the victims of the 1848 revolution who came from Baden. However, in a slyly Simplician manner, it combined both events that were being commemorated. There developed in Renchen a continuing honoring of Grimmelshausen and a certain festival culture, sustained in part by citizens who were able to show their genealogical relationship to the poet. In 1924 they celebrated the three hundredth anniversary of the poet with a dialect folk play by Max Clauss, *Simplicius Simplicissimus,* which was performed at the town's open-air theater. In the same year there was also a commemorative celebration in Gelnhausen.

In 1936 Soest joined in with the "Soester Festspiele," against a Grimmelshausen background or, as the case might be, a background dealing with the hunter of Soest in the version of Raidas's "Volksoper" about Grimmelshausen towns. The "Grimmelshausen-Festtage" of 1941 in Renchen show that it was not difficult for the National Socialists to change these celebrations into "Blut-und-Boden-Veranstaltungen." In Renchen they celebrated the two hundred seventy-fifth anniversary of the poet's death (1951) under different circumstances. There was a parade and an open-air performance of Hermann Streich's dialect folk play *Der Schultheiß von Renchen.* The same is true of Gelnhausen, where they celebrated with an exhibition and a ceremony.

It was not until 1895 that people began to realize that Oberkirch with its suburb of Gaisbach had a claim as the fourth Grimmelshausen town. In the family archives of the Schauenburg family in Gaisbach, someone accidentally found a record with the name of the poet. That provided the impetus for reconstruction of the details of Grimmelshausen's service in the Schauenburg family. Nothing had been known about it up until that time. Gustav Könnecke was the first to publish a corrected biography of the poet (1895). His biography showed that Oberkirch had the honor of being the town in which Grimmelshausen had lived for the longest period of time and where he had written the greatest part of his works. The inn "Zum Silbernen Stern" in the old steward house in Gaisbach, next to St. George's Chapel, where Grimmelshausen served as official and part-time innkeeper, provided Oberkirch with an attractive memorial after the First World War. Beginning in 1940, however, it was used for Busse's National Socialist "Grimmelshausen-Runde" and since 1987 it has been the site of the "Grimmelshausen-Gesprächsrunde" in Oberkirch. The Mooskopf and the Mummelsee have also been included in the Grimmelshausen memorials, since 1951 and 1971 respectively. Since the three hundredth anniversary of the poet's death in 1976 the number of Grimmelshausen memorial sites has continued to increase. In 1977, Franz Burda, a publisher in Offenburg, donated to the city of Renchen a Simplicissimus statue made by the Italian sculptor Giacomo Manzù. It has been placed in front of the city hall. In 1990 the city of Renchen erected, with the help of a donation by the "Grimmelshausen-Freunde" in Renchen, the "Simplicissimus-Haus." It is used for art exhibitions and meetings; there is an ongoing exhibition of modern graphics dealing with Grimmelshausen's works. They have also created the "Grimmelshausen-Literaturpreis." In a kind of noble competition to see who would honor Grimmelshausen more, Oberkirch erected, in the Old City Hall, a Grimmelshausen Museum in 1991. Gelnhausen could no longer keep up; nevertheless, it offers the literary traveler a view of the house where Grimmelshausen was born, identified by a small commemorative plaque. The Thuringian town of Grimmelshausen near Meiningen, the medieval seat of the Grimmelshausen family, has also erected a monument. "Wer den Dichter will verstehen, muß in Dichters Lande gehen" — this proverbial recommendation of Goethe seems to be particularly helpful with reference to Grimmelshausen and his adoptive home, the Ortenau, to Gelnhausen and to the military location of Soest. These locations truly do offer the desired ability to visualize what one reads in Grimmelshausen's printed works.

Translated by Karl F. Otto, Jr. and Christine Dombrowski

Notes

[1] See also the essay in this volume by Christoph Schweitzer that deals with the various editions of the *Simplicissimus*.

[2] See also the essay in this volume by Rosmarie Zeller that deals with the *Ewigwährender Calender*.

Works Cited

Alt, Johannes. *Grimmelshausen und der Simplicissimus.* Munich: Beck, 1936.

Anderson, Susan C. *Grass and Grimmelshausen.* Columbia SC: Camden House, 1987 (Studies in German Literature, Linguistics, and Culture 28).

Battafarano, Italo Michele. "Goethe und Grimmelshausen. Leser, Publikum und mündliche Überlieferung des 'Simplicissimus Teutsch.'" Erster Teil: 1668–1791. *Annali dell'Istituto Universitario Orientale di Napoli. Sezione Germanica* 18 (1975), 2, 91–108.

———. "Das Barock und die Spy Story. Simplicianisches bei John le Carré." *Simpliciana* 9 (1987): 163–69.

———. "Ein Barock-Ec(h)o: Grimmelshausen und Knorr von Rosenroth unter dem Foucault'schen Pendel." *Morgen-Glantz* 1 (1991): 91–96.

———. "Horst Karaseks historischer Roman *Die Stelzer* (1990). Oder wie sich 'ein paar Kunstgriffe bei Grimmelshausen abschauen lassen,' ohne daß die Literaturkritik es merkt." *Simpliciana* 14 (1992): 131–44.

———. "Die *Sinfonia con rosignolo* von Niccolo Castiglioni. Eine musikalische Interpretation des Nachtigallenliedes aus Grimmelshausens *Simplicissimus.*" *Morgen-Glantz* 3 (1993): 235–43.

———. "Erwin Guido Kolbenbeyers und Hans Heinrich Borcherdts Grimmelshausen-Ausgaben im Zeichen nationaler Aufbaustimmung nach dem Ersten Weltkrieg." *Simpliciana* 18 (1996): 217–25.

Bauer, Barbara. "Karl Amadeus Hartmanns Oper *Des Simplicius Simplicissimus Jugend.* Ein Überlebensmodell im nationalsozialistischen Deutschland." *Simpliciana* 10 (1988): 251–99.

Beckmann, Jürgen. "Grimmelshausens Roman *Der abenteuerliche Simplicissimus* im Deutschunterricht. Bausteine zu einer Geschichte seiner Lektüre." In: *Festschrift für Oswald Beck.* Ed. Nikolaus Hofen. Baltmannsweiler: Schneider Hohengehren, 1993. 195–210.

Bircher, Martin. "Grimmelshausen und die Schweiz. Schweizer Künstler als Interpreten des *Simplicissimus.*" *Librarium* 33 (1990): 73–102.

Boeckh, Joachim G. "Grimmelshausen im Preußischen Abgeordnetenhaus." *Neue deutsche Literatur* 8 (1960): 148–51.

Bogner, Ralf Georg. "Rezeptionsgeschichte im Medienwechsel. Grimmelshausens *Bärenhäuter* bei Clemens Brentano, Achim von Arnim, Justinus Kerner und Jakob und Wilhelm Grimm." *Simpliciana* 19 (1997): 29–38.

Breuer, Dieter. "'Kein neuer Simplicissimus' — der satirische Erzähler Christian Weise in seiner Zeit." In: *Christian Weise. Dichter, Gelehrter, Pädagoge.* Ed. Peter Behnke and Hans-Gert Roloff. Bern: Peter Lang, 1994. 185–95. (= Jahrbuch für internationale Germanistik. Reihe A, Kongressberichte, 37)

Bürger, Thomas. "Spätere Ausgaben und Übersetzungen." In: *Simplicius Simplicissimus. Grimmelshausen und seine Zeit.* Ed. Westfälisches Landesmuseum für Kunst und Kulturgeschichte Münster in Zusammenarbeit mit dem Germanistischen Institut der Westfälischen Wilhelms-Universität. Münster: Aschendorff, 1976. 235–36. (= Austellungskatalog)

―――. "Der 'Keusche Joseph' und sein gefährdeter Leser. Eine Marginalie zur Rezeption Grimmelshausens." *Simpliciana* 1 (1979): 79–82.

Einsle, Karlheinz. "Aktualisierende Grimmelshausenrezeption am Beispiel illustrierter Ausgaben der *Courasche*." In: *Europäische Barockrezeption.* Ed. Klaus Garber. Wiesbaden: Harrassowitz, 1991. 771–91.

Enzensberger, Hans Magnus. "Nachwort." In: *Hans Jakob Christoffel von Grimmelshausen: Die Lebensbeschreibung der Erzbetrügerin und Landstörzerin Courasche.* Ed. Engelbert Hegaur. Munich: Deutscher Taschenbuch Verlag, 1962. 145–55.

Fambrini, Alessandro. "Grimmelshausens *Keuscher Joseph* in Schweden. Eine Analyse der Titelblätter." *Simpliciana* 19 (1997): 91–105.

Fechner, Jörg Ulrich. "Rezeption als Interpretation. Hakens *Simplicissimus*-Ausgabe von 1810." *Daphnis* 5 (1971): 677–97.

Gaede, Friedrich. "Grimmelshausen, Brecht, Grass. Zur Tradition des literarischen Realismus in Deutschland." *Simpliciana* 1 (1979): 54–66.

―――. "Barocke Transzendentalpoesie? Grimmelshausen aus der Sicht der Bärenhäuter- und Philistersatire Clemens Brentanos." *Simpliciana* 13 (1991): 407–21.

Gebauer, Hans Dieter. "'Machiavellischer Hocus Pocus.' Eine Quelle zur zeitgenössischen Rezeption der simplicianischen Schriften Grimmelshausens." *Wolfenbütteler Barock-Nachrichten* 4 (1977): 7–9.

Gemert, Guillaume van. "Die Jungfrau von Magdeburg. Walter Mehring und Grimmelshausen." *Morgen-Glantz* 4 (1994): 211–40.

Gerlach, Harald. *Nachrichten aus Grimmelshausen. Gedichte.* Berlin and Weimar: Aufbau, 1984.

Geutikow, Barbara and Kirsten Søholm. "Gesellschaftskritik und karnevalistische Züge in Grimmelshausens *Simplicissimus* und Peter Paul Zahls *Die Glücklichen.*" *AUGIAS* 14 (1984): 21–44.

Grass, Günte. *Das Treffen in Telgte. Eine Erzählung.* Darmstadt and Neuwied: Luchterhand, 1979.

Grimmelshausen, Hans Jacob Christoffel von. *Werke.* Ed. Dieter Breuer. 3 vols. Frankfurt am Main: Deutscher Klassiker Verlag, 1989–1997.

Gustafson, Daryl. "Ludwig Renn — the Simplicissimus of the World War I?" *Simpliciana* 1 (1979): 50–53.

Haberkamm, Klaus. "'Mit allen Weisheiten Saturns geschlagen.' Glosse zu einem Aspekt der Gelnhausen-Figur in Günter Grass' *Treffen in Telgte.*" *Simpliciana* 1 (1979): 67–78.

———. "Verspäteter Grimmelshausen aus der Kaschubei — 'Verspätete Utopie?' Simplicianisches in Grass' *Butt.*" *Simpliciana* 6/7 (1985): 123–38.

Hartmann, Karl Amadeus. *Simplicius Simplicissimus. Drei Szenen aus seiner Jugend.* Nach Hans Jacob Christoph von Grimmelshausen von Hermann Scherchen, Wolfgang Petzet und Karl Amadeus Hartmann. Zürich: Arche, 1989.

Herzog, Urs. "Der Roman auf der Kanzel. Prokop von Templin (um 1608–1680), ein erster Leser von Grimmelshausens 'Simplicissimus.'" *Simpliciana* 6/7 (1985): 99–110.

Hesselmann, Peter. "Zum Grimmelshausen-Bild bei Schriftstellern des 20. Jahrhunderts." *Simpliciana* 4/5 (1983): 173–98.

———. "'Entblösete Brüste' auch in Wolfenbüttel. Grimmelshausens *Keuscher Joseph* und seine Rezeption im 17. und 18. Jahrhundert." *Simpliciana* 11 (1989): 17–33.

———. "Zur Rezeptionsgeschichte Grimmelshausens im Spätbarock. Das Werk Johann Christoph Ettners." *Simpliciana* 12 (1990): 229–66.

———. *Simplicissimus Redivivus. Eine kommentierte Dokumentation der Rezeptionsgeschichte Grimmelshausens im 17. und 18.* Jahrhundert (1667–1800). Frankfurt am Main: Klostermann, 1992. (= Das Abendland NF 20)

Knight, Kenneth G. "*Simplicissimus* und *Mutter Courage.*" *Daphnis* 5 (1976): 699–705.

Koeman, Jakob. *Die Grimmelshausen-Rezeption in der fiktionalen Literatur der deutschen Romatik.* Amsterdam: Rodopi, 1993.

König, Robert. *Deutsche Litteraturgeschichte.* 12th ed. Bielefeld and Leipzig 1882. (First ed. 1878).

Koeppen, Wolfgang. "Grimmelshausen oder Gemein mit jedermanns Angst." In: W. K. *Die elenden Skribenten.* Frankfurt am Main: Suhrkamp, 1981. 9–17.

Koschlig, Manfred. *Grimmelshausen und seine Verleger. Untersuchungen über die Chronologie seiner Schriften und den Echtheitscharakter der frühen Ausgaben.* Leipzig: Akademische Verlagsanstalt, 1939. (= Diss. Berlin 1939 and Palaestra 218)

————. Das Lob des "Francion" bei Grimmelshausen. In: *Jahrbuch der Deutschen Schillergesellschaft* 1 (1957), S. 30–73.

————. "Der 'Französische Kriegs-Simplicissimus' oder: Die 'Schreiberey' des Ulmer Bibliotheksadjunkten Johann Georg Schielen (1633–1684)." *Jahrbuch der Deutschen Schillergesellschaft* 18 (1974): 148–220.

————. "Grimmelshausen und die Gebrüder Grimm. Nachruf auf den 'Barock-Simplicissimus.'" *Daphnis* 5 (1976): 635–76.

————. *Das Ingenium Grimmelshausen und das 'Kollektiv.' Studien zur Entstehungs- und Wirkungsgeschichte des Werkes*. Munich: Beck, 1977.

Kühlmann, Wilhelm. "'Signor Borri' in Straßburg — Zu einer Stelle in der zweiten Continuatio des Barock-'Simplicissimus.'" *Simpliciana* 6/7 (1985): 111–12.

Kunert, Günter. "Deutsche Einfalt. Nach Wiederlesen des *Simplicissimus*." In: G. K. *Diesseits des Erinnerns*. Munich: Hanser, 1982. 163–67.

Kurth-Voigt, Lieselotte. *Zur Simplicissimus-Rezeption in der Frühklassik. Eine Kontroverse aus Anlaß C. J. Wagenseils Roman-Bearbeitung*. Münster: Grimmelshausen-Gesellschaft, 1984. (= Sondergaben der Grimmelshausen-Gesellschaft)

————. "Grimmelshausens 'Simplicissimus' in Aufklärung und Vorklassik." *Simpliciana* 8 (1986): 19–50.

Leighton, Joseph. "Courasche and Moll Flanders: Roguery and Morality." In: *Barocker Lust-Spiegel. Studien zur Literatur des Barock. Festschrift für Blake Lee Spahr*. Ed. Martin Bircher, Jörg-Ulrich Fechner and Gerd Hillen. Amsterdam: Rodopi, 1984. 295–310. (= Chloe 3)

Li, Shu. "Wie und warum übersetzte ich Grimmelshausens *Simplicissimus* ins Chinesische?" *Simpliciana* 4/5 (1983): 137–42.

————. "Aspekte und Probleme der Übersetzung des *Simplicissimus* ins Chinesische." *Simpliciana* 10 (1988): 179–86.

Mannack, Eberhard. "Moderne Schriftsteller als Editoren und Interpreten von Grimmelshausen." In: *Simplicissimus heute*. Ed. Martin Bircher and Christian Juranek. Wolfenbüttel: Herzog August Bibliothek, 1990. 21–34.

————. *Barock in der Moderne. Deutsche Schriftsteller des 20. Jahrhunderts als Rezipienten deutscher Barockliteratur*. Frankfurt am Main, Berne, New York, Paris: Peter Lang, 1991.

Meid, Volker. *Grimmelshausen — Epoche — Werk — Wirkung*. Munich: Beck, 1984. (Arbeitsbücher für den literaturgeschichtlichen Unterricht, Beck'sche Elementarbücher).

———. "Friedrich Christoph Weissers Schalkheit und Einfalt (1822), oder: Der literaturkritische schwäbische Simplicissimus." In: *Literatur und Kultur im deutschen Südwesten zwischen Renaissance und Aufklärung. Festschrift für Walter E. Schäfer.* Ed. Wilhelm Kühlmann. Amsterdam: Rodopi, 1995. 315–27. (= Chloe 22)

Noehles, Gisela. "Text und Bild. Untersuchungen zu den Kupferstichen von 1671 und den nachbarocken Illustrationen zu Grimmelshausen." *Daphnis* 5 (1976): 595–633.

Penkert, Sibylle. "Grimmelshausems Titelkupfer-Fiktionen. Zur Rolle der Emblematik-Rezeption in der Geschichte poetischer Subjektivität." In: *Internationaler Arbeitskreis für Deutsche Barockliteratur. Erstes Jahrestreffen in der Herzog August Bibliothek Wolfenbüttel, 27.-31. August 1973. Vortträge und Berichte.* Wolfenbüttel: Herzog August Bibliothek, 1973. 52–75. (= Dokumente des Internationalen Arbeitskreises für Deutsche Barockliteratur 1)

Petersen, Julius. "Grimmelshausen als Politiker." *Ekkhart. Jahrbuch für das Badner Land* 20 (1939): 33–45.

Preece, Julian. "'Die Schlacht, die schon dagewesen, die immer wieder kommt.' Barocke Geschichte im *Butt* von Günter Grass." *Simpliciana* 16 (1994): 311–22.

Rötzer, Hans Gerd. "Der Schelmenroman und seine Nachfolge." In: *Handbuch des Deutschen Romans.* Ed. Helmut Koopmann. Düsseldorf: Bagel, 1983. 131–50 and 608–10.

Schier, Manfred. "Simplicissimus im preußischen Abgeordnetenhaus." In: *Simplicius Simplicissimus. Grimmelshausen und seine Zeit.* Ed. Westfälisches Landesmuseum für Kunst und Kulturgeschichte Münster in Zusammenarbeit mit dem Germanistischen Institut der Westfälischen Wilhelms-Universität. Münster: Aschendorff, 1976. 217–2. (= Austellungskatalog)

Scholte, Jan Hendrik. "Johann Jacob Christoph von Grimmelshausen und die Illustrationen seiner Werke." *Zeitschrift für Bücherfreunde* 4, 1 (1912): 1–21 and 33–56.

———. "Grimmelshausen und das Barock." In: *Internationale Forschungen zur deutschen Literaturgeschichte.* Julius Petersen zum 60. Geburtstag dargebracht von Herbert Cysarz u.a. Leipzig: Quelle & Meyer, 1938. 69–78.

———. "Grimmelshausens Popularität." In: *Da lacht der Schultheiß von Renchen. Festschrift anläßlich der Grimmelshausentage vom 17. bis 20. August 1951.* Ed. Hermann Streich. Renchen: Stadtverwaltung, 1951. 33–59.

———. "Die Romantik und Grimmelshausen." *Germanisch-Romanische Monatsschrift* NF 3 (1953): 190–200.

Sestendrup, Manfred. *Vom Dichter gewollt. Grimmelshausens Barock-Simplicissimus und seine 20 Textillustrationen.* Renchen: Grimmelshausen-Archiv, 1983.

Sill, Oliver. "Canetti und Grimmelshausen oder 'Die Wirklichkeit der Erinnerung.' Zu einigen Korrespondenzen zwischen Grimmelshausens *Der Abentheurliche Simplicissimus Teutsch* und Elias Canettis *Die gerettete Zunge*." In: *Critica poeticae. Lesarten zur deutschen Literatur*. Ed. Andreas Gößling und Stefan Neuhaus. Würzburg: Königshausen & Neumann, 1992. 243–53.

Simplicissimus heute. Ein barocker Schelm in der Kunst des 20. Jahrhunderts. Ausstellungskatalog. Ed. Martin Bircher u. Christian Juranek. Wolfenbüttel: Herzog August Bibliothek, 1990. (= Malerbuchkatalog der Herzog August Bibliothek 4)

Simplicius Simplicissimus. Grimmelshausen und seine Zeit. Ausstellungskatalog. Ed. Westfälisches Landesmuseum für Kunst und Kulturgeschichte Münster in Zusammenarbeit mit dem Germanistischen Institut der Westfälischen Wilhelms-Universität. Münster: Aschendorff, 1976. (= Ausstellungskatalog)

Spahr, Blake Lee. *The Archives of the Pegnesischer Blumenorden. A Survey and Reference Guide*. Berkeley and Los Angeles: California UP, 1960. (= University of California Publications in Modern Philology 57)

Trappen, Stefan. "*Metzger- und Becker-Streit* — eine vergessene Simpliziade." *Simpliciana* 11 (1989): 9–15.

Umbach, Silke. "Die Wirtin vom Brückenhof. Die Libuschka in Grass' *Das Treffen in Telgte* und ihr Vorbild bei Grimmelshausen: *Die Landstörtzerin Courasche*." *Simpliciana* 14 (1992): 105–29.

Weber, Alexander. "Die Grimmelshausen-Rezeption Friedrich Gundolfs und des George-Kreises." *Euphorion* 90 (1996): 362–81.

Weydt, Günther. "Zum Problem der Wirkungsgeschichte am Beispiel Grimmelshausens." In: *Akten des V. Internationalen Germanisten-Kongresses Cambridge 1975*. Ed. Leonard Forster und Hans-Gert Roloff. Heft 4. Frankfurt am Main: Peter Lang, 1976. 36–41 (= Jahrbuch für Internationale Germanistik. Reihe A. Kongreßberichte 2)

———. *Hans Jacob Christoffel von Grimmelshausen*. 2. ergänzte u. erweiterte Auflage. Stuttgart: Metzler, 1979. (= Sammlung Metzler 99)

Wieckenberg, Ernst-Peter. *Zur Geschichte der Kapitelüberschrift im deutschen Roman vom 15. Jahrhundert bis zum Ausgang des Barock*. Göttingen: Vandenhoeck & Ruprecht, 1969. (= Palaestra 253)

Wimmer, Ruprecht. "Grimmelshausens 'Joseph' und sein unverhofftes Weiterleben." *Daphnis* 5 (1976): 369–413.

———. "Der Herr Facis et (non) Dicis. Thomas Manns Übernahme aus Grimmelshausen." *Thomas-Mann-Jahrbuch* 3 (1990): 13–49.

———. *"Benebenst feinen und neu-inventierten Kupffer-Stücken." Die Illustrationen der posthumen Grimmelshausen-Gesamtausgabe (1683–1713)*. Augsburg: Grimmelshausen Gesellschaft, s.d. (= Sondergabe für die Mitglieder der Grimmelshausen-Gesellschaft V)

Ziegesar, Hertha von. "Grimmelshausen als Kalenderschriftsteller und die Felsseckerschen Verlagsunternehmungen." *Euphorion*. Ergänzungsheft 17 (1924): 50–79.

*"Grimmelshausen money" from Germany's inflation era.
Reprinted from* Simplicius Simplicissimus:
Grimmelshausen und seine Zeit *(1976).*

Celebrating the tricentennial of Grimmelshausen's birth.
Reprinted from Simplicius Simplicissimus: Grimmelshausen
und seine Zeit *(1976).*

II. Critical Approaches

Engraved frontispiece from the first edition of
Springinsfeld *(1670). Reprinted with permission*
of the Herzog August Bibliothek, Wolfenbüttel.

Engendering Social Order: From Costume Autobiography to Conversation Games in Grimmelshausen's Simpliciana

Lynne Tatlock

> *Wenn kein leichtfertiger*
> *Bub wäre/ daß alsdann auch*
> *keine Huren seyn würden*
> (WV 209)

JUST OUTSIDE OF HANAU an officer of the guard interrogates the eponymous hero of *Der abenteuerliche Simplicissmus Teutsch*. Even as the soldiers wonder at the exotic boy, this socially and nationally indeterminate creature — who could have been exhibited at a fair[1] as a Mongol from Siberia or an Eskimo — looks back, nonplussed by the unusual attire of the officer. In a comic and satiric moment, the naïve Simplicius finds himself perplexed, for he does not know whether the officer is a "he" or a "she," for he is wearing his hair and beard in the French style. Not only is the officer's beard sparse and his hair long, but his full trousers look to Simplicius more like a woman's skirt than a man's pants. Ironically, Simplicius, whose own indeterminacy plays a central role in this fictional autobiography, feels compelled to categorize. Unable to make up his mind about the sex of the officer, he finally determines him to be both man and woman. Shortly thereafter, when the officer attempts to confiscate his prayer book, Simplicius falls to the officer's feet, embracing his knees and addressing him as "mein lieber Hermaphrodit" only to be met with the gruff reply, "wer Teufel hat dir gesagt, daß ich Herman heiße?" (55). The context makes clear enough that this illiterate oddball, and not the boy Simplicius, is here the principal object of the author's satiric nationalist barb. In following foreign fashion, this man has relinquished something of his German manhood. At the same time, the very fact of the simpleton's ridiculous confusion obliquely confirms the foundation of the social order — the division between the sexes.

The primacy of the category of gender in the ordering and correction of the social world satirized, as well as reconstructed, in Grimmelshausen's *Simplicissimus* in fact becomes apparent a few chapters earlier in the hermit's catechism of the forlorn and ignorant peasant boy. When the hermit asks Simplicius his name, Simplicius replies that his name is "Boy." We immediately learn, however, that although Simplicius can name his gender assignment, he does not understand its social significance and consequences; language is severed from social knowledge. He does not even know what a mother, father, husband, or wife is. When questioned further, however, he can begin to offer a rudimentary outline of a hierarchically gendered social life on the farm. He knows, for example, with whom his "Meuder" — the woman who gave him the shirt he is wearing — slept at night and he knows that his mother called that person master (25). Nevertheless, his understanding remains at this point in the narrative circumscribed at best. For this naive young simpleton, gender assignment has as yet been of little social consequence and, moreover, he has not attained a level of consciousness and linguistic competence at which he could make sense of even the limited social experience he has had. Not even the first act of social gendering has occurred, for Simplicius does not yet have a name beyond the generic "boy." The hermit performs this task for him when he names him for his salient feature "Simplicius," a designation that genders him, though somewhat ambiguously, as male and comically establishes him as the founding father of a clan of simpletons.[2]

More striking in the hermit's catechism, however, is the order of questioning. Indeed, questions about gendered social life — and specifically gender roles and gender hierarchy within the family — precede the hermit's probe into the state of Simplicius's immortal soul. The hermit seeks to locate Simplicius in a gendered social order, even before he asks whether the boy knows how to pray, specifically, whether he knows how to say an "Our Father." This catechismal sequence suggests that religious instruction can be extrapolated from a stable, gendered, and hierarchically structured social order. And in reconfirming through this catechism the centrality of the paternal, Grimmelshausen echoes the philosophers and moralists of his age — we recall, for example, that in 1667 Grimmelshausen's contemporary, the natural philosopher Samuel von Pufendorf (1632–94) identified paternal authority as the oldest and most honorable form of hegemony (151).

The seventeenth-century wartime Germany of Grimmelshausen's oeuvre lacks precisely such stable social arrangements; indeed, the endangered social order (and, hence, endangered moral order) provides the stuff of the Simplician writings. These works relentlessly employ didactic set pieces and invoke traditional categories — religious, pseudoscientific, and social — as well as allegorical figures, literary tropes and conventions, in an attempt at a textual reassembly of the broken world from its very foundations. However, the unruliness and vicious energy of humankind, or rather the excesses of the early-modern satirical mode, repeatedly break apart the fragile construct. At times sheer narrative delight in recounting transgression in effect overshadows the conservative moral and social message.[3]

Precisely this larger context, that is, the repeated attempt to reassemble the broken world through the imaginary recreation of the gender-stratified social order in which the right man is, so to speak, on top, enables us to put Grimmelshausen's female characters into perspective. Scholars of the 1980s and 1990s, informed by academic feminism and gender studies, have understandably tended, when contemplating the representation of women in Grimmelshausen's work, to focus on his larger-than-life pícara. On the whole, however, they have done so without considering in an extended way how Courage's autobiographical account of her rough-and-tumble life fits together with other Simpliciana.[4] Their scholarship has, nevertheless, proven enormously effective, enabling us to read Courage variously and, sometimes, to borrow Toril Moi's well-known formulation, "against the grain."[5] It now seems useful to reintegrate this pícara into the larger world of Grimmelshausen's literary work by undertaking a broader anatomy of the representation and investigation of gender found therein, one that also takes account of literary genre.

Surprisingly, despite the boom in gender scholarship in early modern European studies over the past fifteen years and despite the ubiquity of the theme in the Simpliciana, scholarship on Grimmelshausen has, aside from the work on Courage, remained largely silent on the subject of gender. This silence may result in part from the fact that, on the face of it, the male point of view dominates so utterly as to make its gendering invisible; or rather, the textual male point of view is obvious and thus unworthy *per se* of scholarly attention. Furthermore, this perspective may seem to some quite simply universal and thus unassailable.

As is by now well understood, however, gender analysis seeks to defamiliarize precisely such universals. It seeks to re-view both masculinity and femininity as multiple, as in flux, as in dynamic relationship with one another, as integral parts of all social systems — and by extension systems of signification — and as culturally and historically determined (Scott, 2). Literary gender analysis seeks to recover the presence and importance of such categories — once largely ignored by scholarship — in literary representation and to tease out a particular culture's historical understanding and instrumentalization of them.

In the following I will explore the autobiographical novels,[6] *Der abenteuerliche Simplicissimus* (1667–69); *Trutz Simplex, das ist Lebensbeschreibung der Ertzbetrügerin und Landstörtzerin Courasche* [*Life History of the Archfraud and Runagate Courasche*, (1670)], hereafter referred to as *Courasche;* and *Springinsfeld* (1670) as invocations and transgressions of categories of gender that graphically express the profound anxiety of a culture still reeling from the effects of thirty years of war and the ensuing social, economic, and political changes. In contrast to most previous studies of gender in Grimmelshausen's works, I do not confine myself to *Courasche.* Courage's autobiography figures in the following investigation as but one of several of the author's extended literary explorations of ruptures in an imagined social world. Such explorations strive to reestablish a male-dominated norm even as they present us with a world in which masculinity is endangered because the world itself is out of kilter.

The very transgressiveness of the dystopian world of Grimmelshausen's novels has fascinated the modern reader-scholar. Occasionally it has obscured the fact that underlying this wayward narrative is always the impetus for restoring order.[7] As Barbara Becker-Cantarino reminds us, "there is an acute awareness of one's gender, gender role, and its limitations: and while there is in the fictional imagination gender inversion and transgression, such playful inversion serves to reinforce existing male norms [. . .]" (43). Grimmelshausen's text itself seems at pains to remind readers of its conservative use value, of the "prodesse" found in a work that sells itself as a "Lust-erweckendes Werck."[8] The motto of the allegorical engraving summarizing the contents of the third volume of the collected works of Grimmelshausen (1684) is one such moment: "Hier findet Warheit sich mit Schertz verdeckt zukauff. Wer Sie nicht sehen kan, der steck die Brillen auff."[9] In other words, the engraving insists that readers themselves are at fault if they cannot perceive the lesson imparted by an entertaining text.

Recognizing the transgressive moments in Grimmelshausen's works, of course, necessitates recalling the gender hierarchy of the cultural surround. Quite simply, the seventeenth century largely privileged men over women, and furthermore, in keeping with the dictates of a religiously based social and moral order, men were expected to guide women who were seen as inherently morally weak. Men had an obligation to keep their wives, daughters, and female servants under control and in the house (Pufendorf, 148–50; Moscherosch; Luther). Women were, moreover, in keeping with Paul's dictum that women remain silent in church (1 Cor 14:34), admonished to refrain from speaking in public. As Grimmelshausen's younger contemporary and imitator Johann Beer (1655–1700) wrote in the preface to his *Simplicianische Welt-Kucker* (1677), "Ich höre daß Frauen-Volck niemahls lieber reden/ als wan sie still schweigen/ dan dadurch kan ich ihre gröste Tugend erkennen" (385). The very fact that Courage occupies center stage for twenty-eight chapters of continuous talk in and of itself brands her in terms of seventeenth-century gender norms as a transgressive figure.

Successful men had of course the additional obligation to keep other men under control, to serve as their rulers, their fathers, their instructors. The absent master of the masterless man or woman who becomes a wandering rogue is thus implicitly male, and his very absence represents a social order in crisis.[10]

Having once unleashed on the malleable and frangible narrative world a passel of masterless men and women — themselves malleable and morally fragile — all homeless vagabonds who are only too ready to tell all, Grimmelshausen seems unable or unwilling to re-house them productively within a stable social order even when they repent their sins.[11] Simplicius renounces the world and ultimately must be confined to an island. A childless Springinsfeld must be killed off. Courage makes it quite clear that she has more to say about her roving life and is by no means under control (130), and the author-narrator-editor feels himself compelled to write a brief addendum to her autobiography in order finally to shut her up.

As I will argue, Grimmelshausen's *Rathstübel Plutonis* published in 1672, two years after *Courasche* and *Springinsfeld,* represents an attempt to overcome precisely the difficulty of reining in and re-integrating his vagrants into a stable order with a prince at the helm who husbands his resources. In switching from the solo autobiographical mode to the genre of the polyphonic *Gesprächspiel* or symposium, Grimmelshausen hits upon a scheme of assemblage that effectively shores up the conservative social order implicit, but not always operative, in his satirical autobiographies. Indeed, *Rathstübel,* which takes place at the time of year when the powers of Simplicius's chalybeate spring reach their zenith, offers an at least temporary cure for the sick society, for the social affliction with which the Simplician writings entered the literary scene — "Es eröffnet sich zu dieser unserer Zeit [. . .] unter geringen Leuten eine Sucht [. . .]" (9). In short, with *Rathstübel Plutonis* Grimmelshausen puts his vagrant characters in their place.

Man on the Move: *Der abenteuerliche Simplicissimus Teutsch/ Das ist: Die Beschreibung deß Lebens eines seltzamen Vaganten*

Elsewhere I have argued for the heuristic value of recognizing and examining the masculine gender of the autobiographical subject of Grimmelshausen's *Der abenteuerliche Simplicissimus*. In this novel Simplicius is unable to construct himself in accordance with the narrative of self of the careerist, socially mobile, self-made man of the seventeenth century (Tatlock, 394–401). As he narrates his life, a sadder but wiser Simplicius repeatedly reveals his incapacity to establish himself and thus make his mark on the world as he roams aimlessly across Europe. Instead, continuous and inconclusive transformation characterizes most of Simplicius's six-book autobiography:

> daß ich an eben demselbigen Ort den Anfang gemacht/ auß einem freien Kerl zu einem Knecht der Liebe zu werden/ daß ich seithero auß einem Officier ein Bauer/ auß einem reichen Bauer ein armer Edelmann/ auß einem Simplicio ein Melchior/ auß einem Witwer ein Ehmann/ auß einem Ehmann ein Gauch und auß einem Gauch wieder ein Witwer worden wäre; Item, daß ich auß eines Bauern Sohn/ zu einem Sohn eines rechtschaffenen Soldaten/ und gleichwohl wieder zu einem Sohn meines Knans worden. (408)

Simplicius's difficulty in achieving a stable social position is in fact prefigured by his issue from and origin in a social order in crisis.

When an older, self-reflective Simplicius complains of a social disease in the opening lines of the novel quoted above, he invokes two interlocking social systems, both of which are hierarchically based, one ostensibly fixed and one permanently in flux — as far as the male is concerned. In the former — the Ständegesellschaft of the early modern period — family origin determines privilege. "Geschlecht" [gender] is submerged in "Geschlecht" [family], that is, the masculine privilege of gender is exercised within the privilege of family. In the latter, ambitious men, unfettered by family origin, remake the world, or at least remake their place in it, be it by establishing themselves as learned professionals in the emergent meritocracy or as participants in the new money economy. Not family, but the masculine enterprise of making one's fortune by employing one's talents — the privilege of masculine gender — enables this reconfiguration. The title of nobility, the marker of privilege, becomes critical to the self-made man only after he has made his fortune. That title serves as seal of his success and guarantor of his admission to the ostensibly static world of the privilege of estate and thus also guarantor of the future of his progeny. As the text will ultimately reveal, the narrator has here identified a disease that signifies the malfunction of both systems, because unworthy men — men with neither pedigree nor talent — aspire to the social privilege of titles of nobility.

Within the six books of *Simplicissimus* our hero experiences a disorderly world at war in which he, as male subject, is unable to profit from the privileges of either system. In keeping with his initial allegorical vision of the *Ständebaum,* he concludes that all worldly endeavor is vain, that cruel Dame World will see to it that no (male) effort is rewarded — male, for this novel displays little interest in any career but the male life story. On the other hand, the privilege of aristocratic birth has not protected him from harm either; he has become the plaything of Fortune. Moreover, at the very moment when he finally secures legal recognition of his origins, the question of his own male heirs is vexed. He has sired an illegitimate child with the lady of easy virtue at the spa — the origins of this son will constitute an ongoing theme of the Simpliciana — and a bastard child with his servant. Meanwhile his wife has given birth to the child of the farm hand, and this child ostensibly stands the best chance of inheriting Simplicius's property and title. Simplicius, able to control neither his sexual impulses nor those of his wife in this disorderly world, has failed to become the father and husband necessary to conserve the very aristocratic order into which he was born. In the end the healthiest spot in the world is the island where he has been able to write his autobiography and thus reconstruct himself. There, he will live in splendid isolation from the company of humankind. He will be free of sexual desire for women, of competition with other men, of the need to regulate others, and of social obligation of any kind.[12] However, as conclusive and otherworldly as this view of Simplicius on the island may seem, we have by no means seen Simplicius for the last time. As we shall see, in *Rathstübel Plutonis* he realizes his male social privilege, indeed comes into his own, after all, within, not apart from, society. As we shall see, in contrast to Courage and Springinsfeld — each gendered object lessons — Simplicius functions in this later work as something of an elder statesman, a man who lives within a social system and who owns a healing chalybeate spring.

When Simplicius summarizes his life in the quotation cited above, he notably does not mention the episode during which he disguises himself as a woman, or, rather, becomes a woman socially. In our context this episode deserves a closer look, for it, too, affirms the centrality of the social division of the sexes, that is, of gender, for the world that Grimmelshausen would implicitly piece together again with his satire even as it destabilizes Simplicius's very positioning vis-à-vis this division. The episode dislocates Simplicius to the other gender, a displacement that the text will shortly counterbalance with the (critically viewed) hypermasculinity of the Hunter of Soest, the next significant guise Simplicius assumes.

Upon the violent death of his surrogate father, the elder Herzbruder, Simplicius determines to rid himself of his fool's garb once and for all. These plans run amok when he fails to find men's clothing during a raid on a village, but instead must be content with women's attire. No sooner has he assembled his woman's disguise, than several men with rape on their mind begin to pursue him. Rape establishes the subordinate position that he must assume as woman. We note here that three years later in *Springinsfeld* the narrator will, with a pun, characterize rape as a woman's becoming a man's woman/wife against her will (104). Simplicius saves himself only by appealing to the mercy of a captain's wife, who makes him her maid. This proves a dubious solution, however, for, as the maid Sabina, Simplicius is immediately caught up in a veritable hurricane of sexual desire, not the least of which is his own. The aging captain's wife, who realizes he is male, enjoys the ambiguous titillation of dressing up the passive boy like a doll and tantalizing him by having him pick fleas from her nude body. The captain, finding "Sabina" all the more beautiful as a result of the fine clothes his wife has given "her," vies with the manservant for her favors, both of them becoming ever more importunate each time Sabina refuses them. Simplicius, more miserable than when wearing his fool's garb, believes that this turn of events fulfills Herzbruder's prophecy that he would be imprisoned if he were to take off the motley; his women's attire in fact holds him prisoner.

When the captain catches his manservant wooing Sabina, he punishes her by throwing her to the stable boys, who then attempt to rape her *en masse*. Just at the moment when they discover Simplicius's biological sex, a constable happens on the scene. Rather than rescuing Simplicius, he takes him prisoner, for a man wearing women's clothing in an army arouses deep suspicion. The military magistrate subjects Simplicius to his perhaps most severe grilling in the entire novel. It quickly becomes clear that Simplicius has transgressed gender codes on two counts: his women's clothing and his ability to perform women's tasks like sewing and cooking. Both his female dress and his woman's skills, as Simplicius himself explains, result from the vicissitudes and irregularities to which the fatherless boy has been subjected in wartime, irregularities that have diverted him from the normative course of a male career under the guidance of a father. Within the text itself, however, his sociological explanation for his deviation falls on deaf ears.

These suspicious circumstances, coupled with his history as fool, lead the authorities to torture him. Any person in his right mind, the magistrate declares, who would wear fool's clothing, any man who would wear women's clothing, must be up to no good. The gender transgression of transvestism requires, it seems, punishment like none of Simplicius's previous infractions. By highlighting the other ambiguities of his brief life, cross-dressing renders him doubly suspect and doubly indictable. He has not studied, but he can read and write. He wears fool's clothes, but has his reason. He attended a witches' Sabbath. His national and familial origins are unknown and, moreover, his whereabouts before he came to Magdeburg are unknown. Such a hugely ambiguous creature sets the full force of the penal system into motion. While the narrative devotes little space to this episode compared with the protracted one in which the governor and his henchmen conspire to turn Simplicius into a fool, the text nevertheless suggests that it constitutes a culmination of ambiguities that can no longer be tolerated. Physical torture will break apart his ambiguous person, just as the governor and his men attempted to shatter his reason.

The narrative requires a catastrophic event, the Battle of Wittstock, to avert impending disaster from Simplicius. While the boy escapes physical torture of his person, the narrative continues the idea of loss of bodily integrity, a bodily integrity linked implicitly to intact and unambiguous genitals. In our context, the description of the carnage of the catastrophic battle that saves Simplicius at the last moment and its juxtaposition to impending torture merits closer attention. It seems more than coincidence that a mass slaughter, a description of men's bodies in pieces, disrupts the narrative here. Grimmelshausen writes of heads separated from torsos, smashed heads, torsos spilling intestines, bodies drained of blood, arms shot off with fingers still wiggling, and thighs robbed of the burden of their bodies (ST 177–78).

This graphic dismemberment can stand in for and magnify Simplicius's own near loss of bodily integrity, first as a result of the attacks he suffers in woman's dress and second as a result of the torture he is about to undergo. Indeed, in the comic episode immediately following the Battle of Wittstock Simplicius, divested of his women's clothes at last yet still vulnerable, finds his genitals, his manhood as the narrator terms it (ST 180), under attack once again, this time from an army of fleas: a battle in miniature.

Ever resilient, Simplicius recovers from all these onslaughts to throw off the ambiguous status of the boy, to insist on proving his manhood despite his lack of a beard (ST 186) and eventually to become the

Hunter of Soest. During this period Springinsfeld joins him, and even as they imperil their immortal souls, they relish the license of negative male behaviors — trickery, theft, fighting, fornicating, idleness, and the seeking of false honor and fame. The novel by no means condones these behaviors; rather it views them as yet another incident of failed socialization and of sinful impulse. A properly gendered male, as Johann Michael Moscherosch (1601–69) insists in his *Insomnis Parentum* (1643) and as the text implies, learns to curb these impulses, to build a home, marry, and produce legitimate offspring.[13] The Hunter of Soest, however, only manages a shotgun wedding which he flees eight days later. In short, in this episode male sex operates without the benefit of appropriate male socialization. In *Springinsfeld,* Simplicius will admonish his former friend that as aging men they can no longer live as they once did in Soest when they ruled over the countryside as their whims dictated (22).

This episode of intense male bonding proves of key importance to later Simpliciana. In fact, Simplicius's homosocial friendship with Springinsfeld becomes something of an open wound; it provides a key site of Courage's dubious revenge on Simplicius personally and on the undisciplined male-dominated world generally.[14]

Woman on Top: *Trutz Simplex: Lebensbeschreibung der Erzbetrügerin und Landstörzerin Courasche*

"Dieser Verräther hat ohne Zweiffel ein groß Schelmstück zu verrichten auf sich genommen/ dann warumb sollte sich sonst ein Gescheider in ein Narrenkleid stecken? oder ein Mannsbild in ein Weiberkleid verstellen?" (ST, 176). If Grimmelshausen had metaphorically donned fool's clothes when he wrote *Simplicissimus,* he metaphorically put on women's clothes when he elected to write a second autobiographical novel. This novel is one with a female narrator, a character whom he terms a monster, a Medusa, and a she-wolf in an addendum that gives a putatively male narrator the opportunity to have the last word. What piece of mischief ("Schelmstück") does Grimmelshausen have in mind then when in a picaresque novel ("Schelmenroman") he assumes the guise of a vicious woman bent on revenge, when he undertakes an extended exploration of inversion? In the following I revisit some aspects that have frequently been explored by Grimmelshausen criticism, but I reframe them in the service of a broader gender analysis.

Courage's dubious career, like Simplicius's, is born in war. No sooner has she put on men's clothing to save her virginity from marauding soldiers than she discovers that, contrary to the expectations of her sex, she loves the sound of the drums of war.[15] Indeed, she wants to be a man so that she can be in the war. Leaving her "feminine" domesticity behind her, she quickly assumes the manners of a male youth and like the young Simplicius finds a position as a manservant to a soldier. Ironically, unable to see through the surface behavior and dress to her biological core, her master and soon-to-be lover takes her for the epitome ("Kern") of a good *valet-de-chambre* (20). She learns to curse and drink like the manliest of men. However, her body betrays her — her sexual desire grows along with her breasts, and, moreover, she lacks an important part.

As in the case of Simplicius, Courage receives a name that in the end genders her female despite her cross-dressing and permanent aspirations to male privilege: Courage. This designation is overdetermined, but in every reading it reminds the reader that the character is biologically female. On the one hand, it signifies lack, that is, her lack of male genitals. When the bellicose fellow attacks the person he takes for a stable boy and reaches for her "Courage," he expects to find a penis and testicles. As later becomes clear, the name "Courage" also hypostatizes the male qualities to which she aspires in battle (53), but which she as a woman does not come by naturally. In these two readings, therefore, Courage bears an ironic name, one that by referring to a lack always reminds us that she is female. However, as the text also makes clear, "Courage" is her own euphemism for female genitalia. We note that she has the temerity not to follow the linguistic conventions of the time, appropriate to the well-socialized person; she calls her genitals "courage" and not "shame" (as in German "Scham" and Latin "pudendum").

On one level, every repeated use of the name Courage amounts to a nastily ironic synecdoche in which this fictitious female autobiographical subject must repeatedly acquiesce to an identity circumscribed by her genitalia. She is her genitals, and more particularly her obvious vulva. She clearly recognizes the insult; she laments that she is never able to divest herself of this name (47–48). However, her story makes abundantly clear that as a woman eight times married — she pursues matrimony relentlessly throughout her life for both social and sexual ends — and as sometime prostitute, she also makes full use of her "Courage."[16] In the end her very genitalia become the instrument of a bitter revenge; they enable her to connect Simplicius to the lowest of the low (57), in fact, the Devil himself. She also thereby nastily seals the bond of Simplicius's and Springinsfeld's homosociality, rendering them brothers-in-law, so to speak. Indeed, Springinsfeld begins his account of his own life by referring to himself as Simplicius's brother-in-law (56). The plot thus supports the claim that the reductive designation fits the person.

Courage both literally and figuratively attempts to wear the pants (38, 41–42) throughout her life. Although she wants to be a man (46), she finds it necessary to face the fact that as a biological woman she must instead procure a man, a pair of pants, as it were, in order to escape rape and conduct business (136). At one point in her checkered career she even considers representing herself as a hermaphrodite (46), that is, an anatomically ambiguous being. She explains, however, that she has no hope of carrying out her plan to represent herself as a hermaphrodite, because her rapacious sexual needs as a woman would necessitate her constantly dropping her disguise and revealing her unambiguous ana- tomical sex; it would necessitate breaking character, as it were. Instead of passing herself off as a hermaphrodite, she lives a hybrid social exis- tence. She wears a thin taffeta skirt over her trousers when she goes into battle, but what is more, she is "gegen dem Feind/ so heroisch als ein Mann/ im Feld so häuslich und zusammenhebig als immer ein Weib" (39).

As she makes repeated sallies into male social territory, she becomes ever more detached from, although well aware of, the gender norms imposed on her biological sex. In other words, when playing her female part, she appears to be in drag. She can cry crocodile tears at will, play the wronged woman and pretend to female virtue to gain her ends. At the same time, she remains untroubled by a core identity that compels her to female roles or female virtue.[17] Grimmelshausen's pícara is handi- capped less by a female core identity than by her anatomy, which makes her both sexually rapacious and ever vulnerable to rape. As Feldman and others have argued, men repeatedly exploit that vulnerability in order to put her in her place in this social order.

On a narrative level, we might usefully understand her to constitute the author's own drag act.[18] As drag act, that is, she provides the author with critical possibility. "Drag," writes Marjorie Garber, "is the theoreti- cal and deconstructive social practice that analyzes these structures [gen- der] from within, by putting in question the 'naturalness' of gender roles through the discourse of clothing and body parts" (151).

While Garber's sense of drag as Western cultural practice does not apply perfectly to the notion of literary drag that I am suggesting here for Grimmelshausen's *Courasche*, it does help us to identify a decon- structive impulse central to both this novel and to *Simplicissimus*. Both when performing the fool and when performing the woman (who imper- sonates men), Grimmelshausen dissects the very foundation of social order.[19] However, within its historical context this satiric impulse should not be mistaken for our contemporary deconstructive mode *per se*, though modern readers might well read, and have read, these texts de-constructively: as we most clearly see in *Rathstübel Plutonis,* Grimmels-hausen's texts do not merely analyze contemporary mores and social arrangements, but through re-constructive writing, or rather fictive talk-ing, aim to reassemble and stabilize the traditional social order.

Courage's finest moment in enacting a gender reversal comes when she virtually enslaves Springinsfeld, Simplicius's buddy, the very friend who had once enabled Simplicius to revel in a newly recovered and affirmed licentious masculinity. This text feminizes Springinsfeld from his first appearance in it when, according to Courage, he looks like a woman who has had an illegitimate child and has no means to feed it (79). Courage, furthermore, allocates to herself the first man Adam's privilege of naming when she calls him "Springinsfeld" after the first command she gives him. As we shall see, Springinsfeld will declare in his own auto-biographical account that Courage saddled ("aufgesattelt," Sp 73) him with the name, a formulation that evokes a well-known early modern trope of role reversal, namely Phyllis riding Socrates like a horse. Springinsfeld's chief virtue seems to be his obedience, and Courage aims principally to secure this obedience, placing him in the position of sub-jection assigned for all time not to men, but to women in seventeenth-century interpretations of Genesis 3,16 and Original Sin. Every article in Courage and Springinsfeld's inverted marriage pact aims at confirming and supporting her power over him and her license to do as she pleases.

Springinsfeld's only hope of regaining the upper hand in their rela-tionship, that is, to gain conjugal rights over her, is to do his manly duty and impregnate her, an impossibility given Courage's perennial infertil-ity — as the narrative makes clear, Courage can at most be pregnant with business possibilities (80). In fact, in the understanding of the time Courage's "unfeminine" qualities and behaviors guarantee her infertility, her inability to realize the role assigned to women in Genesis, to bear children in pain. The physician and apothecary, Johann Christoph Ettner (fl. 1694–1724), for example, warns, in a medical novel that is a store-house of early modern medical lore and practice, that violent anger, to which the female sex is inclined, hinders conception (403). This is of course the very impulse from which Courasche's autobiography is born. Furthermore, as Ettner admonishes his readers, when women behave like men, that is, behave too wildly — move too vigorously, dance, jump, ride, scream, bawl, etc.—they will fail to become pregnant (401–3; Van Ornam 25).

In its understanding of reproduction, especially, the seventeenth century tied socially appropriate behaviors, that is, gender, to anatomy.

Courage, by her transgressions of gendered behavioral codes, also ensures that Springinsfeld will never be able to realize his manhood, that is, father a child. Of course, we might also argue the converse that in failing to live up to male behavioral codes, that is, by not controlling Courage and keeping her quiet, Springinsfeld ensures that Courage will never realize her procreative female destiny.

Man on Bottom: *Der seltzame Springinsfeld . . . Lebens-Beschreibung . . . eines Landstörtzers und Bettlers*

When Springinsfeld reappears in his own autobiography, his condition has altered. Still childless,[20] homeless, and lacking a wife, he now sports a peg leg. This peg leg substitutes for an anatomical lack that figures his sexual impotence — at one point in the narrative he specifically refers to his inability to perform sexually in his older years (112–13)—as well as his more general social lack. Among other things, he has been unable to control his wives and lovers. When Springinsfeld attempts to find his second wife again after another stint in the army, he notes that she will be glad to see this peg leg. She will recognize it as useful for begging; perhaps he also obliquely refers to a useful prosthesis with which he could please his wife sexually, even if he cannot father a child (124). The title engraving makes clear in any case how low Springinsfeld has sunk when it depicts a dog urinating on this very peg leg, the iconographic stand-in for Springinsfeld's genitals.

When questioned by Simplicius, Springinsfeld informs the assembled company that he has no intention of marrying again, for even good women are nothing but trouble and will lead to loss of wealth (55). If, for example, a woman spins, he will have to buy flax and wool and pay a weaver to weave the very yarn she has spun (55). Moreover, he declares, he does not want to be stuck with a passel of brats (55). Indeed, Springinsfeld's avarice extends well beyond miserly hoarding of money: he neither wants to spend the accumulation of ducats he carries hidden on his person nor to spend his seed.

In his dealings with women, Springinsfeld has repeatedly received the short end of the stick. He claims not to know whether he was Courage's husband or her servant (73) and reckons he was both — he both serviced her sexually and otherwise did her bidding — and a fool to boot. Yet, dependent loser that he is, he could only leave this monstrous woman (74) reluctantly. Role reversal characterizes his first official marriage as well: his avaricious wife takes the lead, and he learns to imitate her rather than the reverse (105). His second official marriage begins with a wedding at a fair. As Peter Stallybrass and Alon White argue in

The Politics and Poetics of Transgression, a fair in and of itself can signal the violation of the role reversal of the topsy-turvy world. Springinsfeld's second marriage exhibits such carnivalesque features and deserves a closer look.

Although Springinsfeld had sworn an oath never to leave the free estate of the beggar and never to subjugate himself to a master under the name of an honest citizen, he discovers that for him the much-touted beggar's freedom is illusory at best. Soon after the marriage Springinsfeld finds himself in servitude once more, for his wife and her parents play the master over him (112). However, Springinsfeld's subordination as beggar was signaled and sealed from the outset when he took up a treble violin (tuned an octave above the normal violin) to please his future wife (110). As an honest citizen within an orderly social world he would subordinate himself to a male master; as a beggar he subordinates himself to a woman. The ubiquitous violin figures Springinsfeld's double humiliation: as beggar he must please others with his violin playing; as husband he must please his wife, not the least, sexually — this bawdy sense of the violin and violin playing is confirmed in vulgar language use documented by Bornemann ("Musik").[21]

We know Springinsfeld's second wife only as "die Leierin" (hurdy-gurdy girl). "Leier" too, carries sexual connotations. As vulgar expression for the vulva ("Musik," Bornemann), it figures his second wife synecdochically as twin to Courage; as with Courage, the language of the text reduces Springinsfeld's second wife to her genitalia. Furthermore, the fact that she herself is not simply designated a hurdy-gurdy but rather a player of the hurdy-gurdy suggests the same appropriation of male prerogative that characterizes Courage. The hurdy-gurdy girl is perfectly capable of satisfying herself sexually without Springinsfeld, be it alone[22] or with other sexual partners.

The rest of what the novel graphically condemns as a sinful career illustrates what can happen if women live by their sex alone without the benefit of the decorum that the feminine gender imposes upon them. The narrative doubly enables the licentious behavior of the hurdy-gurdy player, first by giving her an unmanly husband who cannot control her and second by giving her the possibility of making herself invisible and in effect freeing her from the social consequences of her female body. Besides tormenting an abbess, stealing and murdering, the hurdy-gurdy player is able to have sex with men on her terms as for example in the Minolanda episode. Here, she pretends to be a fairy who, like Melusine, can grant the handsome youth who serves as her "husband" progeny, riches, and happiness (128). The hopeful youth obligingly does what the narrator archly calls his work (128), but soon meets with an untimely demise when he betrays the hurdy-gurdy player to the authorities.

Lest readers find her adventures with the invisibility-inducing bird's nest attractive, the text enacts a terrible punishment upon her. It vivisects and makes hypervisible the body whose social consequences she had hoped to escape, "daß man [. . .] Lung und Leber sambt dem Ingeweid in ihrem Leib: Und das Hertz noch zapplen sehen konte" (129). Thereafter, her female body is punished again and burned as appropriate to a witch.

To tell this story, Grimmelshausen donned the garb of an old soldier and beggar, a man whose personal subordination to women magnifies his repeated social subordination to other men in the army and as a beggar on the street. Extreme geographical mobility — neither Simplicius nor Courage wander as far and as often as Springinsfeld — and social instability signify the failure of this male figure. He begins life as the son of a runaway noblewoman and a juggler-tightrope walker, both of whom experience immediate social change as a result of their marriage, an unsanctioned marriage that comes to pass without Springinsfeld's maternal grandfather's blessing.

Even as Springinsfeld seeks to profit from the opportunities for booty in war, he repeatedly changes his rank, forced to assume the station — from drummer to musketeer to pikeman — determined from the outside by whatever prop or weapon he can pillage. He reaches a state of abjection when his horse is shot and falls upon him. Other soldiers take him for dead and rob him, as they would any corpse, of his clothes, the clothes in which he has secreted his money (108). When he awakens to find himself only in his undergarments, he feels as if he has been on the rack and his bodily integrity violated (108–9). His health failing, he believes he has no choice but to beg and having once begged, he determines to continue. At this point, as described above, he meets his perverse destiny in the form of the hurdy-gurdy girl.

In contrast to *Courasche* and *Simplicissimus, Springinsfeld* begins with an extensive frame, namely, an account of yet another male careerist's search for a livelihood and sexual adventure. The frame opens with a double failure that anticipates Springinsfeld's botched life. When Philarchus Grossus von Tromerheim harkens to the appearance of an attractive chambermaid to whom he tries gallantly to offer his (sexual) services and whose master he hopes to serve as a scribe, words fail him — indeed, words fail him in the present of narration as he recalls the experience. Having failed at the very core of his profession, he soon learns that he will neither find the position he seeks nor make time with the pretty chambermaid. He wishes his parents had had him learn another trade, one in which he would not have to flatter other, better-situated men (11). We learn shortly thereafter that not only has he had, while plying his trade, to lick the boots of powerful men, but also to subordinate himself to women, for his greatest accomplishment to date is Courage's vengeful autobiography. In order to save his life when captured by the Gypsies, he was only too glad to take dictation from her (27) and thereby to aid her in seeking revenge against Simplicius. As it turns out, the episode hardly accrues to his glory and Philarchus joins the long list of men whom Courage has bested and betrayed.

Despite this inauspicious beginning, *Springinsfeld* as a literary work aspires more explicitly than the other two autobiographical fictions to an overt reestablishment and reconstruction of a hierarchically gendered social order. Precisely the framing of the individual narrative with a nocturnal conversation among men makes this possible.[23] Although Simplicius appears in the inn with a pilgrim's staff, which might signify a continued wandering life, the text reveals that, contrary to the conclusion of the sixth book of his autobiography, he has returned to society and established himself as "Hausvater," as head of a household. This household consists of his foster parents; his son, the young Simplicius; and a farm hand, who is unusually well-mannered for a man of his station. Philarchus expresses admiring surprise that the once crude and godless Simplicius was able to put his household on such a reputable footing and that he has been able to instill decorum and morals in this rough farm hand.

As the established head of a household, Simplicius appears, furthermore, determined to put aright the disarray he had left behind him in his autobiography, when the matter of his male heir was uncertain. In writing an autobiography to spite Simplicius, Courage asserts that the child she pawned off on Simplicius was the bastard child of her maid and not Simplicius's biological child. As the narrator twice avers, young Simplicius has in the meantime shown by his strong resemblance to his father that he is in fact his father's natural son (29, 50). Nevertheless, Simplicius still believes that the monstrous woman, Courage, is the mother of his child.[24] Philarchus, who as the scribe has advance notice of the content of Courage's autobiography, can deliver the good news that this is not the case (28). In the end, Simplicius pays Philarchus to write down Springinsfeld's autobiography so that the world will know that Simplicius, Jr. is not the child of a whore (132).[25] His son thus receives greater hope of social acceptability as well as salvation.

As the male head of a household, Simplicius can also offer his old friend, the vagabond Springinsfeld, secure shelter for the winter in the hope of persuading him to repent. Philarchus provides a tidy ending for a novel about a wandering male when he reports that having found shelter and with the sure guidance of the now fatherly Simplicius, Springinsfeld repented only to die shortly thereafter childless, but a saved man. Nevertheless, Grimmelshausen resurrects Springinsfeld for a reappearance two years later in a new literary venue, as a participant in a *Gesprächspiel*, a socially sanctioned heterosexual party game of sorts.

"The Order of Things":
Rathstübel Plutonis oder Kunst reich zu werden

Dieter Breuer points in the afterword of the *Deutsche Klassiker* edition of Grimmelshausen's works to the literary debt of *Rathstübel* to the Nuremberg man of letters, Georg Phillip Harsdörffer (1607–1658), whose *Frauenzimmer Gesprächspiele* appeared in eight volumes in the years 1641–49 (Breuer 1024). While Rosmarie Zeller maintains that *Rathstübel* deviates from the *Gesprächspiele* in its lack of playful exchange (Zeller 539), the sexual politics of Harsdörffer's conversation games nevertheless helps to elucidate Grimmelshausen's work.[26]

Harsdörffer's conversation games are remarkable for their representation and promotion of highly literate social interaction that includes women as conversation partners rather than solely as decorative props to facilitate interaction among men (Zeller). Recent feminist scholarship has demonstrated, on the other hand, that although women take part in these conversations, they tend to play a subordinate role in the conversation — figured as educationally inferior, they often merely listen or affirm. Moreover, the contents of the lessons taught by means of these games tend overall to reconfirm the traditional gender hierarchy even while allowing women to gain greater cultural literacy (Wurst, Griesshaber-Weninger). In other words, for the fictive female interlocutors and for the imagined female reader, cultural literacy brings with it a more refined sense and acceptance of women's subordinate position and traditional social roles. Harsdörffer's work thus offers models of social interaction and decorum that secure women's collusion in extant gender arrangements.

Compared with the conversation among three males (additional men and Simplicius's mother are present, but do not speak) that frames Springinsfeld's autobiography, *Rathstübel* stands out not only for its polyphony — there are fourteen participants — but for its inclusion of five women speakers. While in *Springinsfeld* Courage had appeared only as a tightly framed anecdote from the past, she here returns as interlocutor in the same present-tense time of the other speakers. However, even as these five female characters speak, they, like the male characters, are closely regulated by the rules of the game.

Scholarship on Grimmelshausen has pointed out the social orderliness of this conversation as seen, above all, in the title engraving, where the prince occupies the visual center (Breuer 1032). Each contribution to the discussion is numbered, and the characters, with a few notable exceptions, strictly observe a set sequence when contributing. Deviations from the sequence merit a rap of the baton.

Initially the incognito prince provides the narrator with a source of mirth when he officiously takes the lead in organizing the game, banging his baton on the linden tree to call for order (11). However, no one actually questions the prince's authority, even though his true identity remains hidden until the conclusion of the piece. The prince sets the topic of the conversation, determines its rules and twice redirects it so that the game falls into three parts. Once the conversation game begins, the other participants may speak legitimately only when they receive the baton.

Scholars have noted the hierarchy of estate that obtains in this work in contrast to Harsdörffer's *Gesprächspiele* where the characters belong to more or less the same social rank (Breuer 1032). Breuer remarks, for example, on the text's careful attention to social station — from prince to Jew — in the ordering of the conversation, even as, in what he sees as a surprisingly egalitarian turn of things, each person, regardless of social rank, receives a turn to speak (1025). Breuer and others have, however, turned a blind eye to Grimmelshausen's delineation and interweaving of gender codes in this group of speakers. In our context, the ordering in between the prince and the Jew deserves remark, for it secures women's audible presence while confirming their inferior place.

Almaeon, the host and head of the household, immediately receives the baton after the prince has set the rules. For the moment the baton remains within his family: gender appropriately, Almaeon's wife defers to her husband, saying her piece only when he has finished. Age appropriately, the daughter receives the baton after the mother. Contributions by five men of varying rank and profession follow those of the host family. Only then do the other women, Simplicius's foster mother (she occupies position number 10, whereas Simplicius's foster father occupies position number 7) and the actress, speak in order of age, and only the true outsider, the Jew,[27] follows them. Courage and Springinsfeld contribute only one section each, but in their case Grimmelshausen retains an allusion to the well-established gender reversal between the two of them — Courage thus precedes Springinsfeld in the conversation game.

As moderator, the prince appropriates the right to provide commentary, to direct the conversation, and to ask follow-up questions, questions that allow certain characters greater voice in the discussion. We see this, for example, in Simplicius's contribution, numbered 89, where the prince intervenes five times encouraging Simplicius to elaborate. Eventually the prince will give Simplicius the last word. By contrast, the prince never asks a female character a follow-up question; the women generally speak their piece and then fall silent until their turn comes round again.

While the order of the game is three times disrupted, twice by Simplicius's foster-mother and once by Simplicius's foster-father, its rules ensure that a rap of the baton quickly restores order. The person who has spoken out of turn may also later lose a turn, as does Simplicius's foster-mother. The text suggests that the peasants exercise the least self-control, and that, in keeping with gender stereotypes of the time, the female peasant requires greater discipline. Although Courage and Springinsfeld join the conversation circle late in the game and insert themselves in the sequence ahead of others, they speak only when invited to do so and do not indulge in narrative excess as they did in the autobiographical novels when they alone spoke. Each speaks once only, and each contribution is carefully numbered like the rest and thus immediately contained visually. In other words, the text carefully circumscribes the function of these two rapscallions by explaining that they serve as admonitory examples of the evil that comes from sexual license and war (64). This circumscription of their speech and thus of their dangerous allure contributes perhaps to Ken Negus's sense that they "are treated with less severity than they were in their biographies" (120). In other words, there is no need for this text to punish these vagabonds through misadventures. It has over the course of the conversation quite simply put them in their place and diffused their potentially damaging effects on the society created in the work, as well as on the reader reading the text. Especially in the prince's reaction to Courage we see that both she and Springinsfeld serve as gendered object lessons about the evils of men out of control — "O wie manchem geilen Hurenhengst wurde sie das Seil übern Kopff werffen! und ihme also den Lohn seiner viehischen Begierden abstatten" (63–64). While these two vagrants provide contrasting examples of a man and a woman gone bad, in the end Courage constitutes a warning less to women than to men who fail to discipline themselves and their households.

The conversation culminates in Simplicius's lengthy response to the prince's request that Simplicius outline for him the ways in which he would most certainly go to rack and ruin. In this sketch Simplicius, comically playing prime-minister to the state of the prince's person, implicitly equates the moral and physical health of this male person with the well-being of the land. He demonstrates how in the adornment of the body with wigs, rings, gloves, and silk stockings — the very imitation of French fashion that created gender confusion in *Simplicissimus* — the excessive indulgence of his five senses, and the pursuit of costly leisure pastimes like gambling, hunting, and traveling, the prince will "zu andern höhern Dingen undüchtig gemacht werden" (75),[28] not to mention bankrupt himself and his country. Simplicius concludes his clowning sermon on the bad habits of the male person by outlining principles of bad governance, principles rooted in excess that run counter to husbanding a country's resources. He especially warns against the importing and favoring of foreigners to the detriment of natives, starting an unnecessary and unjust war with your neighbors, robbing your subjects of all their money and spending that money abroad.

The prince dutifully declares that he will take to heart the lessons the interlocutors, especially Simplicius, have taught him, that is, he will behave as he must to preserve order and conserve his personal resources and those of his subjects. He then seals the bargain by treating them to a feast and dance that includes everyone, an Arcadian parting view of this mixed company such as is found nowhere in the three autobiographical novels.

Conclusion

In the three central texts of Grimmelshausen's oeuvre, that is, the three autobiographical novels, female characters appear not so much as interesting in their own right, but as part of an extended exploration and reconstruction of gender arrangements. In these novels women and men who cross-dress, women who seek to elude the rule of men, and men who let themselves be ruled by women signify a social order — and hence moral order — generally gone awry that must be brought into line. In the end, men stand at the center of Grimmelshausen's critical vision, and their failure to meet their obligations merits his sharpest barb. Only in the minor work *Rathstübel*, a work that overtly concerns itself with the proper relationship to money, the proper conservation of wealth, does Grimmelshausen manage to set visually and concretely aright the topsy-turvy world of the satires. Here, for the moment at least — aided by the clowning Simplician kibitzer, who stands in for the writer himself, the writer who employs the mode of world upside down — the prince, the headman, is actually present and on top. Indeed, for the few concluding lines of *Rathstübel,* the *locus amoena* of the celebratory feast near Simplicius's curative spa becomes, so to speak, the healthiest spot in the world, a distinction once claimed for the island of Simplicius's world-renouncing retreat (ST 587).

Notes

[1] The reference to a fair constitutes but one of many flags of Simplicius's ambiguity and of the topsy-turvy world his being evokes, a topsy-turvy world that, as has been frequently noted, is characterized by gender role reversal. See, also, Leblans on the significance of the Hanau episode as carnival, esp. 502–10.

[2] The name Simplicius places its bearer in a class of simpletons. Whereas to grammarians the hermit's improvised name for the boy might initially appear to be unsexed inasmuch as it is identical with the neuter comparative form of "simplex," "Simplicius" in fact already explicitly and ironically marks the character as masculine. The name should not be read primarily as meaning "more simple" but as a man's name deriving from the Latin word for simple. Not only does the narrator regularly inflect Simplicius like a masculine noun of the second declension, i.e. like "filius" or "Virgílius," but the ending "-ius" is a masculine suffix used in Roman nomenclature to indicate a male member of the Roman "gens" or clan (Tatlock, 399).

[3] Natalie Davis explains such a dynamic in her seminal essay "Woman on Top," that is, even when transgressive gender reversals are meant to affirm the existing order they also unleash social energy that may have the opposite effect.

[4] Teuscher presents an important exception. He, however, attempts primarily to demonstrate Grimmelshausen's misogyny and not to consider gender arrangements in the light of early modern scholarship.

[5] Toril Moi, *Sexual/ Textual Politics* (1988), qtd. by Van Ornam, 22. See also Feldman, Van Ornam, Arnold, Becker-Cantarino, Berns, Jacobson, Leighton, Solbach, Krebs, and Grewling. While the readings offered by these essays vary considerably, they share an interest in the position of woman in the seventeenth century and in rethinking Grimmelshausen's literary treatment of it. Rainer Hillenbrand makes a valid point when he asserts that some of these interpretations may be misguided in their sympathy with a character whom the text so obviously condemns. They may, in fact, not help us understand what Hillenbrand sees as the "original" intention of the text — students less schooled in the seventeenth century do sometimes tend to read these older texts with the psychologizing habits developed by contemporary reading. Nevertheless, Hillenbrand misunderstands the point of reading against the grain, a theoretical position that clearly informs a number of these articles, that is, deconstructive reading that explores ruptures in the text that enable other meanings — even in their own time. Moreover, he seems blind to the now well-

understood notion that texts always yield multiple readings and that authorial intention, whatever that may be, cannot completely determine understanding — even the understanding of readers contemporary with the author. When he criticizes Solbach's assertion that Courage's rebellion could prove fascinating to a reader as something that could only occur to a modern scholar (190), he fails to read Grimmelshausen's own texts carefully; for these texts repeatedly warn the reader against precisely the allure of the sins they depict. See note 3 on the double effect of inversion.

[6] By autobiographical novels I mean novels written in the first person as if they were the life story of the fictive first-person narrator.

[7] See footnote 5.

[8] See the title pages of the second and third volumes of the collected works (1683–84). Zedler's *Universal-Lexicon* (1732–50), an encyclopedia that summarizes the knowledge of the early modern period, describes "Lust" as something that is put to rest, not something to be aroused (volume 18, columns 1343–46). The formulation "Lust-erweckend" anticipates modern culture in which print culture creates desire rather than fulfilling a specific pre-existing desire.

[9] Engraving preceding the title page of volume 3 (1684) of the collected works (1683–84) in the edition held in the Herzog-August Bibliothek, Lo 2310, in Wolfenbüttel. This engraving is reproduced in *Simplius Simplicissimus. Grimmelshausen und seine Zeit* (127).

[10] Wilhelm von Schröder, for example, writes in his *Fürstlicher Schatz- und Rent-Kammer* (1686) that nothing is more harmful to the common good than the "Mutwillen" of servants (149) and points out that the principal cause of such is the master's failure to manage them properly (155).

[11] For a discussion of Gypsies and beggars in Grimmelshausen's oeuvre in the social context of the seventeenth century, see Jütte. He notes that Grimmelshausen's ideas about these social groups support the existing social order and reflect the spirit of the times, a spirit characterized by a general helplessness vis-à-vis the increasing mass of the poor (131).

[12] I am well aware of the religious significance of this episode, but focus here on a different layer of this complex narrative. In the seventeenth century, of course, the constitution of oneself as male bourgeois subject within a social network is intimately bound to the securing of one's immortal soul.

[13] See esp. 35–62, where Moscherosch clearly addresses his sons, not his daughters. See also chapter 1 (4–28) of Christian Weise's *Politischer Akademicus* for a detailed catalogue of behaviors that sensible and well-brought up young men need to avoid.

[14] I do not mean to imply here that Courage seeks a modern sort of revenge on the male-dominated world, but rather that the author unleashes her as punishment on a world run badly by men, in particular, one in which they give license to their own bestiality. The notion of Courage as punishment is taken up again in *Rathstübel* (see below).

[15] The text contains one oblique reference to a material cause of Courage's gender-norm defying behavior, namely that she was nursed by a wet nurse, who had just born a son. According to seventeenth-century belief, only the mothers of baby girls

should serve as wet nurses to baby girls, lest the infant imbibe a male temperament and character with the mother's milk (Ettner, 727).

[16] In *Rathstübel* she laments her pitiful state in her old age: "in Summa/ der guten Courage ist von ihrer gantzen Courage sonst nichts alß der Namme übrig verblieben [. . .]" (714).

[17] Of course, all women's ability to manipulate gender to men's peril — in crying crocodile tears, for example — is a commonplace in early modern literature, a commonplace that suggests a distinct male bias whenever it appears. The early modern female character, who comments on her fake tears, issues from a male pen and is in effect a man in woman's clothing.

[18] She is Grimmelshausen's grotesque construct, not the attempt to create a believable and nuanced psychological portrait of a woman for which twentieth-century critics occasionally take her for (e.g., Negus).

[19] Judith Butler widely introduced the idea of gender as performance in her *Gender Trouble*. Such a framing of gender enables us to de-naturalize it and to perceive the gap between social expectation and individual inclination.

[20] The text is inconsistent in this matter. Springinsfeld later speaks of his dalliance with two maids "welches in bälde seinen Ausbruch mit Händen und Füßen nemmen würde" (107). In any case, Springinsfeld does not wait around for these corporeal consequences and in his old age is unattached and unaware of offspring.

[21] Bornemann lists the following vulgar expressions relating to the violin: "Streichmusik" for sounds of coitus, "Geigenbogen" for penis, "Griffbrett" for genitals and breast, "Geige" for vagina, and "fiedeln" for coitus.

[22] Bornemann lists "leiern" as a synonym for masturbate ("Musik").

[23] Wiedemann provides an alternative interpretation of this conversation in the inn; he suggests over the course of his argument that this conversation marks a small victory for the common man, inasmuch as the text ensures that not only the educated and socially privileged speak. He also asserts that on another level — Springinsfeld, Simplicius, and Philarchus are flagged as the sole creations of the author — the author reestablishes his own individual experience as sole narrative authority. Wiedemann seems not to have considered the social significance of Simplicius as master of the servant who is also present in the inn, nor the clear exclusion of women as speakers in this conversation among men, which facts speak against a notion of narrative democratization. Although Wiedemann does not consider gender *per se,* both of the above-mentioned points inadvertently support the interpretation of this text as an assertion of male prerogative, as sole authority.

[24] Pufendorf asserts that in the case of a child born out of wedlock, the mother, not the father has power over the child (151). Such legal power would make Courage a double threat.

[25] Of course, contrary to the wording of the text in this passage, precisely the circumstances surrounding Springinsfeld's telling of his life's story, i.e., Philarchus's telling of his story, reveal the origins of Simplicius, Jr., not Springinsfeld's autobiography *per se.*

[26] *Rathstübel* constitutes, according to Zeller, "eher eine gelehrt-satirische Unterhaltung als ein Gesprächspiel in Harsdörfferschen Sinn, das zeigt sich auch daran, daß die Gesprächspartner in ihren Argumenten nicht eigentlich auseinandergehen, sondern nur der Anlaß sind, um Sprichwörter und andere Weisheiten aneinander zu reihen" (539).

[27] The text alludes later to his kosher diet, a diet that sets him apart and nearly precludes his enjoying the concluding festivities.

[28] The word "undüchtig" may suggest a sexual sense as well: a loss of manhood.

Works Cited

Arnold, Herbert A. "Die Rollen der Courasche: Bemerkungen zur wirtschaftlichen und sozialen Stellung der Frau im siebzehnten Jahrhundert." In: *Die Frau von der Reformation zur Romantik*. Ed. Barbara Becker-Cantarino. Bonn: Bouvier, 1980. 86–111.

Battafarano, Italo Michele. "Harsdörffers italiänisierender Versuch durch Integration der Frau das literarische Leben zu verfeinern." In: *Georg Philipp Harsdörffer. Ein deutscher Dichter und europäischer Gelehrter*. Ed. Italo Michele Battafarano. Bern: Lang, 1991. 267–86.

Becker-Cantarino, Barbara. "Dr. Faustus and Runagate Courage: Theorizing Gender in Early Modern German Literature." In: *The Graph of Sex and the German Text: Gendered Culture in Early Modern Europe 1500–1700*. Ed. Lynne Tatlock and Christiane Bohnert. Amsterdam: Rodopi, 1994. 27–44. (= Chloe 19)

Beer, Johann. *Sämtliche Werke. Vol. I: Der Simplicianische Welt-Kucker*. Edited by Ferdinand van Ingen and Hans-Gert Roloff. Bern: Lang, 1981. (= Mittlere Deutsche Literatur in Neu- und Nachdrucken 1)

Berns, Jörg Jochen. "Libuschka und Courasche. I. Teil: Dokumentation. Bemerkungen zu Grimmelshausens Frauenbild." *Simpliciana* 11 (1989): 215–260. "Libuschka und Courasche. Studien zu Grimmelshausens Frauenbild. II. Teil: Darlegungen." *Simpliciana* 12 (1990): 417–41.

Bornemann, Ernest. *Sex im Volksmund. die sexuelle Umgangssprache der Deutschen*. Reinbek bei Hamburg: Rowohlt, 1971.

Breuer, Dieter. "Kommentar. Rathstübel Plutonis." *Hans Jacob Christoffel von Grimmelshausen Werke*. Two vols. Frankfurt / Main: Deutscher Klassiker, 1992. 1022–1062. (= Bibliothek deutscher Klassiker 73)

Butler, Judith. *Gender Trouble: Feminism and the Subversion of Identity*. New York: Routledge, 1990.

Davis, Natalie Zemon. "Woman on Top." In: *Society and Culture in Early Modern France: Eight Essays*. Stanford: Stanford UP, 1975. 124–51.

Ettner, Johann Christoph. *Des Getreuen Eckarths unvorsichtige Heb-amme.* Leipzig: Johann Friedrich Braun, 1715.

Feldman, Linda Ellen. "The Rape of 'Frau Welt': Transgression, Allegory and the Grotesque Body in Grimmelshausen's *Courasche.*" In: *Writing on the Line: Transgression in Early Modern German Literature.* Ed. Lynne Tatlock. Special Issue of *Daphnis* 20 (1991): 61–80.

Garber, Majorie. *Vested Interests: Cross-Dressing and Cultural Anxiety.* New York: Routledge, 1992.

Grewling, Nicole. "'A Woman on her own Account': Courasche und Moll Flanders, ein Vergleich." M.A. thesis. Washington U., 1999.

Griesshaber-Weninger, Christl. "Harsdörffers *Frauenzimmer Gesprächspiele* als geschlechtsspezifische Verhaltensfibel: Ein Vergleich mit heutigen Kommunikationsstrukturen." *Women in German Yearbook* 9 (1993): 49–70.

Grimmelshausen, Hans Christoph von. *Deß Aus dem Grabe der Vergessenheit wieder erstandenen Simplicissimi, Mit kostbaren/ zu dieser Zeit hochwerthen und dero Liebhaber fest an sich ziehenden Waaren an- und ausgefüllter Staats-Kram/ statt deß auf seinen jüngsthin hervorgebenen Lebens-Wandel/ nunmehr ordentlich folgenden Dritten und letzten Theils. Ein überaus curiöses / theils ernstliches/ theils anmuthiges/ und vermittelst wohlausgesonnener Begebenheiten/ Lust-erweckendes Werck/ worinnen/ gleich als in einer hohen Schul/ Die Tugenden belobet/ die Laster getadelt/ ein wohl zu leben guter Vorsatz befestiget/ und mit sonst allerhand erdencklichen Sitten-Lehren an Hand gegangen wird; Auf gethanes Versprechen/ und inständiges Begehren/ zusamt beygefügten netten/ künstlichen Kupfer-Tafeln/ und vor ausgesetzten eines jeglichen Buchs und dessen Capitel Inhalt zeigenden Poetischen Versen / ausgefertiget. Liß mich vornen/ oder hinden/ Du wirst/ was du suchest finden.* Nürnberg: Felßecker, 1684.

———. *Deß possirlichen/ weit und breit bekanten Simplicissimi Sinnreicher und nachdencklicher Schrifften. Zweyten Theils Erstes Buch/ von dem seltzamen Springinsfeld/ Oder Dessen kurtzweiligen/ Lust-erweckenden/ unrecht lächerlichen Lebens-Beschreibung/ Als eines weiland frischen/ wohlversuchten und tapffern Soldaten. Und nachmahlen außmärgelten/ abgelebten/ doch darbey sehr verschlagenen Landstürtzers und Bettlers/ Nach Simplicianischer Anordnung Erstesmal verabfasset 1670. anjetzo aber wieder neu verbässert/ vermehret und auffgelegt Von Philarcho Grosso von Trommenheim.* N.p.: n.p., 1683.

Hillenbrand, Rainer. "Courasche als emanzipierte Frau. Einige erstaunliche Modernitäten bei Grimmelshausen." *Daphnis* 27 (1998): 185–99.

Jacobsen, John W. "A Defense of Grimmelshausen's Courasche." *GQ* 41 (1968): 42–54.

Jütte, Robert. "Vagantentum und Bettlerwesen bei Hans Jacob Christoffel von Grimmelshausen." *Daphnis* 9 (1980): 109–32.

Krebs, Jean-Daniel. "La picara, l'aventurière, la pionnière. Fonctions de l'hêroïne picaresque à travers des figures de Justina, Courage et Moll." *Arcadia* 24 (1989): 239–52.

Leblans, Annie. "Grimmelshausen and the Carnivalesque: The Polarization of Courtly and Popular Carnival in *Der abenteuerliche Simplicissimus.*" *MLN* 105 (1990): 494–511.

Leighton, Joseph. "Courasche and Moll Flanders; Roguery and Morality." In: Barocker *Lust-Spiegel: Studien zur Literatur des Barock. Festschrift für Blake Lee Spahr.* Ed. Martin Bircher, Jörg-Ulrich Fechner, and Gerd Hillen. Amsterdam: Rodopi, 1984. Pp. 295–310. (= Chloe 3)

Luther, Martin. "Eine Predigt vom Ehestand, getan durch D. Martinum Lutherum, seliger. Anno 1525 zu Wittenberg." *Vom ehelichen Leben.* Stuttgart: Reclam, 1978. 63–74. (= Reclams Universalbibliothek 9896)

Mazingue, Etienne. "A propos de Courage et Springinsfeld, et spécialement de leur divorce." In: *Barocker Lust-Spiegel: Studien zur Literatur des Barock Festschrift für Blake Lee Spahr,* ed. Martin Bircher, Jörg-Ulrich Fechner, and Gerd Hillen. Amsterdam: Rodopi, 1984. 311–18. (= Chloe 3)

Moscherosch, Hans Michael. *Insomnis cura parentum. Christliches Vermächnuß oder, Schuldige Vorsorg Eines Trewen Vatters. . . .* [1643]. Halle: Niemeyer, 1893. (= Neudrucke deutscher Litteraturwerke des XVI. und XVII. Jahrhunderts 108–9)

Pufendorf, Samuel von. *Über die Pflicht des Menschen und des Bürgers nach dem Gesetz der Natur* [1673]. Ed. and trans. Klaus Luig. Frankfurt / Main: Insel, 1994. (= Bibliothek des deutschen Staatsdenkens 1)

Schröder, Wilhelm von. *Fürstlicher Schatz- und Rent-Kammer/ ad Augustissimum & Invictissimum imperatorem Leopoldum I Principe M. Triumphantem.* Leipzig: Gerdesius, 1686.

Scott, Joan Wallach. *Gender and the Politics of History.* New York: Columbia UP, 1988.

Simplicius Simplicissimus. Grimmelshausen und seine Zeit. Ausstellungskatalog. Ed. Westälisches Landesmuseum für Kunst und Kulturgeschichte Münster in Zusammenarbeit mit dem Germanistischen Institut der Westfälischen Wilhelms-Universität. Münster: Aschendorff, 1976. (= Ausstellungskatalog)

Solbach, Andreas. "Transgression als Verletzung des Decorum bei Christian Weise, J. J. Chr. v. Grimmelshausen und in Johann Beers *Narrenspital.*" In: *Writing on the Line: Transgression in Early Modern German Literature.* Ed. Lynne Tatlock. Special Issue of *Daphnis* 20 (1991): 33–60.

Stallybrass, Peter, and Alon White. *The Politics and Poetics of Transgression.* Ithaca, NY: Cornell UP, 1986.

Tatlock, Lynne. "Ab ovo: Reconceiving the Masculinity of the Autobiographical Subject." In: *The Graph of Sex and the German Text: Gendered Culture in Early Modern Germany*. Ed. Lynne Tatlock and Christiane Bohnert. Amsterdam: Rodopi, 1994. 383–412. (= Chloe 19)

Teuscher, Gerhart. "'Fromme tugenthaffte Frauen' oder 'arglistiges Weiber-Volck'?" *Jahrbuch für internationale Germanistik* 16 (1984): 94–115.

Van Ornam, Vanessa. "No Time for Mothers: Courasche's Infertility as Grimmelshausen's Criticism of War." *Women in German Yearbook* 8 (1993): 21–45.

Weise, Christian. *Politischer Academicus, Das ist: kurtze Nachricht/ wie ein zukünftiger Politicus seine Zeit und Geld auff der Universität wohl anwenden könne*. Amsterdam: Regenfarb, 1684.

Wiedemann, Conrad. "Die Herberge des alten Simplicissimus. Zur Deutung des *Seltzamen Springinsfeld* von Grimmelshausen." *Germanisch-Romanische Monatsschrift* NS 33 (1983): 394–410.

Wurst, Karin A. "Die Frau als Mitspielerin und Leserin in Georg Philipp Harsdörffers *Frauenzimmer Gesprächspielen*." *Daphnis* 21 (1992): 615–39.

Zedler, Johann Heinrich. *Großes vollständiges Universal-Lexicon aller Wissenschaften und Künste*. Halle / Saale: Zedler, 1732–1750. Here: vol. 18. Cols. 1343–1346.

Zeller, Rosmarie. "Die Rolle der Frau im Gesprächspiel und in der Konversation." In: *Geselligkeit und Gesellschaft im Barockzeitalter*. Pt. 1. Ed. Wolfgang Adam. Wiesbaden: Harrassowitz, 1997. 531–41. (= Wolfenbüttler Arbeiten zur Barockforschung. 28)

Copperplate from a later edition of Springinsfeld *(1684).*
Reprinted with permission of the
Herzog August Bibliothek, Wolfenbüttel.

Engraved copperplate for Simplicissimus Redivivus *(1683).*
Reprinted with permission of the
Herzog August Bibliothek, Wolfenbüttel.

The Poetics of Masquerade: Clothing and the Construction of Social, Religious, and Gender Identity in Grimmelshausen's *Simplicissimus*

Peter Hess

GRIMMELSHAUSEN'S NOVEL *Der Abentheuerliche Simplicissimus Teutsch* opens with the following sentence:

> Es eröffnet sich zu dieser unserer Zeit (von welcher man glaubt/ daß es die letzte seye) unter geringen Leuten eine Sucht/ in deren die Patienten/ wann sie daran kranck ligen/ und so viel zusammen geraspelt und erschachert haben/ daß sie neben ein paar Hellern im Beutel/ ein närrisches Kleid auff die neue Mode/ mit tausenderley seidenen Banden/ antragen können/ oder sonst etwan durch Glücksfall mannhafft und bekant worden/ gleich Rittermäßige Herren/ und Adeliche Personen von uhraltem Geschlecht/ seyn wollen. (9)

Clothing has meaning. It is, as Entwistle points out in her important monograph in 2000, used to express and shape social realities and to construct individual identities (114). As the quotation indicates, people can use clothing to represent themselves as someone they are not. Social status and identities can be manipulated and even forged through certain uses of dress, if identifiable rigid social norms for dress exist within the group. This gives rise to the possibility of play: clothing can be compliant, deceptive, or outright transgressive. Clothing with its almost unlimited and complex options for signification thus allows the individual to play with identities, but, more important, it gives the narrator a useful tool to play with the identity of his characters, as well as with his own. From this perspective, the opening sentence is designed to send a signal to the reader that clothing and its playful and potentially transgressive use will assume a central role in the novel.

Clothing and bodies in *Simplicissimus*, I will argue, engage in an unstable relationship that is a major source signaling the protagonist's unstable identity. Simplicissimus's identity is continuously renegotiated throughout the novel through a mechanism described by Munns and Richards in another context: "Bodies and clothes endlessly redefine each other to forge, adapt, adopt — and deny — varieties of selfhood [. . .]" (Munns and Richards, 9).

This essay explores ways in which "clothing could function to appropriate, explore, subvert, and assert alternative identities and possibilities" (Munns und Richards, 10). It is based on the hypothesis that Grimmelshausen's use of clothing is transgressive throughout the novel: Simplicissimus's clothes are never appropriate in that they do not correspond to his social role (Neri, 69–70). The deceitful use of clothing goes beyond comic relief, as still argued in recent research (Gruenter, 4). Instead, clothing underscores the author's explanation of ethical and moral questions and is equally important as an unstable marker of identity. Masquerading offers the novel's characters "opportunities for dressing above and below status, across genders, and across national/ geographic boundaries" (Munns and Richards, 18). In this way, clothing and its use make statements about an entire society: "Clothes are an index of codes of display, restraint, self-control, and affect-transformation" (Craik, 10; also Elias, 187). My goal is to show that, by making use of the entire range of signification of clothing, including its transgressive and subversive possibilities, Grimmelshausen challenges the "mechanisms of ordering and sense-making" in seventeenth-century German culture (Stallybrass and White, 23).

Clothing as a Social Signifier in Seventeenth-Century Germany

The relationship of textual representation and cultural reality is a complex one (Smith, 321) and needs examination beyond the scope of this study. A considerable amount of scholarship has been published on this issue covering England, France, and the Netherlands, but there is a remarkable absence of work on Germany. Nonetheless, for the European norm of readers which writers like Grimmelshausen no doubt had in mind, textual representations of clothing may not have been a reliable indicator of social norms or fashion trends at the time. However, today's reader should expect that actual fashion trends, social norms, and sumptuary laws operative at the time interacted with and influenced textual representations. For this reason alone, it is important to investigate the real-life social questions that arise from the representation of clothing and its conventions. A novel like that of Grimmelshausen, which displays an understanding of the norms associated with dress, shares the common cultural information with readers of his day that dress can be read in terms of rank, wealth, and gender of the wearer, and that there is a potential for play with identities based on the uneasy relationship between dress and social meaning.

That potential was enhanced by the fact that a piece of clothing represented an enormous material value before the advent of mass production in the Industrial Revolution. Before the eighteenth century, fashion was a privilege of the elites: only a small fraction of the population was able to participate in such alterations of appearance by employing rich materials, strong colors, and lavish styles (Breward, 42; Munns and Richards, 12). The general norm was changelessness, effected by the high cost of clothing, by social stability, and by sumptuary laws pertaining to dress. For the vast majority of the population, participation in fashion trends and thus claims to self-expression through clothing were unrealistic due to the prohibitive cost. That majority, therefore, had a stable appearance as to their clothing that correlated with and signified their ordinary stations in life.

It is not surprising, then, that economic aspects of clothing play a central role in the lengthy article on clothing ("Kleid") in volume 15 of Zedler's *Universallexikon* (1737: 889–97). Zedler gives us a rare glimpse into the every-day reality of clothing and good insight into conventional late seventeenth and early eighteenth-century attitudes toward dress. The prominence of economic aspects of clothing in Zedler's article is remarkable: questions like how clothes are traded, who inherits the clothes of the deceased, and who is given the clothes of executed felons are central points, along with legal transgressions such as the deliberate soiling or destruction of someone else's garments.

Zedler's reality seems to be Grimmelshausen's. References to the material value of clothing are infrequent in *Simplicissimus,* yet, as Zedler made obvious, passing references confirm that the high value of clothing is a given reality. This lets us explain details from the Jäger von Soest episode. Simplicissimus by chance finds red cloth and lining for a coat that he trades for the green cloth he really wants for his new Jäger von Soest uniform. The implication is that he would not have been able to afford his new uniform had it not been for this lucky find (ST 183).

As a more ironic allusion to such material commonplaces, the Schermesser episode in the *Continuatio* further comments on the commercial side of clothing. The anthropomorphized Schermesser actually is a piece of toilet paper, equipped with identity, consciousness, and a gift for keen observation (Busch, 52). As Simplicissimus is about to make final use of it, it tells him its entire life history (514–21), leading up to an unsuccessful plea to spare it. Schermesser reports about its two life cycles: from hemp to the best shirt of a Dutch maiden to a rag and — after reprocessing in a paper mill — from writing paper to packing paper to toilet paper. From this perspective, the Schermesser episode satirizes the rise of a material culture and of an early market economy in the seventeenth century — enhanced by the Thirty Years' War — dominated by commerce where, presumably, life-less objects assume a life of their own.

The details of that life cycle, however, confirm the author's conscious usage of clothing and status. As a piece of clothing, Schermesser shapes the identity of its wearer, the Dutch maiden. While concealing her body from the general public, Schermesser also reveals to the listener how she reveals her body to her many suitors, thus ironically commenting on how such a shirt helps the maiden shape a deceptive identity. Likewise, in a subsequent objective material form as writing paper, Schermesser helps the Zurich merchant maintain a deceptive account of his financial affairs (520–21).

If we assume with Gersch that the *Continuatio* represents a "kommentierendes Widerspiel" to the first five books of the novel (Gersch, 60), then the Schermesser episode should be read as an ironic commentary on how clothing helps Simplicissimus shape and maintain false identities in the novel and more generally on the role of signification of clothing. Here, clothing doesn't just carry meaning, but instead it assumes its own identity, as Schermesser exemplifies. In contrast, while Schermesser as material object has a clear identity and consciousness, the same cannot be said about Simplicissimus, as we will see later. In a case of ironic inversion, Simplicissimus does fit the clothes he is wearing. The point becomes clear: the considerable material value of clothing cannot be separated from its role as signifier, as an almost autonomous social agent.

Grimmelshausen's connection is by no means his alone. This dual role of clothing becomes evident in fashion trends and their discussion by contemporaries (Eisenbart, 93–103). This is particularly true where such trends are criticized, that is where the signification of certain types of clothing is seen as offensive by a subset of the population. Two seventeenth-century fashion trends in particular are widely criticized in this literature: the increasingly effeminate men's wear (wide pants, ruffle collars, frilly bows, loops and ribbons, high heels, long and wavy hair, no facial hair, use of wigs and perfume) (Eisenbart, 102; Garber, 27; Entwistle, 151) and sexually suggestive women's clothing (wide decolletés, open cut shoes, and also very wide dresses (Eisenbart, 101). For the present context, however, the truly unsettling aspect of fashion is that change and changeability is part of its very nature, and that "clothing —

and the changeability of fashion — is an index of destabilization [. . .]"
(Garber, 27). Fashion is a source of inconstancy of Simplicissimus's
world and thus objectionable in a fundamental way (Zedler, 889).

Again, Grimmelshausen's and Zedler's observations fall into a clear
trend in European material culture. The deliberate manipulation of social
meanings attached to clothing begins in the middle of the fourteenth
century and evolves throughout the early modern period; it is achieved
by inventive cutting and new uses of color and texture (Breward, 42; also
Hollander, 31; Cavallaro and Warwick, 135). Even apart from sumptuary
laws, clothes thus become psycho-social agents, acknowledged as
"structures that are simultaneously capable of both hiding and disclosing
bodily attributes and desires" (Cavallaro and Warwick, 128). As we shall
see, the "complementary dynamics of concealment and revelation" (128)
form one of the structural elements in the playful treatment of clothing
in *Simplicissimus,* just as it becomes the foundation for the increased
significance of clothing in texts of the seventeenth century. "Writers and
commentators of the period are keen on emphasizing the explosion of
decorative elements with a taxonomic compulsiveness that vividly evokes
the disappearance of the corporeal beneath ever-increasing superficial
masks" (Cavallaro and Warwick 136).

Not surprisingly, then, Grimmelshausen frequently comments on
fashion trends, occasionally in some detail, albeit usually in a satirical
mode. He satirizes the vain, passing fads of fashionable dress, and he
ridicules women who make a fashion statement by showing much of
their breasts (117), courtiers who always wear the style of the day (292;
also 149), and common people who foolishly try to follow fashion trends
(9). His hero provides the rationale for these judgments: Simplicissimus
is so confused by the stylish appearance of the officer who arrests him at
Hanau that he mistakes the officer for a hermaphrodite (54). However,
soon after, at the directive of the governor of Hanau, Simplicissimus is
stripped and bathed. Then his body is concealed under layers of equally
fashionable dress, make-up, coiffure, and perfume (58–60). This elaborate transformation is described in great detail in what amounts to a
parody of "elite modes of dress" (Breward, 42). Even the novel's first-
person narrator — the old Simplicissimus — ironically refers to this
young transformed Simplicissimus in the third person as a young count
(59). His newly stylish appearance makes his boorish conduct at the
Hanau court even more scandalous because of the intolerable discrepancy between his actions and the identity projected by his noble garments. The experiment that tries to transform Simplicissimus into a
courtier by dressing him like one thus fails miserably. His subsequent

transformation into a calf-like fool is equally misguided, since Simplicissimus has already learned to turn masks to his own advantage. The protagonist has learned that clothes can become the medium of his critique of courtly society (Carbonnel, 65).

The point is reiterated throughout the novel. Clothing, a social signifier laden with polyvalent symbolism, expresses a social reality — factual or imagined. Inversely, clothing is expected to be read accordingly by seventeenth-century society. At the heart of the disorientations of the Hanau episode, for instance, stands the expectation of pre-modern society to be able to determine social standing and origin of a stranger on the basis of clothing (Raudszus, 192). As clothing expresses social rank and wealth, appearance becomes a classifying tool, a means of recognizing markers of rank and wealth of the bearer (Entwistle, 87). Simplicissimus himself expresses this expectation: when he meets Herzbruder again after a long separation, he can tell by the elegant black velvet that his friend now occupies an important position — in contrast to his own lowly position as musketeer. Conforming to their signified roles, Simplicissimus does not speak to him initially for fear that his friend might ignore him because of the social differential (326).

Simplicissimus's clothing, however, can also be read as transgressive in that he makes it impossible for those around him to make correct assumptions about his true identity based on his appearance, a pattern we will be able to identify throughout the novel. This, too, reflects the era's historical practices. The main function of sumptuary laws was to maintain the correlation between rank and wealth on one hand and clothing and general appearance on the other. Such laws preserve the readability of clothes: "Codes of dress are technical devices which articulate the relationship between a particular body and its lived milieu, the space occupied by bodies and constituted by body actions. In other words, clothes construct a personal habitus" (Craik, 4).

In the sense I am pursuing here, sumptuary laws attempt to mark as visible and legible distinctions of rank and wealth in a society that is undergoing rapid changes that blur or even threaten to eliminate these distinctions (Garber, 26). Sumptuary laws and related social commentaries respond to fears about breakdown of economic order or morality and thus serve as a social control mechanism for the lower classes (Entwistle, 90; Sekora), but simultaneously act as seismographs for the perception of social stability. Simplicissimus's world is undergoing such changes. Zedler, for instance, not only repeatedly bemoans the demise of sumptuary laws, but also specifically condemns dressing both below and above status:

In der Kleidung kann man sich durch Mißbrauch versündigen, nemlich durch Kostbarkeit, wenn man mehr darauf wendet, als der Wohlstand und Nothwendigkeit erfordert; durch Ubermuth, wenn sich jemand über seinen Stand kleidet; durch Leichtfertigkeit wider den rechten Zweck der Kleidung, zur Reitzung deren Anschauenden; durch Eitelkeit in leichtsinniger veränderung deren Moden [. . .]. (Zedler, 895–96. Cf. also Zedler, 889, 891–92, and 894)

Garber even sees sumptuary laws as an effort at crisis management to support traditional social norms that are seriously challenged and threatened: "[. . .] class, gender, sexuality, and even race and ethnicity [. . .] are themselves brought to crisis in dress codes and sumptuary regulation" (Garber, 28). Such "crisis management" characterizes the world of the *picaro*. Simplicissimus repeatedly faces sanctions for dressing inappropriately throughout the novel. In each case, as will become evident, the objectionable part of Simplicissimus's transgression is not the violation of sumptuary laws per se, but rather the violation of the social norm that clothing should allow observers to assess rank, status and wealth of an individual. The comment of the narrator in the Magdeburg episode makes it clear that Simplicissimus makes a conscious effort at deception. The threat to social stability ensues because he has no problems convincing people that the qualities falsely represented by his appearance are real (148; also 392–93).

Using dress for purposes of deception is signified in the text as highly transgressive because the social order depends on the readability of dress. Zedler also classifies transgressive clothing as fraud (894). Both authorities assume that the observer has to be able to trust the appearance of a stranger in order to classify him correctly. These texts then reflect what is assumed to be social reality. Until the middle of the eighteenth century, the veracity of appearances is generally accepted (Entwistle, 120). To dress transgressively thus represents a breach of trust, since the observer has no other means to verify the true identity of a stranger. As Shapin convincingly argues, trust is an essential social category in early modern European cultures because of the fundamental lack of other mechanisms to verify an individual's truthfulness (Shapin, 22–27). Montaigne, for instance, sees untruthfulness and the breakdown of trust as the most serious subversion of social order (3). Inversely, distrust is seen as uncivil because it implies dishonesty on the part of the other: there is a social obligation to be trusting (20). Transgressive clothing therefore does not just represent a violation of trust, but it becomes an all-out attack on the social order. The consequences for Grimmelshausen's tale are significant. By wearing transgressive clothing, Simplicissimus is marked for the contemporary reader as a deceptive and untrust-worthy character, with subversive potential. Transgression here, however, is not an act of political protest or social liberation in the sense of Bakhtin, Foucault, and Kristeva. In a world of stable estates, transgres-sion does not render the norm invalid; it rather confirms the validity of the norm. It lies in the very nature of transgression that it depends on norms that remain unchallenged in principle (Hotchkiss, 10).

If indeed we witness in the latter part or the seventeenth century "a gradual wearing down of previous overt strategies of social division and identification in dress" (Breward, 88), both Grimmelshausen's experi-mentation with the signification of clothing and Zedler's hostile reaction can be read as responses to this development. *Simplicissimus's* Jäger von Soest episode exemplifies this sense of transgression against an essentially acceptable norm (183–204). The scene relies on the fact that clothes are social signifiers: they do not hide but rather give shape to the wearer's power. The Jäger von Soest's green uniform expresses a social reality as well as Simplicissimus's aspirations. It is a model case to show how iden-tities, both real and desired, depend on clothing, but the inverse is true in the novel as well. Clothing serves as an important source of identity, as the "Kleider machen Leute" topos indicates (ST, 328; Zedler, 896; Lehmann, 436; Logau III, 5, 35). When Simplicissimus is dressed in much nicer clothing by Herzbruder in book IV, the general belief is expressed that Simplicissimus with different clothes had become a differ-ent person (328). Virginia Woolf put it more succinctly: "[. . .] there is much to support the view that it is clothes that wear us and we them; we may make them take the mould of arm or breast, but they mould our hearts, our brains, our tongues to their liking" (188). It is the green uniform that empowers the Jäger von Soest, that gives him his new identity. He looks more impressive than his commanding officer and consequently feels superior to him. Furthermore, the green uniform allows him to slip into the role of a mischievous and invincible seeker of social justice — a role that is instantly destroyed by the evil Jäger von Werl, who uses the same uniform for his criminal activities and thus attaches a very different meaning to it. Clothing here is like a transplant that would allow him "to fashion a new tailored self" (Cavallaro and Warwick, 132), but in spite of his efforts, Simplicissimus cannot ulti-mately control the signification of his uniform, and the transplant fails. Neither young Simplicissimus the protagonist nor old Simplicissimus the narrator fully understands the subversive potential of this mask: it is doomed because of the increasing resistance of powerful figures around him.

Grimmelshausen's novel thus confirms for Germany what scholars of early modern Europe have assumed: that the meaning of clothing in the early modern era is much more a social construct than a result of individual expression. The existence of sumptuary laws and rigid social norms regarding clothing unleashed various dialectics of conformity and transgression and thus opened a full range of options to express individuality and to construct and to manipulate personal identity, real and imaginary. Ironically, the world of Simplicissimus also clearly lacks the stability and thus depends on role-play as a survival strategy. And here, I will argue, the gap opens between what Grimmelshausen represented and what the seventeenth century experienced, no matter their commonalities. In contrast to seventeenth-century social reality, clothing in the novel actually becomes an unstable marker of identity, and thus an unstable marker for an unstable identity.

Class Identities: Social Transgression

The primary signification of clothing in early modern Europe is in the social area; dress serves as a major identifier to assign social status — real or feigned — to the wearer. In this area, the greatest potential for transgression exists, both in the real world and in Grimmelshausen's novel. As Garber points out, the use of the term "class" is anachronistic with respect to the social formation of early modern Europe: rank and wealth are more useful terms to indicate social status (Garber, 27). The term "rank" is used here to include estate and the German "Stand."

In stating in the first sentence of the novel that many people who dress above their rank pretend to be of noble birth Grimmelshausen serves notice that the protagonist will succumb to this kind of foolishness. Indeed, Simplicissimus on numerous occasions uses fine clothing to augment his prestige and social status. However, as expected, social reality does not follow suit; on the contrary, each attempt to dress above rank has to be abandoned or even ends in disaster.

One such example has already been discussed: the Jäger von Soest episode (183–204 and 223–48). Here, Simplicissimus has assumed the role of social equalizer in an act of self-empowerment that is doomed to fail. It is significant that this is the first time in the novel that Simplicissimus chooses his own clothing and thus has the opportunity to fashion his own identity (Carbonnel, 71). Yet, he ultimately transgresses against the dress code and challenges the privileges of wealth through his green uniform. Ironically, however, his transgressive green uniform cannot unfold its subversive potential because it is itself subverted by the rival

Jäger von Werl. The fact that Simplicissimus will take revenge is irrelevant because he cannot reverse the damage and resume his self-chosen role as Jäger von Soest. Simplicissimus is forced to return to the established social order and to his previous role. The episode is paradigmatic: transgressive dress cannot create a new norm, a new fashion system, because it is impossible for a single individual — the Jäger von Soest — to control its social meaning. Transgression ultimately is unsuccessful, and that outcome confirms the status quo.

This insight is lost on Simplicissimus: he dresses above status whenever he can. Still in Soest, as a private first class, he uses the spoils he had amassed as Jäger von Soest to acquire clothing that is fancier than that of his commanding officers (235 and 236–37). His fashionable appearance does not fail to have an impact on women (237). Bemoaning the fact that he is not a nobleman (237), he even has a coat of arms made for himself — which not by coincidence consists of three masks (237). He thus generates distrust, jealousy and outright hostility among the officers, and he loses the friendship and respect of other privates. Realizing that he is not making friends by displaying pride and avarice, he decides to feign humility and to tone down his clothing until his efforts to become a nobleman are successful (248). Only old Simplicissimus the narrator generates true insight into his inability to subvert the existing code: he concedes the failure of this strategy, and he admits that he should have used his resources to secure a military command, rather than trying to construct an alternate identity around fancy clothing (236–37).

In the first episode in which Simplicissimus dresses above his status, he actually has not done so voluntarily. As mentioned before, the governor of Hanau has him dressed fashionably as a courtier (58–60). The reader, knowing about Simplicissimus's modest roots, views his clothing as transgressive. Ironically, he is not really dressing up: as we find out later in the novel, Simplicissimus in actuality is a nobleman — and the governor's nephew (402), and as such he certainly is entitled to appear as a courtier. Even knowledge of his noble birth would not resolve the problem: the members of the Hanau court do not think of Simplicissimus as a young courtier, and for that reason consider his behavior transgressive. Depending on how we look at the episode, either his clothes or his behavior is transgressive. Interestingly, after Simplicissimus learns about his noble birth, which fulfills a dream held since childhood, he no longer feels the need to dress like a nobleman; from that moment on he prefers peasant's clothing (Müller, 40), which — given his changed reality — is transgressive as well. Simplicissimus shirks all responsibilities that come with his status, including dressing like a nobleman.

Dressing below status thus is equally objectionable. We already discussed Simplicissimus's decision as a soldier in Soest to tone down his clothing in order to create a more humble image of himself (248). The act of dressing below status can take on a more sinister dimension. For example, the Croatian colonel routinely dresses as a peasant. Concealing his true identity allows him to spy on the peasants in order to be able to rob and plunder them more efficiently (138). We see an inverse situation when Simplicissimus meets Jupiter: because of the latter's odd appearance, Simplicissimus suspects that he might be a prince in disguise who spies on his subjects (208). In a different episode, Simplicissimus uses the deliberate disguise of a peddler to get an exorcist ("Teufelsbanner") to reveal the secret of his devil's pact in order to take advantage of him (392–93). In *Simplicissimus,* dressing down is a strategy used to deceive others to gain an advantage, which consistently evokes a negative commentary from the narrator.

Another variation on the problem of clothing and identity is exemplified with borrowed clothes. During an inspection of the Hanau fortress by a Swedish commissioner, for example, Simplicissimus is put into borrowed clothes and given borrowed drums so he would be presentable to the commissioner. The narrator justifies this deceit by drawing the analogy to his own borrowed identity at the time (104).

The Russian episode also develops the theme of borrowed finery. Near the end of the novel, Simplicissimus finds himself stuck in Moscow. By decree of the czar, idle foreigners are forced to leave Russia, but Simplicissimus is not given permission to do so because of his military expertise. After refusing to convert and to accept an estate, he offers to help set up a niter mine. The next day, two servants of the czar bring him a valuable Russian dress (450). When the Swedish colonel, who had lured him to Russia, visits him at the mine wearing his own elaborate Russian dress, it is clear to him that all these ornate dresses are just borrowed from the czar's wardrobe, and that the garments on loan served to deceive him (450). When the Tartars attack, the clothes take on an air of obligation. Simplicissimus is given command over the Russian defending troops (450–52). His orders from the czar simply say that he should prove himself to be the soldier he had pretended to be so His Majesty could recognize him as such (451). He fulfills this task in a richly adorned armored uniform that is also borrowed from the czar (451). Simplicissimus thus creates his own deceptive reality as military commander with the help of a borrowed uniform, and it becomes evident just how much he serves at the czar's pleasure. Thus, both military identity and uniform are borrowed. It cannot surprise us, therefore, that Simplicissimus, after his battlefield victory, has to return his borrowed clothes and along with them his identity as military commander (452).

The remarkable aspect of this episode is that Simplicissimus, who had no previous command experience, is fashioned into a successful military commander simply by being dressed as one. By the same token, he loses his military command and his short-lived identity of a commander when he is stripped of his uniform. As the power is invested in him by virtue of his garments, his power is dismantled in the act of disrobing. As his clothes are just borrowed, so is his identity. The czar thus exercises his absolute power by controlling the garments of his subjects (453).

Clothes for Grimmelshausen thus signify a denser weave of social truths and obligations than was at first apparent. Ownership of clothing has more than a material dimension: it also is a means of controlling identities, one's own or, as in the Russian episode, that of others. To borrow clothes therefore means to borrow an identity. Like dressing above and below status, dressing in borrowed clothes is used as a tool for the deceitful construction of reality. Clothes help construct — and unmask — false identities and forged social realties.

The Ethos of Dress

All episodes discussed so far present clothing on some level as deceitful. The early modern ethical imperative to dress according to status affirms that clothing and the use of clothing do have the ethical dimension that Grimmelshausen highlights. Dressing both above and below status is characterized as deceitful and, therefore, morally reprehensible in *Simplicissimus.* Such scenes exemplify societal attitudes toward socially transgressive dress, as illustrated by Zedler's hostility towards dress that does not properly reflect social status. There are, however more concerns than rank involved with dress. Especially the recurring theme of the hermit's habit helps us to locate Grimmelshausen's message concerning the ethical and moral dimensions of dress.

When Simplicissimus first meets the hermit, the latter's simple outfit with the patched robe is described in detail (22). Due to his own lack of socialization and unstable identity, Simplicissimus fails to recognize the hermit as what he is — ironically the only authentic hermit figure in the novel. In the subsequent chapters, the moral character that corresponds to that appearance is revealed with more precision. The narrator here develops a distinct stereotype of a hermit whose simple dress expresses a noble spirit. In the case of the old hermit, clothing allows one to make assumptions about his character, as the pre-modern reader of epic litera-ture would expect (Raudszus, 203–5). Simplicissimus will try to emulate this model at various junctures in his life — but unsuccessfully, as we will see. A hermit-like dress is worn by only one other figure in the novel, namely by the modest and honest dragoon who captured Simplicissimus at the end of book 2 (182).

After the hermit's death, Simplicissimus puts on his master's habit in imitation of a way of life that the boy cannot comprehend. He just wants to look like his master, believing that this will turn him into a person like him. Furthermore, the habit made from furs offers good protection against the cold (39). He is, of course, wearing the coarse robe incor-rectly on top of his shirt rather than directly on his skin, thus greatly reducing its ascetic and self-denying effect (Neri, 71). His new dress thus indicates that he is not ready to be a hermit and that he is lacking self-knowledge. When he emerges from the forest and approaches Hanau in his hermit's habit, he is not recognized as such in spite of his clothing, because no one sees him as a hermit (54). As his habit is seen as a dis-guise, he is arrested and searched (54) and suspected to be a spy, a luna-tic, a wild man, a spirit, a fool or a miracle (55). The irony lies in the fact that his disguise originates with Simplicissimus's lack of identity. Given the vestimentary norms of the time, the guards of Hanau have to see his disguise as an intentional one — with the obvious negative consequences for Simplicissimus.

The resolution of what a hermit actually is comes slowly. In the three middle books of the novel, the term hermit always is used sarcastically. In Hanau, Simplicissimus, in a phony demonstration of piety, shows the governor how he still prays like a hermit (131). When he lives alone in the forest after fleeing from the Croatians, his life, consisting of stealing food from the farmers in the area, is nevertheless still described as the life of a hermit (141), a life about which he later despairs (142). Simplicissi-mus is too engrossed in his adventures to be concerned with matters of his soul: he is not even interested in maintaining the pretense of a devout life, or in differentiating a holy hermit from a solitary predator.

This lack of vestimentary truth and personal identity only changes at the beginning of book 5, after he rejoins Herzbruder. Herzbruder, after recovering from illness, plans a pilgrimage to Einsiedeln, but at first refuses to take along Simplicissimus because of his godless life (375). Simplicissimus feigns remorse and promises to atone by putting peas into his shoes during the pilgrimage (375). However, when Herzbruder finds out that the peas are cooked, he tells Simplicissimus that he does not want to be friends with an infidel. In response, Simplicissimus engages in some real self-reflection, as he despairs over the lost friendship and the lost innocence he had as a boy in the forest (377). When he reaches Einsiedeln, the issue of truth-telling gets conflated with sooth-saying. A man with divinatory capabilities who is being exorcised accuses Simplicissimus of all kinds of actual sins, including that of having cooked the peas in his shoes (378). Even though the man speaks the truth, the onlookers believe Simplicissimus because they trust that his honorable and respectable robe identifies him as a pilgrim (Müller, 33; 379). Simplicissimus appears to live up to his dress for a moment: shaken and confused, he converts to Catholicism and accepts communion. However, his true motivation, as the narrator admits, is not faith but fear, and soon sloth and shiftlessness take over once again (379–80).

Throughout this episode, Simplicissimus wears the robe of a pilgrim as a deceit. While he goes through all the motions of being a pilgrim, he isn't a pilgrim in mind or spirit. His deceptive dress nonetheless causes bystanders to believe that he is a true pilgrim, even at the cost of an honest man being condemned as a liar. After the public accusations, Simplicissimus misses an opportunity to confess to his sinful ways and to achieve true penance and atonement. While, on the surface, Simplicissimus has reaped a benefit from his transgressive dress, he squanders a chance to purge his soul.

At the end of the novel, Simplicissimus seems to have achieved the spiritual maturation appropriate to that robe. After he is freed from Tartar, Korean, Arabic and Turkish slavery, he acquires a pilgrim's robe (455) and visits many religious sites on his way back to Germany. Since this episode is narrated in broad strokes, there is no conclusive evidence as to the propriety of his dress. Back in Germany, he bemoans his wasted life, which he calls a living death (456). He recognizes that his failure to follow his father's cardinal rule of *nosce te ipsum* (35) caused his downfall (455–56). After his "Adieu Welt" sermon, he decides to become a hermit (463). Still, his commitment is again not complete, unlike that of his father: as the novel closes, he is unsure whether he will remain a hermit for the rest of his life (463). This ironic twist allows us to question the integrity and sincerity of Simplicissimus's decision. Has he really gotten to know himself? If yes, does he realize that he still resists being a hermit?

The *Continuatio* confirms that Simplicissimus's existence as a hermit is a farce. One critic claims that his clothes are not mentioned in this section because he is at inner peace with his existence as a hermit (Müller, 32–33), but the link of clothes with moral duty refutes this claim. While Simplicissimus can keep physical desires like lust and gluttony under control, idleness and sloth dominate his life to invalidate the ethical meaning of his hermit disguise. Yet, his neighbors do not recognize the façade and praise his holiness and his pure hermit's life. The food they bring to him allows him to lead a life of plenty, which makes him even more slothful. He recognizes his hypocritical ways but lacks the resolve to change (473–74). Ironically, Simplicissimus the narrator quotes from patristic literature in order to mediate the hermit's spiritual experience to the reader — something Simplicissimus the protagonist is unable to experience himself (475). However, this underscores which books and which profession are being taken as a disguise. Indeed, the protagonist goes to sleep in violation of one of the hermit's rules — to pray, to fast, to be vigilant — and indulges in an extensive dream on the stereotypical theological question whether avarice or extravagance is the bigger vice. This question, even by the narrator's own admission, has little to do with a hermit's life (475).

He finally recognizes that he does not serve God or humanity through his idle hermit life, and he decides to become a pilgrim again (509). For this reason, he shortens his hermit's robe to give himself the appearance of a pilgrim (509). Knowing about his own godless life, he even asks the local pastor to certify in writing that he indeed was a hermit, thus signaling that he still does not understand that being a hermit is a spiritual condition, not a circumstantial one (510). However, his pilgrim's robe will turn out to be equally deceitful: he acts more like a soldier and thief (510), and he cunningly uses his habit to take advantage of others (510–11). Just as in the Hanau scene at the beginning of the novel (55), people in his surroundings are confused by the discrepancy between appearance and behavior, and they misidentify him as prophet, a curiosity, or the Wandering Jew (511).

The popular notion among critics that Simplicissimus at this point finally finds his identity as pilgrim and that there no longer is a discrepancy between his being and appearance is not supported by the text. The same holds true for the idea that descriptions of clothing no longer are of interest or useful (Carbonnel, 73; Müller, 33) or that the narrative function of the descriptions changes (Müller, 34). While the description of clothing in the *Continuatio* both qualitatively and quantitatively is not as extensive and detailed as in the earlier episodes I have examined, its use continues to be transgressive in that clothing helps construct a false identity.

From this perspective, his pilgrimage, without hat (532) and in the shortened hermit's robe (509 and 542), hardly could be described as a journey towards spiritual purification or a "chemin de croix naturel" (Carbonnel, 72). Simplicissimus is rather driven by the insight that one doesn't get anywhere without money (527). In a cunning move, he rejects alms while denouncing the custom of beggars (532). His feigned moral superiority then persuades his admiring benefactors to treat him to meals and to pay for him to spend the night at the inn. This way, he lives much more comfortably than as a beggar. He also realizes that his disguise as a pilgrim is more successful in the countryside and subsequently avoids cities (534).

Grimmelshausen thus is very careful not to mark this wandering as a positive value. At the inn, the question of his true identity comes up anew (533). Guesses again range from spy, Anabaptist, fool, prophet to the Wandering Jew (534). Only the innkeeper can deter the inquisitive crowd from finding out whether he is circumcised. Even then, Simplicissimus does not reveal who he really is. At a castle where he asks for entry during a rainstorm a few days later, he responds to the request to identify himself with a cryptic riddle: "[. . .] ich seye ein Ball deß wandelbaren Glücks; ein Exemplar der Veränderung/ und ein Spiegel der Unbeständigkeit deß Menschlichen Wesens" (534–35). What on the surface looks like a playful arrangement of baroque literary topoi, contains more than a grain of truth: he is the incarnation of inconstancy and fleeting identity, a principle elaborated in the preceding Baldanders episode (505–7). When pressed by the nobleman's secretary for a straight answer, he merely gives a circumstantial account of his life, which implicates him as the transgressor (535).

Simplicissimus believes that his benevolent treatment is due to his appearance as a god-loving pilgrim (535), but in reality he is the one being deceived. He, too, is being used by having to spend the night in the chamber where the barbering ghost appears. The nobleman wishes to reward Simplicissimus for having successfully tamed the ghost. Simplicissimus refuses, but finally asks him to have a lining sewn into his robe because of the approaching winter (542). Imagining that God looks down on him charitably (543), he decides to conclude his life in humility, pain, and solitude (544). The lining — the German word "Futter" being a homonym of "food" — turns out to be a symbol for temptation. When Simplicissimus discovers that the lining contains numerous coins (544), he decides to keep the money for a pilgrimage to the Holy Land, in violation of the pledge he just had affirmed. Fate intervenes to impose the justice that society could not: during this pilgrimage he ends up shipwrecked on the isolated island near Madagascar.

By persistently raising the question of Simplicissimus's identity and its gap between truth and appearance, behavior and clothes, the narrator achieves a certain symmetry, in terms of both plot development and spiritual development of the protagonist. Both in Hanau and here, he wears a hermit's robe. In both places, his true identity is questioned and even challenged by those around him because they do not trust that his appearance accurately reflects his identity. In the *Continuatio,* the question of identity is resolved when Simplicissimus is asked three times who he really is. Each time, he is evasive, not because he doesn't want to give an answer, but rather because he doesn't know the answer. Thus I would argue here that the level of spiritual development in the *Continuatio* is not significantly different from that at Hanau. He still does not have a deeper understanding of what being a hermit or pilgrim really entails. In both instances, his play-acting is an acquired role, and he has been socialized superficially into believing that this is the role he should be playing in his life. At Hanau, he is beginning to manipulate this role, and in the *Continuatio* he has become a master at it. While Simplicissimus emerges from the involuntary existence as a hermit in a remote forest in the Hanau episode, he is about to leave this world again at this point in the *Continuatio*. He ushers in his final and equally involuntary existence as hermit on a remote island.

After more than one year on the island, Simplicissimus and the carpenter Simon Meron, the only other survivor of the shipwreck, live in a golden age where everything grows without work, like the paradise the first humans experienced (563 and 564). The only source of melancholy that disrupts their paradise is marked appropriately by the author: their clothes are decaying and rotting on their bodies, a sign that their idleness is not spiritually wholesome (564). However, unlike the first humans in paradise, they insist on wearing clothes, like "honest" Christians from Europe (564). In terms of the narrative, however, his refusal to go naked must also be read as a sign that he has not reached his garden of Eden and the status of paradisiacal innocence traditionally associated with nudity (Raudszus, 218).

In the absence of furred, four-legged animals, Simplicissimus and Meron produce clothing out of skin and feathers of large birds. The resulting clothing is not comfortable to wear, not very practical, and it breaks easily (564–65). In an allegorical way, though, these new clothes are quite fitting because they express the way the two feel about themselves and their existence as hermits. Their unstable and uncomfortable clothes represent lack of self-knowledge, unstable identity, discomfort with the hermit's role that they have to this point not understood as a calling, and unsteadiness of the soul. The subsequent clothes made out of palm leaves represent only a slight improvement (565). When Meron dies shortly thereafter from alcohol abuse, Simplicissimus does not grasp the opportunity to seek spiritual healing by becoming a hermit; he is an unfulfilled, lonely man (566). Over the next few pages, we recognize numerous other symptoms for his lack of inner strength and secure faith. His dead comrade appears to him (566–67), he sees his own thoughts as an enemy (567), he fears that the abundance of the island will induce idleness and sloth (566), he forces himself to pray and work every day to fight idleness and illness (567–68), his own labor is futile (568), and he laments the lack of spiritual literature on the island (568). Finally, he starts to experiment with a new approach to his life, using crude neo-platonic thoughts that had come up only once before in a passing reference (123). In an attempt to make sense of his lonely and enigmatic existence on the island, he now views nature, the island being a micro-cosm of the larger whole, as a book in which the divine will reveals itself (568–69).

In the last part of the *Continuatio*, fifteen years after arriving on the island, Simplicissimus has become a wild man, wearing just a loin-cloth made out of palm leaves, with beard and hair reaching belly button and hips (580–81). Still, the narrator, now the Dutch captain Jean Cornelis von Harlem, likens him to Saint Onuphrius, a fourth-century saint who usually is represented with these attributes (Neri, 74; Breuer, 1045). Assuming that his role as a hermit is authentic, as is commonly assumed (Stein, 181–82), his clothing could be called appropriate (Neri, 72). I would argue that he has not reached the consciousness and spiritual purity of a hermit and that therefore his clothes must be regarded as deceptive.

The narrating old Simplicissimus, now object of the narration himself, differs in crucial ways from his paternal role model. Simplicissimus shows no compassion towards the sick Dutch sailors and is unwilling to help them because he is concerned about his own safety (576–77). He rejects the opportunity to return to Europe for all the wrong reasons: he does not want to stay on the island because of the spiritual fulfillment and a sacred path to God it might offer to him. Instead, he stays because the island gives him protection against moral decay, war, corruption, illness, crime and the temptations of the old continent (584). His hermit state is defined negatively, not as a positive vision. At the same time, he refuses to rule out a return to Europe at a later date (578). The island may be simply a stable location — which defines a hermit's existence — physically, but not in his unstable mind. Not surprisingly, the novel concludes with Simplicissimus's request to Cornelis to leave him tools and all kinds of worldly goods, not with an affirmation of faith like that at the end of book 5, and not with positive affirmation of his own place in the world.

Given the common belief that outward appearance represents the inner character (Vincent, 215), Simplicissimus's use of distinctive clothing of a pilgrim or hermit has to be called transgressive. It is evident in the text that Simplicissimus superficially strives to become like his father. However, this son of a hermit is a hermit only in external circumstance, not in essence: he never develops the identity that could be expected from his dress. Müller's hypothesis that only the use of fancy and ornate clothing indicates low points in his moral development must thus be rejected (Müller, 41). I would rather argue that his deceptive use of hermit's and pilgrim's clothing is even more fundamentally indicative of a deep moral and spiritual crisis. In the evolving Puritan mindset in seventeenth century England, moral rectitude was closely linked to plain dress (Entwistle, 94). Conversely, in Reformed eyes, immodest forms of clothing were to be opposed because they indicated excessive pride in appearance, fostered immoral behavior, and ignored or challenged how clothing marked different social ranks (Murdock, 192).

It can be assumed that a German reader held similar expectations — which Simplicissimus obviously does not fulfill. He never restores the lost unity between being and appearance through which he allegedly finds God again, as claimed by Carbonnel (Carbonnel, 74). The tension between claim and authentic reality is never resolved, and Simplicissimus's uneasy relationship with clothing that is associated with the role of a hermit or pilgrim provides substantial evidence of his personal inability to deal with his inheritance. The study of simple clothing in particular helps us understand that there exists a continuous discord between description of character, body, and dress, that Simplicissimus never succeeds in firming up his identity as a hermit, that he never is at peace with himself, that no significant moral and spiritual growth takes place, and that Simplicissimus never ceases to be a restless character without a moral core.

Dress and Gender Identities

I have to this point discussed Simplicissimus's personal transgressions as questions of truth, spiritual condition, or rank. However, a consideration of clothing to account for a performance of gender identity is crucial as well. To be sure, most sumptuary laws in early modern Europe primarily strive to preserve privileges of rank and wealth. Gender is only a secondary concern (Garber, 27; Wurst, 168–72), which is not usually covered in sumptuary legislation (Orgel, 13). Yet obviously, the discussion of styles, types, and colors of garments must be gender-specific. Violations of gender norms for the most part do not appear to be a major concern in comparison to norms governing rank and wealth. As pointed out before, sumptuary laws are most concerned with areas where the threat of transgression and thus the potential for alternate social signification of clothing is greatest. So, what kinds of transgression occur here in performing gender identity?

To begin to get at the answer to this question, gender here must be defined as a matter of culture, as a cultural construct which distinguishes between feminine and masculine gender roles, while sex refers to the biological differences between male and female (Oakley, 16; Entwistle, 142–43). Clothing, as an aspect of culture thus acts as a crucial feature in the production of masculinity and femininity: "[. . .] to be a man or a woman, a boy or a girl, is as much a function of dress, gesture, occupation, social network and personality, as it is of possessing a particular set of genitals" (Entwistle, 143, citing Oakley, 158). In fact, there is "no 'natural' link between the biological categories of 'male' and 'female' and the cultural characteristics of 'masculine' and 'feminine'" (Entwistle, 143). Very instructive for uses of dress as gender identity is the famous example of Catalina de Erauso (1592–1650), who after many years of service as a cross-dressing soldier to the Spanish Crown received a papal dispensation to continue dressing in men's clothing (Perry; Velasco). The definition of gender in the era was therefore not solely based on biological sex but in part is a social construct.

Such willingness to adjudicate gender rules nonetheless seems somewhat surprising today. Early modern Europe, however, knew no privileged discourse, like biology in the nineteenth century, that could even claim to establish a definitive method by which one distinguished male from female (Jones and Stallybrass, 80). Aristotle viewed the female as little more than an incomplete male (Bullough and Bullough, 46). In the Galenic view, the only difference between male and female is heat: the female vagina and male penis are morphologically the same (Jones and Stallybrass, 81; Bullough and Bullough, 49). "[. . .] women were essentially cold men, whose damp bodies contained inverted male genitalia" (Wise, 281; further discussion in Laqueur, 25–28). Consequently, Renaissance medical and biological theories do not offer a stable divide between male and female (Jones and Stallybrass, 81). In practice, then, sexual identity could be treated not as a fixed bodily condition, but rather as relational, as a response to contexts that are always changing (Jones and Stallybrass, 104). The production of gender was differential and local: it varied from state to state, from class to class, from ethnic group to ethnic group (88). However, early modern European culture does not differentiate gender qualities from sexual aspects in principle (Bullough and Bullough, 67). We cannot operate with the modern assumption that gender is a known quantity that is destabilized by transgression — although there are indications for the development of a binary gender system (Jones and Stallybrass, 80).

Manifestations of gender in clothing are quite obvious, but, surprisingly, gender distinctions in clothing in the seventeenth century are often vague (Wise, 282). As already discussed, male fashion is often criticized for being effeminate, while some clothing for women appropriated elements from men's styles: "Some clothes considered appropriate for one sex or the other were in fact a combination of both masculine and feminine garments" (Wise, 282). This resulted in frequent complaints of confusion of status and of gender through fashionable garments (Garber, 27).

This turn to the historical facts will be illuminating Grimmelshausen's framing of gender issues. In spite of the use of clothing to mark social types in *Simplicissimus,* discussions of gender-marked and of female clothing in general are quite rare. Assuming that descriptions of clothing in *Simplicissimus* primarily are intended to pinpoint moments of individual transgression, this is not surprising: early modern German society remained much more concerned with violations of norms relating to rank and wealth than to gender or matters sexual (Hull, 89). Yet, Grimmelshausen was not oblivious to the implications of gendered dress. The Paris episode represents the only passage in the novel where gendered dress is of importance, but there are also instances where clothing challenges assessed gender boundaries that will be discussed in the next section.

Simplicissimus's moving performance as Orpheus makes him known in Parisian circles. Ironically, critics have noted that the Orpheus and Eurydice myth that celebrates "boundless love and conjugal fidelity" enables the sexually excessive adventures of the "beautiful lutenist" turned "consummate lover" — even though he is a recently married man (Schade, 31 and 39). Paradoxically, "Simplicius's physical and vocal beauty [. . .] signals his basic immorality" (40). Inversely, his disfiguring illness at the end of the episode does not turn him into a moral man.

Simplicissimus is lured to the love nest against his will under the pretext of a patron's interest in his lute playing (300–301). In a case of inversion, he has been cast as the powerless part in the sex tryst, while the noble women who request his services remain in control of the situation and even pay him at the end. While they know who he is, they conceal their identity by blindfolding him on the way to their location and by wearing masks. In another reversal, the women use clothing to conceal their identity and thus are empowered by their mask, while Simplicissimus as the target of their transgressive clothing is dominated by it. The real legal correlate is important: keeping themselves masked is essential for the women as revelations of adultery destroyed a noble woman's honor in early modern Germany, much more than a man's (Hull, 84). Thus, the mask does not just conceal the women's identity, it also protects their vulnerability. It allows them to transition safely between their two roles as presumably respectable Parisian upper class women and as women who engage in recreational sex that is not sanctioned by society — a right a nobleman of the time could take for granted.

This transgressive inversion is also marked in other ways. While he admires the beauty of the three women, it will be his beauty that really matters and that drives the events (Schade, 32). Yet after being stripped and bathed, he is forced to wear fine garments of their choosing (304–5). When the three women finally appear to him, they are masked but their breasts are mostly revealed (305). The whole act of disrobing is thus inverted: the face, the only body part that is always visible, now is the only part that is concealed, while the rest of their bodies is freely revealed.

Even the sex act itself is transgressive: here women are portrayed as the active and sexually assertive partners (307), while in early modern German practice, the male is commonly assumed to take the sexual initiative, the female being the passive partner (Hull, 83). This hesitant and passive, traditionally female role is assumed by Simplicissimus, who even thinks of his wife back home (307). Such inversion of sexual roles renders the male powerless and objectified, and it suggests a clear transgression on the part of the aristocratic females. The events of Paris thus parallel the later Schermesser episode: Simplicissimus is objectified as a commodity, as erotic luxury merchandise, ready to assist bodily functions.

There is an apparent price for these aristocratic transgressions. On the way back to Germany, he contracts chicken-pox which he mistakes as syphilis. The illness that is described as punishment disfigures him completely: his hair falls out, his face is scarred, his eyes droop, and he loses his lovely voice (310–11). The loss of his good looks and his lack of attractiveness to women weighs heavily on him. Simplicissimus's scarred face ultimately refers to his corresponding moral unsightliness: he now receives the looks that go along with the moral decay of his character. The illness has given him a permanent mask by taking away his real face. Ironically this mask does not conceal anything, but rather shows him as the person he really is. While the masks of the Parisian women enable their sexual adventures, Simplicissimus's mask precludes further adventures on his part, thus relegating him to a passive, quasi-feminine gender role.

Cross-Dressing

The bounds of masculine and feminine social identities play roles in the novel in one other way: cross-dressing. Early modern gender experimentation was most common during carnival and other events and specific periods of time when inversion of rank and status was acceptable, both in terms of social and gender roles. In England, for example, misrepresentations of gender, cross-dressing, were common on the theater stage, a practice that had no equivalent on the continent. While the evils of cross-dressing where lamented and scorned by moralists, "sumptuary legislation [in England] said nothing about inappropriate garments" (Orgel, 13). In general, Deuteronomy 22,5, which contains an often-quoted prohibition of cross-dressing, appears to have served as a sort of divine sumptuary law (Garber, 28).

Female cross-dressing had been tolerated at various times in various places since the late Middle Ages: it was seen as normal that a female strove to become male — just as a peasant should have wanted to become a noble (Bullough and Bullough, 67; Hotchkiss, 3). On the other hand, Eisenbart attests to a critique of female cross-dressing in German sumptuary laws (Eisenbart, 94). Hostility to male cross-dressing — except on the stage in England — appears to have been widespread (Bullough and Bullough, 75).

In fact, in many parts of Europe, female cross-dressing seems to have been relatively common; we know less about cross-dressing by men. Short-term cross-dressing seems to have been acknowledged as a viable option for women who were struggling to overcome difficult circumstances or were physically in danger during war, riots, or while travelling (Dekker and van de Pol, 2; Trumbach, 125). Long-term cross-dressing was more problematic, as the numerous Dutch cases examined by Dekker and van de Pol show.

Simplicissimus's own cross-dressing experience falls into this pattern, which Grimmelshausen thus seems to affirm as his culture's normal expectation. In a military camp at the gates of Magdeburg, Simplicissimus is tired of his status as fool, and he understands that he needs to get rid of his clothes in order to achieve a new status (167–68). While plundering a village, he is looking for peasants' clothing that would help him escape, but a woman's dress is all he can find (168). The moment, however, he steps out into the street as a woman, he becomes exposed to the perils of life as a woman: soldiers pursue Simplicissimus, but after his pleas to preserve his virginity ("Jungferschaft"), an officer's wife offers her protection. She in turn expresses a sexual interest in Simplicissimus, as do her husband and his servant (168–69). This scenario is what early modern critics of cross-dressing fear most: "women's clothes can serve as transferential objects, kindling a metonymic spark of desire" (Garber, 29), as such crossed attractions will turn the household topsy-turvy.

There is no narrative commentary on the same-sex interest of the officer's wife, and this sub-plot is no longer pursued once the rivalry becomes violent. Significantly, there is ample historical evidence that love affairs between women were not taken seriously in early modern Europe. It was long thought to be impossible for a woman to experience real love and desire for another woman (Dekker and van de Pol, 57; Brown, 6). Furthermore, it did not threaten the patriarchal sexual system (Trumbach, 114).

Grimmelshausen thus prefers to explore this dress transgression as an expression of social powerlessness paralleling the Paris episode. As the sexual advances of all three become more difficult to fend off (169–70), Simplicissimus realizes that he is just as troubled in this new role as in his old one, and that living in a woman's dress has become even more arduous than wearing the costume of a fool. Consequently, he feels truly imprisoned by his disguise (170). His decision to end this transgressive fiction by fleeing in men's clothes comes just at a point when events take care of this. The officer, the spurned lover, turns 'her' over to his sexually deprived solders who are about to gang rape 'her.' The servant, seeing his love-interest humiliated and violated, fights against the hordes in a scene parodistically described as a tournament. While Simplicissimus's transgressive disguise as a woman got him into this trouble, it ironically gets him out of it as well. The disguise is finally dissolved when Simplicissimus's clothes are torn off during the brawl (172).

This cross-dressing incident incorporates an ironic gender inversion. By cross-dressing, Simplicissimus gets himself into exactly the type of situation which motivated real-life women in early modern Europe to cross-dress: to protect themselves against violent acts and specifically against sexual assault (Dekker and van de Pol, 6). While a male disguise frees women from the constraints of their female role, such a gender disguise necessarily diminishes the liberating effect for impersonation for men, since "femininity constricts freedom and lowers social status" (Hotchkiss, 11; Bullough, 1383). Simplicissimus experiences painfully that he is worse off as a woman than he was as a fool, and that there are more confined ranks and stations than his own. Ironically, the constraints of his female role are lifted in the act of disrobing. Once his identity as a man is established, the sexual assault ends.

However, this is not the end of Simplicissimus's troubles. As we have seen before, the forced lifting of a vestimentary disguise raises more suspicions than it resolves as it sparks the crucial question of his trust-worthiness. He is interrogated because of suspicions that he might be a spy or a witch (173), and he is even scheduled for torture and eventual burning at the stake the next day (176). Only the changing fortunes of the war free him from his hopeless situation. The consequences for cross-dressing thus are potentially fatal. Still, as Grimmelshausen portrays it, it is not the violation of gender norms that causes the severity of the punishment, rather it is the deceptive component of his dress, the pretense of a false identity.

The more interesting cross-dressing incident, alluded to briefly before, is the one that isn't. At the beginning of the Hanau episode, young Simplicissimus, still dressed in his odd hermit's habit, is presented to the commanding officer of the guard at Hanau for closer examination and identification. While Simplicissimus is investigated for possibly being a cross-dresser, he himself becomes confused by the appearance of the officer who is wearing the effeminate fashion of the day: braided long hair in the French style, very short, almost invisible beard, and baggy pants that look like a woman's dress (54). Young Simplicissimus is thoroughly confused by his appearance:

> Jch gedachte bey mir selbst/ ist diß ein Mann? so solte er auch einen rechtschaffenen Bart haben/ [. . .]. Jsts aber ein Weib/ warumb hat die alte Hur dann so viel Stupffeln umbs Maul? Gewißlich ists ein Weib/ gedacht ich/ dann ein ehrlicher Mann wird seinen Bart wol nimmermehr so jämmerlich verketzern lassen [. . .]. Und demnach ich also im Zweiffel stunde/ und nicht wuste/ was die jetzige Mode war/ hielte ich ihn endlich vor Mann und Frau zugleich. (54)

This satirical account of the officer's appearance ties into the contemporary critique of effeminate male fashion which is often censured for challenging or crossing gender boundaries (Entwistle, 151). However, effeminacy at the time does not allude to outright transvestism or homosexuality, rather it is seen as self-indulgent and voluptuous, hence "womanish" or enslaved to women (Garber, 27), stressing personal resolve rather than social agency per se. Only in late seventeenth-century England and the Netherlands does effeminacy become the cultural hallmark of the sodomite; before that effeminacy marks the womanizer (van der Meer, 149, 166–69).

As stated before, early modern Europe knows no universally endorsed definition of the biological sexes, and there is no stable divide between male and female (Jones and Stallybrass, 80–81). While the pre-eighteenth-century paradigm begins to firm up a strict binary structure of the genders, generally three biological sexes are thought to exist: male, female, and hermaphrodite (Trumbach, 113). The hermaphrodite represents the third sex: he or she at some point makes a one-time gender choice to fit into the binary gender structure. Early modern hermaphrodites thus can lead a normal gendered existence despite the ambiguity of their sex (Entwistle, 143). For hermaphrodites, the acquisition of masculinity or femininity is not natural or purely biological, it is a cultural process, a result of socialization (Entwistle, 143).

This historical assumption again clarifies the impact of Grimmelshausen's scene. When Simplicissimus classifies the officer as a hermaphrodite, the officer's sexual identity seems clear to him. Given the seventeenth-century fascination with hermaphrodites (Daston and Park, 117), Simplicissimus's interpretation is plausible. Yet, we have to keep in mind that early modern culture was more concerned with gender ambiguity than with sexual ambiguity. In reality, it is the ambivalence surrounding the officer's gender — not clearly dressing as a man or as a woman — that causes the confusion and that has to be seen as transgressive. Simply put, the transgression that Simplicissimus notices is not that the officer is a hermaphrodite, but that he dresses like one, which would cause him to be classified as a transvestite — that his essence does not conform with the social forms signified by his dress. Simplicissimus thus for a brief moment raises the specter of transvestism which according to Garber "came to mark and indeed overdetermine this space of anxiety about fixed and changing identities" (Garber, 32). Simplicissimus's failure to categorize the officer properly represents "not just another category crisis, but — much more disquietingly — a crisis of 'category' itself" (Garber, 32). Simplicissimus is worried about how the officer will behave socially, and how Simplicissimus himself can react. Simplicissimus's error, then, is to confuse sex and gender. Based on appearances, he assigns to the officer the gender of hermaphrodite, not the sex: he is socially ambiguous, not biologically. In early modern thinking, this is an impossibility: if the officer really were a hermaphrodite, gender norms would not allow him to show it through clothing or in any other way.

Grimmelshausen here establishes an important distinction between sex and gender roles — with an implied criticism of traditional conceptions of sex. This becomes even more evident when this episode reaches closure. When Simplicissimus addresses the officer as hermaphrodite, the officer quips back: "wer Teuffel hat dir gesagt/ daß ich Herman heisse?" (55). The fact that he implicitly identifies himself as Herman firmly establishes his gender identity: not only does he have a man's name, but in a pun, which in turn is based on a word play, his name makes a double reference to his masculine identity: "Herr" and "Mann." Ironically, this clarification rekindles the gender confusion we experienced at the beginning of this episode: exactly because his gender identity is established, the officer's transgressive clothing must be read as a challenge to the stability of the gender system.

Conclusion: Undressing the Narrator

Aylett has shown that Simplicissimus's own testimony about himself is unreliable. Grimmelshausen consciously chooses a narrator who is deceptive, a most unreliable witness, and whose credentials as an autobiographer are questionable (Aylett, 1989: 162). The father's eremitic world view leads the son to an internalized optic of his life that is not appropriate. The internalized need to display eremitic qualities leads him to failure and finally causes a self-deceiving account of his own life (Aylett, 1982: 34–84). In this reading, the self-deception becomes obvious at the end of chapter 23 of the *Continuatio* where he concludes his hermit's autobiography from a perspective of deficient self-knowledge.

The analysis I have presented shows that Grimmelshausen works into his text a constant discrepancy between the self-assessment of the narrator and the broader perspective and more comprehensive representation of the protagonist and of the narrator. It is a commonplace to note that old Simplicissimus has not achieved the same level of insight and maturity the author wants to instill and cultivate in the reader (Aylett, 1989: 176). Yet, the fact that the author actually dismisses Simplicissimus as autobiographical narrator and adds three chapters told by a third party, Cornelis, is further evidence for the fact that the author does not trust the narrator. I would suggest that Cornelis's function is to reveal how precisely Simplicissimus the narrator distorts the account of his own life by creating a divergence between the autobiographical account of the hermit and Cornelis's portrayal of Simplicissimus as self-centered and defensive. The dismissal of Simplicissimus as narrator thus demasks the pretense of his life as a hermit, and it unmasks his pretense of enacting the truth of the clothes he wears.

Grimmelshausen takes an extraordinary risk: first, he allows the narrator to construe a partially deceptive account of his life. At the end, however, he revokes his trust in the narrator, which forces the reader to reevaluate the narrator's credibility throughout the novel (Aylett, 1989: 177). I would add that the author increases the distance between himself and his narrator throughout the novel, as his credibility implicitly is questioned more and more by the reader. Inversely, the ironic space between narrator and protagonist disappears as the novel progresses.

The closing moments of the novel thus connect with its beginning where the transgressive use of clothing is established as a major theme. What appears to be a general narrative commentary at the beginning has been sharply refocused on Simplicissimus the protagonist and on Simplicissimus the narrator at the end: Simplicissimus is the transgressor in the novel, and his consistently deceptive use of clothing is the marker for his transgression. Each time he dons transgressive clothing, Simplicissimus, to the contemporary reader, is marked as a deceptive and untrustworthy character.

Throughout the novel, Simplicissimus has used clothing to enact identities — most consistently that of a hermit. While the social norms of the day demanded that clothes reveal the identity of the wearer, Simplicissimus uses clothing to feign identities, thus using clothing to deceive others and to conceal his true identity. Once the reader sees that Simplicissimus transgresses when he changes clothes, his mask becomes transparent, and his clothes now reveal who he really is, which is not what he dresses as. Simplicissimus's clothes thus conceal and reveal at the same time.

If wearing clothes means for the individual to become part of the collective, part of a social order, as scholars have noted (Raudszus, 1), then a transgressive use of clothing has the potential to subvert the social order. It is important to note that this is not acceptable in Grimmelshausen's world: the transgressive use of clothing is never seen as justified. Even when transgressive clothing primarily serves as a survival strategy, the transgressive element ultimately results in negative consequences for the individual who does not fully inhabit the world signified by the clothes. As Simplicissimus's transgressions have negative connotations, so does his resulting challenge to the social order. In this, I am arguing that Grimmelshausen has created a narrative that turns back on itself, since the target of his transgressions appears to be secondary, whether it is social norms, rank, wealth, or gender. Grimmelshausen makes it clear that such transgressions are not opportunities for positive change, but rather have the potential for eroding and debasing the established order.

Viewed from another perspective, however, Grimmelshausen is not interested in social change. The focus of the novel is on Simplicissimus as an individual and on his hapless attempts at defining his social role and fulfilling it. Simplicissimus's inability to dress appropriately at any given time, in other words to own his clothes, point to an ongoing identity issue. His inability to the very end to assume ownership of clothes — and of his body — marks an unstable identity of the protagonist and demasks and undresses the narrative figure. Masquerade serves as an allegory for the elusive construction of identity of Simplicissimus the protagonist and of the old Simplicissimus the narrator. Simultaneously, it erodes and subverts the narrator and the narrative ethos in *Simplicissimus.*

Still, I would argue that the narrative ethos is restored by Cornelis, the narrator of the last three chapters. As captain of a Dutch merchant vessel, he represents the microcosm of an intact world: he is absolutely in charge, but at the same time he feels an absolute obligation towards the ship and his sailors. He fulfills the paternalistic duties of his estate: he behaves nobly, as he must take care of his people — and he concludes Simplicissimus's story with the same ethos.

The clash between the two ethical systems becomes evident when Cornelis asks Simplicissimus to share his resources to cure his ill sailors, which Simplicissimus at first is not willing to do. This egotistical gesture demasks his eremitical posture as a farce: his response is neither noble, nor charitable, nor masculine. He clearly fails his father's charitable legacy, the primary beneficiary of which is Simplicissimus himself: he is but a faint parody of his paternal role model. He appears frozen in effeminate passivity — his masculinity having been questioned for instance in the Paris episode and by his own infertility. The word "mannhafft" (manly) in the very first sentence of the novel according to Tatlock makes reference to "the masculine enterprise of making one's own fortune" — which represents yet another unfulfilled promise (Tatlock, 396). He lives on the island as a godly aristocratic male, but he does not assume responsibility for any of the three roles. He does not earn the privileges of his nobility, he leads a shallow spiritual and religious life, and he does not live an active life associated with masculinity. He is staying on the island based on negative thinking: all other options appear less desirable.

This brings into focus the significance of clothes as markers of Simplicissimus's transgressions. Clothing serves as a steady reminder that Simplicissimus consistently does not recognize his station in life and the duties and obligations that come along with rank, gender, and religious commitment. Simplicissimus therefore in Grimmelshausen's eyes is not a "Schelm," a benign jokester and trickster. He is a man who is wasting his divine gifts, and a man who through his lack of self-knowledge poses a continuous threat to the established order.

Notes

I would like to thank my colleague Katie Arens for her many comments and suggestions.

Works Cited

Aylett, Robert P. T. *The Nature of Realism in Grimmelshausen's "Simplicissimus" Cycle of Novels.* Bern: Lang, 1982. (= Europäische Hochschulschriften. Reihe 1, Deutsche Sprache und Literatur 479)

———. "Lies, Damned Lies, and Simplex's Version of the Truth: Grimmelshausen's Unreliable Narrator." *Daphnis* 18 (1989): 159–77.

Breuer, Dieter. "Stellenkommentar." In: *Hans Jacob Christoffel von Grimmelshausen. Werke.* Volume I, 1. Ed. by Dieter Breuer. Frankfurt: Deutscher Klassiker Verlag, 1989. 794–984 and 1004–48. (= Bibliothek der frühen Neuzeit. Zweite Abteilung: Literatur des Barock 4)

Breward, Christopher. *The Culture of Fashion. A New History of Fashionable Dress.* Manchester: Manchester UP, 1994.

Brown, Judith C. *Immodest Acts. The Life of a Lesbian Nun in Renaissance Italy.* New York: Oxford UP, 1986.

Bullough, Vern L. "Transvestites in the Middle Ages." *Journal of American Sociology* 79 (1974): 1381–1394.

Bullough, Vern L., and Bonnie Bullough. *Cross Dressing, Sex and Gender.* Philadelphia: U of Pennsylvania P, 1991.

Busch, Walter. "Die Lebensbeichte einer Warenseele. Satirische Aspekte der Schermesser-Allegorie in Grimmelshausens 'Continuatio.'" *Simpliciana* 9 (1987): 49–63.

Carbonnel, Yves. "Voyage et vêtement dans *Le Simplicius Simplicissimus* de Grimmelshausen." *Cahiers d'Etudes Germaniques* 9 (1985): 33–75.

Cavallaro, Dani and Alexandra Warwick. *Fashioning the Frame. Boundaries, Dress and Body.* Oxford and New York: Berg, 1998.

Craik, Jennifer. *The Face of Fashion. Cultural Studies in Fashion.* London and New York: Routledge, 1994.

Daston, Lorraine and Katharine Park. "The Hermaphrodite and the Orders of Nature. Sexual Ambiguity in Early Modern France." In: Louise Fradenburg and Carla Freccero (eds.). *Premodern Sexualities*. New York and London: Routledge, 1996. 117–36.

Dekker, Rudolf M. and Lotte C. van de Pol. *The Tradition of Female Transvestism in Early Modern Europe*. New York: St. Martin's Press, 1989.

Eisenbart, Liselotte Constanze. *Kleiderordnungen der deutschen Städte zwischen 1350 und 1700. Ein Beitrag zur Kulturgeschichte des deutschen Bürgertums*. Göttingen: Musterschmidt, 1962. (= Göttinger Bausteine zur Geschichtswissenschaft 32)

Elias, Norbert. *The Civilizing Process*. Oxford: Blackwell, 1978.

Entwistle, Joanne. *The Fashioned Body: Fashion, Dress, and Modern Social Theory*. Cambridge, UK: Polity, 2000.

Garber, Marjorie B. *Vested Interests. Cross-Dressing and Cultural Anxiety*. New York and London: Routledge, 1992.

Gersch, Hubert. Geheimpoetik. *Die* Continuatio des abentheuerlichen Simplicissimi *interpretiert als Grimmelshausens verschlüsselter Kommentar zu seinem Roman*. Tübingen: Niemeyer, 1973. (= Studien zur deutschen Literatur 35)

Gruenter, Rainer. "Simplex Eremita: Zum Einsiedler in Grimmelshausens 'Simplicissimus.'" *Wolfenbütteler Barock-Nachrichten* 18 (1991): 1–10.

Hollander, Anne. *Sex and Suits*. New York: Knopf, 1994.

Hotchkiss, Valerie R. *Clothes Make the Man. Female Cross Dressing in Medieval Europe*. New York: Garland, 1996. (= The New Middle Ages 1)

Hull, Isabel V. *Sexuality, State, and Civil Society in Germany, 1700–1840*. Ithaca and London: Cornell UP, 1996.

Jones, Ann Rosalind and Peter Stallybrass. "Fetishizing Gender. Constructing the Hermaphrodite in Renaissance Europe." In: Julia Epstein and Kristina Straub (eds.). *Body Guards. The Cultural Politics of Gender Ambiguity*. New York: Routledge, 1991. 80–111.

Laqueur, Thomas W. *Making Sex: Bodies and Gender from the Greeks to Freud*. Cambridge: Harvard UP, 1990.

Lehmann, Christoph. *Florilegium politicum*. Lübeck: Jung, 1639. Reprint Bern: Lang, 1986. 434–38. (= Nachdrucke deutscher Literatur des 17. Jahrhunderts 61)

Logau, Friedrich von. *Deutscher Sinn-Getichte drey Tausend*. Breslau: Kloßmann, 1654. Reprint Hildesheim: Olms, 1972.

Meer, Theo van der. "Sodomy and the Pursuit of a Third Sex in the Early Modern Period." In: Gilbert Herdt (ed.). *Third Sex, Third Gender. Beyond Sexual Dimorphism in Culture and History*. New York: Zone Books, 1994. 137–212.

Müller, Klaus-Detlef. "Die Kleidermetapher in Grimmelshausens 'Simplicissimus.' Ein Beitrag zur Struktur des Romans." *Deutsche Vierteljahrsschrift für Literaturwissenschaft und Geistesgeschichte* 44 (1970): 20–46.

Munns, Jessica and Penny Richards (eds.). *The Clothes That Wear Us. Essays on Dressing and Transgressing in Eighteenth-Century Culture.* Newark DE: Delaware UP, 1999.

Murdock, Graeme. "Dressed to Repress? Protestant Clerical Dress and the Regulation of Morality in Early Modern Europe." *Fashion Theory* 4 (2000): 179–200.

Neri, Bianca Maria. "Das typologische Verhältnis zwischen Simplicissimus und dem Einsiedler. Zur allegorischen Funktion des Kleiderwechsel-Motivs in Grimmelshausens Roman." *Simpliciana* 9 (1987): 63–78.

Oakley, Ann. *Sex, Gender and Society.* New York: Harper and Row, 1972.

Orgel, Stephen. "Insolent Women and Manlike Apparel." *Textual Practice* 9 (1995): 5–25.

Ortner, Sherry B. *Making Gender. The Politics and Erotics of Culture.* Boston: Beacon Press, 1996.

Perry, Mary Elizabeth. "From Convent to Battlefield: Cross-Dressing and Gendering the Self in the New World of Imperial Spain." In: Josiah Blackmore and Gregory S. Hutcheson (eds.). *Queer Iberia. Sexualities, Cultures, and Crossings from the Middle Ages to the Renaissance.* Durham NC and London: Duke UP, 1999. 394–419.

Raudszus, Gabriele. *Die Zeichensprache der Kleidung: Untersuchungen zur Symbolik des Gewandes in der deutschen Epik des Mittelalters.* Hildesheim: Olms, 1985. (= Ordo: Studien zur Literatur und Gesellschaft des Mittelalters und der frühen Neuzeit 1)

Schade, Richard E. "Simplicius in Paris: The Allegory of the Beautiful Lutenist." *Monatshefte* 88 (1996): 31–42.

Sekora, John. *Luxury. The Concept in Western Thought, Eden to Smollet.* Baltimore MD: Johns Hopkins UP, 1977.

Shapin, Steven. *Social History of Truth: Civility and Science in Seventeenth-Century England.* Chicago: Chicago UP, 1994.

Smith, Bruce. "Premodern Sexualities." *PMLA* 115 (2000) 318–29.

Squire, Geoffrey. *Dress and Society 1560–1970.* New York: Viking, 1974.

Stallybrass, Peter and Allon White. *The Politics and Poetics of Transgression.* Ithaca: Cornell UP, 1986.

Stein, Alexandra. "Die Hybris der Endgültigkeit oder der Schluß der Ich-Erzählung und die zehn Teile von 'deß Abentheuerlichen Simplicissimi Lebens-Beschreibung.'" *Deutsche Vierteljahrsschrift für Literaturwissenschaft und Geistesgeschichte* 70 (1996): 175–97.

Tatlock, Lynne. "Ab ovo: Reconceiving the Masculinity of the Autobiographical Subject." In: Lynne Tatlock (ed.). *The Graph of Sex and the German Text. Gendered Culture in Early Modern Germany 1500–1700*. Amsterdam and Atlanta: Rodopi, 1994. 383–412. (= Chloe, 19)

Trumbach, Randolph. "London's Sapphists. From Three Sexes to Four Genders in the Making of Modern Culture." In: Julia Epstein and Kristina Straub (eds.). *Body Guards. The Cultural Politics of Gender Ambiguity*. New York: Routledge, 1991. 112–41.

Velasco, Sherry Marie. *The Lieutenant Nun: Transgenderism, Lesbian Desire, & Catalina de Erauso*. Austin TX: U of Texas P, 2000.

Vincent, Sue. "To Fashion a Self: Dressing in Seventeenth-Century England." *Fashion Theory* 3 (1999): 197–218.

Wise, Margaret. "Saint-Balmon, Cross-Dressing, and the Battle of Gender Representation in Seventeenth-Century France." *French Forum* 21 (1996): 281–300.

Woolf, Virginia. *Orlando*. New York: Harcourt Brace, 1928.

Wurst, Karin A. "Gender and Aesthetics of Display: Baroque Poetics and Sartorial Law." *Daphnis* 29 (2000): 159–75.

Zedler, Johann Heinrich. *Grosses vollständiges Universal-Lexicon Aller Wissenschaften und Künste*. 68 vols. Halle and Leipzig: Zedler, 1732–1751. Here, vol. 15 (1737) cols. 889–97.

*Engraved copperplate (the "Phoenix" copperplate) from the frontispiece
of the first edition of* Simplicissimus Teutsch *(1668). Reprinted with
permission of the Herzog August Bibliothek, Wolfenbüttel.*

"To see from these black lines": The Mise en Livre of the Phoenix Copperplate and Other Grimmelshausen Illustrations

Shannon Keenan Greene

> Bey dieser Zeit / ist fast kein Buch verkäuf-
> lich / ohne einen Kuppfertitel welcher dem Le-
> ser desselben Inhalt nicht nur mit Worten /
> sondern auch mit einem Gemähld vorbildet.
> Harsdörffer, *Frauenzimmer Gesprächspiele* (1646),
> Preface to Part VI

> "Liebes Kind / diese bilder können nicht re-
> den / was aber ihr Tun und Wesen sey / kann
> ich auß diesen schwartzen Linien sehen / wel-
> ches man lesen nennet." (ST 31)

A Simplician Model of Reading

WHEN THE ILLITERATE SIMPLICISSIMUS first encounters the texts of the New Testament, in Book I of *Simplicissimus Teutsch* (1668), he apprehends them by way of their illustrations. These he anthropomorphizes, confusing pictures with people. He attempts to speak with the book by speaking with the pictured figures. Yet it is the hermit's corrective response that is particularly striking. Pictures and texts, he explains to the naive Simplicissimus, do not figure in a verbal mode, but are rather to be encountered visually: "[. . .] diese Bilder können nicht reden/ was aber ihr Tun und Wesen sey/ kann ich auß diesen schwartzen Linien sehen/ welches man lesen nennet" (ST 31). From these *black lines* of print, he explains, thereby lending color and shape to the words on the page, one *sees* the actions and essence of the pictures. In other words, one comes to know the pictures, according to the hermit, by viewing a disparate set of pictures; namely, the printed letters on the page.

"To see from these black lines" is thus a Simplician model for read-ing: not the discursive hermeneutics that Simplicissimus himself launched when he began by speaking to the illustrations, but rather a visual en-gagement with books. Where Simplicissimus treats the pictures discur-sively, the lesson to be learned is that it is not the pictures that are to be understood and engaged by means of conversation, but rather the words that are to be understood (viewed, literally), in conjunction with pic-tures.[1] "These black lines" make sense of the pictures. The hermit cor-rects a hermeneutic reading to an emblematic one: it is by way of accompanying words that one sees the actions and essence of pictures.

Grimmelshausen, as he writes *about* reading, seeing, drawing, letters, alphabets, and writing in *Simplicissimus,* sets up an analytic framework that can itself be applied to reading the Grimmelshausen book corpus. In a very concrete sense, the Grimmelshausen corpus consists of books that contain both words and pictures — illustrations — that express the events and meaning of the stories. Because Grimmelshausen himself invites a reading that is also a viewing, it is fruitful to apply this analytic framework, his own, in a reading of his, Grimmelshausen's, texts in conjunction with their illustrations.

There is a *demasking* of language signs implicit in the act of viewing sign vehicles as images. Demasking, removing a mask and showing one's true face, is one of the pictorial elements that can be seen in several of the Grimmelshausen frontispieces. To unmask is to remove artifice and reveal the genuine nature of an object. To view lines of text as black lines, to view them as an illiterate person would, strips letter signs of their function as signs. An illiterate reading of letters is a viewing of letters as pictures; in other words, it is a decipherment of a graphic code according to its nature as image, without knowledge of the arbitrariness of the letter's shapes, the reference they make to a phonemic system, and so forth. Grimmelshausen has drawn attention, through the teachings of the hermit, to the constructed nature of our practices of representation, and he has invited a visual reading.

Simplicissimus follows a path from naiveté to enlightenment. In the course of his adventures, he also emerges from illiteracy to education, finally becoming a writer himself. His authorship unfolds on palm leaves, for lack of paper. The precursor to his autobiography-on-leaves is writing on tree bark, after the death of Simon in the *Continuatio.* Here, he writes and draws simultaneously, writing Biblical passages on some trees and sketching Christian objects on other trees. That writing and pictur-ing occur together is characteristic of Grimmelshausen, and Simplicissi-mus undertakes both in an effort to arrive at a single expression of grief (and of the Christian conquest of grief). To write is to write and picture, and to read is to read both texts and images. Thus, it is not, for Grimmelshausen, simply the case that the illiterate read pictures, and read letters as pictures. Grimmelshausen's model of text and images conjoined extends well into Simplicissimus's literacy, and it extends even to his, Simplicissimus's, practices as a writer.

The Grimmelshausen books allow, rather than resolve, an indecipherability of visuality. We encounter letters and pictures that cannot be read, both in the Simplicissimus story and in the indecipherable images of the open book that is pictured in the Phoenix frontispiece. In Book 1, chapter 19, when his prayer book is discovered on his person, Simplicissimus's writing is proof to the arresting governor that Simplicissimus is not illiterate (not a fool), and therefore not innocent: "zwar kann er kein Narr sein/ weil er so schreibt" (ST 56). The indecipherable script of the hermit's letter, which falls from the book's pages, is interpreted as evidence of Simplicissimus's guilt. Clearly, books, handwritings, and scripts may be transferred from person to person, and ultimately misunderstood. At issue in Simplicissimus's arrest by the governor is the materiality of writing: the birch-tree writing surface, the book carried ("getragen") or worn by Simplicissimus, and the shapes of the scripted letters. Simplicissimus believes that the governor is showing the other officers his book because of its exemplary handwriting. In fact, the governor proffers the book to them as evidence: "blättert er in meinem Büchlein so stark herumb," Simplicissimus explains, "ihnen mein schöne Handschrift zu weisen" (ST 56). Scripted and printed objects (books, papers, and letters — letters in the sense of epistles) figure in terms of the entirety of their physicality: as paper, as ink, as bound pages, and so forth.

On the frontispiece of Grimmelshausen's *Teutscher Michel,* a jester paints *Fraktur* letters onto a canvas. Alan Menhennet writes:

> But there is something odd about the whole thing: the painter is dressed as a Fool or jester. Jesters, we feel, do not paint, at least not in uniform, and painters do not dress themselves up as jesters. And then, the canvas contains not a picture, but words. (Menhennet 1995, 279–80)

In the *Teutscher Michel* frontispiece, words are painted directly onto a canvas, and the image is then printed onto a page. This frontispiece blurs the boundaries of words and pictures, and empowers the satirical jester as the author of this intentional mismatch. To satirize is to paint letters and print pictures, in a topsy-turvy book production authored by a satirist, who himself figures in the *Verkehrte Welt,* the upside-down world of the printed and illustrated book.

The Grimmelshausen model of reading offers an important place for the viewing of a frontispiece. His readers may well have commanded literacy to varying degrees, and an illustration is as much a guide to partially literate readers as it is a promise, and often a summary, to fully literate readers. The *Palma Josephina* (1657) explains that images create anticipation in the reader:

> Fragt aber etwan einer/ für wen oder wohin die Emblemata, Sinn- oder Kennzaichen angesehen? Deme geben wir zur Antwort: Daß sie der vrsachen eingemenget vnnd vndermarcket/ damit der fürwitzig- vnd spitzfindige Leser/ vnder wehrendem lesen/ in etwas ermuntert/ mit grösserem Lust zu lesen fortsetze. (cited in Bircher 574)

Yet the same text also establishes a hierarchy for text and image, explaining that images are merely the condiments on the "banquet table" of reading:

> Der mainung setzet auch der Gastgeb einen Sänff oder anderes Gesältz- auff [. . .] also die Speisen desto lieblicher vnnd angenehmer/ mit grö- sserm Lust-genossen vnd auffgezehret werden. So vil/ von der arth/ weiß und manier/ dises Büchlein/ so wol zu schreiben als zu gebrau- chen. (cited in Bircher 574)

For Harsdörffer, in the preface to part 6 of the *Frauenzimmer- Gesprächspiele,* copperplates represent the content of a book in order to make the book marketable, "verkäufflich," but Harsdörffer does not offer details as to exactly how or why illustrations are appealing to sev- enteenth-century readers. Manfred Koschlig relates how, shortly after its appearance, *Simplicissimus* became entangled in a war of printing rights between Wolf Eberhard Felssecker and Georg Müller. In the printing- rights battle, the Phoenix frontispiece was part of the "content" of *Sim- plicissimus* that Müller appropriated, as payback for an earlier appropria- tion by Felssecker. The original engraved *Simplicissimus* copperplate (both the actual plate, *Platte,* and prints made from it, *Stiche,* are called "copperplates" in English) was not stolen. Without the original plate, the Müller publishing house must have hired someone to recopy, by eye and hand, the design of the Phoenix frontispiece (Koschlig 67–195).

While much book illustration of the mid- to late-seventeenth century is rather more akin to realistic (in art-historical terms: representational) modes of picturing than to emblematic modes, there is a prevalent strain of scholarship that views the activity of literary illustration in this period as emblematic. Thus, Albrecht Schöne asserts that an illustrated text is like an emblem: the *subscriptio,* or text, explicates the *pictura,* that is, the frontispiece. Schöne extends the emblem model even to performed stage plays, in which the visual performance is the *pictura* and the playscript is the *subscriptio.* Here, the emblematic model links baroque writing and picturing in a generalized sense: text and visuality occur simultaneously and play against each other. Within Grimmelshausen scholarship, scholars such as Sibylle Penkert, Alan Menhennet, Jeffrey Ashcroft, and others have proposed emblematic models for understanding the Grimmelshausen illustrations in conjunction with their texts, and conversely, for understanding the Grimmelshausen texts in conjuction with their illustrations.

One cannot help but notice the deictics of the hermit's reading passage: "*these* pictures . . ." as though the hermit is pointing to them, and "*these* lines"; and of course the text which itself gestures toward pictures: "was aber ihr [= der Bilder] Tun und Wesen sey/ kann ich auß diesen schwartzen Linien sehen [. . .]" (ST 31). Grimmelshausen's own formulation of textuality teaches that words are words that point to pictures.

In her study of the Grimmelshausen copperplates, Sibylle Penkert remarks that it was while attending a seminar on Grimmelshausen's *Courage* in 1965 that she arrived at the notion

> dass der Abdruck des Romans ohne sein Kupfer in der ersten Auflage der bekannten Barock-Anthologie weitreichende Konsequenzen für die Interpretation hat, die damit eine *grundsätzliche* Beziehbarkeit von Titelkupfer und Roman aufgäbe. Das impliziert vor allem die *Notwendigkeit* dieser Beziehung. (Penkert, 54–55)

In the style of a marketing taste-test, Penkert has shuffled audience response into two categories: those readers who have read the Grimmelshausen text in which the frontispiece was omitted, and those very different reading experiences in which readers were presented with the Grimmelshausen text and its copperplate illustration side by side. The observation is valuable: interpretive practice is shaped by the illustrations, even though the emblematic meaning of many of the Grimmelshausen images continue to elude us. Indeed, the later 1671 *Simplicissimus* edition (editio D), the "baroque anthology," with its twenty interspersed woodcut illustrations, lends a pious, even unduly pious feel to the work. In this edition, the woodcut illustrations reiterate passages from the text with an often literal interpretation of events in the work, and an engraved meditative directive under which each illustration, and thus each plot event, is subsumed.

The seminar scene as described by Penkert re-enacts, perhaps unwittingly, *Simplicissimus* Book I, chapter 10. Schöne, who has nested baroque illustrated books within the larger category of baroque emblems and emblem-like publications and productions, led the *Courage* seminar at which Penkert came to reflect on the relationship of Grimmelshausen books and pictures. Here, as in the hermit-Simplicissimus scene of the primary book encounter, instructor and student gather to examine words and pictures, and settle on a recognition of their dependence on one another.

What appears to be essential in Grimmelshausen's hermit scene of reading and seeing is the simultaneity of picture and text, a simultaneity that is a *sine qua non* of emblematic presentation and interpretation. Consider the "wolf encounter" from Book I, chapter 6. Knan describes to Simplicissimus what a wolf looks like. Shortly afterward, Simplicissimus encounters a large man with long black-gray hair:

> Er hatte einen wilden Bart/ fast formirt wie ein Schweitzer-Käß/ sein Angesicht war zwar bleich-gelb und mager/ aber doch zimlich lieblich/ und sein langer Rock mit mehr als 1000. Stückern/ von allerhand Tuch überflickt und auffeinandergesetzt/ umb Hals und Leib hatte er ein schwere eiserne Ketten gewunden wie S. Wilhelmus, und sah sonst in meinen Augen so scheußlich und förchterlich auß/ daß ich anfienge zu zittern/ wie ein nasser Hund [. . .]. (ST 22)

Simplicissimus, shaking like a wet dog, mistakes the hermit, dressed as a vagrant, for a wolf: "und weil ich ihn nicht kennete/ konnte ich nichts anders ersinnen/ als dieser alte Greiß müßte ohn Zweiffel der Wolf sein/ davon mir mein Knan kurtz zuvor gesagt hatte" (ST 22). The exact nature of Simplicissimus's mistake is not immediately clear. There is little about the hermit that looks like a wolf. Simplicissimus's error appears to be, at least in part, the assumption that a description will be followed by a visual representation, even where there is no book and a time delay intercedes. He has learned the emblematic structure too well, and mistakenly applies this reading strategy in the absence of a reading context. He takes the wolf description as lemma, introducing a wolf. His presumption is the presumption of an emblematic promise, a pre-figured deictic, and he misses the point that emblems, if they are to function at all, function at the point of simultaneity of word and image: in a codex or broadside. His error lies in a *mise en livre* of verbal-visual input. The joke is that he has here, as elsewhere, mistaken life for books. The description of a wolf cannot summon a wolf, as it might in a controlled narrative.

An Intertextual Illustration

Yet a further remarkable feature of this incident from Book 1, chapter 6 is that it *does* prefigure an image that is yet to come. It prefigures a book image, that is, an illustration of an encounter along the same lines as the meeting of Simplicissimus and the hermit, at a later point in the *Simplicissimus* cycle. The *Springinsfeld* novel, the eighth book in the *Simplician* sequence, appeared in its first edition (1670) with a frontispiece illustration, in which the encounter just described is, one might say, re-staged in new terms. In that frontispiece, a dog is urinating on the artificial limb of Springinsfeld, who is dressed in patched and torn vagrant's clothes. In Simplicissimus's wolf encounter, Simplicissimus likens himself to a dog ("wie ein nasser Hund") and the hermit is dressed as a vagrant in a patched coat. The hermit's oversized crucifix has its correspondence in Springinsfeld's oversized violin.

The woodcut illustration of the wolf encounter in the 1671 edition of *Simplicissimus* misses the spirit of the Book 1, chapter 6 meeting, substituting a pious pilgrim crouching in the woods for what is really a more striking scene of mutual encounter: the "dog" ("wie ein nasser Hund") meets wolf, as Simplicissimus perceives it, or dog meets vagrant, as Grimmelshausen later illustrates.

Technologies of Image Reproduction

As I have argued in my dissertation (18), seventeenth-century book illustrations, particularly book frontispieces, are performative in a number of senses: a performative of promise (a promise as to what topic the book will treat), a performance in the sense of an advertisement (the frontispiece will to some extent determine a book's representation in the marketplace), and a performative in the sense of actually staging the book's contents.

"Das Kunstwerk," according to Walter Benjamin, "ist immer reproduzierbar gewesen" (351):

> Was Menschen gemacht haben, das konnte immer von Menschen nachgemacht werden. Solche Nachbildung wurde auch ausgeübt, von Schülern zur Übung in der Kunst, von Meistern zur Verbreitung der Werke, endlich von gewinnlüsternen Dritten. (351)

Benjamin distinguishes between these kinds of copy processes, and the copy technologies that came later. Copperplate engravings, although Benjamin affords them little discussion, participated in both. They were the single most important reproduction technology of the seventeenth century, enabling, notably, the distribution of diagrams pertaining to the natural sciences. They also played a role in cultural practices that included copying designs from paintings onto copperplates, copying images from other copperplates, altering copperplates by re-engraving them, re-using copperplates in new contexts with new titles, and copying verses or other texts from one copperplate onto another.

For Benjamin, it is the lithograph (an eighteenth-century technique) that inaugurates the age of technologically reproduced art. One makes a lithographic print by applying grease onto a hard surface, and then water, and, finally, ink. Water prevents the absorption of ink, and drawing a design with grease delineates where the water will be repelled, and, thus, ink can be absorbed. Benjamin groups copper techniques, not with lithographs, but together with woodcuts: "Zum Holzschnitt treten im Laufe des Mittelalters Kupferstich und Radierung [etching]" (351). I believe, however, that copperplates and etchings have more in common with what Benjamin characterizes as lithographic reproduction practice than with woodcuts. "Die Graphik," he writes, "wurde durch die Lithographie befähigt, den Alltag illustrativ zu begleiten" (351). Broadsheets were illustrated with copperplates, etchings, and even, sometimes with intentional archaic overtones, woodcuts in the seventeenth century, long before lithographs came to be used.

The loss of aura is, for Benjamin, the crucial characteristic of reproduced art. Copperplate prints have no original, and no ritual use other than mass distribution. In Benjamin's scheme, the actual copperplate, the *Platte,* is not itself an artwork. When the ritual use of art is abandoned, according to Benjamin, the whole social function of art changes. Commercial and political aims usurp the religious-ritualistic purposes of original artworks. Benjamin's work takes a strong stance against reproductions, but also points to its prevalence and importance for scholars of cultural practices, even outside the scope of art history.

It is in his concessions — conceding the importance of reproduced graphics — that Benjamin accommodates graphic technology's ability to mass-distribute a message. In fact, that is his primary critique of graphic reproduction. While Benjamin's distinguishes between some forms of copying (imitation in order to learn/distributing in order to educate, versus reproduction solely for profit), he gives what might perhaps be called short shrift to the continuing creative use of images in contexts in which they are widely reproduced. Book illustrators borrow and refine other illustrator's work, re-use graphics and even alter them by adding new burin incisions to an old *Platte,* and combine image and text in interesting ways, as for the Phoenix copperplate.

The engraved copperplate illustration of the seventeenth century, and its use within seventeenth-century German society, remains to a great degree understudied. Despite recent interest in these prints, frontispieces, author portraits, portraits with verses, broadsides, and other illustrations have been for the most part the particular focus neither of art historians nor of literary historians. John Roger Paas writes:

> Literary historians, untrained in art historical investigation and unaccustomed to drawing material from print collections, are unaware of how much material awaits discovery. Art historians, on the other hand, know the material, but because of their primary concern with describing art historical movements and with attributing works to specific artists they have overlooked the verses (Paas 1988 xiii).

Even for major artists, such as the renowned Dutch printmakers of the seventeenth century, book illustrations have never received the same kind of attention as prints sold as art prints (independent of books). Clifford S. Ackley, in *Printmaking in the Age of Rembrandt,* has called book illustrations (he is speaking of Dutch book illustrations, but the same is true for much of Europe) a "vital" yet "neglected" facet of seventeenth-century art (xvi).

The engravings of a major artist such as Rubens, who "transformed the concept of the title-page" through his subtle and complex designs have only recently begun to be regarded as important seventeenth-century artworks (Judson and van de Velde 26). This expansion of art historians' work into the book is part of a project within early modern, especially Dutch, studies, which aims at coming to a better understanding of the national visual culture as a whole, rather than focusing on a limited number of canonical works. The ways in which European copperplates came to be circulated internationally, as part of the international trade in books, remains almost completely unstudied.

Copperplate and woodcut processes differ from each other. Both have existed since the invention of print, although woodcut technology is much older, and copperplate use is roughly contemporaneous with the emergence of technologies of moveable type. The woodcut was generally the preferred medium of illustration until the seventeenth century, at which time, in Germany, though not in England, the copperplate came to play a dominant role in book illustration. This is in spite of the fact that copperplates are generally more expensive than woodcuts, and financial resources were of course limited during and after the Thirty Years' War. While woodcuts are made by sculpting wood with a knife, an imprecise art in some respects, copperplates are made by engraving a design into a thin sheet of copper using a burin. The burin resembles a pen and is held like a pen; thus, the act of engraving resembles the act of writing. A great deal of precision is possible, and the minute engraved lines may be cross-hatched to create shadows and an illusion of depth. A drawing made with ink or charcoal is generally used as a guide. The engraver carefully copies the artist's design onto a copperplate using a burin. Artist and engraver are often not the same person. In this way, engraving technology works with a doubled hand, and it is a process of reproduction even before the copperplate is inked and pressed.

Whose Hand Guides the Burin?

One of the difficulties with the 1671 illustration of the *Simplicissimus* wolf encounter, the very "literal" illustration in the baroque anthology, is that the illustrator has failed to realize how revealing this scene is for Grimmelshausen's own ideas of pictoriality. The entire sequence of illustrations for that edition renders images so literal in their correspondence to the events in the book that the result is a vulgar, far too literal understanding of the function of illustration. Under the mantra of a single phrase, each illustration arranges the scene at hand as a grouping of figures against a natural background. Missing are the usual Grimmelshausen plays of meaning: the satirical uncertainty, the emblems that resist deciphering, and the collage of parts. Many of the other illustrations, the Grimmelshausen copperplate frontispieces, are far more complex and rife with clues about seventeenth-century pictoriality.

The *Springinsfeld* frontispiece (1670) portrays Springinsfeld outdoors with a wooden leg, in vagrant's attire and holding a violin. Richard E. Schade links this illustration to images of soldiers and of beggars of the early modern era, thereby bringing the image into a standard pictorial genre, to some extent even a frontispiece visual vocabulary of vagrancy (Schade 1987). Alan Menhennet has likewise undertaken to explain the pictorial features of the *Springinsfeld* copperplate:

> The strong downward thrust of the long nose and the rubbery grimace, together with the unusual turn and tilt of the head, produce a sense of near-caricature, of a decided oddness, reinforcing the effect of his socially peripheral status. This is, as the inscriptio has already informed us, "der *seltsame* Springinßfeldt." (1994, 82)

Noehles calls the face "mask-like" (1976a, 16–25). I am less convinced than Menhennet and Noehles that the oddness of design is evidence of an artistic tactic. It appears, rather, to be the careful and slow work of an unskilled amateur. The design is painstakingly created, with careful cross-hatching and evidence of a careful working of details. The folds in the coat, though oversimplified and unrealistic, show a studied attention to following curves. The landscape is well composed and convincingly executed; in my opinion, this landscape background has been copied, probably from another print. Problems abound in the picture. There is a shading emphasis on outline rather than contour. The small dog is too small, the sword is not straight. There are long, straight shadowed areas. The balance — for an experienced artist, this is of particular interest in drawing a man with a straight wooden leg — is ill-conceived, such that Springinsfeld would probably fall forward if he placed his left leg as illustrated. The head angle is strange and not consistent either with comfort or with violin technique. Violinists, for example, know that the chin, rather than the arm, should hold the violin in place. The hand placement as shown will make both position shifts and reaching the strings extremely difficult — and both of these are required to render accurate notes. The right forearm is too short, as is the right ear. The face is elongated and flat, and the eyes are too sharp, too tilted, and too large. The lettering, above, rises, and the word spacing is uneven.

Many of these errors are corrected in the 1684 new engraving, which is certainly from a different and artistically more skilled hand. The violin is held correctly here, and the fingers are positioned consistently with good playing technique. The composition and shading showcase an experienced graphic artist. The dog is especially well drawn, and its proportions, which are natural, help to compose the image.

The cross-hatching, contoured outline, mixed shading, flat long head, and other details abound in the first (error-ridden) *Simplicissimus* Phoenix frontispiece as well as the first (error-ridden) *Springinsfeld* frontispiece, suggesting that a common hand was responsible for executing both drawings. As a part-time professional artist and art instructor, I have tutored beginning artists and taught drawing classes, mostly at a beginner level. In my experience, it is quite unusual for two artists to make all the same drawing errors. The two frontispieces' mixed shading and the flat, long shape of the head, in particular, are highly idiosyncratic in nature. By contrast, darkening an outline is a more usual beginner's error. That a single hand executed both frontispiece drawings cannot, of course, be known from extant evidence. However, a comparison of pictorial "handwritings," with reference to specific pictorial elements, can be extremely fruitful. I am not suggesting that the copper engravings were cut by the same person, but am speaking rather to the composition itself, the drawing from which engravers create a copperplate. Some of these elements of pictorial strategy (or pictorial failings) also characterize sketches attributed to Grimmelshausen, such as the pen-and-ink draw-ings of the Palace Hohengeroldseck, near Baden-Baden (Bayerisches Hauptstaatsarchiv Munich, Plansammlung 11133/54). However, the most telling error is the shape of the heads in the *Simplicissimus* and *Springinsfeld* frontispieces. While these drawings are strikingly similar to each other in this respect, the Hohengeroldseck drawing lacks precisely this element that might have answered, to at least some degree of cer-tainty, the question of Grimmelshausen's artistic participation.

There are no figures in the Hohengeroldseck drawings; only build-ings arranged on the hill. Indeed, there are no known drawings of figures by Grimmelshausen (Noehles 1979, 48). Most of the ink shading of the Hohengeroldseck hill is near its edges, and there are long, straight shad-owed areas at the left. The wall, too, is shaded primarily at its edges. The symmetry is disrupted, and several of the structures are unbalanced. The smaller hill contours near the clustered buildings look very much like the folds in Springinsfeld's frock. The cross-hatching is surprisingly careful for such an unskilled design. The shading is not internally consistent, and the forms that should be foreshortened due to perspective are not fore-shortened at all.

The amateur quality itself points to Grimmelshausen as the artist, "[. . .] wenn man nicht annehmen will, der Verleger Felssecker oder sein Lektor hätte einen Nürnberger Dilettanten mit den Illustrationen beauf-tragt" (Noehles 1979, 49). Yet this lack of skill has a raw freshness of expression which lends charm to the drawings and may have helped to sell books. The artist works the dark areas very meticulously, and there is a delight in detail that emerges from extremely slow and careful work, however unskilled. In the *Simplicissimus* and *Springinsfeld* illustrations, a cartoon-like humor remains despite the compositional complexity of an overworked page.

Jörg Jochen Berns considers it most likely that Grimmelshausen was the "Inventor seiner Titelgraphiken" (Berns 1988, 315), and Menhennet calls the Phoenix illustration "in all probability [Grimmelshausen's] own work" (Menhennet 1995, 278). Noehles emphasizes a Grimmelshausen "hand" characterized by diagonal lines, technical skill, difficulties with perspective and foreshortening, copying from other graphic sources, figure stereotyping, and a pen-and-ink strategy more akin to woodcut strokes than depth-defining copperplate strokes (Noehles 1979, 48). These observations could, of course, describe many sixteenth- and sev-enteenth-century copperplates, and are rather a list of usual drawing practices and errors, not the idiosyncratic errors and strategies one might require in order to argue for the existence of an artistic hand. Except for woodcuts illustrating the *Erster Bernhäuter* and *Gauckel-Tasche,* nearly all the Grimmelshausen frontispieces were engravings or etchings, that is, *Kupferstiche* or *Radierungen,* both of which consist of intaglio designs on a thin metal sheet, usually copper.

In the Phoenix copperplate (the first line of the frontispiece *subscriptio* reads, "Ich wurde durchs Fewer wie *Phoenix* geborn"), the technical parallels to the *Springinsfeld* copperplate are striking. The Phoenix's chin is too large, the face is too flat and long, and the eyes are uneven, just as they were for the *Springinsfeld* copperplate. The masks below are well drawn in profile but the quasi-symmetry of a foreshortened face proves too challenging for the unskilled artist. The artist has little experience drawing human or animal forms from an angle and fails to achieve an anatomical logic (of standing balance, of symmetry, of proportion, or of direction) in the figure. The right foot is not positioned for credible standing, the left shoulder is poorly drawn (in part because only the outline has tone, unlike the forearm). In addition, the horns are too close to the face, the leather strap for the sword hangs awkwardly (it is noteworthy that the sword exceeds the picture frame), and the hoof is near the edge of the stage and does not appear to support the Phoenix's weight. The eyebrows on the masks are uneven, and the images on the pages of the book (the book held open by the Phoenix for the reader) are poorly composed. It is noteworthy that the picture of a sword in the book does not follow the curve of the page into the center. The Phoenix's tail is too darkly shaded in comparison to the rest of the figure, and the logic of the shading for the whole composition is not internally consistent; that is, the implied light source shifts. The musculature of the ram's leg is excellent, except that it is not supporting the creature's weight correctly, which strongly suggests that this leg was copied from another graphic source. The frontispiece to the 1685 edition of Grimmelshausen's collected works corrects these errors; again, this is a reworking that demonstrates more talented artistry, and it is almost certainly from a different hand.

The Agency of the Phoenix

Of the chief interpretations of this figure, a prevalent strain makes reference to the composite monster of Horace's *Ars poetica.* Karl-Heinz Habersetzer cites passages from *Vogelnest I* as well as *Ratio Status* and the *Satyrischer Pilgram* (76–77) to demonstrate that Grimmelshausen was intimately familiar with Horace's *Ars poetica* text. In the *Ars poetica,* a creature composed of mixed parts is summoned as an exemplum of an unpleasant image. The Horatian creature has a man's head, feathers, a fish's lower body, a woman's breasts, and so on; that is to say, it is consistent with Grimmelshausen's Phoenix design. Indeed, such creatures are to be found in nature too, hybridous beings (egg-laying mammals, deciduous conifers) at the thresholds of taxonomic certainties, where nature unravels its own rules.

However, Horace never mentions horns or long ears, nor the finger gesture, nor the book of pictures. Clearly, there is more to the Phoenix figure than Horace's *mixtum compositum*. Schade (1987) asserts that there exists an iconography of the picaresque. By this he means a composition comprised of disparate parts, but one might readily add that this picaresque imagery shares with the literary picaresque an unabashed vagrancy, an outdoorsy readiness, and an eager outlook on adventure, all of which characterize picaresque narratives.

Fritz Halfter in 1924, Hellmut Rosenfeld in 1935, and Walter Ernst Schäfer in 1972 saw, in the Phoenix, horns, ears, hand gesture, and "feet" (one hoof and one webbed foot) a satyr figure, and connected the satyr beast to satirical texts. Halfter was the first to call the creature a satyr (Scholte, in 1912, saw a devil figure in the Phoenix), and was also the first to undertake a thorough study of the images in the open book; that is, the open book which is pictured in the Phoenix copperplate.

Halfter understood the two Phoenix fingers to represent a double pointing toward drawn images: thus the swaddling child image and the tree image, both in the open book, are for Halfter the key iconographic signals. Yet, there is little precedent for seeing the two-finger gesture as a double pointing. Rather, there is precedent for viewing it as a mocking, even obscene gesticulation: a gesture "des 'Eselstechens' oder 'Eselbohrens'—eine im 16./17. Jahrhundert noch landläufig bekannte Spott- und Verhönungsgeste, die sich auch auf anderen Kupfern satirischer Schriften als 'traditionelle Spottgeste des Satyrs' identifizieren lässt" (Habersetzer, 65). Schäfer adds other names for the gesture: "Storch stechen," Italian "fare il corno," and so on, and adds that the gesture was subject to police punishment (208–9). Schäfer, who also likens the Phoenix to a classical Pan figure, looks at the folk origins of the satyr as founder of satire. He adeptly links satirical and moralistic texts as both aiming at scolding sin and urging virtue.

Grimmelshausen's Frontispieces

Both the Phoenix frontispiece and the *Vogelnest I* frontispiece are, according to Berns, satyr-like composite figures with "I" identities (due to

the first-person-singular narrator of the *subscriptio* texts in both frontispieces) that are not identical to the narrators of the two novels. The
question is one of perspective: who speaks for the images, if not the story
narrator? A second question for Berns is the issue of scope. Does the
Phoenix copperplate illustrate just the *Simplicissimus,* or the *Simplicissimus* novel along with the *Continuatio* as well, or does it in fact illustrate
all ten books of the *Simplicissimus* cycle? What appears to be a collection
of different biographies, is, according to Berns, a ten-book inner biography, a "Seelenbiographie," of Simplicissimus. Although Simplicissimus
appears less and less in subsequent novels in physical form, his importance in structuring the other novels of the cycle never wanes, and he
reappears as a giant "Super-Simplicissimus" (Berns 306). Berns concludes that a satirical and satyresque *Über-Ich,* a superego, embodied in
the Phoenix image, controls the whole cycle in a play of onstage masking
and de-masking that ultimately points to Grimmelshausen himself (316–
17). I am less inclined than is Berns to view the *entire* Grimmelshausen
corpus under a scheme of intertextuality, particularly where the illustrations are concerned (although there are notable exceptions, as discussed
in this paper). The woodcuts and copperplates of the Grimmelshausen
corpus point to some of the same issues that figure in seventeenth-
century novels more generally: spatial displacement, social hierarchy (and
disruption of hierarchy), materiality, theatricality, and so on. The Phoenix copperplate does not fit obviously into any particular pictorial genre,
including even the genre of satyrs and satires. Compare this to the *Proximus und Lympida* (1672) frontispiece, an example of a kind of frontispiece pictorial standard that was prevalent in the baroque. The altar-of-
marriage motif, which was popular from about 1640 to about 1670,
forms the frontispiece for the Amsterdam edition of Martin Opitz's
translation of John Barclay's *Argenis* (original 1621, Opitz translation
1626) and other books (such as Zesen's translation of *Lysander und
Kaliste* [1644] and his *Assenat* [1670]) that include a love intrigue or
wedding. Grimmelshausen's *Proximus und Lympida* was also illustrated
in this manner. Jutta Breyl calls this genre an advertising signal ("werbe-
wirksames Signal") for novels in which the theme of marriage figures
prominently (197). Ultimately however, the publisher Felssecker replaced the *Proximus und Lympida* frontispiece with a new copperplate,
in which the characters are more heroically and more romantically pictured, for the posthumous Grimmelshausen collected works.

The *Rathstübel Plutonis* frontispiece is an extraordinary engraving in
which persons of different social stations come to sit together in a demo-
cratic circle, violating the *Ständeklausel,* the literary presumption and

enactment of separated social strata. One might also say that the seated persons are circling like predators; the prey is, of course, money, and the brief tract is in reality a conversation that divulges advice about how to obtain wealth. Berns asserts that the circle of figures in the frontispiece proves that the ten-book cycle is a closed cycle.

Linda Ellen Feldman calls the discursive space of the *Rathstübel* text a Christocentric locus, with the Jewish discussant Aaron at the fringes of the conversation, participating only when threatened with violence. The frontispiece, according to Feldman, visually brands Aaron as an outsider by outfitting him with symbols of his faith and placing him to the speaker's (sinister) left. At issue for Feldman is the need to create a guarantor of Christianity by means of setting up a different and inferior status for Aaron.

After the *Simplicissimus* and *Springinsfeld* frontispieces, it is perhaps the *Courage* frontispiece that is the most provocative and revealing for studies of the seventeenth century. The *Courage* copperplate, in part, portrays reification itself, a representation of materiality that ties into the Phoenix copperplate and its visual display of the book in the gesturing hand of the Phoenix. In the *Courage* copperplate (which exhibits great artistic skill), Courage has joined a Roma (sometimes called Gypsy) band and relinquishes her grooming accessories and cosmetics because her new husband requires it of her. Dressed as a Roma, Courage rides a mule and tosses her cosmetics away into the air. The *Courage* frontispiece is, again, an illustration of vagrancy. In *Vagrant Writing: Social and Semiotic Disorders in the English Renaissance*, Barry Taylor describes the figure of the vagrant and *his* role (Taylor's vagrant is a gendered male) in English literature as follows: "the wandering of the vagabond entails a vagrancy of the signifier — or the surface appearances of social being — from its ground in the signified — the 'natural' hierarchical ordering of rank and status"; the result may be "a pervasive semiotic destabilization, an uncoupling of appearances from reality" (2). For Taylor, the vagrant is always a threat to the elite classes. He threatens not only a social order, in Taylor's understanding, but also an order of language and signification, where an external element reveals as "unnatural" the enactments and assumptions that perform elitism. By contrast, the Grimmelshausen frontispieces catalog vagrants whom we view as equals rather than as societal threats. Just as for the *Rathstübel* frontispiece, it is not clear whether we are seeing a de-stabilization of social ranks in *Courage,* a space for mobility, or a subtle guarantor of stability by means of ousting a dissident force. It appears that Courage does not uncouple appearance from reality here, but disposes of her cosmetics and shows her true appearance. The Grimmelshausen vagrant is genuine, unabashed, and unmasked. The Grimmelshausen vagrant is also resolutely central, in the midst of things, rather than a peripheral destabilizer in the sense of Feldman's or Taylor's arguments.

The Visual Cues of Objects

The *Courage* print deviates from the *Courage* text by also showing objects that are not mentioned in the story. The print exhibits a comb, fan, cosmetic containers, scissors (below in the print), which are consistent with the *Courage* text, but also insects, birds, and monsters (above).[2] Schade, who links Courage riding on a donkey to depictions of melancholy, calls the assemblage in the air a "Satanic realm" or "locus terribilis" (1980, 80). Berns likens these objects to a line of hieroglyphics with allegorical content: "Schon auffälliger sind die allegorischen Signale im Courage-Titelkupfer ausgestellt. Das gilt nicht nur für das Acedia-Programm der Zentralgestalt, der Zigeunerin auf dem distelfressenden Maultier, sondern auch für die seltsamen Flugobjekte und Tiere, die wie eine Hieroglyphenzeile zu Häupten der Vordergrundfiguren schweben" (1988, 316).

Like print, the *Courage* objects are contained in planar space. Whereas the rest of the engraving shows perspective with a vanishing point, the objects and creatures in the sky defy the page's depth. In the Phoenix copperplate, the gathering of objects, the clutter, includes a strewing of masks shown three-dimensionally. Yet it is really the pictures in the book (the book that the Phoenix figure is holding) that function in a two-dimensional display. In the *Courage* print, objects are set onto a flat plane in contrast to the rest of the print, which, as a whole, sets up a logic of three-dimensional depth. In other words, the objects defy the three-dimensional space and appear thrust forward, in the plane of the actual flat paper of the image, foregrounding both the objects and the nature of "objectness" itself. Such a foregrounding thrusts objects, material things, into the view of the reader. I have argued that drawings, such as this one, parallel the seventeenth-century *Vanitas* paintings, which simultaneously condemn, but also resolutely exhibit, material objects (Greene, 1–3).

The illustrations for Gryphius's *Catharina von Georgien* employ similar tactics. Vigilio Castore, who probably etched the illustrations for *Catharina von Georgien,* chose to include in his illustrations a depiction of the play's brief prologue. Bodies, swords, crowns, and scepters are strewn upon the stage in his etching, but they are not strewn with respect to an illusion of depth. The drawing makes use of extreme vanishing points and exaggerated size ratios to create an illusion of three-dimensional space. Yet, the objects on stage are an exception: they are both oddly flattened, and also made to seem as though they are evenly spaced with respect to the plane of the picture itself, rather than with the plane of the stage. The *Courage* objects, too, are evenly spaced with respect to the plane of the page. The effect is an over-presentation of the objects, in terms of both their size and their placement with respect to each other. In a similar manner, the held book in the Phoenix frontispiece illustration displays pictured objects in much the same way: they are flat and non-responsive to bodied, that is, three-dimensional space, much like print itself.

The Book Arranged within the Book

In the Phoenix copperplate, the reified display includes not only drawn imagery, but also a picturing of narrative (in its material nature as a book object), and the Phoenix's gesturing hand is contained in the (pictured) book of the frontispiece much like one of the images. With Fritz Halfter, I question the intent of placing the pictured objects of the Phoenix copperplate in proximity to the Phoenix's hand, although the fingers do not appear to me to be pointing. The Phoenix frontispiece of the 1683–84 edition of Grimmelshausen's collected works (the re-worked frontispiece) does not appear to have assigned importance either to the book images (they are in shadow) or to any kind of pointing function. The finger arrangement as gesture is preserved however, and we can infer that the gesture must, in some ways, have been to the engraver more important than the images in the held book.

Of the many scholars who have commented on the Phoenix print, none has yet remarked on the fact that the finger arrangement, as shown, is not capable of holding the book. I am thinking especially of the placement of the thumb. A book held in this manner would instantly close in upon itself or fall forward. The 1684 engraver has noticed this, and corrected for it. Perhaps the figure's right hand is grasping the book in ways that are not visible to us. In either case, the left hand is *only* gesturing and not holding in any way. Thus, it appears that the mocking, satirizing gesture is of primary importance. The images in the book, only some of which relate to the events in the novel, seem to me less a display of objects in the sense of the *Courage* and *Catharina* illustrations than a picturing of writing itself, writing as laying down pictures on the page, whether of letters or images. This ties into the Simplician model of reading pictures and images together. The hand gesture is an object on display, together with the books' other picturings. The hand that satirizes is also the hand that draws and writes, and is itself included in the book. The hand is exhibited together with the rebus alphabet (the pictures where letters should be) that comprise the pictured book, that is, the book pictured in the Phoenix frontispiece. Clearly, these images are advertising and communicating to illiterate readers and to readers who may seek a visual *summa* of the *Simplicissimus* content: but read in conjunction with Book 1, chapter 10, they also comment on visuality and language in very complex ways.

The Phoenix copperplate is indeed entangled in our reading of the *Simplicissimus* novel, and it provides clues for a Grimmelshausian conception of visual reading. I would like to bring into sharper focus the picturing of the open book from the Phoenix copperplate. Visuality attaches to the *Simplicissimus* text, which itself thematizes visuality by means of at least two levels of the same illustrating gesture. On the one level, the frontispiece is simply, as an illustration, the first page in the book. On another level, the frontispiece illustration itself contains an open book filled with illustrations. A hand gesture points toward the pictured book and exhibits that book to the reader, within a scheme in which viewer and reader are the same. The (pictured) book's images at once illustrate a book but also expose to the reader of *Simplicissimus* the visuality of all books. This reading of black lines is remarkable, because it is in full agreement with the paradigm of text and image laid out in *Simplicissimus,* Book 1, chapter 10. It is a collusion of literacy (the reading of letters as producers of language meaning) and pictorial literacy (the reading of letters as meaningful pictures).

The hand arrangement shapes a gesture (Penkert has read this shape as a letter), which satirizes, "satyrizes," and scorns. The book-in-hand arrangement is a "reading to," a presentation of the book to the viewing scope of the readership. The Phoenix narrator is both the author of his tale and the determiner of the circumstances of its reading. The hand, usually bound up in writing and picturing, is here the facilitator of reading as well.

A visual assortment, a *compositum,* greets the reader of the book in the Phoenix's hand. It is a *mise en livre,* a placement within the book, of an assortment of images. Simplicissimus says elsewhere of *Der keusche Joseph,* "das wäre mein eigene Erfindung nicht/ sondern hätte es auß andern Büchern extrahirt" (ST III, 265). What he expresses here is that his is a book made from parts of books. Similarly, the illustrated open book of the Phoenix frontispiece is a presentation of textuality, and more generally, a presentation of knowledge, by means of a combination of images, which are arranged in a non-linear fashion. Missing is the linear sequencing of letters which characterizes writing. The cuts, parts, and schisms of the Phoenix book images (they are arranged haphazardly), of the Phoenix's body (an amalgam of parts), of the Joseph book ("aus andern Büchern extrahirt"), and of the picaresque form itself (that is, the structure of episodic narrative) comprise iterations of the same combinatory strategy. A "book" is here conceived as an apparatus of moveable, visual signs. In this sense, it recalls the work of a book compositor, who sets the moveable type. In the seventeenth century we see a careful preoccupation with the generative potential of arrangements of numbers and of alphabets (consider also the re-ordered "Versetzung der Buchstaben" of author-names that Grimmelshausen discusses in the "Beschluss" of *Simplicissimus*). In the Phoenix frontispiece, there is a vagrancy (in the sense of a moving and re-arranging) of the very lines of ink that generate signs. When re-arranged, the black lines that constitute letters, numbers, and other signs revert to images. Their presumed collapse is what makes the frontispiece book-within-a-book an effective means by which the *Simplicissimus* text may appear to examine itself. It exposes the book's sign vehicles, its letters, as inked shapes.

Book 1, chapter 10, in which the hermit teaches Simplicissimus to read images in books, brings together not only text and image, but also *Bildung* and *Bildlichkeit*, education and picturing, along the etymological terms of the Old High German *bildunga* that gestures toward *bild* — in its general sense as both *shape* and *shaping* (educating). Chapter 10 follows immediately upon a discussion of the soul as an unwritten tablet (based on Aristotle's *De anima*), in which Simplicissimus explains why the hermit gave him his name.

> Solches alles erwiese ich mit meinem eigenen Exempel/ denn daß ich alles so bald gefasst/ was mir der fromme Einsidel vorgehalten/ ist daher kommen/ weil er die geschlichte Tafel meiner Seelen ganz läer/ und ohn einzige zuvor hinein gedruckten Bildnussen gefunden/ so etwas anders hinein zu bringen hätt hindern mögen; gleichwohl aber ist die pure Einfalt gegen andere Menschen zu rechnen/ noch immerzu bei mir verblieben/ dahero der Einsidel (weil weder er noch ich meinen rechten Namen gewust) mich nur Simplicium genennet (ST I, 29).

What is "pressed" or "printed" therein constitutes the soul; that is to say, a composite of "prints" accumulate in the soul of the experienced person. The soul, like a book, is a "Tafel [. . .] darauff man allerhand notiren kann" (ST I, 29). To be unschooled is to be devoid of inscription (of images, and of writing).

Similarly, *buchstabieren,* the forming of letter shapes, precedes *lesen,* the comprehension of letters and "pictures":

> Nun wolan mein Sohn/ ich will dich lehren/ daß du so wohl als ich mit diesen Bildern wirst reden können/ allein wird es Zeit brauchen/ in welcher ich Geduld/ und du Fleiß anzulegen; demnach schriebe er mir ein Alphabet auff birkene Rinden/ nach dem Druck formirt/ und als ich die Buchstaben kennete/ lernete ich buchstabiren/ folgends lesen/ und endlich besser schreiben/ als es der Einsidel selber konnte/ weil ich alles dem Druck nachmahlet" (ST I, 31).

Simplicissimus has already made the first step toward reading, toward a "Grimmelshausian" reading, when he recognizes the difference between the material line and the encoded line; that is, lines of ink (Linien) and lines of text (Zeilen):

> [The hermit:] "Liebes Kind/ diese Bilder können nicht reden/ was aber ihr Tun und Wesen sey/ kann ich auß diesen schwartzen Linien sehen/ welches man lesen nennet. [. . .]

> [Simplicissimus:] "Wann ich ein Mensch bin wie du/ so müßte ich auch an denen schwartzen Zeilen können sehen/ was du kannst. (ST I, 31)

Notes

[1] Cf. Noehles 1976 "Text und Bild," 605: "Schriftzeichen treten zu den ikonischen Zeichen des Bildes, um in Barock emblematischer Denkweise die Schein-Tautologie des Bildes zu dekodieren."

[2] See the Dürer pen-and-ink nature study *Ein Hase inmitten von Blumen* (1582), which is, I believe, a precedent for this baroque compositional strategy.

Works Cited

Ackley, Clifford S. *Printmaking in the Age of Rembrandt*. Boston: Museum of Fine Arts, 1981.

Ashcroft, Jeffrey. "Ad Astra Volandum: Emblems and Imagery in Grimmelshausen's *Simplicissimus*." *MLR* 68 (1973): 843–62.

Bauer, Conny. "Das Phönix-Kupfer von Grimmelshausens 'Abenteuerlichem Simplicissimus.'" *Text und Kontext* 8 (1980): 43–62.

Benjamin, Walter. *Gesammelte Schriften*. Ed. Rolf Tiedemann and Herman Schweppenhäuser. Vol. 7, 1. Frankfurt: Suhrkamp, 1991.

Berns, Jörg Jochen. 1998. "Erzählte und Erzählende Bilder. Portraittechniken im Simplicianischen Zyklus." *Simpliciana* 20 (1998): 105–22.

———. 1988. "Die 'Zusammenfügung' der Simplicianischen Schriften. Bemerkungen zum Zyklusproblem." *Simpliciana* 10 (1988): 301–25.

Bircher, Martin. *Im Garten der Palme: Katalog einer Sammlung von Dokumenten zur Wirksamkeit der Fruchtbringenden Gesellschaft, mit Beigabe eines Ausstellungskataloges (1991)*. Wiesbaden: Harrassowitz 1998. (= Wolfenbütteler Arbeiten zur Barockforschung 32)

Breyl, Jutta. "'ganz ein ander Buch.' Das Frontispiz zu Grimmelshausens *Proximus und Lympida* als poetologisches Signal." *Simpliciana* 15 (1993): 193–206.

Feldman, Linda Ellen. "Modelling Difference. The Construction of Jewish Identity in Grimmelshausen's *Vogelnest II* and *Rathstübel Plutonis*." *Colloquia Germanica* 28 (1995): 285–306.

Greene, Shannon Keenan. "Dramatic Images. The Visual Performance of Gryphius' Tragedies." Diss. University of Pennsylvania, 1998.

Grimmelshausen, Hans Jacob Christoph von. *Der abentheurliche Simplicissimus Teutsch: und Continuatio des abentheurlichen Simplicissimi*. Ed. Rolf Tarot. 2nd ed. Tübingen: Niemeyer, 1984.

Habersetzer, Karl-Heinz. "'Ars Poetica Simpliciana.' Zum Titelkupfer des 'Simplicissimus Teutsch.'" *Daphnis* 3 (1974): 60–82.

Harsdörffer, Georg Philipp. *Frauenzimmer Gesprächspiele*. Ed. Irmgard Böttcher. 8 vols. Tübingen: Niemeyer, 1968–69. (= Deutsche Neudrucke, Reihe Barock 13)

Heckmann, Herbert. *Elemente des barocken Trauerspiels am Beispiel des "Papinian" von Andreas Gryphius*. Darmstadt: Gentner, 1959. (= Literatur als Kunst)

Judson, J. Richard and Carl van de Velde. *Book Illustrations and Title-Pages.* 2 vols. Philadelphia: Heyden and Son, 1978.

Kaufmann, Jürg. *Die Greuelszene im deutschen Barockdrama.* Zürich: Zürich Verlag, 1968. (= Dissertation, Zürich, 1968)

Koschlig, Manfred. *Grimmelshausen und seine Verleger: Untersuchungen über die Chronologie seiner Schriften und den Echtheitscharakter der frühen Ausgaben.* Leipzig: Akademische Verlagsgesellschaft, 1939. (Reprint New York and London: Johnson, 1967).

Menhennet, Alan. 1995 "Cutting Linguistic Capers. The Title-Sequence of Grimmelshausen's *Teutscher Michel.*" *German Life and Letters* 48 (1995): 277–91.

———. 1994. "Simplician Emblematics? The Title-Sequence of Grimmelshausen's *Springinsfeld.*" *Seventeenth Century* 9 (1994): 77–91.

Michel, Paul. "Eine bisher unbeachtete Vorlage für das Titelkupfer des *Simplicissimus: Der abenteür Hauptman.*" *Simpliciana* 8 (1986): 97–109.

Noehles, Gisela. 1979. "Neues zur Porträtfrage Grimmelshausens. Beobachtungen zu den Illustrationen des 'BarockSimplicissimus.'" *Simpliciana* 1 (1979): 37–47.

———. 1976a. "'Der seltsame Springinsfeld' und sein Illustrator Max Unhold (1885–1964)." In: *Grimmelshausen, Dichter und Schultheiß. Festschrift der Stadt Renchen zur dreihundertjährigen Wiederkehr des Todestages von Johann Jakob Christoph von Grimmelshausen am 17. August 1976.* Renchen: Stadverwaltung, 1976.

———. 1976b. "Text und Bild. Untersuchungen zu den Kupferstichen von 1671 und den nachbarocken Illustrationen zu Grimmelshausen." *Grimmelshausen und seine Zeit. Daphnis* 5 (1976): 595–633.

Paas, John Roger. "Applied Emblematics. The Figure on the *Simplicissimus* Frontispiece and its Places in Popular Devil-Iconography." *Colloquia Germanica* 13 (1980): 303–20.

Penkert, Sibylle. "Grimmelshausens Titelkupfer-Fiktionen." In: *Emblem und Emblematikrezeption. Vergleichende Studien zur Wirkungsgeschichte vom 16. bis 20. Jahrhundert.* Ed. Sibylle Penkert. Darmstadt: Wissenschaftliche Buchgesellschaft, 1978.

Schade, Richard E. 1980. "The *Courage*-Frontispiece. Gypsy, Mule, and Acedia." *Simpliciana* 3 (1980): 73–93.

———. 1987. "Junge Soldaten, alte Bettler. Zur Ikonographie des Pikaresken am Beispiel des 'Springinsfeld'-Titelkupfers." *Chloe* 5 (1987): 93–112.

———. 1989. "Ehezucht Emblematics? In Praise of Marriage. The Frontispiece of Grimmelshausen's *Proximus und Lympida.*" *MLN* 104 (1989): 519–30.

————. 1991. "Text and Image. Representation in Grimmelshausen's *Continuatio*." *German Quarterly* 64 (1991): 138–48.

Schäfer, Walter Ernst. "Der Satyr und die Satire. Zu Titelkupfern Grimmelshausens und Moscheroschs." In: *Rezeption und Produktion zwischen 1570 und 1730. Festschrift für Günther Weydt*. Ed. Wolfdietrich Rasch, Hans Geulen, and Klaus Haberkamm. Bern and Munich: Francke, 1972. 183–232.

Scholte, J[an]. H[endrik]. "Johann Jacob Christoph von Grimmelshausen und die Illustrationen seiner Werke." *Zeitschrift für Bücherfreunde* 4 (1912): 33–57.

Schöne, Albrecht. *Emblematik und Drama im Zeitalter des Barock*. Munich: Beck, 1964.

Sestendrup, Manfred. *Vom Dichter gewollt. Grimmelshausens "Barock-Simplicissimus" und seine 20 Textillustrationen*. Renchen: Grimmelshausen-Archiv, 1983.

Spahr, Blake Lee. *Andreas Gryphius. A Modern Perspective*. Columbia, SC: Camden House, 1993.

Taylor, Barry. *Vagrant Writing. Social and Semiotic Disorders in the English Renaissance*. Toronto: Toronto UP, 1991.

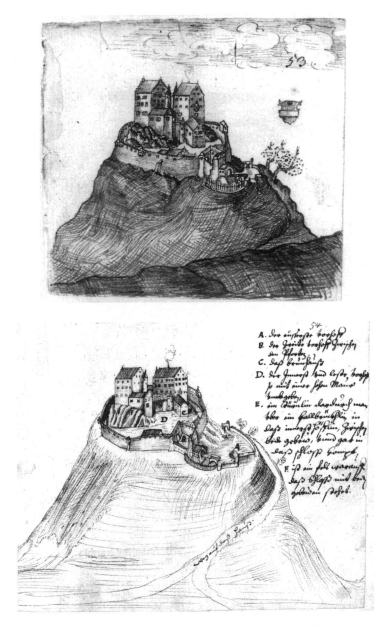

Grimmelshausen's sketches of Schloß Hohengeroldseck.
Reprinted with permission of the
Bayerisches Hauptstaatarchiv, Munich.

The Search for Freedom: Grimmelshausen's Simplician Weltanschauung

Alan Menhennet

THERE IS NO SUCH THING AS Simplician*ism*. It would be quite feasible, if a little tiresome for both writer and reader, to distill from Grimmelshausen's writings a systematic account of his "thinking" on a wide variety of topics. There are treatises on social and governmental "policy" (*Ratio Status* [1670]), on language (*Teutscher Michel* [1672]), and on the acquisition of wealth (*Rathstübel Plutonis* [1672]. The *Satyrischer Pilgram* and the *Verkehrte Welt* (1672), the latter of which owes much to the Alsatian author of the *Gesichte* of Philander von Sittewaldt, Johann Michael Moscherosch (1601–1669), show him as a comprehensive and severe satirist of human frailty. The novels, in addition, range over most aspects of seventeenth-century life. Yet in creating such an account, we would run the risk of losing sight of what makes Grimmelshausen most accessible and precious to us. And that is his "Simplician" way of looking at, and finding freedom and humor in, a real world, which, like most of his contemporaries, he found something of a prisonhouse and vale of tears and yet at the same time infinitely fascinating. Our aim, therefore, is the evocation of an attitude rather than the definition of a philosophy.

The image of Grimmelshausen that emerged from the latter would be somewhat less exciting, probably, than his known biography might lead one to expect. His childhood, and education, had been rudely interrupted at age thirteen, by the sack of Gelnhausen after the Battle of Nördlingen. He had known, and shared, the "low life." He had experienced his share of knocks, and even after he had pulled himself up by his bootstraps and re-assumed the aristocratic "von" that his baker-grandfather had felt inappropriate to his station, occupied a somewhat precarious position between the noble and moneyed and the "low" layers of society. Much of Baroque literature is courtly, in ethos if not literally in origin, but he could say with justice: "An grosser Herren Höffen bin

ich zwar nicht sonderlich bekant" (VW 13). While he retained an understanding of the peasant's viewpoint, he was no revolutionary. He endorsed the "God-given" social order.[1] He was a good, orthodox Catholic
Christian, but no bigot. He was less than reverential, at times, to the
Church's representatives, many of whom show a regrettable tendency to
worldly deviousness and pride, and excessive confidence in their own
spiritual authority.[2] Further, he is a conscientious, no doubt reasonably
efficient administrator, neither a courtier nor a tribune of the people, not
an out-and-out intellectual, but an intelligent and well-read man. He
despised ignorance and stupidity, but also the arrogant (and often
equally stupid) display of the educated sophisticate.[3]

Simplicity, in Grimmelshausen, can be the comic folly that derives
from ignorance, but it is also the hallmark of the most positive hero in
the whole Simplician corpus, the "Einsiedel" (hermit) in *Simplicissimus.*
The Christianity he teaches the young Simplex, by precept and example,
is practical in character, devoid of all theological subtlety — and none the
worse for that. He sends Simplicius out into the world with three brief
"commandments": know thyself, avoid bad company, and remain constant. Such simple and pithy brevity, the author makes clear, is vastly
preferable to "ein langes Geplauder" or "eine lange Sermon" (ST 35)
which you can understand but have difficulty in remembering. Grimmelshausen sometimes adopts, ironically, the literary role of "*Ignorant,*" but
would have been mortally offended to be taken seriously![4] The one
example of successful lyricism in all his work, the "Nachtigallenlied," a
vigil-hymn sung by the hermit in *Der abentheurliche Simplicissimus* (ST
I, 7), succeeds precisely because it is designed (or rather, assembled) as
a symbolic expression of simple Christian devotion. He is attracted by
the simple and practical religious life of the Anabaptists (ST V, 19),
though their "heresy" disqualifies them as role models. Alongside the
"Einsiedel," the saintly Proximus, whose disregard for earthly riches
recalls that of "die Einsidler in der Aegyptischen Wildnus" (PL 55),[5] can
stand as a model hero. Not that long-term separation from the world —
for all that the latter was full of snares and temptations — appealed to
him as a final answer. Simplicissimus comes finally to rest in the "Welt,"
not the "Wald"; the attraction of the eremitical life as a symbolic ideal
recurs in both "heroic" novels, but Dietwald and Amelinde come back
to the world, and Proximus achieves a godly life "mitten in der unruhi-
gen, gottlosen Welt" (PL 84). Grimmelshausen was capable of stylistic
elegance when appropriate, and he was not above making a display of his
own learning, whether it be on the more contemporary issue of witchcraft or on ancient history (ST II, 18 and DA 9–177). In addition, he

equipped with commendatory verses in all proper Baroque form those novels to which he signed his own name. Still, his preferred approach was that summed up in the expression "teutsch," that is, sensible, straightforward, and relatively plainspoken, as demonstrated by the Simplicissimus figure in his *Rathstübel Plutonis*.

He saw the Thirty Years' War, as did many others at the time, as a punishment sent from God (WV II, 278–818) and beyond the wit of man to alleviate. He shares the ideals of the deranged "Jupiter," and his criticism of political and religious divisions in Germany. In that regard, the Jupiter-figure can be seen as fulfilling at the national and political level the satirical role performed at the private and social by the naïve and still uncorrupted Simplicissimus himself in Hanau. He is the fool who criticizes the faults of his "betters," to the extent that his very folly is called in question, the simple man who exposes the folly of the "wise" (ST 217). As in the case of the young Simplicius, the theme of folly is multi-layered. The plan points out what ought to be, but the proposed method of execution (ST III, 4–6) is impractical, and at times faintly ridiculous. The "Teutscher Held" is clearly a Utopian fantasy, and perhaps in part, at least, a satire of the chiliastic tendencies that were currently abroad, and the "Kingly god" lets himself down definitively when he lets down his trousers to get rid of the fleas that are plaguing him (ST 218).[6] In general, while he obviously cannot ignore the War, since it creates the conditions in which his characters live, Grimmelshausen shows only a limited interest in its main issues, events and characters. There are some set-piece battle descriptions (Wittstock in *Simplicissimus* ([II: 27] and Lützen in *Springinsfeld* [14]), and the leading actors in the drama are occasionally mentioned, but they exist only at the fringe of the main action. One of the few occasions on which the mention of one of the figures that acted on the historical stage, as opposed to the Simplician world, is more than merely "passing," is that of the downfall of Albrecht von Wallenstein (1583–1634). This is a classic case of a real-life Baroque "Trauerspiel,"[7] but its importance, in the context of the *Springinsfeld* (81), is simply that Springinsfeld's regiment has to swear a new oath of allegiance.

Grimmelshausen did not delve deeply into philosophical issues, and he was certainly no forerunner of the Enlightenment. The framework within which he viewed the world was that provided by Christianity. With a certain tendency towards conservatism, perhaps, he shared the attitudes and prejudices common in his day. He was still unwilling to dismiss "superstitions" such as the belief in witchcraft (ST II, 18)[8] or to embrace liberal attitudes towards Jews[9] or women.[10] All this, and more, could go into the portrait of Herr von Grimmelshausen (one imagines he would insist on the "von"). It might even be quite interesting to meet this person. One wonders, though, whether by doing so, one would be meeting the real "author" of *Der abentheurliche Simplicissimus,* or gaining insights that would help us greatly in penetrating to its essence. If we extrapolate an ideological "content" from the published works we find a man who was, in an untimely fashion, ripped from a settled home background, denied a full formal education, and thrown into the maelstrom of the Thirty Years' War. Yet this same man worked his way back to become, by his own efforts, "honestus et magno ingenio et eruditione."[11] However, this would not necessarily give us the "Simplician author"(WV II, 148) of books that we read now, not for their erudition or mastery of Baroque rhetoric, but for the life that teems within them. We could well be better served by a more circuitous route which, entirely within the Simplician spirit, would result in a product that would be more untidy, but also more inclusive, than the systematic method.

Superimposed, apparently, on the design of the title-engraving of Grimmelshausen's *Simplicianischer Zweyköpffiger Ratio Status,* just above the ruler-figure with the two heads that represent respectively the good and the bad approach (David and Saul, respectively) to the question of self-preservation, there is a winged head. Unlike the pictures in the top and bottom panels (Jonathan and Joab), which complement the message of the central figure, this head bears no discernible relationship to the "Materi," as Grimmelshausen calls it (RS 54) of *raison d'état.* Curt Hohoff has speculated that it may even be a self-portrait (6).[12] That may or may not be the case; either way, it is possible, perhaps even probable that the function of this apparent intruder is to give graphic expression to that element in the work that is represented in the title by the word "Simplicianisch." This adjective should be seen as applying, not so much to a person, as to a persona. It is true that in the dedicatory epistle, Grimmelshausen has identified this as a work by the "author" (cf. Menhennet 179–81) of *Der abentheurliche Simplicissimus,* Samuel Greifnson vom Hirschfeld (RS 5–6). Still, he has identified his civil self (that is, the "Schultheiß" of Renchen) as author on the title page, and he has signed himself accordingly at the end of the dedication. This is not, then, a work by Simplicissimus. Whether or not it was written before the appearance of *Simplicissimus* in 1668, Grimmelshausen wishes, in 1670, to reflect onto a "serious" subject some of the glory of his bestseller. This work, deemed fit to bear his own name, and dedicated to a nobleman who knew him, is also supposed to reflect onto that serious subject a little of the character of the *Simplicissimus* novel. He accomplishes this reflection (of glory and character) by subjecting the novel to a process of Simplicianization. This process, as in the case of the second version of the *Keuscher Joseph* (also 1670), consists essentially in the grafting-on, as the winged head seems to be grafted on, of a certain amount of material whose connection with the original subject can only be described as extremely loose.

Loose connections, however, are in themselves "Simplician," as is the impression of variegation to which such a process inevitably gives rise. That variegation has to be part of our Grimmelshausen image. That image includes the "Schaffner" in Gaisbach and the local magistrate in Renchen, the solid and respectable citizen, if not particularly highly placed on the hierarchical social ladder. At the same time, he is the free spirit who may not entirely identify himself with Till Eulenspiegel (cf. Menhennet 16, 66, 125). Nevertheless, he has more than a little in him of the humor and lack of respect for solemn form that abounds in that work, and in the tradition of the "Schwank" to which it belongs. He accepted the social order, but at the same time retained a measure of inner independence. This emerges most forcefully, perhaps, in the older Simplicissimus's reaction, in *Vogelnest I,* to the unmerited rejection of his son. Both court and cloister are "prisons," and he and his son can get on without them: "If a man does not wish to be my Lord, I am under no obligation to serve him" (WV I, 106).

The comic view of life does not mix with the formal system, which is why this essay cannot afford to be thoroughly systematic. For in that case, the Simplician spirit would evaporate, and we would be left with only the serious and sober Grimmelshausen, who did, of course, exist. A comic framework can quite naturally embrace seriousness, whereas the reverse is much less likely. Too often, in portraits of the man and writer (which, in the absence of letters, diaries and detailed philosophical statements means much the same thing), the humor, which is always acknowledged, seems in some way to be a welcome, but essentially superficial garnishing of the dish. It is a way of simply entertaining, or of sweetening the satirical pill. The horizon of the comic world-view encompasses the comic and the serious, the metaphysical and the physical. It is our contention that this view provides a more satisfactory basis for the coexistence of the "lustig" and "nützlich" principles so often named together on Grimmelshausen's title pages than does the more one-sidedly moralistic "satirical" formula.[14] This does not attempt to resolve the dualism by merging the two. Instead it removes the sense of disruptive contradiction by finding a way in which they can be accommodated in the same landscape without compromising their own identities.

A careful examination of the head in the *Ratio Status* engraving reveals that it, too, is dualistic, or perhaps a better expression might be "lacking in integration." It seems like a composite, made up of two half-heads, one garlanded, one crowned, the former having long hair, the latter, short. From the position of the nose, it would seem that we are looking from the side, from that of the eyes, that we are looking, and being looked at, head-on. It seems possible to trace the line of a joint, running more or less down the center, particularly through the mouth. Especially when one takes the wings into account, it reminds one of the variegated composite figure that appears in the frontispiece of the *Simplicissimus*. There is a scheme, but there is also a degree of freedom to roam. It is that freedom of which Grimmelshausen avails himself in his introduction to, and narration of, the story of Sabud, which has no biblical basis,[15] and is, as he himself openly declares, an "appendage" that has no connection with the theme of *Ratio Status*. The story turns out to be the story of a nagging wife, one whose milieu, style and tone become progressively more homely, racy, in a word, Simplician, than those of Saul, David, Jonathan and Joab. Rather than attempt the "fusion" of which Angel Valbuena y Prat speaks in the case of *Don Guzmán de Alfarache*,[16] Grimmelshausen has simply and openly stepped sideways; not, though, into a different world, for the comic vision insists on the unity as well as the variety of its world, and on the right of many themes, moods, and styles to belong together within it.

The world is, in accordance with the serious Baroque world-view, which still preserved many core medieval concepts in it, a "verkehrte Welt." Grimmelshausen treated this theme at length in a treatise of 1672 which, though it claims the "Simplician" title, leans uncharacteristically strongly in the "aufferbaulich" direction.[17] However, apparent chaos and inconsequentiality are also features of the comic vision of the world. This is perhaps the quality that is most obviously apparent in the process that makes the potentially merely satirical into the more positively Simplician. The method that underpins the "Simplicianization" of the *Ratio Status* is one example of such a tendency: the author boldly, almost defiantly announces his intention to disregard the "proper form" of a rounded and finished discourse. He adds an appendage "zum Beschluß" (RS 55), irrespective of the fact that he has on the previous page, already written a pretty "conclusive" conclusion (54, lines 10–29) consigning the "Machiavellist" to eternal damnation. That, of course, is the non-Simplician "author" speaking.[18] Yet another spirit, a spirit of inconsequentiality, begins to enter the work at this point, and to affect the author's attitude. Cheek-by-jowl with a solemn condemnation of "Machiavellian" self-seeking founded on biblical authority, he deposits a freely invented tale which moves from the discursive to the narrative and proceeds from a style and milieu which can be called courtly, to a domestic setting in which a high-born lady descends to the level of an inquisitive, pestering wife,[19] and finally to an amusing animal language appropriate to poultry (RS 62)[20] and on being told by Herod, the dog, how Abisag is nagging Sabud, asks scornfully why he doesn't give her a good beating: "If I were in his shoes, I'd tan her hide good and proper" (RS 62–63). This assertion of comic coexistence is at its most blatant in the final section of the *Bart-Krieg*[21] but it underlies also the varied content and flexible structure of the Simplician corpus as a whole. The "conclusion" of *Ratio Status* also reads like an assertion of the freedom of the author who disregards the logic of the subject in favor of the much looser logic of Life. Having, as it were, "re-opened" the book in order to tack on a further section, he simply announces that "I will now conclude," though he is in fact not so much "concluding" as simply stopping. He inserts the word "Ende," and then leaves the reader effectively in mid-air, just as one is, of course, when life is not shaped and controlled.

The sense of freedom is an important component in the make-up of the "Simplician author," and in the outlook on life to which this concept corresponds. We must not be seduced into talking, anachronistically, of something that belongs to more modern times. As one would expect in an age, the ideology of which is based on the teachings of the Church, true freedom could be found only by transcending "The World." The freedom of (as opposed to freedom from) this world "macht die grösten Sclaven" writes (of all people!) Christian Hoffmann von Hofmannswaldau (II, 797). Aegidius Albertinus could assert: "Wir allesambt seyndt gleichsam gefangne in der Babylonischen Gefengnus dieser Welt" (306). Freedom was widely seen as dangerous. Youth, in particular, was a time during which individual freedom needed to be strictly curbed: "ein sehr grosses und gefehrliches ungewitter," says the same author, and a parent who wishes to protect his children from the snares of the devil ". . . muß jhnen die freyheit benemmen" (173). Again, we find Grimmelshausen, in his serious philosophizing mode, concurring with this orthodox view. In the *Continuatio*, he describes "die unbesonnene Jugend" coming to grief, like the young animals when they are first let out into the fields in spring, when they find themselves "aus der Eltern Augen in der lang erwünschten Freyheit" (490). As he tries to persuade Springinsfeld to abandon the "free life" and think instead of his eternal welfare, Simplicius surely speaks for Grimmelshausen, or at least for the "older and wiser" Grimmelshausen who, in 1670, sees the need for order and an ordered life.

And we, too, see that his advice is sensible and moral. Yet there is another voice, one that is a vital component of the Simplician way of thinking, and that in fact makes itself heard through the even older reprobate Springinsfeld, who still wishes to live free, "on the road." He sees Simplicius as a Bible-thumper, a moralizing preacher purveying "Münchs Possen" (Sp 131).

In the same way, the Gypsy life is regularly condemned by Grimmelshausen, both through the account of the life of the *Ertzbetrügerin und Landstörtzerin Courasche,* and in the lucubrations of Philarchus in *Springinsfeld.* Yet even this severe critic cannot suppress a certain positive appreciation of both the way in which this "Lumpen-Gesindel" orders its republic and of the freedom of its life-style:

> Bey diesen Leuthen findet durchaus einige Traurigkeit / Sorg oder Bekümmernus keinen Platz; sie ermahnten mich an die Marder und Füchse / welche in ihrer Freyheit leben (Sp 34).

The lives of the itinerant "professions" — Gypsies and beggars — who operated outside, or at best on the fringes of social, and moral order, were not to be admired or envied. Still, one envied them perhaps just a little, as it was not easy, in the seventeenth century, to find freedom within that order.[22] Their own hyperbolic claims to be the only true possessors of "die edle Freyheit," and to the enjoyment of a "Herren-Leben" (WV I, 21 and 23) one must, of course, take with a pinch of salt. Still, they do have a certain symbolic validity. Without in any way constituting an endorsement of what is a life of thievery outside society, the flexible Simplician framework allows the expression, even through the pompous persona of Philarchus Grossus von Tromerheim, or of the moralizing nest-bearer in *Vogelnest I,* of the presence in Gypsies and beggars of a spiritual quality of "inner freedom"[23] which may not cancel out the reprehensible aspects of a life of crime and disorder, but can be seen as coexisting with them, and, in a different context, could have real value.

Courage even tells Philarchus that her way of life is preferable to that of "a Lord" under a great Prince (WV I, 34–35). We do not need to see this as literally true, in order to appreciate that here again, the ethos of freedom is being celebrated. Even in the case of Olivier the "Merodebruder," something of this spirit subsists. Grimmelshausen, indeed, likens these people to the Gypsies, and comments that they live "wie die Frey-Herren" (ST 331–332). Olivier is the most villainous character in the book, but even he can be the vehicle for something positive. His arguments may be "Machiavellian," but that does not prevent us from seeing that he sometimes has a point, not only in satirical observation of the faults of civil society, for example the "vornehme Standes-Persohn" who has oppressed his subjects, yet escaped punishment at the hands of the law. We know he is no romantic Robin Hood, but he, too, represents a facet of the theme of freedom: "Ich bin eines recht auffrichtigen Gemüts / und treibe diese Manier zu leben / frey offentlich ohne allen Scheu."[24] He is not, of course, "aufrichtig" in absolute moral terms, but he is comparing his roguery, in Simplician style ("auff gut Alt-Teutsch"), to that of the usurer who acts "unter dem Deck-Mantel Christlicher Lieb" (ST, 338). One ought, of course, not to approve of his immoral character, and dislike of the discipline of the Dutch army. Still, alongside this, there does seem to be a plea for some recognition of the humanity of the soldier in his remark: "da wurden wir eingehalten wie die Mönche / und solten züchtig leben als die Nonnen" (ST, 353). One remembers Kipling's phrase about "single men in barracks."

Grimmelshausen has certainly not broken the mold of the serious, religion-based Baroque value-system, in which an "Eternal" dimension of reality and truth stands in unchallenged priority over against a "Temporal" one, with the principle of the *vanitas mundi* clearly established. Without wishing in any way to impugn the seriousness of the "serious" works, or the serious episodes and reflections in the Simplician novels, such as the "Farewell to the World" in *Simplicissimus* (V, 24), we still feel the need to draw an ideological line between him and Andreas Gryphius (1616–1664). Grimmelshausen as the author of a martyr tragedy seems somehow an inconceivable proposition. Certainly, he presents images of a more or less ascetic, anti-worldly piety in figures like the "Einsiedel" and Proximus, and he wants us to take them seriously. Still, it is surely clear, in *Simplicissimus*, that we are meant to see the hermit as an ideal figure, albeit helpful as such to the mere human embroiled in real life, rather than a real one. Even in the heroic context of *Proximus und Lympida*, the feeling one has is that all this saintliness, while infinitely admirable, is not real, but super-real. A kind of aureole seems to emanate from Proximus, and to set him apart:

> auß des Proximi holtseeligem Angesicht leuchtet ich weiß nit was vor ein sonderbarer Glantz welcher eine klare anzeigung gab/ deren in ihm verborgenligenden Tugenden und göttlichen Gaben; welches ihn dan vom Modesto ein grosses underschiede. (PL 91)

While Grimmelshausen is able to sustain the "serious," at least semi-heroic format and style, including rhetorical structures, reasonably well, there are moments when a certain strain begins to make itself felt. There is a different spirit, not so much striving to undermine the serious, as to find for itself a small corner of freedom within it. The main signs are involuntary discrepancies between style and milieu. Thus Dietwalt's grandmother takes the orphaned princes under her wing "wie ein sorg-fältige Gluckhenne" (DA 70), and the hero and heroine, in fighting the good Christian fight, know that they will need to survive "etliche kleine Scharmützel mit uns selbsten" (DA 51). Kenneth Hayens writes that in such works, Grimmelshausen "practically denies himself" the use of popular proverbs (65). Relatively speaking, perhaps, one can concede the truth of this, but proverbial expressions do appear from time to time, and to incongruous effect, as when in *Ratio Status,* Joab kills Absalon: "Dieser Politicus wuste das Sprichwort/ Eyer in die Pfannen/ so werden keine Junge daraus" (RS 51).[25] This is unlikely to be a deliberate attempt at a comic effect. Humor, or to be more precise, the comedy of life, has no place in the heroic context, and when it occurs in *Ratio Status,* it is, as we have seen, separated off in an appendix, introduced with an overt shifting of perspective that is characteristically Simplician.

In the Simplician works proper, it coexists easily with seriousness. An example is the description of the torture inflicted on the young lad's "Knan" (in fact his foster-father) by the soldiers who raid the farm. As the author's introductory remarks make clear, this is intended both as an individual incident, and as a symbolic one, representative of the "cruelties" perpetrated "in diesem unserm Teutschen Krieg." The house is ransacked and ravaged, and the soldiers then turn their attentions to the human beings, who are treated no less brutally. Every soldier has his own ingenious way of inflicting pain, and consequently, every peasant "seine sonderbare Marter." It is, up to that point, a description of unrelieved negativity, though the formality of its rhetorical structure is tempered by an earthy, vigorous style that distinguishes it as something more than merely a standard Baroque accumulation. The Simplician character emerges fully when attention is turned to the fate of the "Knan," who has his bare feet smeared with damp salt, which the family goat then licks off, tickling him "daß er vor lachen hätte zerbersten mögen." It is the boy's reaction that is decisive. He does not understand what is going on, and so responds spontaneously to what seems an irresistibly comic spectacle: "das kam so artlich/ daß ich Gesellschafft halber/ oder weil ichs nicht besser verstunde/ von hertzen mit lachen muste" (ST, 19). We, the readers, are aware that something serious, indeed reprehensible, is going on, even though we feel some degree of inherent comic incongru-ity between the ideas of torture and uncontrollable laughter. The image of the boy, in his ignorance, joining in the forced hilarity with spontane-ous laughter of his own makes this a truly comic moment for us as well. Our amusement does not undermine our appreciation of the "tragic" character of the situation that is being described. We do, however, rec-ognize a deeper comic irony that arises out of life itself, its essentially varied and "mixed" nature, which throws up all kinds of sometimes incongruous juxtapositions, against which the systematic philosopher, or the consistently tragic writer, rages in vain.

Grimmelshausen has not hidden his moral disapproval of the brutal-ity of the soldiers in the above example, any more than he does in the case of the gang-rape inflicted on the central figure in *Courasche* (chapter 12). Alongside this, and in no way canceling it out, he expresses his sense of the ridiculousness of the position into which she is put, in an image taken from the store of that lively, proverbial language of which he is so fond. He pictures her "leaping and spluttering like a donkey that has had of handful of thorns or nettles tied under its tail" (63).[26] A darker and bitterer, but still authentic instance of this Simplician method of uninte-grated juxtaposition is afforded by the episode in which, on the battle-field at Nördlingen, Springinsfeld murders in cold blood a wounded Swedish officer who has begged for his help as a "brother." There can be, and is, no justification for this act which, taken independently, could be seen as justifying the phrase "homo homini lupus" which Friedrich Gaede has applied to this figure: the inhumanity of man. This is, though, an isolated moment, and not a basis for a systematic interpretation under the aegis of Thomas Hobbes. It stands alongside a moment of under-standable, if not particularly charitable, human reaction. The word "brother" awakens in Springinsfeld, whose ambition to become an offi-cer himself will never be realized, and perhaps also in the class-conscious author as well, the memory of deep wounds inflicted in the past:

> Ja; gedachte ich/ jetzt bin ich dein Bruder/ aber vor einer Viertel Stund hettest du mich nicht gewürdigt/ nur ein eintziges Wort mir zusprechen/ du hettest mich dann etwan einen Hund genant (Sp, 82–83).

Two different perceptions, two discrete fragments of life, stand side by side. The one does not justify, or even explain the other: Springins-feld, the mercenary soldier, acts by the "rules" and when he finds that the other man is on the other side, has no compunction about killing him and robbing his dead body. In this case, the mood is bleak rather than comic, but the logic, insofar as there is logic, is still that of the strange combinations that life can produce. This structural principle of juxtaposition reaches its apogee in Grimmelshausen's *Ewig-während er Calender,* in which texts on a series of logically disparate "matters" are printed in columns, one alongside the other. Grimmelshausen's introductory remarks seem to imply that the work can be read "across" as well as "down," and to give the lie to the idea that this is simply a gesture of despair at the lack of coherence ("Widersprüchlichkeit") of the abundance of material with which real life confronts us.[27]

If one is to accept that logic, and refrain from the attempt to harmonize the discrepancies out of existence, a breadth of vision, and an acceptance of untidiness and apparent inconsistency is called for. This might be said to be analogous with Shakespeare's willingness to confront us with a drunken porter in the scene immediately following the murder of Duncan in *Macbeth.* He does this, not so much with "comic relief" in mind, as in reflection of the fact that in the nature of things, different people live side by side in different worlds. Similarly, in recognition of the fact that even a single mind can have many mansions, he creates a murderer who can show genuine poetic sensitivity as he lies in wait for Banquo.[28] There is an endorsement, here, for the reality of real life, with all its defects and inconsistencies. We do not find that in the realism of the everyday, which aims to make coherent sense of reality, nor in the transcendentally oriented heroic tragedy or novel (nor, for that matter, in Grimmelshausen's own "heroic" novels).

The "Simplician author" shows even greater respect for religious and moral values, but not at the cost of devaluing his characters' humanity. Thus, while he bemoans the fact that Simplicissimus gives in to the immoral demands of the lady in Paris ("Ich war *leyder* ein Mensch," [*my emphasis*], he treats the force of the lady's corporeal beauty and his hero's humanity in responding to it, with full sympathy:

> [ich] fand ein solch wolproportionirte Creatur/ und zwar von solcher Lieblichkeit/ daß ich wol ein Ploch hätte seyn müssen/ wenn ich keusch hätte darvon kommen sollen" (ST 307).

Regret at human frailty stands alongside respect for human reality, and an ability, which he shares with another great storyteller, Geoffrey Chaucer, to inhabit that reality and savor its vitality to the fullest. The lady stands here for Vice, and the man for fallible mankind, but they are no allegories. Fornication is a sin, and sexuality a net spread by the devil. Nonetheless, it is also a human attribute and a human need. Courasche is the living embodiment of "das Thier/ das Zöpff hat" (ST 266), perhaps even "Frau Welt." Still, when she says, in her inimitably earthy way, "I have never been so finicky as to deny an honest fellow a ride when he was desperate" (74), she becomes a vehicle for the voice of frail, but authentic humanity.

The transcendental perspective does not, in the Simplician world, render the immanent reality pale and transparent. The elaborate and formal, witty Baroque figurative style is not absent, but it is not allowed to slow the pace too greatly, or dilute the commitment to solid reality with its tendency to intellectual abstraction. Thus the young Simplex's killing of the lice that have been tormenting him (II, 28) is elegantly and amusingly rendered, in a Baroque mini-allegory, in terms of a battle. The "swords" he uses are also firmly attached to his thumbs, and the slaughter brutal and bloody: "[. . .] ein solches Würgen und Morden [. . .] daß mir gleich beyde Schwerder an den Daumen von Blutt triefften/ und voller todten Cörper/ oder vielmehr Bälg hiengen" (II 28). There is certainly allegory to be found in this Simplician world, but it is usually adulterated with real, individual life. It is narrated with storytelling pace and brio, as for example in the "Schermesser" episode in the *Continuatio*.[29] By contrast, the long allegory which renders Lympida's defeat by "invincible Cupid," in spite of all the "Wehr und Waffen" she fetches out of the "Schatz- und Rustkammer ihrer Gottes Forcht" (PL 72–73), seems, the longer it goes on, to move further and further away from the object into indulgent contemplation of its own ingenuity. These formal features mirror the central problem of reality and its "meaning," if indeed we can speak of such a thing, for our life on this planet. As far as its implications for the narrative artist are concerned — and we must remember that this, in Grimmelshausen's case, is the source of almost all our evidence — Rolf Tarot has formulated the question as "das Woraufhin des Entworfenseins der Wirklichkeit" (256). In simple terms, this means the purpose for which the writer sketches out a plan of reality. Tarot denies that what he accepts as the "durchgehende Allegorik oder Sinnbildlichkeit" of the Simplician corpus is in conflict, as Müller-Seidel believes it is, with the idea of realism (Tarot 258–60). This seems a tenable position, as long as one thinks of realism in formal terms. However, when one is asking, as we must here, whether a represented reality has "meaning," or better, perhaps, validity qua reality, the fact that the allegorical tendency has the capacity seriously to undermine that validity is surely undeniable. Dream-visions, for example, such as that of the "Ständebaum" dream in *Simplicissimus* (ST I 15–18), or the vision of Hell in the *Continuatio* (C 1–5), lift us out of the earthly, and on to the "eternal" dimension. The fantastic figure of Baldanders (C 505–8) is clearly "not real."

These episodes and others do reflect Grimmelshausen's world-view as one constructed from a transcendental and ultimately religious perspective. Nevertheless, the respect for mere terrestrial reality of which we have spoken penetrates, by virtue of the fact that the abstraction endemic to allegory is not allowed to dominate, even into this area. This is true also of the "symbolic" passages, such as that of the "Gauckeltasche" in *Der seltzame Springinsfeld* (chapter 7). It is clearly meant to reiterate the message, which crops up periodically in the Simplician corpus, of the "satirical" value of Grimmelshausen's storytelling. While we cannot take the market-place scene as literally "real," it is realized, in the narration, so graphically and concretely, that we cannot take it as "unreal" either. We do not, that is, nor should we, refrain from savoring the vital and real existence of Springinsfeld, that includes his animal-imitations "biß auff das forchterlich Geheul der Wölffe," the six-hundred-strong crowd "die vor Verwunderung Maul und Augen auffsperrten," Simplicius as "Marktschreyer," with his authentic vernacular patter, or the red-nosed drunk "der allbereit mit Kupffer anfieng zuhandeln" (Sp 42). The verb "savor" is important. It is enjoyment of the vitality of living reality coursing in one's own veins, the feeling that the meaning of being is being itself, which is at the heart of the particular "lustig" quality that distinguishes Grimmelshausen's "Simplician" perception of the world from, and lifts it above, that of his merely satirical predecessors, such as Johann Balthasar Schupp (1610–1661)[30] and Johann Michael Moscherosch (1601–1669)[31] both of whose works were well known to Grimmelshausen and influenced him.

It is no accident that, as the opening chapter of *Simplicissimus* and the whole of the *Courasche,* in particular, testify, Grimmelshausen was a consummate ironist. He even gives us ironic snapshots of himself, or at least of men in his line of business. We have, for example, the "Schaffner" in *Springinsfeld,* who does not know what a hoe is (chapter 2). We have the callow young "Rentmeister" in *Das wunderbarliche Vogelnest* (39), who makes up for the lack of hair on his face with "seine erschreckliche Parüque unter deren er herfür guckt wie eine Eul die kläpffen wil."[32] That he was more than willing to engage with reality is clear enough, but the designation "realist," as applied to him, has proved to be problematic. Certainly, as a writer, he is not content to portray reality in the straightforward manner of a Johann Beer (cf. Alewyn). Nor does he do so in the mood of practical normality that we associate with the "plain style" of Daniel Defoe.[33] In Simplician mode, at any rate, he tends towards the "seltsam" and the "curious." It is at that point that the element in his writing that can be called truly "lustig" begins to make itself felt. It is not always in a mood of outright hilarity, but rather with a certain imaginative detachment. That suggests that the Simplician attitude to the world, out of which the corresponding "Art" or "Manier" arises, is a way of reconciling himself with the world, or rather his undoubted enjoyment of its vitality with his awareness of its defects.

He accepts ideals, and can render their beauty in a "pure" form, as in the case of the "Einsiedel" in *Simplicissimus*. However, this pure state belongs to the "Wald," not the "Welt." He accepts the real world too, as we have said, and while he satirizes its faults, he does not, in all probability, expect to cure them through satire, and is certainly not willing to cut off the head as a remedy for the headache. The ability to "laugh" at the world, which means neither frivolity nor a never-ending string of funny stories, is a way of preserving at least his own independent balance. He had, no doubt, to preserve his self-esteem by performing a difficult balancing-act in his social relationships, with the aristocrats under whom, and the peasants over whom he had been set, and with the world of writers and intellectuals in which he had not been truly "accepted." An uneasy, sometimes resentful awareness of this emerges at times in his writings.[34] Mentally, at least, one can detach oneself from, and stand "above," even "play" ironically with, a reality that fascinates, but to which one cannot entirely commit oneself. The ideal cannot be "realized" without destroying reality, but it can be preserved inwardly. Thus the meanness of the notary of ("pro forma") Cologne is dignified, not in itself, but in the Simplician perception, by a playful, humorous exaggeration: "[wir] kriegten auff den Tisch [. . .] nur das jenige [Fleisch]/ so acht Tag zuvor von der Studenten Tafel getragen/ von denselben zuvor überall wol benagt/ und nunmehr vor Alter so grau als Mathusalem worden war [. . .]" (ST 284). The writer, here, is not the "character," the "odd vagrant" who is buffeted by fortune and has to live by his wits as best he can, but the settled Simplicissimus who appears in the *Teutscher Michel* (which has already announced a polished and ironic, as well as a satirical attitude on its title page),[35] presiding over a "lustige Gartengesellschaft" (chapter 8). A similar aura surrounds the Simplicius of the *Rathstübel Plutonis*,[36] a man at ease with his place in society, treated with respect, and capable of taking a relaxed view of the world around him. He even has as a companion, in the latter work, the actress Coryphaea, who has, characteristically, chosen a life as an itinerant ("Reisende"), that guarantees her "die edle Freyheit" (RP 26 and 67). One fears that in "real" terms, both of these portraits are mere wish-fulfillment on the part of a man for whom life is still full of bumps, bruises and constraints. It is a consolation that they can be seen as evidence of the mental emancipation that also underlies the Simplician style, and the Simplician Weltanschauung.

Notes

[1] Cf. in particular the passage in which the "Knan" is reproved for complaining about the burdens imposed on the peasantry by the other classes of society. Grimmelshausen is not entirely unsympathetic, but God's "Ordnung" is not to be disturbed (RP 59).

[2] The regimental chaplain at Philippsburg, for example (ST IV, 11), described, not without irony, as a "recht frommer Seelen-Eiferer," threatens the "recht wilder" Simplicissimus with fearful punishments, culminating in the dragging of his corpse, for burial, "auff den Schind-Wasen bey die Cadavera deß verreckten Viehs." While the passage clearly indicates the author's awareness of the seriousness of his hero's sinful state, the cleric, with his "heiliger Seelen-Eyfer" comes out of the episode looking rather ridiculous. He asks, nay begs Simplicissimus to let him have a hare he has trapped, but the latter refuses, on the grounds that the creature, having caught itself in a snare and hung itself, does not deserve burial in consecrated ground. Courasche is spiritually a fool, steeped in sin, but we cannot but enjoy her teasing of the "Herren Geistliche" in her opening chapter. Cf. also the "gottloser Geistlicher" who attempts to seduce a peasant woman in Part One of Das wunderbarliche Vogelnest (45–46), and the malicious monks who conspire against the Young Simplicius (ibid. 90–94). There are of course also good monks, who maintain true Christian simplicity (94).

[3] For example, his attacks on "Sprachhelden" in the Teutscher Michel, the two students who have to be saved from robbers by an "ungelehrter Idiot" in the Wunderbarlicher Vogel-Nest I (49–57), or "Jupiter" in Der abentheurliche Simplicissimus, a "Phantast [. . .] der sich überstudirt / und in der Poeterey gewaltig verstiegen" (ST III, 3). Simplicius's rather unreasonable carping at Zesen's Assenat in the Vogelnest I (100–104) may also be fueled by resentment at slights, real or imagined, received from the intellectual establishment.

[4] Compare his assertion in the "Glückwünschender Zuruff" appended to Dietwalt und Amelinde (100): "Der den Simplicem gemachet ist fürwar ein kluger Kopff."

[5] For the influence of this tradition on Grimmelshausen, especially the figure of St Antony, cf. Ilse-Lore Konopatzki, Grimmelshausens Legendenvorlagen, Berlin: Erich Schmidt, 1965.

[6] For the "royal" image of Jupiter, see Günther Weydt, Nachahmung und Schöpfung im Barock. Studien um Grimmelshausen, Berne-Munich: Francke, 1968, p. 246. It may well be that the nautical telescope carried by the man is a "travestied" version of the scepter in the hand of the god (ibid.) but . . . it is a travesty!

[7] In another context, Grimmelshausen is capable of seeing it in this light: the man who aspires to topple the Emperor and whose corpse is eventually dragged through the town on a manure-cart "aller Welt zum Spott," presents a fine example of *vanitas* (RP 65).

[8] Cf. the references to the "unseelige," or "unglückselige" "Congregation der Hexen" in *Springinsfeld* (Sp 60) and *Vogelnest II* (WV II, 277).

[9] The money-grubbing stigma is reflected, for example, in *Springinsfeld:* "mein Weib konnte auch den Juden-Spieß so wol führen als ein sechtzigjähriger Bürger von Jerusalem hätte thun mögen" (Sp 105). The nest-bearer resolves, on the promptings of his conscience, to steal only from Jews, and never again from a Christian, "er hätte denn ärger als ein Jud seyn müssen / dergleichen ich mir nimmer zu finden getraute / und solte ich gleich alle Winckel der Welt außlauffen" (WV, I 83). The treatment of the Jews and their faith in the "Esther" episode in *Vogelnest II* (13–20) shows a marked lack of sympathy.

[10] See A. Menhennet, *Grimmelshausen the Storyteller. A Study of the Simplician Novels,* Columbia SC: Camden House 1997, 54–55 and 129–32. The treatment of Sabud's wife Abisag in *Ratio Status* (see below) is another example. For a robustly argued positive view (which in the end I cannot share) of Grimmelshausen's principal female character, see John W. Jacobson, "A Defense of Grimmelshausen's Courasche," *GQ* 41(1968) 42–54.

[11] That is how he was described, after his death, in the local church records. For Grimmelshausen's erudition and its likely sources, see Weydt 1968, 20–43.

[12] Hohoff prints an enlargement of this section of the engraving that is easier to read than the reproduction in the *Gesammelte Werke.*

[14] Satire, representing the serious side of Grimmelshausen's nature, is, of course, a component of the Simplician mixture, but it is not a formula that can totally contain it. In the opening chapter of the *Continuatio,* in which the author looks back to the original novel before he looks forward, we feel that is trying, in the interest of literary respectability, to shoe-horn a broad, spreading foot into a neat, but narrow glass slipper. This is perhaps the best-known of several statements of the satirical formula.

[15] Zabud is mentioned simply as "King's Friend" among Solomon's officers in 1 Kings, 4, with no further details. Abishag the Sunammite disappears from the biblical narrative after Adonijah's failed attempt to gain her for his wife.

[16] "Introduccion" to *La novela picaresca española,* Madrid 1943, xvii.

[17] See further W. Welzig, "Ordo und verkehrte Welt bei Grimmelshausen," *ZfdPh* 78 (1959): 424–30 and 79 (1960): 133–41.

[18] A Simplician treatment, which we shall in due course examine more thoroughly, can be found in the portrait (ST IV, 15–17) of Olivier the "Merodebruder." He twice (338 and 339) calls Machiavelli in aid in his argument with Simplicius.

[19] One cannot, somehow, imagine Lympida or Amelinde scolding their husbands or sulking as Abisag does! However, they are heroic stereotypes. The troublesome

spouse is a satirical stereotype, of course, but here it is, in Simplician fashion, given real narrative life and individuality.

[20] "[. . .] potz 1000 Säck voll Regen-Würm und allerley Kräuter-Samen!" (for "Sakramente").

[21] See Menhennet, 58 and further on "conclusiveness," Menhennet, 109–15.

[22] Cf. Robert Jütte, "Vagantentum und Bettlerwesen bei Hans Jacob Christoffel von Grimmelshausen," *Daphnis* 9 (1980), 109: "Der Freiheitsraum des einzelnen Menschen in der frühneuzeitlichen Gesellschaft war eng umgrenzt."

[23] WV I, 20: "ihr fröhlich Gelächter/ ohngebundene Geberden und freye Reden gaben mir die grosse innerliche Freyheit ihrer Gemüther zu erkennen."

[24] An interesting parallel is the way in which the Australian bushrangers could acquire a certain gloss of "romantic" freedom. "By making the bush his new home," says Robert Hughes, "[the absconder] renamed it with the sign of freedom." Cf. R. H., *The Fatal Shore. A History of the Transportation of Convicts to Australia 1787–1868* (1986), London: Folio Society, 1998, 224.

[25] Cf. *Simplicissimus:* to his companion's plea that he spare the children, Olivier replies: "Eyer in die Pfannen/ so werden keine Junge drauß" (ST 358).

[26] Grimmelshausen uses the same image in picturing a schoolboy chastised by his teacher in the *Teutscher Michel* (22).

[27] Zeller (31): "Die Fülle des Wissens und die Erkenntnis seiner Widersprüchlichkeit führt offenbar zu einer tiefen Unsicherheit."

[28] Shakespeare, *Macbeth,* Act 2, sc. 3, 1–40 and Act 3, sc. 2, 4–7.

[29] ST chapters 11–12; discussed at length in Menhennet, 41–45.

[30] He was both a cleric and academic; see especially his *Der Freund in der Not.*

[31] He was both a scholar and an administrator. His *Gesichte Philanders von Sittewald* (1642) is strongly echoed in the satirical parts of Grimmelshausen's work, most notably, perhaps, in the criticism of the "Alamodewesen," the neglect of simple "German" virtues and cultivation of all things foreign, including foreign vocabulary, that is a prominent characteristic of the Baroque age. Grimmelshausen's *Teutscher Michel* is a good example of this, though here too, Simplician, storytelling element enlivens the drier satire. Cf. Menhennet, 1986, 646–54.

[32] Very much the same image is used in the both touching and comic description that Simplicissimus gives of himself after the death of the hermit: amid the "natürliche Verwirrung" of his unkempt hair, "[sahe ich] darunter herfür mit meinem bleichen Angesicht wie ein Schleyer-Eul die knappen [that is "schnappen"] wil" (ST 53).

[33] I hope to develop this theme myself in a forthcoming essay.

[34] Cf. for example the prefatory exchange between "Momus"; and "Greifnson" in the *Satyrischer Pilgram,* or the claim, in the self-penned "Glückwünschender Zuruff" appended to *Dietwalt und Amelinde,* that this work will win him recognition "bey dem gelehrten Volck," a clear indication that four years later, and after the success of *Simplicissimus,* he was still an outsider, still no more than "ein geringer Dorf-

Schultes," in the words of Quirin Moscherosch's famous letter of 1673 to Sigmund von Birken (quoted by Weydt, *Nachahmung und Schöpfung*, 306), and at best something of a "card" (a "Dauß-Eß").

[35] A work that contains criticism of the bombastic display of the "alamode" cult of the foreign, proclaims itself as "Simplicissimi Pralerey und Gepräng . . . jedermänniglichen / wanns seyn kan / ohne Lachen zu lesen erlaubt." There is also a clear irony in the title page of the *Gauckel-Tasche*, which, with a side-glance at the market-place scene in *Springinsfeld*, is advertised as ". . . allen denen nöhtig und nützlich / die auf offenen Märckten gern einen Umbstand herbey brächten" (*Kleinere Schriften* 11).

[36] There is no questioning of the formal priority in the social scale afforded to the nobleman Secundatus, but Simplicius is the dominant personality, and is even permitted to address Secundatus with the familiar "Du," on the strength of his "Simplician" credentials!

Works Cited

Albertinus, Aegidius. *Hirnschleiffer*, ed. L. S. Larsen. Stuttgart: Hiersemann, 1977. (= Bibliothek des Literarischen Vereins in Stuttgart 299)

Alewyn, Richard. *Johann Beer. Studien zum Roman des siebzehnten Jahrhunderts*, Leipzig: Mayer & Müller, 1932. (= Palaestra 181)

Gaede, Friedrich. "Homo homini lupus et ludius est," *Deutsche Vierteljahrsschrift für Literaturwissenschaft und Geistesgeschichte* 57 (1983): 240–58.

Hayens, Kenneth. *Grimmelshausen*, Oxford-Edinburgh: Oxford UP, 1932.

Hohoff, Curt. *Johann Jacob Christoph von Grimmelshausen in Selbstzeugnissen und Bilddokumenten*. Reinbek bei Hamburg: Rowohlt, 1978.

Hofmann von Hoffmanswaldau, Christian. *Deutsche Übersetzungen und Getichte*, ed. F. Heiduk. Two volumes. Hildesheim and New York: Olms, 1984.

Hughes, Robert. *The Fatal Shore. A History of the Transportation of Convicts to Australia 1787–1868*. London: Folio Society, 1998.

Jacobson, John. W. "A Defense of Grimmelshausen's Courasche." *German Quarterly* 41 (1968): 42–54.

Jütte, Robert. "Vagantentum und Bettlerwesen bei Hans Jacob Christoffel von Grimmelshausen." *Daphnis* 9 (1980): 109–31.

Konopatzki, Ilse-Lore. *Grimmelshausens Legendenvorlagen*, Berlin: Schmidt, 1965. (= Philologische Studien und Quellen 28)

Menhennet, Alan. 1986. "The Simplicianische Manier in a Satirical Context: Grimmelshausen's *Teutscher Michel*." *MLR* 81 (1986): 646–54.

———. 1997. *Grimmelshausen the Storyteller. A Study of the "Simplician" Novels*. Columbia SC: Camden House, 1997.

Tarot, Rolf. "Grimmelshausens Realismus." In: *Rezeption und Produktion zwischen 1570 und 1730. Festschrift für Günther Weydt zum 65. Geburtstag.* Ed. Wolfdietrich Rasch, Hans Geulen and Klaus Haberkamm. Bern: Francke, 1972. 233–65.

Weydt, Günther. 1968. *Nachahmung und Schöpfung im Barock. Studien um Grimmelshausen,* Bern and Munich: Francke, 1968.

———. 1971. *Johann Jacob Christoffel von Grimmelshausen.* Stuttgart: Metzler, 1971. (= Sammlung Metzler 99)

Welzig, Werner. "Ordo und verkehrte Welt bei Grimmelshausen." *Zeitschrift für deutsche Philologie* 78 (1959): 424–30 and 79 (1960): 133–41.

Zeller, Rosmarie. "Die 'ordentliche Unordnung' in Grimmelshausens *Ewigwährender Calender.*" *Simpliciana* 16 (1994): 117–36.

Contributors

ITALO MICHELE BATTAFARANO, born 1946 in Taranto, has been Professor of German Literature in Italy (Ordinarius für Deutsche Literatur in Italien) since 1980. He is editor of the book series *IRIS* and of the journal *Morgen-Glantz*. He is the founder of the Knorr von Rosenroth Gesellschaft (1990), over which he currently presides, and the co-founder of the Grimmelshausen-Gesellschaft (1977). He has published the following books: *Grimmelshausen-Bibliographie 1666-1972* (1975); *Da Müntzer a Gaismair* (1979); *Von Andreae zu Vico* (1979); *Spees Cautio Criminalis* (1993); *Glanz des Barock* (1994); *L'Italia ir-reale* (1995); *Die im Chaos blühenden Zitronen: Identität und Alterität in Goethes "Italienischer Reise"* (1999); *Von Linden und roter Sonne: Deutsche Italien-Literatur im 20. Jahrhundert* (2000, with Hildegard Eilert). In addition, he has edited the following books: *Friedrich von Spee* (1988); *Italienische Reise — Reisen nach Italien* (1988); *Il picaro nella cultura europea* (1989); *Georg Philipp Harsdörffer* (1991); *Tomaso Garzoni* (1991); *Begrifflichkeit und Bildlichkeit der Reformation* (1992); *Deutsche Aufklärung und Italien* (1992); *Über-Setzen: Eine unendliche Aufgabe* (1993); *L'Italia nella poesia tedesca contemporanea* (1997). He has also edited *Christian Knorr von Rosenroth: Conjugium Phoebi et Palladis* (2000).

DIETER BREUER studied in Mainz and Münster and received his Dr. phil. in Mainz with a dissertation dealing with novels of the German Baroque. Since 1969 he has been a member of the Germanistisches Institut of the RWTH, Aachen. His Habilitationsschrift deals with literature from Upper Germany during the period 1565-1650, as a result of which he was awarded the "Venia legendi" for modern German literary history. He held a guest professorship in Vienna (1980) and shortly thereafter became a university professor in Germany (1982). He has published many books and articles on topics dealing with Early Modern German Literature, including literary history, religion and church membership, the history of the book, of verse, and of literary censorship, and Grimmelshausen. In addition, he has publications on the Catholic Enlightenment, Goethe, Eichendorff, Hasenclever, regional aspects of the modern, and the Nibelungenlied. For a more complete listing of works, see www.germanistik.rwth-aachen.de. He has also edited both Grimmels-hausen (three volumes 1989-97) and Walter Hasenclever (eight volumes 1990-97).

SHANNON KEENAN GREENE received her Ph.D. in Germanic Languages and Literatures from the University of Pennsylvania, and has taught at the University of Pennsylvania and Bryn Mawr College. She has also studied at McMaster University (Ontario, Canada) and Tübingen University. Her dissertation engages copperplate engravings in Gryphius's published books as theatrical enactments of his dramas. Her research examines materiality, performativity, and image in German baroque publications. She is presently a freelance artist and author, and resides in Swarthmore, Pennsylvania.

KLAUS HABERKAMM, Dr. phil., is Professor at the Institute for German Philology II (Neuere deutsche Literatur) at the Westfälische Wilhelms-Universität in Münster in Westfalen. Since 1975 he has also been Adjunct Professor in the Department of German at the Johns Hopkins University and has been a guest professor at several universities in Europe as well. He has published extensively on seventeenth-century literature, especially on Grimmelshausen, and on literature after 1945, especially Frisch. He is also the co-editor of several research journals. A more complete list of his publications can be found at http://www.uni-muenster.de/DeutschePhilologie2/HOMEHABE.htm

PETER HESS is Associate Professor of Germanic Studies at The University of Texas at Austin. He received his Ph.D. at the University of Michigan, Ann Arbor. He has published books on Harsdörffer's poetics (*Poetik ohne Trichter,* 1986) and on the epigram (*Epigramm,* 1989). He has written articles on early modern rhetoric, topics, poetics, and translation, as well as articles on numerous writers of the seventeenth century. He is currently preparing an edited volume on definitions of sex and gender in early modern Germany. Other projects include a study on Grimmelshausen's picaresque novels and on representations of the New World in early modern German literature and art.

ALAN MENHENNET is Professor Emeritus of German at the University of Newcastle, Newcastle upon Tyne, United Kingdom. Over the years he has published articles and books on a wide range of topics, including many Baroque authors, Klopstock, Wieland, femininity in the novel, and later authors as well, e.g., Joseph Roth. He also has considerable expertise as a translator. His recent investigative study of Grimmelshausen (*Grimmelshausen the Storyteller* [1997]) was very well received. At approximately the same time this volume appears, Menhennet will be publishing his latest work, *The Historical Experience in German Drama from Gryphius to Brecht* (also with Camden House).

KARL F. OTTO, JR. is Professor of Germanic Languages and Literatures at the University of Pennsylvania (Philadelphia). He received his Ph.D. from Northwestern University. He has published books, editions, and bibliographies on Philipp von Zesen (1972), *Die Sprachgesellschaften des 17. Jahrhunderts* (1972), *Opitz' Schäferei von der Nymfen Hercinie* (1976), Zesen's *Gesellschaftsschriften* (1985), the Klesch family (1996, with Jonathan Clark), and on Friedrich Scherertz's emblems (2000). He has also written articles on numerous figures from German Baroque Literature (especially Zesen and members of his *Sprachgesellschaft* as well as on women in the *Sprachgesellschaften*) and on methodological and pedagogical topics. He is currently working on major bibliographical projects dealing with the casual poetry of the seventeenth century in Nürnberg and Hamburg.

CHRISTOPH E. SCHWEITZER is Professor emeritus at the University of North Carolina at Chapel Hill. He received his Ph.D. at Yale University. His most recent book is entitled *Men Viewing Women as Art Objects* (1998). He has edited several other books, including Lessing's *Nathan der Weise* (1970 and 1984), Pastorius's *Deliciæ Hortenses* (1982), Albertinus's *Verachtung dess Hoflebens* (1986), *Early and Miscellaneous Letters of J. W. Goethe* (1992), Carovè's *Kinderleben* (1995) and, along with James Hardin, volumes 90, 94, and 97 in the *Dictionary of Literary Biography*. His articles deal with Antonio de Guevara, Grimmelshausen, the picaresque, Johannes Scheffler, Lessing, Goethe, Sarah Austin, Schiller, Dorothea Schlegel, E. T. A. Hoffman, and Theodor Storm as well as with early German-American literature. He is currently preparing the edition of an anonymous 1783 pamphlet, entitled *Wahrheit und Guter Rath, an die Einwohner Deutschlands, besonders in Hessen*.

ANDREAS SOLBACH is Professor of German and Film and Theater Studies at the Johannes Gutenberg-Universität Mainz. He took his Ph.D. from Harvard University and has taught at Universität Dortmund and the University of Toronto. His work is mostly concentrated in the field of early modern literature, and includes the books *Gesellschaftsethik und Romantheorie, Evidentia und Erzähltheorie,* and *Johann Beer*. His other interests include narratology, film and theater studies, and cultural studies. One volume of studies in rhetoric and literature, a monograph on the early work of Anna Seghers, and on the rhetoric of unreliable narration is presently prepared for the press. Solbach is also the co-founder and president of the Internationale Andreas Gryphius-Gesellschaft.

LYNNE TATLOCK, Hortense and Tobias Lewin Distinguished Professor in the Humanities at Washington University in St. Louis, received her Ph.D. from Indiana University. She has published widely on German literature and culture from the seventeenth century to the present. Her research on seventeenth-century German letters has focused largely on the early novel and its reponses to, and participation in, contemporary events and social change. Her publications include *The Graph of Sex and the German Text: Gendered Culture in Early Modern Germany 1500-1700* (co-editor 1994), *Seventeenth-Century German* (editor, 1993), *Writing on the Line: Transgression in Early Modern German Literature* (editor, 1991), *Konstruktion: Untersuchungen zum Roman der Frühen Neuzeit* (editor, 1990), as well as articles on Catharina Regina von Greiffenberg and on the midwife Justine Siegemund.

ROSMARIE ZELLER is Professor für Neuere Deutsche Literatur at the University of Basel (Switzerland). Her Dr. phil. is from the University of Zürich, and her dissertation dealt with Harsdörffer. Her Habilitationsschrift on poetics of the drama was accepted at the University of Basel (1988). Her major publications deal with questions of genre in narrative literature of the seventeenth century, with Grimmelshausen, Knorr von Rosenroth, with the transmission of knowledge of the natural sciences in literary texts, and with the novel in Switzerland after 1945.

Index

Aaron (character), 348

Abisag, 365

Abrahanel, Jehuda. *See* Ebreo,
Leone

Abrahanel, Jizchaq, 106

Absolon, 368

Aceeeffghhiillmmnnoorrssstuu, 3

Ackley, Clifford S., 341

Adair, Monte, 250

Adam, 281

adaptations of Grimmelshausen's
works: *Wechsel des Glücks und
Unglücks* (1756), 30; *Der [. . .]
weltberufene Simplizius v.
Einfaltspinsel* (1790), 30

"Adjeu Welt," 31, 148, 312, 367

Albertinus, Aegidius, 16, 45, 100,
104, 147–56, 158–60, 365

Albertinus, Aegidius, works by:
*Christi vnsers Herrn Königreich
vnd Seelengejaidt,* 100; *Gusman
von Alfarche,* 45, 147, 150–56,
158–60; *Verachtung des
Hoflebens und Lob des
Landlebens,* 148

Albertus Julius, 239

Alciatus, Andreas, 105

Aleman, Mateo, 94, 147, 149–50,
152–53, 156, 158, 160–61

Aleman, Mateo, works by:
Guzmán de Alfarache, 147,
149–51, 158–61, 364

Alewyn, Richard, 372

Alfarche, 157

allegory and allegorical forms, 93–
142, 256

Allgemeine Literatur-Zeitung, 247

Almaeon, 287

Alsace, 359

Alt, Johannes, 6

Amadis, 148

Amazon, 69

Amelinde, 218–19, 360

America, 150, 186

Amsterdam, 120, 347

Anabaptists (Hungarian), 6–7, 52,
158, 314, 360

anagram, 4, 53–54, 216, 248,
352

Anderle, Jiri, 245

Andreae, Johann Valentin, 108

Andreae, Johann Valentin, works
by: *De Christiani Cosmoxeni
Genitvra, Ivdicium,* 107

Apollo, 120–21, 135

apophthegmata, 17

Aquarius, 138

Arabia, 57, 312

Aries, 175

Aristotle, 318

Arnim, Achim von, 242–43

Arnim, Achim von, works by:
Isabella von Ägypten, 242–43;
*Philander unter streifenden
Soldaten und Zigeunern,* 242

Asaneth, 214

Ashcroft, Jeffrey, 337

astrology and astrological
structure, 8, 12, 17–18, 93–
142, 189

Augsburg, 45

Augustine, St., 52, 104

Augustine, St., works by:
Confessions, 52

Avarus (or avarice), 53, 65–66,
74, 155, 313

Aylett, Robert P. T., 325–26

Babylon, whore of, 78, 104
Bacon, Francis, 189
Bacon, Francis, works by:
  *Von Unterhaltung und
  Gesprächen,* 189
Baden, 257
Bakhtin, 306
Baldanders, 314, 372
Banquo, 370
Barclay, John, 347
Barclay, John, works by:
  Argenis, 347
Bärenhäuter, Der (opera), 244
Barlach, Ernst, 245
Baroque literature, 1, 15, 46, 52,
  93, 95, 314, 359, 361, 371
Basilia, 221–22
Basle, 132, 173, 177
Battafarano, Italo Michele, 18,
  33, 182
Bauer, Barbara, 181–82, 244
Baumann, Hans, 244
Baumann, Hans, works by:
  *Der Bärenhäuter: Ein
  Soldatenspiel,* 244
Bayreuth, 251
Beau Alman (Beau Alleman)
  [= Simplicius Simplicissimus],
  6, 74, 157, 236
Becher, Johannes R., 246
Becher, Johannes R., works by:
  Grimmelshausen 1625–1676,
  246
Bechtold, Artur, 248
Becker-Cantarino, Barbara, 272
Beer, Johann, 162, 236–37, 252–
  53, 273, 372
Beer, Johann, works by:
  Kurzweilige Sommertäge, 237;
  Narren-Spital, 237; *Pokazi,*
  236; *Simplicianischer Welt-
  Kucker,* 236, 273; *Teutsche*

Winternächte, 237; *Weiber-
  Heckel,* 236
Beer, Johann Christoph, 37, 233
Bella, 242
Bender, Wolfgang, 26, 39, 249
Benjamin (brother of Joseph),
  216
Benjamin, Walter, 339–40
Berberi, 36
Berghaus, 7, 9–10, 17
Berlin, 248, 255
Berns, Jörg Jochen, 167, 170,
  344, 346–49
Bible, 98–100, 158; Old
  Testament, 98, 240; New
  Testament, 98, 333
Bibliothek des Literarischen
  Vereins (Stuttgart), 26
Bircher, Martin, 245, 336
Birken, Sigmund von, 29, 251
Bismarck-Schönhausen, Otto von,
  9
Black Forest, 97, 132, 185
Blankenburg, Friedrich von, 253
Bobertag, Felix, 25, 34, 249
Bohemia, 68–69
Book of Nature (*Buch der Natur*),
  57, 98, 100
Borcherdt, Hans Heinrich, 26,
  33–34, 248–49, 256
Bornemann, Ernest, 283
Brandsteller, Christian, 180, 184–
  87
Brecht, Bertold, 245
Brecht, Bertold, works by:
  *Mutter Courage und ihre
  Kinder,* 245–46
Breisach, 131–32
Brentano, Clemens, 241, 243–44
Brentano, Clemens, works by:
  *Geschichte und Ursprung des
  ersten Bärnhäuters,* 243;
  *Märchen von dem Schulmeister
  Klopstock,* 241 (*see also Zeitung
  für Einsiedler*)

Breslau, 252
Breuer, Dieter, 18, 27, 34–38, 177, 187, 201, 249, 256, 286–87, 316
Breughel, Pieter, 99, 105
Breward, Christopher, 301, 303, 306
Breyl, Jutta, 347
Brockhaus (publisher), 248
Brown, Judith C., 322
Bruck, Arthur Moeller van den, 255
de Bry (brothers), 239
Buchholtz, Andreas Heinrich, 16
Buchner, August, 100
Bullough, Bonnie, 318–19, 321
Bullough, Vern L., 318–19, 321, 323
Bülow, Karl Eduard von, 3, 25, 31, 248
Bundespost, Deutsche, 8
Burda, Franz (publisher), 258
Bürger, Thomas, 249
Burgundy, 80
Busch, Walter, 301
Busse, Erich, 256, 258

Calderón le la Barca, Pedro, 147
Calderón le la Barca, Pedro, works by: La vida es sueño, 147
calendar, 17–18
calendar, Roman, 170–71, 177
calendar stories. See Kalendergeschichten
Canard, Monsieur, 234
Capricorn, 137–38
Capuchins, 251
Carbonnel, Yves, 304, 307, 313, 317
Carpathian Mountains, 238
Cassirer, Ernst, 110
Castore, Vigilio, 349
Catholicism and Roman Catholic Church, 2, 9–10, 33, 71, 99, 156, 174, 211–12, 224, 251, 254, 312, 360, 365
Cavallaro, Dani, 303, 306
Cervantes Saavedra, Miguel de, 106, 148, 153
Cervantes Saavedra, Miguel de, works by: Don Quijote, 148, 153, 158; Rinconete y Cortadillo, 153
Chaldean system of planets, 7, 139, 142
Charles V, Emperor, 148
Chaucer, Geoffrey, 370
chronogram, 169
Chronos, 127
Circe, 100
Claasen, Udo, 245
Clauss, Max, 257
Clauss, Max, works by: Simplicius Simplicissimus, 257
clothes or clothing, 18, 157
Coler, Johann, 171
Colleville, Maurice, 250
Cologne, 7, 123, 133, 244, 373
Conigliani, Camilla, 250
Constance, 38
Constance, Lake, 26
constancy, 7
Constantinople, 238
converso, 156
copperplate engravings, 8, 13, 18, 28, 32–33, 35, 94, 142, 154, 233, 272, 333–53, 364
Cornelis von Harlem, Jean, 316, 325–26
Cornelius, 242–43
Coryphaea, 373
Cotta (publisher), 243; Morgenblatt für gebildete Stände, 243
Counterreformation, 150
Courasche (Courage), 10–12, 14, 46, 49–50, 52–56, 66–78, 81–83, 94–95, 103, 128, 138, 150–51, 159–61, 242, 271–72,

273, 275, 278–85, 287–88, 348, 366, 370
Craik, Jennifer, 300, 304
Creidius, Hartmann, 101, 104, 109
Creidius, Hartmann, works by: *Danck- Buß- vnd Bet-Altar,* 101, 109
Croats or Croatians, 138, 309, 311
Cupid, 371
cycle of novels, 1, 8, 11–12, 45, 47, 49–51, 53–57, 64, 66–67, 74, 77–78, 82–84, 96, 103, 108–9, 111, 127, 170, 201–2, 220, 232, 234–35, 256, 347–48
Cyprus, 238
Cysarz, Herbert, 255

Dame World, 71–73, 103, 275, 371
Danes, 76
Dante Alighieri, 139
Dante Alighieri, works by: *Divina Commedia,* 99
Daston, Lorraine, 324
David, 16, 207–8, 210, 362, 364
Defoe, Daniel, 239, 372
Defoe, Daniel, works by: *Robinson Crusoe,* 30, 239, 253
Dekker, Rudolf M., 321–22
Delrio, Antonio Martino, 71
Delrio, Antonio Martino, works by: *Disquisitiones Magicae,* 71
Democritus, 48
Dèttore, Ugo, 250
Deuteronomy, 321
Deutscher Klassiker Verlag, 27, 34
dialect (Nürnberg), 232
dialect (Upper Hessian), 232
Dietwalt, 218–19, 360, 368
Dietzin, Justina, 161
docere et delectare, 202

Domagalla, Leo, 137
Don Buscon, 231
dtv (publisher), 33
Duncan, 370
Duncker, Albert, 257
Dürer, Albrecht, 7

Ebreo, Leone, 106–7
Ebreo, Leone, works by: *Dialoghi d'amore,* 106–7
Echtermeyer, Theodor, 3–4, 248
Egypt, 14, 238
Eichenberg, Fritz, 245
Eichendorff, Joseph, Freiherr von, 241
Eichendorff, Joseph, Freiherr von, works by: *Ahnung und Gegenwart,* 241–42; *Dichter und ihre Gesellen,* 242; *Eine Meerfahrt,* 242
Einsiedeln, 60, 97, 311–12
Eisenbart, Liselotte Constanze, 302, 321
Elias, Norbert, 300
Elter, Johann Burkhard von, 2
emblems, 96, 142, 337–38
Endinger Forest, 118, 131
Endter (publisher), 231–32
England, 300, 317, 321, 323–24, 341
Enlightenment, 93–94, 107, 240–41, 252, 361
Entwhistle, Joanne, 299, 302, 304–5, 317–18, 323–24
Entwicklungsroman, 7, 51, 59
Enzensberger, Hans Magnus, 254
epics, 1
epigram, 189
Eraclitus, 48
Erasmus von Rotterdam, 46
Erauso, Catalina de, 318
Erbauunsgroman, 202, 206
Erler-Samaden, Erich, 245
Eros, 67

Eschenbach, Wolfram von, 1, 8, 16, 255
Eschenbach, Wolfram von, works by: *Parzival*, 8, 16, 255
Eskimo, 269
Essarts, Herberay des, 147
Ettner von Eiteritz, Johann Christoph, 252, 281
Ettner von Eiteritz, Johann Christoph, works by: *Der unwürdige Doktor*, 252; *Der verwegene Chirurgus*, 252
Eulenspiegel, 243
Eulenspiegel, Till, 363
Europe, 12, 52, 54, 57–58, 63–64, 68, 84, 162, 240–41, 274, 307, 315–18, 321–22, 324
Eurydice, 319

Faber du Faur, Curt von, 5, 7, 146, 197–99
fairy tale, 13
Falk, Adalbert, 9
Falsetta rediviva inpunita, 239
Falsette, 239
Falsette, 239
Fechner, Jörg-Ulrich, 31
Feldges, Matthias, 100, 103
Feldman, Linda Ellen, 348–49
Felssecker, Adam Jonathan (grandson of Wolff Eberhard), 29, 235
Felssecker, Johann Jonathan (son of Wolff Eberhard), 29, 235
Felssecker, Wolff Eberhard, 5, 25, 27–30, 39, 231–36, 246, 254, 336, 347
feminism, 18
Fénélon, François, 220
Fénélon, François, works by: *Télémaque*, 220
Ficino, Marsilio, 106
Fillion, Johann, 27
First World War, 33, 255, 258
Florence (Florentine), 106

fool, 5–7, 113
Fortuna (Fortune), 133, 209, 275
Foucault, 306
France, 16, 31, 64, 218, 237–38, 300
Franciscans, 148
Francisci, Erasmus, 180
Franck, Sebastian, 45
Frankfurt, 26, 97, 236, 244, 246, 249
"Frauenfeindlichkeit," 11
Freytag, Gustav, 98
frontispiece. *See* copperplate engravings
Fuchshaim, Melchior Sternfels von, 4, 10, 30, 53–54, 152, 157, 182, 246
furor poeticus, 103, 207

Gaede, Friedrich, 369
Gaisbach, 2, 258, 363
Ganymed, 105
Garber, Marjorie, 280, 302–5, 307, 317, 319, 321–24
Garzoni, Tomaso, 103–4, 171–72, 174, 176–77, 179–82, 185, 187, 203
Garzoni, Tomaso, works by: *Piazza Universale* (*Allgemeiner Schauplatz*), 14, 97, 100, 171, 180–81, 203
Gauckel-Tasche, 371
Gelnhausen, 2, 15, 257–58, 359
Gemini, 132, 134
gender, construction of, 18
Genesis (Bible), 281
Genuth, Sara Schechner, 181
German (language), 14, 168
Germania, 9
Germanists, early, 3
Germany, 6–7, 33, 162, 180, 256, 270, 300, 307, 312, 320, 341
Gersch, Hubert, 93–94, 302
Gesprächspiel, 13, 188, 273, 286

Goethe, Johann Wolfgang von, 1,
29, 38, 253, 255, 258
Goethe, Johann Wolfgang von,
works by: *Faust,* 255; *Hans
Wursts Hochzeit oder der Lauf
der Welt,* 253; *Leiden des
jungen Werthers,* 29, 38
Golden Age (of Dutch painting),
99
Golden Age (of Spanish
Literature), 147
Goldschmitt, Bruno, 245
Gonella, 231
Gongora, Luis de, 147–48
Gongora, Luis de, works by: *Las
soledades,* 148
Goodrick, Alfred Thomas, 250
Gorgias, 204
Gorgo, 107
Göttingen, 253
Gottsched, Johann Christoph,
246, 252
Gottsched, Johann Christoph,
works by: *Critische Dichtkunst,*
252; *Die Vernünftigen
Tadlerinnen,* 252
Gracián, Baltasar, 148
Gracián, Baltasar, works by: *El
criticón,* 148
Grass, Günter, 162, 246
Grass, Günter, works by: *Die
Blechtrommel,* 162; *Das Treffen
in Telgte,* 246
Greece, 97
Greene, Shannon Keenan, 8, 18
Greif[e]nson, 4, 236, 251–53
Grellmann, Heinz Moritz, 172
Griesshaber-Weninger, Christl,
286
Grillandus, Erasmus (pseud.), 238
Grillandus, Erasmus (pseud.),
works by: *Der Politische . . .
Simplicianische Hasen-Kopff,*
238
Grimm Brothers, 243

Grimm Brothers, works by: *Der
Bärenhäuter,* 243; *Kinder- und
Hausmärchen,* 243; *Der Teufel
Grünrock,* 243; *Des Teufels
rußiger Bruder,* 243
Grimmelshausen (town), 258
Grimmelshausen, Johann Jacob
Christoffel von, discussion of
editions and translations, 246–
51; list of critical editions, 39–
41; list of first editions and
translations, xi–xiv
Grimmelshausen, Johann Jacob
Christoffel von, works by:
*Der Abenteuerliche Simpli-
cissimus Teutsch,* 1–11, 13,
17–18, 25–35, 37–38, 45–
48, 53–54, 56–57, 59, 61,
65–67, 76–77, 79, 93, 95–
97, 99, 103, 111, 113, 115,
118, 123–24, 127, 133, 135,
138–39, 141, 147, 150, 152–
56, 158–61, 167, 169, 184–
85, 201–3, 207, 216–17,
231–37, 239–41, 244–45,
247–48, 251–57, 269–70,
272, 274–75, 278, 280, 284,
289, 299–328, 332 (copperplate), 333–34, 336, 338–39,
342–44, 347–48, 351, 360,
362, 364, 367, 371–73
Anhang, 235
Bartkrieg, 13, 235, 365
Beernhäuter, 12, 170, 239,
242–43, 245, 345
Continuatio, 26–27, 33–36, 45,
47–48, 54, 56–59, 65, 77,
79, 101, 105, 128, 155–56,
158, 161, 186, 202, 233,
239, 242, 253–54, 301–2,
312–13, 315–16, 325, 334,
347, 365, 371
Courasche, 10–14, 18, 26, 32–
33, 35, 38, 44 (copperplate),
45, 49, 52, 54–56, 67, 77,

79, 94, 96, 103, 110, 124, 138, 147, 152, 159, 161, 170, 185, 202, 234–35, 239, 242, 245, 247, 251–53, 272–73, 278–82, 284, 337–38, 348–50, 366, 369, 372

Dietwalt und Amelinde, 15–16, 35, 201–2, 216–18, 220, 222, 224

Ewig-während er Calender, 7, 13, 17, 27, 38–39, 101, 105, 107, 110, 121–23, 125, 128–30, 132, 136–37, 166 (copperplate), 167–90, 196–99 (sample pages), 231, 232, 235, 252, 370

Extract, 235

Galgen-Männlin, 14, 170, 242, 252

Gaukel-Tasche, 7, 12–13, 170, 345

Keuscher Joseph, 14–15, 35, 38, 114, 135, 201–3, 205, 207, 212–13, 215–18, 224, 235, 240, 252–53, 351, 363

Keuscher Joseph, translations of, into Swedish, 15

Musai, 14, 39, 201, 235

Proximus und Lympida, 15–16, 200 (copperplate), 201, 216–18, 220, 222, 224, 347, 367

Rathstübel Plutonis, 13, 16, 38, 242, 273, 275, 281, 286–90, 347–48, 359, 361, 373

Ratio Status, 16–17, 202, 207, 209, 211–13, 216, 218, 222, 224, 228 (copperplate), 345, 359, 362, 364–65, 368

Satyrischer Pilgram, 14, 45, 47, 202–5, 207–8, 211–16, 218, 222, 224, 251–53, 345, 359

Simplicissimus Redivivus, 92, 298 (copperplate)

Springinsfeld, 8, 11–12, 14, 18, 26, 32, 45, 48, 50, 52, 54,

56, 68, 77–79, 82–83, 127–28, 147, 152, 159–61, 170, 185, 202, 234, 242, 245, 247, 268 (copperplate), 272–73, 276, 278, 282–87, 297 (copperplate), 339, 342–45, 348, 361, 366, 372

Stoltzer Melcher, 13

Teutscher Michel, 13–14, 29, 234, 335, 359, 373

Verkehrte Welt, 13, 252, 336, 359, 362

Wunderbarliches Vogelnest (I and / or II), 11–13, 26, 29, 34–35, 45, 47, 50, 55, 66, 74, 83, 101–3, 105, 111, 116, 119, 121, 123–24, 139, 146 (copperplate), 170, 234–35, 237, 245, 252, 345–46, 363, 366, 372

Grimmelshausen-Festtage, 257

Grimmelshausen-Freunde, 258

Grimmelshausen-Gesellschaft e.V., 256

Grimmelshausen-Gesprächsrunde, 258

Grimmelshausen-Literaturpreis, 258

"Grimmelshausen money" (illustration), 265

Grimmelshausen-Runde, 256, 258

Gruenter, Rainer, 300

Grufensholm, Erich Stainfels von, 4

Gryphius, Andreas, 349, 367

Gryphius, Andreas, works by: *Catharina von Georgien,* 349–50

Gueintz, Christian, 27

Guevara, Antonio de, 31, 148

Guevara, Antonio de, works by: *Menosprecio de corte y alabanza de aldea,* 148. *See also* "Adjeu Welt"

Guinea, 33
Gundolf, Friedrich, 255
Guru, E. G., 250
Gusman, 153–55, 157, 159–61, 231
Gusmändl, 157
Guzmán, 161
Guzman, Don Iohan de, 157

Haberkamm, Klaus, 7–8, 10, 17–18, 32, 38, 95, 102, 105–6, 169, 173, 178
Habersetzer, Karl Heinz, 8, 345–46
Haken, [Johann] Christian Ludwig, 30–31, 241, 254
Haken, [Johann] Christian Ludwig, works by: *Der Held des neunzehnten Jahrhunderts,* 241
Halfter, Fritz, 346, 350
Hamburg, 236
Hanau, 5, 124, 135–38, 141, 154, 156–58, 244, 269, 303–4, 308–9, 311, 313, 315, 323, 361
Happel, Eberhard Werner, 239–40
Happel, Eberhard Werner, works by: *Grösseste Denckwürdigkeiten der Welt,* 240
Harlem. *See* Cornelis von Harlem, Jean
Harsdörffer, Georg Philipp, 11, 13–14, 100, 180, 286–87, 333, 336
Harsdörffer, Georg Philipp, works by: *Frauenzimmer Gesprächspiele,* 286–87, 333, 336
Hartmann, Johann Ludwig, 252
Hartmann, Karl Amadeus, 244
Hartmann, Karl Amadeus, works by: *Des Simplicius Simplicissimus Jugend,* 244
Hassenpflug, 4

Hayens, Kenneth, 368
Hayn, Johann Rosenbach vom, 17, 114, 118, 171, 176, 179–80, 182, 185
Hayn, Johann Rosenbach vom, works by: *Astrologia naturalis,* 181; *Stern-Kunst,* 114
hedgehog, 124
Hegenbarth, Josef, 245
Heidelberg, 243
Heiligenvitae, 52
Heisig, Bernhard, 245
Helikanus, 241
Heliodor, 190
Henninger, Catharina, 2
Hercules, 102, 108
Hermes, 121
hermit, 5–6
Hertenfels, Simon Leugfrisch von, 4
Herzbruder, 60, 62–63, 97, 113–18, 124, 126–35, 138, 140, 158, 276, 304, 306, 311
Herzog August Bibliothek, Wolfenbüttel, 44, 92, 166, 196, 200, 228, 268, 297–98, 332
Heselhaus, Clemens, 95–97, 99, 108
Hess, Peter, 18
Hesselmann, Peter, 96, 100, 104, 235–37, 247, 250–51
Hessia, 2, 257
Hieronymus. *See* Jerome, St.
Hildebrand, Wolfgang, 129, 134, 181
Hildebrand, Wolfgang, works by: *Planeten-Buch,* 181
Hindemith, Paul, 244
Hirschfeld, Samuel Greiffnsohn von, 4, 15, 362
Historie von dem keuschen Jüngling Joseph in einer Comödie vorgestellet, 240
Hobbes, Thomas, 369
Hoffmann (publisher), 232

Hoffmann von Hofmannswaldau, Christian, 365
"höfisch-historischer Roman," 15, 189–90, 201
Hohengeroldseck, Schloß, 344, 357 (illustration)
Hohoff, Curt, 362
Hölderlin, Friedrich, 255
Holland. *See* Netherlands
Holland, Wilhelm Ludwig, 25, 248–49
Hollander, Anne, 303
Holy Land, 238, 314
Homer, 46, 99
Honoria, 16, 221–22
Horace, 345–46
Horace, works by: A*rs poetica,* 345
Hotchkiss, Valerie R., 306, 321, 323
Hugenfels, Israel Fromschmidt von, 4
Hull, Isabel V., 319–20
Humanism, 94
humility, 15
Hungary, 238
Hunziker, Max, 245

Ida, 242
"Idealroman," 15
inconstancy, 7
Indagine, Johannes von. *See* Hayn, Johann Rosenbach vom
Index librorum prohibitorum, 10
Indian Ocean, 53
Ingen, Ferdinand van, 169
Italy, 7, 152

Jäger von Soest [= Simplicius Simplicissimus], 5–6, 66, 75, 118, 124, 157, 257, 276, 278, 301, 306–8
Jäger von Werl [= Olivier], 118, 124, 306, 308

Jahrbuch, Grosses astrologisches, 231
Jäjerken, det [= Simplicius Simplicissimus], 157
Janco (and Janko), 54, 56, 68
Jauss, Hans Robert, 109
Jensen, Anton, 242
Jerome, St., 104
Jerusalem, 10, 46, 150
Jesuits, 71, 104, 148
Jew or Wandering Jew, 55, 106, 153, 156, 287, 313–14, 361
Joab, 16, 207–8, 362, 364, 368
Jöcher, Christian Gottlieb, 252–53
Jöcher, Christian Gottlieb, works by: *Allgemeines Gelehrten-Lexikon,* 252–53
Jonathan, 16, 207–8, 362, 364
Jones, Ann Rosalind, 318–19, 324
Jöns, Dietrich, 101, 105
Joseph (Gen., v. 37–50), 14–15
Joseph (figure in the novel), 114, 202, 213–16, 219, 352
Josephus, Flavius, 209
Judson, J. Richard, 341
Julus (or extravagance), 26, 36, 53, 65, 74, 155, 313
Jupiter, 5, 7, 97, 107, 120–24, 127, 130–31, 133, 135, 137, 139–42, 158, 240–41, 254–55, 309, 361
Justina Dietzin Picara, 150

Kalendargeschichten, 17, 93, 167, 188
Kamimura, Kiyonobu, 250
Kästner, Abraham Gotthelf, 253
Keller, Adalbert von, 26, 249
Kelletat, Alfred, 32–36
Kempis, Thomas à, 206
Kempis, Thomas à, works by: *Imitatio Christi,* 206
Kepler, Johannes, 130

Kepler, Johannes, works by:
  Prognosticum, 130
Kerner, Justinus, 244
Kerner, Justinus, works by: *Der
  Bärenhäuter im Salzbade: Ein
  Schattenspiel,* 244
Kiel, 252
Kipling, Rudyard, 367
Kircher, Athanasius, 104
Kircher, Athanasius, works by:
  Oedipus Aegyptiacus, 104
Kladderadatsch, 10
Klee, Johann Ludwig, 3–4
Klemm, Walter, 245
Kley, Henrich, 250
Klinger, Max, 245
Klinger, Max, works by:
  Intermezzi, 245
Knab, Armin, 242
Knan, 5, 35, 48–49, 59, 77, 126,
  138, 178–80, 184–87, 232,
  338, 368
Knopf, Jan, 94
Knopf, Ludwig, 167
Koch, Erduin Julius, 253
Koch, Erduin Julius, works by:
  *Compendium der Deutschen
  Literatur-Geschichte,* 253
Koeman, Jakob, 240, 243
Kögel, Rudolf, 25, 249
Kolbenheyer, Erwin Guido, 33
"Komm Trost der Nacht," 35,
  241–42, 248, 360
König, Robert, 254–55
König, Robert, works by: *Deutsche
  Litteraturgeschichte,* 254
Könnecke, Gustav, 13, 137, 258
Koreans, 312
Kornmann, Heinrich, 108–9
Kornmann, Heinrich, works by:
  Mons Veneris, 108
Koschlig, Manfred, 29, 37, 232–
  33, 248, 252, 256, 336
Kraaz, Gerhart, 245
Kristeva, 306

Küffer, Johann (the Younger), 3
Kugelmann, 231
Kulturkampf, 9, 33
Kurth-Voigt, Lieselotte E., 30
Kurz, Heinrich, 25, 34, 249
Kurz, Hermann, 3, 248

Laquer, Thomas W., 318
Lateinschule, 2
Latin, 2, 179
Lauremberg, Johann, 180
Lazarillo, 148–49, 151, 157, 161
Lazarillo de Tormes, 45, 148–49,
  151, 157
Lázaro. *See* Lazarillo
Lehmann, Christoph, 306
Leibniz, Gottfried Wilhlem, 93,
  252
Leipzig, 27, 246–48, 251
Leipzig, University of, 107
Lemke, Gerhard, 8
Leontin, 242
Lesage, Alain René, 253
Lesage, Alain René, works by: *Gil
  Blas,* 253
Lessing, Gottfried Ephraim, 30,
  253
Libuschka (*see also* Courasche),
  49, 56, 68, 72, 77
Lippstadt, 32, 111, 125, 133,
  141, 158
literature, classical (antiquity), 2
literature, classical (German), 1
literature, medieval, 1
literature, world, 1, 45, 93
littera Pythagorae. See Y-sign
locus amoena, 290
locus terribilis, 349
Logau, Friedrich von, 306
Lope de Vega, Felix, 147
López de Úbeda, Francisco, 94,
  151, 161
López de Úbeda, Francisco,
  works by: *Pícara Justina,* 94,
  151, 161; translations of, into

German (*see Justina Dietzin Picara*)
Lorenz, 237
Lorraine, 80
Lorris, Guillaume de, 109
Lorris, Guillaume de, works by: *Rosenroman,* 109
Louis XIV (France), 13
Louvre, 111
Löwenhalt, Johann Rompler von, 2
Lucifer, 53, 65, 74, 155
Ludwig, 237
Lugowski, Clemens, 256
Luther, Martin, 98–99, 272
Lützen, Battle of, 361
Luxembourg, 80
Lycosthenes, Conrad Wolfhardt, 177
Lycosthenes, Conrad Wolfhardt, works by: *Prodigiorum ac ostentorum Chronicum* [Book of Miracles], 177
Lydia, 36
Lympida, 16, 223–24, 371

Machiavelli, 16, 64, 133, 207, 209–10, 213–14, 219, 364, 367
Macke, August, 245
Madagascar, 314
Madrid, 157, 159
Magdeburg, 62, 114, 127, 131–33, 138, 277, 305, 321
magic, 14
mandrake root, 14, 242
Mann, Thomas, 162, 203, 246
Mann, Thomas, works by: *Doktor Faustus,* 246; *Felix Krull,* 162; *Joseph und seine Brüder,* 203
Manzù, Giacomo, 258
Marcus Aurelius, 148
Mars, 7, 60, 67, 96, 108–9, 120–22, 139, 141
Martí, Juan, 147, 149–50, 152

Martyrologium, 173
Mathusalem, 373
Matthäus, Klaus, 171
Matthew, Gospel of, 102
Medusa, 278
Meer, Theo van der, 324
mehrfacher Schriftsinn, 95–99, 101–4, 107
Meid, Volker, 2, 8, 11, 15, 17, 33, 248, 254–55
Meiningen, 258
Meisterlied, 217
Meistersinger, 37
Melanchthon, Philipp, 2
Melcher, 13, 186
Melusine, 283
memento mori, 99
Mendelssohn, Arnold, 244
Menhennet, Alan, 18, 335, 337, 342, 344, 362–63
Mercury, 7, 67, 121, 123, 127–35, 139–41
Merode-Brüder, 131–32, 134–35, 159, 366
Meron, Simon, 315, 334
Messmahl, Signeur, 4
Meuder, 5, 77, 126, 185–87, 232
Meusebach, Karl Hartwig Gregor von, 3–4
Mexía, Petrus, 178, 181, 188–89
Mexía, Petrus, works by: *Silva de varia leccion,* 178, 181, 188
Meyer, Elard Hugo, 9, 33
Michelangelo, 105
Michelangelo, works by: Cavalieri papers, 105
Michelsen, Peter, 169
Middle Ages, 16, 93–95, 98, 122, 321
migrations, great (Völkerwanderungen), 16
Miki, Nikada, 250
Milan, 80
Milton, John, 139
Minolanda, 283

Mirandola, Pico della, 106
miscellanies, 188–89
Mochizuki, Ichie, 250
Modestus, 16, 221–23, 367
Modestus (the younger), 221
Momus, 204–5, 215
Moi, Toril, 271
Mongol, 269
Monpelgart, 27
Montaigne, Michel, 305
Montalvo, 147
Montalvo, works by: *Amadís de Gaula,* 147
Moon, 7, 121, 139–40, 174
Mooskopf, 258
Morgenblatt für gebildete Stände. See Cotta (publisher)
Morhof, Daniel Georg, 252
Morhof, Daniel Georg, works by: *Unterricht von der Teutschen Sprache und Poesie,* 252
Moscherosch, Johann Michael, 3, 8, 14, 148, 240, 242, 272, 278, 359, 372
Moscherosch, Johann Michael, works by: *Gesichte Philanders von Sittewald,* 8, 148, 240, 242, 359; *Insomnis Parentum,* 278
Moscherosch, Quirin, 29, 251
Moscow, 309
Motte-Foque, Friedrich de la, 242
Motte-Foque, Friedrich de la, works by: *Das Galgenmännlein,* 242
Müller, Ernst E., 26–27, 37
Müller, Georg, 25, 27, 38, 336
Müller, Klaus-Detlev, 157, 308, 312–13, 317
Müller-Seidel, Walter, 108–9, 371
Mummelsee, 6–7, 112, 158, 161, 184, 252, 258
Munich, 45, 147, 244, 252, 344, 357; Bayerisches Hauptstaatsarchiv, 344, 357
Munns, Jessica, 300–301

Münster in Westphalia, 139, 256
Murdock, Graeme, 317
Musai, 14, 114, 214–16

"Nachtigallen-Lied." *See* "Komm Trost der Nacht"
Napoleon, 31, 241, 254
narrative stance, 4, 8, 46, 49–51, 53–59, 61, 63–66, 74, 78–79, 120, 325
National Socialists, 255–58
Near East, 152
Negus, Ken, 288
Neri, Bianca Maria, 300, 311, 316
nest, bird's, 12
Netherlands, 13, 80, 120, 147, 237, 300, 324
Neudrucke deutscher Literaturwerke, 26–27
Neville, Henry, 239
Neville, Henry, works by: *The Isle of Pines,* 239
Newton, Sir Isaac, 93
Nibelungenlied, 1
Nielsen, Morton, 15
Niemeyer Verlag, 34, 39
Nizami (Persian poet), 139
Noehles, Gisela, 250, 342, 344
Nördlingen, Battle of, 359, 369
Norrköping, 251
Nosce te ipsum, 5, 312, 360
novel, relationship of, to biography, 45–84
novel, structure of the, 5–8, 10, 12, 217
Nürnberg (Nuremberg), 14, 25, 27, 37, 100, 235, 251, 286

Oakley, Ann, 318
Oberkirch(en), 2, 56, 84, 258
Odysseus, 100, 214
Offenburg, 2, 256, 258
Ohly, Friedrich, 98, 108–9
Olearius, Adam, 14

Olivier, 17, 32, 53, 61–66, 74–
75, 80, 116–18, 127–34, 140,
159, 366
Onuphrius, St., 316
Opitz, Martin, 100, 347
ordo, 72
Orgel, Stephen, 318, 321
Orontaeus, 223
Orpheus, 156, 319
Ortenau, 258
Otto, 242
Ottoman Empire, 16, 238
Ovid, 99

Paas, John Roger, 8, 341
Palatinate, Prince Elector of the,
251
Palma Josephina, 336
Pan (mythological god), 346
Paradeis and paradise, 52, 58,
156–57, 237, 315
Paris, 6, 28, 32, 111, 125, 141,
156–57, 239, 319–20, 322,
326, 370
Park, Katharine, 324
Parliament, Prussian (Landtag), 9,
32, 255
Pasch, Georg, 252
Passow, Wilhelm Arthur, 3–4,
257
Paul, works by: *Epistle to the
Corinthians* (I), 273; *Epistle to
the Galatians,* 98
Pencz, Georg, 7
Penkert, Sibylle, 8, 250, 337–38,
351
Pérez, Andreas, works by: *Pícara
Justina,* 10, 110
Perry, Mary Elizabeth, 318
Perseus, 107
perspectives. *See* narrative stance
Perus, Jan, 231
Petersen, Julius, 255–56
Petrat, Gerhardt, 171
pharaoh, 14, 214–15

phoenix, 333, 335–36, 340, 343–
52
Phyllis, 281
picaresque novels and picaresque
tradition, 1, 4, 8, 10, 45, 52,
71, 76, 94, 119, 140, 147–62,
189, 202, 217, 237, 239, 253,
270, 278, 280, 305, 346, 352
Pisces, 139
planets and planetary structure, 7–
8, 13, 17–18
Plato, 100, 106, 204
Plato, works by: *Gorgias,* 204
Pliny, 243
Pliny, works by: *Historia
naturalis,* 243
Plutarch, 108
Plutarch, works by: *de audienda
Poetica,* 108
Pol, van de, Lotte C., 321–22
Politicus, 231
Portugal, 55, 106
Potiphar, 214
Praetorius, Johannes, 14, 251
Prague, 238–39
Printz, Wolfgang Caspar, 252
Procopius von Templin, 251
Procopius von Templin, works by:
Encaeniale, 251; *Patrociniale,*
251
prodesse et delectare, 206, 272
Prophecy and prophecy motif, 8,
93–42
Proximus, 16, 220–24, 360, 367
Prussia, 10
pseudonym, 4
Pufendorf, Samuel von, 270, 272
Puritan revolution, 65

Quevedo y Villegas, Francisco de,
59, 148, 150
Quevedo y Villegas, Francisco de,
works by: *Los sueños,* 148; *La
vida del buscón,* 148, 150
Quijote, Don, 34

Raidas, 257
Ramsey, Governor, of Hanau, 5,
136, 158, 303, 308, 335
ratio status, 207–15, 218–19
Raudszus, Gabriele, 304, 311,
315, 326
Rebhu, Jan, 236
Reclam, Philipp jun. (publisher),
33, 38
Reformation, 14
Rehder, Helmut, 7, 134, 139
Reichard, Heinrich, 246
Renaissance, 99, 106, 318
Renchen, 3–4, 56, 61, 230, 255,
257–58, 265–66, 362–63
Reuter, Christian, 162, 243
Reuter, Christian, works by:
Schelmuffsky, 162, 243
Revolution, French, 240
Revolution, Industrial, 301
Revolution of 1848, 257
Rhine, Upper, 56, 63, 77, 132
Richards, Penny, 300–301
Riehl, Wilhelm Heinrich, 242
Riemer, Johann (*see* Grillandus,
Erasmus), 238
Rist, Johann, 180, 183
Rist, Johann, works by: *Märtzens-
Unterredungen,* 180, 183
Robin Hood, 367
Rohner, Jan, 167
Roman Empire, Eastern, 16
Romanticism and Romantic
authors, 3, 31, 236, 240–48,
253–54
Rosenau, Ferdinand, 242
Rosenau, Ferdinand, works by:
Vizlipuzli, 242
Rosenfeld, Hellmut, 346
Rosgarten (publisher), 38
Rosinante, 34
Rothenburg, 252
Ruben (brother of Joseph), 213
Rubens, Peter Paul, 341
Russia, 184, 309

"Rüstige, der." *See* Rist, Johann

Sabina, 157, 276
Sabud, 207, 364–65
Sachs, Hans, 14, 217
Sagittarius, 137
Saine, Thomas, 29
St. Victor, Hugo von, 104
Salamanca, 149
Salomon, Temple of, 104
Salzburg, 251
Samuel, 209
Saracenus (Sarasin), Johannes
Carolus, 107
satire, 6
Saturn, 7, 109, 121, 125, 127–
31, 135, 137–41
Saudi Arabia, 238
Sauerbruch, Hans, 245
Sauerbrunnen, 61, 97, 184–85
Saul, 16, 207–10, 362, 364
Savoy, 80
Schade, Richard E., 319–20, 342,
346, 349
Schäfer, Walter Ernst, 217, 346
Schauenburg, Hans Reinhard
von, 2
Schauenburg, Maria Dorothea
von, 15
Schauenburg, Philipp Hannibal
von, 15
Schauenburg family, 258
Scheiding, Fritz, 242
Schermesser, 301–2, 320, 371
Schielen, Johann Georg, 237
Schielen, Johann Georg, works
by: *Deß Französischen Kriegs-
Simplicissimi Lebens-Lauff,* 237
Schiller, Friedrich von, 1, 106
Schloß Hoya, 73, 76
Schmidt-Wolfratshausen, Kare,
245
Scholasticism, 95, 100
Schnabel, Johann Gottfried, 239

Schnabel, Johann Gottfried, works by: *Wunderliche Fata* [= *Insel Felsenburg*], 239
Schöne, Albrecht, 337–38
Schöninghs deutsche Textausgaben, 32
Scholte, Jan Hendrik, 6, 26, 35–38, 169, 233, 235, 248–50, 256, 346
Schorlemer-Alst, Baron von, 9–10
Schottelius, Justus Georg, 100
Schrepffeisen, 13, 231
Schulz-Behrend, Georg, 250
Schupp, Johann Balthasar, 372
Schweitzer, Christoph E., 11, 18
secularization, tendency toward, 104, 107
Sedlmayr, Hans, 99, 105
Sekora, John, 304
Selicha, 213–14
Sehmsdorff, Michael Reculin von, 4, 53
Selhammer, Christian, 251
sensus duplex, 95–96, 98, 100, 105–6, 110, 112
Sephira, 240
sermon and its relationship to literature, 59–60
Sestendrup, Manfred, 250
Shakespeare, William, 370
Shakespeare, William, works by: *Macbeth*, 370
Shapin, Steven, 305
Shu, Li, 250
Siberia, 269
Sidney, Sir Philip, works by: *Arcadia*, 8
Siebenbürgen, 238
Sieveke, Franz Günter, 26, 39, 249
Simpliciana, 256
Simplicissimus (doctor), 233, 235
Simplicissimus (journal title), 245
Simplicissimus Redivivus (1743), 238

Simplicissimus Redivivus, der [. . .] sich noch in dem Kriege befindliche, 239
Simplicius Simplicissimus (father), 4–7, 11–14, 17, 28, 35, 37, 46–50, 52–54, 56–63, 65–68, 71, 74–75, 77–84, 95, 111–19, 123–24, 126–29, 131–38, 141–42, 148, 153–61, 169–71, 175–76, 178–79, 183–87, 231, 236–39, 241, 244, 253, 269–70, 273, 275–79, 281–82, 284–86, 288, 290, 300–317, 319–27, 333–35, 338–39, 347, 351, 353, 360–63, 365–66, 370–73
Simplicius Simplicissimus (son), 14, 54, 77, 79, 111–12, 158, 180, 182, 184–86, 189, 231, 241, 275, 285
Smith, Bruce, 300
Socrates, 281
Sodmann, Timothy, 169, 232
Soest, 54, 66, 75, 125, 130–31, 257–58, 278, 308–9. *See also* "Jäger von Soest"
Soester Festspiele, 257
Solbach, Andreas, 17–18
Sophie, Duchess of Hannover, 251–52
Sorel, Charles, 252
Sorel, Charles, works by: *Francion*, 252
South Sea islands, 52
Spahr, Blake Lee, 8, 29
Spain, 147, 149, 152, 156, 162
Spangenberg, Wolfhart, 243
Spangenberg, Wolfhart, works by: *Ganskönig*, 243
Spee, Friedrich von, works by: *Cautio Criminalis*, 71
Speer, Daniel, 237
Speer, Daniel, works by: *Simplicianischer/ Lustig-Politischer Haspel-Nannß*, 237; *Ungarischer oder Dacianischer*

Simplicissimus, 237; *Türckischer Vagant,* 237
Speier, Hans, 250
"Spielende, der." *See* Harsdörffer, Georg Philipp
Spinola, Ambrosius, 80
Spinoza, Baruch, 106
spiritus familiaris, 36, 82–83, 242
Sprachgesellschaft (*see also* individual societies), 3, 14
Springinsfeld, 12, 14, 46, 50, 52–54, 66, 70, 74, 77–83, 118, 124, 160, 273, 275, 278–79, 281–89, 342–43, 361, 365–66, 369, 372
Stadler, Ernst, 245
Stadler, Ernst, works by: *Simplicius wird Einsiedel,* 245
Stallybrass, Peter, 282, 300, 318–19, 324
Steckborn (Switzerland), 240
Stein, Alexandra, 316
Stockholm, 2515
Strasbourg, 3, 238
Strasbourg, Gottfried von, 1
Straßburgischer Staats-Simplicius, 238
Streich, Hermann, 257
Streich, Hermann, works by: *Der Schultheiß von Renchen,* 257
Streller, Siegfried, 106, 256
structure. *See* "novel, structure of the"
structure, tripartite, 204
Sturmdorff, Urban von Wurmsknick auff, 216
Suhl, 1
Sulsfort, German Schleifheim von, 4, 25, 153
Sulzer, 253
Sulzer, works by: *Allgemeine Theorie der Schönen Künste,* 253
Sun, 7, 109, 120–21, 135, 137–39

Switzerland (Swiss), 52, 60, 77, 132
Sylvander, 216

Tabori, Georg, 246
Tabori, Georg, works by: *Mutters Courage,* 246
Tannengesellschaft, Aufrichtige, 3
Tarot, Rolf, 26–27, 34–37, 249, 256, 371
Tartars, 309, 312
Tasso, Torquato, 46
Tatlock, Lynne, 18, 274, 327
Taylor, Barry, 348–49
Theil am Rhein, 132
Thirty Years' War, 1–2, 4, 6, 11, 31–33, 45, 47, 50, 54, 56–57, 60, 67, 69, 76–77, 103, 155, 158, 161, 203, 237, 248, 254, 272, 302, 341, 361–62, 368
Thomasius, Christian, 94, 252
Thomasius, Christian, works by: *Monats-Gespräche,* 252
Thuringia, 1, 258
Tieck, Ludwig, 3, 25, 31, 240, 247–48, 253
Tieck, Ludwig, works by: *Der Runenberg,* 242; *Ein Tagebuch,* 240; *Zerbino oder die Reise nach dem guten Geschmack,* 241
Tormes (river), 149
Trappen, Stefan, 38
Treuer, Gotthilf, 108
Treuer, Gotthilf, works by: *Deutscher Dädalus,* 108
Treves, Angelo, 250
Trommenheim (auf Griffsberg), Philarchus Grossus von, 4, 53–54, 74, 76–79, 81–82, 84, 284–86, 366
Trumbach, Randolph, 321–22, 324
Turks, 238, 312

Ugo, Bianca, 250

Ulenhart, Niclas, 153
Ulenhart, Niclas, works by:
    See Cervantes, Rinconete y
    Cortadillo
Ullenburg, 3
Ulm, 237
Unold, Max, 245
Uppsala, 251
Ursula (daughter of Meuder and
    Knan), 187
utopia, 6–7, 58, 61, 161, 361

Valbuena y Prat, Angel, 364
Valentin, Jean, 94
Van Ornam, Vanessa, 281
Velasco, Sherry Marie, 318
Velasquez, Diego Rodriguez de
    Silva y, 105
Velde, Carl van de, 341
Venator, Balthasar, works by:
    Reise-Beschreibung nach der
    obern neuen Monds-Welt, 26;
    Seltzame Traum-Geschicht, 26
Venus, 7, 67, 108–11, 121–22,
    125, 135, 139–40
Venus-Berg, 111, 125, 141
Vermeer, Jan, 99, 105
via equestris, 95
via pedestris, 95
Vienna, 68
vierfacher Schriftsinn. See
    mehrfacher Schriftsinn
Villingen, 132
Vincent, Sue, 317
violin (fiddle), 12
Virgil, 46, 99
Virgo, 132
virtues, Christian, 5–6
vita activa, 107
Voss, Johan Heinrich, 243
Vulcan, 109, 122

Wackenroder, Wilhelm Heinrich,
    253

Wagenseil, Christian Jacob, 30,
    246, 253
Wagenseil, Christian Jacob, works
    by: Der abentheuerliche
    Simplicissimus (1785), 246
Wagner, Matthäus (publisher),
    237
Wagner, Richard, 244
Wagner, Siegfried, 244
"der Wahn betrügt," 12, 29–30,
    32, 234
Wallenstein, Albrecht von, 126,
    361
war. See Thirty Years' War; First
    World War
War of Austrian Succession, 239
Warmund, 218–19
Warwick, Alexandra, 303, 306
Weber, A. Paul, 245
Weimar, 133, 135
Weimar, Duke of, 135
Weise, Christian, 240, 251
Weise, Christian, works by: Die
    drey ärgsten Ertz-Narren, 240
Weissen, Friedrich Christoph,
    247–48
Weltanschauung, 18
Werl, 131. See also Jäger von Werl
Westphalia, 131–32
Westphalia, Peace of, 2
Wette, Hermann, 244
Weydt, Günther, 2, 7–10, 13, 17–
    18, 32, 38, 125, 135, 139–40,
    153, 169, 232, 256
White, Alon, 282, 300
Wieckenberg, Ernst-Peter, 233
Wilhelminian Empire, 254
Wimmer, Ruprecht, 169, 184,
    235, 240, 250
Winkler Verlag, 33
Wise, Margaret, 318–19
witchcraft and witch hunt, 71–74,
    78, 82–83, 361
Wittstock, 132

Wittstock, Battle of, 62–63, 131, 277, 361
Wolfenbüttel. *See* Herzog August Bibliothek, Wolfenbüttel
Woolf, Virginia, 306
Wundergeschichten Calender, 28, 169, 231–33
Wurst, Karin, 286, 317

Y-sign, 95–96, 102
Yale University Library, 37, 146, 197–99

Zaenker, Karl, 150
Zedler, Johann Heinrich, 4, 107, 252, 301, 303–6, 310
Zedler, Johann Heinrich, works by: *Universal-Lexikon aller Wissenschaften und Künste,* 107, 252, 301
Zeiller, Martin, 180
Zeitung für Einsiedler, 243
Zeller, Rosmarie, 17–18, 286
Zesen, Philipp von, 100, 203, 240, 251–52, 347
Zesen, Philipp von, works by: *Assenat,* 15, 203, 240, 252, 347; *Assenat,* translations of, into Danish, 15; translations by: *Lysander und Kaliste,* 347
Ziegesar, Hertha von, 169, 232
Ziegler von Kliphausen, Heinrich Anselm, 240
Ziegler von Kliphausen, Heinrich Anselm, works by: *Helden Liebe der Schrift Alten Testaments,* 240
Zieglschmid, 256
zodiac, signs of the (*see also* individual signs), 174–76, 187, 231
Zollikofer [Zolekhofer], Lucas, 189
Zongari. *See* Garzoni, Tomaso
Zuckerbastel, 153

Zum Rappen, 111–12
Zum schwarzen Roß, 111–12
Zum silbernen Stern, 2, 258
Zurich, 302